FLORIDA STATE
UNIVERSITY LIBRARIES

AUG 9 2000

TALLAHASSEE, FLORIDA

THE THEORY OF MONETARY AGGREGATION

CONTRIBUTIONS TO ECONOMIC ANALYSIS

245

Honorary Editor:
J. TINBERGEN†

Editors:
R. BLUNDELL
D. W. JORGENSON
J. -J. LAFFONT
T. PERSSON

ELSEVIER
Amsterdam – Lausanne – New York – Oxford – Shannon – Singapore – Tokyo

THE THEORY OF MONETARY AGGREGATION

Edited by

William A. BARNETT
Washington University, St. Louis, U.S.A.

and

Apostolos SERLETIS
University of Calgary, Calgary, Canada

2000

ELSEVIER
Amsterdam – Lausanne – New York – Oxford – Shannon – Singapore – Tokyo

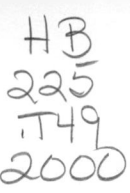

ELSEVIER SCIENCE B.V.
Sara Burgerhartstraat 25
P.O. Box 211, 1000 AE Amsterdam, The Netherlands

© 2000 Elsevier Science B.V. All rights reserved.

This work is protected under copyright by Elsevier Science, and the following terms and conditions apply to its use:

Photocopying
Single photocopies of single chapters may be made for personal use as allowed by national copyright laws. Permission of the Publisher and payment of a fee is required for all other photocopying, including multiple or systematic copying, copying for advertising or promotional purposes, resale, and all forms of document delivery. Special rates are available for educational institutions that wish to make photocopies for non-profit educational classroom use.

Permissions may be sought directly from Elsevier Science Rights & Permissions Department, PO Box 800, Oxford OX5 1DX, UK; phone: (+44) 1865 843830, fax: (+44) 1865 853333, e-mail: permissions@elsevier.co.uk. You may also contact Rights & Permissions directly through Elsevier's home page (http://www.elsevier.nl), selecting first 'Customer Support', then 'General Information', then 'Permissions Query Form'.

In the USA, users may clear permissions and make payments through the Copyright Clearance Center, Inc., 222 Rosewood Drive, Danvers, MA 01923, USA; phone: (978) 7508400, fax (978) 7504744, and in the UK through the Copyright Licensing Agency Rapid Clearance Service (CLARCS), 90 Tottenham Court Road, London W1P 0LP, UK; phone (+44) 171 631 5555; fax: (+44) 171 631 5500. Other countries may have a local reprographic rights agency for payments.

Derivative works
Tables of contents may be reproduced for internal circulation, but permission of Elsevier Science is required for external resale or distribution of such material. Permission of the Publisher is required for all other derivative works, including compilations and translations.

Electronic Storage or Usage
Permission of the publisher is required to store or use electronically any material contained in this work, including any chapter or part of a chapter.

Except as outlined above, no part of this work may be reproduced, stored in a retrieval system or transmitted in any form or by any means, electronic, mechanical, photocopying, recording or otherwise, without prior written permission of the Publisher. Address permissions requests to: Elsevier Science Rights & Permissions Department, at the mail, fax and e-mail addresses noted above.

Notice
No responsibility is assumed by the Publisher for any injury and/or damage to persons or property as a matter of products liability, negligence or otherwise, or from any use or operation of any methods, products, instructions or ideas contained in the material herein. Because of rapid advances in the medical sciences, in particular, independent verification of diagnoses and drug dosages should be made.

First edition 2000

Library of Congress Cataloging in Publication Data

The theory of monetary aggregation / edited by William A. Barnett and Apostolos Serletis.
   p. cm. -- (Contributions to economic analysis ; 245)
  Includes bibliographical references and index.
  ISBN 0-444-50119-3 (alk. paper)
   1. Index numbers (Economics) 2. Monetary policy. 3. Money supply. I. Barnett, William A. II. Serletis, Apostolos. III. Series.

HB225 .T49 2000
332.4'15--dc21

00-034082

ISBN: 0 444 50119 3

⊚ The paper used in this publication meets the requirements of ANSI/NISO Z39.48-1992 (Permanence of Paper).

Printed in The Netherlands.

INTRODUCTION TO THE SERIES

This series consists of a number of hitherto unpublished studies, which are introduced by the editors in the belief that they represent fresh contributions to economic science.

The term 'economic analysis' as used in the title of the series has been adopted because it covers both the activities of the theoretical economist and the research worker.

Although the analytical methods used by the various contributors are not the same, they are nevertheless conditioned by the common origin of their studies, namely theoretical problems encountered in practical research. Since for this reason, business cycle research and national accounting, research work on behalf of economic policy, and problems of planning are the main sources of the subjects dealt with, they necessarily determine the manner of approach adopted by the authors. Their methods tend to be 'practical' in the sense of not being too far remote from application to actual economic conditions. In addition they are quantitative.

It is the hope of the editors that the publication of these studies will help to stimulate the exchange of scientific information and to reinforce international cooperation in the field of economics.

The Editors

Contents

Preface W. Erwin Diewert	xxiii
Editors' Introduction William A. Barnett and Apostolos Serletis	xxix

PART 1: MONETARY INDEX NUMBER THEORY AND THE PRICE OF MONEY

SECTION 1.1: EDITORS' OVERVIEW OF PART 1 William A. Barnett and Apostolos Serletis	3
SECTION 1.2: DERIVATION OF THE USER COST OF MONETARY SERVICES	6
Chapter 1: The User Cost of Money William A. Barnett	6
1 Introduction	6
2 Assumptions and Notation	7
3 Derivation	9
SECTION 1.3: THE PRICE OF MONETARY SERVICES AND ITS USE IN MONETARY INDEX NUMBER THEORY	11
Chapter 2: Economic Monetary Aggregates: An Application of Index Number and Aggregation Theory William A. Barnett	11
1 Introduction	12
2 Objectives	13

3	The Consumer's Decision		16
	3.1	Intertemporal Allocation	16
	3.2	The User Cost of Monetary Assets	20
	3.3	Supernumerary Quantities	20
	3.4	Conditional Current Period Allocation	22
4	Preference Structure over Financial Assets		23
	4.1	Blocking of the Utility Function	23
	4.2	Multi-stage Budgeting	23
5	Recursive Estimation Approach		25
6	Passbook Savings		26
	6.1	C.E.S. Specification	26
	6.2	Theoretical Index Number Properties	28
	6.3	Results with Passbook Savings	29
7	Transaction Balances		31
	7.1	Specification	31
	7.2	Estimates	33
	7.3	Functional Index Numbers	34
8	Implications of Estimates		34
9	Empirical Selection of Blocking		35
	9.1	Conditions on Elasticities of Substitution	35
	9.2	Empirical Evidence	36
10	Statistical Index Numbers		38
	10.1	Definition	38
	10.2	Example	40
11	Conclusion		45
	Appendix: Duality		47

Chapter 3: The Microeconomic Theory of Monetary Aggregation
William A. Barnett

49

1	Introduction		49
2	Consumer Demand for Monetary Assets		51
	2.1	Finite Planning Horizon	51
	2.2	Infinite Planning Horizon	53
	2.3	Income Taxes	54
3	Supply of Monetary Assets by Financial Intermediaries		55
	3.1	Properties of the Model	58
	3.2	Separability of Technology	59
4	Demand for Monetary Assets by Manufacturing Firms		60
	4.1	Separability of Technology	62
5	Aggregation Theory Under Homogeneity		63

	5.1 The Consumer	64
	5.2 The Manufacturing Firm	66
	5.3 The Financial Intermediary	72
	5.4 Summary of Aggregator Functions	74
	5.5 Subaggregation	75
6	Index Number Theory Under Homogeneity	76
	6.1 The Consumer and the Manufacturing firm	76
	6.2 The Financial Intermediary	78
7	Aggregation Theory Without Homotheticity	80
	7.1 The Consumer and the Manufacturing Firm	81
	7.2 The Financial Intermediary	85
8	Index Number Theory Under Nonhomogeneity	86
	8.1 The Consumer and the Manufacturing Firm	86
	8.2 The Financial Intermediary	87
	8.3 Subaggregation	87
9	Aggregation Over Consumers and Firms	88
10	Technical Change	90
11	Value Added	92
12	Macroeconomic and General Equilibrium Theory	94
	12.1 The Utility Production Function	95
	12.2 Velocity Function	96
13	Conclusion	98

Chapter 4: Understanding the New Divisia Monetary Aggregates   **100**
William A. Barnett

1	Introduction	100
2	The Divisia Index	101
3	The Weights	103
4	Is it a Quantity or Price Index?	105
5	Stocks Versus Flows	107
6	Conclusion	108

PART 2: INDEX NUMBER THEORY

SECTION 2.1: EDITORS' OVERVIEW OF PART 2   **111**
William A. Barnett and Apostolos Serletis

SECTION 2.2: GENERAL INDEX NUMBER THEORY — 113

Chapter 5: Divisia Indices — 113
William A. Barnett

1. Aggregation Theory 113
   1.1 Structure of the Economy 113
   1.2 Aggregator Functions 114
   1.3 Exact Aggregator Functions 114
2. Index Number Theory 114
   2.1 Functional Index Numbers 114
   2.2 Statistical Index Numbers 114
3. Divisia Index 115
   3.1 Continuous Time 115
   3.2 Discrete Time 115
4. Dual Price Indices 116

Chapter 6: Divisia Monetary Aggregates — 117
William A. Barnett

1. The Economic Decision 118
2. The Divisia Index 119
3. Applications 120
4. Structural Change 121
5. Regulation 122
6. Controllability 122
7. Conclusion 123

SECTION 2.3: MONETARY INDEX NUMBER THEORY — 125

Chapter 7: The Optimal Level of Monetary Aggregation — 125
William A. Barnett

1. Introduction 125
2. The Earlier Literature 126
3. The Divisia Quantity Index 128
   3.1 The Definition 128
   3.2 The Effects of Interest Rate Changes 129
4. Graphical Comparisons of the Divisia and Simple Sum Aggregates 130
5. The Stages in the Selection Procedure 133

5.1	Stage 1: Selection of Admissible Component Groupings	133
5.2	Stage 2: Selection of an Index Number Formula	138
5.3	Stage 3: Selection of an Optimal Level of Aggregation	140

6 Available Empirical Evidence 142
   6.1 Component Groupings 142
   6.2 Divisia Aggregation versus Simple Sum Aggregation 143
   6.3 Comparisons Across Levels of Aggregation 144
7 Conclusion 148

Chapter 8: New Concepts of Aggregated Money   150
   William A. Barnett

1 The User Cost of Money 151
2 Aggregation Theory 152
3 Index Number Theory 153
4 Velocity of the Index 154
5 Liquidity Characteristic 156
6 Rates of Return 158
7 Conclusion 159

PART 3: EXTENSIONS OF INDEX NUMBER THEORY

SECTION 3.1: EDITORS' OVERVIEW OF PART 3   163
   William A. Barnett and Apostolos Serletis

SECTION 3.2: EXTENSIONS TO SECOND MOMENTS   167

Chapter 9: A Dispersion-Dependency Diagnostic Test for Aggregation Error: With Applications to Monetary Economics and Income Distribution   167
   William A. Barnett

1 Introduction 168
2 The Divisia Index Number Theory 170
   2.1 The Divisia Mean 170
   2.2 Stochastic Index Number Theory 172

	2.3	The Divisia Second Moments	172
3	Granger Causality	174
	3.1	The Specification	174
	3.2	The Causality Results	176
4	Reduced Form Equations	177
	4.1	Model without Divisia Second Moments	177
	4.2	Model with Divisia Second Moments	181
5	Aggregation Error in Aggregation over Consumers	186
	5.1	Gorman's Conditions	186
	5.2	The Specification	187
	5.3	The Results	191
6	Conclusions	193
Appendix A: Data Appendix	194

SECTION 3.3: EXTENSIONS TO RISK — 195

3.3.1: MONETARY AGGREGATION THEORY UNDER RISK — 195

Chapter 10: Exact Aggregation Under Risk — 195
William A. Barnett

1	Introduction	195
2	Microfoundations of Consumer Demand for Money	196
	2.1 Introduction	196
	2.2 Existence of a Monetary Aggregate for the Consumer	198
	2.3 The Solution Procedure	201
	2.4 Deceptive Simplifications	204
	2.5 Monetary Policy	205
3	The Risk-Neutral Case	206
4	A Generalization	207
5	Strong Separability in Currency	209
6	Conclusions	211
Appendix A: Proof of Consumer's Aggregation Theorem	212
Appendix B: Demand for Monetary Assets by Manufacturing Firms	213
	B.1 The Model	213

　　　　　B.2　Existence of a Monetary Aggregate for the
　　　　　　　Firm 215

**Chapter 11: Monitoring Monetary Aggregates Under
　　　　　　　Risk Aversion　　　　　　　　　　　　　　217**
　　　　　*William A. Barnett, Melvin Hinich, and
　　　　　Piyu Yue*

　　1　Introduction 217
　　　　1.1　Objectives 217
　　　　1.2　Methodology 220
　　　　1.3　A Moral of the Story 222
　　　　1.4　Illustration 223
　　2　Microfoundations of Consumer Demand for Money . . 223
　　　　2.1　Introduction 223
　　　　2.2　The Shocks 225
　　　　2.3　Consumer Demand for Monetary Assets 225
　　　　2.4　Existence of a Monetary Aggregate for the
　　　　　　　Consumer 227
　　3　The Risk Neutral Case 228
　　4　Data and Specification 230
　　5　Estimation 231
　　6　Results 237
　　7　Another Example 237
　　8　Conclusions 238
　　Appendix A:　The Hinich Bispectral Approach 240
　　　　A.1　Definitions and Background 240
　　　　A.2　The Test Method 240
　　　　A.3　Computation of the Test Statistics 241

**3.3.2: MONETARY INDEX NUMBER THEORY UNDER
　　　　RISK　　　　　　　　　　　　　　　　　　　　245**

**Chapter 12:　CAPM Risk Adjustment for Exact
　　　　　　　Aggregation Over Financial Assets　　　245**
　　　　William A. Barnett, Yi Liu, and Mark Jensen

　　1　Introduction 246
　　　　1.1　Money in the Utility Function 248
　　2　Consumer Demand for Monetary Assets 250
　　　　2.1　The Decision 250

	2.2 Existence of a Monetary Aggregate for the Consumer	251
3	The Perfect-Certainty Case	252
4	New Generalized Divisia Index	253
	4.1 User Cost of Money Under Risk Aversion	253
	4.2 Generalized Divisia Index Under Risk Aversion	257
5	CCAPM Special Case	258
6	Magnitude of the Adjustment	262
7	Generation of Simulated Data	263
	7.1 Introduction	263
	7.2 Parameterized Model of Preferences	263
	7.3 Euler Equations	265
	7.4 Solving the Euler Equations	266
8	Conclusion	271
	Appendix A: Consumer's Aggregation Theorem	272

Chapter 13: Stochastic Volatility in Interest Rates and Nonlinearity in Velocity   274
William A. Barnett, and Haiyang Xu

1	Introduction	274
2	Assumptions and Theoretical Specifications	276
3	Money Velocity With No Nominal Risk	280
4	Money Velocity With Nominal Interest Risk	282
5	Empirical Results	288
6	Conclusion	290
	Appendix A: Proof of Proposition 1	291
	Appendix B: Aggregation over First Order Conditions	292

SECTION 3.4: EXTENSIONS TO CAPITALIZED MONEY STOCK AGGREGATION   296

Chapter 14: A Reply to Julio J. Rotemberg   296
William A. Barnett

1	Introduction	296
2	The Economic Stock of Money	297
3	Implications for Simple Sum Aggregation	299
4	The Economic Stock of Money and the Divisia Monetary Aggregate	300
5	Uses of the Stock and the Flow Monetary Aggregates	302
6	Other Comments	303

6.1	Nested Hierarchies of Aggregates	303
6.2	Benchmark Rate	304
6.3	Long-run versus Short-Run Applications	305
6.4	Aggregation over Economic Agents	305
6.5	The Use of Coherent Demand Systems	305
7	Conclusion	306

Chapter 15: Partition of M2+ as a Joint Product: Commentary   307
William A. Barnett, and Ge Zhou

1	Introduction	307
2	Challenges Presented to Economic Theory	308
3	Historical Background	308
4	Ferrari Sports Cars	309
5	What to Do Next	310
6	The Theory	310
7	'Ancient' History	313
8	The Data	313
9	The Results	314
10	Where is All of This Going?	318

PART 4: CONSUMER MONETARY AGGREGATION UNDER PERFECT CERTAINTY

SECTION 4.1: EDITORS' OVERVIEW OF PART 4   323
William A. Barnett and Apostolos Serletis

SECTION 4.2: GENERAL INDEX NUMBER THEORY   325

Chapter 16: New Indices of Money Supply and the Flexible Laurent Demand System   325
William A. Barnett

1	Introduction		326
	1.1	Overview	326
	1.2	The Divisia Monetary Aggregates	326
	1.3	The Laurent Demand System	327

2	The New Monetary Quantity Index Numbers	329
	2.1 Aggregation Theory	329
	2.2 Index Number Theory	330
	2.3 The User Cost of Money	331
3	Behavior of the Divisia Monetary Aggregates	332
4	The Demand System	337
5	Functional Approximation Methods	338
	5.1 Definition of Second-Order Approximation	338
6	The Taylor Series Approximation	340
	6.1 Analytic Function Theory	340
	6.2 Behavior of the Remainder Term	341
	6.3 Conclusion	342
7	The Laurent Series Expansion	343
8	The Specifications	344
	8.1 The Generalized Leontief Model	344
	8.2 The Full Laurent Model	345
	8.3 The Minflex Laurent Model	346
9	Estimation	348
	9.1 Data and Restrictions	348
	9.2 Results	350
10	Conclusions	352
	10.1 Conclusions Regarding Monetary Aggregation	352
	10.2 Conclusions Regarding the Laurent Expansion Approach to Modeling	353
	10.3 Areas for Further Research	353
	Appendix A: Diewert's Definition of Second-Order Approximation	353
	Appendix B: Analytic Function Theory	355
	Appendix C: Properties of the Laurent Expansion	357
	Appendix D: Local Flexibility of the Minflex Laurent Model	358
	Appendix E: Global Theoretical Regularity Conditions for the Full Laurent Model	359

Chapter 17: The New Divisia Monetary Aggregates   360
William A. Barnett

1	Introduction	360
2	History and Objectives	361
3	The Divisia Monetary Quantity Index	363
4	Granger Causality and Prediction Risk Reduction	365
5	Velocity	368
6	Money Demand Functions	372

		6.1	Specification	372
		6.2	Empirical Results	373
	7	Reduced-Form Equations		378
		7.1	The Equations	378
		7.2	Results	380
		7.3	Divisia Second Moments	380
		7.4	Controllability	380
	8	Conclusion		383

Appendix A: Error Structure Analysis and Demand for Money Function Estimates 384

Appendix B: Divisia Second Moments 387

Chapter 18: Consumer Theory and the Demand for Money 389
William A. Barnett, Douglas Fisher, and Apostolos Serletis

1	Introduction		389
2	The Definition of Money		392
3	The Microeconomic Theory of a Monetary Economy		397
	3.1	The Aggregation-Theoretic Approach to Money	400
	3.2	Index Number Theory and Monetary Aggregation	402
	3.3	The Links Between Aggregation, Index Number Theory, and Monetary Theory	403
	3.4	Understanding the New Divisia Aggregates	408
	3.5	The Optimal Level of Monetary Subaggregation	409
4	Econometric Considerations		410
	4.1	Approximating the Monetary Services Subutility Function	413
	4.2	An Example	415
5	Empirical Dimensions		416
	5.1	Empirical Comparisons of Index Numbers	416
	5.2	Empirical Results for the Demand System Approach	418
6	Extensions		421
7	Conclusions		426

PART 5: DEMAND AND SUPPLY SIDE MONETARY AGGREGATION BY FIRMS AND FINANCIAL INTERMEDIARIES

SECTION 5.1: EDITORS' OVERVIEW OF PART 5   431
     William A. Barnett and Apostolos Serletis

SECTION 5.2: PRODUCTION AND SUPPLY SIDE   433

Chapter 19: The Regulatory Wedge Between the Demand-Side and Supply-Side Aggregation-Theoretic Monetary Aggregates   433
     William A. Barnett, Melvin J. Hinich, and Warren E. Weber

  1 Introduction 434
     1.1 The Issue 434
  2 Demand-Side Monetary Aggregation and Index Number Theory 435
     2.1 Aggregation Theory 435
     2.2 Index Number Theory 437
  3 Supply-Side Monetary Aggregation and Index Number Theory 438
     3.1 Aggregation Theory 438
     3.2 Index Number Theory 440
  4 The Regulatory Wedge 440
  5 Dynamic Behavior 443
     5.1 Data 443
     5.2 Estimating spectra 444
     5.3 Cross-spectral Estimation 445
     5.4 The Hilbert Transform Estimator 447
  6 Steady State Behavior 450
  7 Conclusion 452

Chapter 20: Financial-Firm Production of Monetary Services: A Generalized Symmetric Barnett Variable-Profit-Function Approach   454
     William A. Barnett and Jeong Ho Hahm

  1 The Model 456
     1.1 A Brief Overview of the Literature 456
     1.2 An Alternative Approach to the Modeling of Financial Firms 458
     1.3 Separability of Technology and Supply-Side Monetary Aggregation 462

	2	Separability Testing	464
	3	Data and Some Measurement Problems	470
	4	Empirical Results	474
	5	Concluding Remarks	480

SECTION 5.3: EXTENSIONS TO RISK   482

Chapter 21: Financial-Firms' Production and Supply-Side Monetary Aggregation Under Dynamic Uncertainty   482
William A. Barnett and Ge Zhou

1	Theoretical Model		486
2	Supply-Side Monetary Aggregation and a Weak Separability Test		494
	2.1	Supply-Side Aggregation	495
	2.2	Flexibility, Regularity and Weak Separability	497
3	Empirical Application		505
4	Empirical Results		509
5	The Regulatory Wedge		523
6	The Errors-in-the-Variables Problem		526
7	Conclusions		528

Chapter 22: Estimating Policy-Invariant Deep Parameters in the Financial Sector When Risk and Growth Matter   530
William A. Barnett, Milka Kirova, and Meenakshi Pasupathy

1	Introduction		530
	1.1	The Lucas Critique	531
	1.2	The Barnett Critique	532
	1.3	The Two Critiques Combined	533
2	Financial Intermediaries		534
	2.1	Financial Firm's Production	535
	2.2	Output Aggregation	538
	2.3	Testing for Weak Separability	539
	2.4	Empirical Application	542
	2.5	Results	545
3	Manufacturing Firms		547
	3.1	The Model	548
	3.2	Demand-Side Monetary Aggregation and Weak Separability	550

       3.3 Flexible Functional Form Specification and Regularity
            Conditions 551
       3.4 Data and Results 552
   4 Consumers 554
   5 Conclusions 556

PART 6: MONETARY POLICY WITH EXACT MONETARY AGGREGATION

SECTION 6.1: EDITORS' OVERVIEW OF PART 6 561
William A. Barnett and Apostolos Serletis

SECTION 6.2: MONETARY POLICY 563

Chapter 23: Recent Monetary Policy and the Divisia Monetary Aggregates 563
William A. Barnett

   1 Introduction 563
   2 The Tightness of Money 565
   3 Statistical Index Number Theory 566
   4 Economic Aggregation Theory 568
   5 Monetary Aggregation 569
   6 Conclusions 575

Chapter 24: Which Road Leads to Stable Money Demand? 577
William A. Barnett

   1 The Broken Road 577
       1.1 September 26, 1983 577
       1.2 September 26, 1983 Once Again 578
       1.3 The 'Monetarist Experiment' of November 1979 to
            August 1982 580
   2 The Low Road 582
       2.1 Where is the Low Road? 582
       2.2 The Price of Money 583
       2.3 Ancient History 584

	2.4	We All Are Suffering from Delusions	584
	2.5	Income and Velocity	585
	2.6	Functional Form	585
	2.7	Evaluation of the Low Road	586
3	The High Road		587
	3.1	The Dependent Variable	587
	3.2	The Independent Variables	588
	3.3	Model Structure	589
4	Misunderstandings		590
5	Conclusion		592

SECTION 6.3: MACROECONOMIC POLICY — 593

Chapter 25: Perspective on the Current State of Macroeconomic Theory — 593
William A. Barnett

1	Introduction		594
2	Definition of Macroeconomics		595
3	Aggregation Theory		596
4	Dimension Reduction		598
5	Keynesian Discretion versus Open Loop Rules		599
6	Non-Linear Dynamics		600
7	Consequences		601
	7.1	Time Inconsistency	601
	7.2	Non-Linear Dynamics	602
	7.3	Distribution Effects	603
8	Conclusion		604

DATA APPENDIX

SECTION A.1: EDITORS' OVERVIEW OF APPENDIX — 609
William A. Barnett and Apostolos Serletis

SECTION A.2: ST. LOUIS FEDERAL RESERVE BANK DATA — 610

Appendix A: Introduction to the St. Louis Monetary Services Index Project *Richard G. Anderson, Barry E. Jones, and Travis D. Nesmith*	610
Consolidated References	617
Index by Name	649
Index by Subject	655

Preface to
The Theory of Monetary Aggregation

W. Erwin Diewert
University of British Columbia

W. T. Foster wrote the following lines as a start to his preface of Irving Fisher's classic study, *The Making of Index Numbers*:

> "To determine the pressure of steam, we do not take a popular vote; we consult a gauge. Concerning a patient's temperature, we do not ask for opinions: we read a thermometer. In economics, however, as in education, though the need for measurement is as great as in physics or in medicine, we have been guided in the past largely by opinions. In the future, we must substitute measurement. Toward this end, we must agree upon instruments of measurement. That is the subject of this book."

The above lines are also an appropriate introduction to the present book, edited by William Barnett and Apostolos Serletis. The present book is a collection of papers by Barnett and his co-authors (E. Offenbacher, P. Spindt, A. Serletis, M. Hinich, P. Yue, Y. Liu, M. Jensen, H. Xu, G. Zhou, D. Fisher, W. E. Weber, J. H. Hahm, M. Kirova, and M. Pasupathy). Each paper has better measurement as its central theme and hence this book follows in the tradition of Irving Fisher, who also tried to improve economic measurement. In what follows, when I refer to Barnett, this should be understood as a shorthand notation for Barnett and his co-authors, when appropriate.

Barnett's basic research program has been to integrate monetary theory into macroeconomics starting with microeconomic theory and then using index number and aggregation theory to go from microeconomics to macroeconomics. Barnett has also used modern econometric techniques to estimate demand and supply functions for money and test for the existence of various monetary aggregates. More specifically, some of the major theoretical contributions of Barnett, which appear in this book, are: (i) producer and consumer user costs for money are rigorously derived and used as the appropriate prices for monetary components; (ii) the insertion of real balances into neoclassical utility and production functions is rigorously justified using the work of Fischer, Feenstra, and others; (iii) when aggregating commodities, superlative index number formulae are used; (iv) flexible functional forms for utility and production functions are consistently used throughout the book; (v) modern developments in testing for the existence of weakly separable aggregates are used to test for the existence of various monetary aggregates; and (vi) the usual consumer and producer models are extended to include *risk* in a fundamental way. I would also like to note the contribution made in chapters 3 and 19 where Barnett points out that the existence of bank reserve requirements creates a regulatory wedge in the user cost of money. That is, the reserve requirement acts like a capital tax on the bank and thus the user cost of money will be different on the supply (or bank) side of the market compared to the demand side of the market. This point creates a tremendous difficulty for macro models or applied general equilibrium models: there is no unique price that can equilibrate the demand and supply of money!

In addition to the above theoretical contributions, Barnett compares the performance of his superlative indexes, which use monetary user costs, with simple sum monetary aggregates, which do not use user costs. In chapter 24, he notes that Milton Friedman predicted that a resurgence of inflation would inevitably follow the explosion that occurred in the simple sum aggregates for the U. S. from late 1982 to mid 1983. Friedman also predicted that once the inevitable inflation began, the Federal Reserve would tighten monetary policy in a manner that would produce a recession. However, on the very same day that Friedman made his prediction, Barnett went on the record with a dramatically different forecast based on his superlative Divisia monetary indexes (which showed no monetary explosion). In fact, Friedman's predicted inflation and subsequent recession did not occur.

It is also interesting to observe what happened during the immediately preceding period. The following quotation, taken from pages 581-582 of chapter 24, explains how the different measurement techniques led to very different numerical estimates of money supply growth and to the mistakes in policy between 1979 and 1982 that produced the recession of 1982:

> "As I reported in Barnett (1984), the growth rate of simple sum M2 during the period of the 'monetarist experiment' averaged 9.3%, while the growth rate of Divisia M2 during the period averaged 4.5%. Similarly, the growth rate of simple sum M3 during the period averaged 10%, while the growth rate of Divisia M3 during the period averaged 4.8%. This period followed double digit growth rates of all simple sum and Divisia monetary aggregates. In short, believers in simple sum monetary aggregation, who had been the advocates of the 'monetarist experiment,' were put in the embarrassing position of witnessing an outcome (the subsequent recession) that was inconsistent with the intent

of the prescribed policy and with the behavior of the simple sum aggregates during the period. This unwelcome and unexpected outcome rendered vulnerable those economists who advocated a policy based upon the assumption of a stable simple sum demand for money function.

Friedman's very visible forecast error on 26 September 1983 followed closely on the heels of the end of the monetarist experiment in August 1982 and the recession that it produced. The road buckled and collapsed below the monetarists and those who believed in stable simple sum demand for money functions. Those two associated groups have never recovered.

But the recession that followed the monetarist experiment was no surprise to anyone who had followed the Divisia monetary aggregates, since those aggregates indicated that a severe deflationary shock had occurred. To those who were using data based upon valid index number and aggregation theory, rather than the obsolete simple sum monetary aggregates, the road remained smooth — no bumps, no breaks. Nothing unexpected had happened."

The above quotation shows that measurement matters! It is a topic that is dear to my heart, having labored in the measurement field for some 25 years. Thus it is perhaps no surprise that I am very enthusiastic about the basic Barnett research program: there is a substantial overlap in our research agendas. I too have worked with user costs, aggregation theory, flexible functional forms, tests for separability, and superlative index numbers. In Diewert (1974c), I derived a very simple user cost formula for non-interest bearing money, but I did not deal with interest bearing monetary assets and I did not deal adequately with the problem of converting nominal balances into real balances. The path breaking works of Fischer (1974), Samuelson and Sato (1984), and Feenstra (1986) on this tough problem were not yet available at that time. After this early attempt to integrate money into consumer theory, I never wrote another paper on this topic, although my former students — Donovan, Epstein, Feenstra, Hancock, and Kohli — have all made important contributions in this area of research. To further differentiate the research products of Barnett and Diewert, I note that, in addition to being the master of monetary user cost theory, Barnett has very substantial skills as an econometrician and macroeconomist — skills that I lack!

Barnett is very generous in this book about giving me credit for unifying the statistical (or test) approach to index number theory with the economic approach based on weakly separable aggregator functions. I would like to take this opportunity to point out that I was not the first to note the link of statistical agency index number formulae with functional forms for aggregator (utility or production) functions. In Diewert (1976, p. 116), I referred to Byushgens, Konüs, Frisch, Wald, Afriat, and Pollak as early pioneers in making this connection. However, these early researchers did not have the concept of a flexible functional form at their disposal, so they could not determine which exact index number formula might be "best" from the viewpoint of the approximation properties of the corresponding aggregator function. Barnett is well aware of this point, but I do not want others to be confused about the nature of my contribution to the literature.

What is a possible future research agenda that might flow out of this book? It seems to me that there are a number of basic problems that need additional research.

- There is a need to examine more closely the problem of deriving the "right" price deflator for monetary balances. The "right" deflator depends on one's theory of how money enters the constraints of the consumer's and producer's constrained maximization problems. Moreover, the producer model of Fischer (1974) and the consumer model of Feenstra (1986) are both highly aggregated, and there is a need to generalize their deflator results to higher dimensionality models.

- Chapters 10, 11, 12, and 21 all deal with the extension of riskless consumer and producer models to situations where the consumer or producer make decisions under uncertainty. This is very innovative work, which I applaud, but these chapters use an expected utility approach. Starting with Allais (1953), various researchers, including for example, Machina (1982), Mehra and Prescott (1985), and Chow and Epstein (1989), have noted various paradoxes associated with the use of the expected utility approach. Using the state contingent commodity approach to choice under risk that was pioneered by Blackorby, Davidson, and Donaldson (1977), Diewert (1993) tried to show that the expected utility framework led to a relatively inflexible class of functional forms to model preferences over uncertain alternatives. Diewert showed that a much more flexible class of functional forms can be obtained by moving to nonexpected utility models that are counterparts to the choice over lotteries models of the type pioneered by Dekel (1986), Chew (1989), Epstein and Zin (1990, 1991), and Gul (1991). Epstein and Zin (1990), Epstein (1992), and Diewert (1993, 1995b) showed that these more flexible models can explain many of the choice under uncertainty paradoxes, including the equity premium puzzle of Mehra and Prescott (1985). Thus there is a need for the Barnett research agenda to be extended to a nonexpected utility approach. A related problem in this uncertainty area that needs further research is the problem of determining the firm's preference for risk utility function, given that the owners of the firm might have rather diverse risk preferences.

- There is a need to solve the problem raised in chapter 19 where the price of money on the supply side of the market is not equal to the corresponding price on the demand side. Actually, this problem is a special case of a wider problem, which may not have a satisfactory solution. The wider problem is this: if our macro model or applied general equilibrium model of the economy distinguishes more than one class of consumer or more than one class of producer (e.g., industries or firms are distinguished), then the index number commodity aggregates for the household and production sectors constructed by statistical agencies *will never match up*. In other words, the composition of aggregate "food" consumption by say, the elderly, will never be *precisely* equal to the composition of aggregate "food" consumption by say, single person working households. This means that the aggregate "food" equation for the economy will never add up precisely; i.e., the physical balancing of commodity supply and demand that input-output analysis attempts to do cannot be done *precisely*.

Before closing, I would like to discuss a few additional points that struck me as I read the manuscript.

- At times Barnett is somewhat critical of the monetary authorities for not adopting a user cost approach to the price of monetary services while he praises statistical agencies like the Bureau of Labor Statistics for producing consumer price indexes that are closer to the ideal indexes that economic theorists might prefer. However, while some statistical agencies may be willing to construct user costs for housing (or use a rental equivalence approach as the BLS does), most statistical agencies are just as opposed to constructing user costs for other consumer durables as the monetary authorities are opposed to constructing user costs for monetary components. Why is this? It is because statistical agencies feel that user costs are not *objective* or *reproducible*. In constructing a user cost, various choices have to be made about the appropriate depreciation rate, the appropriate interest rate, whether expected or ex post capital gains should be included, whether tax considerations should be included and so on. Since there is usually no single unambiguous choice for all of these components of a user cost, the agency is open to a charge of being nonobjective, and of course different statisticians will make different choices, and so the resulting user cost will not be reproducible. Of course, as an economic theorist, I am not as worried about this lack of objectivity problem as the statistician since

I believe that reasonably objective procedures could be worked out. In addition, it is worth observing that the greatest problems in measuring depreciation rates — the dependency upon usage rates, maintenance, and wear-and-tear — are not relevant to financial and monetary assets. However, it is important for theorists to recognize the concerns of the practitioners.

- This leads us to Barnett's interesting discussion on page 401 below on why government statistical agencies shy away from using econometrics in their procedures. Barnett points out that there are many possible econometric specifications (both of functional forms and of stochastic specifications) that could be used to address a particular problem, and there are many methods of statistical estimation (and of model selection). Thus statistical agencies will have difficulty in justifying an econometric model to persons untrained in econometrics. In other words, the use of econometrics these days is inherently *nonreproducible*: different econometricians will come up with different models (including functional forms, stochastic specification, model selection criterion, and method of estimation) and possibly, very different results. I believe that this *nonreproducibility* problem is even worse today than it was two decades ago due to the widespread use of the Generalized Method of Moments (GMM) method of estimation, which requires the researcher to choose a set of instrumental variables. As far as I can determine, there is no *objective* way for researchers to choose these instruments. In many cases, the choice of instruments will affect the results obtained, so GMM has just added to the *nonreproducibility* problems associated with the use of econometric techniques. Let me add here that I am not advocating throwing out econometrics; I am just pointing out that there is a problem out there (the lack of reproducibility problem) that the econometric literature has not adequately addressed.

- On page 566 and elsewhere, Barnett refers to the statistical or test approach to index number theory that was pioneered by Irving Fisher (1911, 1922). Readers who might be interested in more recent work on the test or axiomatic approach to index number theory could refer to Diewert (1992b) and Balk (1995).

To conclude, I note that Barnett and Serletis have nice introductions to each major section of the book, which will give the reader an overview of each section's content. For the reader who is not familiar with the Barnett approach, I recommend reading chapters 18, 23, 24, and 25 first. These chapters lay out much of the practical importance of the Barnett research philosophy and will serve to motivate further reading of the book.

Editors' Introduction to Volume

William A. Barnett and Apostolos Serletis

The fields of aggregation theory and index number theory are vast and have been growing. Certain landmark publications have been critical to the current state of the art. Of particular note are:

- Irving Fisher's (1922) famous book on index numbers,

- A. Konüs's (1924) derivation of the true cost of living index,

- Francois Divisia's (1925) derivation of the Divisia index,

- S. Malmquist's (1953) derivation of the Malmquist index,

- Dale Jorgenson's (1967) derivation of the user cost (rental price) of capital, and

- Erwin Diewert's (1976) unification of index number theory and aggregation theory.

In recent years, there has been a resurgence of interest in index number theory and aggregation theory, since the two previously divergent fields have been successfully unified. The underlying aggregator functions are the building blocks of economic theory. Those fundamental aggregator functions are weakly separable subfunctions of utility, cost, distance, and production functions. The derivation of index numbers based upon their ability to track those aggregator functions is now called the "economic theory of index numbers."

Modern economic index number theory was introduced into monetary and financial economics by William Barnett (1980a), who is a coeditor of this volume. He merged the economic theory of index numbers with monetary theory, and argued for a new microeconomic and aggregation-theoretic approach to monetary economics. The new approach involves use of the aggregator functions of neoclassical monetary theory and the construction of "superlative" non-parametric approximations to those functions. The result is aggregated data and models such that the aggregation theory that produced the data is consistent with the theory that produced the models within which the data is used. Without internally consistent nesting of aggregator functions within models, inferences become incoherent. In addition, the index number approximations to those aggregator functions must track those functions accurately.

Clearly these new developments in the field of monetary and financial economics would not have been possible without the earlier results in general index number theory, aggregation theory, and durable goods theory.

This book comprises a focussed and unified collection of the most important publications in monetary and financial aggregation by Barnett and his co-authors. The two coeditors of this volume have organized the papers into logical sections, with unifying introductions and overviews. The result is a systematic development of the state of the art in monetary and financial aggregation theory, covering:

- derivation of the user cost price of monetary services,
- exact aggregation of monetary assets on the demand and supply sides,
- general equilibrium of all economic agents' demands and supplies,
- dynamic solution of the exact system, and
- extension to monetary aggregation under risk.

Fisher's (1922, p. 29) book had already concluded over 75 years ago that: "The simple arithmetic [index] should not be used under any circumstances. The simple arithmetic average produces one of the very worst of index numbers, and if this book has no other effect than to lead to the total abandonment of the simple arithmetic type of index number, it will have served a useful purpose."

Clearly by that criterion, Fisher's book was successful in all areas other than monetary and financial aggregation. But disillusionment is now widespread with the simple sum monetary aggregates and their arithmetic average interest rate and opportunity cost aggregates. This book demonstrates that this disillusionment is well founded.

In some ways, the developments contained in this book were objectives of early research by Milton Friedman and his workshop participants at the University of Chicago. In fact, Friedman and Anna Schwartz (1970, pp. 151-152) criticized simple-sum monetary aggregation and discussed the possibility of generalizing the conventional monetary aggregates to index numbers: "This (summation) procedure is a very special case of the more general approach. In brief, the general approach consists of regarding each asset as a joint product having different degrees of 'moneyness,' and defining the quantity of money as the weighted sum of the aggregate value of all assets."

With monetary and financial assets yielding interest, we shall see in this book that the components of monetary aggregates are indeed joint products and that application of modern aggregation and index number theory requires aggregation over imperfect substitutes to be nonlinear. But a weighted sum of component levels is a linear aggregator and implies perfect substitutability. When components are imperfect substitutes, aggregator functions are strictly concave, and index numbers must be able to track those aggregator functions.

Research by Friedman and his associates preceded developments in index number and aggregation theory that have been critical to the derivation of monetary and financial index number and aggregation theory. Nevertheless, it is interesting to see what Friedman and his students attempted to do in this area. See Friedman and Schwartz (1970, pp. 151-154) for a list of dissertations and related research produced by that group.

As illustrations of the economic theory of monetary aggregation, this book includes relevant empirical articles applying the theory of monetary aggregation to:

- problems in monetary policy,

- econometric modeling of money demand and supply,

- modeling and estimation of Euler equations,

- measurement of regulatory wedges in financial markets, and

- testing for stability of the economy's structure.

The included applied papers demonstrate that many of the empirical and policy puzzles in the area of monetary and financial economics disappear when simple sum monetary aggregates are replaced by index numbers that are coherent with the relevant theory

This book's results are heavily dependent upon the literature on microeconomic theory, index number theory, aggregation theory, and durables demand and supply, but not at all dependent upon any macroeconomic school of thought (e.g., monetarist, real business cycle, or Keynesian). Aggregation theory and index number theory are logically prior to any and all macroeconomic theories and are equally as relevant to all traditions in macroeconomics.

The following table provides an overview of the structure of the book. Prior to each section, there is an introduction highlighting some of the more important contributions of that section and briefly summarizing each chapter. The table identifies the organization of the book, including the clustering of chapters into sections and subsections, and locates the pages on which the section introductions can be found.

TABLE 1
Section and Subsection Structure, and Page Location of Editors' Introduction to Each Section

Section and Subsection Structure	Introduction Location

PART 1: MONETARY INDEX NUMBER THEORY AND THE PRICE OF MONEY

    Section 1.1: Editors' Overview of Part 1 .... p. 3

    Section 1.2: Derivation of the User Cost of Monetary Services

        • Chapter 1

    Section 1.3: The Price of Monetary Services and its Use in Monetary Index Number Theory

        • Chapters 2, 3, 4

PART 2: INDEX NUMBER THEORY

    Section 2.1: Editors' Overview of Part 2 .... p. 111

    Section 2.2: General Index Number Theory

        • Chapters 5, 6

    Section 2.3: Monetary Index Number Theory

        • Chapters 7, 8

PART 3: EXTENSIONS OF INDEX NUMBER THEORY

    Section 3.1: Editors' Overview of Part 3 .... p. 163

    Section 3.2: Extensions to Second Moments

        • Chapter 9

    Section 3.3: Extensions to Risk

        Section 3.3.1: Monetary Aggregation Theory under Risk

            • Chapters 10, 11

        Section 3.3.2: Monetary Index Number Theory under Risk

            • Chapters 12, 13

    Section 3.4: Extension to Capitalized Money Stock Aggregation

        • Chapters 14, 15

EDITORS' INTRODUCTION   xxxiii

PART 4: CONSUMER MONETARY AGGREGATION UNDER PERFECT CERTAINTY

    Section 4.1: Editors' Overview of Part 4 .... p. **323**

    Section 4.2: Consumer Money Demand

- Chapters 16, 17, 18

PART 5: DEMAND AND SUPPLY SIDE MONETARY AGGREGATION BY FIRMS AND FINANCIAL INTERMEDIARIES

    Section 5.1: Editors' Overview of Part 5 .... p. **431**

    Section 5.2: Production and Supply Side

- Chapter 19, 20

    Section 5.3: Extensions to Risk

- Chapters 21, 22

PART 6: MONETARY POLICY WITH EXACT MONETARY AGGREGATION

    Section 6.1: Editors' Overview of Part 6 .... p. **561**

    Section 6.2: Monetary Policy

- Chapters 23, 24

    Section 6.3: Macroeconomic Policy

- Chapter 25

DATA APPENDIX

    Section A.1: Editors' Overview of Appendix .... p. **609**

    Section A.2: St. Louis Federal Reserve Bank Data

- Chapter 26

Part 1: Monetary Index Number Theory and the Price of Money

Section 1.1: Editors' Overview of Part 1

William A. Barnett and Apostolos Serletis

The following table contains a brief summary of the contents of each chapter in Part 1 of this book. This section of the book contains the economic theory, aggregation theory, and index number theory that are fundamental to the rest of the book.

Part 1 Section Contents
Monetary Index Number Theory and the Price of Money

Chapter Number	Chapter Title	Contents
1	The User Cost of Money	Barnett's original derivation of the formula for the user cost of monetary services.
2	Economic Monetary Aggregates: An Application of Index Number and Aggregation Theory	The fundamental paper on monetary aggregation and index number theory on the consumer demand side.
3	Microeconomics of Monetary Aggregation	The state of the art in monetary aggregation and index number theory under perfect certainty for consumers and firms, including extensions to the nonhomothetic case and to supply side aggregation theory over inside money produced by financial intermediaries.
4	Understanding the New Divisia Monetary Aggregates	Explanation of the correct interpretation of index-number-theoretic monetary aggregates, answers to often asked questions, and correction of frequent misunderstandings.

Chapter 1:

Chapter 1 contains Barnett's original derivation of the user cost price of monetary services for a consumer. Without this result on the "price of money," the research in the rest of the book would not have been possible. The resulting formula appears as equation (3) in Chapter 1. The extension to include taxation of interest income appears in equation (4) of Chapter 2.

Chapter 2:

Chapter 2 contains the paper that first applied rigorous index number and aggregation theory to monetary economics. The theory used in that chapter applies to consumer demand for monetary services. The chapter assumes that consumers are price takers and that the user cost prices of monetary assets are among the prices taken as given by consumers. However, the chapter's results do not depend upon an assumption of market clearing. The results are explicitly demand side, and are produced both from economic aggregation theory, by econometric estimation of aggregator functions, and from index number theory, by nonparametric approximation of unknown aggregator functions.

The formula for the discrete time Divisia (Törnqvist) monetary quantity index is acquired and supplied in equation (17) of Section 10.1. The Fisher ideal monetary quantity index also is supplied in Section 10.1, and now is called the "monetary services index" (MSI) by the Federal Reserve. See the appendix at the end of this book regarding availability of that MSI data from the St. Louis Federal Reserve Bank. The appendix to Chapter 10 provides the theory that defines the exact user cost price aggregate that is dual to the exact quantity aggregate.

The chapter's empirical results demonstrate that the paradoxes regarding velocity behavior during the 1970s disappear, when monetary aggregates are produced from index number theory, rather than from simple summation.

Chapter 3:

Chapter 3 extends the results in Chapter 2 to the case of nonhomotheticity of category utility functions and derives the analogous results for firm demand for monetary services and financial intermediary supply of monetary services. The chapter contains extensive use of duality theory to provide the user cost price aggregates that are dual to the exact monetary quantity index numbers. All results in the chapter assume perfect certainty.

This chapter is a fundamental source of theoretical results on monetary aggregation theory, on both the demand and supply side and for aggregation over both quantities and user cost prices. It is recommended that readers of this book use Chapter 3 as a reference source for theory and formulas needed

Editors' Overview of Part 1 5

throughout the book, except in those chapters providing the extensions to risk.

Chapter 4:

Chapter 4 should be read carefully by anyone seriously interested in this subject, even though that chapter contains no new results. Misunderstandings and misinterpretations of the Divisia monetary aggregates have been common and frequent among economists not well versed in index number theory and its connection with microeconomic aggregation theory. These misinterpretations are usually associated with confusion of marginal utilities, average utilities, and total utilities in the derivation of the Divisia index. That derivation is provided in equations (1)-(5) of this chapter.

Those sources of confusion are entirely analogous to the ones producing the "diamonds versus water paradox" of undergraduate microeconomics textbook fame. Chapter 4 addresses the most common of those misunderstandings and provides the kind of fundamental economic intuition needed to interpret and use the Divisia monetary aggregates and their "weights" correctly.

Section 1.2: Derivation of the User Cost of Monetary Services

Chapter 1

The User Cost of Money

*William A. Barnett**

Prior imputations of a price to monetary asset services have not been based upon an explicit assumption structure or an explicit model. We rigorously derive a unique user cost formula for that price; our results are consistent with Donovan's (1977) formula.

1 Introduction

In the money demand literature there has long been interest in the subject of imputing a 'price' to monetary assets. That price usually has been viewed to be some unknown function of the price level, the own interest rate, the rate of change of the price level, and a discount rate. Recent literature has increased the potential importance of such an imputation by modeling the

---

*Reprinted from *Economics Letters*, 1, William A. Barnett, "The User Cost of Money," pp. 145–149, Copyright (1978), with permission from Elsevier Science. It has been slightly edited for this book to correct a typographical error that appeared in the original journal article and to render the notation in chapter 1 to be consistent with the notation in chapter 2.

demands for monetary assets jointly within conventional demand systems.[1] All such conventional demand system approaches require the imputation of a 'price' to each good. We shall rigorously derive a unique user cost ('equivalent rental') price imputation for interest-bearing or non-interest-bearing money.

Donovan (1977) acquired such a user cost imputation through general economic reasoning without the use of a model and under the assumption that the 'services' of financial assets are proportional to the stocks with a unitary proportionality constant. However it is difficult to determine the assumptions implicit in his argument without a model, and it is difficult to recognize the class of models to which his result is applicable. Furthermore, there is always the possibility of unrevealed error in sophisticated results acquired without a formal mathematical model. We construct a general and widely applicable consumer decision model, and we prove that Donovan's formula provides the correct and unique user cost monetary asset price imputation within that model. We make no assumptions regarding the functional relationship between stocks and their service flows.

We shall derive the user cost of monetary assets from a rigorous Fisherine intertemporal consumption expenditure allocation model. Since the model is formulated in discrete time, a structure of assumptions is required regarding the timing of interest rate and price changes and of portfolio transactions. Although we shall not fix the time interval, it could be set at one day, since interest rarely is paid more frequently than daily. In most applications, the resulting discrete time model could be viewed as approximating a continuous time model, since discrete time data in empirical studies usually corresponds to substantially longer time intervals.

2 Assumptions and Notation

We define time period t to be the time interval $[t, t+1)$, closed on the left and open on the right. Hence the instant of time t is included in interval t, but the instant $t+1$ is not. We assume that consumption of goods can proceed continuously throughout any time interval, although our model will use only the total (integral) of that consumption for any time period. Stocks of monetary assets and bonds are constant during each period, and can change only at the end of an interval. Hence during period t, any changes in holdings occurring at instant $t+1$ are not seen until the initial instant of interval $t+1$. In short, all portfolio transactions take place at the boundaries between intervals.

---

[1] See, e.g., Bisignano (1974), Chetty (1969), Clements (1976), Donovan (1977), and Parkin, Cooper, Henderson and Danes (1975).

Interest on bonds and on monetary assets is paid at the end of each period. Since the end (right-hand boundary) of period t is included in period $t+1$, but not in period t, interest paid for asset holdings during period t cannot be consumed until period $t+1$. Interest rates, prices, and wage rates remain constant within the interior of each period, but can change discretely at the boundaries of periods. Hence capital gains (or losses) resulting from changes in market bond yields can take place only at the boundaries of periods. Consumers are assumed to sell all bond holdings at the end of each period and to buy new issues, so that the market value equals the face value of bonds within the interior of each period, and the new issue interest rate equals the seasoned rate.

We treat labor supply as exogenously determined, and we assume that labor supplies, $(L_t, \ldots, L_{t+T})$, during all periods of the consumer's planning horizon are blockwise weakly separable from all other arguments of his utility function, so that we can use the subutility function defined only over the other arguments. Let t be the current period (or equivalently the instant of time at the start of the period). In effect, the instant at the start of each period indexes the period. Let T be the length of the planning period, so that the consumer currently plans through all periods, s, in $\{s : t \leq s \leq t+T\}$. We now define our variables:

$\mathbf{x}_s$ = vector of per capita (planned) consumptions of goods and services (including those of durables) during period s.

$\mathbf{p}_s$ = vector of goods and services expected prices and of durable goods expected rental prices during period s.

m_{is} = planned per capita real balances of monetary asset i during period s $(i = 1, \ldots, n)$.

r_{is} = the expected nominal holding period (including capital gains and losses) yield on monetary asset i during period s $(i = 1, \ldots, n)$.

A_s = planned per capita real bond holdings during period s.

R_s = the expected (one-period holding) yield on bonds during period s.[2]

L_s = per capita labor supply during period s.

w_s = the wage rate during period s.

---

[2]We here define A_s to be bonds and R_s their holding period yield only to simplify exposition. In theory and in practice, A_s is called the benchmark asset, which is a pure investment. Since the pure investment produces only financial yield and no other services, the expected benchmark rate of return must exceed that on monetary assets that also provide services. For further discussion, see footnote 12 in chapter 2. For an explanation of how the benchmark yield is computed in the United States by the Federal Reserve Bank of St. Louis, see Anderson, Jones, and Nesmith (1997c, p. 75).

3 Derivation

We shall let u be the representative consumer's utility function. Assuming continuous replanning, we can write the consumer's decision problem during each period s ($t \leq s \leq t+T$) within his planning horizon as

$$\max u(m_t, \ldots, m_{t+T}; x_t, \ldots, x_{t+T}; A_{t+T}/p^*_{t+T}),$$
subject to

$$p^*_s x_s = w_s L_s + \sum_{i=1}^{n}[(1+r_{i,s-1})p^*_{s-1}m_{i,s-1} - p^*_s m_{is}] \quad (1)$$
$$+ [(1+R_{s-1})A_{s-1} + K_s - A_s].$$

The real value of assets carried over (endowed) from the prior planning period is

$$\sum_{i=1}^{n}(1+r_{i,t-1})m_{i,t-1} + (1+R_{t-1})A_{t-1},$$

and the real value of the consumer's provisions for later planning periods is

$$\sum_{i=1}^{n}(1+r_{i,t+T})m_{i,t+T} + (1+R_{t+T})A_{t+T}.$$

Let

$$\rho_s = \begin{cases} 1, & s = t, \\ \prod_{u=t}^{s-1}(1+R_u), & t+1 \leq s \leq t+T. \end{cases}$$

Then ρ_s is the discount factor for discounting period s transactions. Observe that $\rho_s \neq \prod_{u=t}^{s}(1+R_u)$, since R_s is not paid during $[s, s+1)$, but rather at the start of $[s+1, s+2)$.

Solve (1) for A_s and write the resulting equation for each s between t and $t+T$. Then back substitute for A_s starting from A_{t+T} working down to A_t, always substituting the lower subscripted equation into the next higher one. Completion of the sequence of back-substitutions results in the single wealth constraint,

$$\sum_{s=t}^{t+T}(\mathbf{p}'_s/\rho_s)\mathbf{x}_s + \sum_{s=t}^{t+T}\sum_{i=1}^{n}\left[\frac{p^*_s}{\rho_s} - \frac{p^*_s(1+r_{is})}{\rho_{s+1}}\right]m_{is}$$
$$+ \sum_{i=1}^{n}\frac{p^*_{t+T}(1+r_{i,t+T})}{\rho_{t+T+1}}m_{i,t+T} + \frac{p^*_{t+T}}{\rho_{t+T}}A_{t+T}$$

$$= \sum_{s=t}^{t+T} (w_s/\rho_s) L_s + \sum_{i=1}^{n}(1+r_{i,t-1})p^*_{t-1}m_{i,t-1}$$
$$+(1+R_{t-1})A_{t-1}p^*_{t-1}. \qquad (2)$$

Equation (2) states that the discounted value of goods consumption plus the discounted user cost (equivalent rental price) evaluated monetary asset holdings plus the discounted cost of passing on $\mathbf{m}_{t+T} = (m_{1,t+T}, \ldots, m_{n,t+T})$ to the next planning period plus the discounted cost of passing on A_{t+T} to the next planning period equals discounted total labor income plus the nominal value of assets carried over (endowed) from the prior planning period. The consumer now can be viewed as maximizing utility subject to the single wealth constraint (2).

From (2) we see immediately that the user cost (equivalent rental price) of m_{is} is
$$\frac{p^*_s}{\rho_s} - \frac{p^*_s(1+r_{is})}{\rho_{s+1}}.$$

Finally the current period user cost, p_{it}, of m_{it} is
$$p_{it} = p^*_t \frac{R_t - r_{it}}{1+R_t}, \qquad (3)$$

which is the Donovan's (1977) user cost formula.[3]

---

[3] If we were further to assume that the utility function is blockwise weakly separable, with m_t comprising one block, then a single period model of monetary asset demand would exist in which all prices would be user costs of the form (3). Also observe that although (3) does not depend directly upon inflation rates, the nominal interest rates within the formula can be expected to respond to expected inflation rates. Furthermore, since the well known user cost formula for non-monetary durables services does depend inversely upon the expected inflation rate, it follows that the user cost of monetary assets relative to durables increases as the expected inflation rate increases.

Section 1.3: The Price of Monetary Services and its Use in Monetary Index Number Theory

Chapter 2

Economic Monetary Aggregates:
An Application of Index Number
and Aggregation Theory

*William A.Barnett**

> The debate over what should be counted as money is between people who do not know and people who do not know that they do not know.
>
> John Kenneth Galbraith (1979, p. 90)

---

*Reprinted from the *Journal of Econometrics*, 14, William A. Barnett, "Economic Monetary Aggregates: An Application of Index Number and Aggregation Theory," pp. 11–48, Copyright (1980), with permission from Elsevier Science. The views expressed herein are solely those of the author and do not necessarily represent the views of the Board of Governors of the Federal Reserve System. This research was partially supported by National Science Foundation Grant SOC 76-84459. I have benefited from comments on this research by William Brainnard, Kenneth Clements, David Humphrey, Donal Donovan, Donald Hester, Franco Modigliani, Robert Rasche, Henri Theil, Peter Tinsley, and participants at the University of Chicago's Econometrics Symposium and at the 1979 European Econometric Society Meetings in Athens.

1 Introduction

Monetary policy is related to the behavior of indices of the quantity, 'price' and velocity of money. Yet, for such aggregates to be useful, they must have meaning and must be measurable. This raises troublesome methodological questions. What is money? Is it a 'good' whose quantity can be measured, or is it just a vector of different characteristics (liquidity, means of payment, etc.)? Do currency and time deposits possess identical 'moneyness' so that their quantities can be aggregated linearly and with equal weights to acquire a meaningful quantity aggregate? If money is a meaningful good, then what is its price? Can more than one monetary aggregate jointly have meaning? We shall explore these issues using aggregation theory and index number theory.

Although not previously applied to money demand, the literature on aggregation theory exists *precisely* for the purpose of providing rigorous and unique answers to the sort of questions listed above. We apply aggregation theory to the construction and estimation of economic aggregates for passbook accounts across institution types and then to nested aggregation over transaction balances.[1] We show that passbook accounts at different institution types are close substitutes and hence can be aggregated linearly. But aggregation by simple summation is rejected, since the coefficients of the linear function are unequal. Substitutability between passbook savings and transaction balances is found to be low. Hence nonlinear aggregation is required to approximate the economic aggregate over savings and transaction balances.[2] We provide similar empirical results for time deposits and large certificates of deposit.

Since the beginning of this century a highly respected and increasingly sophisticated literature has been under development on statistical index number theory. While aggregation theory results in exact aggregator functions depending upon unknown (but estimable) parameters, statistical index number theory results in *parameter-free* approximations to aggregator functions. Index number theory provides the basis for the index numbers published by nearly every governmental agency in the world (other than the central banks).[3] In the latter sections of this paper, we explore the implications of

---

[1] Economic aggregates are also called functional, true, or exact aggregates. The other well known class of aggregates consists of statistical indices, which approximate functional aggregates.

[2] Our results also suggest that passbook accounts at commercial banks provide greater services than passbook accounts in savings and loans or mutual savings banks, since the economic aggregate weights passbook accounts at commercial banks more heavily than passbook accounts at savings and loans or at mutual savings banks. Similarly transaction balances are far more heavily weighted than passbook accounts.

[3] See Barnett (1982b).

statistical index number theory for the construction of monetary quantity index numbers, and we advocate the use of the Törnqvist-Theil Divisia index to measure the quantity of money.

During the past decade there has been much concern about the apparent destabilization of velocity.[4] In fact the problem arose primarily because of the long-run substitution effect resulting from rising own rates on unregulated monetary assets relative to the own rates on rate-regulated monetary assets. But the value of an *economic* aggregate (by its definition) *cannot* change as a result of internal substitution effects. Hence the money market substitution effects destabilizing velocity should be completely internalized by proper aggregation over the money market.

When *any* reputable index number formula is used, we find that the velocity of money *is* increasingly stabilized as the level of aggregation is increased, but the velocity of the usual simple sum index is destabilized by aggregation beyond an intermediate level. Furthermore, on direct empirical grounds, Barnett and Spindt (1979), and Barnett, Offenbacher, and Spindt (1984) have shown that the Törnqvist-Theil Divisia index *dominates* the simple sum index, *regardless* of the indexes' monetary components or of the final targets. The primitive simple sum index of money supply is *severely* defective, as should be no surprise to anyone who is familiar with any portion of the past half century of literature on aggregation and index number theory.

2 Objectives

Suppose we should wish to construct a monetary quantity index defined over the components of M_2. In economic aggregation theory, economic agents (consumers and producers) then must be able to treat M_2 as the quantity of a meaningful single good in their decisions. Economic agents must be able to select their desired aggregate quantity of M_2 without regard to its composition. The allocation of M_2 over its component elements then could be accomplished in a later second stage decision, conditionally upon the prechosen aggregate level of M_2. Varying the relative quantities of currency and time deposits within M_2 while holding the aggregate M_2 level constant must not affect tastes or technology over any other goods. If this condition is satisfied, economic agents, can possess stable preferences and technology over M_2 and other goods. If M_2 is not a good in this fundamental sense, then tastes or technology over M_2 and other goods will appear to shift whenever the relative proportions of the components of M_2 change.

If the concept of money has meaning, then it follows that an aggregate of monetary assets must exist which is treated by the economy *as if* it were

---

[4]See, e.g., Enzler, Johnson and Paulus (1976) and Goldfeld (1976).

a single good, which we thereby can call 'money'. Such an aggregate is a function (of its component monetary quantities) which is separable from the economy's structure. *That* concept of money is the subject of aggregation theory and is the concept relevant to policy, since both aggregation theory and policy postulate the appearance of a monetary aggregate as a *meaningful* stably defined variable in the economy's structure. Without the appropriate separability conditions, any aggregate is inherently arbitrary and spurious and does not define an economic variable.

It can be shown that when a functional quantity aggregate exists for a consumer, that aggregate itself must possess the known properties of a utility function, and that utility function must possess certain additional special properties (homotheticity and weakly separable nesting within the consumer's full utility function). Then, when the aggregate quantity index is held constant, the 'utility of money' is necessarily held constant independently of its composition. As has been observed by Samuelson and Swamy (1974, p. 568): 'The fundamental point about an economic quantity index, which is too little stressed by writers, Leontief and Afriat being exceptions, is that it must itself be a cardinal indicator of ordinal utility.' The conditions for economic aggregation over goods demanded by firms are the analogous conditions on production functions, and the form of aggregator functions and index numbers is identical for firms and consumers. To simplify the discussion, we present the theory and results in terms of consumer decisions.[5]

Irving Fisher (1922) provided a list of desirable properties for economic price and quantity indices. Ragnar Frisch (1930) proved that when the number of goods exceeds unity, no index number formula can satisfy all of those properties. However, Samuelson and Swamy (1974, p. 566) have shown that if price and per capita quantity data is assumed to fall on neoclassical demand functions (rather than to be unrestricted independent variables, as

---

[5]The utility approach to consumer money demand modeling is currently the basis for rapidly expanding empirical research in the literature. Consider, for example, Chetty (1969), Bisignano (1974), Diewert (1974), Parkin, Cooper, Henderson, and Danes (1975), Clements (1976), Donovan (1977), Phlips (1978), Offenbacher (1979), and Clements and Nguyen (1980). Early advocates of the utility approach include Friedman and Patinkin.

The utility approach is based upon implicit modeling rather than the explicit modeling used in the transactions demand or portfolio analysis approaches. In an economic (rather than empirical) sense, the utility approach is a reduced form approach which models, restricts, and characterizes the results of the consumer's decisions without the need to consider the explicit structure of the decision. The resulting approach has the merit of unifying the modeling of the demand for all money market instruments within a single framework without the need to explore the detailed and different structures of the consumer's decisions within each sector of the money market.

It would be preferable to aggregate within each relevant sector (firms, wealthy households, etc.) separately, and then over the sector aggregates. But adequate data currently is not available by sector.

assumed by Frisch), then the economic quantity and dual price indices discussed above, 'do meet the spirit of all of Fisher's criteria in the only case in which a single index number of the price of cost of living makes economic sense'. Furthermore, economic aggregates can be constructed at multiple levels of monetary aggregation in such a manner that the indices are nested. As a result, internal contradictions cannot arise at varying levels of aggregation. We shall use only such economic quantity and dual price indices (or statistical approximations to them), and we shall accept the assumptions necessary and sufficient for the existence of a hierarchy of nested aggregates.

The economic quantity index cannot be known exactly without knowledge of the representative consumer's utility function, since the economic quantity index depends upon and is defined in terms of consumer preferences.[6] Conventional accounting practices generate economic indices only to the degree that those indices imply plausible preference orderings over components. Yet, all current monetary quantity indices are constructed from simple addition of components. *If* those indices measure economic variables, then it follows that the variables have been generated by a utility function for financial assets possessing the same simple unweighted summation form used in constructing the index. But such a utility function requires the goods over which it is defined to be perfect substitutes in identical ratios. In other words, the components of the quantity index must be indistinguishable to the consumer.[7]

We frequently seek information about the 'price' of money. In various studies, the price of money has been viewed as an interest rate, an index of interest rates, the rate of change of prices, the price level, or an index of some subset of those subindices. We derive the Jorgensonian user cost (equivalent rental price) of money. Furthermore, when we aggregate over monetary assets, we can aggregate over those user costs (in parallel with aggregation over quantities) by using the theory of economic price indices. Once the consumer's preference structure has been estimated, the 'price' and the quantity of the aggregate are simultaneously implied as duals.[8]

---

[6] In this paper we postulate the existence of a representative consumer, although we argued against that practice in Barnett (1979b). We use a community utility function here because of its usefulness as a means of imposing functional regularity on demand systems, rather than out of any conviction that such a community utility function actually need exist. However, there is some empirical and theoretical evidence that, under some conditions, the behavior of aggregate consumption data may be approximated by a consistent and transitive preference ordering. See Dixon (1975), Maks (1978), and Donovan (1979).

[7] In the existing simple sum M_2, for example, the consumption characteristics of one dollar of currency must be *identical* to those of one dollar of long-term small time deposits. The violation of aggregation theory increases as the level of aggregation increases, since the higher the level of aggregation the less substitutable the components of the aggregates become.

[8] These indices satisfy the accounting identity of equality between expenditure and the product of quantity and price, and the consumer can be shown to behave in a rational

In section 3 we define the consumer's intertemporal decision problem, derive the user cost of monetary assets, and derive the consumer's current period monetary asset allocation problem. In section 4 we block the consumer's current period monetary asset utility function, and we present the consumer's resulting multistage budgeting procedure along with the implied functional quantity and price aggregates. In section 5 we present our recursive estimation and recursive functional aggregation procedure, which works its way up the utility tree. In sections 6, 7, and 8 we present our results with passbook accounts and transaction balances and reject aggregation by summation. In section 9 we present a procedure for empirical selection of a more extensive blocking of preferences, and we discuss some preliminary results. In section 10 we define *parameter-free* statistical index numbers that can approximate the functional aggregates, and we construct an example; we plot the velocity of the resulting quantity index. We conclude by advocating use of the Divisia parameter-free statistical index number to measure the quantity of money. We reject further use of the obsolete simple sum index.

3 The Consumer's Decision

3.1 Intertemporal Allocation

In this section we shall derive the Jorgensonian user cost (equivalent rental price) of monetary assets from a rigorous Fisherine intertemporal consumption expenditure allocation model. Since the model is formulated in discrete time, a structure of assumptions is required regarding the timing of interest rate and price changes and of portfolio transactions.[9]

We define time period t to be the time interval $[t, t+1)$, closed on the left and open on the right. Hence the instant of time t is included in interval t, but the instant $t+1$ is not. We assume that consumption of goods can proceed continuously throughout any time interval, although our model will use only the total (integral) of that consumption for any time period. Stocks of monetary assets and bonds are constant during each period, and can change only at the end of an interval. Hence during period t, any changes in holdings occurring at instant $t+1$ are not seen until the initial instant of interval

---

manner relative to the aggregate good whose price and quantity have been defined. This rationality obtains both relative to the aggregates and relative to their components, and consumers' decisions at all levels of aggregation are consistent with a single joint rational choice criterion.

[9]Although we shall not fix the time interval, it could be set at one day, since interest on savings deposits rarely is paid more frequently than daily. For our purposes a daily discrete time model could be viewed as approximating a continuous time model, since our average quarterly data corresponds to a substantially longer period.

The Consumer's Decision

$t+1$. In short, all portfolio transactions take place at the boundaries between intervals.

Interest on bonds and on monetary assets is paid at the end of each period. Since the end (right hand boundary) of period t is included in period $t+1$, but not in period t, interest paid for asset holdings during period t cannot be consumed until period $t+1$. Interest rates, prices, and wage rates remain constant within the interior of each period, but can change discretely at the boundaries of periods. Hence capital gains (or losses) resulting from changes in market bond yields can take place only at the boundaries of periods.

We treat labor supply as exogenously determined, and we assume that labor supplies, $L_t, \ldots, L_{t+T}$, during all periods of the consumer's planning horizon are blockwise weakly separable from all other arguments of his utility function, so that we can use the subutility function defined only over the other arguments.

Let t be the current period (or equivalently the instant of time at the start of the period).[10] Let T be the length of the planning horizon, so that the consumer currently plans through all periods, s, in $\{s : t \leq s \leq t+T\}$. We now define our variables:[11]

- $\mathbf{x}_s$ = vector of per capita (planned) consumptions of goods and services (including those of durables) during period s.
- $\mathbf{p}_s$ = vector of goods and services expected prices and of durable goods expected rental prices during period s.
- m_{is} = planned per capita real balances of monetary asset i during period s $(i = 1, \ldots, n)$.
- r_{is} = the expected nominal holding period (including capital gains and losses) yield on monetary asset i during period s $(i = 1, \ldots, n)$.
- A_s = planned per capita real bond holdings during period s.
- R_s = the expected (one-period holding) yield on bonds during period s.[12]
- L_s = per capita labor supply during period s.
- w_s = the wage rate during period s.

---

[10] In effect, the instant at the start of each period indexes the period.

[11] We require planned to equal actual values only during the current period t.

[12] As will be seen in the formulation of the consumer's decision problem below, R_s, is the expected one-period holding (including realized or unrealized capital gains or losses) yield (during period s) on assets accumulated to transfer wealth between multi-period planning horizons rather than to yield liquidity or other services during the current period. As a result, A_s will enter the consumer's utility function only during period $s = t+T$, and A_s need not necessarily be bond holdings. We use the word 'bonds' (also sometimes referred to as the benchmark asset in this context) to simplify exposition. The benchmark asset's one-period holding yield during period s is defined to contain all premiums available in the market for foregoing the services provided by monetary assets. Note that the holding period used in defining R_s must be the same as that of r_{is}, which is a short rate.

We let u_t be the representative consumer's current intertemporal, T-period, utility function. We assume that u_t is weakly separable in each period's consumption of goods and monetary assets, so that u_t can be written in the form

$$\begin{aligned} u_t &= u_t(\mathbf{m}_t, \ldots, \mathbf{m}_{t+T}; \mathbf{x}_t, \ldots, \mathbf{x}_{t+T}; A_{t+T}) \qquad (1) \\ &= U_t(v(\mathbf{m}_t), v_{t+1}(\mathbf{m}_{t+1}), \ldots, v_{t+T}(\mathbf{m}_{t+T}); \\ &\quad V(\mathbf{x}_t), V_{t+1}(\mathbf{x}_{t+1}), \ldots, V_{t+T}(\mathbf{x}_{t+T}); A_{t+T}), \end{aligned}$$

for some monotonically increasing, linearly homogeneous, strictly quasiconcave functions, $v_{t+1}, \ldots, v_{t+T}, V, V_{t+1}, \ldots, V_{t+T}$.[13] The function, v, is monotonically increasing and strictly quasiconcave, but not necessarily linearly homogeneous.[14] The function U_t also is monotonically increasing.

Dual to the functions, V and V_s $(s = t+1, \ldots, t+T)$, there exist current and planned true cost of living indices, $p_t^* = p(\mathbf{p}_t)$ and $p_s^* = p_s^*(\mathbf{p}_s)$ $(s = t+1, \ldots, t+T)$.[15] Those indices will be used to deflate all nominal quantities to real quantities, as in the definitions of m_{is} and A_s above.

Assuming replanning at each t, we write the consumer's decision problem during each period s $(t \leq s \leq t+T)$ within his planning horizon as to choose $(\mathbf{m}_t, \ldots, \mathbf{m}_{t+T}; \mathbf{x}_t, \ldots, \mathbf{x}_{t+T}; A_{t+T}) \geq 0$ to

$$\max u_t(\mathbf{m}_t, \ldots, \mathbf{m}_{t+T}; \mathbf{x}_t, \ldots, \mathbf{x}_{t+T}; A_{t+T}),$$

subject to

$$\begin{aligned} \mathbf{p}_s' \mathbf{x}_s &= w_s L_s + \sum_{i=1}^{n}[(1 + r_{i,s-1})p_{s-1}^* m_{i,s-1} - p_s^* m_{is}] \qquad (2) \\ &\quad + [(1 + R_{s-1})p_{s-1}^* A_{s-1} - p_s^* A_s]. \end{aligned}$$

The real value of assets carried over (endowed) from the prior planning period is

$$\sum_{i=1}^{n}(1 + r_{i,t-1})m_{i,t-1} + (1 + R_{t-1})A_{t-1},$$

---

[13] Observe that $v_t = v$ and $V_t = V$ independently of t for the current period t. Also observe that u_t can be acquired as a 'derived' utility function from the 'true' utility function, which does *not* depend upon monetary assets. The derivation postulates the existence of an arbitrary time-using transactions technology. See Arrow and Hahn (1971, p. 350). Quirk and Saposnik (1968, p. 97) further argue that if such a derived utility function does not exist, then no money will be held in equilibrium.

[14] We later shall assume that v is linearly homogeneous in supernumerary quantities.

[15] For a discussion of the relevant duality theory, see the appendix. The true cost of living index for a weakly separable block of goods equals expenditure on those goods divided by the (category) indirect utility function for those goods.

The Consumer's Decision

and the real value of the consumer's provisions for later planning periods is

$$\sum_{i=1}^{n}(1+r_{i,t+T})m_{i,t+T} + (1+R_{t+T})A_{t+T}.$$

Let

$$\rho_s = \begin{cases} 1, & s = t \\ \prod_{u=t}^{s-1}(1+R_u), & t+1 \le s \le t+T+1. \end{cases}$$

Then ρ_s is the discount factor for discounting period s transactions. Observe that $\rho_s \ne \prod_{u=t}^{s}(1+R_u)$, since R_s is not paid during $[s, s+1)$, but rather at the start of $[s+1, s+2)$. In problem (2), $(\mathbf{m}_t, \mathbf{x}_t)$ is actual consumption of goods and monetary assets during period t, while $(\mathbf{m}_{t+1},\ldots,\mathbf{m}_{t+T}; \mathbf{x}_{t+1},\ldots,\mathbf{x}_{t+T})$ is planned consumption of goods and monetary assets.[16]

Solve (2) for A_s and write the resulting equation for each s between t and $t+T$. Then back substitute for A_s starting from A_{t+T} and working down to A_t, always substituting the lower subscripted equation into the next higher one. Completion of the sequence of back-substitutions results in the single wealth constraint

$$\sum_{s=t}^{t+T}(\mathbf{p}'_s/\rho_s)\mathbf{x}_s + \sum_{s=t}^{t+T}\sum_{i=1}^{n}\left[\frac{p^*_s}{\rho_s} - \frac{p^*_s(1+r_{is})}{\rho_{s+1}}\right]m_{is}$$
$$+ \sum_{i=1}^{n}\frac{p^*_{t+T}(1+r_{i,t+T})}{\rho_{t+T+1}}m_{i,t+T} + \frac{p^*_{t+T}}{\rho_{t+T}}A_{t+T}$$
$$= \sum_{s=t}^{t+T}(w_s/\rho_s)L_s + \sum_{i=1}^{n}(1+r_{i,t-1})p^*_{t-1}m_{i,t-1}$$
$$+ (1+R_{t-1})A_{t-1}p^*_{t-1}. \qquad (3)$$

The consumer now can be viewed as maximizing utility subject to the single wealth constraint, (3), which is interpreted in Barnett (1978).

---

[16] Since we assume replanning each period and permit u_t to vary over time, the consumer's behavior is bound only by his decisions regarding current period consumption. Actual consumption patterns need not evolve in agreement with prior plans. However, further restrictions (stationary preferences, intertemporal strong separability, and constant rate of time preference) could be imposed upon u_t to assure that the sequence of current consumption quantities evolves over time in agreement with plans whenever correct expectations exist for all variables that are not under the consumer's control. Agreement between actual and planned consumption paths is not necessary to the estimation of our model.

3.2 The User Cost of Monetary Assets

From (3) we see immediately that the user cost (equivalent rental price) of m_{is} is

$$\pi_i^s = \frac{p_s^*}{\rho_s} - \frac{p_s^*(1+r_{is})}{\rho_{s+1}}. \tag{4}$$

Finally the current period user cost, π_{it}, of m_{it} reduces to

$$\pi_{it} = \frac{p_t^*(R_t - r_{it})}{1+R_t}.\text{[17]}$$

Correcting the formula for taxation, we get

$$\pi_{it} = \frac{p_t^*(R_t - r_{it})(1-\tau_t)}{1+R_t(1-\tau_t)}, \text{[18]} \tag{5}$$

where τ_t is the marginal income tax rate. Observe that financial asset i is a free good if $r_{it} = R_t$, and observe that the current period user costs of financial assets are independent of expectations. We shall use formula (5) to compute the user costs of financial assets.

It is interesting to observe that although (5) does not depend directly upon inflation rates, the nominal interest rates within the formula can be expected to respond to expected inflation rates. Furthermore, since the well-known user cost formula for non-monetary durables services does depend inversely upon the expected inflation rate, it follows that the user cost of monetary assets relative to durables increases as the expected inflation rate increases. Hence consumers will respond to increased inflationary expectations by substituting consumer durables for monetary assets.

3.3 Supernumerary Quantities

We have not assumed linear homogeneity of v, since that assumption would be unnecessarily strong for our purposes. However in this section we assume a form of marginal homogeneity that will be required for aggregation.

---

[17] It can be shown that π_{it} is the monetary asset analog of the well-known Jorgensonian user cost (rental price) of durable consumer goods. See Donovan (1978).

[18] User costs commonly are viewed as the prices of the services of durables rather than of their stocks. See Donovan (1978). In that interpretation, services are assumed to be proportional to stocks, and units of quantities and prices are assumed to have been chosen such that the proportionality constants are one. Hence user-cost evaluated stocks (stocks multiplied by corresponding user costs) are expenditures on the services of the stocks.

Observe that our model is not a disequilibrium stock adjustment model. Since we assume continuous optimal adjustment, consumers optimally select quantities consumed for their services.

The Consumer's Decision

We assume that v depends upon $\mathbf{m}_{t-1}$ as well as upon $\mathbf{m}_t$. This assumption introduces no complications into the earlier sections, since the consumer selected $\mathbf{m}_{t-1}$ during the prior planning horizon and hence $\mathbf{m}_{t-1}$ is given and fixed during the current horizon. We further assume that there exist constants, $\boldsymbol{\delta} = (\delta_1, \ldots, \delta_n)'$, and a linearly homogeneous function, u, such that $v(\mathbf{m}_t; \mathbf{m}_{t-1}) = u(\mathbf{y}_t)$, where $\mathbf{y}_t = (y_{1t}, \ldots, y_{nt})'$ and $y_{it} = m_{it} - \delta_i m_{i,t-1}$. In short, we assume the existence of proportional habit formation in current (but not future planned) consumption.[19] In the language of the habit formation literature, $\mathbf{y}_t$ is supernumerary consumption of monetary assets and $\delta_i m_{i,t-1}$ is the quantity of monetary asset i consumed out of habit (independently of current interest rates or income) during period t.

From (1), (3), (4), and (5), we see that the consumer's intertemporal decision problem can be rewritten as to choose $(\mathbf{y}_t, \mathbf{m}_{t+1}, \ldots, \mathbf{m}_{t+T}; \mathbf{x}_t, \ldots, \mathbf{x}_{t+T}; A_{t+T}) \geq \mathbf{0}$ to

$$\max U_t(u(\mathbf{y}_t), v_{t+1}(\mathbf{m}_{t+1}), \ldots, v_{t+T}(\mathbf{m}_{t+T}); \quad (6)$$
$$V(\mathbf{x}_t), V_{t+1}(\mathbf{x}_{t+1}), \ldots, V_{t+T}(\mathbf{x}_{t+T}); A_{t+T})$$

subject to the single wealth constraint

$$\sum_{s=t}^{t+T} (\mathbf{p}'_s/\rho_s) \mathbf{x}_s + \sum_{i=1}^{n} \pi_{it} y_{it} + \sum_{s=t+1}^{t+T} \sum_{i=1}^{n} \pi_i^s m_{is}$$
$$+ \sum_{i=1}^{n} \frac{p_{t+T}^*(1+r_{i,t+T})}{\rho_{t+T+1}} m_{i,t+T} + \frac{p_{t+T}^*}{\rho_{t+T}} A_{t+T}$$
$$= \sum_{s=t}^{t+T} (w_s/p_s) L_s + \sum_{i=1}^{n} [(1+r_{i,t-1})p_{t-1}^* - \delta_i \pi_{it}] m_{i,t-1}$$
$$+ (1+R_{t-1}) A_{t-1} p_{t-1}^*. \quad (7)$$

We now have established the model and assumption structure needed to apply aggregation theory to monetary aggregation. If we must use aggregates, a case can be made for accepting whatever assumptions are required to render economic aggregates meaningful. If we cannot accept the assumptions, we have no economic aggregates at all. As Samuelson and Swamy (1974, p. 592) conclude: 'One must not expect to be able to make the naive measurements that untutored common sense always longs for; we must accept the sad facts of life, and be grateful for the more complicated procedures economic theory devises.'

---

[19] The theoretical implications of habit formation have been considered by Pollak (1976).

3.4 Conditional Current Period Allocation

Our assumptions on the homogeneous blockwise weakly separable structure of the intertemporal utility function, (6), are sufficient for consistent two-stage budgeting. Hence by Green's (1964) Theorem 4 it follows that the consumer can maximize utility, (6), subject to the wealth constraint, (7), in two stages. In the first stage, the consumer selects aggregate monetary asset expenditure (supernumerary expenditure for the current period), aggregate consumer goods expenditure for each period within his planning horizon, and his terminal bond holdings, A_{t+T}.[20] In the second stage, he allocates current aggregate monetary asset expenditure and current aggregate consumer goods expenditure over individual current period monetary assets and consumer goods.

The second-stage allocation decision over individual current period supernumerary monetary assets is to select $\mathbf{y}_t$ to

$$\max u(\mathbf{y}_t) \qquad (8)$$

subject to

$$\boldsymbol{\pi}_t^{*'} \mathbf{y}_t = M_t^*, \qquad (9)$$

where $\pi_{it}^* = \pi_{it}/p_t^*$ is the real current period user cost of monetary asset i, $\boldsymbol{\pi}_t^* = (\pi_{1t}^*, \ldots, \pi_{nt}^*)'$, and M_t^* is the real value of aggregate supernumerary monetary asset holdings allocated to the current period in the consumer's first-stage decision. Observe that $\pi_{it}^* = (R_t - r_{it})(1 - \tau_t)/[1 + R_t(1 - \tau_t)]$ independently of p_t^*.[21]

We model the conditional current period monetary asset allocation decision, (9), in sections 4 through 9 of this paper, and we explore its implications for aggregation.[22]

---

[20] The chosen bond holdings are to be carried forward to the start of his next planning horizon.

[21] The choice between the real values, π_{it}^* and M_t^*, and the corresponding nominal values, π_{it} and M_t, is arbitrary, since p_t^* can be canceled out of each side of the budget constraint in the nominal case. This observation is just a restatement of the well-known homogeneity of demand.

We further could multiply the budget constraint through by $[1 + R_t(1 - \tau_t)]/(1 - \tau_t)$ in order to use $R_t - r_{it}$ as prices. The simplified formulation then would correspond with that of Klein (1974) and Offenbacher (1979).

[22] We treat M_t^* as exogenous, although M_t^* actually may be endogenous. Although nearly all of the demand systems literature estimates such conditional current period demand, we nevertheless should recognize the possibility of simultaneous bias in the estimates.

4 Preference Structure over Financial Assets

4.1 Blocking of the Utility Function

Suppose that $\mathbf{y}_t$ contains only total transaction balances and passbook savings deposits at three institution types, and we seek to aggregate passbook savings deposits over institution types and to nest that aggregate within an aggregate of all of the components of $\mathbf{y}_t$. We partition the vector, $\mathbf{y}_t$, such that $\mathbf{y}_t = (y_{1t}, \mathbf{y}'_{2t})'$, where y_{1t} is per capita real supernumerary transaction balances and $\mathbf{y}_{2t}$ is a vector of per capita real supernumerary passbook account deposits. We correspondingly partition $\boldsymbol{\pi}^*_t$ and $\boldsymbol{\delta}$ such that $\boldsymbol{\pi}^*_t = (\pi^*_{1t}, \boldsymbol{\pi}^{*'}_{2t})'$ and $\boldsymbol{\delta} = (\delta_1, \boldsymbol{\delta}'_2)'$.

We assume that the utility function, $u(\mathbf{y}_t)$, can be written in the blockwise weakly separable form

$$u(\mathbf{y}_t) = \mu(y_{1t}, u_2(\mathbf{y}_{2t})), \qquad (10)$$

with the function u_2 being linearly homogeneous. As discussed below, these conditions are both necessary and sufficient for the existence of the economic aggregates we seek.[23]

Back substituting (7) into (6), observe the way in which we have nested weakly separable blocks within weakly separable blocks. We have established a fully nested utility tree. As a result we can acquire a rational multi-stage budgeting procedure, in which the structured utility function itself defines the relevant theoretical quantity index at each stage, and duality theory defines the corresponding functional price index.[24]

In the next section we elaborate on the multi-stage budgeting properties of decision (6) and the implications for quantity and price aggregation.

4.2 Multi-stage Budgeting

Our assumptions on the properties of u are sufficient for a two-stage solution of the decision problem (9).[25] We define that two-stage decision in this section.

---

[23]This conclusion, based upon Green's (1964) Theorem 4, assumes that $\mathbf{y}_t$ is held exclusively by consumers. For firms, the analogous conditions would be applied to the production functions.

[24]Other financial assets (repurchase agreements, money market mutual funds, Treasury bills, commercial paper, etc.) could be included in the analysis by increasing the dimension of $\mathbf{y}_t$, partitioning it into more than two subsectors, and blocking u into multiple blocks accordingly.

[25]Recall that decision (9) itself was defined as the second stage of a two-stage decision. Hence we now are acquiring multi-stage budgeting rather than just two-stage budgeting. Our separability conditions are also sufficient for modeling structural change through the use of the household production function approach. That approach introduces production

Let $\Pi_{2t}^* = \Pi_2(\pi_{2t}^*)$ be a function of the user costs π_{2t}^*. The first stage of the two-stage decision is to select y_{1t} and Y_{2t} to solve

$$\max_{(y_{1t}, Y_{2t})} u(y_{1t}, Y_{2t}),$$

subject to

$$\pi_{1t}^* y_{1t} + \Pi_{2t}^* Y_{2t} = M_t^*. \tag{11}$$

From the solution to problem (11), the consumer determines aggregate supernumerary consumption of real passbook account services, $\Pi_{2t}^* Y_{2t}$.

In the second stage, the consumer allocates $\Pi_{2t}^* Y_{2t}$ over consumption of the services of passbook accounts at individual institution types. He does so by solving the decision problem:

$$\max_{\mathbf{y}_{2t}} u_2(\mathbf{y}_{2t}),$$

subject to

$$\pi_{2t}^{*'} \mathbf{y}_{2t} = \Pi_{2t}^* Y_{2t}. \tag{12}$$

It follows from Green's (1964) Theorem 4 that there exists some function, Π_2, such that the solution for $\mathbf{y}_t$ to problem (9) is the same as the solution for $\mathbf{y}_t$ acquired from the two-stage decision, (11) and (12), for any theoretically admissible values of M_t^* and π_t^*. It furthermore can be shown that if we use that function, Π_2, in (11), then $Y_{2t} = u_2(\mathbf{y}_{2t})$ at the solution values for Y_{2t} and $\mathbf{y}_{2t}$ to the two-stage decision. We shall say that $Y_{2t} = u_2(\mathbf{y}_{2t})$ is the economic (or functional) quantity aggregate (or index) corresponding (or dual) to the economic (or functional) user cost aggregate (or index), $\Pi_{2t}^* = \Pi_2(\pi_{2t}^*)$. We shall call u_2 the quantity aggregator function, and we shall call Π_2 the user-cost (or price) aggregator function.

In general, the quantity aggregator function is the corresponding (category) utility function. We show in the appendix that the corresponding price (user cost) index is equal to expenditure, $\Pi_{2t}^* Y_{2t}$, divided by the (category) indirect utility function (induced by the direct utility function, u_2).

This two-stage decision process is two-stage budgeting, and can be extended to n-stage budgeting simply by nesting weakly separable blocks within weakly separable blocks, etc., in the analogous manner. The result that follows from such nesting is purely mathematical and need not be related to actual multistage decision processes. We need only observe that the consumer acts 'as if' he were making his decision in stages, if his preferences are nested.

---

functions which model the production of monetary services from monetary asset portfolios. See Barnett (1977b).

The price index, Π_{2t}^*, and the quantity index, Y_{2t}, are economic price and quantity indices. As can be seen from problem (11), those indices have all of the properties of quantities and prices of actual goods (whether or not aggregates).[26]

5 Recursive Estimation Approach

The consumer is viewed as making his budgeting decisions from the top of the tree down, as he decentralizes his budgeting to lower levels of aggregation; but we can estimate the entire implied model recursively from the bottom up. We begin at the bottom of the tree and estimate the most disaggregated demand decisions. We compute the implied price (user cost) and quantity indices, based upon the utility functions we have estimated, and we then move up to estimate the next level using the just-computed price aggregates as instrumental variables. This approach to recursive estimation of utility trees has been developed by Barnett (1977a), Fuss (1977), and Anderson (1979). Our data consists of quarterly average values from the first quarter of 1970 to the first quarter of 1978. The data sources are described in Barnett (1981b, Chapter 7).

Recall that the current period monetary asset allocation problem, (9), is defined conditionally upon the consumer price index, p_t^*, which is dual to (and therefore derivable from) the consumer goods current period utility function, V. Hence to apply this instrumental variables approach most fully, we should estimate the function, V, defined over the consumer goods sector, prior to estimating u, defined over the monetary asset sector. But aside from p_t^*, we seek no other information from the consumption sector. Hence the cost of strict adherence to the recursive instrumental variables approach is excessive in the case of computation of p_t^*.

As a result, we use a statistical index rather than a functional index for p_t^*. Statistical price indices can depend upon quantities as well as prices, but cannot depend upon unknown parameters.[27] We assume that $V(\mathbf{x}_t) = (\mathbf{x}_t' \mathbf{B} \mathbf{x}_t)^{1/2}$ locally for some square matrix, $\mathbf{B}$, of unknown parameters. That specification can provide a quadratic approximation to any aggregator function. Diewert (1976) has shown that if a representative consumer exists, then the Fisher Ideal statistical price index (geometric mean of the Laspeyres and Paasche indices) is always equal to the true value of the functional index, p_t^*,

---

[26] In particular, observe that the consumer acts as if actual aggregate goods existed. Also observe that quantity indices depend exclusively upon quantities, and that price indices depend exclusively upon prices. Furthermore, the budget constraint of problem (12) shows that the product of a dual price index and its corresponding quantity index always equals actual expenditure on the goods within the aggregate.

[27] Statistical indices are introduced more rigorously in section 10.

regardless of the values of the parameters in the matrix, **B**. We shall use the Fisher Ideal price index for p_t^*.[28]

Having computed p_t^*, we begin our empirical ascent up the utility tree. Recalling the form of equation (10), we begin by estimating u_2. Then $u_2(\mathbf{y}_{2t})$ becomes the economic quantity index used with y_{1t} in the next (higher) stage. We compute the implied price index dual to u_2 and estimate the demand system generated by μ. The procedure could be carried to any level of aggregation, but will be terminated at μ.

6 Passbook Savings

6.1 C.E.S. Specification

In the current subsection we present our specification for passbook savings conditional demand, which is the solution to decision (12). Since $\mathbf{m}_{2t}$ is a vector, we implicitly have segmented passbook deposits into categories. We let $\mathbf{m}_{2t} = (m_{21t}, m_{22t}, m_{23t})'$, where m_{21t} = real per capita holdings of commercial bank passbook accounts, m_{22t} = real per capita holdings of savings and loan passbook accounts, and m_{23t} = real per capita holding of mutual savings bank passbook accounts.[29] We then write tth period supernumerary real per capita holdings in passbook account category i as $y_{2it} = m_{2it} - \delta_{2i} m_{2i,t-1}$.

To clarify our notation, we replace the subscript 2 with p (for passbook). Then $u_p(\mathbf{y}_{pt}) = u_2(\mathbf{y}_{2t})$, etc. The C.E.S. specification for u_p is

$$u_p(y_{pt}) = \left[\sum_{i=1}^{3} \alpha_i y_{pit}^\beta\right]^{1/\beta}$$

$$= \left[\sum_{i=1}^{3} \alpha_i (m_{pit} - \delta_{pi} m_{pi,t-1})^\beta\right]^{1/\beta},$$

where $\boldsymbol{\alpha} = (\alpha_1, \alpha_2, \alpha_3)'$ and β are parameters satisfying $\beta < 1$ and $\boldsymbol{\alpha} \geq \mathbf{0}$.[30] In decision (12) we let $E_{pt}^* = \Pi_{2t}^* Y_{2t}$, which is total user-cost-evaluated ex-

---

[28] In computing the Fisher Ideal index, we use the Bureau of Labor Statistics' CPI as the Laspeyres index and the Commerce Department's Implicit Price Deflator as the Paasche Index. Some approximation error exists in the use of the CPI as the Laspeyres index, although the error is small. See Triplett (1976).

[29] Lack of appropriate data prevented us from using credit union passbook deposits.

[30] While more flexible utility functions exist than the C.E.S., they did not appear to be appropriate to our objectives. Our approach estimates a demand system that is integrable to a marginally homothetic utility function and has known closed form representations both for the demand system and for the utility function. The model also is a generalization of the simple sum utility function which provides the conventional quantity indices. The C.E.S. satisfies all of those objectives and is a very substantial generalization of the simple sum

penditure allocated to passbook account services, determined from the prior allocation stage (one level higher in the utility tree).

The solution to (12) is the demand system

$$m_{pit} = \delta_{pi} m_{pi,t-1} + \frac{\bar{\alpha}_i \pi_{pit}^{*\bar{\beta}}}{\pi_{pit}^* \sum_k \bar{\alpha}_k \pi_{pkt}^{*\bar{\beta}}} \left(E_{pt}^* - \sum_k \pi_{pkt}^* \delta_{pk} m_{pk,t-1} \right), \quad (13)$$

where

$$\bar{\alpha}_i = \alpha_i^{1/(1-\beta)} \quad \text{and} \quad \bar{\beta} = \beta/(\beta-1),$$

with

$$\bar{\boldsymbol{\alpha}} = (\bar{\alpha}_1, \bar{\alpha}_2, \bar{\alpha}_3)' > \mathbf{0} \quad \text{and} \quad \bar{\beta} < 1.$$

The vector of parameters $\bar{\boldsymbol{\alpha}}$ is not jointly identified, since the demand system is homogeneous of degree zero in $\bar{\boldsymbol{\alpha}}$. Hence we impose the identifying restriction $\sum_i \bar{\alpha}_i = 1$.[31]

We seek to estimate (13) in a form that will impose all theoretical restrictions. We do so by transforming the parameters into other parameters that are free of inequality restrictions. We then impose our restrictions by substitution. We can acquire the maximum likelihood estimates (M.L.E.) of the transformed parameters and then acquire the unique M.L.E.'s of the original restricted parameters by using the invariance property of the M.L.E. In particular, we substitute the transformation $\bar{\alpha}_j = \gamma_j^2$ ($j = 1, 2, 3$) to impose $\bar{\alpha}_j \geq 0$, and we estimate the unrestricted parameters $\gamma = (\gamma_1, \gamma_2, \gamma_3)'$. Since $\bar{\beta} < 1$ defines an open set, that restriction (or any other such strict inequality restriction) cannot be imposed. We replace $\bar{\beta} < 1$ with the approximation $\bar{\beta} \leq 0.9$. We then substitute the transformation $\bar{\beta} = 1.9 - \cosh \theta$ into (13) and estimate the unrestricted parameter θ.

Since $\mathbf{y}_{pt} > \mathbf{0}$, it follows that for any i, we must have $m_{pit} > \delta_{pi} m_{pi,t-1}$ for all t. Since passbook deposits never changed by more than 20% between quarters in our data, a sufficient condition for the inequality would be $\delta_{pi} \leq 0.8$ for all $i = 1, 2, 3$. We shall impose that sufficient condition. In addition, we require that $\boldsymbol{\delta}_p \geq \mathbf{0}$.[32] We jointly impose all of these restrictions on $\boldsymbol{\delta}_p$

---

function. Since the simple sum aggregate is widely used, it could be impractical (at this stage of research) to consider a quantity index more general than the C.E.S. Furthermore, the use of a common elasticity of substitution appears reasonable with our passbook savings data. At higher levels of aggregation, a more flexible functional form would be required.

[31] We do so by estimating (13) with the normalization $\bar{\alpha}_3 = 1$, and then renormalizing the resulting estimates to get $\sum_i \bar{\alpha}_i = 1$. The choice of normalization is arbitrary; we can renormalize at will.

[32] Although theory does not require this restriction, the logic of the multi-stage budgeting process becomes more difficult to interpret when $\boldsymbol{\delta}_p$ contains negative elements. In addition, our prior views on $\boldsymbol{\delta}_p$ impute low probability to negative elements of $\boldsymbol{\delta}_p$, and

by substituting the transformations $\delta_{pit} = 0.4(1 + \sin\phi_i)$ for $i = 1, 2, 3$, and estimating the unrestricted vector $\phi = (\phi_1, \phi_2, \phi_3)'$.

Multiplying (13) by π^*_{pit}/E^*_{pt} to acquire desired expenditure shares, $w^*_{pit} = \pi^*_{pit}m_{pit}/E^*_{pt}$, and making all of the parameter substitutions described above, we acquire our model for the consumer's desired expenditure shares. Since adjustment costs may exist, we permit actual expenditure shares, w_{pit}, to differ from desired expenditure shares, w^*_{pit}, in accordance with the partial adjustment scheme: $w_{pit} = \lambda w^*_{pit} + (1 - \lambda)w_{pi,t-1}$, where $0 \leq \lambda \leq 1$. We use the same adjustment rate, λ, for each institution type to assure that the budget constraint will be satisfied in actual expenditure shares as well as in desired budget shares. In addition, equality of adjustment rates appears plausible for passbook accounts at different institution types. Performing all of these transformations on (13), we have our passbook deposits allocation model. We take x_{pit}, $i = 1, 2, 3$, as endogenous and E^*_{pt} and π^*_{pit}, $i = 1, 2, 3$, as exogenous. We adopt a conventional additive error structure without serial correlation.[33]

6.2 Theoretical Index Number Properties

We now consider the properties of the functional price and quantity index numbers for passbook savings, when aggregation over institution types is to be consistent with the C.E.S. consumer preferences specified in the previous section.

The functional quantity index is the utility level itself. Normalizing the index to equal 1.0 at the first observation, we acquire the normalized functional quantity index $Q_p(\mathbf{y}_{pt}) = u_p(\mathbf{y}_{pt})/u_p(\mathbf{y}_{p1})$.[34] The nominal functional price index that is dual to our C.E.S. specification of u_p is $\pi_p(\boldsymbol{\pi}_{pt}) = (\sum_{i=1}^{3} \bar{\alpha}_i \pi_{pit}^{\bar{\beta}})^{1/\bar{\beta}}$, where $(\bar{\boldsymbol{\alpha}}, \bar{\beta})$ are as defined in the previous section. The corresponding normalized nominal user-cost price index is $P_p(\boldsymbol{\pi}_{pt}) = \Pi_p(\boldsymbol{\pi}_{pt})/\Pi_p(\boldsymbol{\pi}_{p1})$.[35]

Barnett (1977a) has found that negative estimates of δ_p tend to have low precision and hence to be statistically indistinguishable from zero at conventional levels of significance.

[33] Serially correlated disturbances did not appear to be a potential problem, since our specification contains lagged values both of quantity demanded (through habit formation) and of expenditure shares (through partial adjustment).

[34] A functional quantity index must be linearly homogeneous in its arguments. While u_p is linearly homogeneous in $\mathbf{y}_{pt}$, u_p is not homogeneous in $\mathbf{m}_{pt}$ unless $\delta_{pi} = 0$ for all i. Hence u_p cannot strictly be viewed as an aggregator function for $\mathbf{m}_{pt}$ when some δ_{pi} is nonzero, although $u_p(\mathbf{y}_{pt})$ is always the functional quantity aggregate for the supernumerary quantities, $\mathbf{y}_{pt}$.

[35] The corresponding real price indices are $\Pi_p(\boldsymbol{\pi}^*_{pt})$ and $P_p(\boldsymbol{\pi}^*_{pt})$. If we were to require an index of *total* (rather than per capita) supernumerary nominal balances, we could compute $Q_p(\mathbf{y}_{pt})$ using total passbook deposit data in place of the per capita real balances, $\mathbf{m}_{pt}$, in

We seek to consider the limiting case in which $\alpha_1 = \alpha_2 = \alpha_3$ and $\beta = 1$. In that case the functional quantity index equals the simple sum of its components. Since the elasticity of substitution, σ, equals $1/(1-\beta)$, we see that $\sigma \to \infty$ as $\beta \to 1$. Hence the special case we are considering is that of three 'goods' (or, more appropriately, services) that are perfect substitutes in equal proportions, i.e. indistinguishable goods. When $\beta = 1$ (but the α_i's are not necessarily equal), the functional quantity index acquires the form of a Laspeyres-type (fixed weight linear) quantity index. The functional price index that is dual to the Laspeyres quantity index is the Leontief price index, $\Pi_p(\boldsymbol{\pi}_{pt}) = \min\{\pi_{pit}/\alpha_i : i = 1, 2, 3\}$.[36] Hence if the monetary quantity index is the usual simple sum index (so that $\alpha_1 = \alpha_2 = \alpha_3$), then the corresponding price index is just the minimum user cost.

6.3 Results with Passbook Savings

The parameter estimates for eq. (13) using passbook data and joint maximum likelihood (FIML) estimation are displayed in Table 1 with standard errors in parentheses and with γ_3 normalized to equal one.[37] The estimates of ϕ_1 and (ϕ_2, ϕ_3) imply boundary solutions for δ_{p1} and $(\delta_{p2}, \delta_{p3})$ at their lower and upper bounds, respectively. Transforming back to the original parameters of $u_p(\mathbf{y}_{pt})$, we find that the implied joint maximum likelihood estimates are $\hat{\beta} = 0.62$ and $\boldsymbol{\alpha} = (0.55, 0.26, 0.20)'$, where $\boldsymbol{\alpha}$ has been renormalized such that $\sum_{i=1}^{3} \alpha_i = 1$.

Precisions (t-ratios) are generally high. The implied elasticity of substitution, σ, equals 2.66, which is very high.[38] We can see just how high that value is by observing that σ is monotonically increasing in β, and β must lie between $-\infty$ and 1. Clearly $\hat{\beta} = 0.62$ is very close to the upper bound of 1, at which the utility function (and hence the functional quantity index) is linear and demand functions become set valued correspondences.[39]

Thus we see that passbook accounts at different institution types are highly substitutable, and a simple linear quantity index may be a reasonable approximation to the theoretical quantity index. However the simple sum

---

the definition of $\mathbf{y}_{pt}$. The result would be identical to computing $Q_p(\mathbf{y}_{pt})$ with population and p_t^* fixed at index year levels, since those fixed index year levels would be cancelled out of the numerator and denominator of $Q_p(\mathbf{y}_{pt})$.

[36] See Samuelson and Swamy (1974, p. 574).

[37] The standard errors were computed from Theorem 4 of Barnett (1976). The data is described in Barnett's (1981b, Chapter 7).

[38] This elasticity is the short run elasticity of substitution, as is relevant to the aggregator function and hence to aggregation and index number theory. Regarding the long-run utility function, see Pollak (1976).

[39] Observe from $\hat{\lambda}$ that the estimated quarterly adjustment rate from desired to actual shares is about 21%.

index requires equal weights in the linear index, and $\hat{\alpha}_1$ differs substantially from $\hat{\alpha}_2$, which does approximately equal $\hat{\alpha}_3$.[40] The tail area of the asymptotic likelihood ratio test of equal α_i's is less than 0.00001. Since that tail area is well below 0.05, we reject the hypothesis of equal α_i's.[41]

TABLE 1
Parameter Estimates.[a]

θ_1	ϕ_1	ϕ_2	ϕ_3	γ_1	γ_2	λ
1.94	$-\pi/2$	$\pi/2$	$\pi/2$	3.83	1.43	0.206
(0.24)	(1.31)	(0.35)	(0.27)	(0.18)	(0.06)	(0.06)

[a] Standard errors in parentheses.

A functional quantity index measures the quantity of a properly aggregated economic 'good'. Since α_1 clearly exceeds α_2 or α_3, we see that commercial bank passbook accounts contribute more heavily to that meaningful economic 'good' than mutual savings bank or savings and loan passbook accounts. An explanation may lie in the fact that commercial bank passbook accounts possess all of the basic consumption characteristics of the other two types, but greater liquidity through the 'one-stop-banking' property made available during routine trips to the bank to deposit funds into checking accounts.[42] If funds were transferred from savings and loan passbook accounts to commercial bank passbook accounts, our functional quantity index would increase, evidently to reflect the economy's increased liquidity. The usual sum index would not change.[43]

---

[40] If $\alpha_1 = \alpha_2 = \alpha_3$ with $\beta = 1$, then $u(\mathbf{y}_{pt})$ is a linear function of the usual simple sum index, $\sum_{i=1}^{3} m_{pit}$. But with unequal α_i's, our economic quantity index is a linear function of $\sum_{i=1}^{3} \alpha_i m_{pit}$, not of the simple unweighted sum.

[41] To test the hypothesis of a simple sum aggregate, we should test the hypothesis that $\beta = 1$ jointly with the hypothesis of dual intensity parameters (α_i's). However the likelihood function is not uniquely defined when $\beta = 1$, since demand functions become set valued in that case. Hence a likelihood ratio test is not applicable. We could construct an approximate test by testing the hypothesis that $\beta = 0.999$, at which demand remains a point valued function.

[42] Aggregation theory does not attach a name (such as 'moneyness' or 'liquidity') to the functional quantity index. However our use of user costs does dictate that the quantity index is the quantity of services provided by the components of the aggregate. Hence it may not be unreasonable to deduce that commercial bank passbook accounts appear to provide greater 'monetary services' than passbook accounts at the other two institution types.

[43] We also observed that computed values of the normalized functional quantity index,

There appears to be information contained in the fact that δ_{p1} is at its lower bound, while δ_{p2} and δ_{p3} are large. Recall that $\delta_{pi}m_{pi,t-1}$ is a vector of quantities consumed out of habit (or for 'subsistence') regardless of the variations in user costs or in total consumption expenditure within the sample period. Evidently commercial bank passbook accounts contain actively managed primary balances, while mutual savings bank and savings and loan passbook accounts contain a greater percentage of less actively managed secondary balances and saved consumer reserve funds.[44]

7 Transaction Balances

7.1 Specification

We now progress to the next level of the utility tree in (10) to estimate μ. We again use a C.E.S. utility function.[45] We specify μ to be C.E.S. in two goods: real per capita supernumerary transactions balances, y_{1t}, and the economic real per capita supernumerary passbook savings aggregate, $u_{pt} = u_p(\mathbf{y}_{pt})$.[46] We introduce no additional habit formation at this level of aggregation (in

---

$Q_p(\mathbf{y}_{pt})$, and the normalized user-cost price index, $P_p(\boldsymbol{\pi}_{pt})$, tended to move in opposite directions, as would be expected from movement along a demand curve. This result is not surprising since Regulation Q cannot decrease the user cost of passbook account deposits to below the equilibrium price, although the regulation can raise the user cost to above the equilibrium level. Hence an excess supply but not an excess demand can exist in the passbook account market. We therefore can expect the data always to lie on the demand function, even when the market is out of equilibrium. In addition, governmental rate setting tends to minimize simultaneous bias in estimators that condition upon exogenous user costs.

[44] When integrability conditions are imposed, as we have done, it is common for some of them to be binding. Hence the existence of binding regularity conditions is not surprising. Nevertheless, it is also possible that the boundary solutions on the habit formation parameters may have resulted from the joint use of the habit formation dynamics and partial adjustment dynamics. Despite the fact that all of the model's parameters are identified, the data may not contain sufficient information to permit distinguishing adequately between the two sources of dynamic consumer behavior.

[45] At this level of aggregation, it no longer would be reasonable to assume that elasticities of substitution are constant between all monetary assets. But we now have only two 'goods' and hence only one elasticity of substitution. The flexibility of the C.E.S. specification therefore still remains satisfactory for our purposes. Furthermore a constant finite elasticity of substitution, even between all monetary assets, would be more reasonable than the uniformly infinite elasticities of substitution implied by the usual simple sum indices.

[46] Transaction balances are measured as the sum of M_1 plus NOW accounts (at all institution types) plus share drafts at credit unions plus demand deposits at mutual savings banks. Offenbacher's (1979) results suggest that currency and demand deposits do not satisfy the conditions for aggregation by summation. However separate treatment of those two components required imputation of separate own rates to each. In this paper we avoid such ambiguous and controversial imputations. Hence we condition upon summed transaction balances as an elementary good.

y_{1t} and the aggregate u_{pt}), since habit formation already is built into $u_p(\mathbf{y}_{pt})$ through the specification of $\mathbf{y}_{pt}$, and since we expect short-run Engel curves in y_{1t} to pass through the origin.[47]

We impute to m_{1t} the user cost price, (5), with the own rate set equal to zero. We impute to the supernumerary passbook aggregate, $u_p(\mathbf{y}_{pt})$, the dual user-cost functional price index, $\Pi_{pt} = \Pi_p(\boldsymbol{\pi}_{pt})$. We do not introduce adjustment dynamics at this level of aggregation. Since transaction balances turnover rates are high, we believe that adjustment to the desired transaction balances share in monetary asset consumption is rapid.[48]

The utility function is of the C.E.S. form

$$\mu(y_{1t}, u_{pt}) = \mu(m_{1t}, u_{pt}) = (\alpha_1 m_{1t}^\beta + \alpha_2 u_{pt}^\beta)^{1/\beta},$$

where $(\alpha_1, \alpha_2, \beta)$ are parameters satisfying $\beta < 1$ and $(\alpha_1, \alpha_2) > \mathbf{0}$.

The conditional decision problem at this level of aggregation is to choose (m_{1t}, u_{pt}) to

$$\max \mu(m_{1t}, u_{pt}) \qquad (14)$$

subject to

$$m_{1t}\pi_{1t}^* + u_{pt}\Pi_p(\boldsymbol{\pi}_{pt}^*) = E_t^*,$$

where E_t^* is user-cost-evaluated expenditure allocated to the services of real transaction balances and of real supernumerary passbook savings deposits during the current period.

We define the expenditure share of transaction balances in E_t^* to be $w_{1t} = m_{1t}\pi_{1t}^*/E_t^*$. The share of supernumerary passbook deposits then is $w_{pt} = 1 - w_{1t}$. After employing parameter transformations analogous to those in section 6.1, we find that the solution to (14) can be written in the form

$$w_{1t} = \frac{\gamma_1^2 \Pi_{1t}^{*(1.9 - \cosh\theta)}}{\gamma_2^2 \pi_{1t}^{*(1.9 - \cosh\theta)} + \gamma_2^2 \Pi_{pt}^{*(1.9 - \cosh\theta)}}, \qquad (15)$$

and

$$w_{pt} = 1 - w_{1t},$$

---

[47] Observe therefore that $y_{1t} = m_{1t}$ and that μ is homothetic in real per capita transaction balances and in aggregate real per capita supernumerary (not total) passbook savings deposits.

[48] Combining both stages of the decision over transaction balances and passbook savings deposits, we find that consumers are viewed as allocating expenditure over transaction balances and passbook savings deposits (either jointly or through the equivalent two-stage decision) by utility maximization (with habit formation in passbook savings preferences) to acquire desired consumption levels. The desired level of transaction balances then is purchased without lags. In addition the desired level of current total user-cost-evaluated expenditure on passbook savings deposits services is actually consumed, but its distribution over institution types differs from the desired allocation in accordance with the linear partial adjustment mechanism used in section 6.1.

Transaction Balances

where $\Pi^*_{pt} = \Pi_p(\boldsymbol{\pi}^*_{pt})$.

Let $\widehat{\Pi}^*_{pt}$ be the value of $\Pi_p(\boldsymbol{\pi}^*_{pt})$ with the parameters of Π_p replaced by their estimates acquired in section 6.3. We replace Π^*_{pt} with $\widehat{\Pi}^*_{pt}$, normalize γ_2 to equal 1.0, and estimate (15) with an additive disturbance term.[49]

Letting ε_t ($t = 1, \ldots, T$) be the additive error in equation (15), we introduce first-order autocorrelation by specifying that $(\varepsilon_2, \ldots, \varepsilon_T)$ is a sample from a stationary scalar autoregressive stochastic process satisfying the stochastic difference equation $\varepsilon_t = \rho \varepsilon_{t-1} + u_t$, where the sequence $\langle u_t : t = 2, \ldots, T \rangle$ consists of independently and identically distributed normal random variables with mean zero.[50] The parameter ρ is subject to the constraint $-1 \leq \rho \leq 1$. To impose that restriction, we let $\rho = \sin \psi$. We eliminate that equality by substitution and estimate the unconstrained parameter, ψ.[51]

7.2 Estimates

The resulting maximum likelihood estimates of (γ_1, θ, ψ) are presented in Table 2. Transforming back to the original parameters of u, we find that $\hat{\beta} = -2.53$, $\hat{\rho} = 0.96$, and $(\hat{\alpha}_1, \hat{\alpha}_2) = (0.77, 0.23)$, where (α_1, α_2) have been renormalized to sum to one.[52] The implied elasticity of substitution is $1/(1 - \hat{\beta}) = 0.28$. Substitutability between transaction balances and passbook savings deposits is far lower than between passbook accounts at different institutions types. The elasticity of substitution of 0.28 is too low and the precision of its estimator is too high to justify a linear approximation (requiring infinite elasticity of substitution) to μ.

---

[49] Fuss (1977) has considered the properties of such nested estimation procedures.

[50] The same value, ρ, is used in defining the error structure for each of the two demand equations derived from (14). That procedure follows from Berndt and Savin (1975) when no serial correlation of disturbances exists across equations.

[51] To estimate (15) with the additive autoregressive disturbance, ε_t, we use the following transformation. Let the right-hand side of (15) be written as $f(\boldsymbol{\pi}^*_{1t}, \Pi^*_{1t}; \gamma_1, \theta)$, so that

$$w_{1t} = \rho w_{1,t-1} - [f(\boldsymbol{\pi}^*_{1t}, \Pi^*_{pt}; \gamma_1, \theta) - \rho f(\boldsymbol{\pi}^*_{1,t-1}, \Pi^*_{p,t-1}; \gamma_1, \theta)].$$

If we add ε_t to the right-hand side of (15), then it follows that the disturbance to be added to the right-hand side of the transformed equation is $\varepsilon_t - \rho \varepsilon_{t-1} = u_t$. So we can estimate the transformed equation using maximum likelihood estimation with a conventional disturbance, u_t.

[52] Our estimate of the intensity parameter, α_1, is more than three times our estimate of α_2. Hence we might deduce that transaction balances, m_{1t}, contribute to our monetary asset economic quantity aggregate more heavily than our nested passbook deposits aggregate, u_{pt}. However one should be cautious about viewing the intensity parameters as simple weights in this case, since μ is a nonlinear function rather than a linear weighted average.

TABLE 2
Parameter estimates.[a]

θ	γ_1	ψ
0.597	1.20	1.29
(0.22)	(0.17)	(0.17)

[a] Standard errors in parentheses.

7.3 Functional Index Numbers

In the present section, our highest level aggregator function is μ. Hence our highest level economic quantity aggregate is $u_t = \mu(m_{1t}, u_p(\mathbf{y}_{pt}))$. The nominal dual user cost aggregate is

$$\Pi(\pi_{1t}, \Pi_{pt}) = (\bar{\alpha}_1 \pi_{1t}^{\bar{\beta}} + \bar{\alpha}_2 \Pi_{pt}^{\bar{\beta}})^{1/\bar{\beta}},$$

where

$$\bar{\alpha}_i = \alpha_i^{1/(1-\beta)} \quad \text{and} \quad \bar{\beta} = \beta/(\beta - 1).$$

In summary, we have acquired the following nested pair of quantity and nominal dual user cost indices, with all indices normalized to equal 1.0 in the first quarter. For passbook accounts we have the maximum likelihood estimate of the normalized functional quantity index, $Q_p(\mathbf{y}_{pt})$, and its nominal dual user cost index, $P_p(\boldsymbol{\pi}_{pt})$. For our higher level ($M_2$-type) monetary asset aggregate we have the maximum likelihood estimate of the normalized functional quantity index,

$$Q(m_{1t}, \mathbf{y}_{pt}) = \frac{\mu(m_{1t}, u_p(\mathbf{y}_{pt}))}{\mu(m_{11}, u_p(\mathbf{y}_{p1}))},$$

and its nominal dual user cost index,

$$P(\pi_{1t}, \Pi_{pt}) = \frac{\Pi(\pi_{1t}, \Pi_p(\boldsymbol{\pi}_{pt}))}{\Pi(\pi_{11}, \Pi_p(\boldsymbol{\pi}_{p1}))}.$$

8 Implications of Estimates

While passbook accounts at different institutions are excellent substitutes, we find no evidence to support equal weighting of the accounts across institutions. Although a simple linear (Laspeyres-type) index of passbook deposits may be useful, the conventional unweighted sum index should be understood to be based upon accounting practice rather than upon any economically meaningful index number construct. If one sought no more than total dollar deposits in passbook accounts in all institution types, the use of simple summation would be dictated tautologically by an accounting identity.

The simple sum index in economics corresponds to the degenerate limiting special case of preferences having linear indifference curves at 45 degree angles, and the corresponding dual price index is the poorly behaved Leontief fixed coefficients index. In our case, consumers would use passbook accounts in only one institution type, unless all institutions paid the exact same interest rate. If all institutions did pay the exact same interest rate, then the budget constraint would lie on top of a linear indifference curve, and consumers would not care how they allocated funds over institution types. No unique solution would exist. But in fact commercial banks pay lower interest rates than the other two institution types, yet acquire stable non-zero deposits. Since passbook accounts across institution types do provide very similar services, we should expect to find even poorer support for the simple sum index at higher levels of aggregation within the money market, and that conclusion generally is supported by our results with transaction balances at the next aggregation level.

When we pass to a higher level of aggregation to incorporate transaction balances into our monetary aggregate, the possibility of a useful linear approximation, even with unequal coefficients, disappears. Transaction balances and passbook savings are not perfect substitutes and possess an elasticity of substitution of only 0.28. The usual simple sum monetary quantity index is rejected. The current M_2 aggregate provides useful accounting information on commercial bank liability structure, but is badly designed as an economic monetary quantity index. The use of simple sum monetary quantity aggregates as economic indices of the quantity of monetary services should be discontinued.

9 Empirical Selection of Blocking

9.1 Conditions on Elasticities of Substitution

In section 4.1, we selected our homothetic weakly separable blocking of the current period conditional utility function, u, on a priori grounds. That blocking then dictated the components of each subindex and index at all levels of aggregation within our hierarchy of aggregates. Conditionally upon that blocking, we have determined in sections 6, 7, and 8 that the form of the aggregator function over the components of each index precludes use of aggregation by simple summation. In the current section we briefly consider the possibility of formally testing for the blocking itself, rather than solely for the form of the preblocked utility (aggregator) function.

We begin with the current period monetary asset utility function, $u(\mathbf{y}_t)$, for the vector of real supernumerary per capita holdings, $\mathbf{y}_t$, of all monetary assets in the economy. We seek a partitioning, $\mathbf{y}_t = (\mathbf{y}'_{1t}, \ldots, \mathbf{y}'_{Mt})'$, such that u can be written in the blockwise weakly separable form

$$u(\mathbf{y}_t) = \mu(u_1(\mathbf{y}_{1t}), u_2(\mathbf{y}_{2t}), \ldots, u_M(\mathbf{y}_{Mt})), \tag{16}$$

with u_k linearly homogeneous for all $k = 1, \ldots, M$. The existence of such a homogeneous weakly separable blocking is necessary and sufficient for the existence of consistent quantity aggregation (to the functional quantity aggregates, $u_1(\mathbf{y}_{1t}), u_2(\mathbf{y}_{2t}), \ldots, u_M(\mathbf{y}_{Mt})$.[53] Clearly our earlier a priori blocking, (10), was a special case of (16) with one dimensional $\mathbf{y}_{1t}$ and with $M = 2$.

Necessary and sufficient conditions for that homogeneous weakly separable blocking are that the elasticity of substitution between any component of $\mathbf{y}_{kt}$ (for fixed $k = 1, \ldots, M$) and any (supernumerary) monetary asset *not in* $\mathbf{y}_{kt}$ be independent of the element of $\mathbf{y}_{kt}$ selected. We shall refer to those conditions on elasticities of substitution as the *Aggregation Conditions*. Systematic testing for those conditions with monetary assets has not yet been undertaken and is a promising area for future research.[54] However Barnett's (1981b) Chapter 7 contains elasticity of substitution estimates (without formal separability hypothesis tests) between many categories of monetary assets. The conclusions suggested (at unknown statistical significance levels) by comparisons of those elasticity of substitution estimates follow.

9.2 Empirical Evidence

Referring to Barnett's (1981b) Chapter 7, we observe the following. Over the past decade substitutability among passbook accounts at the three institution types (commercial banks, S&Ls, and MSBs) has risen substantially and to high level ($\hat{\sigma} = 2.66$ jointly). In addition substitutability is high between small time deposits at S&Ls and MSBs ($\hat{\sigma} = 12.82$). However substitutability is low between time deposits at commercial banks and at either of the two thrift institutions.[55] In general, substitutability within the many diverse

---

[53] The conditions could be substantially weakened by dropping the homogeneity condition, if we permit Fisher's factor reversal test to be violated.

[54] A testing approach potentially applicable to that problem is contained in Denny and Fuss (1977).

[55] Those individuals who purchase small time deposits at commercial banks perceive them to possess properties that are, in some ways, significantly different from those of small time deposits at S&Ls or MSBs. This result is not surprising since those individuals who purchase small time deposits at commercial banks generally are locked into the lower

groups of financial assets considered in Barnett (1981b) has tended to rise over the past decade. However, with the exception of the two cases just described, substitutability between financial assets has remained *very* low.[56]

We now consider the implications of those elasticity of substitution estimates for the selection of the components of aggregates. From Barnett (1981b), we find that the elasticities of substitution between passbook accounts at different institution types are far higher than the elasticities of substitution between passbook accounts at any one of those institution types and any other financial asset. Hence any aggregate (such as the old M-2 index) which contained passbook accounts at some but not at all institution types would violate the Aggregation Conditions. Similarly we find that any aggregate containing small time deposits at S&Ls must also contain small time deposits at MSBs. In short, the empirical evidence in Barnett (1981b) tends to support aggregation of like-assets over institution types, as proposed in Barnett, Beck, Ettin, Kalchbrenner, Lindsey, Porter, Simpson, and Tinsley (1979).

In sections 6, 7, and 8, we considered the separate question of whether aggregation over *given* components can be accomplished by simple summation. Aggregation by summation is a special case of linear aggregation. The necessary and sufficient conditions on elasticities of substitution for linear aggregation are infinite elasticities of substitution between all components *within the aggregate*. We call those conditions the *Linearity Conditions*. The frequently very low elasticities of substitution found in Barnett (1981b) further strengthen our rejection of the Linearity Conditions in sections 6, 7, and 8.

It should, however, again be observed that our inferences drawn from Barnett (1981b), without formal statistical testing, are highly tentative. Our conclusions in this section should be viewed as suggestive of areas for future research through systematic hypothesis testing with models specifically designed for that purpose.

---

yields paid by the commercial banks, as a result of the penalty structure imposed on early redemption. In fact it would be difficult to understand why anyone would hold commercial bank small time deposits if he considered them to be close substitutes for small time deposits at thrift institutions.

[56] Earlier published studies of substitutability between monetary assets have all indicated very low substitutability between monetary assets. Hence our results are in general agreement with the earlier findings, and our finding of current high substitutability between passbook accounts at the three institution types and between small time deposits at thrift institutions are thereby strengthened by contrast.

10 Statistical Index Numbers

10.1 Definition

In the prior sections, we have been using aggregation theory. In aggregation theory, aggregator functions are utility functions for consumers and production functions for firms. Aggregator functions provide the foundations of aggregation theory, and hence their existence and properties are important in understanding aggregation. By estimating aggregator functions in the prior sections, we have acquired information regarding the components of consistent aggregates, and we have determined that aggregator functions defined over financial assets cannot be adequately approximated by simple summation. Aggregation theory itself then would leave us with the alternative of using the actual nonlinear aggregator function in aggregating over monetary assets.

However, as we have seen, functional quantity aggregators depend upon the quantities of the component goods and upon *unknown* parameters. Estimates of the unknown parameters depend upon the specified model, the data, and the estimator. Hence aggregator functions, although important in theory and in hypothesis testing, are not generally useful in constructing index numbers which are publishable as data by governmental agencies. For precisely that purpose, the theory of statistical index numbers has been developed. We introduce and then use that highly practical theory in this section.

A functional quantity aggregator depends only upon component quantities and unknown parameters. Functional quantity aggregators cannot depend upon prices, and the definition of a functional quantity aggregator does not depend upon maximizing behavior by economic agents. On the other hand, statistical index numbers do *not* depend upon any unknown parameters, but quantity index numbers can depend upon component prices as well as upon component quantities, and the definition of *exact* statistical index numbers does depend upon the maximizing behavior of economic agents. In brief, the introduction of prices (and maximizing behavior in the exact case) into index number theory permits us to dispense with the unknown parameters that exist in the aggregator functions. The merits of the resulting index numbers are not dependent upon any specialized properties of the aggregator function (such as linearity of the function).

A quantity index between periods $t-1$ and t, $Q(\boldsymbol{\pi}_{t-1}, \boldsymbol{\pi}_t; \mathbf{m}_{t-1}, \mathbf{m}_t)$, is a function of the vectors of prices (user costs) in periods $t-1$ and t, $\boldsymbol{\pi}_{t-1} > \mathbf{0}$ and $\boldsymbol{\pi}_t > \mathbf{0}$, and the corresponding quantity vectors, $\mathbf{m}_{t-1} > \mathbf{0}$ and $\mathbf{m}_t > \mathbf{0}$.[57]

---

[57] Given a quantity index, the corresponding price index can be computed from Fisher's weak factor reversal test. See Diewert (1976, p. 115).

Diewert defines such an index to be exact for a given aggregator function, f, if $Q(\pi_{t-1}, \pi_t; \mathbf{m}_{t-1}, \mathbf{m}_t) = f(\mathbf{m}_t)/f(\mathbf{m}_{t-1})$ whenever $\mathbf{m}_t > \mathbf{0}$ is the value of $\mathbf{m} > \mathbf{0}$ which maximizes $f(\mathbf{m})$ subject to $\pi'_t \mathbf{m} \leq \pi'_t \mathbf{m}_t$. In other words, an index number is exact if it exactly equals the aggregator function whenever the data is consistent with microeconomic maximizing behavior.[58] Since the aggregator function depends only upon quantities, the index number is a quantity index number despite the existence of prices in its formula.

Two particularly noteworthy contributions exist in the recent literature on index numbers. Hulten (1973) has proved that in continuous time the Divisia index is always exact for *any* consistent (blockwise homothetically weakly separable) aggregator function.[59] Hence no index number can be better than the Divisia in continuous time. Although no always-exact index numbers are known in the discrete time case, Diewert (1976) has constructed an elegant theory of superlative index numbers in discrete time. Diewert defines an index number to be 'superlative' if it is exact for some aggregator function, f_s, which can provide a second-order approximation to any linearly homogeneous aggregator function. We call such an index number Diewert-superlative.

Fisher (1922) advocated the following quantity index number, called the Fisher Ideal index:

$$Q_t^F = Q_{t-1}^F \left[\frac{\left(\sum_{i=1}^{N} \pi_{it} m_{it}\right)\left(\sum_{i=1}^{N} \pi_{i,t-1} m_{it}\right)}{\left(\sum_{i=1}^{N} \pi_{it} m_{i,t-1}\right)\left(\sum_{i=1}^{N} \pi_{i,t-1} m_{i,t-1}\right)} \right]^{1/2}.$$

Törnqvist (1936), and subsequently Theil (1967), advocated the following quantity index number, called the Törnqvist-Theil Divisia index:

$$Q_t^T = Q_{t-1}^T \prod_{i=1}^{N} \left(\frac{m_{it}}{m_{i,t-1}}\right)^{(1/2)(s_{it}+s_{i,t-1})},$$

---

[58] In this paper we do not consider the sophisticated issue of aggregating over economic agents. Relevant references are Muellbauer (1976), Dixon (1975), Barnett (1979a, 1979b), and Maks (1978). The form of the index numbers does not depend upon whether the aggregator function is a utility function or a production function. If distributional data were available on shares held by firms (vs. households) or by different categories of wealth holders, that information could be incorporated directly into the index number. See Theil (1967, ch. 5) for an information theoretic interpretation of the resulting index numbers.

[59] The Divisia index is the line integral defined by the differential

$$d\log Q = \sum_{i=1}^{N} s_i d\log q_i, \quad \text{where} \quad s_i = p_i x_i / \mathbf{p}'\mathbf{x}.$$

where $s_{it} = \pi_{it}m_{it}/\sum_{k=1}^{N}\pi_{kt}m_{kt}$. Taking logarithms of each side, observe that

$$\log Q_t^T - \log Q_{t-1}^T = \sum_{i=1}^{N} s_{it}^*(\log m_{it} - \log m_{i,t-1}), \tag{17}$$

where $s_{it}^* = (1/2)(s_{it} + s_{i,t-1})$. The same index numbers result, regardless of whether the aggregator functions are utility functions or production functions.

Diewert (1976) has proved that both the Fisher Ideal and Törnqvist-Theil Divisia indices are Diewert-superlative. In addition, as can be seen from (17), the Törnqvist-Theil Divisia index provides a discrete time approximation to the optimal continuous time Divisia index. In fact the Törnqvist-Theil Divisia index can be derived by numerical integration of the Divisia line integral. The Törnqvist-Theil Divisia index and the Fisher Ideal index are highly reputable throughout all segments of the current literature on index numbers, both for their statistical and economic properties.

As a quantity index, the Törnqvist-Theil Divisia index is more widely used than the Fisher Ideal index, since eq. (17) permits a natural interpretation of the index. Observe that the growth rate of the index is a weighted average of the growth rates of the components. The weights are the share contributions of each component to the total value of the services of all components. Because of the availability of that transparently clear interpretation, we advocate use of the Törnqvist-Theil Divisia index to measure the quantity of money at all levels of aggregation (higher than M_1).

10.2 Example

In this section we consider the case of an aggregate having the following components: transaction balances, passbook savings at the three institution types and at credit unions, small time deposits at the three institution types, and negotiable and nonnegotiable large C.D.'s at commercial banks. The components were selected on the basis of ready availability of the data rather than as a proposal.[60] The collection of components will be called M_3. Table 3 displays the GNP velocity of the Törnqvist-Theil Divisia index, of the Fisher Ideal index, and of the simple sum index for seasonally adjusted data. Velocity is normalized to be one in the first quarter. Observe that the velocities of the Fisher Ideal and Törnqvist-Theil Divisia indices are identical to three decimal places, so that the choice between those two indices is of no

---

[60]The proper procedure for selecting components is described in section 9, but we seek only an example in the current section.

importance.[61]

However the ordinary simple sum index differs substantially from the two Diewert-superlative indices. In addition the range of values of the velocity of the sum index (0.201) is more than twice that of the superlative indices (0.089). The velocities of the simple sum and Divisia indexes for M_3 are plotted in Figure 1. The Divisia and Fisher ideal indexes are too close to be plotted.

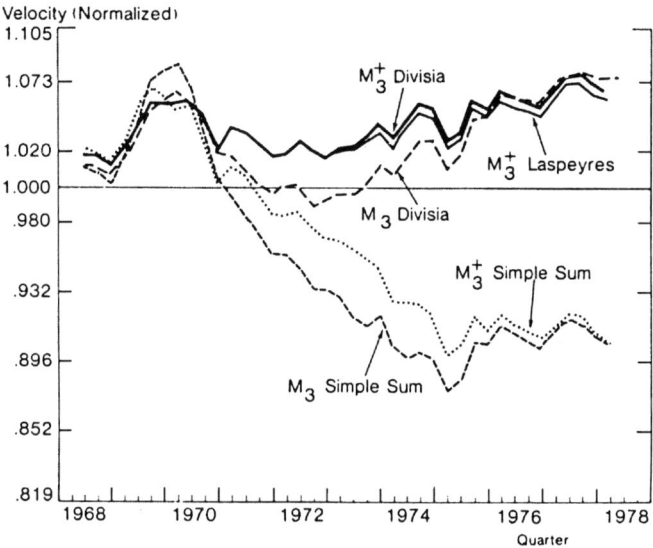

Figure 1: Seasonally adjusted velocity (normalized).

The velocity of the simple sum index continues declining secularly from 1972(3), while the velocity of the Divisia index rises. Our aggregate does not include many money market instruments such as RP's, treasury bills, commercial paper, money market funds, etc., while our aggregate includes many assets subject to governmental rate regulation. Hence we should expect substitution (disintermediation) to occur out of our aggregate and into such substitutes during periods of rising interest rates and high inflation, if our M_3 index approximates an economic monetary good. In such cases velocity

---

[61] This phenomenon resulted from the fact that each is a Diewert-superlative index number. Hence if an aggregator function exists and maximizing behavior obtains, then the two indices can differ only by a third-order remainder term. In addition, each of the two indices should agree with the unknown aggregator function equally as well as they agree with each other, since the remainder term is of the same order in either case.

should *rise*. Clearly the declining velocity of the simple sum index is very misleading.

TABLE 3
GNP VELOCITIES (SEASONALLY ADJUSTED DATA)

Quarter	Fisher Ideal	Törnqvist-Theil Divisia	Simple Sum
1968(1)	1.0000	1.0000	1.0000
1968(2)	1.0141	1.0141	1.0141
1968(3)	1.0131	1.0131	1.0094
1968(4)	1.0088	1.0088	1.0027
1969(1)	1.0174	1.0174	1.0188
1969(2)	1.0311	1.0312	1.0385
1969(3)	1.0524	1.0525	1.0713
1969(4)	1.0570	1.0571	1.0793
1970(1)	1.0626	1.0626	1.0825
1970(2)	1.0574	1.0574	1.0671
1970(3)	1.0473	1.0472	1.0412
1970(4)	1.0231	1.0229	1.0072
1971(1)	1.0219	1.0217	0.9975
1971(2)	1.0123	1.0121	0.9846
1971(3)	1.0041	1.0037	0.9726
1971(4)	0.9997	0.9993	0.9617
1972(1)	1.0031	1.0027	0.9611
1972(2)	1.0013	1.0009	0.9553
1972(3)	0.9919	0.9916	0.9419
1972(4)	0.9942	0.9939	0.9407
1973(1)	0.9998	0.9996	0.9365
1973(2)	0.9977	0.9976	0.9241
1973(3)	1.0061	1.0060	0.9205
1973(4)	1.0172	1.0171	0.9240
1974(1)	1.0104	1.0103	0.9065
1974(2)	1.0234	1.0233	0.9019
1974(3)	1.0348	1.0347	0.9043
1974(4)	1.0339	1.0338	0.8997
1975(1)	1.0170	1.0169	0.8823
1975(2)	1.0263	1.0262	0.8895
1975(3)	1.0517	1.0516	0.9116
1975(4)	1.0555	1.0554	0.9127
1976(1)	1.0670	1.0668	0.9209
1976(2)	1.0681	1.0680	0.9206
1976(3)	1.0661	1.0660	0.9163
1976(4)	1.0608	1.0607	0.9097
1977(1)	1.0709	1.0707	0.9164
1977(2)	1.0815	1.0814	0.9237
1977(3)	1.0801	1.0800	0.9197
1977(4)	1.0766	1.0765	0.9128
1978(1)	1.0733	1.0732	0.9057

Comparing Figure 1 with the ten-year government bond rate in Figure 2, we see that variations in the velocity of the Divisia index make economic sense; the interest elasticity of money demand has the right sign. Internalizing further money market substitution by aggregating over additional money market instruments can be expected further to stabilize the velocity of the superlative index. The substitution effect (*defined* to hold utility constant) of a change in the relative prices of components *within* an aggregate *cannot* change the value of an economic quantity aggregate (utility level)!

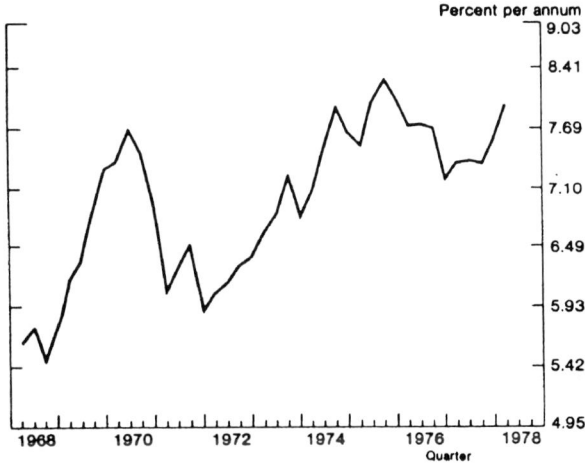

Figure 2: Ten-year government bond rate.

In contrast, the trend in velocity of the simple sum index would suggest that, in response to rising interest rates and rising inflationary expectations, monetary asset holders have increased the fraction of GNP allocated to consumption of the services of the lowest yielding (largely rate controlled) sector of the market.[62] Disintermediation thereby would appear (misleadingly) to have proceeded within the money market in the wrong direction. It is not surprising that simple sum aggregates frequently provide conflicting information.

The computational reason for the divergence between the Divisia and the simple sum indexes can be seen from eq. (17).[63] The Törnqvist-Theil Divisia

---

[62] Since GNP does not include the user-cost-evaluated services of durables or of monetary assets, our conclusion is based upon the use of GNP as an approximation to the corresponding theoretical national product concept.

[63] It is tempting to conclude that the reason the velocity of the Diewert-superlative index tracks the government bond rate is the fact that the Diewert-superlative index depends upon interest rates. However the index is constructed to approximate the aggregator function, which depends only upon quantities and therefore not upon R_t.

index (or therefore, approximately, any Diewert-superlative index) weights transaction balances more heavily than any of the other components of the aggregates, since transaction balances provide the largest share of monetary services, s_{it}. An economic reason for the heavy weighting of transaction balances is that their liquidity contributes heavily to monetary services. But the velocity of transaction balances has been rising rapidly in recent years. Hence the inadequate weighting of transaction balances in the simple sum M_3 has permitted velocity to be drawn down by the substitution effect of the increasing relative price (user cost) of transaction balances relative to less liquid monetary substitutes.

To further verify our interpretation, we now incorporate elements of the unregulated money market into M_3 to create M_3^+. We incorporate dealer and directly placed commercial paper, repurchase agreements (RP's) of commercial banks with the non-bank public, bankers' acceptances, and negotiable Treasury securities with less than one year remaining to maturity. In Figure 1, we plot the velocity of M_3^+, with M_3^+ computed as a simple sum index, as a Divisia index, and as a chained Laspeyres index. We continue to normalize all velocities to equal 1.0 in the first quarter.

Clearly internalizing those additional segments of the money market has further stabilized the velocity of the Divisia index. The velocity of the simple sum index continues to trend in the wrong direction. The Laspeyres index is seen to provide a far better approximation than the simple sum index, despite the fact that the Laspeyres index provides only a first-order approximation to the value of the aggregator function.[64] The slight variations remaining in the velocity of the Divisia index continue to correlate with the ten-year bond rate and to reflect the fact that some elements of the unregulated money market remain outside of the aggregate.[65]

Further information regarding the comparison between the simple sum and the Törnqvist-Theil Divisia index of money supply has been provided by Barnett and Spindt (1979), and Barnett, Offenbacher, and Spindt (1984). They used information theory to compute the information gained about various final targets (GNP, the inflation rate, etc.) from knowledge of the rate of growth of a measure of the money supply. They found that, regardless of the targets used or of the components included in the aggregate, the Törnqvist-Theil Divisia index dominated the sum index computed using the *same* monetary components. In addition, the gains in information acquired by going

---

[64]The Divisia indices provide a second-order approximation.

[65]An entirely rigorous conclusion would be based upon the observation that the velocity of the Diewert-superlative index reveals (to the second-order) movements along the aggregator function and therefore movements of the underlying economic aggregate. Hence Figure 1 indicates that the velocity of the simple sum index has been moving in the wrong direction, in the sense of moving in the direction opposite to that of the economic aggregate.

from the sum to the Törnqvist-Theil Divisia index frequently were extremely large.

The simple sum index is a Laspeyres quantity index with the weights erroneously set to be equal. Clearly the arbitrary weighting destroys the index's critical independence of substitution effects (within the aggregate), and hence the simple sum index *cannot* approximate the economic aggregate.

11 Conclusion

In computing monetary quantity indices, the simple sum index number formula is not satisfactory. The aggregates should be computed as Törnqvist-Theil Divisia indices. The components of the aggregates should be selected to satisfy the conditions for consistent aggregation described in section 9. These conclusions apply so long as the indices are to be used as quantity indices of monetary services, as required in economics. Simple summation would provide valid indices of the stock of nominal monetary wealth, as required in national accounting, or indices of bank liability structure, as required in bank accounting, but *not* valid structural economic variables.

The discussion in this paper has related to the economic theories of aggregation and index numbers. However, there is also a statistical theory of index numbers, which does not depend upon economic theory for its foundations. Statistical index number theory considers the ability of index numbers to pass certain classical tests, such as factor reversal and circulatory tests. During the past decade, results from both approaches have converged on the Törnqvist-Theil Divisia and Fisher Ideal indices as being clearly among the best, and advocates of both the economic and statistical approaches view the simple sum index as being among the very worst index numbers ever devised.[66]

According to Fisher, the two worst statistical properties that an index number can possess are called 'bias' and 'freakishness'. Regarding the simple sum (or equivalently the arithmetic average) index, which Fisher called his Formula 1, Fisher (1922, p. 363) observed: 'There are two objections to Formula 1, the simple arithmetic, *viz.*: (1) that it is 'simple', and (2) that it is arithmetic! — that it is at once freakish and biased. In the case of Sauerbeck's index number, for instance, the bias alone reaches 36 percent!'

In our case we found that the simple sum index dismally failed to internalize the long-run substitution effects that have occurred within the money

---

[66] As we have observed, Hulten's and Diewert's work strongly supports the economic foundations of the Törnqvist-Theil Divisia and Fisher Ideal indices. In addition Fisher (1922) and Theil (1967) strongly support those same indices on the basis of their statistical index number properties.

markets during the past decade, and Barnett and Spindt (1979), and Barnett, Offenbacher, and Spindt (1984) found that much component information is unnecessarily lost when monetary components are aggregated by simple summation.[67] These results are consistent with our empirical rejection of aggregator function constraints that are necessary for economic aggregation by simple summation. As Fisher (1922, p. 361) long ago deduced correctly: 'The simple arithmetic (Formula 1) should not be used under any circumstances.'[68]

We conclude with the following quotation from Fisher's (1922, p. 29) classical book, written over half a century ago:

> 'The simple arithmetic average is put first merely because it naturally comes first to the reader's mind, being the most common form of average. In fields other than index numbers it is often the best form of average to use. But we shall see that the simple arithmetic average produces one of the very worst of index numbers, and if this book has no other effect than to lead to the total abandonment of the simple arithmetic type of index number, it will have served a useful purpose.'[69]

---

[67] For an overview of additional ongoing research in this area, see Barnett, Offenbacher and Spindt (1981).

[68] At the time that this paper was published, we believed that the index called arithmetic average (Formula 1 or Carli index) by Fisher was proportional to the simple sum (Formula 51 or Dutot index). We thought that the arithmetic average index was the simple sum divided by the number of components. But recently Erwin Diewert has pointed out to us that the two indexes are deflated in a noncomparable manner, and hence the properties of the two indexes are not identical. The statements quoted in this paper from Fisher (1922) about the arithmetic average index should not be imputed to the simple sum. For example, while the arithmetic average index is "biased" and "freakish," the simple sum index is "freakish" and "haphazard" in Fisher's terminology. Nevertheless, the two indexes share the same common fundamental flaw relative to aggregation theory: both are not even a first order approximation to an arbitrary aggregator function. As one might expect, there is no shortage of negative statements about the simple sum in Fisher (1922), who took the simple sum even less seriously than the arithmetic average. In fact continuing on to the next sentence, this particular quotation from Fisher (1922, p. 361) becomes: "The simple arithmetic (Formula 1) should not be used under any circumstances, being always biased and usually freakish as well. Nor should the simple aggregative (Formula 51) ever be used; in fact this is even less reliable."

[69] As explained in the previous footnote, the arithmetic average index in Fisher (1922) is not proportional to the simple sum index. But Fisher viewed the arithmetic average as a more worthy target for criticism, since he viewed the simple sum as an even worse index and as considerably less reputable, when his book was published in 1922.

Conclusion

12 Appendix: Duality

A quantity aggregator function and its corresponding price aggregator function are duals. The mathematics of function duals is not the subject of this paper and will not be discussed in detail below. Nevertheless, those familiar with classical duality relationships will recognize the foundations for the following observation. We begin with the two stage decision of section 4.2.

Dual to the (quantity aggregator) function $u_p(\mathbf{y}_{pt})$ exists the function $\Pi_p(\boldsymbol{\pi}_{pt})$ such that the identity $u_p(\mathbf{y}_{pt})\Pi_p(\boldsymbol{\pi}_{pt}) = \mathbf{y}'_{pt}\boldsymbol{\pi}_{pt}$ will hold whenever $\mathbf{y}_{pt}$ is the solution to the problem

$$\min_{\mathbf{y}_{pt}} \mathbf{y}'_{pt}\boldsymbol{\pi}_{pt},$$

subject to

$$u_p(\mathbf{y}_{pt}) = k_1,$$

where k_1 is a positive constant.

This duality relationship demonstrates that knowledge of the function u is sufficient for determination of the function Π_p. Hence we need only estimate the conditional demand system solving (12) to estimate Π_p and therefore to compute estimates of the passbook real user cost index, $\Pi_{pt}^* = \Pi_p(\boldsymbol{\pi}_{pt}^*)$. We thereby can acquire Π_{pt}^* without estimating the higher level utility function, μ, of eq. (10). Hence in (14) we were thereby justified in treating Π_{pt}^* as given and recursively estimating the utility tree from the bottom up. In fact it can be shown that $\Pi_p(\boldsymbol{\pi}_{pt}^*)$ is just real expenditure on passbook account services, $\mathbf{y}'_{pt}\boldsymbol{\pi}_{pt}^*$, divided by the indirect utility function corresponding to $u_p(\mathbf{y}_{pt})$. Since preferences are assumed to be homogeneous of degree one, it follows that the resulting function, Π_p, depends only upon $\boldsymbol{\pi}_{pt}^*$ (and is independent of expenditure on passbook account services).

The function Π_p is homogeneous of degree 1. Hence $\Pi_p(\boldsymbol{\pi}_{pt}^*) = \Pi_p(\boldsymbol{\pi}_{pt})/p_t^*$. As a result, we can compute the real value of the user-cost price aggregate, $\Pi_p(\boldsymbol{\pi}_{pt})/p_t^*$, by using real user costs, $\boldsymbol{\pi}_{pt}^*$, as arguments for Π_p. Thus our earlier observation that our estimates do not depend upon the use of p_t^* is verified.

It is interesting to observe that this nesting process immediately can be carried to a higher level to acquire a user cost index for the economic aggregate over passbook accounts and transaction balances taken jointly. Since economic quantity aggregates always are utility functions, the quantity aggregate immediately is seen to be $u_t = \mu(m_{1t}, u_p(\mathbf{y}_{pt})) = \mu(m_{1t}, u_{pt})$. We define the dual user-cost index by observing that dual to the function (quantity index) $\mu(m_{1t}, \mu_{pt})$ exists a function (price index) $\Pi(\pi_{1t}, \Pi_{pt}) = \Pi(\pi_{1t}, \Pi_p(\boldsymbol{\pi}_{pt}))$ such that the identity

$$\mu(m_{1t}, u_{pt})\Pi(\pi_{1t}, \Pi_{pt}) = m_{1t}\pi_{1t} + u_{pt}\Pi_{pt} = m_{1t}\pi_{1t} + \mathbf{y}'_{pt}\boldsymbol{\pi}_{pt}$$

will hold whenever (m_{1t}, u_{pt}) is the solution to the problem

$$\min_{(m_{1t},u_{pt})} (m_{1t}\pi_{1t} + u_{pt}\Pi_{pt}),$$

subject to

$$\mu(m_{1t}, u_{pt}) = k_2,$$

where k_2 is a positive constant.

By Fisher's factor reversal test (equality of expenditure to the product of the price and quantity index), the price (user-cost) index dual to a functional quantity index must equal total expenditure on the aggregated assets divided by the indirect category (conditional) utility function defined on those assets. Because of our linear homogeneity assumption on category utility functions, total expenditure cancels out of the quotient leaving a functional price index depending solely upon prices.

Chapter 3

The Microeconomic Theory of Monetary Aggregation

William A. Barnett *

> In recent decades there has been a resurgence of interest in index numbers resulting from discoveries that the properties of index numbers can be directly related to the properties of the underlying aggregator functions that they represent. The underlying functions — production functions, utility functions, etc. — are the building blocks of economic theory, and the study of relationships between these functions and index number formulas has been referred to by Samuelson and Swamy (1974) as the economic theory of index numbers.[1]

1 Introduction

The use of economic index number theory was introduced into monetary theory by Barnett (1980a, 1981b). His merger of economic index number theory with monetary theory was based upon the use of Diewert's approach to producing 'superlative' approximations to the exact aggregates from consumer demand theory.[2] As a result, Barnett's approach produces a Diewert-superlative measure of the monetary service flow perceived to be received by consumers from their monetary asset portfolio. However, aggregation and index number theory are highly developed in production theory as well as in consumer demand theory. Substantial literatures exist on aggregation over factor inputs demanded by firms, aggregation over multiple product outputs

---

*Originally published in *New Approaches to Monetary Economics*, William A. Barnett and Kenneth Singleton (eds.), Cambridge Universtiy Press, 1987, pp. 115–168. Reprinted with the permission of Cambridge University Press. This research was partially supported by National Science Foundation grant SOC 8305162.

[1] Caves, Christensen, and Diewert (1982a, p. 73).

[2] For empirical applications, see Barnett (1980b, 1981a, 1982a, 1983a, 1984); Barnett, Offenbacher, and Spindt (1984); Barnett and Spindt (1979, 1982); Serletis (1984, 1987a); Ewis and Fisher (1984, 1985); Barnett, Hinich, and Weber (1986); Cockerline and Murray (1981b); Serletis and Robb (1986); Marquez (1986); Ishida (1984); and Swofford and Whitney (1986). For a survey of the theory, see Barnett (1982b, 1983b) and Barnett, Offenbacher, and Spindt (1981).

produced by firms, and aggregation over individual firms and consumers. In addition, substantial literatures exist on exact measurement of value added by firms and of technical change by firms. All of these literatures are potentially relevant to closing a cleared money market in an exact aggregation-theoretic monetary aggregate. In this paper, we establish the relationship between monetary theory and all of the above listed areas of aggregation and index number theory. These results are relevant to building and using theoretical or empirical macroeconomic models possessing an aggregated money market.

The demand for money is both by firms and consumers. Hence we present the aggregation and index number theory relevant to demand by firms as well as by consumers. The supply of money is partially produced by financial intermediaries. As a result, we present the aggregation and index number theory relevant to aggregation over the multiple outputs of such financial firms. Because there has been considerable technological change in the industry in recent years, a theory relevant to measuring technological change within a financial firm is presented. In addition, because the impact of changes in outside money on the economy is likely to depend upon value added by financial intermediaries, the theoretical and approximation approaches relevant to measuring value added by such firms are also presented.

In this paper, the models of monetary asset demand by consumers and by firms, as well as the model of monetary asset supply by financial intermediaries, are based upon commonly used neoclassical formulations. In addition, the results in aggregation and index number theory used in this paper are well established and widely known in their respective literatures. Besides surveying the relevant results from those literatures, the primary objective of this paper is algebraically to formulate and manipulate the presented theories of monetary consumption, factor demand, and production in a manner that provides immediate direct relevancy to the existing results in the literatures on aggregation and index number theory.

Because a government sector is not introduced, the financial firm, the consumer, and the manufacturing firm modeled herein are not imbedded in a macroeconomic model. The reason is that the results surveyed and developed here are applicable to macroeconomic modeling regardless of the nature of the model's transmission mechanism or of any policy implications that might be suggested by a full macroeconomic model. There are as many ways to imbed these results into a macroeconomic model as there are ways to build a macroeconomic model.

2 Consumer Demand for Monetary Assets

In this section we formulate a consumer's decision problem over consumer goods and monetary assets. The decision will be structured in a manner that provides immediate applicability of the relevant literature on economic aggregation over consumer goods. Hence the existing results in economic aggregation and index number theory will be directly usable.

Two versions of the decision problem will be provided. The first version will use a finite planning horizon and will be an extension of Barnett's (1978, 1980a, 1981b) formulation. The second version will use an infinite planning horizon and will be shown to produce the same aggregation theoretic results as the finite-horizon version. The reason is that both versions produce the same current period aggregator function over monetary assets, and both versions produce the same user cost formulas for monetary assets.

2.1 Finite Planning Horizon

The following variables are used in consumer c's decision problem, formulated in period t for periods $t, t+1, \ldots, s, \ldots, t+T$, where T is the number of periods in the consumer's planning horizon:

$\mathbf{x}_s$ = vector of planned consumption of goods and services during period s;
$\mathbf{p}_s$ = vector of goods' and services' expected prices and of durable goods' expected rental prices during period s;
$\mathbf{m}_s$ = vector of planned real balances of monetary assets during period s;
$\mathbf{r}_s$ = vector of expected nominal holding period yields of monetary assets;
A_s = planned holdings of the benchmark asset during period s;
R_s = the expected one-period holding yield on the benchmark asset during period s;
L_s^c = planned labor supply during period s;
$\bar{L}_s = k - L_s^c$ = planned leisure demand during period s, where k = total hours available per period;
w_s = the expected wage rate during period s;[3] and
I_s = other expected income (government transfer payments, profits of owned firms, etc.) during period s.

The benchmark asset is defined to provide no services other than its yield

---

[3] If the expected demand for the consumer's labor is not equal to planned supply, then w_s is the expected shadow price of leisure. See Barnett (1980a, 1981a).

R_s, which motivates holding of the asset solely as a means of accumulating wealth. As a result, R_s is the maximum expected holding period yield in the economy in period s; and the benchmark asset is held to transfer wealth between multiperiod planning horizons, rather than to provide liquidity or other services.

The consumer's intertemporal utility function in period t is[4]

$$u_t = u_t(\mathbf{m}_t, \ldots, \mathbf{m}_{t+T}; \bar{L}_t, \ldots, \bar{L}_{t+T}; \mathbf{x}_t, \ldots, \mathbf{x}_{t+T}; A_{t+T}). \tag{1}$$

We assume that u_t is blockwise weakly separable as follows.

$$u_t = U_t(u(\mathbf{m}_t), u_{t+1}(\mathbf{m}_{t+1}), \ldots, u_{t+T}(\mathbf{m}_{t+T}); \bar{L}_t, \ldots, \bar{L}_{t+T};$$
$$v(\mathbf{x}_t), v_{t+1}(\mathbf{x}_{t+1}), \ldots, v_{t+T}(\mathbf{x}_{t+T}); A_{t+T}). \tag{2}$$

The functions $u, u_{t+1}, \ldots, u_{t+T}, v, v_{t+1}, \ldots, v_{t+T}$ are called category subutility functions. Then, dual to the functions v and v_s ($s = t+1, \ldots, t+T$), there exist current and planned true cost of living indexes, p_t^* and p_s^* ($s = t+1, \ldots, t+T$), that can be used to deflate nominal to real values.[5]

Assuming continuous replanning at each t, the consumer's decision is to choose $(\mathbf{m}_t, \ldots, \mathbf{m}_{t+T}, \bar{L}_t, \ldots, \bar{L}_{t+T}; \mathbf{x}_t, \ldots, \mathbf{x}_{t+T}; A_{t+T})$ to maximize u_t subject to the $T+1$ budget constraints

$$\mathbf{p}'_s \mathbf{x}_s = w_s L_s^c + \sum_{i=1}^{n}[(1 + r_{i,s-1})p_{s-1}^* m_{i,s-1} - p_s^* m_{is}]$$
$$+ [(1 + R_{s-1})p_{s-1}^* A_{s-1} - p_s^* A_s] + I_s \tag{3}$$

for $s = t, t+1, \ldots, t+T$ and with $\bar{L}_s = k - L_s^c$. The consumer's initial nominal wealth in period t is $\sum_{i=1}^{n}(1 + r_{i,t-1})p_{t-1}^* m_{i,t-1} + (1 + R_{t-1})p_{t-1}^* A_{t-1}$.

Let $(\mathbf{m}_t^*, \ldots, \mathbf{m}_{t+T}^*, \bar{L}_t^*, \ldots, \bar{L}_{t+T}^*; \mathbf{x}_t^*, \ldots, \mathbf{x}_{t+T}^*; A_{t+T}^*)$ be the solution to that constrained optimization problem. Following the procedures in Barnett (1980a, 1981b), it then can be shown that $\mathbf{m}_t^*$ is also the solution for $\mathbf{m}_t$ to the following current period conditional decision:

$$\text{maximize } u(\mathbf{m}_t) \text{ subject to } \boldsymbol{\pi}'_t \mathbf{m}_t = y_t, \tag{4}$$

---

[4]Regarding the existence of this derived utility function, into which the consumer's transactions technology has been absorbed, see Arrow and Hahn (1971), Phlips and Spinnewyn (1982), and Samuelson and Sato (1984). In the most general case, the derived utility function containing money could also include prices of consumer goods. Additional assumptions, which we implicitly make, limit that price dependency to the price level deflator used to deflate nominal to real balances of money in the derived utility function. To our knowledge, no one has ever empirically investigated dependency of the derived utility function upon relative prices of consumer goods.

[5]See Barnett (1980a, 1981b).

where $\boldsymbol{\pi}_t = (\pi_{1t}, \ldots, \pi_{nt})'$ is the vector of monetary asset nominal user costs

$$\pi_{it} = p_t^* \frac{R_t - r_{it}}{1 + R_t} \tag{5}$$

and $y_t = \boldsymbol{\pi}_t' \mathbf{m}_t^*$. We could convert from the nominal user costs $\boldsymbol{\pi}_t$ to the real user costs $\boldsymbol{\pi}_t^*$ by dividing the budget constraint of (4) by p_t^* to obtain

$$\text{maximize } u(\mathbf{m}_t) \text{ subject to } \boldsymbol{\pi}_t^{*\prime} \mathbf{m}_t = y_t^*, \tag{6}$$

where $y_t^* = y_t/p_t^*$ and $\boldsymbol{\pi}_t^* = \boldsymbol{\pi}_t/p_t^*$. The function u is assumed to be monotonically increasing and strictly concave. Decision problem (6) is in the form of a conventional consumer decision problem, and hence the literature on aggregation theory and index number theory for consumers is immediately available.

2.2 Infinite Planning Horizon

In this section, we reformulate the consumer's decision problem using an infinite planning horizon. We show that the same current-period conditional decision problem, (6), is acquired. As a result, the existing literature on aggregation and index number theory will remain relevant.

We replace the finite planning horizon intertemporal utility function (2) by the infinite horizon intertemporally separable utility function

$$u_t = \sum_{s=t}^{\infty} \left(\frac{1}{1+\xi}\right)^{s-t} U(u(\mathbf{m}_s), \bar{L}_s, \mathbf{x}_s), \tag{7}$$

where ξ is the consumer's subjective rate of time preference, assumed to be constant to assure Strotz consistent planning.[6] The consumer selects the sequence $(\mathbf{m}_s, \bar{L}_s, \mathbf{x}_s)$, $s = t, t+1, \ldots$, to maximize (7) subject to the sequence of constraints (3) for $s = t, t+1, \ldots$. The upper limit $t+T$ to the planning horizon no longer exists. Again R_s must exceed r_{is} for all i, because A_s is not in the utility function and hence would not otherwise be held.

Construct the Lagrangian, Λ, and differentiate with respect to A_t, $\mathbf{x}_t$, and $\mathbf{m}_t$ to acquire the following first-order conditions for constrained maximization at t:

$$\partial \Lambda / \partial A_t = -\lambda_t + \lambda_{t+1}(1 + R_t) = 0, \tag{8}$$

$$\partial \Lambda / \partial x_{it} = \partial U / \partial x_{it} - \lambda_t p_{it} = 0, \tag{9}$$

---

[6] The same current-period conditional decision would result if ξ were not constant. As a result, Strotz consistency produces no loss in generality in our aggregation-theoretic results. If intertemporal separability were not assumed, expectations could be endogenized through rational expectations, as in Attfield and Browning (1985).

$$\partial \Lambda / \partial m_{it} = \partial U / \partial m_{it} - \lambda_t p_t^* + \lambda_{t+1} p_t^*(1 + r_{it}) = 0, \qquad (10)$$

where λ_t and λ_{t+1} are two of the Lagrange multipliers in the sequence $(\lambda_t, \lambda_{t+1}, \lambda_{t+2}, \ldots)$ of Lagrange multipliers in Λ. Substituting (8) into (10) to eliminate λ_{t+1}, we obtain

$$\partial U / \partial m_{it} = \lambda_t \pi_{it}, \qquad (11)$$

where π_{it} is as in (5).

Hence, from (11), we have that

$$\frac{\partial U / \partial m_{it}}{\partial U / \partial m_{jt}} = \frac{\pi_{it}}{\pi_{jt}}, \qquad (12)$$

or

$$\frac{\partial u / \partial m_{it}}{\partial u / \partial m_{jt}} = \frac{\pi_{it}^*}{\pi_{jt}^*}. \qquad (13)$$

Now for $s = t, t+1, \ldots$ let $(\mathbf{m}_s^*, \bar{L}_s^*, \mathbf{x}_s^*)$ maximize (7) subject to (3), and let

$$y_t^* = \boldsymbol{\pi}_t^{*\prime} \mathbf{m}_t^*. \qquad (14)$$

Then the first-order conditions for the solution to problem (6) are (13) and (14). Hence $\mathbf{m}_s^*$ solves problem (6). As a result, we again find that we can use the conventional neoclassical decision (6), and thereby all of the existing literature on aggregation over goods consumed.

2.3 Income Taxes

The results in Sections 2.1 and 2.2 do not explicitly incorporate taxes. Nevertheless all of those results would remain valid if we convert to after-tax yields as follows. Let τ_t be the consumer's marginal tax rate on interest earned from the benchmark asset, and let τ_{it} be the consumer's marginal tax rate on monetary asset i. Then the nominal user cost (5) becomes

$$\pi_{it} = p_t^* \frac{R_t(1 - \tau_t) - r_{it}(1 - \tau_{it})}{1 + R_t(1 - \tau_t)}, \qquad (5a)$$

which in turn becomes

$$\pi_{it} = p_t^* \frac{(R_t - r_{it})(1 - \tau_t)}{1 + R_t(1 - \tau_t)} \qquad (5b)$$

if $\tau_{it} = \tau_t$ for all i.

In the latter case, we can return to using (5) instead of (5b) to acquire $\pi_{it}^* = \pi_{it}/p_t^*$, when $\boldsymbol{\pi}_t^*$ is to be used in decision (6). To do so, we need only replace y_t^* by $[1 + R_t(1 - \tau_t)]y_t^*/[(1 - \tau_t)(1 + R_t)]$, since we then would only have multiplied both sides of the budget constraint of (6) by $[1 + R_t(1 - \tau_t)]/[(1 - \tau_t)(1 + R_t)]$.

3 Supply of Monetary Assets by Financial Intermediaries

Monetary assets are generally either primary securities, such as currency or Treasury bills, or assets produced through the financial intermediation of financial firms. In this section, we develop a model of production by financial intermediaries under perfect certainty.[7] It will be shown that the model can be manipulated into the conventional neoclassical form of production by a multiproduct firm. As a result, the existing literature on output aggregation becomes immediately applicable to the construction of a neoclassical money supply function for aggregated money.

Consider a financial intermediary which makes only one kind of loan, yielding R_t, and produces (through financial intermediation) a vector $\boldsymbol{\mu}_t$ of real balances of monetary assets.[8] The firm uses c_t real units of excess reserves, in the form of currency, as a factor of production in producing $\boldsymbol{\mu}_t$ during period t.[9] Real balances such as $\boldsymbol{\mu}_t$ and c_t are defined to equal nominal balances divided by p_t^*, which was defined in Section 2.1. The firm also uses the vector $\mathbf{L}_t$ of labor quantities and the vector $\mathbf{z}_t$ of other factor quantities. The vector of reserve requirements is $\mathbf{k}_t$, where k_{it} is the reserve requirement applicable to μ_{it} and $0 \leq k_{it} \leq 1$ for all i.

The firm's efficient production technology is defined by the transformation function $F(\boldsymbol{\mu}_t, \mathbf{z}_t, \mathbf{L}_t, c_t; \mathbf{k}_t) = 0$. The firm's technology can be equivalently defined by its efficient production set (also called the production possibility efficient set)

$$S(\mathbf{k}_t) = \{(\boldsymbol{\mu}_t, \mathbf{z}_t, \mathbf{L}_t, c_t) \geq 0 : F(\boldsymbol{\mu}_t, \mathbf{z}_t, \mathbf{L}_t, c_t; \mathbf{k}_t) = 0\} \qquad (15)$$

or by its production correspondence F, defined such that

$$G(\mathbf{z}_t, \mathbf{L}_t, c_t; \mathbf{k}_t) = \{\boldsymbol{\mu}_t \geq 0 : (\boldsymbol{\mu}_t, \mathbf{z}_t, \mathbf{L}_t, c_t) \in S(\mathbf{k}_t)\}. \qquad (16)$$

If $(\mathbf{z}_t, \mathbf{L}_t) = 0$ then no financial intermediation takes place, no value added exists, and no loans are made. In short, in that case the firm is acting as

---

[7] Because risk premia will be left in all yields, a certainty equivalence assumption could be viewed as implicit. The explicit incorporation of expected profit maximization would greatly complicate the analysis to follow.

[8] In practice, R_t should be 'the marginal cost of borrowing an additional dollar for one period' [see Diewert (1980a, pp. 476–7)].

[9] We treat monetary assets produced by financial intermediation to be outputs of financial intermediaries, and we thereby implicitly assume that the user costs of such assets are positive. Hancock (1985, 1986) postulates that some such assets can be inputs to financial intermediaries if the corresponding user costs are negative. That possibility is not excluded by the formulation presented below, although we shall not explicitly discuss the probably unusual case of negative user costs.

a vault, so that all of $\sum_i p_t^* \mu_{it}$ is reserves, and hence excess reserves are $p_t^* c_t = \sum_i \mu_{it}(1 - k_{it})p_t^*$.

The transformation function F is strictly quasiconvex in $(\boldsymbol{\mu}_t, \mathbf{z}_t, \mathbf{L}_t, c_t)$. In addition, $\partial F/\partial L_{it} < 0$, $\partial F/\partial z_{it} < 0$, and $\partial F/\partial c_t < 0$, because $\mathbf{L}_t, \mathbf{z}_t$, and c_t are inputs. Conversely, $\partial F/\partial \mu_{it} > 0$ because $\boldsymbol{\mu}_t$ are outputs.[10] All factors $\mathbf{z}_t$ are purchased at the start of period t for use during period t, and the firm must pay for those factors at the start of the period. The exception is labor $\mathbf{L}_t$, which receives its wages at the end of the period t for labor quantities supplied to the firm during period t. Interest on produced monetary assets $\boldsymbol{\mu}_t$ is paid at the end of the period, and interest on loans outstanding during period t is received at the end of period t.

Because our model contains only one kind of primary market loan, yielding R_t, the federal funds rate must therefore also equal R_t. However, the discount rate, being regulated, can differ from R_t. Let R_t^d be the discount rate during period t, and define $\bar{R}_t = \min\{R_t, R_t^d\}$. We assume that required reserves are never borrowed from the Federal Reserve, but could be borrowed in the federal funds market.[11] Excess reserves can be borrowed from either source. As a result, if $R_t^d < R_t$ then all excess reserves will be borrowed from the Federal Reserve and there are no free reserves. If $R_t^d > R_t$, then there is no borrowing from the Federal Reserve and free reserves equal excess reserves. In addition, in that case the percentage of excess reserves borrowed from the federal funds market is indeterminate, because the opportunity cost of not lending free reserves at R_t is equal to the cost of borrowing free reserves from the federal funds market at R_t. For the same reason, the percentage of required reserves borrowed in the federal funds market is indeterminate in both cases. If $R_t^d = R_t$, then all of the following are indeterminate: the percentage of required reserves or of excess reserves borrowed in the federal funds market, the percentage of excess reserves borrowed from the Federal Reserve, and the level of free reserves.

We now proceed to determine the level of variable profits at the end of period t. Suppose that $R_t \leq R_t^d$, so that $\bar{R}_t = R_t$. Then variable revenue from loans is

$$\left(\sum_i \mu_{it}p_t^* - \sum_i k_{it}\mu_{it}p_t^* - c_t p_t^* - \mathbf{q}_t' \mathbf{z}_t\right) R_t, \tag{17}$$

where $\mathbf{q}_t$ is the price of the factors $\mathbf{z}_t$. If z_{it} is a durable variable factor, then $\mathbf{q}_t$ is its user cost. However, if $R_t > R_t^d$, so that $\bar{R}_t = R_t^d$, then variable

---

[10] If the user cost of μ_{it} were negative for some $i = j$, then $\partial F/\partial \mu_{jt}$ would become nonpositive because μ_{jt} would become an input. In that probably rare case, μ_{jt} could be removed from $\boldsymbol{\mu}_t$ and treated as a component of $\mathbf{z}_t$.

[11] This assumption of 'perfect moral suasion' could easily be weakened or removed.

revenue from loans is

$$\left(\sum_i \mu_{it} p_t^* - \sum_i k_{it} \mu_{it} p_t^* - \mathbf{q}_t' \mathbf{z}_t\right) R_t - c_t p_t^* R_t^d. \tag{18}$$

Hence, in either case, variable revenue from loans is

$$\left[\sum_i (1 - k_{it}) \mu_{it} p_t^* - c_t p_t^* - \mathbf{q}_t' \mathbf{z}_t\right] R_t + c_t p_t^* (R_t - \bar{R}_t). \tag{19}$$

Variable cost that must be paid out of variable revenue is

$$\sum_i \mu_{it} p_t^* \rho_{it} + \mathbf{q}_t' \mathbf{z}_t + \mathbf{w}_t' \mathbf{L}_t, \tag{20}$$

where $\mathbf{w}_t$ is the vector of wage rates corresponding to labor quantities $\mathbf{L}_t$, and $\boldsymbol{\rho}_t$ is the vector of yields paid by the firm on $\boldsymbol{\mu}_t$. Observe that $\mathbf{w}_t' \mathbf{L}_t$ appears in (20), but not in (19), because $\mathbf{w}_t' \mathbf{L}_t$ is not paid until the end of the period and therefore is not subtracted out of loan quantities placed at the beginning of the period.

Variable profit received at the end of period t is acquired by subtracting (20) from (19).[12] If we then divide by $1 + R_t$ in order to discount variable profits to the beginning of period t, we find that the present value of period t variable profits is

$$\begin{aligned} P(\boldsymbol{\mu}_t, \mathbf{z}_t, \mathbf{L}_t, c_t; p_t^*, \mathbf{q}_t, R_t, R_t^d, \boldsymbol{\rho}_t, \mathbf{w}_t, \mathbf{k}_t) \\ = \boldsymbol{\mu}_t' \boldsymbol{\gamma}_t - \mathbf{q}_t' \mathbf{z}_t - \mathbf{L}_t' \mathbf{w}_t / (1 + R_t) - \gamma_{ot} c_t, \end{aligned} \tag{21}$$

where the nominal user cost price of produced monetary asset μ_{it} is

$$\gamma_{it} = p_t^* \frac{(1 - k_{it}) R_t - \rho_{it}}{1 + R_t} \tag{22}$$

and the nominal user cost price of excess reserves (real balances of currency) is

$$\gamma_{ot} = p_t^* \frac{\bar{R}_t}{1 + R_t}. \tag{23}$$

The corresponding real user costs are γ_t / p_t^* and γ_{ot} / p_t^*.[13]

---

[12] Observe that fixed factors, including financial capital, are not relevant to the determination of variable profit.

[13] Observe that those derived user cost formulas, after some manipulation, become equivalent to those used by Hancock (1985, 1986), although her method of measuring the discount rate is not consistent with the above theory that produced results (22) and (23). She also incorporated explicit transactions costs into the formula.

If we write the vector of all variable factor quantities as $\alpha_t = (\mathbf{z}'_t, \mathbf{L}'_t, c_t)'$ and the vector of corresponding factor prices as $\boldsymbol{\beta}_t = (\mathbf{q}'_t, \mathbf{w}'_t/(1+R_t), \gamma_{ot})'$, it becomes evident that variable profits take the conventional form

$$P_t = \boldsymbol{\mu}'_t \boldsymbol{\gamma}_t - \boldsymbol{\alpha}'_t \boldsymbol{\beta}_t, \qquad (24)$$

and the firm's variable profit maximization problem takes the conventional form of selecting $(\boldsymbol{\mu}_t, \boldsymbol{\alpha}_t) \in S(\mathbf{k}_t)$ to maximize (24). Hence the existing literature on output aggregation for multiproduct firms becomes immediately applicable to aggregation over the produced monetary assets $\boldsymbol{\mu}_t$ and to measuring value added and technological change in financial intermediation.

3.1 Properties of the Model

Observe that variable revenue can be written in the form

$$\boldsymbol{\mu}'_t \boldsymbol{\gamma}_t = \boldsymbol{\mu}'_t \boldsymbol{\pi}^b_t - \frac{p^*_t R_t \mathbf{k}'_t \boldsymbol{\mu}_t}{1+R_t}, \qquad (25)$$

where

$$\pi^b_{it} = p^*_t \frac{R_t - \rho_{it}}{1+R_t} \qquad (26)$$

has the same form as the monetary asset user cost formula (5) for consumers' π_{it}. Clearly π^b_{it} in (26) would equal γ_{it} if $\mathbf{k}_t = \mathbf{0}$. As a result, it is evident that $p^*_t R_t \mathbf{k}'_t \boldsymbol{\mu}_t/(1+R_t)$ is the present value (at the beginning of the period) of the tax $p^*_t R_t \mathbf{k}'_t \boldsymbol{\mu}_t$ 'paid' by the financial intermediary (at the end of the period) as a result of the existence of reserve requirements. The tax is the foregone interest on uninvested required reserves.

The solution to the firm's variable profit-maximization problem is its factor demand functions for $\boldsymbol{\alpha} = (\mathbf{z}'_t, \mathbf{L}'_t, c_t)'$ and its supply functions for its multiple products $\boldsymbol{\mu}_t$. Derived demand is thereby produced for high-powered (base) money. That derived demand, in real terms, is

$$h_t = c_t + \sum_i k_{it} \mu_{it}. \qquad (27)$$

The financial firm's nominal demand for high-powered money is $p^*_t h_t$.

Stockholder capital (net worth) is a fixed factor during period t and hence does not enter the variable cost function. Since stockholder capital is not reservable, all stockholder capital will go into loans at yield R_t. If capital is paid the competitive rate of return, then all of the yield on the investment of stockholder capital will be paid to stockholders as dividends and hence will not affect either total or variable economic profits. However, the investment of stockholder capital will augment total accounting profits and will contribute to the total stock of loans in the economy.

3.2 Separability of Technology

If the user costs γ_t all moved proportionally, then we could use Hicksian aggregation to aggregate over the firm's joint monetary supplies $\boldsymbol{\mu}_t$. But since that proportionality assumption is not typically reasonable for monetary asset user costs, aggregation over outputs is possible only if outputs are separable from inputs in the financial firm's technology. Hence, in order to establish the existence of an output aggregate, we shall assume that there exist functions f and H such that[14]

$$F(\boldsymbol{\mu}_t, \mathbf{z}_t, \mathbf{L}_t, c_t; \mathbf{k}_t) = H(f(\boldsymbol{\mu}_t; \mathbf{k}_t), \mathbf{z}_t, \mathbf{L}_t, c_t). \tag{28}$$

It seems likely that $\mathbf{k}_t$ would enter F only through f, as in (28). However, this analysis could easily be extended to the case in which $\mathbf{k}_t$ also enters H as independent arguments.

There will exist a function g such that

$$f(\boldsymbol{\mu}_t; \mathbf{k}_t) = g(\mathbf{z}_t, \mathbf{L}_t, c_t) \tag{29}$$

is the solution for $f(\boldsymbol{\mu}_t; \mathbf{k}_t)$ to[15]

$$H(f(\boldsymbol{\mu}_t; \mathbf{k}_t), \mathbf{z}_t, \mathbf{L}_t, c_t) = 0. \tag{30}$$

The function $f(\boldsymbol{\mu}_t; \mathbf{k}_t)$ is called the factor requirements function because it equals the right-hand side of (29), which is the minimum amount of aggregate input required to produce the vector $\boldsymbol{\mu}_t$. The function $g(\mathbf{z}_t, \mathbf{L}_t, c_t)$ is the production function because it equals the left-hand side of (29), which is the maximum amount of aggregate output that can be produced from the inputs $(\mathbf{z}_t, \mathbf{L}_t, c_t)$. Hence f is both the factor requirements function and the outputs aggregator function, while g is both the output production function and the inputs aggregator function.

We assume that f is convex and linearly homogeneous in $\boldsymbol{\mu}_t$. In addition, it follows — from our assumptions on the derivatives of the transformation function F — that g is monotonically increasing in all of its arguments and that f is monotonically increasing in $\boldsymbol{\mu}_t$. We assume that g is locally strictly concave in a neighborhood of the solution to the first-order conditions for variable profit maximization. In addition, it follows — from the strict quasiconvexity of the transformation function F — that g is globally strictly quasiconcave.

---

[14] For the theoretical implications of that assumption for technology, see Denny and Pinto (1978), Hall (1973), and Shephard (1970, p. 275).

[15] The existence of g follows from the implicit function theorem and our assumptions on the transformation function F. See footnote 2 of Brown, Caves, and Christensen (1979).

4 Demand for Monetary Assets by Manufacturing Firms

In addition to consumer demand for monetary assets, there also is demand for monetary assets by manufacturing firms. In this section we formulate the decision problem of such a manufacturing firm when monetary assets enter the firm's production function.[16] The firm is assumed to maximize the present value of its profits flow subject to its technology. The firm's intertemporal technology, over its T-period planning horizon, is defined by its transformation function

$$\Omega(\boldsymbol{\delta}_t, \ldots, \boldsymbol{\delta}_{t+T}, \boldsymbol{\varepsilon}_t, \ldots, \boldsymbol{\varepsilon}_{t+T}, \boldsymbol{\kappa}_t, \ldots, \boldsymbol{\kappa}_{t+T}) = 0, \qquad (31)$$

where, for $t \leq s \leq t+T$:

$\boldsymbol{\delta}_s$ = vector of planned production of output quantities during period s;
$\boldsymbol{\varepsilon}_s$ = vector of planned real balances of monetary assets held during period s; and
$\boldsymbol{\kappa}_s$ = vector of planned use of other factors during period s.

The firm's technology can be equivalently defined by its efficient production set

$$\begin{aligned}\Gamma = \{(\boldsymbol{\delta}_t, \ldots, \boldsymbol{\delta}_{t+T}, \boldsymbol{\varepsilon}_t, \ldots, \boldsymbol{\varepsilon}_{t+T}, \boldsymbol{\kappa}_t, \ldots, \boldsymbol{\kappa}_{t+T}) : \\ \Omega(\boldsymbol{\delta}_t, \ldots, \boldsymbol{\delta}_{t+T}, \boldsymbol{\varepsilon}_t, \ldots, \boldsymbol{\varepsilon}_{t+T}, \boldsymbol{\kappa}_t, \ldots, \boldsymbol{\kappa}_{t+T}) = 0\}.\end{aligned} \qquad (32)$$

The transformation function Ω is assumed to be strictly quasiconvex. In addition, $\partial\Omega/\partial\delta_{is} > 0$, $\partial\Omega/\partial\varepsilon_{is} < 0$, and $\partial\Omega/\partial\kappa_{is} < 0$.

The firm's decision problem is formulated in period t for periods $t, t+1, \ldots, s, \ldots, t+T$, where T is the number of periods in the firm's planning

---

[16] Since manufacturing technology does not depend upon money balances, our production function is actually a derived production function acquired by absorbing the firm's transactions technologies in factor markets into the production function. The existence of such a derived production function follows from the same analysis used to prove the existence of a derived utility function containing monetary balances. See Arrow and Hahn (1971), Phlips and Spinnewyn (1982), and Samuelson and Sato (1984). For explicit derivations of the derived production function based upon a Baumol-Tobin transactions model or a vending-machine model, see Fischer (1974). Fischer (1974, p. 532) concludes that real balances can be entered into production or utility functions unless a 'deeper explanation of the demand for money' is needed. Since we are not seeking to explain why people demand money, but rather how they behave when money has value, we have no need for deeper explanation for motives.

Demand for Assets by Firms

horizon. During period s, the firm's profits are

$$\Psi_s = \delta'_s \nu_s - \kappa'_s \zeta_s + \sum_i [(1+r_{i,s-1})p^*_{s-1}\varepsilon_{i,s-1} - p^*_s \varepsilon_{is}], \tag{33}$$

where

ν_s = vector of output expected prices, and
ζ_s = vector of expected prices of the factors κ_s.

To simplify the notation, we assume that consumers and manufacturing firms have access to the same monetary assets, so the expected nominal holding period yields on ε_s can be viewed as being r_s (defined in Section 2.1). Real balances ε_t are defined to equal nominal balances divided by p^*_t (also defined in Section 2.1).[17]

The discounted present value of the firm's profit flow during the $T+1$ periods plus the discounted present value of the firm's monetary asset portfolio at the end of the planning horizon is

$$\Psi^* = \sum_{s=t}^{t+T} (\Psi_s/\theta_s) + (1/\theta_{t+T+1}) \sum_i p^*_{t+T} \varepsilon_{i,t+T}(1+r_{i,t+T}), \tag{34}$$

where the discount factor is θ_s, such that $\theta_s = 1.0$ for $s = t$ and

$$\theta_s = \prod_{a=t}^{s-1}(1+R_a) \quad \text{for} \quad t+1 \leq s \leq t+T+1.$$

We now substitute (33) into (34) and rearrange the terms, grouping together those terms with common time subscripts. The result is

$$\Psi^* = \sum_{s=t}^{t+T} \delta'_s \bar{\nu}_s - \sum_{s=t}^{t+T} \kappa'_s \bar{\zeta}_s - \sum_{s=t}^{t+T} \varepsilon'_s \eta_s + \sum_{i=1}^{n}(1+r_{i,t-1})p^*_{t-1}\varepsilon_{t-1}, \tag{35}$$

---

[17]This definition is greatly simplifying because it permits use of the same price index, p^*_t, for the manufacturing firm as for the consumer. We shall do the same thing with the financial firm's output in the next section. Thus the same price deflator applies to consumer monetary asset demand, manufacturing firm monetary factor demand, and financial firm output demand. Unfortunately this assumption is not based upon solid theoretical foundations; in principle, a different price deflator should be used in each of the three cases. Our only defense is that perhaps the three theoretically correct deflators may not differ that much. However, our deflator is theoretically correct only for the consumer, since we produced p^*_t from consumer duality theory. For rigorous treatment of firm input and output deflators, see Fisher and Shell (1972, essay 2; 1979; 1981).

where $\bar{\nu}_s = \nu_s/\theta_s$ and $\bar{\zeta}_s = \zeta_s/\theta_s$ are the discounted present values of the prices ν_s and ζ_s respectively, and where the user cost of ε_{is} is

$$\eta_{is} = (p_s^*/\theta_s) - (1 + r_{is})p_s^*/\theta_{s+1}. \tag{36}$$

Because $\sum_{i=1}^{n}(1 + r_{i,t-1})p_{t-1}^*\varepsilon_{t-1}$ is wealth endowed from the previous planning horizon, that contribution to present wealth is fixed. Hence the discounted present value of variable profits is

$$\Psi_v^* = \sum_{s=t}^{t+T}\delta_s\bar{\nu}_s - \sum_{s=t}^{t+T}\kappa_s'\bar{\zeta}_s - \sum_{s=t}^{t+T}\varepsilon_s'\eta_s, \tag{37}$$

which is in conventional form. In addition, the user cost η_{is} in the current period $s = t$ is

$$\eta_{it} = p_t^*\frac{(R_t - r_{it})}{1 + R_t}, \tag{38}$$

which is in familiar form [see equations (4) and (26)]. With the conventional decision problem of maximizing variable profit (37) subject to (31), we have immediate access to the existing literature on aggregation over factors of production, enabling us to aggregate over monetary assets ε_t demanded by the manufacturing firm.

The approach used above to derive the user cost formula η_{is} is analogous to that used for physical capital by Diewert (1980a, p. 47). The same result would be acquired from the approach of Coen and Hickman (1970, p. 298), because the first-order conditions for maximization of (37) subject to (31) include the condition that the marginal rate of substitution between ε_{is} and ε_{js} be $-\eta_{is}/\eta_{js}$. Using the observations of Diewert (1980a, pp. 478–9), extension of the above results to include taxes is straightforward. See Coen and Hickman (1970, p. 299) for discussion of the approaches to dealing with such further potential complications as differences between borrowing and lending rates, the existence of more than one lending rate, differences in taxation rates, risk-induced dependency upon debt/equity ratios, and so on. The extension of the above result to an infinite planning horizon is immediate by allowing $T \to \infty$ in (35).

4.1 Separability of Technology

For the same reason discussed in (16), we shall require that technology be separable, although here separability will be assumed in current monetary assets used as inputs (by the manufacturing firm) rather than in monetary assets produced as outputs (by the financial intermediary). In particular, we assume that there exist functions a and B such that

$$\Omega(\delta_t, \ldots, \delta_{t+T}, \varepsilon_t, \ldots, \varepsilon_{t+T}, \kappa_t, \ldots, \kappa_{t+T})$$
$$= B(\delta_t, \ldots, \delta_{t+T}, a(\varepsilon_t), \varepsilon_{t+1}, \ldots, \varepsilon_{t+T}, \kappa_t, \ldots, \kappa_{t+T}). \quad (39)$$

In that case, the function $a(\varepsilon_t)$ is called a category subproduction function.

Let $(\delta_t^*, \ldots, \delta_{t+T}^*, \varepsilon_t^*, \ldots, \varepsilon_{t+T}^*, \kappa_t^*, \ldots, \kappa_{t+T}^*)$ be the solution to maximizing (37) subject to (31), and let $b_t = \varepsilon_t^{*\prime} \eta_t$. Then it follows that ε_t^* must also be the solution for ε_t to the current period conditional decision:

$$\text{maximize } a(\varepsilon_t) \text{ subject to } \eta_t' \varepsilon_t = b_t, \quad (40)$$

which is in the same form as (4) for the consumer. In addition, if we divide both sides of the constraint in (40) by p_t^* then we obtain the following decision, which is in the same form as (6):

$$\text{maximize } a(\varepsilon_t) \text{ subject to } \eta_t^{*\prime} \varepsilon = b_t^*, \quad (41)$$

where $\eta_t^* = \eta_t/p_t^*$ and $b_t^* = b_t/p_t^*$. The function $a(\varepsilon_t)$ is assumed to be monotonically increasing and strictly concave in ε_t. The large literature in aggregation and index number theory based upon the conventional consumer decision, of form (6), is immediately applicable to decision (41) and hence to aggregation over ε_t.

Numerous simplifying assumptions were made in Sections 2, 3, and 4. Although these assumptions are common in the conventional neoclassical literature, extension of these results to include (for example) uncertainty and differences in taxation rates would be useful. A list of areas needing such extensions in the conventional approach can be found in Diewert (1980b, p. 265).[18]

5 Aggregation Theory Under Homogeneity

The theory of aggregation over goods directly produces unique, exact results when the aggregator function is linearly homogeneous. In that case, the growth rates of the aggregation-theoretic price and quantity aggregates are independent of selected reference levels for utility, prices, or quantities. In addition, the dual quantity and price aggregates then behave in a manner indistinguishable from that of an elementary good. In this section, we discuss that most elegant of situations. In Section 6, we present recent theory relevant to aggregation in the nonhomothetic case.

---

[18] Some of those extensions can be found in Part 3 of this book.

5.1 The Consumer

Here we seek to produce the exact aggregation theoretic aggregate over the monetary asset quantities $\mathbf{m}_t$ of Section 2. As shown in Barnett (1980a, 1981b), the exact quantity aggregate is the level of indirect (i.e., optimized) utility

$$M_t^c = \max\{u(\mathbf{m}_t) : \boldsymbol{\pi}_t'\mathbf{m}_t = y_t\}, \tag{42}$$

so u is the aggregator function that we assume to be linearly homogeneous in this section. Dual to any exact quantity aggregate, there exists a unique price aggregate, one that aggregates over the prices of the goods. Hence there must exist an exact nominal price aggregate over the user costs $\boldsymbol{\pi}_t$, and there must also exist the corresponding real (user cost) price aggregate over $\boldsymbol{\pi}_t^*$. As shown in Barnett (1980a, 1981b), the consumer behaves relative to the dual pair of exact quantity and price aggregates as if they were the quantity and price of an elementary good. As a result, the exact aggregate is empirically indistinguishable from an elementary good.

One of the properties that an exact dual pair of price and quantity aggregates satisfies is Fisher's 'factor reversal' test, which states that the product of an exact quantity aggregate and its dual exact price aggregate must equal actual expenditure on the components. Hence if $\Pi^c(\boldsymbol{\pi}_t)$ is the exact user cost aggregate dual to M_t^c, then $\Pi^c(\boldsymbol{\pi}_t)$ must satisfy

$$\Pi^c(\boldsymbol{\pi}_t) = y_t / M_t^c. \tag{43}$$

Since (43) produces a unique solution for $\Pi^c(\boldsymbol{\pi}_t)$, we could use (43) to define $\Pi^c(\boldsymbol{\pi}_t)$. In addition, if we replace M_t^c by the indirect utility function that is defined by (42) and use the linear homogeneity of u, we can show that $\Pi_t^c = \Pi^c(\boldsymbol{\pi}_t)$ defined by (43) does indeed depend only upon $\boldsymbol{\pi}_t$, and not upon $\mathbf{m}_t$ or y_t. See Barnett (1983b) for a version of that proof. The conclusion produced by that proof can be written in the form

$$\Pi^c(\boldsymbol{\pi}_t) = \left[\max_{\mathbf{m}_t}\{u(\mathbf{m}_t) : \boldsymbol{\pi}_t'\mathbf{m}_t = 1\}\right]^{-1}, \tag{44}$$

which clearly depends only upon $\boldsymbol{\pi}_t$.

Although (43) provides a valid definition of Π_t^c, a direct definition (not produced indirectly through M_t^c and Fisher's factor reversal test) is more informative and often more useful. The direct definition depends upon the cost (or expenditure) function E, defined by

$$E(u_0, \boldsymbol{\pi}_t) = \min_{\mathbf{m}_t}\{\boldsymbol{\pi}_t'\mathbf{m}_t : u(\mathbf{m}_t) = u_0\}, \tag{45}$$

which equivalently can be acquired by solving the indirect utility function equation (42) for y as a function of $u_0 = M_t^c$ and π_t. It can be proved [see, e.g., Shephard (1970, p. 144)] that

$$\Pi^c(\pi_t) = E(1, \pi_t) = \min_{\mathbf{m}_t}\{\pi_t'\mathbf{m}_t : u(\mathbf{m}_t) = 1\}, \qquad (46)$$

which is often called the unit cost or price function. The unit cost function is the minimum cost of attaining unit utility level for $u(\mathbf{m}_t)$ at given user cost prices π_t. Clearly, (46) depends only upon π_t. Hence by (43) and (46), we see that $\Pi^c(\pi_t) = y_t/M_t^c = E(1, \pi_t)$.

Equation (46) is the most informative expression for Π_t^c. For example, it is immediately evident from (46) that Π^c is linearly homogeneous in π_t. Hence the real user cost aggregate is $\Pi_t^{c*} = \Pi^c(\pi_t/p_t^*) = \Pi^c(\pi_t)/p_t^*$. In addition, we can see from (46) that (M_t^c, Π_t^c) must satisfy Fisher's factor reversal test. The demonstration of that result follows. Observe first that

$$\begin{aligned} M_t^c \min_{\mathbf{m}_t}\{\pi_t'\mathbf{m}_t : u(\mathbf{m}_t) = 1\} &= \min_{\mathbf{m}_t}\{\pi_t'(M_t^c\mathbf{m}_t) : M_t^c u(\mathbf{m}_t) = M_t^c\} \\ &= \min_{\mathbf{m}_t}\{\pi_t'(M_t^c\mathbf{m}_t) : u(M_t^c\mathbf{m}_t) = M_t^c\}, \quad (47) \end{aligned}$$

where the last equality follows from the linear homogeneity of u. If we let $\hat{\mathbf{m}}_t = M_t^c\mathbf{m}_t$, then

$$M_t^c \min_{\mathbf{m}_t}\{\pi_t'\mathbf{m}_t : u(\mathbf{m}_t) = 1\} = \min_{\hat{\mathbf{m}}_t}\{\pi_t'\hat{\mathbf{m}}_t : u(\hat{\mathbf{m}}_t) = M_t^c\}. \qquad (48)$$

Hence, by (46), we obtain from (48) that

$$M_t^c\Pi_t^c = \min_{\hat{\mathbf{m}}_t}\{\pi_t'\hat{\mathbf{m}}_t : u(\hat{\mathbf{m}}_t) = M_t^c\}. \qquad (49)$$

However, expenditure minimization (at the optimized value M_t^c of utility) is a necessary condition for utility maximization. Hence the right-hand side of (49) will be actual expenditure on the services of $\mathbf{m}_t$, and therefore (49) is Fisher's factor reversal test. A more formal proof, not explicitly including monetary assets, is available in Shephard (1970, p. 93).

In addition, (42) and (46) provide easy interpretations of (M_t^c, Π_t^c). From (42), we see that M_t^c is the consumer's optimized utility level from monetary assets held during period t. Hence M_t^c is the consumer's perceived service flow from his selected $\mathbf{m}_t$. In order similarly to interpret Π_t^c, observe from (45) and (49) that $E(M_t^c, \pi_t) = M_t^c\Pi_t^c$. Differentiating both sides with respect to M_t^c, we see immediately that

$$\Pi_t^c = \partial E(M_t^c, \pi_t)/\partial M_t^c. \qquad (50)$$

Hence Π_t^c is the marginal cost to the consumer of consuming another unit of aggregate monetary services, M_t^c.

It is interesting to observe that we could work in reverse to derive (46) from Fisher's factor reversal test, (49). In particular, if we *define* Π_t^c by (49), we could then use (48) to acquire (46) as a conclusion. Alternatively, we could start with (49) and simply let $M_t^c = 1$ to acquire (46) immediately.

The duality between M_t^c and Π_t^c is evident from (42) and (46), which use dual decision problems. In addition, the duality between M_t^c and Π_t^c permits us to get back and forth between them easily. The indirect method would be through (43). But we also can derive either M_t^c or Π_t^c directly in terms of the other. As can be seen from (42), the quantity aggregator function is u, because M_t^c is equal to $u(\mathbf{m}_t^*)$ when $\mathbf{m}_t^*$ is the consumer's chosen (constrained utility-maximizing) choice for $\mathbf{m}_t$. Hence we see immediately that we can derive the user cost price aggregate directly from the corresponding quantity aggregator function from either (44) or (46). Conversely, the quantity aggregate $M_t^c = u(\mathbf{m}_t^*)$ can be derived directly from the price aggregator function Π^c, because

$$u(\mathbf{m}_t^*) = \left[\max_{\boldsymbol{\pi} \geq 0}\{\Pi^c(\boldsymbol{\pi}) : \boldsymbol{\pi}'\mathbf{m}_t^* = 1\}\right]^{-1}. \tag{51}$$

See Diewert (1981, equation 4).

We now have the fundamental aggregation-theoretic tools for aggregating over goods within the decision of a consumer. The reason that M_t^c and Π_t^c are called exact aggregates is that (M_t^c, Π_t^c) can be used to decompose the consumer's decision into a two-stage budgeting process. In the first stage, M_t^c is treated as an elementary good with price Π_t^c within the intertemporal utility maximization decision. In particular, M_t^c appears in place of $u(\mathbf{m}_t)$ within the intertemporal utility function U_t. Having solved for M_t^c in the first stage, the consumer then solves for $\mathbf{m}_t$ from the second-stage decision (4), with y_t determined from $M_t^c\Pi_t^c$. For all possible nonnegative values of prices and wealth, the two-stage decision will produce the same solution as the original complete decision defined in section 2.1 or 2.2. Hence (M_t^c, Π_t^c) are behaviorally indistinguishable from the quantity and price of an elementary good. The details of the two-stage budgeting theorem are available in Barnett (1980a, 1981b) and Green (1964, Theorem 4).

5.2 The Manufacturing Firm

Since the decision problems (6) and (41) are in the same form, the aggregation theory in Section 5.1 for consumer demand for monetary assets is immediately applicable to aggregation over monetary assets demanded by a manufacturing firm. The only change is in the interpretation of the quantity aggregator function. With a consumer, the quantity aggregator function is the category subutility function u. With a manufacturing firm, the quantity aggregator function is the category subproduction function $a(\varepsilon_t)$. Clearly, the quantity aggregator function in both cases is the objective function of the corresponding conditional decision problem, (6) or (41).

In the case of demand by a manufacturing firm, however, a particularly interesting interpretation of the derivable two-stage budgeting process is available, as has been observed by Blackorby, Primont, and Russell (1978, p. 210). Restating their interpretation of separable factor demand in terms of monetary asset demand, the following becomes available under our assumptions. Instead of maximizing profits directly in a single joint decision, the firm can produce the same optimum solution by decentralizing its monetary portfolio decisions to a financial 'division' or department, which is instructed to maximize its financial services with a fixed allocated budget b_t. In other words, the financial division is asked to select its monetary portfolio ε_t by solving decision problem (40). In order for that decentralized decision to be solvable, the firm's corporate office must be able to determine the optimal level of monetary expenditure b_t to be supplied to the financial division before it solves problem (40). It can be shown that the firm can produce that correct prior solution for b_t from its first-stage decision problem. That first-stage decision requires knowledge of the firm's exact monetary user cost aggregate $\Pi_t^f = \Pi^f(\eta_t)$, which can be acquired by the financial division from the right-hand side of (44) or of (46) when the symbols (functions or variables) from the consumer's decision are replaced in the obvious manner by the corresponding symbols from the firm's decision. That correspondence between symbols is the one acquired by replacing decision (6) with decision (41).

In summary, the firm could operate in the following decentralized manner. The financial division uses (44) or (46) to acquire Π_t^f, which the financial division supplies to the firm's corporate office. The corporate office then solves the firm's first-stage decision to acquire the profit-maximizing budget b_t to be allocated to financial services. Having received b_t, the financial division then selects the optimal portfolio of monetary assets ε_t by solving problem (40) to maximize monetary services M_t^f available from the fixed budget. The result is exact profit maximization by the firm. The resulting exact monetary quantity aggregate, as with the consumer, is (42) (with the obvious change of symbols between consumers and firms). Observe that the monetary quantity aggregate M_t^f is the optimized level of the financial division's objective function, and hence is the optimized monetary asset service flow.

In the above decentralized two-stage decision, we have identified the second-stage decision to be decision problem (40), which is solved conditionally upon b_t. However, we have not formally defined the first-stage ('corporate office') decision, which is needed to determine the profit maximizing portfolio services budget b_t. That first-stage decision is to select $(\boldsymbol{\delta}_t^*, \ldots, \boldsymbol{\delta}_{t+T}^*, M_t^f, \boldsymbol{\varepsilon}_{t+1}^*, \ldots, \boldsymbol{\varepsilon}_{t+T}^*, \boldsymbol{\kappa}_t^*, \ldots, \boldsymbol{\kappa}_{t+T}^*)$ to maximize the discounted present value of variable profits

$$\Psi^* = \sum_{s=t}^{t+T} \boldsymbol{\delta}_s \bar{\boldsymbol{\nu}}_s - \sum_{s=t}^{t+T} \boldsymbol{\kappa}_s' \bar{\boldsymbol{\zeta}}_s - \sum_{s=t+1}^{t+T} \boldsymbol{\varepsilon}_s' \boldsymbol{\eta}_s - M_t^f \Pi_t^f, \tag{52}$$

subject to

$$B(\boldsymbol{\delta}_t, \ldots, \boldsymbol{\delta}_{t+T}, M_t^f, \boldsymbol{\varepsilon}_{t+1}, \ldots, \boldsymbol{\varepsilon}_{t+T}, \boldsymbol{\kappa}_t, \ldots, \boldsymbol{\kappa}_{t+T}) = 0. \tag{53}$$

Having solved that decision, involving the aggregated quantity M_t^f and price Π_t^f, the optimal budget for financial services is immediately available as $b_t = M_t^f \Pi_t^f$.

The consumer's two-stage decision can be interpreted in an analogous manner, but with the quantity aggregator function u viewed as the consumer's transactions technology.

5.2.1 The two-stage decentralized decision

The fact that two-stage decentralization is possible, and that it always produces the firm's profit-maximizing solution for all values, is easily proved when the two-stage decision is restated in a different form. Since that result previously has been proved only for single-output firms, we now provide the proof for multiple-output firms. The proof is a straight-forward extension of Shephard's (1970, pp. 144–6) result with a single-output technology. In this section, we assume that the second-stage decision (the financial division's decision) is to minimize cost at fixed output of monetary services. Hence the corporate office, after solving the first-stage decision, supplies M_t^f to the financial division, which then minimizes cost subject to $a(\boldsymbol{\varepsilon}_t) = M_t^f$. In our previous equivalent interpretation, the corporate office supplies $b_t = M_t^f \Pi_t^f$ to the financial division, which then maximizes $a(\boldsymbol{\varepsilon}_t)$ subject to the condition that cost cannot exceed b_t.

We shall need the firm's full intertemporal variable cost function

$$C(\boldsymbol{\delta}_t, \ldots, \boldsymbol{\delta}_{t+T}, \bar{\boldsymbol{\zeta}}_t, \ldots, \bar{\boldsymbol{\zeta}}_{t+T}, \boldsymbol{\eta}_t, \ldots, \boldsymbol{\eta}_{t+T})$$
$$= \min_{(\boldsymbol{\kappa}_t, \ldots, \boldsymbol{\kappa}_{t+T}, \boldsymbol{\varepsilon}_t, \ldots, \boldsymbol{\varepsilon}_{t+T})} \left\{ \sum_{s=t}^{t+T} \boldsymbol{\kappa}_s' \bar{\boldsymbol{\zeta}}_s + \sum_{s=t}^{t+T} \boldsymbol{\varepsilon}_s' \boldsymbol{\eta}_s : B(\boldsymbol{\delta}_t, \ldots, \boldsymbol{\delta}_{t+T}, \right.$$
$$\left. a(\boldsymbol{\varepsilon}_t), \boldsymbol{\varepsilon}_{t+1}, \ldots, \boldsymbol{\varepsilon}_{t+T}, \boldsymbol{\kappa}_t, \ldots, \boldsymbol{\kappa}_{t+T}) = 0. \right\}. \tag{54}$$

Observe that (54) is acquired by minimizing all of the firm's variable factor costs. In contrast, the subcost function $E(a_0, \boldsymbol{\eta}_t)$, defined by the production analog to (45), is acquired by minimizing only the firm's monetary service costs. In particular, that subcost function is

$$E(a_0, \boldsymbol{\eta}_t) = \min_{\boldsymbol{\varepsilon}_t}\{\boldsymbol{\eta}'_t \boldsymbol{\varepsilon}_t : a(\boldsymbol{\varepsilon}_t) = a_0\}. \tag{55}$$

Let

$$\boldsymbol{\delta} = (\boldsymbol{\delta}'_t, \ldots, \boldsymbol{\delta}'_{t+T})', \quad \bar{\boldsymbol{\zeta}} = (\bar{\boldsymbol{\zeta}}'_t, \ldots, \bar{\boldsymbol{\zeta}}'_{t+T})', \quad \boldsymbol{\eta} = (\boldsymbol{\eta}'_t, \ldots, \boldsymbol{\eta}'_{t+T})',$$
$$\boldsymbol{\kappa} = (\boldsymbol{\kappa}'_t, \ldots, \boldsymbol{\kappa}'_{t+T})', \quad \boldsymbol{\varepsilon} = (\boldsymbol{\varepsilon}'_t, \ldots, \boldsymbol{\varepsilon}'_{t+T})', \quad \text{and } \bar{\boldsymbol{\nu}} = (\bar{\boldsymbol{\nu}}'_t, \ldots, \bar{\boldsymbol{\nu}}'_{t+T})'.$$

We now prove the following theorem, which is needed to prove the consistency of the two-stage decision.

Theorem 1

$$C(\boldsymbol{\delta}, \bar{\boldsymbol{\zeta}}, \boldsymbol{\eta}) = \min_{(\boldsymbol{\kappa}, a_0, \boldsymbol{\varepsilon}_{t+1}, \ldots, \boldsymbol{\varepsilon}_{t+T})} \Big\{ \boldsymbol{\kappa}\bar{\boldsymbol{\zeta}} + E(a_0, \boldsymbol{\eta}_t) $$
$$+ \sum_{s=t+1}^{t+T} \boldsymbol{\varepsilon}'_s \boldsymbol{\eta}_s : B(\boldsymbol{\delta}, a_0, \boldsymbol{\varepsilon}_{t+1}, \ldots, \boldsymbol{\varepsilon}_{t+T}, \boldsymbol{\kappa}) = 0 \Big\}.$$

Proof: Define $(\boldsymbol{\kappa}^*, \boldsymbol{\varepsilon}^*)$ to solve the minimization problem in (54), so that

$$C(\boldsymbol{\delta}, \bar{\boldsymbol{\zeta}}, \boldsymbol{\eta}) = \boldsymbol{\kappa}^* \bar{\boldsymbol{\zeta}} + \boldsymbol{\varepsilon}^{*'} \boldsymbol{\eta} \tag{56}$$

with

$$B(\boldsymbol{\delta}, a(\boldsymbol{\varepsilon}^*_t), \boldsymbol{\varepsilon}^*_{t+1}, \ldots, \boldsymbol{\varepsilon}^*_{t+T}, \boldsymbol{\kappa}^*) = 0; \tag{57}$$

and define $(\hat{\boldsymbol{\kappa}}, \hat{a}_0, \hat{\boldsymbol{\varepsilon}}_{t+1}, \ldots, \hat{\boldsymbol{\varepsilon}}_{t+T})$; such that

$$\min_{(\boldsymbol{\kappa}, a_0, \boldsymbol{\varepsilon}_{t+1}, \ldots, \boldsymbol{\varepsilon}_{t+T})} \Big\{ \boldsymbol{\kappa}'\bar{\boldsymbol{\zeta}} + E(a_0, \boldsymbol{\eta}_t)$$
$$+ \sum_{s=t+1}^{t+T} \boldsymbol{\varepsilon}'_s \boldsymbol{\eta}_s : B(\boldsymbol{\delta}, a_0, \boldsymbol{\varepsilon}_{t+1}, \ldots, \boldsymbol{\varepsilon}_{t+T}, \boldsymbol{\kappa}) = 0 \Big\}$$
$$= \hat{\boldsymbol{\kappa}}'\bar{\boldsymbol{\zeta}} + E(\hat{a}_0, \boldsymbol{\eta}_t) + \sum_{s=t+1}^{t+T} \hat{\boldsymbol{\varepsilon}}'_s \boldsymbol{\eta}_s \tag{58}$$

with

$$B(\boldsymbol{\delta}, \hat{a}_0, \hat{\boldsymbol{\varepsilon}}_{t+1}, \ldots, \hat{\boldsymbol{\varepsilon}}_{t+T}, \hat{\boldsymbol{\kappa}}) = 0; \tag{59}$$

but suppose that

$$\kappa^{*\prime}\bar{\zeta} + \varepsilon^{*\prime}\eta \neq \hat{\kappa}\bar{\zeta} + E(\hat{a}_0, \eta_t) + \sum_{s=t+1}^{t+T} \hat{\varepsilon}'_s \eta_s. \tag{60}$$

Define $\hat{\varepsilon}_t$ to solve the minimization problem in (55) when $a_0 = \hat{a}_0$, so that

$$E(\hat{a}_0, \eta_t) = \eta'_t \hat{\varepsilon}_t \tag{61}$$

with

$$a(\hat{\varepsilon}_t) = \hat{a}_0. \tag{62}$$

Then, by (59) and (62), we have that

$$B(\delta, a(\hat{\varepsilon}_t), \hat{\varepsilon}_{t+1}, \ldots, \hat{\varepsilon}_{t+T}, \hat{\kappa}) = 0, \tag{63}$$

so $(\hat{\kappa}, \hat{\varepsilon}_t, \hat{\varepsilon}_{t+1}, \ldots, \hat{\varepsilon}_{t+T})$ is feasible for the minimization problem in (54). Hence, by the definition of $(\kappa^*, \varepsilon^*)$, we see that

$$\kappa^{*\prime}\bar{\zeta} + \varepsilon_t^{*\prime}\eta_t + \sum_{s=t+1}^{t+T} \varepsilon_s^{*\prime}\eta_s < \hat{\kappa}'\bar{\zeta} + \hat{\varepsilon}'_t \eta_t + \sum_{s=t+1}^{t+T} \hat{\varepsilon}'_s \eta_s. \tag{64}$$

Let $a_0^* = a(\mathbf{e}_t^*)$. Then, by (57), we have that

$$B(\delta, a_0^*, \varepsilon_{t+1}^*, \ldots, \varepsilon_{t+T}^*, \kappa^*) = 0,$$

so $(\kappa^*, a_0^*, \varepsilon_{t+1}^*, \ldots, \varepsilon_{t+T}^*)$ is feasible for the minimization problem in (58). But by (54), ε_t^* must minimize $\eta'_t \varepsilon_t$ subject to

$$B(\delta, a(\varepsilon_t), \varepsilon_{t+1}^*, \ldots, \varepsilon_{t+T}^*, \kappa^*) = 0. \tag{65}$$

Also, by the monotonicity of B in $a(\varepsilon_t)$ and by (57), it follows that (65) is true if and only if $a(\varepsilon_t) = a_0^*$. Hence ε_t^* must minimize $\eta'\varepsilon_t$ subject to $a(\varepsilon_t) = a_0^*$, which is the minimization problem in (55). So

$$E(a_0^*, \eta_t) = \eta'_t \varepsilon_t^*. \tag{66}$$

By the feasibility of $(\kappa^*, a_0^*, \varepsilon_{t+1}^*, \ldots, \varepsilon_{t+T}^*)$ in the minimization problem in (58) and by the definition of $(\hat{\kappa}, \hat{\varepsilon}_t, \hat{\varepsilon}_{t+1}, \ldots, \hat{\varepsilon}_{t+T})$, it follows that

$$\hat{\kappa}'\bar{\zeta} + E(\hat{a}_0, \eta_t) + \sum_{s=t+1}^{t+T} \hat{\varepsilon}'_s \eta_s < \kappa^{*\prime}\bar{\zeta} + E(a_0^*, \eta_t) + \sum_{s=t+1}^{t+T} \varepsilon_s^{*\prime}\eta_s.$$

Combining that result with (61) and (66), we contradict (64). □

Producing the firm's decentralized two-stage decision problem is now straightforward. First observe from the production analog of (59) that

$$\Pi_t^f(\eta_t)a_0 = E(a_0, \eta_t),$$

which is just Fisher's factor reversal test. From Theorem 1 we therefore have that

$$C(\delta, \bar{\zeta}, \eta) = \min_{(\kappa, a_0, \varepsilon_{t+1}, \ldots, \varepsilon_{t+T})} \left\{ \kappa'\bar{\zeta} + \Pi_t^f(\eta_t)a_0 + \sum_{s=t+1}^{t+T} \varepsilon'_s \eta_s : \right.$$

$$\left. B(\delta, a_0, \varepsilon_{t+1}, \ldots, \varepsilon_{t+T}, \kappa) = 0 \right\}. \quad (67)$$

The firm maximizes profits by solving for the output levels δ to maximize $\delta\nu - C(\delta, \bar{\zeta}, \eta)$. Hence it follows from (67) that the firm can maximize profits by selecting $(\delta^*, \kappa^*, a_0^*, \varepsilon_{t+1}^*, \ldots, \varepsilon_{t+T}^*)$ to

$$\text{maximize} \quad \delta\nu - \kappa'\bar{\zeta} - \Pi_t^f(\eta_t)a_0 - \sum_{s=t+1}^{t+T} \varepsilon'_s \eta_s$$

$$\text{subject to} \quad B(\delta, a_0, \varepsilon_{t+1}, \ldots, \varepsilon_{t+T}, \kappa) = 0, \quad (68)$$

which is the first stage decision.

In the second stage, the firm's corporate office instructs the financial division to purchase a_0^* quantity units of monetary services at minimum cost. The financial division then selects the monetary asset portfolio ε_t^* to solve the decision problem on the right-hand side of (55) with a_0 set at a_0^*. At this point the firm has optimally solved its full profit-maximization problem, because $(\delta^*, \kappa^*, \varepsilon_t^*, \varepsilon_{t+1}^*, \ldots, \varepsilon_{t+T}^*)$ is the profit-maximizing input-output vector.

Recall that a necessary condition for profit maximization is that ε_t^* solve problem (32). Hence it follows from the production analog of (42) that the firm's solution value for $a_0^* = a(\varepsilon_t^*)$ must equal its exact monetary quantity aggregate

$$M_t^f = \max\{a(\varepsilon_t) : \eta_t'\varepsilon_t = b_t\}. \quad (69)$$

The corresponding exact economic price aggregate clearly is $\Pi_t^f(\eta_t)$.

The above two-stage decomposition of the firm's profit-maximization decision provides the reason for defining M_t^f and $\Pi_t^f(\eta_t)$ to be the firm's exact monetary quantity and price aggregates. However, that decomposition can also be used as a means for estimating the firm's technology in two stages. See Fuss (1977).[19]

---

[19] Fuss's procedure also requires use of the fact that homogeneous separability of a production function implies corresponding homogeneous separability of the cost function.

5.3 The Financial Intermediary

The aggregation theory relevant to aggregating over the outputs of the multi-product financial firm is analogous to that for aggregation over the financial inputs of the manufacturing firm, but with the manufacturing firm's cost function replaced by the financial firm's revenue (or 'benefit') function. In this manner we can produce a two-stage decision for the financial intermediary. In the first stage the firm solves for profit-maximizing factor demands and the profit-maximizing level of aggregate financial assets produced. In the second stage, the revenue-maximizing vector of individual financial asset quantities supplied is determined at fixed aggregate financial asset quantity supplied.

To display that decomposition of the firm's profit-maximization decision, we start by defining the relevant revenue functions. The financial firm's revenue function is

$$R^*(\boldsymbol{\alpha}_t, \boldsymbol{\gamma}_t; \mathbf{k}_t) = \max_{\boldsymbol{\mu}_t}\{\boldsymbol{\mu}_t'\boldsymbol{\gamma}_t : f(\boldsymbol{\mu}_t; \mathbf{k}_t) = g(\boldsymbol{\alpha}_t)\}, \tag{70}$$

which is the revenue function analog of the manufacturing firm's cost function (54). The firm selects $\boldsymbol{\alpha}_t$ to maximize variable profits

$$P_t = R^*(\boldsymbol{\alpha}_t, \boldsymbol{\gamma}_t, \mathbf{k}_t) - \boldsymbol{\alpha}_t'\boldsymbol{\beta}_t. \tag{71}$$

However, by Shephard's (1970, p. 251) Proposition 83, it follows that there exists a linearly homogeneous output price aggregator function Γ such that[20]

$$R^*(\boldsymbol{\alpha}_t, \boldsymbol{\gamma}_t; \mathbf{k}_t) = \Gamma(\boldsymbol{\gamma}_t)g(\boldsymbol{\alpha}_t). \tag{72}$$

Hence the financial firm's variable profits can alternatively be written as

$$P_t = \Gamma(\boldsymbol{\gamma}_t)g(\boldsymbol{\alpha}_t) - \boldsymbol{\alpha}_t'\boldsymbol{\beta}_t. \tag{73}$$

The firm's first-stage decision is to select $\boldsymbol{\alpha}_t^*$ to maximize (73). Substituting the optimized input vector $\boldsymbol{\alpha}_t^*$ into $g(\boldsymbol{\alpha}_t)$, the firm can compute the optimum aggregate monetary asset quantity supplied, M_t^b. In stage two of the decentralized decision, M_t^b is substituted into (70) to replace $g(\boldsymbol{\alpha}_t)$, and the maximization problem in (70) is solved to acquire the optimum vector of individual monetary assets $\boldsymbol{\mu}_t$ produced. Observe that the intermediary's supply function for its monetary aggregate is produced from stage one alone.

---

[20] An analogous result exists for the firm's inputs. Under our assumptions of separability and homogeneity of the output aggregator function, Hall (1973) has shown that the firm's cost function is separable, such that $C(\boldsymbol{\mu}_t, \boldsymbol{\beta}_t; \mathbf{k}_t) = f(\boldsymbol{\mu}_t, \mathbf{k}_t)P(\boldsymbol{\beta}_t)$, where $P(\boldsymbol{\beta}_t)$ is the factor price aggregate.

Clearly, the exact economic output quantity aggregate for the financial firm is
$$M_t^b = f(\boldsymbol{\mu}_t^*; \mathbf{k}_t), \tag{74}$$
when $\boldsymbol{\mu}_t^*$ is the profit-maximizing vector of monetary assets produced; the corresponding output price aggregate is
$$\Gamma_t^b = \Gamma(\boldsymbol{\gamma}_t). \tag{75}$$

Fisher's output reversal test states that $M_t^b \Gamma_t^b$ must equal actual revenue from production of $\boldsymbol{\mu}_t^*$. That condition is satisfied as a result of (70), (72), and the fact that $f(\boldsymbol{\mu}_t^*; \mathbf{k}_t)$ must equal $g(\boldsymbol{\alpha}_t)$ at $\boldsymbol{\alpha}_t = \boldsymbol{\alpha}_t^*$. Also observe from (70) and (72), with $g(\boldsymbol{\alpha}_t)$ set equal to 1.0, that the output price aggregate is equal to
$$\Gamma(\boldsymbol{\gamma}_t) = \max_{\boldsymbol{\mu}_t}\{\boldsymbol{\mu}_t' \boldsymbol{\gamma}_t : f(\boldsymbol{\mu}_t; \mathbf{k}_t) = 1\}, \tag{76}$$
which is the unit revenue function. The unit revenue function is the maximum revenue that can be acquired from the production of one unit of the output monetary aggregate, $M_t^b = f(\boldsymbol{\mu}_t; \mathbf{k}_t)$. The linear homogeneity of Γ is clear from (76). In addition, the unit revenue function is convex and increasing in $\boldsymbol{\gamma}_t$.

It is easily shown that — instead of maximizing $\boldsymbol{\mu}_t' \boldsymbol{\gamma}_t$ subject to
$$f(\boldsymbol{\mu}_t; \mathbf{k}_t) = g(\boldsymbol{\alpha}_t^*)$$
to acquire the stage-two solution for $\boldsymbol{\mu}_t^*$ — we could equivalently define the stage-two decision to be the selection of $\boldsymbol{\mu}_t^*$ to minimize the aggregate factor requirement $f(\boldsymbol{\mu}_t; \mathbf{k}_t)$ subject to
$$\boldsymbol{\mu}_t' \boldsymbol{\gamma}_t = \Gamma(\boldsymbol{\gamma}_t) g(\boldsymbol{\alpha}_t^*).^{21}$$

As a result, we can rewrite (74) to obtain
$$M_t^b = \min_{\boldsymbol{\mu}_t}\{f(\boldsymbol{\mu}_t; \mathbf{k}_t) : \boldsymbol{\mu}_t' \boldsymbol{\gamma}_t = \Gamma(\boldsymbol{\gamma}_t) g(\boldsymbol{\alpha}_t^*)\}, \tag{77}$$
while our earlier statement of the stage-two decision produces the equivalent result that
$$M_t^b \Gamma(\boldsymbol{\gamma}_t) = \max_{\boldsymbol{\mu}_t}\{\boldsymbol{\mu}_t' \boldsymbol{\gamma}_t : f(\boldsymbol{\mu}_t; \mathbf{k}_t) = g(\boldsymbol{\alpha}_t^*)\}. \tag{78}$$

Comparing (76) and (77), we can see the clear duality between the decision problems. As usual, the exact quantity and price aggregates of economic theory are true duals.

---

[21] The proof uses (72) to equate the first-order conditions for both decisions.

Equation (76) defines the unit revenue (output price aggregator) function in terms of the factor requirement (output quantity aggregator) function. The converse is also possible as a result of the fact that

$$f(\mu_t^*; k_t) = \left[\min_{\gamma_t \geq 0} \{ \Gamma(\gamma_t) : \mu_t^{*'} \gamma_t = 1 \} \right]^{-1},$$

which is the output analog to (51).[22]

5.4 Summary of Aggregator Functions

The aggregation theory presented above demonstrates that a unique correct monetary quantity and price aggregator function exists for each of the three economic agents (the consumer, the manufacturing firm, and the financial intermediary) when the aggregator function is linearly homogeneous. We summarize below the aggregator function found in each case.

In the consumer case, the monetary quantity aggregate is given by (42). If $\mathbf{m}_t^*$ is the consumer's optimal portfolio that solves the decision problem on the right-hand side of (42), we see that the exact monetary quantity aggregate is $M_t^c = u(\mathbf{m}_t^*)$, so u is the monetary quantity aggregator function. The corresponding dual user-cost price aggregate is given by $\Pi^c(\boldsymbol{\pi}_t)$, defined in (46), where Π^c is the unit cost function dual to the category utility function u. So the price aggregator function is the unit cost function.

In the case of the manufacturing firm, the exact monetary quantity aggregate is given by (69). Hence if $\boldsymbol{\varepsilon}_t^*$ is the firm's optimal portfolio that solves the decision problem on the right-hand side of (69), then the firm's exact monetary quantity aggregate is $M_t^f = a(\boldsymbol{\varepsilon}_t^*)$, so the category production function a is the monetary quantity aggregator function. The corresponding dual user-cost price aggregate is given by $\Pi^f(\boldsymbol{\eta}_t)$, where Π^f is the unit cost function dual to the category production function a. So the price aggregator function again is the unit cost function.

In the case of the financial intermediary, the exact monetary quantity aggregate is given by (74), (77), or (78). Hence if $\boldsymbol{\mu}_t^*$ is the firm's profit-maximizing vector of monetary assets produced, then $M_t^b = f(\boldsymbol{\mu}_t^*; \mathbf{k}_t)$ is the firm's exact monetary supply quantity aggregate, so the input requirement function f is the firm's monetary quantity aggregator function. The corresponding dual monetary price aggregate is $\Gamma(\boldsymbol{\gamma}_t)$, defined in (76). So the financial intermediary's output price aggregator function is its unit revenue function Γ.

---

[22] For the proof, see Diewert (1976, equation 3.2).

5.5 Subaggregation

In Section 5.4 we provided a single monetary quantity aggregator function for each economic agent. This quantity aggregate in each case aggregates over all of the monetary assets demanded or supplied by the economic agent. However, exact subaggregates also exist if the quantity aggregator functions in Section 5.4 are weakly separable in a subvector of the monetary assets demanded or supplied, and if those subfunctions are linearly homogeneous. The resulting weakly separable subfunction is an exact aggregator function over its subvector of monetary asset components, and the corresponding unit cost or unit revenue function is the dual user-cost price aggregate. By nesting weakly separable blocks within weakly separable blocks, a hierarchy of nested exact aggregates can be produced. See Barnett (1980a, 1981b) for the construction of such a hierarchy of exact monetary assets for a representative consumer.

The two-stage decision described above can be extended into an n-stage decision for an n-level hierarchy of nested monetary aggregates. The fact that the n-stage decision produces the optimal solution for the economic agent can be proved from induction, using the results for the corresponding two-stage decision. The theory of multistage recursive aggregation has been developed in detail by Blackorby, Primont, and Russell (1978).

By nesting weakly separable blocks within weakly separable blocks to produce recursive subaggregation, the consumer's utility function produces a 'utility tree' [see, e.g., Barnett (1980a, 1981b)]. The analogous structure for the manufacturing firm's production function is a 'production tree.' In that case, the firm can optimize factor intensities within branches and then optimize between subset intensities conditionally upon the fixed preselected intensities within branches [see, e.g., Berndt and Christensen (1973)]. Whenever a quantity aggregator function is itself weakly separable into subfunctions, the subfunctions are themselves quantity aggregator functions at a lower level of aggregation. If those subfunctions are linearly homogeneous, then the price (unit cost or unit revenue) function is also correspondingly weakly separable. The resulting subfunctions of the price function are the price (unit cost or unit revenue) functions dual to the corresponding quantity aggregator functions.[23] See Diewert (1980a). Hence all of the quantity and price aggregator functions are easily produced at all applicable levels of aggregation.

---

[23] In addition, for a consumer the indirect utility function — written in terms of expenditure normalized prices — is also correspondingly weakly separable. The subfunctions are the indirect utility functions dual to the corresponding quantity aggregator functions.

6 Index Number Theory Under Homogeneity

The results in Section 5 provide unique exact economic aggregator functions for aggregating over monetary assets demanded or supplied by each of the three classes of economic agents. Each of the resulting monetary quantity aggregates depends only upon the component monetary asset quantities and the form of the aggregator function. To use such an aggregate, it is necessary to select a parameterized econometric specification for the aggregator function and estimate its parameters. Estimating aggregator functions and exploring their properties plays an important role in the aggregation theory literature. For many purposes, however, the most useful aggregates are those produced without the need to estimate unknown parameters. In that case, nonparametric approximations to the unknown aggregator functions are needed. The production of such nonparametric approximations is the subject of index number theory.

Index number theory eliminates the need to estimate unknown parameters by using both prices and quantities simultaneously, along with approximation techniques often resembling revealed preference theory, in order to estimate economic quantity aggregates that depend only upon quantities and not prices. Similarly, index number theory uses both prices and quantities simultaneously in order to approximate economic price aggregates that depend only upon prices and not quantities.

6.1 The Consumer and the Manufacturing Firm

Solution of the decision problem (6) is a necessary condition (with the appropriate selection of notation) for optimal portfolio choice for either the consumer or the manufacturing firm, and the exact monetary aggregate is the optimized value of the objective function in either case. Hence the approximation theory relevant to producing a nonparametric approximation to the exact aggregate is the same in both. Therefore, we present the index number theory only for the consumer in this section. The corresponding results for the manufacturing firm could be acquired immediately by changing notation in the obvious way.

If $\mathbf{m}_t^*$ is acquired by solving (6), then $u(\mathbf{m}_t^*)$ is the exact monetary aggregate M_t^c. In continuous time, $M_t^c = u(\mathbf{m}_t^*)$ can be tracked without error [see Barnett (1983b) for a proof] by the Divisia index, which provides M_t^c as the solution to the differential equation

$$d\log M_t^c/dt = \sum_i s_{it} d\log m_{it}^*/dt, \qquad (79)$$

where $s_{it} = \pi_{it} m_{it}^*/y_t = \pi_{it}^* m_{it}^*/y_t^*$ is the ith asset's share in expenditure on the total portfolio's service flow. Note that $\mathbf{m}_t^*$ in (79) must continually solve (6) for (79) to hold.

In continuous time, under our assumptions the Divisia index is perfect. There is no remainder term in its approximation [see, e.g., Hulten 1973)], regardless of the form of the unknown function u. In discrete time, however, many different approximations to (79) are possible, because $\mathbf{s}_t = (s_{1t}, \ldots, s_{nt})'$ need not be constant during any given time interval. With annual data, differences between such approximations can be substantial. The most popular discrete time approximation to the Divisia index is the Törnqvist-Theil approximation (often called the Törnqvist index), which is just the Simpson's rule approximation:

$$\log M_t^c - \log M_{t-1}^c = \sum_i \bar{s}_{it}(\log m_{it}^* - \log m_{i,t-1}^*), \qquad (80)$$

where $\bar{s}_{it} = \dfrac{1}{2}(s_{it} + s_{i,t-1})$. By using the Simpson's rule average shares, $\mathbf{s}_t^* = (\bar{s}_{it}, \ldots, \bar{s}_{nt})'$, the index (80) has obvious appeal as a discrete time approximation to the Divisia index (79). Hence in discrete time we shall call (80) simply the Divisia index.

Recently, a very compelling reason has appeared for using (80) as the discrete time approximation to the Divisia index. Diewert (1976) has defined a class of index numbers, called 'superlative' index numbers, which have particular appeal in producing discrete time approximations to $M_t^c = u(\mathbf{m}_t^*)$. Diewert defines a superlative index number to be one that is exactly correct for some quadratic approximation to u. The discrete Divisia index (80) is in the superlative class because it is exact for the translog specification for u. The translog is quadratic in the logarithms. As a result, if the translog specification is not exactly correct then the discrete Divisia index (80) has a third-order remainder term in the changes, since quadratic approximations possess third-order remainder terms. With weekly or monthly monetary asset data, the Divisia index (80) is accurate to within three decimal places, which is smaller than the data's roundoff error [see Barnett (1980a)].[24]

The Fisher ideal index is another popular element of Diewert's superlative class, and was proposed for use with monetary data, along with the Divisia index, by Barnett (1980a, 1981b). The Fisher ideal index is exact for the square root of the quadratic specification for u. Usually the Fisher ideal and Divisia indexes are identical (to within roundoff error) with monetary data.[25] Nevertheless, on theoretical grounds the Divisia index is now the preferred

---

[24] In addition, Star and Hall (1976) derived an analytic expression for the error in the discrete Divisia approximation to the exact continuous time Divisia index. They found that the error is always small if the shares do not fluctuate wildly.

[25] An exception is when a new asset is introduced. Special procedures, involving the

selection from the superlative class by index number theorists, largely as a result of its uniquely attractive properties in the nonhomothetic case (to be discussed in Section 8 below).

When the quantity aggregate M_t^c is acquired from the Divisia index, the dual user-cost price index, called the implicit Divisia price index, is acquired from Fisher's factor reversal test $\Pi_t^c = y_t/M_t^c$. Since relative user costs usually vary more than relative quantities, use of the Divisia index to produce the quantity aggregate, with the price aggregate produced from factor reversal, is preferable to the converse. See Allen and Diewert (1981). When M_t^c is produced from the discrete Divisia index, it is easily shown that the implicit Divisia price index, produced from factor reversal, is superlative in the Diewert sense.

6.2 The Financial Intermediary

The financial intermediary's output aggregation is produced from a decision which does not have the same form as the decision that produced the Divisia index for the consumer or manufacturing firm. Monetary output aggregation is produced by solving the financial intermediary's second-stage decision for $\boldsymbol{\mu}_t^*$ and substituting it into f to acquire $M_t^b = f(\boldsymbol{\mu}_t^*; \mathbf{k}_t)$. That second-stage decision is to select $\boldsymbol{\mu}_t$ to

$$\text{maximize} \quad \boldsymbol{\mu}_t' \boldsymbol{\gamma}_t \quad \text{subject to } f(\boldsymbol{\mu}_t; \mathbf{k}_t) = M_t^b. \tag{81}$$

The following theorem proves that the Divisia index tracks M_t^b without error in continuous time, so long as $\boldsymbol{\mu}_t^*$ is continually selected to solve (81) at each instant, t.

Theorem 2 *If $\boldsymbol{\mu}_t^*$ solves (81) continually at each instant $t \in T_0$, then for every $t \in T_0$*

$$d\log M_t^b/dt = \sum_i s_{it}^b d\log \mu_{it}^*/dt,$$

where the ith asset's share in the financial intermediary's revenue from production of monetary services is $s_{it}^b = \gamma_{it}\mu_{it}^*/\boldsymbol{\gamma}_t'\boldsymbol{\mu}_t^{*'}$.

Proof: The first-order conditions for solution to (81) are

$$\gamma_{it} = -\lambda \partial f/\partial \mu_{it} \tag{82}$$

and $f(\boldsymbol{\mu}_t^*; \mathbf{k}_t) = M_t^b$, where λ is the Lagrange multiplier.

---

imputation of a reservation price, are needed in that case. See Diewert (1980a, sec. 8.6). In addition, special procedures are needed to deal with seasonality. See Diewert (1980a, sec. 8.7).

Compute the total differential of f to acquire

$$df(\boldsymbol{\mu}_t; \mathbf{k}_t) = \sum_i \frac{\partial f}{\partial \mu_{it}} d\mu_{it}.$$

Substitute (82) to find, at $\mu_t = \mu_t^*$, that

$$\lambda df(\boldsymbol{\mu}_t^*; \mathbf{k}_t) = -\sum_i \gamma_{it} d\mu_{it}^*. \tag{83}$$

But by summing (82) over i and solving for λ, we have that

$$\lambda = -\frac{\boldsymbol{\mu}_t^{*\prime} \boldsymbol{\gamma}_t}{\boldsymbol{\mu}_t^{*\prime} \partial f / \partial \boldsymbol{\mu}_t}. \tag{84}$$

Substitute (84) into (83) and rearrange to obtain

$$d\log f(\boldsymbol{\mu}_t^*; \mathbf{k}_t) = \frac{\boldsymbol{\mu}_t^{*\prime} \partial f / \partial \boldsymbol{\mu}_t}{f(\boldsymbol{\mu}_t^*; \mathbf{k}_t)} \sum_i \frac{\gamma_{it}}{\boldsymbol{\mu}_t^{*\prime} \boldsymbol{\gamma}_t} d\mu_{it}. \tag{85}$$

But since f is linearly homogeneous in $\boldsymbol{\mu}_t$, we have from Euler's equation that

$$\boldsymbol{\mu}_t^{*\prime} \partial f / \partial \boldsymbol{\mu}_t = f(\boldsymbol{\mu}_t^*; \mathbf{k}_t). \tag{86}$$

Substituting (86) into (85), we obtain

$$d\log f(\boldsymbol{\mu}_t^*; \mathbf{k}_t)/dt = \sum_i s_{it}^b d\log \mu_{it}^*/dt,$$

where $s_{it}^b = \gamma_{it} \mu_{it}^* / \boldsymbol{\gamma}_t' \boldsymbol{\mu}_t^*$. □

Hence the Divisia index is equally as applicable to aggregating over the monetary assets produced by the financial intermediary as over the monetary assets purchased by the consumer or manufacturing firm. In addition, Simpson's rule again produces the Törnqvist-Theil discrete time approximation

$$\log M_t^b - \log M_{t-1}^b = \sum_i \bar{s}_{it}^b (\log \mu_{it}^* - \log \mu_{i,t-1}^*), \tag{87}$$

where $\bar{s}_{it}^b = \frac{1}{2}(s_{it}^b + s_{i,t-1}^b)$. Furthermore, if the input requirement function f is translog, then the discrete Divisia index (87) is exact in discrete time [see Diewert (1976, p. 125)]. Hence (87) is a superlative index number. The reason for preferring the Divisia index over the other superlative indexes will be evident from the nonhomothetic case below.

While the Divisia monetary quantity index takes the same form for all three economic agents, the financial firm's monetary output aggregate nevertheless is distinguishable from the monetary aggregates for the consumer or manufacturing firm, because only the financial intermediary's aggregate depends upon reserve requirements $\mathbf{k}_t$. The financial intermediary's monetary asset user costs $\boldsymbol{\gamma}_t$ each depend directly in (22) upon the 'reserve requirement tax' produced by nonzero $\mathbf{k}_t$ with no interest paid on required reserves. But the financial intermediary's monetary quantity aggregator function f also depends upon $\mathbf{k}_t$. Hence the Divisia quantity index for the financial intermediary depends upon $\mathbf{k}_t$ both through the effect on $\boldsymbol{\gamma}_t$ and also upon $f(\boldsymbol{\mu}_t^*; \mathbf{k}_t)$, which the Divisia index seeks to track. As a result, the Divisia monetary quantity index for the financial intermediaries tends to internalize the effects of changes in reserve requirements.

Having produced the output quantity aggregate from the Divisia index, the dual price aggregate is produced from output reversal,

$$\Gamma_t = \boldsymbol{\mu}_t^{*'} \boldsymbol{\gamma}_t / M_t^b. \tag{88}$$

The user-cost price index produced in that manner is called the implicit Divisia price index. The resulting price index is superlative in the Diewert sense, as is easily shown from (88) and the fact that M_t^b is superlative.

7 Aggregation Theory Without Homotheticity

As we have seen in Sections 4 and 5, aggregation theory and index number theory provide readily derived results when aggregator functions are linearly homogeneous. However, linear homogeneity is a strong assumption, especially for a consumer.[26] As a result, despite the elegance of the theory produced under linear homogeneity, extension of aggregation and index number theory to the nonhomothetic case can be very important empirically. As concluded by Samuelson and Swamy (1974, p. 592):

> "Empirical experience is abundant that the Santa Claus hypothesis of homotheticity in tastes and in technical change is quite unrealistic. Therefore, we must not be bemused by the undoubted elegances and richness of the homothetic theory. Nor should we shoot the honest theorist who points out to us the unavoidable

---

[26] It can be shown that an aggregator function is linearly homogeneous if and only if the elasticity of substitution — between a given good outside the separable block and a good within the block — is independent of the good within the block.

truth that in nonhomothetic cases of realistic life, one must not expect to be able to make the naive measurements that untutored common sense always longs for; we must accept the sad facts of life, and be grateful for the more complicated procedures economic theory devises."

This section deals with the most promising of those more complicated procedures devised by economic theory.

The quantity and price aggregates presented in previous sections were produced from duality theory under the assumption that the category utility (or production) function defined over the component quantities is linearly homogeneous. However, in recent years it has been shown in the literature on duality theory that the quantity and price aggregates produced under that homogeneity assumption are special cases of a more general pair of dual functions that are applicable without any homotheticity assumptions on tastes or technology. In this section we provide the more general aggregation theory, as it applies to the three economic agents postulated in Sections 2, 3, and 4.

7.1 The Consumer and the Manufacturing Firm

As we have seen in the homogeneous case, the monetary aggregation theory applicable to the manufacturing firm is identical to that of the consumer, since the decision problems producing the aggregates are identical. All of the monetary aggregation theory for both economic agents is produced by the second-stage decision problem (4): The conditional portfolio decision (4) for the consumer is converted to the manufacturing firm's conditional portfolio decision (40) by a simple change of notation. Hence, in this section we shall use (4) with the understanding that the appropriate change of notation would be used if our results were applied to the manufacturing firm rather than the consumer. However, we now no longer assume that u is linearly homogeneous, or even homothetic.

As we have seen, under linear homogeneity of u, the quantity aggregator function is the category subutility function u itself. However, if u is not linearly homogeneous, u clearly cannot serve the role of the quantity aggregator function because a quantity aggregator function that is not linearly homogeneous does not make sense. If every component quantity is growing at the same rate, then any sensible quantity aggregate would have to grow at that same rate. But that is the definition of linear homogeneity. Hence the theoretically appropriate quantity aggregator function should be linearly homogeneous in the component quantities $\mathbf{m}_t$, and should reduce to the category subutility function u in the special case of linearly homogeneous u. The corresponding price aggregator function should be the true dual to the quantity aggregator function, should be linearly homogeneous in the component prices, and should reduce to the unit cost function (46) in the case of linearly homogenous category subutility u. It has been shown in recent literature that the duals that best serve those purposes are the distance function at fixed utility level (as the quantity aggregate) and the cost function at fixed utility level (as the dual price aggregate). When normalized to equal one at base-period prices and utility, the result is the aggregation-theoretic Malmquist quantity index and the Konüs true-cost-of-living index, respectively.

Before we can present these results, we must define the distance function, $d(u_0, \mathbf{m}_t)$, at u_0. That function can be defined in implicit form to be the solution to the equation

$$u(\mathbf{m}_t/d(u_0, \mathbf{m}_t)) = u_0 \qquad (89)$$

for preselected fixed reference utility level u_0.[27] Equation (89) has an interesting geometric interpretation. We see that $d(u_0, \mathbf{m}_t)$ is the factor by which $\mathbf{m}_t$ must be deflated to reduce (or increase) the utility level to the fixed reference level u_0. In other words, we move along the direction of the $\mathbf{m}_t$ vector until we intersect the isoquant $u(\mathbf{m}_t) = u_0$; then $d(u_0, \mathbf{m}_t)$ measures how far that intersection point is from the point $\mathbf{m}_t$. While (89) defines the distance function in terms of the utility function, we also can do the converse, since the utility function is the solution for u to $d(u, \mathbf{m}_t) = 1$.

The distance function (at fixed u_0) is indeed linearly homogeneous, monotonically increasing and strictly concave in $\mathbf{m}_t$, even when u is not linearly homogeneous. Hence, when u is linearly homogeneous, u has exactly the same properties that d always has, regardless of whether or not u is linearly homogeneous. In addition, when u actually is linearly homogeneous, the distance function becomes proportional to the utility function. Hence, when u is linear homogeneous, the quantity aggregate produced from the distance function will always grow at exactly the same rate as the quantity aggregate $u(\mathbf{m}_t^*)$ that we already have derived in the case of linearly homogeneous u. This fact is easily seen by observing that linear homogeneity of u implies that $u(\mathbf{m}_t)/d(u_0, \mathbf{m}_t) = u(\mathbf{m}_t/d(u_0, \mathbf{m}_t))$, which equals u_0 by (89). Hence $d(u_0, \mathbf{m}_t) = u(\mathbf{m}_t)/u_0$, which is proportional to $u(\mathbf{m}_t)$ at fixed u_0.

In order to acquire the dual price aggregate, we need only observe the following two relationships, which follow from equations (92) and (93) in Deaton and Muellbauer (1980, p. 55):

$$d(u_0, \mathbf{m}_t) = \min_{\boldsymbol{\pi}_t}\{\boldsymbol{\pi}_t'\mathbf{m}_t : E(u_0, \boldsymbol{\pi}_t) = 1\} \qquad (90)$$

---

[27]The equivalent direct definition is $d(u_0, \mathbf{m}_t) = \max_{\kappa}\{\kappa : u(\mathbf{m}_t/\kappa) \geq u_0\}$.

and
$$E(u_0, \pi_t) = \min_{\mathbf{m}_t}\{\pi'_t \mathbf{m}_t : d(u_0, \mathbf{m}_t) = 1\}. \tag{91}$$

Equations (90) and (91) demonstrate that the distance function d and the cost function E are duals.[28] As we therefore might expect, the price aggregate in general is the cost function, as a function of π_t, at fixed reference utility level u_0.

At fixed reference u_0, the cost function has all of the correct properties for a price aggregator function, including linear homogeneity in π_t. In addition, the cost function is monotonically increasing and concave in π_t. Hence, regardless of whether or not u is linearly homogeneous, the cost function has all of the same properties that the unit cost function has when u is linearly homogeneous. In addition, if category subutility really is linearly homogeneous, we get the same price aggregate growth rates by using the cost function as we did in Section 5 when we used the unit cost function, since the two functions are then proportional to each other. That result follows from (48) by setting M_t^c equal to u_0; the proportionality constant becomes u_0. Observe that both the exact quantity aggregate produced by the distance function and the exact price aggregate produced by the cost function are entirely ordinal, because each is invariant to monotonic transformations of utility.

In order for the duality defined in (90) and (91) to be perfect, we also need the distance and cost functions to satisfy factor reversal, when consumer decisions are made optimally. Gorman (1976) has shown this to be the case.[29] Following earlier work by Afriat, Gorman defines the price vector π_t and the quantity vector $\mathbf{m}_t$ to be 'conjugate' at category subutility level u_0, if the cheapest way to reach u_0 at prices π_t is a vector proportional to $\mathbf{m}_t$. Gorman proved that if $\tilde{\pi}_t$ and $\tilde{\mathbf{m}}_t$ are conjugates in that sense, then

$$M^c(\tilde{\mathbf{m}}_t; u_0)\Pi^c(\tilde{\pi}_t; u_0) = \tilde{\mathbf{m}}'_t \tilde{\pi}_t, \tag{92}$$

where the exact monetary aggregate is

$$M^c(\mathbf{m}_t; u_0) = d(u_0, \mathbf{m}_t) \tag{93}$$

and the exact dual monetary user-cost aggregate is

$$\Pi^c(\pi_t; u_0) = E(u_0, \pi_t). \tag{94}$$

Clearly, (92) is factor reversal at $(\tilde{\mathbf{m}}_t, \tilde{\pi}_t)$.[30]

---

[28] Also, d and E have some interesting and useful derivative properties. See Deaton (1979, p. 394).

[29] Also see Deaton (1979) for a clear presentation of the relevant theory.

[30] In addition, Malmquist (1953, p. 234) has shown that reference utility level u_0 always exists such that the Malmquist and Konüs indexes satisfy factor reversal. The proof is reproduced in Diewert (1981, p. 177).

In aggregation theory, exact economic *aggregates* are converted to exact economic *indexes* by dividing by a base period value of the aggregate. The natural ways thereby to convert (93) and (94) into exact economic indexes are

$$M^{mc}(\mathbf{m}_{t_2}, \mathbf{m}_{t_1}; u_0) = d(u_0, \mathbf{m}_{t_2})/d(u_0, \mathbf{m}_{t_1}) \tag{95}$$

and

$$\Pi^{kc}(\boldsymbol{\pi}_{t_2}, \boldsymbol{\pi}_{t_1}; u_0) = E(u_0, \boldsymbol{\pi}_{t_2})/E(u_0, \boldsymbol{\pi}_{t_1}). \tag{96}$$

The price index $\Pi^{kc}(\boldsymbol{\pi}_{t_2}, \boldsymbol{\pi}_{t_1}; u_0)$ is the famous Konüs (1924) true-cost-of-living index. The dual quantity index $M^{mc}(\mathbf{m}_{t_2}, \mathbf{m}_{t_1}; u_0)$ is the Malmquist index, proposed in consumer theory by Malmquist (1953) and later in producer theory by Moorsteen (1961).

At this point, it is clear why the case of linear homogeneity of u is so important. Without linear homogeneity of utility, the exact quantity and price aggregator functions M^{mc} and Π^{kc}, although unique and based upon very elegant duality theory, nevertheless depend upon a reference utility level u_0; and the index provides no information about how to choose the reference utility level. The base period need not be t_1, or t_2. Hence the aggregation theory is equally applicable for any selection of u_0. It can be shown that M^{mc} and Π^{kc} are independent of u_0 if and only if category utility is linearly homogeneous [see Diewert (1981, sec. 3)]. Otherwise the exact economic monetary quantity and price aggregates depend upon the reference utility surface relative to which the indexes are defined.

Although the Konüs true-cost-of-living index has long been recognized to be the correct price index in economic aggregation theory, recognition that the Malmquist quantity index is the correct dual quantity index has been more recent. Previously, the quantity index commonly viewed to be exact was the Allen index

$$M^{ac}(\mathbf{m}_{t_2}, \mathbf{m}_{t_1}; \boldsymbol{\pi}_0) = E(u(\mathbf{m}_{t_2}); \boldsymbol{\pi}_0)/E(u(\mathbf{m}_{t_1}); \boldsymbol{\pi}_0). \tag{97}$$

whereas the Malmquist quantity index depends upon an undefined value for u_0, the Allen quantity index depends upon an undefined value for the reference user-cost price vector $\boldsymbol{\pi}_0$, which need not be the prices at either t_2 or t_1. Although the Allen index is now primarily of historical interest only, we nevertheless shall see that our choice of a statistical (nonparametric) quantity index number will be the same, regardless of whether it is viewed to be an approximation to the exact parametric Malmquist index or to the Allen index.[31] It is also interesting to observe that in the case of linearly homogeneous utility, the Malmquist and Allen indexes are equal.

---

[31] The primary defect of the Allen index is the fact that it is not linearly homogeneous in $\mathbf{m}_t$. Diewert (1981, p. 174).

7.2 The Financial Intermediary

As may be expected from our results in the homogeneous case, the results in Section 7.1 for the consumer and manufacturing firm apply also to aggregation of financial intermediary output with a nonhomogeneous factor requirement function, if we replace the cost function by its output analogue, the revenue function, and if we replace the category subutility function u [or $a(\varepsilon_t)$ for the manufacturing firm] by its output analogue, the factor requirements function.

By analogy to (89), define the financial firm's output distance function implicitly to be the value of $D(\boldsymbol{\mu}_t, \boldsymbol{\alpha}_t, \mathbf{k}_t)$ that solves

$$f(\boldsymbol{\mu}_t/D(\boldsymbol{\mu}_t, \boldsymbol{\alpha}_t; \mathbf{k}_t); \mathbf{k}_t) = g(\boldsymbol{\alpha}_0), \tag{98}$$

for preselected reference input vector $\boldsymbol{\alpha}_0$.[32] Then the exact monetary quantity output aggregate for the financial intermediary is

$$M^b(\boldsymbol{\mu}_t; \boldsymbol{\alpha}_0, \mathbf{k}_t) = D(\boldsymbol{\mu}_t, \boldsymbol{\alpha}_0; \mathbf{k}_t), \tag{99}$$

and the corresponding Malmquist economic output quantity index is

$$M^{mb}(\boldsymbol{\mu}_{t_2}, \boldsymbol{\mu}_{t_1}; \boldsymbol{\alpha}_0, \mathbf{k}_t) = D(\boldsymbol{\mu}_{t_2}, \boldsymbol{\alpha}_0; \mathbf{k}_t)/D(\boldsymbol{\mu}_{t_1}, \boldsymbol{\alpha}_0; \mathbf{k}_t). \tag{100}$$

The corresponding dual Konüs monetary output price index is produced by replacing the cost function in Section 7.1 by its output analogue, the revenue function (70). Hence the true output price aggregate is

$$\Gamma(\boldsymbol{\gamma}_t; \boldsymbol{\alpha}_0, \mathbf{k}_t) = R^*(\boldsymbol{\alpha}_0, \boldsymbol{\gamma}_t; \mathbf{k}_t), \tag{101}$$

and the corresponding Konüs true financial output price aggregate is

$$\Gamma^k(\boldsymbol{\gamma}_{t_2}, \boldsymbol{\gamma}_{t_1}; \boldsymbol{\alpha}_0, \mathbf{k}_t) = R^*(\boldsymbol{\alpha}_0, \boldsymbol{\gamma}_{t_2}; \mathbf{k}_t)/R^*(\boldsymbol{\alpha}_0, \boldsymbol{\gamma}_{t_1}; \mathbf{k}_t). \tag{102}$$

Again we find that, in the case of nonhomogeneity (of f), the exact economic output price and quantity aggregates and indexes depend upon an undefined choice. In this case, that choice is of the reference input vector $\boldsymbol{\alpha}_0$. The dependency upon $\boldsymbol{\alpha}_0$ disappears if and only if the factor requirement function is linearly homogeneous, in which case the results above reduce to those in Section 5.3.

The duality results analogous to (90) and (91) are

$$D(\boldsymbol{\mu}_t, \boldsymbol{\alpha}_0; \mathbf{k}_t) = \max_{\boldsymbol{\gamma}_t}\{\boldsymbol{\gamma}_t'\boldsymbol{\mu}_t : R^*(\boldsymbol{\alpha}_0, \boldsymbol{\gamma}_t; \mathbf{k}_t) = 1\} \tag{103}$$

and

$$R^*(\boldsymbol{\alpha}_0, \boldsymbol{\gamma}_t; \mathbf{k}_t) = \max_{\boldsymbol{\mu}_t}\{\boldsymbol{\gamma}_t'\boldsymbol{\mu}_t : D(\boldsymbol{\mu}_t, \boldsymbol{\alpha}_0; \mathbf{k}_t) = 1\}. \tag{104}$$

---

[32] The equivalent direct definition is $D(\boldsymbol{\mu}_t, \boldsymbol{\alpha}_t; \mathbf{k}_t) = \min_{\kappa}\{\kappa : f(\boldsymbol{\mu}_t/\kappa; \mathbf{k}_t) \leq g(\boldsymbol{\alpha}_0)\}$.

8 Index Number Theory Under Nonhomogeneity

There are a number of published approaches to producing nonparametric approximations to the Malmquist or Allen quantity index. Yet virtually all of them result in selection of the discrete (Törnqvist) Divisia index. In fact, it is the nonhomogeneous case in which the Divisia index stands out as being the uniquely best element of Diewert's superlative class. When Denny asked whether it is possible to acquire superlative indexes other than the Divisia in the nonhomothetic case, Diewert (1980c, p. 538) replied: "My answer is that it may be possible, but I have not been able to do it." More recently, Caves, Christensen, and Diewert (1982b, p. 1411) have proved that the (discrete) Divisia index "is superlative in a considerably more general sense than shown by Diewert. We are not aware of other indexes that can be shown to be superlative in this more general sense."

8.1 The Consumer and the Manufacturing Firm

Perhaps the first rigorously proved theoretical results on nonparametric approximation in the nonhomothetic case are those of Theil (1968) and Kloek (1967). Their result produces the following conclusion in our case. Suppose that $\mathbf{m}_{t_i}$ is the consumer's utility-maximizing monetary asset portfolio at user-cost prices $\boldsymbol{\pi}_{t_i}$ and at expenditure $\boldsymbol{\pi}'_{t_i}\mathbf{m}_{t_i}$ (with $i = 1$ or 2), and let $\boldsymbol{\pi}_0$ be the vector having $(\pi_{t_1 k}\pi_{t_2 k})^{1/2}$ at its kth component. Then the (discrete) Divisia index provides a second-order approximation to the Allen quantity index, eq. (97).

More recently Diewert (1976, pp. 123–4) has proved that the discrete Divisia index is exact for the Malmquist quantity index (95) under a specific choice for the distance function and the reference utility level. In our case, those assumptions would be that: the distance function d is generalized translog; $\mathbf{m}_{t_i}$ is the consumer's utility-maximizing monetary asset portfolio at user-cost prices $\boldsymbol{\pi}_{t_i}$ and at expenditure $\boldsymbol{\pi}'_{t_i}\mathbf{m}_{t_i}$ (with $i = 1$ or 2); and the reference utility level u_0 is $(u_1 u_2)^{1/2}$, where $u_1 = u(\mathbf{m}_{t_1})$ and $u_2 = u(\mathbf{m}_{t_2})$. Since the translog specification can produce a second-order approximation to any distance function, we see that the Divisia index produces a second-order approximation to any Malmquist quantity index if the reference utility level is selected in accordance with Diewert's theorem.

In addition, it has recently been shown that the Divisia index is not only exact for a generalized translog distance function, but remains appropriate even when tastes or technology are changing over time. The Divisia index is a chained index which measures changes relative to the previous period, rather than relative to a fixed base period. As a result, it has always been believed that the Divisia index would work well with shifting tastes or technology, since chained indexes adjust rapidly to the latest form of a shifting aggregator function.[33] However, Caves, Christensen, and Diewert (1982a,b) have recently found a precise relationship between the Divisia quantity index and a shifting aggregator function. In particular, their result shows that if u shifts between periods t_1 and t_2 then the Divisia index accurately produces the log change in aggregate consumption (or factor demand, for the manufacturing firm) of monetary services by the consumer, if the distance function is generalized translog in both periods t_1 and t_2 such that the second-order terms in $\mathbf{m}_t$ have the same coefficients in both periods. The result does not require constancy of the remaining coefficients or homotheticity of u.

Any of the above results can be used to prove that the implicit Divisia user-cost price index, produced from the Divisia quantity index and factor reversal, possesses the same approximation properties relative to the Konüs true-cost-of-living index that the Divisia quantity index possesses relative to the Malmquist (or Allen) quantity index. Also, the results imputed above to consumer monetary portfolio aggregation clearly are immediately applicable to manufacturing firm monetary portfolio demand. We need only replace the consumer's category subutility function u with the manufacturing firm's category subproduction function a.

8.2 The Financial Intermediary

All of the results described in section 8.1 are equally applicable to providing nonparametric ('statistical') approximations to the financial intermediary's monetary asset output Malmquist quantity index, eq. (100), and its dual Konüs user-cost price aggregate, eq. (102). All that is needed is to replace the input distance function d by the output distance function D, and the cost function E by the revenue function R^*. See Diewert (1976, p. 125; 1980a, p. 463) and Caves, Christensen, and Diewert (1982b, sec. 3).

8.3 Subaggregation

In Section 5.5, we discussed the theory of exact subaggregation in economic aggregation theory. The resulting utility or production tree can produce recursive aggregation over increasingly broad aggregates — for example, from Divisia M1, to Divisia M2, to Divisia M3, to Divisia L. However, the aggregation theory is in terms of exact aggregator functions, recursively nested. The question naturally arises as to whether statistical index numbers, such as the

---

[33] See, e.g., Samuelson and Swamy (1974, p. 587) and Diewert (1976, footnote 16).

Divisia index, can be nested within each other to produce Divisia indexes of Divisia indexes at successively higher levels of aggregation.

If, for example, Divisia indexes of Divisia indexes are Divisia indexes of the original components, then the Divisia index would be called consistent in aggregation. A statistical index that has the property of consistency in aggregation is the Vartia (1976) index. However, the Vartia quantity index has the extremely unattractive property of not being invariant to rescaling of the prices in either period. Similarly, the Vartia price index does not increase at the same rate as second-period prices, when all second-period prices are inflated by a common rate. The Vartia index is also not a superlative index. However, the Divisia index is almost consistent in aggregation, since the Divisia index of Divisia indexes differs from the Divisia index over the original components only by an error of the third order. These results apply in discrete time, regardless of whether the category subutility or category subproduction function is linearly homogeneous.

Of course, in continuous time the Divisia index is exactly consistent in aggregation in the homogeneous case, because the Divisia index then is exact at all levels of aggregation for any aggregator function. There are no remainder terms.

9 Aggregation Over Consumers and Firms

The aggregation theory presented above is for individual decision makers: either one consumer, one manufacturing firm, or one financial intermediary. We have not discussed aggregation over individual decision makers, although a large literature exists on the subject. In this section we cite a few of the more useful results in that literature, and present one particularly interesting result that is specific to the Divisia index.

The subject of aggregation over consumers has been heavily researched, and the results are well known. The most important of those results are surveyed in Barnett (1983a, 1983b) and will not be repeated here. Two different literatures exist on aggregation over firms. One literature resembles that for aggregation over consumers, but a more specialized literature exists on the derivation of production transformation surfaces for an industry or the entire economy. Sato (1975) has provided an excellent survey of that literature.[34] One of his more interesting results (1975, p. 283) is that a constant-returns-to-scale economy-wide production function exists if there is a social utility function. As a result, aggregation over consumers can itself produce perfect aggregation over firms. Other results on aggregation over firms are surveyed in Diewert (1980a, pp. 464–70). Particularly useful

---

[34] He derives an industry production transformation surface on p. 282.

results are those of Bliss (1975, p. 146) and Debreu (1959, p. 45), who found that if all firms are competitive profit maximizers, then the group of firms can be treated as a single firm maximizing profits subject to the sum of the individual firm's production sets. That result provides a very simple means of aggregating over firms.

All of the theory presented above is directly linked to deterministic microeconomic and aggregation theory. However, the Divisia index can be acquired in another manner, one that easily permits aggregation over goods, consumers, and firms jointly. This approach, called the *atomistic* approach and championed by Theil (1967) and Clements and Izan (1984), treats the expenditure weights in the Divisia index as the probabilities of drawing the corresponding quantity log changes. Then the Divisia quantity index is just the mean of the distribution of log changes. To see how easily we can thereby also aggregate jointly over economic agents, consider the case of demand for monetary assets by the consumer and the manufacturing firm. In continuous time, the consumer's Divisia monetary quantity index can be written in differential form as

$$d \log M_t^c = \sum_i s_{it}^c d \log m_{it}^*, \qquad (105)$$

where $s_{it}^c = \pi_{it} m_{it} / \pi_t' \mathbf{m}_t$ can be interpreted as the probability of drawing $d \log m_{it}^*$ in a random sampling from the population of monetary asset growth rates at t by consumer i. The analogous Divisia index for the manufacturing firm is

$$d \log M_t^f = \sum_i s_{it}^f d \log \eta_{it}, \qquad (106)$$

where $s_{it}^f = \eta_{it} \varepsilon_{it} / \eta_t' \varepsilon_t$.

Now let Π_t^c be the implicit Divisia user-cost aggregate produced from M_t^c and factor reversal, and let Π_t^f be the implicit Divisia user-cost aggregate produced from M_t^f and factor reversal. Let $W_t^f = \Pi_t^f M_t^f / (\Pi_t^f M_t^f + \Pi_t^c M_t^c)$ and $W_t^c = \Pi_t^c M_t^c / (\Pi_t^f M_t^f + \Pi_t^c M_t^c)$. Then the shares (W_t^f, W_t^c) can be interpreted as probabilities, so that we can define the Divisia quantity M_t^{fc} aggregated over both the firm and consumer by

$$d \log M_t^{fc} = W^f d \log M_t^f + W^c d \log M_t^c. \qquad (107)$$

Substituting (105) and (106) into (107), we find that

$$\begin{aligned} d \log M_t^{fc} &= \sum_i \frac{\eta_{it} \varepsilon_{it}}{\Pi_t^f M_t^f + \Pi_t^c M_t^c} d \log \eta_{it} \\ &+ \sum_i \frac{\pi_{it} m_{it}}{\Pi_t^f M_t^f + \Pi_t^c M_t^c} d \log m_{it}. \end{aligned} \qquad (108)$$

Clearly (108) is itself a Divisia index, since

$$\sum_i \frac{\eta_{it}\varepsilon_{it}}{\Pi_t^f M_t^f + \Pi_t^c M_t^c} + \sum_i \frac{\pi_{it} m_{it}}{\Pi_t^f M_t^f + \Pi_t^c M_t^c} = 1,$$

so (108) is a share-weighted average of log changes. But (108) aggregates *simultaneously* over monetary assets demanded by both the consumer and the manufacturing firm. This procedure is equally applicable to aggregation over monetary assets demanded by many consumers and firms. The approach is most advantageously used to aggregate over monetary assets demanded by different pre-aggregated groups of asset holders (e.g., firms, rich consumers, other consumers, etc.) when the ability to decompose the aggregate into the group subaggregates could be useful. Prior aggregation within the groups could be in accordance with the methods mentioned earlier in this section.

10 Technical Change

It has frequently been argued that substantial technical change occurred in the banking industry over the past decade. The potential existence of technological innovation in that industry has sometimes been viewed as a complicating factor in financial modeling and in monetary policy. However, aggregation theory and index number theory are directly relevant to measuring technical change. In fact, a long literature exists on that subject. In this section, we discuss some of those results that are most relevant to measuring technical change in the banking industry. We shall do so in terms of the technology of our financial intermediary.

When technical change is possible, the financial intermediary's production function is

$$M_t^b = g(\boldsymbol{\alpha}_t, t), \qquad (109)$$

where $\boldsymbol{\alpha}_t$ is the vector of factor inputs and

$$M_t^b = f(\boldsymbol{\mu}_t; \mathbf{k}_t) \qquad (110)$$

is the exact economic quantity aggregate over monetary asset outputs $\boldsymbol{\mu}_t$. Technical change in production of aggregate monetary output is thereby equivalent to a shift in technology in (109) over time, so $g(\boldsymbol{\alpha}_t, t)$ must have time as an argument. In accordance with Ohta's (1974) definition, the primal (as opposed to dual) rate of change of total factor productivity is

$$\partial \log g(\boldsymbol{\alpha}_t, t)/\partial t \mid_{\boldsymbol{\alpha}_t},$$

which measures the rate of disembodied technical change.[35]

---

[35] Also see Berndt and Khaled (1979). The dual rate of total cost diminution is $-\partial \log C^b(\boldsymbol{\mu}_t, \boldsymbol{\beta}_t, t)/\partial t \mid_{\boldsymbol{\mu}_t, \boldsymbol{\beta}_t}$, which is used in Diewert (1980b, sec. III).

Technical Change

Consider first the simplest case, which is neutral technological progress. Then there must exist a function $\phi(t)$ of time such that (109) can be written

$$M_t^b = \phi(t)g(\boldsymbol{\alpha}_t), \qquad (111)$$

with variation in $\phi(t)$ producing parallel translations of isoquants. In discrete time, according to Ohta's definition, the rate of disembodied technical change is the log change of (111) with $\boldsymbol{\alpha}_t$ held constant:

$$(\log M_{t+1}^b - \log M_t^b)\,|_{\alpha_t} = \log(\phi(t+1)/\phi(t)). \qquad (112)$$

Substituting (111) into (112), we obtain

$$(\log M_{t+1}^b - \log M_t^b)\,|_{\alpha_t} = \log(M_{t+1}^b/M_t^b) - \log(g(\boldsymbol{\alpha}_{t+1})/g(\boldsymbol{\alpha}_t)). \qquad (113)$$

If the input aggregator function (or output production function) g is linearly homogeneous, then

$$\log(g(\boldsymbol{\alpha}_{t+1})/g(\boldsymbol{\alpha}_t)) = \log g(\boldsymbol{\alpha}_{t+1}) - \log g(\boldsymbol{\alpha}_t) \qquad (114)$$

can be measured by the discrete Divisia index over growth rates of input quantities $\boldsymbol{\alpha}_t$. Since the index is superlative, the error is third-order. If the output aggregator function f is also linearly homogeneous, then

$$\log(M_{t+1}^b/M_t^b) = \log M_{t+1}^b - \log M_t^b \qquad (115)$$

can be measured by the discrete Divisia index over growth rates of output quantities $\boldsymbol{\mu}_t$. Hence we can see from (113), (114), and (115) that the rate of technical change can be measured by the difference between two Divisia indexes, one aggregating over growth rates of output quantities and the other aggregating over growth rates of input quantities. In continuous time, the result measures the total rate of disembodied technical change exactly.[36] If f and g are both translog, then the result is also exact in discrete time.[37]

Since we explicitly assumed output separability when we defined the technology of the financial intermediary in Section 3, we do so in the above derivation as well. However, it is worth observing that the result can be adapted to the case of nonseparability [see Diewert (1976, pp. 127-9)]. The results also can be generalized to the case of nonhomothetic g and f; see Caves, Christensen, and Diewert (1982a, b). In that case, technical progress is defined in

---

[36] For a proof, see Diewert (1981, p. 20) or Diewert (1980b, pp. 261-2).

[37] Sometimes $\phi(t) - 1$ is treated as the rate of technical progress. In that case, there is said to be technical progress if $\phi(t) > 0$ or technical regress if $\phi(t) < 0$. Clearly from (111), we see that $\phi(t)$ can be computed from the ratio of the output Divisia index level to the input Divisia index level.

terms of Malmquist input and output indexes. When the distance functions used to define the Malmquist input and output indexes are translog, the rate of technological change again is measured exactly in terms of Divisia input and output indices.

For a discussion of nonneutral technical change, see Jorgenson and Lau (1975). In that case, the Divisia index still measures aggregate monetary output by the financial intermediary (regardless of the technical progress), but measurement of the technical progress itself requires estimation of the firm's technology, containing an index of technological change.

11 Value Added

In monetary theory, outside money plays an important role because outside (or high-powered, or base) money is net wealth, whereas the potential wealth effect of inside money is often viewed as offset by equal liabilities corresponding to each such asset. Although outside money certainly is uniquely important in many ways, it seems worth observing that there is value added produced by the banking industry. So long as primary factors of production other than base money are employed in that industry, the banking industry produces net services that were not embodied in the industry's employment of outside money. In this section we discuss the measurement of value added for our financial intermediary.

Partition the financial intermediary's input vector α_t so that $\alpha_t = (\alpha'_{1t}, \alpha'_{2t})'$, where α_{1t} is quantities of primary inputs (such as labor, capital, and land), and α_{2t} is quantities of intermediate inputs (such as materials).[38] Partition the factor-price vector correspondingly so that $\beta_t = (\beta'_{1t}, \beta'_{2t})'$. Then the financial intermediary's technology can be written as

$$M_t^b = g(\alpha_{1t}, \alpha_{2t}). \tag{116}$$

Let the firm's maximum variable profit level at given α_{1t} be

$$V_t = V(\alpha_{1t}, \beta_{2t}, \gamma_t), \tag{117}$$

which is the firm's variable profit function conditional upon α_{1t}. As a function of α_{1t} at fixed prices, V has all of the usual properties of a neoclassical production function. Sato (1975) calls

$$V_{t_0, t_1} = V(\alpha_{1t_0}, \beta_2^*, \gamma^*) / V(\alpha_{1t_1}, \beta_2^*, \gamma^*) \tag{118}$$

---

[38] In some models all production by every firm is value added. In that case, all firms are completely vertically integrated, so no intermediate inputs exist. See Sato (1975, p. 280).

the true index of real value added, which depends upon the selection of the reference prices $(\boldsymbol{\beta}_2^*, \boldsymbol{\gamma}^*)$.[39]

In order to provide a nonparametric (statistical) approximation to (118), assume constant returns to scale. Also assume that V is translog and select $(\boldsymbol{\beta}_2^*, \boldsymbol{\gamma}^*)$ to be the geometric means of those prices in periods t_0 and t_1. Diewert (1980a, p. 459) then has shown that (118) equals the discrete Divisia quantity index for aggregating over the primary inputs.

The need to select the reference prices $(\boldsymbol{\beta}_2^*, \boldsymbol{\gamma}^*)$ becomes unnecessary if and only if g is separable, so that (116) can be written

$$M_t^b = G(\zeta(\boldsymbol{\alpha}_{1t}), \boldsymbol{\alpha}_{2t}). \tag{119}$$

In that case, V can be written[40]

$$V_t = V_1(\boldsymbol{\alpha}_{1t}) V_2(\boldsymbol{\beta}_{2t}, \boldsymbol{\gamma}_t). \tag{120}$$

So clearly

$$V_{t_0,t_1} = V_1(\boldsymbol{\alpha}_{1t_0}) / V_1(\boldsymbol{\alpha}_{1t_1}), \tag{121}$$

which does not depend upon reference prices. The function V_1 has all of the properties of a conventional neoclassical production function. However, in this case $\zeta(\boldsymbol{\alpha}_{1t})$ is itself a category subproduction function, so we can more directly define the value added index to be[41]

$$V^*_{t_0,t_1} = \zeta(\boldsymbol{\alpha}_{1t_0}) / \zeta(\boldsymbol{\alpha}_{1t_1}). \tag{122}$$

If ζ is translog, then the discrete Divisia index is exact for either (122) or (121), so the discrete Divisia index provides a second-order approximation for $V^*_{t_0,t_1}$ or V_{t_0,t_1} for any ζ. In continuous time, the Divisia index is always exact for $\zeta(\boldsymbol{\alpha}_{1t})$, which is value added. Clearly high-powered money is all value added if and only if $\boldsymbol{\alpha}_{1t}$ contains only high-powered money.

The source of the term 'value added' can be found in the accounting conventions for measuring value added. The accounting convention, called 'double deflation,' requires the very restrictive assumption that (119) can be written in the form

$$M_t^b = \zeta_1(\boldsymbol{\alpha}_{1t}) + \zeta_2(\boldsymbol{\alpha}_{2t}). \tag{123}$$

Clearly $\zeta_1(\boldsymbol{\alpha}_{1t})$ is value added, since it is added to $\zeta_2(\boldsymbol{\alpha}_{2t})$ to get M_t^b. In that case, Sims (1969) has proved that value added is measured exactly by a Divisia index.

---

[39] Also see Diewert (1980a) and Bridge (1971, pp. 324–43). The variable profit function in real terms measures real income originating within the firm.
[40] See Lau (1978b, sec. 2).
[41] See Denny and May (1978).

12   Macroeconomic and General Equilibrium Theory

In terms of its relationship with final targets of policy, the demand-side Divisia monetary aggregates are the most relevant. Those aggregates measure the economy's monetary service flow, as perceived by the users of monetary assets. As a result, it might seem that we would be interested only in the consumer and manufacturing firm, whose decisions are analogous and pose little difficulty. This convenient situation would arise, for example, if we were seeking monetary aggregates to be used as indicators. Frequently, however, money plays a more complex role in economics. For example, a money market appears in most macroeconomic models and in many recent general equilibrium models. Policy simulations with macroeconometric models usually require a modeled money market. In addition, targeting a monetary aggregate requires information about the supply function for the aggregate. All of these objectives would be facilitated if the supply-side Divisia monetary aggregates from the financial firm, along with the transmission mechanism from central bank instruments, were incorporated into a full model of the economy. Producing a cleared money market in a Divisia monetary aggregate along with a transmission mechanism operating through that market is an objective toward which the above research is tending. However, much research remains before such a closed model could be constructed.

If a model included only a demand-side Divisia monetary aggregate, then closing a complete model would require modeling the supply of every component in the Divisia monetary aggregate. Market clearing then would occur at the level of disaggregated component quantities, which then could be substituted into the Divisia demand monetary aggregate. While the resulting aggregate could be informative and useful, much of the potential simplification is lost by the need to produce completely disaggregated supply functions. However, incorporating both supply and demand aggregates in a model — which would be needed to produce a market for an aggregate — has been given very little consideration in aggregation theory. Many difficult issues arise. What do we do if the financial firm's technology is separable in different blockings of monetary assets from those that appear in the consumer's utility function or the manufacturing firm's technology? How do we deal with the fact that currency and primary monetary securities appear as components of the consumer's and manufacturing firm's monetary demand aggregate, but not as components of the financial firm's monetary output aggregate? What happens to the ability to close the money market if homotheticity applies on one side of the money market while nonhomotheticity requires use of a Malmquist index on the other side of the market?

One potential problem is immediately evident from the results in prior sections. The user-cost prices of monetary assets produced by the financial intermediary are different from those for the consumer (or manufacturing firm). The reason is the existence of reserve requirements, which produce an implicit tax on financial intermediaries. The tax does not affect the user cost of the same assets for consumers or manufacturing firms. Income taxes produce similar 'wedges' between user costs on the supply and demand sides of the money markets. As a result, even when the markets for every component are cleared, the Divisia demand and corresponding Divisia supply aggregate need not be equal because the different user costs can produce different weights, although all corresponding component quantities nevertheless may be equal.

Another potential problem results from the fact that in parts of some macroeconomic models, monetary wealth rather than the monetary service flow is relevant. This could be the case, for example, in producing an argument of a consumption function. Then it is necessary to compute the expected discounted present value of the service flow.[42] The expected service flow in a future period is measured by its expected Divisia index. For a discussion of the appropriate use of capital stocks and capital service flows, see Usher (1980, pp. 17–18).

We do not propose here to imbed our three economic agents (along with a government sector) into a closed model, since we view that objective as a subject for future research. However, we do present a few simple results relevant to the use of monetary aggregation theory within macroeconomics.

12.1 The Utility Production Function

The supply of money function used in monetary theory often has not been a neoclassical supply function, in the traditional sense. Instead, the supply of money function often has been an equilibrium condition or reduced-form equation relating money to the monetary base through a multiplier.[43] As seen from our model of the financial intermediary, the relationship between such an equation and monetary production technology is not clear. In fact, although high-powered money is a factor of production for the financial in-

---

[42]See section 3.4 of this book.

[43]Such equations often have been associated with Brunner and Meltzer (1964) and Johannes and Rasche (1979). In fact, a strong case can be made on econometric grounds for that sort of procedure with all durable goods. See Deaton and Muellbauer (1980, pp. 350–1), who advocate solving a two-equation durable demand and supply system to produce the single-equation specification to be estimated. In our case, we thereby would solve for the market-clearing value for the dual user-cost aggregate. That solution function then would be substituted back into either the demand or supply function for the quantity aggregate.

termediary, the total monetary base (which also includes currency held by the consumer and manufacturing firm) does not appear in the financial intermediary's decision. Problems produced by this fact have been discussed by Saving (1977, p. 294). In addition, as described above, the demand Divisia aggregate need not equal the corresponding supply Divisia aggregate.

Nevertheless, a straightforward interpretation can be given to the conventional multiplier-type 'supply' function as a utility production function. As defined by Samuelson (1968), a utility production function is acquired by replacing the quantities in a utility function by their reduced-form equations. By applying that procedure to the consumer's monetary category subutility function and analogously to the manufacturing firm's monetary category subproduction function, equations can be produced describing the equilibrium monetary service flows as functions of exogenous variables, including central bank instruments.[44] In continuous time, Sato (1975, p. 283) has shown that the left-hand side of a utility production function can be measured exactly by a Divisia index.[45]

12.2 Velocity Function

The aggregation theory provided above can be used to derive the velocity function. The separability of the utility function in (2) can be used to produce a current period category utility function of the form $\nu(u(\mathbf{m}_t), v(\mathbf{x}_t), \bar{L}_t)$. Then a consistent current period conditional decision can be defined. That decision is to select $(\mathbf{m}_t, \mathbf{x}_t, \bar{L}_t)$ to

$$\text{maximize } \nu(u(\mathbf{m}_t), v(\mathbf{x}_t), \bar{L}_t) \text{ subject to } \boldsymbol{\pi}_t'\mathbf{m}_t + \mathbf{p}_t'\mathbf{x}_t + w_t\bar{L}_t = Y_t^*, \quad (124)$$

where Y_t is total current period expenditure on goods, monetary services, and leisure. The variable Y_t is preallocated from a prior-stage intertemporal allocation decision.[46]

However, decision (124) can itself be solved in two stages. The first stage is to solve for $(M_t^c, X_t, \bar{L}_t)$ to

$$\text{maximize } \nu(M_t^c, X_t, \bar{L}_t) \text{ subject to } M_t^c\Pi_t^c + p_t^*X_t + w_t\bar{L}_t = Y_t \quad (125)$$

where X_t is the goods quantity aggregate over $\mathbf{x}_t$. The solution function for M_t^c will be of the form

$$M_t^c = \Psi(Y_t, \Pi_t^c, p_t^*, w_t). \quad (126)$$

---

[44] For related discussion see Saving (1977, pp. 300–1).
[45] Sato also recommends specifying the right-hand side as a linearly homogeneous production function, so that all variables can be measured in per capita terms.
[46] See Barnett (1980a, 1981b).

If ν is linearly homogeneous, then (126) can be written in the form

$$M_t^c = Y_t \Phi(\Pi_t^c, p_t^*, w_t) \tag{127}$$

or

$$M_t^c (\Phi(\Pi_t^c, p_t^*, w_t))^{-1} = Y_t, \tag{128}$$

so that $(\Phi(\Pi_t^c, p_t^*, w_t))^{-1}$ is velocity relative to the 'income' variable Y_t.

For some purposes it would be useful to solve (125) conditionally upon $\bar{L}_t$ with $w_t \bar{L}_t$ subtracted from both sides of the constraint in (125). Then the income variable would become $Y_t^* = Y_t - w_t \bar{L}_t$, and w_t would not appear as a variable in velocity. In addition, ν could be the current period utility function for a representative consumer under the conditions for aggregation over consumers. Since the second-stage decision for the manufacturing firm is analogous to that for the consumer, (128) could be produced even after aggregation over consumers and manufacturing firms jointly.

It is particularly interesting to observe that the velocity function depends only on the tastes of consumers and the technology of manufacturing firms. The velocity function does not depend upon the technology of the financial firm, or upon Federal Reserve policy, or upon the money multipliers. As a result, the velocity function is not affected by structural change in the banking sector. In contrast, the velocity of the monetary base depends jointly upon money demand and money supply, and hence is affected by structural change in the banking industry.

When applying the aggregation and index number theory presented in this paper to produce macroeconomic results (such as the above results on velocity), it is critically important to assure that the behavioral theory upon which the index numbers are based is consistent with one's model. Many examples of such inconsistency exist in the literature on monetary aggregation.[47] For example, the official simple sum monetary aggregates are consistent with aggregation theory if and only if the components are indistinguishable perfect substitutes. Yet many models in which the official aggregates are used are structured in a manner inconsistent with that assumption.

A more recent example is the aggregate M_Q, proposed by Spindt, which uses the Fisher ideal index to produce a monetary aggregate and a velocity aggregate. However, turnover rates — rather than the user cost prices appearing in the usual Fisher ideal index — are treated as dual to quantities. The theory on which Spindt's aggregates are based is presented in Spindt (1985b). Nevertheless, it is easily seen from the theory in Sections 5 and 6 above that his results are consistent with the relevant index number theory [including Diewert's (1976) theory, used by Spindt (1985b)] *only if* economic

---

[47] See Barnett (1990) for some examples.

agents solve one of the following two possible decision problems:

$$\text{select } \mathbf{m}_t \text{ to maximize } M(\mathbf{m}_t) \text{ subject to } \mathbf{m}'_t\mathbf{v}_t = p_t^* X_t \qquad (129)$$

or

$$\text{select } \mathbf{v}_t \text{ to maximize } V(\mathbf{v}_t) \text{ subject to } \mathbf{m}'_t\mathbf{v}_t = p_t^* X_t, \qquad (130)$$

where $\mathbf{v}_t$ is the vector of turnover rates corresponding to the vector of monetary asset quantities $\mathbf{m}_t$. The resulting monetary aggregate is $M(\mathbf{m}_t)$ and the resulting velocity aggregate is $V(\mathbf{v}_t)$. Either of the above two behavioral hypotheses would be consistent with Spindt's use of index number theory. In addition, if either of those two decision problems is applicable, and if M and V are linearly homogeneous, it follows from factor reversal that $M(\mathbf{m}_t)V(\mathbf{v}_t) = p_t^* X_t$, which is the 'quantity equation.'

However, it is not at all clear how either of those two decisions could be imbedded in a sensible way into a jointly rational decision over goods and monetary assets (for either a consumer or firm) under any kind of separability assumption. In addition, if (129) is solved, then $\mathbf{v}_t$ must be treated as exogenous to the decision maker. Alternatively, if (130) is solved, then $\mathbf{m}_t$ must be treated as exogenous to the decision maker. Neither possibility is reasonable, since both turnover rates $\mathbf{v}_t$ and monetary asset quantities demanded $\mathbf{m}_t$ are in actuality selected by monetary asset holders.

The source of this problem in Spindt's work is the fact that he used Diewert's (1976) result that the Fisher ideal index is exact for the square root quadratic aggregator function; but Spindt overlooked the fact that Diewert's proof applies only for optimizing behavior. With the use of turnover rates rather than user costs, the optimizing behavior required for use of Diewert's theorem must be either (129) or (130).

Without rigorous internally consistent behavioral theory, a Fisher ideal index in monetary quantities and turnover rates (as opposed to the prices, which fall directly out of the existing aggregation and index number theory) is just an arbitrary combination of component quantities and turnover rates. An infinite number of such functions of monetary quantities and turnover rates exist, and they can produce any arbitrary growth rate for the aggregate from the same component data. As a result, Spindt's aggregate is entirely arbitrary. In short, rolling one's own index number, without access to the 100-year-old cumulative literature on quantity and price (not turnover rate) indexes, is a hazardous venture.

13 Conclusion

This paper has provided many aggregation-theoretic results relevant to producing rigorous microeconomic foundations for monetary economics and

Conclusion

macroeconomics. A logical next step in this evolving research would be to imbed aggregation theory in a full macroeconomic model. However it is clear that this next step is a big one. Introducing the relevant aggregation theory throughout a full model of the economy is likely to be a formidable theoretical task. For example, producing comformable aggregation on both sides of each market with market clearing in aggregates raises theoretical problems for which existing literature provides little guidance.

The literature on aggregation theory typically has taken the position that only one side of each market is relevant to each application of aggregation theory.[48] The literature then applies aggregation theory only to that relevant side of the market. However, when determining the transmission mechanism of monetary policy, no one side of any market is the sole correct side. Much work remains to be done before microeconomics and macroeconomics can be unified through the application of their logical link: aggregation theory.

---

[48] See, e.g., Brown (1980, pp. 377–432).

Chapter 4

Understanding the New Divisia Monetary Aggregates

*William A. Barnett**

> The Federal Reserve Board's staff has released the back data on its Divisia monetary aggregates (Barnett and Spindt, 1982). However, the earlier publications on the theoretical foundations and empirical support for those aggregates were directed at an audience of professional aggregation theorists. The current paper provides interpretive information for potential data users, who need not have prior knowledge of formal aggregation theory. Particular emphasis is placed on the need for proper understanding of the Divisia weights and of their source in theory.

1 Introduction

The official monetary aggregates are computed as simple sums of component quantities. Yet simple sum aggregation implies perfect substitutability between components, and the components of the monetary aggregates are far from perfect substitutes. Barnett (1980a; 1981b, chapter 7) has derived a monetary quantity index number based upon the Divisia index, which requires no assumptions on substitutability between components. The back data on those new aggregates were released by the Federal Reserve Board in Barnett and Spindt (1982).

However, the many published papers and books on the subject of those aggregates have been written for an audience of professional aggregation theorists.[1] Potential users of the new data series sometimes have found that their questions do not appear directly to be answered by the existing published literature, since that literature does not provide the interpretive information that a nonspecialist would require. The purpose of this paper is to present the underlying theory in a form that would permit a potential user to

---

*Originally published in the *Review of Public Data Use*, now called the *Journal of Economic and Social Measurement* (1983), pp. 7–23. The research on this paper was partially supported by NSF grant SOC8305162.

[1] Two exceptions are Barnett (1982b) and Barnett, Offenbacher, and Spindt (1981). Also see Barnett and Spindt (1979).

2 The Divisia Index

Difficulties in understanding the Divisia monetary aggregates can almost invariably be traced to misunderstandings of the Divisia 'weights.' In order to understand those weights, the source of the Divisia index number itself must be understood. The following discussion presents that source in terms of easily understood microeconomic theory.

Suppose the economy's transactions technology (or the 'representative consumer's' utility function) over monetary assets is $Q(\mathbf{x})$, where $\mathbf{x}$ is the vector of n component asset quantities. In aggregation theory, $Q(\mathbf{x})$ then is the economic quantity aggregate. The aggregation theoretic procedure for selecting the n component assets is described in Barnett (1982a).

Take the total differential of Q to get

$$dQ(\mathbf{x}) = \sum_{i=1}^{n} \frac{\partial Q}{\partial x_i} \, dx_i. \tag{1}$$

Since $\partial Q/\partial x_i$ contains the unknown parameters of the function Q, we shall replace each of those marginal products (or marginal utilities) by $\lambda p_i = \partial Q/\partial x_i$ which is a first-order condition for expenditure constrained maximization of Q, where λ is the Lagrange multiplier and p_i is the user-cost price of asset i. We then get

$$\frac{dQ(\mathbf{x})}{\lambda} = \sum_{i=1}^{n} p_i \, dx_i, \tag{2}$$

which has no unknown parameters on the right-hand side.

In order for a quantity aggregate to be useful, it must be linearly homogeneous. In fact, if there is one case in which the correct growth rate of an aggregate is entirely obvious, it is in the case in which all components are growing at the same rate. As required by linear homogeneity, we would certainly expect that the quantity aggregate then would grow at that same rate. Hence we shall assume Q is linearly homogeneous.

Define $P(\mathbf{p})$ to be the dual price index satisfying Fisher's factor reversal test, $P(\mathbf{p})Q(\mathbf{q}) = \mathbf{p}'\mathbf{q}$. In other words, define $P(\mathbf{p})$ to equal $\mathbf{p}'\mathbf{q}/Q(\mathbf{q})$, which can be shown to depend only upon $\mathbf{p}$, when Q is linearly homogeneous.[2]

---

[2] The proof replaces $Q(\mathbf{q})$ by the correponding indirect utility function, factors $m = \mathbf{p}'\mathbf{q}$ out of the indirect utility function, and cancels m out of the numerator and denominator of the expression for $P(\mathbf{p})$.

Then the following lemma holds.

Lemma 1 $\lambda = 1/P(\mathbf{p})$.

Proof. Let $m = \mathbf{p}'\mathbf{q}$, and let $\mathbf{q} = \mathbf{D}(m, \mathbf{p})$ be the solution to maximization of $Q(\mathbf{q})$ subject to $\mathbf{p}'\mathbf{q} = m$. By the linear homogeneity of $Q(\mathbf{q})$, we know that there must exist $\phi(\mathbf{p})$ such that $\mathbf{D}(m, \mathbf{p}) = \phi(\mathbf{p})m$. Substituting for $\mathbf{q}$ into $Q(\mathbf{q})$, we get that

$$Q(\mathbf{q}) = Q(\phi(\mathbf{p})m) = mQ(\phi(\mathbf{p})). \tag{3}$$

Since $\lambda = \partial Q/\partial m$, we have from Equation (3) that $\lambda = Q(\phi(\mathbf{p}))$. In addition, from $Q(\mathbf{q})P(\mathbf{p}) = m$, and, from Equation (3), we have that $P(\mathbf{p}) = 1/Q(\phi(\mathbf{p}))$. Hence $\lambda = 1/P(\mathbf{p})$. □

From Equation (2) we therefore find the following:

$$P(\mathbf{p})dQ(\mathbf{x}) = \sum_{i=1}^{n} p_i \, dx_i. \tag{4}$$

Manipulating Equation (4) algebraically to convert to growth rate (log change) form, we find that

$$d \log Q(\mathbf{x}) = \sum_{i=1}^{n} w_i \, d \log x_i, \tag{5}$$

where $w_i = p_i x_i/m$ is the ith asset's value share in total expenditure on monetary asset services. Equation (5) is the Divisia index in growth rate terms. In short, the growth rate of the Divisia index, $Q(\mathbf{x})$, is the share weighted average of the growth rates of the components. The index was originated by the French economist, François Divisia (1925).

Finally in order to be able to apply (5) to monetary aggregation, we need the user cost of each monetary asset.[3] Barnett (1978; 1980a) proved that the user cost of monetary asset i is

$$p_i = f(p^*, R)(R - r_i), \tag{6}$$

where $f(p^*, R) = p^*/(1 + R)$, p^* is the true cost of living index, r_i is the own yield on asset i, and R is the maximum expected holding-period yield available in the economy.[4] Substituting (6) into (5), we see that $f(p^*, R)$ cancels out of the numerator and denominator of each share, and hence $f(p^*, R)$

---

[3] We also need a finite change approximation to (5). The Törnqvist-Theil approximation used by Barnett (1980a; 1981b, Chapter 7) is very accurate in discrete time.

[4] The use of the true cost of living index over consumer goods prices to deflate nominal to real monetary balances is not without controversy. For example, under some assumptions the price index deflator should include the user costs of monetary assets as well as the prices of consumer goods, but these deep matters are beyond the current scope of this research.

does not appear in the Divisia index formula. As a result, we could use the following simpler form of the user-cost prices:

$$p_i = R - r_i. \tag{7}$$

Clearly, (7) is just the interest foregone (and therefore opportunity cost) of holding asset i.

Barnett's (1980a; 1981b, chapter 7) Divisia monetary aggregates are acquired by using (7) for the user-cost prices in the Törnqvist-Theil discrete time approximation to (5). As we now shall see, interpretation of the behavior of the Divisia monetary aggregates is not difficult when the derivations of (5) and (7) are kept in mind.

3 The Weights

The most widely asked questions regarding the Divisia monetary aggregates relate to the 'weights' and to the relationship between the weights and interest rates. In this section we shall consider that subject in light of the derivation in the last section.

If r_i is high, as, for example, has sometimes been the case for money market funds, then p_i is low in (7). Hence, if the yield on money market funds were high and *if* the 'weight' attached to money market funds in a monetary aggregate were its user cost, then money market funds would have little influence on the aggregate. Observations of that sort have occasionally led to misunderstandings of the Divisia aggregates. However, the user costs are *not* the weights. As can be seen from (4), the prices weight the marginal component changes, dx_i, to get the dollar value of the marginal change in the aggregate, $P(\mathbf{p})dQ(\mathbf{x})$. This elementary fact, which follows directly from microeconomic theory, does not apply either to the growth rate or to the level of the quantity aggregate. In addition, the role of prices in (4) applies only at the margin.

The role of prices at the margin should be no surprise, since the relationship between prices and marginal utilities or marginal products is well known. The fallacies that can arise from misinterpreting the role of prices in economics are also well known. For example, the familiar diamonds and water paradox illustrates that high price and therefore high marginal utility do not necessarily imply high utility. In fact, if a utility function is strictly concave, then marginal utility and total utility are *inversely* related. Hence, if we view $Q(\mathbf{x})$ as a utility function, we see that low user-cost price of money market funds [and therefore low marginal utility, as reflected in (4)] does *not* imply low contribution of money market funds to total utility, $Q(\mathbf{x})$.

If we look at (5) rather than (4), we see the source of the common interpretation of the shares, w_i, as being the Divisia weights. This interpretation is useful, both because (5) does define the Divisia index and also because (5) illustrates that the shares weight component *growth rates* to get the *growth rate* of the aggregate. Since the growth rates of monetary aggregates are the most closely watched properties of the aggregates' time paths, the Divisia share weights are important. But note that each share depends upon *all* prices and *all* quantities. This observation further emphasizes the fact that the user-cost prices are not the weights. In fact without knowing the own price elasticity of demand for asset i, it is impossible to predict the direction of the change in w_i, when p_i increases. Hence high or rising p_i need not imply high or rising w_i. For example if $Q(\mathbf{x})$ were Cobb-Douglas, then w_i would be independent of p_i.

As weights, the value shares are far more meaningful than the user costs. The user costs are *prices*. Every quantity index contains prices in its weights. The Laspeyres, Paasche, and Fisher-ideal quantity indices all contain prices in their weights. Although each such index uses the same vector of prices, each index certainly does not have the same weights.

Nevertheless, the value shares, w_i, also need to be interpreted with care, when viewed as 'weights.' If understood clearly in terms of their role in weighting growth rates in (5), the shares are indeed weights. However, in common usage, the term 'weight' frequently refers to the contribution of the *level* of a component to the level of the aggregate. The shares do not serve that role for the Divisia index. In fact, in the Divisia index and in general aggregation theory, no such level weights exist. When components are not perfect substitutes, economic aggregates always are non-linear and therefore cannot be completely strongly separable ('additive'). Without additivity, the concept of weights in levels has no meaning.

To see this problem, suppose the economic quantity aggregate, $Q(\mathbf{x})$, is completely additive, so that it can be written in the form

$$Q(\mathbf{x}) = \sum_{i=1}^{n} f_i(x_i) \tag{8}$$

for some f_i $(i = 1, \ldots n)$. Then we equivalently can write

$$Q(\mathbf{x}) = \sum_{i=1}^{n} A_i(x_i) x_i, \tag{9}$$

where $A_i(x_i) = f_i(x_i)/x_i$ is the *average* product (or average utility) of asset (or good) i. Clearly, $A_i(x_i)$ also is the weight imputed to component quantity level x_i to get the level of the aggregate $Q(\mathbf{x})$. Since the user costs measure *marginal* products (or marginal utilities), the user costs do not measure the aggregation theoretic level weights $A_i(x_i)$. Furthermore, unless $Q(\mathbf{x})$ can be written in the form (8), $Q(\mathbf{x})$ *cannot* be written as a weighted average of component levels, as in (9). Yet most misunderstandings of the Divisia monetary aggregates result from viewing the user costs as the level weights $A_i(x_i)$ in (9). Clearly both (9) and therefore the resulting level weights $A_i(x_i)$ usually do not exist, and, even when they do, the level weights $A_i(x_i)$ do not equal the user costs. Furthermore, the level weights do not equal the shares w_i.

In short, misunderstandings of the Divisia monetary aggregates generally stem from confusing marginal products (or user costs) with average products (or level weights, when they exist) or with growth rate weights (or value shares). Understanding of the derivation and discussion above should permit potential users of the Divisia aggregates to avoid such easily made errors.

Finally, to summarize all of the above in one equation, we shall solve the differential equation (5) for the level of the index, $Q(\mathbf{x})$. First we rewrite (5) as the explicit differential equation

$$\frac{d\log Q(\mathbf{x}(t))}{dt} = \sum_{i=1}^{n} w_i(t) \frac{d\log x_i(t)}{dt}, \qquad (10)$$

where $\mathbf{x}(t)$, $t \in T$, is the time path of the asset quantities and $w_i(t)$, $t \in T$, is the time path of the ith value share. Clearly, $w_i(t) = p_i(t)x_i(t)/\mathbf{p}(t)'\mathbf{x}(t)$, where $\mathbf{p}(t)$, $t \in T$, is the time path of the user-cost prices.

Solving the differential equation (10) for $Q(t)$, we get

$$Q(t) = \exp \int_{\tau=0}^{t} \left[\sum_{i=1}^{n} w_i(\tau) \frac{d\log x_i(\tau)}{d\tau} \right] d\tau. \qquad (11)$$

In discrete time, we would use the Törnqvist-Theil approximation to the line integral (11). The recursive form of that approximation is given in Barnett (1980a; 1981b, chapter 7). Inspecting (11), we see that $Q(t)$ does not have the simple linearly weighted form of (9). Reading 'weights' into a deeply nonlinear function such as (11) clearly is a hazardous enterprise.

4   Is it a Quantity or Price Index?

A deeper understanding of the Divisia index is acquired when one realizes that the weights and even the user-cost prices are really not there at all. One should learn to see through the weights and user costs to the fact that the resulting index equals $Q(\mathbf{x})$, which depends *only* upon quantities. Clearly the only arguments of $Q(\mathbf{x})$ are the quantities, $\mathbf{x}$. No prices appear as arguments of Q. In short $Q(\mathbf{x})$ is a quantity index, not a price index.

The paradox that may appear to be evident from the appearance of prices on the right-hand side of (5) is easily explained through the derivation of (5) from (2). The prices were used to eliminate the marginal products from (2), so that no unknown parameters would exist in the index. However, the marginal products depend only upon quantities, and hence the right-hand side of (5) continues to track the quantity aggregate on the left-side exactly.

Once one has recognized the fact that the Divisia quantity index measures $Q(\mathbf{x})$, which contains no prices, one can see that the Divisia monetary aggregates are easily controlled. Federal Reserve policy instruments affect the economy's equilibrium value for $Q(\mathbf{x})$, which measures a true structural economic variable. Since the Divisia monetary aggregates accurately measure $Q(\mathbf{x})$, a stable relationship can be expected to exist between Federal Reserve instruments (such as the monetary base or nonborrowed reserves) and the Divisia monetary aggregates. Since the simple sum aggregates do not measure $Q(\mathbf{x})$, we cannot expect to find a stable relationship between Federal Reserve instruments and the simple sum aggregates. These theoretical conjectures have been verified empirically by Barnett, Offenbacher, and Spindt (1984), and Barnett (1983a).

The prices in (5) affect $Q(\mathbf{x})$ only to the degree that changes in prices induce changes in component quantities, $\mathbf{x}$, affecting $Q(\mathbf{x})$. Similarly prices appear in revealed preference theory despite the fact that the preferences being revealed are defined only over quantities. Nevertheless, if the Federal Reserve were to adopt the Divisia monetary aggregates as policy targets, it is conceivable that some aspects of the targeting and control procedures might require forecasting of the share weights, w_i ($i = 1, \ldots, n$), rather than direct forecasting of $Q(\mathbf{x})$. However, it would be preferable to treat the Divisia monetary aggregates themselves as elementary variables, and target or forecast them directly, rather than to operate indirectly through the weights.

Nevertheless, since quantities and own prices tend to move in opposite directions along demand curves, value shares tend to be more stable over time than either prices or quantities alone. Hence the value shares can more easily be forecasted than either component quantities or prices alone. In fact, a no-change extrapolation, which uses the current period shares as next period's shares, is usually hard to beat (see, e.g., Parks, 1969, for such a comparison). Hence even the simplest means of forecasting the Divisia share weights is likely to result in far less weighting error than the use of the greatly inaccurate simple sum weighting scheme.

Finally the relative ease of controlling the Divisia monetary aggregates is increased by the existing institutional arrangements in the money markets. The simple sum aggregates, at high levels of aggregation, heavily weight high yielding money substitutes, which typically are backed by either zero or low reserve requirements. The Divisia monetary aggregates, on the other hand, frequently impute lower weights to such high yielding component assets. Hence the problems of controlling component assets having low reserve requirements is less serious for the Divisia than the simple sum aggregates. When treated directly as an elementary variable, the Divisia quantity aggregates are more heavily reserve backed than the simple sum aggregates computed over the same components.

5 Stocks Versus Flows

The Divisia monetary aggregate over $\mathbf{x}$ measures $Q(\mathbf{x})$. With the prices, $\mathbf{p}$, measured as user costs rather than stock prices, $Q(\mathbf{x})$ measures the service flow produced by $\mathbf{x}$. The simple sum aggregates measure the stock. This result also can be seen by exploring the mathematical relationship between (5) and the simple sum aggregate.

To determine that relationship, we need only write $Q(\mathbf{x}(t)) = \sum_{i=1}^{n} x_i(t)$ and take the time derivative of $\log Q(\mathbf{x}(t))$ in continuous time. We find that we again get (10), but with the shares equaling $w_i^* = x_i / \sum_{j=1}^{n} x_j$. Hence in continuous time the Divisia aggregates reduce to the simple sum aggregates when all prices are equal. That simple sum special case can be acquired in one of two ways. One method would be to use $Q(\mathbf{x})$ as a service flow measure under the assumption that all components are perfect substitutes in identical units. In that case all equilibrium user-cost prices would be equal. The other method would be to treat $Q(\mathbf{x})$ as an accounting (as opposed to economic) stock aggregate.[5] In that case, each monetary asset would be a 'numeraire' good with price of one dollar.

The relationship between the Divisia aggregates and service flows can further be seen through the form of the user-cost prices, (7). The theory views the services of monetary assets as being of two types: investment services and other services, such as transactions services. At the margin, r_i fully values the investment services of asset i. The other marginal services are valued by $R - r_i$, which measures the potential investment services foregone by holding asset i at yield r_i, when R was potentially available on an asset providing nothing but investment services. In cases of rate regulated assets, the own market yield, r_i, may not fully measure the asset's investment yield. An implicit rate of return then is needed, as is used for demand deposits in the new Divisia monetary aggregates (see Barnett and Spindt, 1982).

---

[5] Regarding the measurement of the economic stock, see Section 3.4 of this book.

6 Conclusion

Divisia quantity indexes inherently are no more complicated or mysterious than Laspeyres or Paasche price indices. In theory the only significant difference is that Laspeyres and Paasche index numbers provide first-order approximations, while Divisia (or Fisher ideal) index numbers provide second-order approximations. The Labor Department's CPI is a Laspeyres index, and the Commerce Department's implicit price deflator is a Paasche index.[6] Yet few users of the CPI or the implicit price deflator concern themselves with the aggregation theoretic foundations of Laspeyres or Paasche index numbers. Rather such users have become accustomed to treating each index as a price aggregate with properties learned from experience.

Once users have become accustomed to the Divisia monetary aggregates and their historical behavior, the aggregation theoretic source of the Divisia monetary aggregates are likely again to become a matter of interest only to specialists in aggregation theory. But until experience with the behavior of the Divisia aggregates becomes widely distributed over potential users, the theoretical considerations presented above are likely to be the most readily accessible source of interpretive information regarding the behavior of the Divisia monetary aggregates.

---

[6] Since the original publication of this paper, the Commerce Department has converted to chained Fisher ideal indexes.

PART 2:

Index Number Theory

Section 2.1: Editors' Overview of Part 2

William A. Barnett and Apostolos Serletis

The following table contains a brief summary of the contents of each chapter in Part 2 of this book.

Part 2 Section Contents
Index Number Theory

Chapter Number	Chapter Title	Contents
5	Divisia Indices	An encyclopedia entry providing a concise source of background on the general Divisia index.
6	Divisia Monetary Aggregates	Another encyclopedia entry providing a concise source of information on the Divisia monetary index.
7	The Optimal Level of Monetary Aggregation	Explains the logical sequence of steps in producing monetary aggregates that are consistent with theory, including the relevant clustering criterion for grouping assets into components of a theoretically admissible aggregate.
8	New Concepts of Aggregated Money	An explanation of various competing approaches for aggregating monetary assets, including a procedure for extracting characteristic services.

Chapters 5 and 6:

These chapters contain background from the general field of index number theory. Chapters 5 and 6 both are encyclopedia entries. Chapter 5 is background on the Divisia index itself, while Chapter 6 is background on the application of the Divisia index to monetary aggregation.

Chapter 7:

Chapter 7 provides the logical sequence of steps in the production and use of index numbers, beginning with clustering of components through tests of blockwise weak separability. Following the identification of an admissible weakly separable block of components, the chapter explains the procedure for aggregation over the clustered components through the use of index numbers providing satisfactory tracking of the unknown theoretical aggregator function. Finally the chapter discusses the choice among nonunique theoretically admissible aggregates, when more than one component group is weakly separable. An example is the case of nested recursive tree structures.

The chapter emphasizes the importance of conducting each step of the procedure in the correct order, as opposed to the methodologically improper procedure of producing aggregates to make some applied macroeconomic theory or point of view work well. The latter circular procedure accounts for many of the most unfortunate abuses of scientific methodology in economics. Data production and aggregation must be prior to use. The valid procedure for data production in aggregation and index number theory is independent of and unbiased by the final use.

The paper concludes with empirical results comparing the simple sum monetary aggregates with aggregates produced in accordance with valid index number theory.

Chapter 8:

Chapter 8 contrasts the Divisia monetary aggregates, which measure the aggregate flow of monetary services, with the indexes produced from Theil's (1976) more complicated preference independence transformation approach. Theil's approach can be viewed as the converse of Lancaster's (1971) consumption characteristics approach. Theil's approach untangles individual service types and measures each separately. The result can be the measurement of one particular source of monetary service, such as "liquidity" or "means of payment." In contrast, the Divisia index removes nonmonetary service motives, such as investment return, and measures the aggregate of all remaining monetary services not removed.

There is a derivable connection between the two approaches, which complement each other.

Section 2.2: General Index Number Theory

Chapter 5

Divisia Indices

*William A. Barnett**

The Divisia index is a highly regarded continuous-time statistical index number. In addition, discrete-time approximations to the Divisia index are among the best available discrete-time statistical index numbers. Index numbers acquire their link with economic theory through the aggregator functions of aggregation theory, since index numbers can be viewed as approximations to aggregator functions.

1 Aggregation Theory

1.1 Structure of the Economy

Aggregation theory is a branch of economic theory. In economic theory, the structure of an economy is defined by the tastes (utility functions) of consumers and the technology (production functions) of firms. Let there be n consumers and N firms. Let f_i, $i = 1, \ldots, n$, be the utility function of the ith consumer, and let f_i, $i = n+1, \ldots, n+N$, be the production function (possibly vector-valued) of the ith firm. Then the structure of the economy is defined by $\{f_i : i = 1, \ldots, n+N\}$.

---

*Originally published in Kotz and Johnson (eds.), *Encyclopedia of Statistical Sciences* 1982, 412–414. Reprinted by permission of John Wiley & Sons, Inc.

1.2 Aggregator Functions

Let $\mathbf{x}_i$ be the vector of arguments of f_i for economic agent (firm or consumer) i. Then $\mathbf{x}_i$ consists of consumer goods, if i is a consumer, or factors of production, if i is a firm. For some economic agent, i, let there exist functions, g_{ij} ($j = 1, \ldots, k$) and F_i and a partition of $\mathbf{x}_i$, $\mathbf{x}_i = (\mathbf{x}'_{i1}, \ldots, \mathbf{x}'_{ik})'$, such that $f_i(\mathbf{x}_i) = F_i(g_{i1}(\mathbf{x}_{i1}), \ldots, g_{ik}(\mathbf{x}_{ik}))$ for all feasible $\mathbf{x}_i$. Then for economic agent i, g_{ij} is defined to be the 'quantity aggregator function' over the components $\mathbf{x}_{ij}$, and $g_{ij}(\mathbf{x}_{ij})$ is the economic quantity aggregate over the components $\mathbf{x}_{ij}$.

1.3 Exact Aggregator Functions

An aggregator function or its corresponding economic aggregate is called 'exact' or 'consistent' if the aggregator function is linearly homogeneous. It can be shown [see, e.g., Green (1964, Theorem 4)] that economic agents behave as if exact economic aggregates were elementary goods. The specification of an aggregator function is defined to be 'flexible' if it can provide a second-order approximation to any arbitrary aggregator function. Examples include the quadratic and translog specifications.

2 Index Number Theory

2.1 Functional Index Numbers

To approximate an aggregator function, a specification commonly is selected having unknown parameters. If the parameters are estimated empirically and the unknown parameters are replaced by their estimates, the resulting estimated function (normalized to equal 1 in a fixed base year) is called a 'functional index number.' Although such index numbers are valuable in research, their dependence upon estimated parameters commonly discourages their publication as data by governmental agencies.

2.2 Statistical Index Numbers

Statistical index numbers provide parameter-free and specification-free approximations to economic aggregates. An economic quantity aggregate, $g_{ij}(\mathbf{x}_{ij})$, depends upon the component quantities, $\mathbf{x}_{ij}$, and upon the unknown function, g_{ij}. A statistical quantity index depends upon the component quantities, $\mathbf{x}_{ij}$, and also upon the corresponding prices, $\mathbf{p}_j$, but not upon any unknown parameters or functions. The inclusion of prices in statistical quantity indices permits the index (under conventional economic behavioral assumptions) to reveal information regarding the current point, $g_{ij}(\mathbf{x}_{ij})$, on the aggregator function, i.e., the current value of the aggregate. Statistical index numbers cannot provide information regarding the form or properties (such as substitution elasticities) of the aggregator function, g_{ij}, itself.

Statistical index numbers are characterized by their statistical properties and by their economic properties. The classical source on the statistical properties of statistical index numbers is Fisher (1922). See also Theil (1967). The economic properties of statistical index numbers are defined in terms of the indices' abilities to approximate economic aggregates.

A particularly desirable economic property of a statistical index number is the ability of the index always to attain the current value of a 'flexible' aggregator function. A statistical index number possessing that property is called 'superlative.' [See Diewert (1976).]

3 Divisia Index

3.1 Continuous Time

Let us fix (i,j). To simplify the notation, now drop the subscripts i and j from $\mathbf{x}_{ij}$ and $\mathbf{p}_j$. Our data then are $(\mathbf{x}, \mathbf{p})$. In continuous time, $(\mathbf{x}, \mathbf{p}) = (\mathbf{x}(t), \mathbf{p}(t))$ is a continuous function of time.

The Divisia (1925) quantity index, $Q(t)$, is the line integral defined by the differential

$$d\log Q(t) = \sum_{k=1}^{M} s_k(t) d\log x_k(t),$$

where M is the dimension of the vector $\mathbf{x}$, and $s_k = p_k x_k / \mathbf{p}'\mathbf{x}$ is the expenditure share of good k in total expenditure, $\mathbf{p}'\mathbf{x}$, on the M goods. In short, the growth rate of the Divisia index is defined to be the weighted average of the growth rates of the components, where the weights are the corresponding expenditure value shares, $\mathbf{s} = (s_1, \ldots, s_M)'$, of the components.

The statistical properties of the Divisia index are provided by Richter (1966). Hulten (1973) has shown that under the conditions sufficient for the existence of a consistent aggregator function, the Divisia index line integral is path independent and the resulting Divisia index always exactly attains the current value of the economic aggregate.

3.2 Discrete Time

In discrete time Törnqvist (1936) and Theil (1967) have proposed the following approximation to the Divisia index:

$$\log Q_t - \log Q_{t-1} = \sum_{k=1}^{M} s_k^* (\log x_{kt} - \log x_{k,t-1}),$$

where $s_k^* = (1/2)(s_{k,t}+s_{k,t-1})$ is the average of the current expenditure value share, $s_{kt} = p_{kt}x_{kt}/\mathbf{p}_t'\mathbf{x}_t$, and the lagged share, $s_{k,t-1}$.

The Törnqvist-Theil approximation to the Divisia index does not possess all of the properties proved for the continuous-time Divisia index by Hulten (1973). In fact, no known discrete-time statistical index is capable of attaining the current value of every economic aggregate without error. However, the Törnqvist-Theil Divisia index does fall within Diewert's class of 'superlative' index numbers. The magnitude of the error of the approximation generally is very small. Applications of the Törnqvist-Theil Divisia index are discussed in Theil (1967) and Barnett (1980).

4 Dual Price Indices

In economic theory, price and quantity aggregator functions are dual's. Hence the discussion on quantity aggregation above applies directly to price aggregation. While the price aggregator function dual to quantity aggregator function is unique, two price index numbers can be acquired from a statistical quantity index. One price index can be acquired by interchanging prices with quantities in the quantity index. In the case of the Divisia index, we get

$$d\log P(t) = \sum_{k=1}^{M} s_k(t) d\log p_k(t)$$

in the continuous-time case, and

$$\log P_t - \log P_{t-1} = \sum_{k=1}^{M} s_k^*(\log p_{kt} - \log p_{k,t-1})$$

in the Törnqvist-Theil discrete-time case. Another price index can be acquired by dividing actual total expenditure on the components by the quantity index number.

If the two methods result in the same price index, the index number formula is said to satisfy Fisher's factor reversal test, or in the more modern terminology to be self-dual. The Divisia index in discrete time is not self-dual, although the magnitude of the discrepancy commonly is very small

Chapter 6

Divisia Monetary Aggregates

William A. Barnett[*]

Aggregation theory and index-number theory both have histories dating back to the turn of the century. The use of the techniques from those fields to generate official government data began in the 1920s, and nearly all economic data have subsequently been generated by methods developed in those literatures.

Nevertheless, one conspicuous exception remains. The monetary quantity aggregates supplied by nearly every central bank in the world are not based on index-number or aggregation theory, but are rather the simple sums of the components. The Divisia monetary aggregates, originated by Barnett (1980a), remedy this problem by applying economic index-number theory.

The problem with using the exact aggregates of aggregation theory for constructing official data is that they depend on unknown aggregator functions, which typically are utility, production, cost, or distance functions. Such functions must first be econometrically estimated. Hence the resulting exact quantity and price indexes become estimator- and specification-dependent. This dependency is troublesome to governmental agencies, which therefore view aggregation theory as strictly a research tool.

Statistical index-number theory, on the other hand, provides quantity and price indexes which are computable from quantity and price data, without first estimating unknown functions. Such index numbers, whether price or quantity indexes, always depend jointly on all prices and all quantities, but not on any unknown parameters. The exact aggregates of aggregation theory, however, depend on unknown parameters, and either solely on quantity data (if a quantity aggregate) or solely on price data (if a price aggregate). In a sense, index-number theory trades joint dependency on prices and quantities for independence of unknown parameters. Examples of such statistical index numbers are the Laspeyres, Paasche, Divisia, and Törnqvist indexes. Despite their obvious usefulness, these statistical index numbers could not be derived until recently from aggregation-theoretic microeconomic theory. As a result, statistical index numbers were judged primarily by their known 'good' and 'bad' properties, none of which were their order of approximation to the exact

---

[*]Originally published in David Glasner (ed.), *Business Cycles and Depressions, An Encyclopedia* (1997), 173–177.

aggregates of aggregation theory.

The absence of a direct link between aggregation theory and index-number theory caused some aggregation theorists to view index-number theory as ad hoc and lacking solid theoretical foundations, and also caused a tremendous proliferation of index-number formulas in index-number theory. Although most reputable index numbers usually move closely together, the multitude of index numbers reinforced the impression that index-number theory was ad hoc.

Until recently, the link between statistical index-number theory and microeconomic aggregation theory was even weaker for aggregating monetary quantities than for aggregating other quantities. The problem (only recently solved when Barnett (1978, 1980a) derived formulas for the user cost for demanded monetary services and in 1987 for supplied monetary services) was that quantity indexes depend on prices as well as quantities, and the 'price' of a monetary asset's services is not clearly defined. An early implicit attempt to apply index-number theory to monetary aggregation was Hutt (1963, p. 92), and his index is noteworthy since recently a similar index has been advocated by Rotemberg (1991).

The loose link between index-number theory and aggregation theory was reinforced when Diewert (1976) defined the class of 'superlative' index numbers. Statistical index-number theory became part of microeconomic theory, as aggregation theory had been for decades. Barnett's results on the user cost of the services of monetary assets set the stage for introducing index-number theory into monetary economics.

1 The Economic Decision

Consider a decision problem over monetary assets that illustrates the capability of the Divisia monetary aggregates in theory. The decision problem will be defined so that the relevant literature on economic aggregation over goods is immediately applicable.

Let $\mathbf{m}_t$ be the vector of real balances of monetary assets during period t, r_t be the vector of nominal holding-period yields for monetary assets during period t, A_t be the planned holdings of the benchmark asset during period t, and R_t be the expected one-period holding yield on the benchmark asset during period t. The benchmark asset is defined to provide no services other than its yield, R_t, so that the asset is held solely to accumulate wealth. Thus, R_t is the maximum expected holding-period yield in the economy in period t.

In practice, the benchmark yield is computed by maximizing over the yield-curve-adjusted holding-period yields on all of the monetary assets on which the central bank has data. Usually, some other yields are also included within the set of rates of return over which that upper envelope is computed. Since this maximization is repeated each period, the asset that serves the role of the benchmark asset can change each period.

Let y_t be the real value of total budgeted expenditure on monetary services during period t. The optimal portfolio allocation decision is:

$$\text{maximize } u(\mathbf{m}_t) \\ \text{subject to } \boldsymbol{\pi}_t' \mathbf{m}_t = y_t, \tag{1}$$

where $\boldsymbol{\pi}_t = (\pi_{1t}, \ldots, \pi_{nt})'$ is the vector of monetary asset real user costs, and

$$\pi_{it} = \frac{R_t - r_{it}}{1 + R_t}. \tag{2}$$

This function u is the decision-maker's utility function, assumed to be monotonically increasing and strictly concave. The decision problem (1) is a constrained-optimization problem, so that results from the literature on aggregation theory and index-number theory for consumers are immediately applicable. The user-cost formula (2), derived by Barnett (1978), measures the foregone interest or opportunity cost of holding monetary asset i, when the higher yielding benchmark asset could have been held.

The exact monetary aggregate of economic theory is the utility level associated with holding the portfolio and hence is the optimized value of the objective function of the decision:

$$M_t = u(\mathbf{m}_t) \tag{3}$$

2 The Divisia Index

Although equation (3) is exactly correct, it depends upon the unknown utility function, u. Nevertheless, statistical index-number theory enables us to track M_t exactly, without estimating the unknown function u.

If $\mathbf{m}_t^*$ is derived by solving equation (3), then $u(\mathbf{m}_t^*)$ is the exact monetary aggregate M_t. In continuous time, $M_t = u(\mathbf{m}_t^*)$ can be tracked exactly (Barnett 1983b) by the Divisia index, which solves the differential equation

$$\frac{d \log M_t^c}{dt} = \sum_i s_{it} \frac{d \log m_{it}^*}{dt}, \tag{4}$$

for M_t^c, where $s_{it} = \pi_{it} m_{it}^*/y_t$ is the i'th asset's share in expenditure on the total portfolio's service flow. As a formula for aggregating over quantities of perishable consumer goods, that index was first proposed by Francois Divisia

(1925) with market prices of those goods in place of the user costs in equation (4).

In continuous time, the Divisia index, under conventional neoclassical assumptions, is perfect. However, in discrete time, many different approximations to equation (4) are possible. The most popular is the Törnqvist-Theil approximation (often called the Törnqvist index), which is just the Simpson's rule approximation:

$$\log M_t - \log M_{t-1} = \sum_i \bar{s}_{it}(\log m_{it}^* - \log m_{i,t-1}^*), \qquad (5)$$

where $\bar{s}_{it} = (1/2)(s_{it} + s_{i,t-1})$. In discrete time we shall call equation (5) simply the Divisia index.

A compelling reason for using equation (5) as the discrete-time approximation to the Divisia index is that Diewert (1976) has defined a class of *superlative* index numbers, which have particular appeal in producing discrete-time approximations to $M_t^c = u(\mathbf{m}_t^*)$. Diewert defines a superlative index number to be one that is exactly correct for some quadratic approximation to u. The discrete Divisia index (5) is superlative. With weekly or monthly monetary data, the Divisia index (5) is accurate to within three decimal places, which typically is smaller than the round-off error of the data (Barnett 1980a).

3 Applications

A number of important extentions and applications recently have appeared. Serletis (1991a), Belongia and Chalfant (1989), Swofford and Whitney (1987), and Hancock (1985) have produced some high-quality applications of this literature. Hancock's work deals with supply-side aggregation, while the work by the others is on the demand side. Ewis and Fisher (1985) introduced foreign-currency substitution into monetary aggregation theory and applied the resulting microeconomic foundations empirically. Hancock (1985) introduced transaction costs into the supply-side user costs, and Barnett, Hinich, and Weber (1986) tested the statistical significance of the regulatory wedge, produced by the nonpayment of interest on required reserves. Poterba and Rotemberg (1987) and Barnett, Hinich, and Yue (1991) have extended the theory to the case of risk aversion.

Ishida (1984) investigated the performance of the Divisia monetary aggregates as a substitute for the Bank of Japan's official simple-sum monetary aggregates. The dynamic behavior of the Divisia monetary aggregates has been studied by Barnett and Chen (1988), and Barnett, Hinich, and Yue

(1991). Barnett, Offenbacher, and Spindt (1984) used Granger-causality testing and other conventional comparisons of monetary assets to compare the Divisia with the simple-sum monetary aggregates.

In some applications, monetary wealth rather than the monetary service flow is relevant. It is necessary to compute the expected discounted present value of the service flow. The expected service flow in a future period is measured by its expected Divisia index. The simple-sum aggregates can be derived from discounting only if the investment yield is discounted to present value along with nominal expenditure on the service flow. However, the interest yield on an asset has never been viewed as a monetary service in macroeconomic theory. For the formula for the discounted service flow (net of the investment yield), see Barnett, Hinich, and Yue (1991).[1]

Barnett, Fisher, and Serletis (1992) have surveyed the voluminous available empirical results, which now are available from many countries and using many empirical criteria. However, certain of these empirical criteria (structural change, regulation, and controllability) seem to be particularly relevant to the objectives of this survey.

4 Structural Change

A major issue in monetary economics recently has been whether structural change affects the stability of the demand-for-money and supply-of-money functions. The weight of the evidence is that using Divisia monetary aggregates instead of simple-sum aggregates produces functions that are much more stable than the functions produced from the simple-sum aggregates, but at the cost of greater interest elasticity. When Divisia monetary data are used, the economic variables in the models explain the demand for and supply of monetary services adequately, and tests for structural change reject the hypothesis of shifts in the economy's structure. When simple-sum monetary data are used, the interest elasticities of the demand and supply functions are usually lower than those found with the Divisia data, but the functions estimated with simple-sum monetary-aggregate data are subject to recurring unexplained structural shifts.

It is perhaps not surprising that greater explanatory power of economic variables tends to increase elasticities to variations in those variables and conclusions about structure based on the simple-sum aggregates probably untenable. The structural innovations usually observed in money markets are widely viewed to have been triggered by spikes in nominal interest rates caused by surges in inflationary expectations. However, nominal interest rates already are variables in the equations purported to have shifted. Since, by

---

[1] In this book, see Section 3.4 regarding the economic capital stock of money.

definition, structural shifts are produced by omitted variables, to attribute a functional shift to a shift in an included variable is self-contradictory. Divisia data do not involve this inconsistency.

5 Regulation

There are circumstances under which simple-sum aggregation is justifiable over certain subsets of monetary aggregates, although never over an aggregate that includes currency as a component. Paradoxically, the breadth of the span of assets over which simple-sum aggregation is justified increases as regulation either becomes very tight or is totally abandoned.

Simple-sum aggregation can be justified only over those assets which have nearly equal user costs, since the Divisia index converges to the simple-sum index as the user costs approach each other. Under severe regulation of all monetary assets, the benchmark asset's yield may be very large relative to the own rates of return on monetary assets. If so, even though the own rates of the monetary components may differ, their user costs nevertheless may be nearly equal. The Divisia index can then be approximated by the simple-sum index. The considerable evidence that demand deposits have always yielded a substantial implicit rate of return to corporate depositors makes it doubtful this was ever true in the United States. Even if once true, that time is now long past.

Under total deregulation, the rates of return on many monetary assets tend to converge, since rate differentials and the corresponding differentiation of the competing monetary products have to some degree been produced by regulation. Similar yielding, closely substitutable, deregulated assets may be aggregated by simple summation. But since currency's yield is zero, the user cost of currency is much greater than that of such deregulated monetary assets. Hence, no subgrouping of monetary assets that can be aggregated by simple summation under deregulation can include currency.

6 Controllability

Procedures for controlling the Divisia monetary aggregates are necessarily fundamentally different from those for controlling the simple-sum aggregates. The simple-sum aggregates do not enter into the decisions of any economic agents, and hence are not variables within the structure of the economy. The Divisia monetary aggregates, on the other hand, track exact aggregation-theoretic monetary aggregates [which are separable functions, $M_t = u(\mathbf{m}_t)$, of the component asset quantities, as in equation (3) above] and hence measure variables that satisfy the existence condition for a structural variable. Only when the component assets in $\mathbf{m}_t$ are perfect substitutes, so that $u(\mathbf{m}_t)$ is a simple sum, does the simple-sum aggregate appear within the structure of the economy as a separable subfunction, and hence only then does the simple-sum index satisfy the existence condition for an economic aggregate.

The only possible way to control the sum of imperfect substitutes is to control each individual component asset. The imposition of reserve requirements on component assets — a tendency which has been growing in recent years in the U.S. — is intended precisely to allow such direct controllability of each component asset. While the same method is equally as applicable to controlling the Divisia aggregates, direct control over components is not necessary. Any procedure that alters the economy's general equilibrium will alter the economic variables being equilibrated. Since the Divisia monetary aggregates do indeed measure such separable structural variables, control of the Divisia monetary aggregates can operate on the aggregate itself, as if it were an elementary asset. In fact, in economic aggregation theory, an aggregate is defined to be exact, if and only if economic agents act as if the aggregate were an elementary variable.

Whether the money supply should be controlled is a separate issue requiring consideration of the properties of the entire macroeconomy. The theory and empirical evidence above demonstrate only that a control procedure operating directly on the monetary aggregate is available with the Divisia aggregates, but not with the simple-sum aggregates.

Whether or not the money supply is deliberately controlled by the central bank, the Divisia monetary aggregates can serve as indicators. Since the simple-sum aggregates do not measure service-flow variables within the economy's structure, the simple-sum aggregates discount to present value both expenditure on the monetary service flow and also the investment yield from interest-yielding monetary components. The confounding of fundamentally different motives explains why the simple-sum aggregates have no counterpart in the structure of the economy.

7 Conclusion

Much progress in monetary aggregation theory has recently been made. Much remains to be done. The basic issue is that only economic aggregates measure structural variables within the economy. The simple-sum monetary aggregates are just accounting identities, not economic aggregates. The Divisia monetary aggregates are economic aggregates, and hence are relevant to understanding the behavior of economic time series. In fact, the only economic data in which deterministic chaos has yet been detected are the Divisia monetary aggregates, which are sufficiently free from noise to permit detection of the underlying nonlinear determinism below the noise (Barnett and Chen 1988). Links to national and international sources of data on Divisia monetary aggregates can be found on the World Wide Web at URL location: http://wuecon.wustl.edu/~barnett/.

Section 2.3: Monetary Index Number Theory

Chapter 7

The Optimal Level of Monetary Aggregation

*William A. Barnett**

1 Introduction

In this paper, I have three objectives: (1) to describe the aggregation theoretic procedure for selecting the optimal monetary aggregate, (2) to survey the available empirical evidence for information on the optimal aggregate, and (3) to describe the procedures that should be followed to complete a redefinition of the monetary aggregates. Although all of the Federal Reserve Board's current official aggregates are rejected as targets, some newer aggregates are found to be substantially preferable to the official aggregates.

The Federal Reserve Board's staff recently completed the official redefinition of its monetary aggregates in a manner largely unrelated to aggregation and index number theory. My own research in recent years has sought to remedy that shortcoming. Except for monetary aggregates, most of the data provided by governmental agencies are constructed in accordance with aggregation and index number theory.[1] Since aggregation theory can be applied to

---

*Reprinted by permission from the *Journal of Money, Credit, and Banking*, Vol. 14, No. 4 (November 1982). Copyright 1982 by Ohio State University Press. All rights reserved.

[1] While those agencies do use index numbers from index number theory, the implementation of those index numbers sometimes is far removed from the views of professional

monetary aggregation,[2] I constructed new monetary aggregates that are consistent with the economic theory.[3] Recently the empirical properties of those aggregates and the official aggregates have been compared.[4] The new aggregates were generally found to perform better than the official aggregates. The historical data for the new aggregates have recently been released by the Federal Reserve Board in Barnett and Spindt (1982), and regular monthly updates are available upon request.

My past research on the subject was directed towards improving upon the monetary aggregates at each level of aggregation. Comparisons were always between my aggregates and the official simple sum aggregates at each given level of aggregation. Comparisons *across* levels of aggregation were not considered. In this paper I carry the theory one step further to the selection of the optimal levels of monetary aggregation. I then reconsider the existing empirical results to determine the information that they contain regarding the optimal aggregation level.

2 The Earlier Literature

The fact that simple sum monetary aggregation is unsatisfactory has long been recognized, and there has been a steady stream of attempts at weakening the perfect substitutability assumption by constructing weighted average monetary aggregates.[5] Since those weighted averages were not directly based upon aggregation and index number theory, there is a continuum of such potential weighting schemes. However economic aggregation and index number theory recently has been applied to monetary aggregation by Barnett (1980a), who constructed monetary aggregates based upon Diewert's (1976) class of 'superlative' quantity index numbers. The new aggregates released in Barnett and Spindt (1982) are Divisia quantity indices, which are elements of the superlative class.

---

academic index number theorists. For example, government agencies' views regarding user cost pricing of durables often diverge from those of academic index number and aggregation theorists.

[2]Barnett (1980a) and Barnett (1981b, chap. 7).

[3]In that painstaking and lengthy procedure, I was assisted by Paul Spindt. The approach has also been adopted by Cockerline and Murray (1981a) at the Bank of Canada in constructing index numbers of the Canadian money supply. Regarding Divisia monetary aggregates data from other countries, see chapter 18 and the appendix to this book.

[4]See Barnett (1980a, 1981b, 1983a), Barnett and Spindt (1979, 1982), Barnett, Offenbacher, and Spindt (1984), Barnett, Spindt, and Offenbacher (1980b).

[5]See, for example, Hawtrey (1930), Gurley (1960, p. 7–8), Friedman and Meiselman (1963, p. 185), Kane (1964), Ford and Stark (1967), Chetty (1969, 1972), Friedman and Schwartz (1970 p. 151–52), Steinhauer and Chang (1972), Lee (1972), Bisignano (1974), Moroney and Wilbratte (1976), and Barth, Kraft, and Kraft (1977).

Since simple sum aggregation is clearly inappropriate at high levels of aggregation, most economists have never placed much faith in the broader aggregates. An exception is Milton Friedman, who has been a strong advocate of M2. Nevertheless, Friedman and Schwartz, (1970, pp. 151–152) have clearly described the problem with high level simple sum aggregates:

> "This [simple summation] procedure is a very special case of the more general approach. In brief, the general approach consists of regarding each asset as a joint product having different degrees of 'moneyness,' and defining the quantity of money as the weighted sum of the aggregated value of all assets, the weights for individual assets varying from zero to unity with a weight of unity assigned to that asset or assets regarded as having the largest quantity of 'moneyness' per dollar of aggregate value. The procedure we have followed implies that all weights are either zero or unity.
>
> The more general approach has been suggested frequently but experimented with only occasionally. We conjecture that this approach deserves and will get much more attention than it has so far received."

In fact, the problem also was known to earlier economists, who recognized the relevancy of index number theory to its solution. See Hawtrey (1930).

By equally weighting components, simple sum aggregation can badly distort an aggregate. If one wished to obtain an aggregate of transportation vehicles, one would never aggregate by simple summation over the physical units, of, say, subway trains and roller skates. Instead one could construct a quantity index using weights that depend upon the *values* of the different modes of transportation. As a further example of this point, suppose the money supply were measured by the Federal Reserve's current highest level simple sum aggregate, L. It includes most of the national debt of short and intermediate maturity. All of that debt could be monetized (bought and paid for with freshly printed currency) without increasing either taxes or L, since the public would simply have exchanged component securities in L for currency.[6] However, the new Divisia index over the components of L would not treat this transfer as an exchange of 'pure money' for 'pure money.' Instead Divisia L would rise at about the same rate as the inflation in prices that would result from this action.

At the opposite extreme, many problems associated with policies that target low level aggregates, such as M1B, result from the inability of those

---

[6] This example requires a 100 percent reserve system.

aggregates to internalize pure substitution effects occurring within the economy's transactions technology, because the aggregation is over such a small subset of the factors of production in that transactions technology.

The traditionally constructed high level aggregates (such as M2 or M3) implicitly view distant substitutes for money as perfect substitutes for currency. Rather than capturing only part of the economy's monetary services, as M1B does, the broad aggregates swamp the included monetary services with heavily weighted nonmonetary services. Nevertheless, the need remains for an aggregate that captures the contributions of all monetary assets to the economy's flow of monetary services.

3 The Divisia Quantity Index

3.1 The Definition

In this section I define the Divisia monetary quantity index and describe the procedure for computing it.

Before the Divisia index formula can be computed, the user cost price of each component monetary asset must be computed, since the price of the services of a durable, such as money, is its user cost. The formula for the user cost price of a monetary asset is provided in section 5.2 below. However, a simplification is possible. All of the factors in the formula for the ith asset's user cost, π_i, can be shown to cancel out of the Divisia index except for $R-r_i$, where for any given time period, r_i is the own rate of return on asset i and R is the expected maximum holding period yield available in the economy during that period.[7]

The growth rate of the Divisia quantity index is a weighted average of the growth rates of the component quantities.[8] The weights are the corresponding user-cost evaluated *value shares*. Since those value shares represent the contributions of the components to expenditure on the services of all of the

---

[7]Barnett and Spindt (1982) contains details on the computation of the own rates and the computation of a proxy for R.

[8]The mathematical formula for the aggregate (see Barnett (1981b)) is defined as follows. Let Q_t be the value of the aggregate during period t, and let $G(Q_t)$ be the growth rate of Q_t between period $t-1$ and t. Let $q_{it}(i=1,\ldots,n)$ be holdings of monetary asset i during period t, and let $G(q_{it})$ be the growth rate of monetary asset i between periods $t-1$ and t. Let p_{it} be the user cost of asset i during period t. Let

$$S_{it} = \frac{p_{it}q_{it}}{\sum_j p_{jt}q_{jt}}$$

equal the expenditure share on the services of monetary asset i, and let $S_{it}^* = (1/2)(S_{it} + S_{i,t-1})$. Then the rate of growth of the Divisia quantity aggregate, Q_t, is the weighted average of the growth rates of the component quantities, with the average shares, S_{it}^*

components, use of those shares as weights for the corresponding component quantity growth rates makes intuitive sense. However, it should be observed that the functional form of the Divisia index, *and therefore the form of the weights*, results from a formal mathematical proof in the index number literature, not from intuition.[9] It is important to recognize that the user costs *are not the weights*, but rather are the *prices* used along with all of the quantities in computing the weights. Each weight depends upon *all prices and all quantities*.[10] In fact if the own price elasticity of demand of asset i is greater than one, then changes in the asset's own rate of return will induce changes in the asset's weight *in the same direction.*

It can be shown that the simple sum aggregates are a special case of the Divisia aggregates. If all own rates of return on all monetary assets are the same, then the growth rates of the Divisia indices reduce to the growth rates of the corresponding simple sum aggregates.[11] The assumption of always equal own rates could be justified, if all component monetary assets were perfect substitutes. In fact, over ten years of accumulated empirical research results reported in the published literature overwhelmingly suggest that substitutability between different monetary assets is low,[12] and of course all component own rates of return are not the same.

3.2 The Effects of Interest Rate Changes

If the interest rate on a component monetary asset is changed (resulting in a change in the user cost), asset holders will respond by substituting towards the assets with relatively decreased user costs (increased own yield). The Divisia monetary quantity index will change only if the approximated economic quantity aggregate changes. As discussed in section 5.2, the eco-

---

$(i = 1, \ldots, n)$, being the weights. More formally we have

$$G(Q_t) = \sum_{i=1}^{n} S_{it}^* G(q_{it}).$$

[9]See Diewert (1976) and Hulten (1973). The index has been proved to be exact for any aggregator function (the true economic aggregate) in continuous time (in which case the level of the index is a line integral) and for the translog aggregator function in discrete time. The Divisia index also is a second order approximation to any aggregator function in discrete time.

[10]The weights are the values of S_{it}^* in note 7.

[11]This result is exactly true in continuous time and approximately true in discrete time.

[12]This conventional view has been further verified by Barnett's (1980a, 1981b) empirical study with recent data.

nomic quantity aggregate is necessarily a utility (or production) function.[13] Hence the aggregate will change only if the change in relative prices results in a change in utility (or, equivalently, in the monetary asset service flow). Equivalently, the index number will change only if the change in the interest rate has an 'income effect.' Any quantity index number constructed from index number theory will perfectly internalize pure 'substitution effects,' which, by definition, occur at constant utility levels (and therefore constant levels of monetary service flows). Hence, the aggregate *will not* change, when it *should not* change. The simple sum aggregate, on the other hand, does not internalize pure substitution effects. Interest rate changes cause shifts in a simple sum aggregate even when there has been no change in the utility level and hence no change in monetary service flows.

4 Graphical Comparisons of the Divisia and Simple Sum Aggregates

The extensive available graphical comparisons between the behavior of the Divisia and simple sum monetary aggregates are scattered over various sources. In this section, some of the more interesting graphical comparisons from those sources are collected together and discussed jointly.

The first charts of the behavior of the Divisia aggregates appeared in Barnett (1980a) and Barnett and Spindt (1979). One of those charts is reproduced below as Figure 1. That figure contains plots of the velocity of M3 and of M3$^+$, which roughly corresponds to the aggregate now called L. Velocity is plotted in each of those cases with the monetary aggregate alternatively computed as a simple sum or as a Divisia quantity index. With M3$^+$ the Laspeyres quantity index also is used.

The velocity of the Divisia aggregates can be seen to follow a path that closely resembles that of the interest rate cycle from 1968 to 1978. Hence velocity appears to be a stable function of the interest rate. In addition, the Laspeyres quantity index moves much more closely to the Divisia index than to the simple sum index. By contrast, the velocity of the simple sum aggregates can be seen to trend downwards in a manner that violates prior theoretical views regarding the behavior of velocity during periods of rising interest rates and inflationary expectations. Substitution (disintermediation) appears to go in the wrong direction.

Similar time series plots for the multiplier between the monetary base and the monetary aggregates were presented in Barnett and Spindt (1982). The

---

[13]If the utility or production function is not linearly homogeneous, the economic quantity aggregator function is the distance function, as explained in chapter 3 of this book. But in this chapter, we do not use that extension of the theory.

Graphical Comparisons

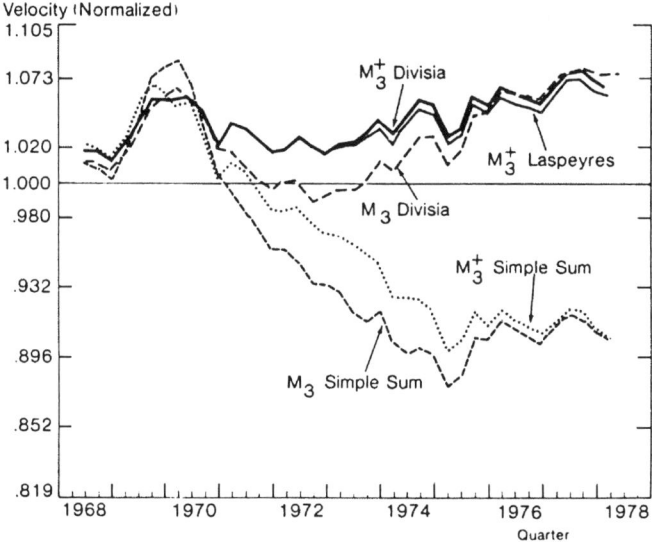

Figure 1: Income velocity of monetary aggregate, quarterly, 1968.II–1978.I, normalized in 1968.I.

most interesting of those graphs is reproduced in Figure 2, which contains the monetary base multiplier for both simple sum and Divisia L. As is evident from Figure 2, the base multiplier for Divisia L is relatively stable over the long run, and the cycles in the multiplier negatively correlate with the interest rate cycle. The long-run multiplier for the simple sum aggregate is far from stable. These results with the high level aggregates are particularly important, since the high level Divisia aggregate is designed to capture the total contributions of all monetary assets to the economy's monetary service flow.

Since an interest rate is not a dimension of either Figure 1 or 2, the precise nature of the functional relationship with interest rates is not entirely clear from those graphs. In addition, Figure 1 terminates in 1978, and it would be interesting to see whether the relationship to the interest rate cycle continued through 1981. We can explore those questions from the cross-plots against interest rates that were presented in Barnett, Offenbacher, and Spindt (1984). Four of those plots are reproduced in Figures 3–6.

Figures 3 and 4 contain cross-plots of the velocity of M3 against a bond rate. Three plotting symbols are used to differentiate between three time periods. Since function shifts in money markets are widely reported to have

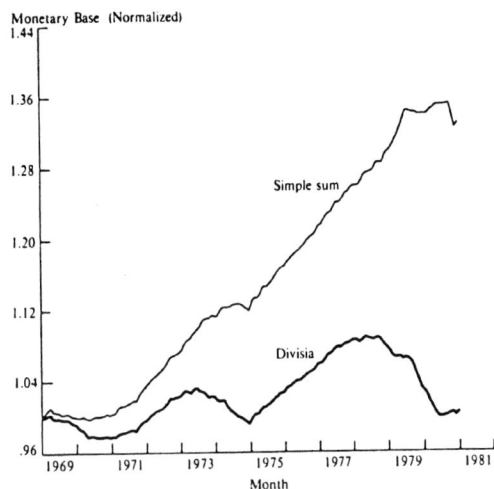

Figure 2: Base multiplier for monetary aggregate L, 1969.I–1980.XII, monthly, normalized in 1969.I.

occurred in mid-1974, comparison of the results before and after mid-1974 are particularly interesting. Figure 3 contains the results when M3 is computed as a simple sum. The expected shift is very evident. Figure 4 contains the analogous plot when M3 is computed as a Divisia aggregate. No significant function shift is evident. A stable nearly linear function of only one explanatory variable is revealed by the plot. The demand appears to be stable and easily modeled.

Figures 5 and 6 contain analogous plots for the base multiplier of M3, although each axis now measures the deviation from a linear time trend. For policy purposes, controllability of an aggregate through the use of the base as instrument is unaffected by the need to extrapolate a data series by a fixed time trend, and of course no-trend is just a special case of a linear trend. Hence in Figures 5 and 6, linear time trends were subtracted out of all data series before the plots were constructed. Figure 5 contains the cross-plot for the base multiplier against a bond rate when M3 is computed as a simple sum. A very dramatic shift occurred in the functional relationship in mid-1974. Before mid-1974, the function is parabolic. After mid-1974 an intersecting linear function appears. Figure 6 contains the same plot when M3 is computed as a Divisia aggregate. A stable linear relationship is revealed. Hence Divisia M3 is evidently controllable through the use of the base.

In the next section I briefly summarize some basic principles from ag-

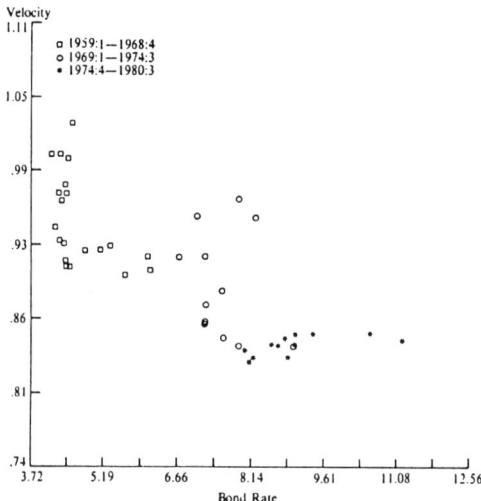

Figure 3: Simple sum M3 velocity versus Moody's AAA corporate bond rate, quarterly, 1959.I–1980.III.

gregation and index number theory as those principles relate to monetary aggregation.

5 The Stages in the Selection Procedure

In economic theory the optimal aggregate is acquired through a three-stage selection procedure. The selection criteria used at each stage are distinct and cannot be interchanged. As we shall see, the deficiencies in the official aggregates result from the fact that the third-stage criteria alone were used to select the aggregates, although those criteria are inappropriate in either of the first two stages.

5.1 Stage 1: Selection of Admissible Component Groupings

The first stage in the selection of an optimal aggregate is the determination of all theoretically admissible sets of component assets. Aggregates then can be constructed over *only* those sets. To acquire those admissible sets, we first must acquire the separable subsets of the set of all monetary components, $M = \{m_i : i = 1, \ldots, N\}$, where there are N monetary components, m_i.

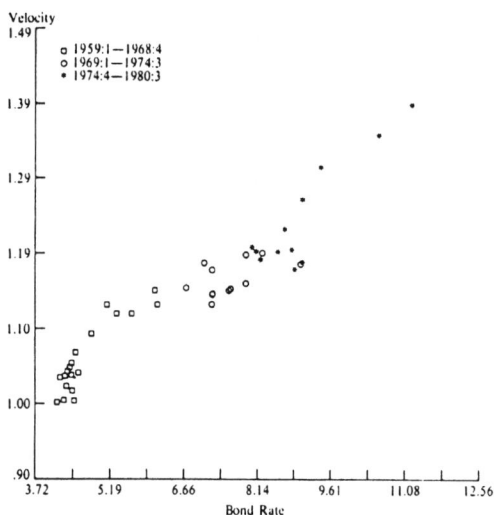

Figure 4: Divisia M3 velocity versus Moody's AAA corporate bond rate, quarterly, 1959.I–1980.III.

We now define the conditions for a separable subset, which we shall call a separable component group.

Condition 1. Let C be a subset of M, so that C is itself a set of (not necessarily all) component monetary assets. Then C is a separable component group if and only if the marginal rate of substitution between any two assets in C is independent of the quantity of any good or asset not in C.[14]

Condition 1 is necessary and sufficient for a subfunction of the assets in C alone to be factorable out of utility or production functions. The value of that factored subfunction, which is called the economic aggregate, depends only upon the assets in C and is independent of the quantities consumed or held of any other goods or assets. Without condition 1, no stable preferences or transactions technology can exist over elements of C alone, and hence goods or assets not in C will act as missing shift variables in the demand for any aggregates constructed over assets in C alone.

We shall call condition 1 the *Existence condition*, since it defines the condition under which an economic aggregate exists in aggregation theory. However existence alone is not sufficient for an aggregate to behave like an elementary good. To acquire that result we need the following stronger con-

---

[14]Condition 1 is the definition of a weakly separable block in aggregation theory.

The Stages in the Selection Procedure

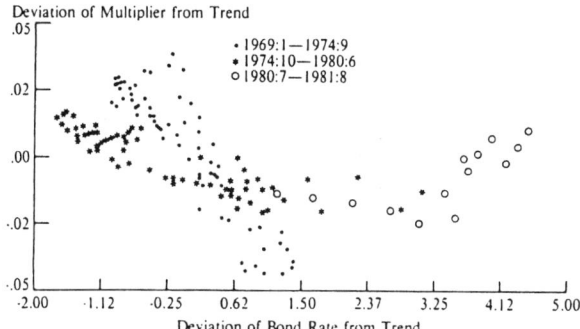

Figure 5: Deviation from time trend of simple sum M3 base money multiplier versus deviation from time trend of Moody's Baa corporate bond rate, monthly, 1969.I–1981.VIII.

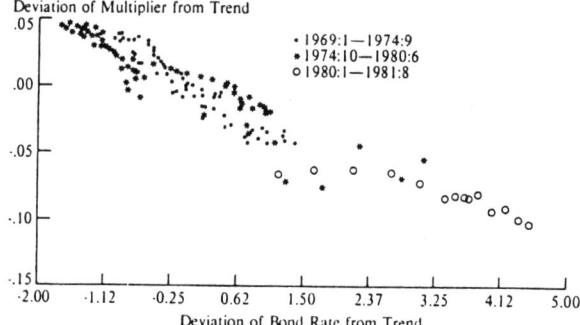

Figure 6: Deviation from time trend of Divisia M3 base money multiplier versus deviation from time trend of Moody's Baa corporate bond rate, monthly, 1969.I–1981.VIII.

dition, which we shall call the *Consistency condition*.[15]

Condition 2. An admissible component group, C, is a consistent component group, if the elasticity of substitution between any component asset in the group and any good or asset not in the group is independent of the good or asset that is not in the group.[16]

Condition 2 implies condition 1, but the converse is not true. Every consistent component group is separable, but not every separable component group is consistent. Although some aspects of aggregation theory can be applied with only satisfaction of condition 1, condition 2 substantially simplifies interpretation and use of an aggregate.[17] Condition 2 is acquired by imposing linear homogeneity on the economic aggregate that condition 1 assures exists over the assets in C. It would be very curious indeed if linear homogeneity of an aggregate failed; in such a case, the growth rate of the aggregate would differ from the growth rates of the components, even if all components were growing at the same rate.

Neither condition 1 nor condition 2 has meaning unless the concept of substitutability between assets has meaning. We need the existence of a utility function or production function containing monetary assets (with or without other goods) as arguments. The existence of a transactions technology would suffice.

If our objective were to explain why people hold money, then assuming that monetary assets enter utility or production functions would be assuming away the problem. However for our purposes, we can assume that money has positive value in equilibrium. Under that assumption, it has been proved in general equilibrium theory that money must enter into a derived utility or production function.[18] Hence conditions 1 and 2 can be defined relative to that derived function.[19]

In order for an aggregate to serve the role of 'money' in the economy, we

---

[15]See, for example, Green (1964, theorem 4).

[16]Condition 2 defines a linearly homogeneous, weakly separable block in aggregation theory.

[17]Examples using only condition 1 can be found in Barnett (1980a) and Barnett (1981b, chap. 7).

[18]See Arrow (1971) and Quirk and Saposnik (1968, p. 97). A widely used special case of the general equilibrium result arises if money acquires its usefulness by entering a transactions constraint. In that case the derived utility function is the Lagrangian containing both the original elementary utility function (which does not contain money) and the constraint defined by the transactions technology. See Phlips and Spinnewyn (1982), whose approach applies regardless of whether money does or does not yield interest.

[19]There is still the problem of aggregating over individual economic agents (households and firms). For a survey of that literature, see Barnett (1981b, pp. 306–7). For a new approach to the problem, see Barnett (1979b). For a well-known directly relevant approach, see Muellbauer (1975), Phlips and Spinnewyn (1982). For recent surprisingly favorable empirical results on aggregation over economic agents, see Varian (1983a).

would expect the components to satisfy another restriction. In addition to satisfying condition 2, the components should satisfy the following condition, which we shall call the *Recursiveness condition*.[20]

Condition 3. The components of each aggregate must include currency (legal tender) and must not include any good or asset that is not a 'monetary asset.'

Although aggregation theory provides no definition of 'monetary asset,' the identity of the 'money market' is no less widely understood than the identity of the durables market or the recreational goods market. In attaching a name to an aggregate, such as food or money, a prior definition of the components' domain must be selected.

Aggregation theory itself does not dictate use of condition 3. In principle, we would lose nothing by dropping condition 3. However in practice the number of component groups that would satisfy condition 2 is likely to be very large. Although the condition 2 component groups would always contain the 'best' group (or groups) for any particular purpose, the empirical research needed to choose between such a large class of component groups could be difficult and expensive. Condition 3 applies conventional views from monetary theory to restrict further the number of admissible component groups. In particular, condition 3 restricts the domain of possible components to 'monetary assets' and requires the collection of admissible component groups to be nested about 'hard core money,' defined here by its legal tender property. Researchers applying the procedures outlined in this paper could tighten or loosen the restrictiveness of condition 3 as needed to accommodate the scope (i.e., ambitiousness) of the research, with the limiting (most ambitious) case being elimination of condition 3 entirely.

The component groups that satisfy both conditions 2 and 3 comprise a family of completely nested sets. Hence aggregation is perfectly recursive as we pass to increasingly high levels of aggregation over those nested groups. We shall call a set of components that satisfies both conditions 2 and 3 a *consistent recursive component group*.

When we seek an aggregate to serve the role of 'money' in the economy, as would be acquired for a monetary target or for the variable 'money' in a model, we shall require the components of the aggregate to comprise a consistent recursive component group. If we were seeking only an indicator, the prior imposition of condition 3 would generally not be justified, and we could perhaps even do without condition 2. We therefore shall say that a set of components that is separable is *admissible for an indicator*.[21] We

---

[20] The condition results in a recursively nested functional structure for the aggregator function in aggregation theory. See Barnett (1977a, 1980a).

[21] For further discussion on the subject of monetary indicators, see Brunner (1967), Brunner and Meltzer (1969), and Hamburger (1970).

shall say that a set of components that is also consistent and recursive is *admissible for a monetary variable.* Since the primary objective of this paper is determination of the optimal monetary variable, indicators will not be explored in detail. In the monetary asset case, I derived the precise test for condition 2 in Barnett (1980a) and in Barnett (1981b, chap. 7).[22]

I summarize the results of this section with a statement of the solution to the stage 1 problem in monetary aggregation.

Step 1. Determine those sets of monetary assets that satisfy both conditions 2 and 3.

5.2 Stage 2: Selection of an Index Number Formula

Having determined the admissible component groupings, we next must determine a formula to be used for computing the aggregates over the components of each admissible group. In the Federal Reserve Board's current official aggregates, the formula is simple summation of the component quantities. The aggregation formula is called the aggregator function, and the necessary and sufficient conditions for a linear aggregator function are the following:

Condition 4. The aggregator function is linear if and only if the component goods (or assets) are perfect substitutes.

We shall call condition 4 the *Linearity Condition.* Clearly the components of the monetary assets are not perfect substitutes. Hence the aggregates cannot be computed from simple summation or from any other linear formula. When components are not perfect substitutes, a nonlinear aggregator function is needed. The aggregate acquired from the nonlinear function is called the 'economic aggregate.'[23]

To use a nonlinear aggregator function directly, we would have to specify the form of the function and then estimate its parameters. Alternatively index number theory provides parameter-free approximations to the economic aggregates of aggregation theory. Economic quantity aggregates depend upon quantities and unknown parameters, but not prices. However quantity *index numbers* depend upon quantities and prices, but not unknown parameters.

---

[22]The component groups used in constructing the Federal Reserve Board's official monetary aggregates, M1B, M2, M3, and L, were not acquired by testing for either condition 1 or condition 2. Some of those component groups are probably inadmissible either for indicators or for monetary variables. For example, Series E bonds and nonnegotiable, consumer-type, small time deposits are probably not elements of any admissible monetary asset component group, although they may be elements of an admissible group of components for an intermediate-term-bond aggregate.

[23]If m is the vector of components and if f is the aggregator function, then $f(m)$ is the economic aggregate.

Hence quantity index numbers dispense with unknown parameters by introducing prices. Diewert (1976) has defined the class of 'superlative' index numbers, which provide very high quality approximations to economic aggregates.

In constructing a superlative monetary quantity index number, the selection of the index number from among those in the superlative class is of little importance, since all of the index numbers within the class move very closely together.[24] However, they all jointly diverge from the simple sum index.[25] My monetary aggregates are constructed from the Divisia index.[26] That index has the most easily understood form of any of the index numbers in Diewert's superlative class and hence is potentially the most useful to policymakers.

The selection of the prices to be used in the index number formula is important. If user cost (or 'rental') prices are used in an aggregate of durables, such as monetary assets, then the resulting quantity index measures the *service flow* generated by the component durable goods. The formula for the user cost price of a monetary asset was derived by Barnett (1978, 1980a).[27]

I summarize the conclusions of this section with a statement of the solution to the stage 2 problem in monetary aggregation.

Step 2. Using user cost prices for each component asset, compute a superlative quantity index over each of the admissible groups of component assets acquired from step 1.

---

[24] The difference with monetary data is in the fifth decimal place.

[25] As a result, the simple sum index is entirely disreputable in the index number literature. Fisher (1922) found that the simple sum index was the very worst index that he was able to devise. The simple sum index was the only index that possessed both of the bad properties that he defined: bias and freakishness, and he found the size of the bias to exceed 35 percent of the level of the index. Fisher (1922, p. 29) observed that "the simple arithmetic average produces one of the very worst of index numbers, and if this book has no other effect than to lead to the total abandonment of the simple arithmetic type of index number it will have served a useful purpose." Fisher (1922, p. 36) concluded that "the simple arithmetic [index] should not be used under any circumstances."

[26] Actually I use the Törnqvist-Theil discrete time approximation to the Divisia index, which is a continuous time index. See Barnett (1980a).

[27] The nominal user cost of monetary asset i for a discrete time period is $\pi_i = p^*(R - r_i)(1-\tau)/[1+R(1-\tau)]$, where p^* is the true cost of living index, r_i is the own rate of return on asset i, R is the expected maximum holding yield available in the economy during that period, and τ is the marginal tax rate. Also see Donovan (1978). For details regarding measurement of the user costs, see Barnett and Spindt (1982). In some cases implicit rates of return must be used in computing the interest rates in the formula for π_i, especially when the own rate of return on an asset is subject to governmental rate regulation. An implicit imputation is also used in the measurement of R. The Divisia quantity index has been found to be robust to those imputations within the plausible ranges of error in the imputations.

5.3 Stage 3: Selection of the Optimal Level of Aggregation

Having completed step 2, we have a hierarchy of nested aggregates. We now must select among them.

Each element of our hierarchy of monetary quantity index numbers approximates a perfect economic aggregate. In aggregation theory every household and firm in the economy can be shown to behave *as if* a consistent aggregate is an elementary good.[28] Hence no information is lost by using a consistent aggregate, if the variables about which we seek information are not themselves variables in the aggregate. Since the component monetary quantities and interest rates are not likely to be final targets of policy, we have nothing to lose by using the highest level aggregate among those that are in the admissible hierarchy.

The question now arises as to whether we have anything to lose by using an admissible aggregate *other than* the highest level aggregate, and we do indeed. By using a lower level aggregate, we are omitting factors of production from the economy's transactions technology. Furthermore, as the level of aggregation decreases, the number of price aggregates contained in the demand function increases.[29] As a result, modeling the demand for the aggregate becomes more difficult, and if any of the explanatory variables is omitted, the function will appear to shift in an unstable fashion. However the economic aggregates of aggregation theory can be shown to internalize pure substitution effects *perfectly*.

In short, the highest level admissible aggregate from step 2 provides a properly weighted measure of the total service flow of all of the money market's separable components. We now can state the final step in the procedure for choosing the optimal monetary aggregate.

Step 3. Select the highest level aggregate from among those generated by step 2.

However, at this point it may be wise to hedge our bets. While aggregation theory does tell us to use only the nested admissible aggregates provided by step 2, my advocacy of the highest of those aggregates on theoretical grounds depends upon a nontrivial assumption: equilibrium in the market for every

---

[28]The solution to each economic agent's full decision is the same as the solution to a multistage decision. The consistent aggregates are the variables in each stage of the multistage budgeting procedure except for the last stage. The variables in the last stage are the elementary goods from the original full decision. See Green (1964, theorem 4).

[29]This result follows from duality theory. There is a price aggregate that is dual to the quantity aggregate over each group of components satisfying condition 2. The demand for automobiles, depends upon the price of automobiles, fuel, housing, etc.; but the price of Ford Pintos depends upon the price of VW Rabbits, Toyota Corollas, Exxon regular gasoline, etc.

component asset. As Cagan (1982) has observed, the economy's disequilibrium dynamics can affect differently the information content of aggregates at different levels of aggregation.

Aggregates generated by step 2 at each level of aggregation will properly measure the total service flow produced by the components, regardless of whether interest rates are market determined or are set by regulation, and regardless of whether the markets for components are or are not in equilibrium. Hence the aggregates produced by step 2 remain the valid aggregate monetary variables. But the validity of step 3 depends upon an equilibrium assumption and is therefore conclusive only in the long run.[30]

The importance of the theoretical conclusion (step 3) should be an increasing function of the weight that we place upon the objective of controlling the long-run (equilibrium) inflation rate. I conclude this section with a statement of the short-run disequilibrium alternative to step 3.

Step 3a. From *among the admissible aggregates* provided by step 2, select the one that empirically works best in the application in which the aggregate is to be used.

Observe that step 3a *cannot* be accomplished without prior completion of steps 1 and 2. However, the Federal Reserve Board's official aggregates were constructed from research that related *solely* to step 3a. Step 1 was never conducted, and step 2 was violated by the use of simple sum aggregation.

Step 1 is needed to assure the existence of behaviorally stable aggregates over the component groups, and step 2 is needed to assure that the computed aggregates provide high quality approximations to the unknown behaviorally stable aggregates.[31] By violating step 2, the official aggregates cannot approximate behaviorally stable aggregates, and by using components that need not satisfy step 1, the official aggregates permit all forms of spurious and unstable relationships during the application of step 3a. In short, the procedure used in selecting the official aggregates virtually eliminates the possibility of imputing meaning or replicable explanatory or predictive ability to the movements of the aggregates, since the economy cannot act as if the official aggregates are variables in the economy's structure.

Movements of the official aggregates could have stable relationships with actual structural variables, such as the inflation rate, only if the aggregates' components were perfect substitutes, so that step 2 would be satisfied, and

---

[30] However it is perhaps unlikely that this problem would be serious with aggregates satisfying conditions 1 and 2, since the markets for those components are among the best and fastest adjusting in the economy. Nevertheless the components of the current official aggregates include some very illiquid assets having long maturities and heavy early redemption penalties. Hence until the components are properly regrouped in accordance with step 1, step 3 cannot be viewed as conclusive on theoretical grounds alone.

[31] See Green (1964, theorem 4).

if step 1 were satisfied by a combination of chance and superior judgement. Clearly the violation of step 2 is more serious than the violation of step 1, since the perfect substitutability condition needed for satisfaction of step 2 with simple sum aggregation could not have been satisfied by chance. In addition, if step 2 had been applied, the possibility would have been increased that the component groupings that were selected from step 3a would also have satisfied step 1.

In the next section I report on the results of a search of the empirical evidence relevant to proper use of step 3a.

6 Available Empirical Evidence

6.1 Component Groupings

My earlier work on the empirical behavior of the monetary aggregates was directed towards comparison of my Divisia monetary aggregates with the Federal Reserve's official simple sum aggregates. Those comparisons required use of the same component groups with Divisia aggregation as with simple sum aggregation. Hence I either could have selected my own groupings from step 1 and computed both simple sum and Divisia aggregates over those same component groups, or I could have computed Divisia aggregates over the component groups used with the Federal Reserve's official simple sum aggregates. In my earlier work, I selected the latter alternative.[32] I thereby put step 1 into abeyance and pursued the more important immediate objective of questioning the official use of the simple sum aggregates.

In each comparison of simple sum versus Divisia aggregation, I used the same components for each aggregation method but never compared results with different component groups. Hence none of my earlier work included comparisons between different levels of aggregation. In the present paper I explore the selection of the optimal level of monetary aggregation.[33]

---

[32] That alternative permitted comparisons with the official simple sum aggregates on their own ground, since the official aggregates were constructed with the component groups that appeared to provide the best possible empirical behavior with simple sum aggregation. The second reason for using the official grouping was that it avoided questioning official procedures in two areas simultaneously: the selection of the component grouping (step 1) and the selection of the quantity index number for aggregating over the component groups (step 2). But more importantly, the Federal Reserve Board's failure to apply step 2 appeared to be a far worse source of policy error than the Bederal Reserve Board's failure to apply step 1.

[33] It should first be observed, that such comparisons (with the existing component groupings) are inherently biased in favor of simple sum M2 and simple sum M3. The reason is that the circularity in the Federal Reserve Board's definition procedure was more severe with M2 and M3 than with M1B or L. The dominant principle used in defining M1B was

6.2 Divisia Aggregation versus Simple Sum Aggregation

Before comparing levels of aggregation, I briefly summarize the results on comparing Divisia versus simple sum monetary aggregation.[34] Table 1 contains a table of conclusions from all of the existing studies on the subject.[35]

Since simple sum and Divisia M1B move more closely together than the simple sum and Divisia aggregates at higher levels of aggregation, the power of the tests comparing simple sum and Divisia monetary aggregation increases as the level of aggregation increases.[36] Hence in the construction of Table 1 the choice between simple sum and Divisia aggregation was based upon the tendency of one index to dominate the other as the level of aggregation increases. Although the choice at the lowest levels of aggregation sometimes was not clear, the dominant aggregation method always became clear as the level of aggregation increased. In Table 1 an x is placed below the aggregation method that dominated relative to each comparison criterion.

Divisia aggregation dominated simple sum aggregation, except with the single equation portfolio model demand for money function. However in that case the demand equation for the simple sum aggregate was meaningless, since the lagged endogenous variable swamped all of the other explanatory variables in the equation. As a result, there was really no demand equation

---

the collection together of transactions balances. The dominant principle used in defining L was the collection together of all elements of the money market. Although questionable choices sometimes were made in those regards, including aggregation over some highly illiquid assets, the dominant principles in construction of M1B and L bear some relationship to conditions 1, 2, and 3. Hence, one could expect the components of M1B and L to approximate groups that would be admissible if step 1 were completed using subjective prior views on elasticities of substitution.

However M2 and M3 were constructed in an entirely circular fashion by seeking groupings, admissible or otherwise, that result in simple sum aggregates with attractive empirical properties relative to policy criteria. But as discussed at the end of the last section, those criteria should not be applied until the meaningful, admissible, aggregated monetary variables have been acquired from completion of both steps 1 and 2. The principle applied in selection of the components of M2 and M3 was the maximization of spurious correlation. Hence simple sum aggregates constructed over *admissible* groups at levels of aggregation between M1B and L would not perform as well as M2 and M3 relative to the policy criteria used in constructing M2 and M3 (at least over the sample period used in the original selection of M2 and M3).

[34] The results are summarized from the sources listed at the bottom of the table.

[35] Included among the comparison procedures was information theoretic comparison of simulations with the Federal Reserve's quarterly (FMP) model. However that procedure was limited to comparison between simple sum and Divisia M2, since the only Divisia monetary aggregate currently available within the FMP model is Divisia M2.

[36] Divisia and simple sum M1B differ as a result of the explicit rate of return paid on some transaction balances, such as NOW accounts, and also as a result of the imputation of an implicit rate of return on demand deposits in accordance with Startz (1979).

for the simple sum aggregate at all. The conclusion to be reached from Table 1 is clear. Step 2 is empirically verified: a superlative monetary quantity index, such as the Divisia, should be used.

6.3 Comparisons Across Levels of Aggregation

In order to acquire the results presented in this section, I reconsidered the research results that generated Table 1 for the purpose of determining which aggregate did best relative to each criterion. In other words, I performed step 3a. Strictly speaking it would be best to consider only Divisia (or other superlative) quantity indexes in order to approximate the step 2 aggregates as well as possible with the available official component groupings. However the fact is that the simple sum monetary aggregates remain the official aggregates. I therefore searched for the optimal aggregate jointly over both the Divisia aggregates and the inadmissible, but still official, simple sum aggregates.[37]

In Tables 2–4, I list the aggregate, whether Divisia or simple sum, which worked best relative to each criterion. The superscript D after an aggregate designates a Divisia aggregate. All other aggregates are simple sums. Table 2 contains the conclusions based upon information theory. Shannon's information content measure was used to determine the information acquired relative to various policy targets by conditioning upon knowledge of a monetary aggregate (in the same or a previous period). The three targets considered are listed across the top of the table. The left-hand column lists the time lag between observation of the monetary aggregate and determination of the information gained about the target. The monetary aggregate listed in each case is the one possessing the highest information content relative to the designated target.[38]

Table 3 contains the aggregates that performed best relative to the forecasting and stability properties of relevant estimated functions.[39] The functions considered were the demand for money function, the velocity function (containing an interest rate or user cost variable), and a reduced form equa-

---

[37] Nevertheless the conclusions regarding the optimal level of aggregation would not have been affected appreciably if the simple sum aggregates had been excluded from the search. Generally when high (or low) levels of aggregation worked best with simple sum aggregation, the same was true for Divisia aggregation.

[38] The results are based upon the empirical distribution function of the data. The cited sources also include results that are conditional upon the Federal Reserve's quarterly model or upon an ARIMA process. However the results with the model are available only at one level of aggregation, and the ARIMA approach complicates interpretation of comparisons across levels of aggregation.

[39] When more than one aggregate appear in the table as 'best,' they are nearly as good relative to the selection criterion.

tion. The sources from which these results were deduced are listed in the table's footnotes.

Table 4 contains the analogous results deduced from a search of papers using other comparison criteria. Finally Table 5 provides an overview of the results in Tables 2–4. In order to construct Table 5, I counted the number of times that each aggregate was a best performer in Tables 2–4.

TABLE 1
Score Card

Criterion	Source	Simple Sum Aggregates	Divisia Aggregates
Index number theory	1, 2, 3, 4, 5, 7		x
Aggregation theory	1, 2, 3, 4, 5, 7		x
Base multiplier	9, 12		x
Velocity behavior	1, 4, 8, 9, 10, 12		
a. Plausibility			x
b. Function stability			x
Demand for money function			
a. Double log fixed coefficients	8, 9		
1. Plausibility of estimates		mixed	
2. Stability tests			x
3. Forecasting simulations			x
b. Portfolio model fixed coefficients	8		
1. Plausibility of estimates		unacceptable	
2. Stability tests		x	
3. Forecasting simulations		x	
c. Stochastic coefficients	9		
1. Stability test			x
Information theory	4, 8, 9, 10, 11		
a. Naive forecasting			x
b. Time series forecasting			x
c. FMP model forecasting			x
Causality tests	8, 9		
a. Pierce-Haugh			x
b. Sims			x
c. Bivariate			x
Reduced form	8, 9		x
Second moment cyclical stability	8, 9		x
Fit of joint monetary asset demand system	6		x

NOTE: The sources of the results summarized in this table are identified by the following numbers: (1) Barnett (1980a), (2) Barnett (1982b), (3) Barnett (1980b), (4) Barnett (1981b, chap. 7), (5) Barnett (1981a), (6) Barnett (1983a), (7) Barnett, Offenbacher, and Spindt (1981), (8) Barnett, Spindt and Offenbacher (1981), (9) Barnett, Spindt and Offenbacher (1984), (10) Barnett and Spindt (1979), (11) Barnett, Offenbacher, and Spindt (1984), (12) Barnett and Spindt (1982).

TABLE 2
AGGREGATES HAVING MAXIMUM INFORMATION CONTENT

	Target		
Lag	$\dot{x}^*$	$\dot{p}^*$	u^*
Contemporaneous	L^D	$M3^D$	M2
1 month	$M2^D$	$M3^D$	M2
3 months	L^D	$M3^D$	$M2^D$

NOTE: The targets are defined as follows: $\dot{x}^*$ is the growth rate of personal income, $\dot{p}^*$ is the rate of change of the Fisher ideal price index (approximated by the geometric mean of the CPI and the Commerce Department's personal consumption deflator), and u^* is the unemployment rate for males aged 25 or older. These results were deduced from the information contents reported in Barnett (1981b, chap. 7), Barnett and Spindt (1979), Barnett, Offenbacher, and Spindt (1984), and Barnett, Spindt and Offenbacher (1981, 1984). Also see Tinsley, Spindt and Friar (1980) for related theory and results. The data were monthly from 1969.I to 1979.XII.

TABLE 3
AGGREGATES PERFORMING BEST IN ESTIMATED DEMAND, VELOCITY, AND REDUCED FORM EQUATIONS

	Forecasting		Stability
Equation	RMSE	Mean Error	
Fixed coefficient demand for money*	M2	$M2^D$	L^D
Stochastic coefficient demand for money†	—	—	$M3^D$
Velocity function‡	—	—	L^D, $M3^D$
Reduced form, constrained*	L^D	$M2^D$, L^D	L^D
Reduced form, unconstrained*	L^D, M2	M3	L^D

NOTE. The forecasting results are based upon growth rate forecast errors in percentage points per year. RMSE is the root mean squared error of forecasts. The stability test in the stochastic coefficients case tests for a constant valued process. In the other cases, the stability test tests for a shift in mid-1974. All data are quarterly from 1959.III to 1980.IV. The constraint imposed on the constrained reduced form is a necessary condition for superneutrality. The source codes used in the notes below are defined in the note to Table 1. A dash in the table indicates that no results are available.
* The sources used to deduce these results are Barnett (1980a, 1981b). The specification is Goldfeld's (1976).
†The source used to deduce this result is Barnett (1981b). The specification is Goldfeld's (1976).
‡ The sources used to deduce these results are Barnett (1979a), Barnett (1980b), Barnett (1981b), Barnett, Offenbacher, and Spindt (1981).

It could be argued that for each purpose the aggregate that is best for that particular purpose should be used. However the determination of the aggregate that is truly best for any one purpose is not an easy task.[40] Furthermore, aggregation theory implies that there is a unique optimal admissible monetary aggregate, at least in the long run.

---

[40] Undoubtedly any of the results in Tables 2–4 could be altered by changing the sample

TABLE 4
Aggregates Performing Best Relative to Other Criteria

Criterion	Test	Best Aggregate
Granger causality*	Haugh-Pierce test, 8 quarter lag	L^D
	Haugh-Pierce test, 12 quarter lag	$M2^D$
	Sims test	L^D
	Direct test	$L^D, M2^D$
Cyclical variability of index quality†	Divisia quantity variance stability	L^D
Controllability‡	Base multiplier stability	L^D
Cagan's best target§	Stability of velocity trend	$M1B^D$

NOTE: The source codes used in the notes below are defined in the note to Table 1.
* The sources used to deduce these results are Barnett (1980a, 1981b). The data are quarterly from 1959.I to 1979.IV. For the proper interpretation of Granger causality, see Schwert (1979).
† The sources used to deduce these results are Barnett (1980a, 1981b). The data are quarterly from 1969.I to 1979.IV.
‡ The sources used to deduce these results are Barnett (1981b), and Barnett, Offenbacher, and Spindt (1981). The data are monthly from 1969.I to 1981.VIII.
§ Cagan's result is in Table 1 of Cagan (1982). The data are quarterly from 1969.I to 1980.IV.

From Figure 5, it is clear that a conspicuously high percentage of the existing evidence favors Divisia L. That result is greatly strengthened by three facts: (1) the results support our theoretical selection from step 3, (2) the results are biased in favor of simple sum M2 and M3, as discussed in section 5.3, and (3) in our monthly memoranda at the Federal Reserve Board on the behavior of the aggregates, we have found the broadest Divisia aggregate consistently and accurately to reflect our prior views regarding the 'tightness' of money. Furthermore, the ability of the broadest Divisia aggregates to stabilize the velocity function and the monetary base multiplier is dramatic, as illustrated in section 4 above.

Cagan's results, listed in Table 4, favor Divisia M1B. Cagan's criterion is minimization of velocity variability about a time period. However, in Table 3 Divisia M3 and Divisia L are listed as best relative to my stability of velocity criterion. The difference in conclusions results from the fact that the explanatory variable in Table 3 is an interest rate (or user cost). The explanatory variable in Cagan's velocity function is time.

---

period or the approach to selection of the best aggregate. For example, it is unlikely that the results with the demand for money functions would be entirely robust to changes in the specification over the vast array of demand for money function specificiations that exist in the literature.

TABLE 5
Number of Times that Each Aggregate was Best Performer in Tables 2-4

Component Group	Divisia Aggregation	Simple Sum Aggregation
M1B	1	0
M2	6	4
M3	5	1
L	14	0

It is widely argued that zero interest elasticity of the velocity of money is not necessarily a desirable property.[41] In fact it has been argued frequently that high interest elasticity is a desirable property for a monetary aggregate.[42] There is certainly nothing in economic theory that would dictate an inelastic demand function. Nevertheless, to the degree that controversy may still exist on this subject, Divisia M1B should be used for some purposes.

The simple sum aggregates fail every admissibility condition. Simple sum M3 and L, in particular, are far removed from anything that might reasonably be viewed as being 'money.' The available evidence, including Cagan's (1982), favors Divisia over simple sum M1B, although movements of simple sum M1B frequently are not very different from those of Divisia M1B. As a result, simple sum M1B may not be too bad as a proxy for the generally preferable Divisia M1B. Simple sum M2 may have some value as an indicator. Cagan (1982) finds merit in M2 as an advance indicator. In addition the results in Table 2 provide some evidence favorable to the possible use of simple sum M2 as an indicator of real (rather than nominal) variables: in particular, unemployment. Simple sum M2 perhaps should remain available as a possible indicator, at least until all admissible groups have been identified by testing for conditions 2 and 3. When all admissible aggregates have been generated by step 3, I would expect that no further potential use would remain for any simple sum aggregate.

7 Conclusion

Those components that would not be in any admissible group generated by step 1 should be eliminated from all of the aggregates. Such assets would probably include those with long maturities and those with substantial early

---

[41] For example, Friedman (1969, p. 155) states that "In my opinion no 'fundamental issues' in either monetary theory or monetary policy hinge on whether the estimated elasticity can for most purposes be approximated by zero or is better approximated by $-.1$ or $-.5$ or -2.0, provided it is seldom capable of being approximated by $-\infty$."

[42] See, for example, note 23 and section 4 of Friedman (1981).

redemption penalties, such as government savings bonds and small time deposits. Targeting of simple sum M1B and M2 should be terminated, but there may be some merit to their continued computation and publication.

The current simple sum M1B target should be replaced by Divisia M1B. The current simple sum M2 target should be replaced by Divisia L. I expect that experience with those two targets would eventually lead to the dominance of Divisia L as the policy target.

The components of Divisia L should permanently be defined to include all of the money market. Then new money market assets would be incorporated immediately, by definition of the aggregate. The procedure would be analogous to that used in computing GNP, which also has implicitly defined components. Introduction of new assets would not result in discrete shifts in Divisia L, since the weight attached to a new component would be very low during the period of its initial introduction.[43]

The components of Divisia M2 and Divisia M3 should be redefined to comprise admissible groups generated by step 1. The determination of those groups could become the source of considerable research for experts in testing for separable functional structures.[44] At present it is not even known whether any admissible aggregates exist at levels of aggregation between M1B and L. If they do exist, it is not clear what roles they could appropriately play in policy, other than as variables in models, or possibly as indicators.

Research on the possible policy use of the monetary base should be expanded. As observed in Table 1, Divisia L is the aggregate with the highest long run stability of its base multiplier. This fact demonstrates the controllability of Divisia L, which weights only reservable assets heavily. However the result also may suggest that, at least in the long run, the base may itself have some merit as a target or indicator. There also appears to be much room for theoretical research on the mechanism that results in the stability of the long-run multiplier between the base and Divisia L.[45] Since Divisia L is the aggregate most clearly resembling the one that would be provided by step 3, the long-run relationship between the base and Divisia L may be more than just a coincidence.[46]

---

[43] This result follows from the fact that own yields on new assets are usually high when the asset evolves. Hence the user cost price is low. Since the quantity is also low during those periods, the share weight in the Divisia index is very low. For the procedure needed to introduce new assets into an aggregate, see Diewert (1980a, sec. 8.6).

[44] The tests could be conducted using the translog, Barnett's (1983a) Laurent demand system, or Gallant's (1981) Fourier demand system.

[45] In addition, the multiplier is a stable function of an interest rate in the short run.

[46] Additional favorable evidence on the base can be found in Hamburger (1980) and Brunner (1979).

Chapter 8

New Concepts of Aggregated Money

*William A. Barnett, Edward Offenbacher, and Paul Spindt**

The Federal Reserve Board's recent redefinition of its monetary aggregates followed three years of intensive Board staff research on monetary aggregation.[1] While the new aggregates ultimately were selected along conventional lines, some of the staff's research was oriented towards more fundamental changes in monetary aggregation methods. This paper reviews such proposals, which are based upon the rigorous application of index number and aggregation theory and of principal components analysis in the construction of economic monetary aggregates.

The usefulness of aggregation and index number theory in acquiring price indices is widely known. The theory of the true cost of living index is an application of aggregation theory. Examples of applied index number theory include the Commerce Department's implicit price deflator, which is a Paasche index, and the Labor Department's consumer price index, which is a Laspeyres index. Somewhat less well known is the fact that dual to the theory of economic price aggregates and indices is a theory of economic quantity aggregates and indices. An example of a highly reputable quantity index is the Divisia quantity index.

The monetary aggregates traditionally are thought to measure the supplied quantity of an economic good called 'money.' Whenever monetary aggregates are used in the context of economic theory (rather than as simple accounting identities), the theory of economic quantity aggregation is specifically applicable. However, published monetary aggregates in all countries have always been computed as simple sums. But as Fisher (1992, p. 29) observed in the conclusion to his classic treatise on index number theory, "the simple arithmetic average produces one of the very worst of index numbers, and if this book has no other effect than to lead to the total abandonment

---

*Originally published in the *Journal of Finance* (1981), 497–505. The views expressed herein are solely those of the authors and do not necessarily represent the views of the Board of Governors of the Federal Reserve System. This research was partially supported by National Science Foundation Grant SOC 76-84459. We are deeply indebted to the conference session's discussant of this paper, W. Erwin Diewert, for volunteering to cede his allocated journal space to us so that the paper could take its current extended form.

[1] See Barnett, Beck, Ettin, Kalchbrenner, Lindsey, Porter, Simpson, and Tinsley (1979) and the subsequent formal redefinition.

of the simple arithmetic type of index number, it will have served a useful purpose." With an example of the simple sum index, Fisher (1922, p. 363) found that "the bias alone reaches 36 percent." Although index number theory has not yet found its way into the monetary theory literature, all of the literature on index number theory and aggregation theory for the past half century supports the result long ago deduced by Fisher (1922, p. 361) that the "simple arithmetic [index] should not be used under any circumstances."[2] The authors' research surveyed herein provides the foundations for construction of monetary aggregates through the rigorous application of economic aggregation and index number theory.

1 The User Cost of Money

Economic quantity aggregates depend upon relative prices as well as upon component quantities. If the price of each component of the monetary aggregates were one dollar, then relative prices would never change. However, money is a durable good, and the one dollar price of a unit of its stock is applicable only for an infinite holding period.[3] Our concern is with the flow of monetary services generated by that stock during a finite holding period. At the end of the finite holding period, the monetary asset remains in existence, and therefore the asset's lifetime services, valued at the price of the stock, have not yet been fully consumed. Within each time period, the quantity of services provided by a monetary asset (during that finite holding period) is an economic variable entering the economy's structure, and it is those services that we seek to aggregate over monetary assets. The price of those services is the user cost of 'rental price' of the monetary asset.

Until recently the form of the user cost function for monetary assets was not known. This fact had hindered the application of aggregation theory to monetary aggregation. However, Donovan (1978) has deduced the user cost formula (in discrete time) by analogy with the consumer durables case, and Barnett (1978, 1980a) has acquired the same result through a rigorous mathematical proof. Hence the way now is open to application of aggregation theory in constructing monetary aggregates.

The user cost formula is constructed as follows. Let p_t^* be the true cost of living index during period t; let R_t be the maximum available expected one period holding yield during period t; let r_{it} be the own rate of return on asset i $(i = 1, \ldots, N)$ during period t; and let τ_t be the marginal tax

---

[2]For corrections to inaccurate representations in this paper about Fisher's statements regarding the simple sum index, see footnotes 68 and 69 in chapter 2 of this book.

[3]Regarding measurement of the economic capital stock of money, see section 3.4 of this book.

rate during period t.[4] Then the user cost of the services of monetary asset i during period t is

$$\pi_{it} = h(R_t, \tau_t, p_t^*)(R_t - r_{it}),$$

where $h(R_t, \tau_t, p_t^*) = p_t^*(1-\tau_t)/[1+R_t(1-\tau_t)]$. Since $h(R_t, \tau_t, p_t^*)$ does not depend upon the selection of good i, that factor will be seen to cancel out of our monetary quantity indices. Hence we equivalently could view $R_t - r_{it}$ alone as the user cost.

2 Aggregation Theory

Aggregation theory is a branch of economic theory. In economic theory the structure of the economy is defined by the tastes (utility functions) of consumers and the technology (production functions) of firms. In aggregation theory, an economic aggregate exists if a function of the components of the aggregate can be factored out of the economy's structure in such a manner that the economy depends upon the components only through that function. We then say that the structure is weakly separable in the components.[5] The resulting function factored out of the structure is called an aggregator function. The current economic (or 'functional') quantity aggregate is acquired by evaluating the aggregator function at the current values of its components.

Aggregation theory provides us with three capabilities. (1) We can test for weakly separable (factorable) blockings of monetary assets to select the components of economic monetary aggregates. (2) Having determined the existence and components of the aggregates, we then can test for their functional form. (3) We also can compute the values of the aggregates. The last of the three capabilities is the least useful, since the value of the economic aggregate depends upon unknown parameters, which must be estimated. Data series depending upon unknown parameters are generally not suitable for publication by government agencies. As discussed in the next section, index number theory provides a means of avoiding the unknown parameters problem arising in aggregation theory.

The first two capabilities of aggregation theory have been applied to monetary data. In applying the first capability, Barnett (1981b, chapter 7) has found empirical evidence supporting the Board's new procedure of aggregating like assets over different institution types (such as passbook savings over

---

[4] For a recent discussion of the after tax user cost formula, see Dutkowsky (1999).

[5] For all of aggregation theory to be applicable, the functions also must be linearly homogeneous. A rigorous statement of the weak separability and homogeneity conditions is contained in Green's (1964) Theorem 4 and in Barnett (1980a). For complications that can result from aggregation over households and firms, see Barnett (1979a) and section 9 of chapter 3 in this book.

commercial banks and thrift institutions). Of particular interest is Barnett's (1980a) application of the second capability of aggregation theory. He tested for the simple summation form for the aggregator function and *rejected* the hypothesis.[6]

This conclusion should be no surprise. A necessary (but not sufficient) condition for simple summation aggregation is perfect substitutability between components. Over a decade of empirical evidence on elasticities of substitution between monetary assets heavily supports the conclusion of generally low substitutability between many of the components of the monetary aggregates. Having determined that simple summation aggregation must be rejected, we should consider more reputable indices.

3 Index Number Theory

As mentioned in the previous section, the aggregator functions of aggregation theory contain unknown parameters. Index number theory exists to permit us to approximate the current point on the aggregator function without knowledge of, or estimates of, the unknown parameters. The 'statistical' index numbers of index number theory are *parameter free* and depend only upon the data.

A quantity aggregator function in aggregation theory depends upon quantities and unknown parameters, but not upon prices. A statistical quantity index number in index number theory depends upon both quantities and prices, but not upon unknown parameters. An important recent paper by Diewert (1976) has united index number theory and aggregation theory by identifying a class of statistical index numbers which not only perform well relative to the properties deemed desirable in statistical index number theory, but also provide high quality approximations to values of the economic quantity aggregates of aggregation theory.

For purposes of monetary quantity aggregation, the (Törnqvist-Theil discrete time approximation to the) Divisia index is our preferred choice from that attractive class of index numbers.[7] As Barnett (1980a) has shown, selection between reputable index numbers (such as the Divisia or Fisher ideal indices) is of little empirical importance, since the difference between their growth rates is negligible (although their divergence from the simple sum index is large). However, interpretation of the Divisia index is attractively

---

[6] Barnett's test requires that monetary services (and thereby the real balances that produce those services) appear in a utility function. Such a derived utility function must exist if money is to have positive value in equilibrium. See Quirk and Saposnik (1968, p. 97) and Arrow and Hahn (1971, p. 350).

[7] See Barnett (1980a, 1982b) for further details on the form and use of the Divisia index with monetary data.

transparent, as could be important in any policy applications, and the Divisia index possesses a particularly desirable limiting property as measurement frequency increases and continuous time is approached. In addition, as has been shown by Diewert (1978), Divisia subindices can be nested (to within a second order approximation) within higher level Divisia indices.

The Divisia index is defined as follows. Let m_{it} be (nominal or real; total or per capita) balances of monetary asset i during period t. Let $s_{it} = \pi_{it} m_{it} / \sum_{k=1}^{N} \pi_{kt} m_{kt}$, and let $s_{it}^* = (1/2)(s_{it} + s_{i,t-1})$. Then the Divisia quantity index, Q_t, over the components m_{it} ($i = 1, \ldots, N$) during period t is defined such that

$$\log Q_t - \log Q_{t-1} = \sum_{i=1}^{N} s_{it}^* (\log m_{it} - \log m_{i,t-1}).$$

Barnett (1980a) and Barnett and Spindt (1979) have shown that the velocity of Divisia monetary aggregates is particularly well behaved. As substitution is internalized through aggregation, the index is increasingly stabilized, with the remaining variation correlating with the interest rate. Those results are reproduced in the next section. The puzzling behavior of the demand for money in the United States (including the widely publicized 'shifts' in the demand for money function) disappears when Divisia aggregation (or any other reputable form of aggregation) is used. In addition, Barnett and Spindt (1979), Barnett, Offenbacher, and Spindt (1984) have applied information theory to compare the Divisia index with the simple sum index. They found that the Divisia index's information content *dominates* that of the simple sum index for each of their choices of components for the monetary aggregate and for each of their choices of targets for policy.

4 Velocity of the Index

In this section we consider the case of an aggregate (M_3) having the following components: transaction balances, passbook savings at the three institution types and at credit unions, small time deposits at the three institution types, and negotiable and non-negotiable large C.D.'s at commercial banks. The velocity of the conventional simple sum index (labeled 'M_3 simple sum') and of the (Törnqvist-Theil) Divisia index (labeled 'M_3 Divisia') are plotted in Figure 1.

While the velocity of the Divisia index rises, the velocity of the simple sum index declines secularly from 1972(3). The Divisia index weights transaction balances more heavily than any of the other components of the aggregate, since transaction balances provide the largest share of monetary services. But

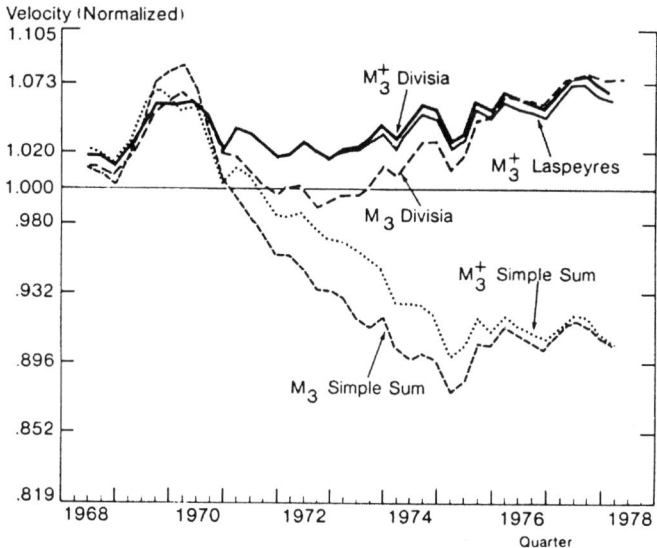

Figure 1: Seasonally adjusted velocity, normalized.

the velocity of transaction balances has been rising rapidly in recent years. Hence the inadequate weighting of transaction balances in the simple sum M_3 has permitted velocity to be drawn down by the substitution effect of the increasing relative price (user cost) of transaction balances relative to less liquid monetary substitutes.

The aggregate does not include many negotiable money market instruments, although many assets subject to governmental rate regulation are included. We should therefore expect substitution (disintermediation) to occur out of this aggregate into unregulated substitutes during periods of rising interest rates and high inflation, if M_3 approximates an economic good. That is, velocity should *rise*. Comparing Figure 1 with the ten-year government bond rate in Figure 2, we see that when the Divisia index is used, the interest elasticity of money demand has the right sign. Internalizing more money market substitution by aggregating over additional money market instruments can be expected to stabilize further the velocity of the Divisia index, since economic aggregation perfectly internalizes substitution effects between components [see Barnett (1980a)].

To further verify our interpretation, we incorporate elements of the unregulated money market [dealer and directly placed commercial paper, repurchase agreements (RP's) of commercial banks with the non-bank public,

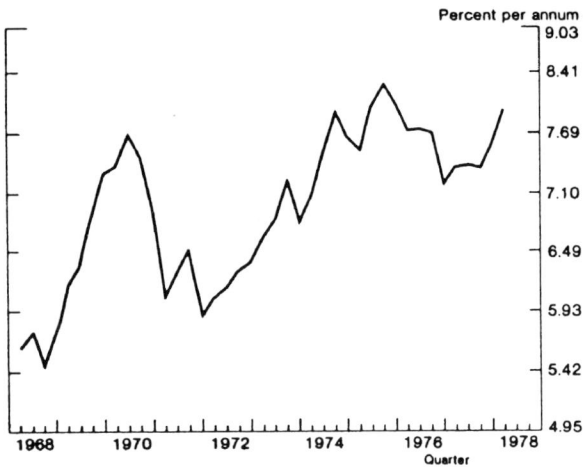

Figure 2: Ten year government bond rate.

bankers' acceptances, and negotiable Treasury securities with less than one year remaining to maturity] into M_3 to create M_3^+. In Figure 1 we plot the velocity of M_3^+, with M_3^+ computed as a simple sum index (labeled 'M_3^+ simple sum'), as a Divisia index (labeled 'M_3^+ Divisia'), and as a chained Laspeyres index (labeled 'M_3^+ Laspeyres'). Internalizing these segments of the money market further stabilizes the velocity of the Divisia index. The velocity of the simple sum index continues to trend in the wrong direction. The Laspeyres index is seen to provide a far better approximation than the simple sum index, despite the fact that the Laspeyres index provides only a first-order approximation to the value of the underlying economic aggregator function. The slight variations remaining in the velocity of the Divisia index continue to correlate with the ten-year bond rate, since some elements of the unregulated money market remain outside of the aggregate.

The simple sum index is a Laspeyres quantity index with the weights erroneously set to be equal. Clearly the erroneous weighting destroys the index's critical independence of substitution effects (within the aggregate), and hence the simple sum index *cannot* approximate the economic aggregate.

5 Liquidity Characteristic

When the user cost of monetary services is imputed to the components of a Divisia monetary aggregate, the resulting quantity index is an index of the quantity of services provided by the aggregate. The index then evaluates an economic structural variable, as is required in monetary policy. However, for some specialized research purposes, measurement of only one of the elementary services provided by the assets can be more informative. In such cases, transformation to elementary consumption characteristics is required.

Lancaster (1971) has postulated that market goods are functions of elementary consumption characteristics. In monetary theory, we might expect that those characteristics would include 'liquidity' and perhaps 'means of payment' and 'store of value.' In some cases one of those characteristics may be of independent interest. Lancaster's formulation views market goods as being functions of measurable characteristics, while we seek to deduce consumption characteristic quantities from measurement of market goods. Theil (1976, chapters 12–13) has provided a means of computing such an inverse of the Lancaster transformation under the plausible (if not necessary) assumptions that elementary consumption characteristics are preference independent (strongly separable) and that the number of characteristics does not exceed the number of goods.

In principle, Theil's transformation can be applied to any estimated integrable demand system (at a point) to reveal the basic preference independent consumption characteristics (at least at that point). In addition to generating the characteristics, the transformation provides the income elasticities of each characteristic and the composition matrix of share contributions of each market good to each consumption characteristic. The income elasticities and composition matrix can be computed at each data point, since the properties of the preference independent goods are usually not constant over time.

Since Theil's methodology is intended to be general, the transformation alone is not capable of attaching a name ('flavor,' 'nutrition,' 'liquidity,' etc.) to the revealed consumption characteristics. However, the income elasticities and composition matrices generally provide sufficient information to permit deduction of the identities of most, if not all, of the revealed consumption characteristics. Since the quantities of the revealed consumption characteristics depend upon estimated parameters and upon the specification of a demand system in market goods, the resulting indices of revealed consumption characteristics are not usable for publication as quantity data by governmental agencies. Nevertheless, the information provided by the elementary consumption characteristics can be informative for some research purposes.

Offenbacher (1980b) has estimated a household demand system for monetary assets with holdings by firms subtracted out. He applied Theil's preference independence transformation and found that one of the elementary consumption characteristics appeared to be liquidity, which was the dominant characteristic.[8]

In applications in which *data* on the supply of economic monetary services is required, as is true in monetary policy, the Divisia index described in Section 3 should be preferred. When knowledge solely of the liquidity characteristic of the components of that aggregate is required, the preference independence transformation can be applied, as has been illustrated by Offenbacher (1980b).

6 Rates of Return

The real user cost of a monetary asset depends upon the one period holding yield of that asset and the maximum available expected one period holding yield on any asset. All of the above methods depend upon availability of user costs and therefore on those own rates and the maximum rate. Issues exist in the operational definition of those rates.

The explicit rate of return on demand deposits (other than NOW accounts) is zero in the United States. But an implicit rate of return is received by many firms holding demand deposits. In principle, that implicit rate of return should be evaluated and used in a Divisia index of monetary services to the degree that the implicit return is itself not in the form of a 'monetary service'.[9]

In addition, an implicit rate must be imputed to demand deposits, if the substitutability between currency and demand deposits is to be estimable. Offenbacher (1980a) imputed to demand deposits both the full competitive rate and 40% of that rate and estimated the translog model in monetary assets.[10] He found that substitutability between currency and demand deposits is very low in both cases. Unless 40% of the competitive rate greatly overestimates the non-monetary-services implicit return to demand deposits, Offenbacher's result implies that even transaction balances should be aggregated by Divisia aggregation rather than by simple summation. The proper implicit rate imputation to demand deposits remains an important open issue.

In addition, two reputable competing methods exist for computing the

---

[8] Another characteristic appeared to be store of value 'for a rainy day.'

[9] A nonmonetary service paid to a demand deposit holder could be better-than-market terms on a commercial loan. For further discussion of this issue, see Offenbacher (1980c) and Barnett (1980b).

[10] Startz (1979) estimates the implicit return at about 50% of the competitive rate. Interestingly, firms' share in demand deposits is about 40%. Hence 40% of the competitive rate is a potentially attractive imputation. Interest bearing NOW accounts did not exist at the time that this original article was published.

maximum available expected holding period yield.[11] The selection between those two methods remains another open issue. Recent work on these issues is described in Barnett, Offenbacher and Spindt (1984). However, such data refinements are always possible and pose no fundamental problems in implementing aggregation theory.

7 Conclusion

Simple sum monetary aggregates are appropriate for accounting purposes, as in monitoring the liability structure of banks. But when monetary aggregates are used as economic variables, the aggregate should be computed using appropriate methods from aggregation or index number theory. For such purposes, the parameter-free (Törnqvist-Theil) Divisia index is particularly well suited.

When a single component of monetary services (such as 'liquidity') must be isolated for research purposes, the preference independence transformation can be used.

---

[11] Term structure theory, rational expectations theory, and perfect arbitrage dictate use of the maximum available short rate (plus a probably small maturity premium). However, recent work by Shiller (1979) dictates maximization over available rates at all maturities. Our recent empirical work marginally supports Shiller's result, although our results are robust to either selection. The measurement of this "benchmark rate" has been considered in many papers, some of which are discussed elsewhere in this book. An excellent source is the Federal Reserve of St. Louis study referenced in the appendix to this book.

PART 3:

EXTENSIONS OF INDEX NUMBER THEORY

Section 3.1: Editors' Overview of Part 3

William A. Barnett and Apostolos Serletis

The following table contains a brief summary of the contents of each chapter in Part 3 of this book. This section contains extensions of the theory to the case of aggregation error, heterogeneous agents, and risk. The chapter also derives the discounted monetary capital stock implied by the aggregation theoretic measurement of the monetary service flow.

Part 3 Section Contents
Extensions of Index Number Theory

Chapter Number	Chapter Title	Contents
9	A Dispersion-Dependency Diagnostic Test for Aggregation Error: with Applications to Monetary Economics and Income Distribution	Introduces the use of Divisia second moments for cases in which the usual Divisia first moment is not adequate.
10	Exact Aggregation under Risk	Extends aggregation theory to the case of risk, so that first order conditions become Euler equations.
11	Monitoring Monetary Aggregates under Risk Aversion	Econometrically applies the extended theory of monetary aggregation under risk.
12	The CAPM Risk Adjustment for Exact Aggregation over Financial Assets	Extends index number theory to the case of risk, and derives the risk adjustment to user costs required for consistency with Euler equation models.
13	Stochastic Volatility in Interest Rates and Nonlinearity in Velocity	Explores inference errors regarding velocity and money demand behavior, when the risk adjustment to user costs is overlooked.

Chapter Number	Chapter Title	Contents
14	A Reply to Julio J. Rotemberg	Derives the economic capital stock of money implied by the Divisia index's service flow, and resolves the paradox produced by the need to pay the simple sum price for the stock's joint product.
15	Partition of M2+ as a Joint Product: Commentary	Explores the empirical behavior of the the-. oretical monetary capital stock and compares with the behavior of the simple sum aggregate, by untangling the joint product.

Chapter 9:

Chapter 9 considers the implications of violations of aggregation assumptions made in earlier chapters. Violations of assumptions regarding aggregation over economic agents are considered, as well as violations of assumptions regarding aggregation over goods and assets. It is found that consistency with theory no longer remains possible, if aggregation is limited to the use of the Divisia first moment (the "Divisia index"). Divisia second moments then appear from the theory, and only disappear again if the violated assumptions are reimposed.

How to use the Divisia second moments, when needed, is derived and illustrated in applications.

Chapter 10:

Chapter 10 extends the theory of microeconomic quantity and price aggregation to the case of risk. In the earlier literature on quantity and price aggregation, as used in Chapter 3, the theoretical existence of exact aggregates is proved through the use of nested two stage budgeting theorems and duality theory. The objective is to identify an aggregator function such that the economic agent can be proven to behave as if the aggregate is indistinguishable from an elementary good. But under risk, two stage budgeting theorems do not work, and most duality theory does not apply.

In Chapter 10 behavioral equivalence of a weakly separable aggregate is successfully proven under risk, without the use of two stage budgeting or duality. The resulting fundamental theorem of quantity aggregation is Theorem 4 for consumers in that chapter and Theorem B1 for firms in the chapter's appendix. Policy relevance of the exact aggregate is proven in Section 2.5 of the chapter. In addition, in Section 4 it is proven that no generalization of the Divisia index for exact tracking is needed if risk applies only to future prices and interest rates. Generalization is needed only when there is risk regarding contemporaneous prices or interest rates.

Editors' Overview of Part 3

In Section 5 of the chapter, the CE ("currency equivalent") index of Rotemberg (1991) and Rotemberg, Driscoll, and Poterba (1995) is proven to be a nested special case of the Divisia index, when currency is strongly separable from other monetary assets.

Chapter 11:

Using the theory from Chapter 10 on the existence of an exact monetary aggregate under risk, Chapter 11 uses generalized method of moments to estimate the parameters of the resulting Euler equations. Tastes are specified by a nested constant elasticity of substitution utility function in goods and money. Substitution of the econometrically estimated parameters back into the monetary quantity aggregator function produces the estimated exact monetary aggregate under risk. The simple sum and Divisia indexes (unadjusted for risk) are compared in terms of their ability to track the estimated exact aggregator function.

Chapter 12:

In Chapter 11, the monetary quantity aggregate produced from aggregation theory depends upon the parametric specification of the aggregator function and the choice of econometric estimator. The objective of index number theory is to track unknown aggregator functions nonparametrically. Chapter 12 extends the Divisia index through the introduction of a risk adjustment such that the resulting extended Divisia index exactly tracks the unknown aggregator function, when contemporaneous interest rates are not known with certainty and economic agents are risk averse. The ordinary Divisia index is shown to be a special case attained under perfect certainty.

The risk adjusted user costs are defined in Definition 1 and derived and provided in Theorem 1. The resulting risk-adjusted Divisia monetary aggregate is derived and provided in Theorem 2. If the same weights and the same formula are used to aggregate over user costs, rather than over monetary quantities, Theorem 2 provides the risk adjusted Divisia user cost index. If the simplifying assumptions of consumption capital asset pricing theory are accepted, the risk adjustment becomes equation (27).

In the latter sections of that chapter, the magnitude of the adjustment is investigated by solving the Euler equations numerically.

Chapter 13:

Having determined the correct extension of aggregation theory and index number theory for risk, it is interesting to ask about the nature of the inference errors that could be produced by ignoring the extension and using methods based upon the assumption of perfect certainty. Chapter 13 investigates the induced appearance of velocity instability that could be produced by making that error, and finds that some of the literature's findings of velocity instability could have been generated by failure to use proper risk adjustment in velocity function stability tests.

An interesting and useful formula first defined and derived in this paper is the aggregation-theoretic exact interest rate index that is dual to the exact monetary aggregate. The formula can be found in equation (5) in this chapter. The paper also establishes the relationship between the exact interest rate aggregate and the exact user cost price aggregate, which measures aggregate foregone interest (opportunity cost), rather than aggregate interest received.

Chapter 14:

The prior chapters all deal with monetary services as flows, rather than the implied economic capital stock of money produced by discounting that flow to present value. Chapter 14 derives the economic monetary capital stock. The resulting formula is provided in equation (2). The simple sum monetary asset stock is proven to be a joint product equal to the sum of the discounted expected investment yield of the monetary assets and the economic monetary stock defined by equation (2). That economic money stock, measuring monetary wealth, is shown to equal the discounted present value of the expected Divisia index's monetary service flow. The CE index is proven to be a special case attained under stationary expectations.

Chapter 15:

Chapter 15 empirically applies the decomposition of the simple sum joint product stock into its economic monetary capital stock and the discounted investment yield. Since many monetary assets now produce substantial interest yield, the gap between the economic monetary capital stock and the simple sum stock is found to be large. It is found that misusing the simple sum stock in an economic model requiring the economic monetary capital stock can produce misleading results.

Section 3.2: Extensions to Second Moments

Chapter 9

A Dispersion-Dependency Diagnostic Test for Aggregation Error: With Applications to Monetary Economics and Income Distribution

William A. Barnett and Apostolos Serletis[*]

> It is well known that specification error within a model's equations can produce a remainder term consisting of higher-order terms. We find similarly that specification error from inexact aggregation over goods or over economic agents can produce within a model an additive remainder term: but it consists of higher-order moments of the distribution of component growth rates, for aggregation over goods, or it consists of higher-order moments of the distribution of income, for aggregation over consumers. We use this result to create diagnostic tests for aggregation error in causality testing, reduced form modeling, and consumer demand system modeling. We apply the tests to monetary data.

---

[*]Reprinted from the *Journal of Econometrics*, 43, William A. Barnett and Apostolos Serletis, "A Dispersion-Dependency Diagnostic Test for Aggregation Error: With Applications to Monetary Economics and Income Distribution," pp. 5–34, Copyright (1990), with permission from Elsevier Science. This research was partially supported by National Science Fondation grant SES 8305162.

We call our approach dispersion-dependency diagnostic testing (DDT), and we advocate application of DDT to all modeling and forecasting procedures in econometrics as an effective diagnostic treatment for aggregation error.

1 Introduction

In economic aggregation theory, economic agents behave as if exact aggregates were elementary goods. In particular, economic agents behave in a manner such that the time paths produced for the exact aggregation-theoretic aggregates could have been produced from rational optimizing behavior defined directly over the aggregates. Hence the exact aggregation-theoretic aggregates are behaviorally indistinguishable from elementary goods. Under the assumptions and construction procedures that produce such exact aggregates, the dispersion of component growth rates contains no information about the economy, if one already has conditioned upon the information contained in the aggregates themselves. The dispersion of variables within the exact aggregates contains information only relative to variables allocation within the aggregate. Hence, for macroeconomic purposes, the dispersion about the mean of components of an exact economic aggregate contains no information at all. The basic principle of exact aggregation holds, regardless of whether the aggregation is over component goods or over economic agents.

Nevertheless, there are circumstances under which dispersions within aggregates can have macroeconomic effects. In particular, few economists believe that all of the assumptions made in their models are exactly correct. At best, we assume that the assumptions are sufficiently realistic to produce useful approximations. As a result, there is always reason to be concerned about the effects of the approximation errors created by differences between one's assumptions and reality. In the theory of aggregation over goods, approximation errors produce dependency upon higher-order moments of component growth rates. In fact, there is a subfield of aggregation theory which deals explicitly with stochastic aggregation, so that higher-order moment measures are directly implied by the first moment measure which produces the level of the exact aggregate itself.[1] Similarly in the theory of aggregation over consumers, aggregation error is reflected in dependency upon higher-order moments of the income distribution. In either case, dependency solely upon first moments is achieved only if exact aggregation holds.

In this paper we apply the methods of stochastic aggregation theory to produce the dispersion measures that correspond to the Divisia index. Since the Divisia index is itself a mean, the relevant dispersion measures are the

---

[1] See, e.g., Clements and Izan (1987) and Theil (1967).

Introduction

corresponding Divisia second moments. We then explore the macroeconomic effects of those dispersion measures through the use of some standard tests, such as reduced form estimation, causality testing, and demand for money function estimation, when the Divisia index is used to aggregate over monetary assets. Of course, if all component growth rates were equal, there could be no room for approximation error from aggregation. However, the dispersion of component monetary asset growth rates is usually sufficiently large for Divisia second moments to have potentially important macroeconomic effects, if the assumptions needed for perfect aggregation are not exactly correct.

Just as exact aggregation over goods produces independence of second and higher-order moments of component quantity growth rates, exact aggregation over economic agents produces independence of second and higher-order moments of the total expenditure distribution. Gorman's well-known conditions (linear Engel curves parallel over consumers) for the existence of a representative consumer produce aggregate demand that depends upon prices and per capita total expenditure ('income') alone: i.e., upon the first moment of the total expenditure distribution. Attempts to weaken Gorman's conditions therefore generally have required the incorporation of some moment or property of the expenditure distribution other than, or in addition to, the first moment. See, e.g., Muellbauer (1975, 1976), Berndt, Diewert, and Darrough (1977), Gorman (1981), Jorgenson, Lau, and Stoker (1982), Lau (1977, 1982), Stoker (1986), and Lewbel (1987, 1988).[2] In fact, the primary role of aggregation theory in macroeconomics traditionally has been to assume away income distribution effects. In the final section of this paper, we incorporate the Divisia total expenditure variance explicitly into a system of consumer demand functions as a means of testing for exact aggregation over consumers.

Hence we see that the Divisia variance over component growth rates or over the income distribution can be used to test for exact aggregation over economic agents or over goods, respectively. If conditions for exact aggregation over goods and agents are not acceptable, then inclusion of the Divisia second moments of component growth rates and of total expenditure can be used to incorporate into one's model the remainder term produced by inexact aggregation ('aggregation error' or 'aggregation bias').

Corresponding to the Divisia quantity variances that we introduce into monetary economics and apply in this paper, there also exist Divisia variances of prices and Divisia covariances between quantities and prices. Although we introduce those moments and the relationship between them in this paper, we do not apply them empirically in this paper. A logical direction for future

---

[2] Stoker's quantile test is especially interesting, since Stoker provides measures of the power of his test.

research in this area would be empirical implementation of those additional Divisia covariances and variances. Further generalization could be acquired by also introducing third and higher-order Divisia moments in cases in which the power of the Divisia second-moment test is not high, as for example when there is insufficient variability in the Divisia second moments within the data sample.

It is well known that specification error produced from an inexact model can be reflected by the existence of an induced additive remainder term, which can be investigated or modeled (e.g., semiparametrically) to improve upon a model or to explore a model's approximation capabilities. The methodological innovation provided by this paper is the observation that specification error produced from inexact aggregation over goods or over economic agents is analogously reflected in the existence of an induced additive remainder term within any model that uses that inexact aggregation. While specification error within a model's equations typically is reflected in higher-order terms in the model's variables, we find that specification error produced from inexact aggregation over goods or individuals is reflected in higher-order moments over component growth rates or over income distribution, respectively. We provide a means of utilizing such higher-order additive moments to test for aggregation error. We call our approach dispersion-dependency testing (DDT), which we advocate as an effective diagnostic treatment for aggregation error.[3]

2 The Divisia Index Number Theory

2.1 The Divisia Mean

In the literature on quantity aggregation, the most widely used quantity index is the Divisia index, which has been shown to track *any* aggregation-theoretic exact aggregator function with *no error at all* in continuous time. This remarkable result holds, no matter what the form of the unknown exact aggregator function may be, so long as the assumptions necessary for the existence of an exact aggregator function hold. In discrete time, the famous

---

[3]It perhaps should be observed that linearity of the model is neither necessary nor sufficient for dependency upon only first moments. Distribution effects can arise in linear as well as in nonlinear models. This observation is true both in the case of aggregation over goods and aggregation over economic agents. In fact, all of the models used in the applications in this paper are linear, including the consumer demand system. Furthermore, the dependence upon second moments observed in Theil's (1954) seminal book was produced in all cases from linear models.

Törnqvist approximation, Q_t, to the Divisia index is defined such that

$$\log Q_t - \log Q_{t-1} = \sum_{i=1}^{n} \bar{s}_{it}(\log m_{it} - \log m_{i,t-1}), \qquad (1)$$

for observations $t = 1, \ldots, T$ and for quantity m_{it} of component good i during period t. Clearly the growth rate of the aggregate is the weighted average of the growth rates of the component quantities, where the Divisia 'weights' are $\bar{s}_i$, $i = 1, \ldots, n$. Those weights, in turn, are defined to be the expenditure shares averaged over the two periods of the change. In particular, let π_{it} be the price of component good i during period t, and define the expenditure share of good i during period t to be $\pi_{it} m_{it} / \sum_{j=1}^{n} \pi_{jt} m_{jt}$. Then $\bar{s}_{it}$ is defined such that

$$\bar{s}_{it} = \frac{1}{2}(s_{it} + s_{i,t-1}), \quad i = 1, \ldots, n. \qquad (2)$$

If good i is a durable good, the price becomes its user cost. Barnett (1978, 1980a) has proven that the real user cost for monetary asset is

$$\pi_{it} = (R_t - r_{it})/(1 + R_t), \qquad (3)$$

where r_{it} is the own expected holding-period yield on monetary asset i and R_t is the benchmark yield, which is the maximum expected holding-period yield available in the economy.[4] When equation (3) is used as the price of asset i during period t and m_{it} is the quantity of component monetary asset i during period t, then equation (1) defines the Divisia monetary aggregate, first proposed by Barnett (1980a, 1981b). Clearly the Divisia monetary aggregate is an elementary and direct application of the well-known aggregation theory supporting the use of the Törnqvist-Divisia index to track arbitrary quantity aggregator functions.

For an overview of the economic theory relevant to Divisia monetary aggregation, see Barnett (1987). For a general overview of index number theory, see Diewert (1976, 1980a). It should be observed carefully that the 'weights' are *not* produced in an ad hoc fashion or through any intuitive concept of 'weights'. The entire formula (1) is directly derived mathematically as the Simpson's rule discrete time approximation to the famous Divisia line integral in continuous time, which in turn is just a transformation of the first-order conditions for constrained optimization. Hence the Divisia index and its discrete time approximation are themselves part of neoclassical economic theory itself. Since we shall be dealing exclusively with discrete time, we shall refer to the Törnqvist discrete time approximation, equation (1), as

---

[4] The nominal user cost is π_{it} multiplied by the true cost of living index.

2.2 Stochastic Index Number Theory

Theil (1967) has observed that an interesting stochastic interpretation of the Divisia index exists. He observed that the Divisia weights, $\bar{s}_{it}$, are nonnegative and sum to 1.0, when summation is with respect to i at fixed t. Hence we can treat the component growth rates as drawn randomly from a population such that the right-hand side of (1) becomes an expectation. Then the growth rate of the Divisia index on the left-hand side of (1) is simply the mean growth rate of the components, when the mathematical expectation is taken with respect to the probability distribution, $\bar{s}_{it}$ ($i = 1, \ldots, n$).

Since we thereby see that the Divisia index is a first moment, we can appeal to Theil's sampling analogy to define the Divisia second moments.

2.3 The Divisia Second Moments

To simplify the notation, let D be the log change operator, so that $Dz_t = \log z_t - \log z_{t-1}$. Then equation (1) can be rewritten as

$$DQ_t = \sum_{i=1}^{n} \bar{s}_{it} Dm_{it}. \tag{4}$$

Clearly the corresponding Divisia quantity growth rate variance is

$$K_t = \sum_{i=1}^{n} \bar{s}_{it} (Dm_{it} - DQ_t)^2. \tag{5}$$

Since the Divisia user cost growth rate index (mean) is

$$D\Pi_t = \sum_{i=1}^{n} \bar{s}_{it} D\pi_{it}, \tag{6}$$

it follows that the Divisia user cost growth rate variance is

$$J_t = \sum_{i=1}^{n} \bar{s}_{it} (D\pi_{it} - D\Pi_t)^2 \tag{7}$$

---

[5] In addition, the Divisia index in continuous time tracks any aggregator function without error, although the Törnqvist discrete time approximation has a third-order remainder term in its approximation, where the third-order remainder term is in the differences. But so long as the time intervals are not very long, the third-order remainder term typically is zero to three decimal places.

and that the Divisia price-quantity growth rate covariance is

$$\Gamma_t = \sum_{i=1}^{n} \bar{s}_{it}(Dm_{it} - DQ_t)(D\pi_{it} - D\Pi_t). \tag{8}$$

Similarly we can define the Divisia growth rate mean and variance of the expenditure shares. The Divisia share growth rate mean is

$$DS_t = \sum_{i=1}^{n} \bar{s}_{it} Ds_{it} \tag{9}$$

and the Divisia share growth rate variance is

$$\psi_t = \sum_{i=1}^{n} \bar{s}_{it}(Ds_{it} - DS_t)^2. \tag{10}$$

If component quantities do not all grow at the same rate during period t, and if component user cost prices do not grow at the same rate during period t, and if the assumptions (blockwise weak separability) necessary for perfect aggregation are not exactly satisfied, all of the moments defined in this section, along with the first moment defined in section 2.1, may jointly contain useful information about macro behavior.[6] In this paper we investigate the information contained solely in the Divisia quantity growth rate mean (1) and variance (5) jointly. A similar study investigating the information contained in the other first and second moments defined above could be useful. In fact, Theil (1967, p. 155) has shown that the Divisia second moments [(5), (7), (8), and (10)] are related by the equality

$$K_t = \psi_t - J_t - 2\Gamma_t. \tag{11}$$

Hence equation (12) can be used to decompose the Divisia quantity growth rate variance, which is the subject of this paper, into the other Divisia second moments.

---

[6] If in addition to blockwise weak separability we have linear homogeneity of the resulting category utility or production function, then the Divisia index tracks that category function itself. If we have weak separability but not linear homogeneity, then the exact aggregator function becomes the distance function instead of the category function. In the latter case, the Divisia index tracks the distance function (which, when normalized, is called the Malmquist index) instead of the category utility or production function. See Barnett (1987).

3 Granger Causality

3.1 The Specification

In this section, we report on the results of tests for Granger causality from the Divisia first- and second-order growth rate moments of money to income.[7] There are two specifications of the time series relationship that can be used in testing for Granger causality. In the trend stationary specification the relationship between the time series is assumed to be in levels, while in the difference stationary specification the relationship is assumed to be in differences. We use the trend stationary specification. In particular, we use

$$z_t = a_0 + \sum_{i=1}^{r} a_i z_{t-i} + \sum_{j=1}^{s} b_j Q_{t-j} + \sum_{l=1}^{k} c_l K_{t-l} + dt + u_t, \qquad (12)$$

where z_t is nominal GNP during period t, Q_t is a given Divisia monetary aggregate (i.e., Divisia mean) during period t, K_t is the corresponding Divisia monetary quantity growth rate variance during period t, and u_t is a stochastic disturbance assumed to be white noise. The data is quarterly, so the time periods are quarters. The parameters in the specification are a_0, a_i, b_j, c_l, and d. In equation (12) we have applied DDT for aggregation error through the incorporation of the term $\sum_{l=1}^{k} c_l K_{t-l}$.[8]

Before the test statistic, η, can be computed, it is necessary to select a procedure for choosing the lag lengths, r, s, k. In the literature on causality testing, the lag lengths often are chosen to have the same value, and lag lengths of 4, 6, or 8 are the ones most often used for the common value of r, s, and k. However, that approach is potentially problematic, since Granger-causality tests are often very sensitive to the order of the lags. One procedure for resolving that source of arbitrariness in the test is the use of Akaike's (1969a, 1969b) Final Prediction Error (FPE) criterion for selecting the maximum likelihood solution for the triple (r, s, k).[9] In using the

---

[7] For earlier causality tests between the Divisia monetary aggregates, not including the Divisia second moments, and income, see Serletis (1988a).

[8] DDT stands for dispersion-dependency diagnostic testing.

[9] By this method, the value of (r, s, k) is selected to minimize the value of FPE, where FPE is defined to be the product of $(n+r+s+k+1)/(n-r-s-k-1)$ and SSR/n. Note that the values of r, s, and k are not set to be equal to each other under this procedure. As can be seen from the construction of the value of FPE, the procedure balances the degrees of freedom used, as implied by the multiplicative factor, and the fit of the equation, as implied by SSR. An alternative, but less well-known, procedure is that of Schwarz (1978). Although not used here, the Schwarz criterion, in our opinion, has considerable merit when the FPE criterion selects long lag lengths. However, in our results the FPE criterion never selected a lag length exceeding 4.

FPE criterion, we adopted the Caines, Kang, and Sethi (1981) procedure for introducing independent variables in a stepwise manner.

The results of the causality tests are displayed in Table 1 for the arbitrary customary lag lengths of 4, 6, and 8 quarters and for the FPE 'optimal' lag length. The FPE optimal lag lengths are displayed in parentheses in the FPE lags column of Table 1. To test, for example, whether Q_t causes z_t in the Granger sense, we follow the usual procedure as follows. We first estimate equation (12) by ordinary least squares and obtain the unrestricted sum of squared residuals, SSR_u. We then estimate (12) again by ordinary least squares, but with the imposition of the restrictions that $b_j = 0$ for all $j = 1, \ldots, s$. The result of the latter regression is the computation of the restricted sum of squares, SSR_r. The test statistic, η, then is the ratio of $(\text{SSR}_r - \text{SSR}_u)/s$ to $\text{SSR}_u/(n - r - s - k - 1)$. Under our assumption of white noise disturbances, η is asymptotically distributed as an F-distribution with numerator degrees of freedom s and denominator degrees of freedom $n - r - s - k - 1$, where n is the number of observations.[10] The roles of Q_t and K_t are reversed in another F-test to see whether K_t causes z_t.

The results with the following test statistics are provided in Table 1. The statistic η_1 is the asymptotic F-test statistic for the null hypothesis that the Divisia monetary (first-moment) index does not Granger-cause GNP, when the coefficients of the Divisia variance are maintained all to equal zero.[11] The statistic η_2 is the test statistic for the null hypothesis that the Divisia monetary (mean) index does not Granger-cause GNP, when the coefficients of the Divisia variance are not restricted to equal zero.[12] The statistic η_3 is the test statistic for the null hypothesis that the Divisia monetary (mean) index and variance jointly do not Granger-cause GNP.[13] The statistic η_4 is the test statistic for the null hypothesis that the Divisia monetary variance does not Granger-cause GNP, when the coefficients of the Divisia monetary (mean) index are not restricted to equal zero.[14]

---

[10] The subtraction of one degree of freedom in $n - r - s - k - 1$ results from the existence of a constant in equation (12).

[11] More explicitly, in a regression of z on lagged values of itself and of Divisia first moments and on time, the coefficients of the Divisia first moments are zero under the null.

[12] More explicitly, in a test of the hypothesis that in a regression of z on lagged values of itself and of Divisia first and second moments and on time, the coefficients of the Divisia first moments are zero under the null.

[13] More explicitly, in a regression of z on lagged values of itself and of Divisia first and second moments and on time, the coefficients of the Divisia first and second moments are zero under the null.

[14] More explicitly, in a regression of z on lagged values of itself and of Divisia first and second moments and time, the coefficients of the second moments are zero under the null.

TABLE 1
Tests of causality from Divisia monetary first and second moments to nominal GNP[a].

Component Group	Test Statistic	8 lags	6 lags	4 lags	FPE lags
Divisia M1	η_1	3.165[b]	2.697[b]	3.908[b]	5.453[b]
		[0.007]	[0.025]	[0.007]	[0.002](2, 3, 0)
	η_2	1.434	1.449	1.903	5.453[b]
		[0.193]	[0.188]	[0.083]	[0.002](2, 3, 0)
	η_3	2.203	2.253	3.697[b]	5.453[b]
		[0.057]	[0.059]	[0.010]	[0.002](2, 3, 0)
	η_4	0.229	0.420	0.164	N.A.[c]
		[0.982]	[0.860]	[0.955]	
Divisia M2	η_1	2.444[b]	3.556[b]	4.168[b]	13.106[b]
		[0.031]	[0.006]	[0.005]	[0.000](2, 1, 4)
	η_2	2.366[b]	2.481[b]	3.064[b]	20.414[b]
		[0.021]	[0.017]	[0.007]	[0.000](2, 1, 4)
	η_3	3.163[b]	3.389[b]	5.927[b]	4.204[b]
		[0.010]	[0.009]	[0.000]	[0.002](2, 1, 4)
	η_4	1.845	1.270	1.716	1.784
		[0.108]	[0.294]	[0.163]	[0.147](2, 1, 4)
Divisia M3	η_1	2.045	2.837[b]	3.724[b]	11.759[b]
		[0.067]	[0.020]	[0.010]	[0.001](2, 1, 4)
	η_2	1.566	2.242[b]	3.274[b]	23.316[b]
		[0.142]	[0.029]	[0.005]	[0.000](2, 1, 4)
	η_3	1.612	3.088[b]	6.305[b]	4.876[b]
		[0.164]	[0.014]	[0.000]	[0.001](2, 1, 4)
	η_4	1.061	1.464	2.398	2.766[b]
		[0.416]	[0.217]	[0.064]	[0.037](2, 1, 4)
Divisia L	η_1	1.924	2.773[b]	3.508[b]	11.201[b]
		[0.085]	[0.022]	[0.013]	[0.001](2, 1, 4)
	η_2	1.638	2.052[b]	2.635[b]	18.400[b]
		[0.120]	[0.046]	[0.018]	[0.000](2, 1, 4)
	η_3	1.701	2.721[b]	5.052[b]	3.881[b]
		[0.140]	[0.027]	[0.001]	[0.004](2, 1, 4)
	η_4	1.248	1.239	1.592	1.867
		[0.307]	[0.309]	[0.192]	[0.131](2, 1, 4)

[a] The data is quarterly from 1970:2 to 1984:4. The triple in parentheses contains the FPE optimal lag order of the trivariate autoregressive processes. Numbers in brackets are tail areas (P-values) of the asymptotic F-test.
[b] Statistics would reject no causality at the 0.05 level.
[c] Hypothesis η_4 is listed as N.A. (not applicable) for Divisia M1 with the FPE lags, since the FPE lags in that case impose the null, so that the null and maintained hypotheses are identical.

3.2 The Causality Results

Since the fixed lag of 8 quarters is so much larger than any of the FPE lags, we tend to discount the results acquired with the 8 quarters fixed lag. With the other lag lengths, it is clear that the conventional Granger-causality te. between Divisia money and GNP, with the Divisia variances deleted fro. the test, always result in acceptance of causality from money to GNP at al. levels of monetary aggregation. When the Divisia variance is included in the specification, the Divisia mean continues to Granger-cause GNP at all levels of monetary aggregation, both alone (statistic η_2) and jointly with the Divisia variance (statistic η_3). The sole exception is the univariate test at the lowest level of monetary aggregation, M1. However, from the results with η_4 it appears that the Divisia variance alone does not Granger-cause GNP when lags in the Divisia monetary mean also are in the specification.

In conclusion, it appears that both the Divisia mean and variance contain some Granger-causal influence relative to GNP, but that the influence from the Divisia mean, which can stand on its own as causal, is much stronger than that of the Divisia variance, which can pass the Granger-causality test only jointly with the Divisia mean. These results are consistent with the theory, which demonstrates that the Divisia variance measures only the remainder produced by the approximation error in the Divisia monetary (mean) index, when the assumptions necessary for error-free perfect aggregation are not exactly true. Although our results provide no strong evidence of aggregation error, perhaps the one case that may merit further investigation is the M3 case, since the M3 Divisia variance was itself causal under hypothesis η_4, when FPE lags were used.

4 Reduced Form Equations

4.1 Model without Divisia Second Moments

Another basis for assessing the importance of the Divisia variance is a study of its performance in St. Louis-type reduced form equations. These equations relate the growth rate of nominal GNP to current and lagged money growth rates and the current and lagged values of a fiscal policy variable.

The specification adopted here is from Tatom (1981), with the strike variable and the relative price of energy deleted from the model. Let D be the annual percentage change operator. Then the model takes the form

$$Dz_t = a_0 + \sum_{i=0}^{3} b_i DQ_{t-i} + \sum_{i=0}^{3} c_i Dg_{t-i} + u_t, \qquad (13)$$

where Dz_t is the annualized growth rate of nominal GNP during quarter t, DQ_t is the annualized growth rate of a Divisia (first-moment) monetary aggregate during quarter t, Dg_t is the annualized growth rate of cyclically adjusted federal expenditures during quarter t, and u_t is a white noise disturbance. The percentage change form of the variables has the desirable effect of producing residuals that are consistent with the white noise assumption on the disturbances. Our sample period is quarterly from 1970:1 through 1984:4. We estimate the parameters using ordinary least squares.

TABLE 2
Estimates of the Unconstrained St. Louis-type Reduced Form Equation.[a]

Coefficients	Divisia M1	Divisia M2	Divisia M3	Divisia L
a_0	−0.003	0.028	0.024	0.013
	(−0.1)	(1.1)	(0.9)	(0.4)
b_0	0.306	−0.112	−0.031	0.052
	(1.3)	(−0.7)	(−0.1)	(0.2)
b_1	0.526[b]	0.333	0.268	0.289
	(2.4)	(1.9)	(1.4)	(1.3)
b_2	0.583[b]	0.337[b]	0.363[b]	0.400
	(2.9)	(2.0)	(2.0)	(1.9)
b_3	−0.206[b]	−0.040	−0.091	−0.108
	(−1.0)	(−0.2)	(−0.5)	(−0.5)
c_0	0.036	0.086	0.077	0.026
	(0.4)	(1.1)	(1.0)	(1.1)
c_1	0.066	0.094	0.102	0.119
	(0.8)	(1.2)	(1.3)	(1.5)
c_2	−0.092	−0.027	−0.019	−0.013
	(−1.2)	(−0.3)	(−0.2)	(−0.1)
c_3	0.106	0.134	0.152[b]	0.151[b]
	(1.4)	(1.8)	(2.0)	(2.0)
Summary statistics				
R^2	0.276	0.290	0.264	0.263
SDR	0.044	0.044	0.044	0.044
DW	1.680	1.837	1.770	1.764
DE	51	51	51	51

[a] Sample period quarterly 1970:1–1984:4. Numbers in parentheses are t-statistics.
[b] Significance at the 0.05 level.

The parameters of equation (13) are estimated both with and without the constraint that the sum of the b_i coefficients is equal to 1.0. This constraint is necessary for steady state (long-run) superneutrality. The results are summarized in Table 2 without the superneutrality constraints and in Table 3 with

Reduced Form Equations

the superneutrality constraints. We use the following notational conventions in the table: R^2 is the adjusted squared multiple correlation coefficient, SDR is the standard error of the regression, DW is the Durbin-Watson statistic, and DF is the degrees of freedom.

TABLE 3
Estimates of the Constrained St. Louis-Type Reduced Form Equation.[a]

Coefficients	Divisia M1	Divisia M2	Divisia M3	Divisia L
a_0	0.009	−0.016	−0.025	−0.022
	(0.5)	(−0.8)	(−1.3)	(−1.1)
b_0	0.250	0.022	0.126	0.161
	(1.3)	(0.1)	(0.7)	(0.8)
b_1	0.460^b	0.440^b	0.380	0.374
	(2.7)	(2.5)	(2.0)	(1.8)
b_2	0.529^b	0.436^b	0.448^b	0.468^b
	(3.1)	(2.4)	(2.4)	(2.2)
c_0	0.036	0.126	0.118	0.114
	(0.4)	(1.6)	(1.4)	(1.5)
c_1	0.068	0.133	0.148	0.150
	(0.9)	(1.6)	(1.8)	(1.9)
c_2	−0.090	0.001	0.022	0.015
	(−1.2)	(0.2)	(0.2)	(0.1)
c_3	0.108	0.151	0.180^b	0.169^b
	(1.4)	(1.9)	(2.2)	(2.2)
Summary statistics				
R^2	0.490	0.480	0.469	0.440
SDR	0.044	0.046	0.047	0.045
DW	1.690	1.537	1.507	1.643
DF	52	52	52	52

[a] Sample period quarterly 1970:1–1984:4. Numbers in parentheses are t-statistics.
[b] Significance at the 0.05 level.

Tables 4 and 5 contain various test statistics and forecasting results with the reduced form model. The statistics and simulated forecasting results in Table 4 are without the superneutrality constraints, and the statistics and forecasting results in Table 5 are with the superneutrality constraints imposed.[15] The reported test statistics are the following: η_1 is the Chow test

---
[15] Strictly speaking, superneutrality refers to the lack of any effect of inflation on the level of real output, although our usage is consistent with the custom in reduced form equation modeling.

statistic for half-sample parameter constancy, η_2 is the test statistic for the hypothesis that the coefficients of Dg_t are zero, and η_3 is the test statistic for the hypothesis that the coefficients of DQ_t are zero. Each of those three test statistics has the F-distribution, with the relevant number of degrees of freedom, under the test's null.[16]

TABLE 4
HYPOTHESIS TESTS AND SIMULATED FORECASTING WITH THE UNCONSTRAINED ST. LOUIS-TYPE REDUCED FORM EQUATION.[a]

Hypothesis Tests	Divisia M1	Divisia M2	Divisia M3	Divisia L
η_1	0.718	1.163	1.152	1.310
	[0.689]	[0.342]	[0.349]	[0.260]
η_2	1.392	1.607	1.730	1.856
	[0.249]	[0.186]	[0.157]	[0.132]
η_3	3.809^b	4.122^b	3.537^b	3.515^b
	[0.008]	[0.005]	[0.012]	[0.013]
Forecasting				
RMSE	5.613	4.783	4.974	5.253
Mean error	−0.025	−0.010	0.007	−0.010

[a] The sample period used in the hypothesis tests is quarterly 1970:1–1984:4. The simulated forecasts were produced using parameters estimated for a 1970:1–1980:4 sample period while simulating from 1981:1 through 1984:4. Numbers in brackets are tail areas (p-values) of the tests. The RMSE is the root mean squared error of the forecasts.
[b] Rejection of the null at the 0.05 level.

By conventional standards, the estimates seem reasonable. They support the view that monetary actions exert a larger influence on economic activity than do fiscal actions, that the response of economic activity to monetary actions is in general more predictable than the response to fiscal influence, and that the influence of monetary actions on economic activity occurs faster than that of fiscal actions. There is no evidence of half-sample parameter nonconstancy, and although we cannot come close to rejecting the hypothesis that the coefficients of the fiscal variable are zero, we reject the hypothesis that the coefficients of the monetary variables are zero.

---

[16] For test statistic η_1, the degrees of freedom of the F-distribution under the null are $(9, 42)$ without the superneutrality constraints and $(8, 44)$ with the constraints. For test statistic η_2, the degrees of freedom are $(4, 51)$ without the constraints and $(4, 52)$ with the constraints. For test statistic η_3, the degrees of freedom are $(4, 51)$ without the constraints and $(3, 52)$ with the constraints.

TABLE 5
Hypothesis Tests and Simulated Forecasting with the Constrained St. Louis-Type Reduced Form Equation.[a]

Hypothesis Tests	Divisia M1	Divisia M2	Divisia M3	Divisia L
η_1	0.762	1.942	1.787	1.695
	[0.637]	[0.077]	[0.105]	[0.126]
η_2	1.435	2.112	2.458	2.510
	[0.235]	[0.092]	[0.056]	[0.052]]
η_3	16.026[b]	12.267[b]	11.896[b]	10.447[b]
	[0.000]	[0.000]	[0.000]	[0.000]
Forecasting				
RMSE	5.271	4.936	5.558	5.473
Mean error	−0.024	0.008	0.010	−0.002

[a] The sample period used in the hypothesis tests is quarterly 1970:1–1984:4. The simulated forecasts were produced using parameters estimated for a 1970:1–1980:4 sample period while simulating from 1981:1 through 1984:4. Numbers in brackets are tail areas (p-values) of the tests. The RMSE is the root mean squared error of the forecasts.
[b] Rejection of the null at the 0.05 level.

In producing the forecasting experiments, the sample period used in parameter estimation was 1970:1 through 1980:4, while the simulated forecasts were from 1981:1 through 1984:4. The evidence on the optimal level of aggregation for forecasting is mixed, although it is clear that the lowest level of aggregation, M1, produced the poorest forecasts of GNP relative to both criteria (RMSE and mean error) reported in the table.

4.2 Model with Divisia Second Moments

Equation (13) omits the Divisia second moments. The following equation generalizes equation (13) to condition upon the information contained in the time path of the dispersion of component monetary asset growth rates:

$$Dz_t = a_0 + \sum_{i=0}^{3} b_i DQ_{t-i} + \sum_{i=0}^{3} c_i Dg_{t-i} + \sum_{i=0}^{3} d_i K_{t-i} + u_t, \quad (14)$$

where K_t is the Divisia growth rate variance of the monetary components contained in the Divisia monetary aggregate, Q_t. We have applied DDT for aggregation error through the inclusion of the term $\sum_{i=0}^{3} d_i K_{t-i}$ in the model. Tables 6 and 7 contain the estimates of the parameters of equation (14) with and without imposition of the superneutrality restrictions on the b_i's. Tables 8 and 9 contain the test statistics and forecasting results from the restricted and unrestricted equations.

TABLE 6
Estimates of the Unconstrained Augmented St. Louis-type Reduced Form Equation.[a]

Coefficients	Divisia M1	Divisia M2	Divisia M3	Divisia L
a_0	0.042	−0.054	−0.130	−0.184[b]
	(1.0)	(−0.7)	(−1.5)	(−2.0)
b_0	0.330	−0.151	−0.098	−0.003
	(1.4)	(−0.8)	(−0.5)	(−0.0)
b_1	0.648[b]	0.457[b]	0.442[b]	0.531[b]
	(2.9)	(2.4)	(2.2)	(2.2)
b_2	0.640[b]	0.316	0.389	0.434
	(3.0)	(1.6)	(1.9)	(1.8)
b_3	−0.219	0.059	0.029	0.070
	(−1.0)	(0.3)	(0.1)	(0.3)
c_0	0.046	0.121	0.148	0.175[b]
	(0.6)	(1.5)	(1.8)	(2.1)
c_1	0.048	0.121	0.173	0.207[b]
	(0.6)	(1.4)	(1.9)	(2.3)
c_2	−0.117	−0.021	0.001	0.025[b]
	(−1.4)	(−0.2)	(0.1)	(2.9)
c_3	0.112	0.159[b]	0.180[b]	0.186[b]
	(1.4)	(2.0)	(2.3)	(2.3)
d_0	−0.001	−0.002	−0.002	−0.001
	(−0.3)	(−0.2)	(−0.2)	(−0.1)
d_1	0.001	0.008	0.013	0.014
	(0.3)	(1.1)	(1.8)	(1.8)
d_2	−0.002	−0.004	0.001	0.002
	(−0.4)	(−0.6)	(0.1)	(0.3)
d_3	−0.007	0.008	0.007	0.008
	(−1.4)	(1.3)	(1.0)	(1.1)
Summary statistics				
R^2	0.338	0.337	0.343	0.357
SDR	0.044	0.044	0.044	0.043
DW	1.789	1.903	1.903	1.950
DF	47	47	47	47

[a] Sample period quarterly 1970:1–1984:4. Numbers in parentheses are t-statistics.
[b] Significance at the 0.05 level.

The inclusion of the Divisia variances does affect the performance of the equation. Although the residual variances are only slightly decreased, the adjusted R^2s are clearly increased. In addition, when the Divisia variances are included the fit tends slowly to improve as the level of monetary aggregation increases, although that tendency was not evident when the Divisia variances were not included in the model. More importantly, the hypothesis that the coefficients of the fiscal policy variable are zero is now rejected except with the Divisia M1 and M2 aggregates, and in the latter case only when long-run superneutrality is not imposed. The hypothesis that the coefficients of the Divisia monetary aggregates are zero is still rejected throughout. The

TABLE 7
ESTIMATES OF THE CONSTRAINED AUGMENTED
ST. LOUIS-TYPE REDUCED FORM EQUATION.[a]

Coefficients	Divisia M1	Divisia M2	Divisia M3	Divisia L
a_0	0.061	-0.131^b	-0.199^b	-0.175
	(1.7)	(-2.9)	(-3.5)	(-3.2)
b_0	0.220	-0.073	-0.043	-0.010
	(1.1)	(-0.4)	(-0.2)	(-0.0)
b_1	0.524^b	0.532^b	0.499^b	0.523^b
	(2.9)	(2.9)	(2.6)	(2.3)
b_2	0.538^b	0.373^b	0.426^b	0.428
	(3.0)	(2.0)	(2.1)	(1.8)
c_0	0.049	0.156^b	0.183^b	0.171^b
	(0.6)	(2.0)	(2.4)	(2.3)
c_1	0.057	0.148	0.202^b	0.203^b
	(0.7)	(1.8)	(2.4)	(2.4)
c_2	-0.112	-0.001	0.025	0.021
	(-1.4)	(-0.1)	(0.3)	(0.2)
c_3	0.115	0.165^b	0.191^b	0.184^b
	(1.5)	(2.1)	(2.4)	(2.4)
d_0	-0.002	0.000	-0.000	-0.001
	(-0.4)	(0.0)	(0.0)	(-0.1)
d_1	0.002	0.010	0.015^b	0.014
	(0.4)	(1.4)	(2.1)	(1.9)
d_2	-0.001	-0.002	0.003	0.002
	(-0.3)	(-0.4)	(0.3)	(0.2)
d_3	-0.006	0.010	0.009	0.008
	(-1.3)	(1.6)	(1.3)	(1.2)
Summary statistics				
R^2	0.527	0.562	0.580	0.540
SDR	0.044	0.044	0.044	0.043
DW	1.792	1.803	1.853	1.949
DF	48	48	48	48

[a] Sample period quarterly 1970:1–1984:4. Numbers in parentheses are t-statistics.
[b] Significance at the 0.05 level.

conclusion regarding fiscal policy is particularly striking, since there are more variables in the model than previously. The increased precision (and therefore statistical significance) of the fiscal policy variable, despite the increased number of variables in the model, is evidence of specification error in the model without DDT.

In addition to η_1, η_2, and η_3 the following two test statistics are also reported: η_4 is the test statistic for the hypothesis that the coefficients of the Divisia mean and variance are jointly zero, and η_5 is the test statistic for the hypothesis that the coefficients of the Divisia second moments alone are zero. The statistics η_4 and η_5 both have the F-distribution under their respective null hypotheses.[17]

TABLE 8
HYPOTHESIS TESTS AND SIMULATED FORECASTS WITH THE UNCONSTRAINED AUGMENTED ST. LOUIS-TYPE REDUCED FORM EQUATION.[a]

Hypothesis Tests	Divisia M1	Divisia M2	Divisia M3	Divisia L
η_1	0.816	0.816	0.786	0.703
	[0.640]	[0.640]	[0.669]	[0.747]
η_2	1.634	2.141	2.793^b	3.213^b
	[0.181]	[0.090]	[0.036]	[0.020]
η_3	4.555^b	4.095^b	4.621^b	4.996^b
	[0.003]	[0.006]	[0.003]	[0.001]
η_4	2.465^b	2.450^b	2.528^b	2.705^b
	[0.025]	[0.026]	[0.022]	[0.015]
η_5	1.093	0.833	1.406	1.702
	[0.370]	[0.511]	[0.246]	[0.165]
Forecasting				
RMSE	5.531	5.538	5.395	5.523
Mean error	−0.019	−0.022	−0.017	−0.024

[a] The sample period used in the hypothesis tests is quarterly 1970:1–1984:4. The simulated forecasts were produced using parameters estimated for a 1970:1–1980:4 sample period while simulating from 1981:1 through 1984:4. Numbers in brackets are tail areas (p-values) of the tests. The RMSE is the root mean squared error of the forecasts.
[b] Rejection of the null at the 0.05 level.

We strongly reject the hypothesis that the coefficients of the Divisia mean and variance jointly are zero, but we usually cannot reject the hypothesis that the coefficients of the Divisia variances alone are zero. However, with the latter hypothesis, possible exceptions to our conclusion arise at the two highest (M3 and L) levels of aggregation, at which the coefficients of the Divisia second moments are significantly different from zero when long-run superneutrality is imposed.

The reduced form equations (13) and (14) both performed rather well relative to the usual criteria. However, to the degree that inclusion of the Divisia variances produced gains, it appears that the gains increase somewhat as the level of aggregation increases. Since aggregation error is likely to be greatest at the highest levels of aggregation, the potential gain from

---

[17] For test statistic η_1, the degrees of freedom of the F-distribution under the null are (13, 34) without the superneutrality constraints and (12, 36) with the constraints. For test statistic η_2, the degrees of freedom are (4, 47) without the constraints and (4, 48) with the constraints. For test statistic η_3, the degrees of freedom are (4, 47) without the constraints and (3, 48) with the constraints. For test statistic η_4, the degrees of freedom are (8, 47) without the constraints and (7, 48) with the constraints. For test statistic η_5, the degrees of freedom are (4, 47) without the constraints and (4, 48) with the constraints.

incorporating the dispersion measure at the highest levels of aggregation is as expected. But since those gains, even at the highest levels of aggregation, are rather modest, the reduced form results do not provide evidence of major aggregation error in the Divisia monetary aggregates, although some minor evidence was detected.[18]

TABLE 9
HYPOTHESIS TESTS AND SIMULATED FORECASTS WITH THE CONSTRAINED AUGMENTED ST. LOUIS-TYPE REDUCED FORM EQUATION.[a]

Hypothesis Tests	Divisia M1	Divisia M2	Divisia M3	Divisia L
η_1	0.970	0.947	0.891	0.793
	[0.493]	[0.513]	[0.563]	[0.654]
η_2	1.674	2.780^b	3.926^b	3.803^b
	[0.171]	[0.037]	[0.007]	[0.009]
η_3	15.769^b	10.350^b	10.065^b	8.772^b
	[0.000]	[0.000]	[0.000]	[0.000]
η_4	7.373^b	7.066^b	7.775^b	6.518^b
	[0.000]	[0.000]	[0.000]	[0.000]
η_5	0.939	2.268	3.184^b	2.605^b
	[0.449]	[0.075]	[0.021]	[0.047]
Forecasting				
RMSE	5.314	5.305	5.555	5.497
Mean error	−0.022	−0.023	−0.015	−0.023

[a] The sample period used in the hypothesis tests is quarterly 1970:1–1984:4. The simulated forecasts were produced using parameters estimated for a 1970:1–1980:4 sample period while simulating from 1981:1 through 1984:4. Numbers in brackets are tail areas (p-values) of the tests. The RMSE is the root mean squared error of the forecasts.
[b] Rejection of the null at the 0.05 level.

---

[18] Alternatively it is possible that the growth rate (rather than the level) of the Divisia second moments may have explanatory power on the right-hand side of the reduced form equation. In that case, instead of conditioning the reduced form equation directly upon the information contained in the distributed lag on K_t, the reasoning begins at the underlying structural model. Since the structural model initially depends upon each individual component and thereby upon their distribution, the structural model can depend upon all moments of the distribution of component growth rates. As a result, the reduced form also can depend upon all moments of that distribution, if the separability conditions for exact aggregation are not met. Under that reasoning, a first-differenced reduced form could depend upon a distributed lag on DK_t as well as on DQ_t. We tried that alternative specification of our augmented reduced form equation, but the results were not substantively different from those acquired by not differencing K_t. Hence we report only the results with a distributed lag directly on K_t.

5 Aggregation Error in Aggregation over Consumers

5.1 Gorman's Conditions

The tests reported above are relevant to incorporation of the remainder term that arises when the conditions for exact aggregation over goods, or in our case monetary assets, do not hold. In this section we consider the remainder term that arises when the conditions for exact aggregation over consumers do not hold. We shall find that a Divisia second moment again captures that source of potential aggregation error, although now the Divisia second moment is of the distribution of total expenditure ('income') over consumers, rather than of the dispersion of quantity growth rates over components. The fact that a second moment captures the relevant form of aggregation error in each case should be no surprise, since it is well known in aggregation theory that aggregation is exact if and only if distribution effects have no macro effects.

Consider aggregation of consumer demand functions over consumers. Although each individual's demand function system depends only upon a single income measure, namely the income of that consumer, the aggregate demand system acquired after summing over the demand systems of all consumers depends upon the income of every consumer. Hence the aggregate demand system depends upon the economy's complete income distribution. If every consumer receives exactly the same income, then the income distribution can be characterized entirely by its mean, so that the dependency upon higher-order moments of the income distribution is eliminated. But the assumption of equal income shares is not reasonable. As a result, the approach that typically has characterized nearly all applied econometric research, as well as most theoretical research in macroeconomics, has been to assume the existence of a representative consumer. In this section we use the Divisia variance of total expenditure distribution to explore the representative consumer hypothesis as well as a weaker version of that hypothesis.

The conditions for the existence of a representative consumer were originated by Gorman. The idea behind his conditions is the following. Suppose every consumer's Engel curves for every good are linear. Those Engel curves need not pass through the origin, since the lower boundary of each consumer's survival set need not include the origin. Hence the Engel curves are linear down to their intersection with the boundary of the survival set, but the Engel curves are not defined below that boundary. Hence the extension of the Engel curves to the zero-income point could produce a nonzero intercept. Furthermore, suppose that the slopes of those linear Engel curves can be different for different goods, but that for any given good the slopes must be the same across consumers. Under those assumptions, everyone's Engel curves are a vertical translation of everyone else's Engel curves. We now have made all of Gorman's assumptions.

To see how those assumptions work, consider a redistribution of income between two consumers. For example, suppose we take some income from the richer of the two consumers and give that income to the poorer consumer. Since both consumers have the same marginal propensity to consume any given good, the redistribution will have no effect on aggregate demand of any good. The decrease in consumption of each good by the richer consumer will be exactly offset by an identical increase in consumption of that good by the poorer consumer. There are no distribution effects. Only the mean of the income distribution has any effect on any market. As has been observed by Muellbauer (1975, 1976) and by Berndt, Diewert, and Darrough (1977), violation of Gorman's condition will produce dependency of market demand upon the second moment, and perhaps higher moments of the total expenditure distribution. In this section, we explicitly incorporate a potential dependency upon the Divisia growth rate variance of the total expenditure distribution to permit us to investigate the size of the remainder term produced by possible violations of Gorman's conditions. Although Gorman's linearity decision can be defended locally as a linear approximation to arbitrary Engel curves, Gorman's parallelism assumption is very strong, and hence the possibility of dependence upon the Divisia growth rate variances is very real.

5.2 The Specification

The consumer demand model that we use to investigate dependency upon the Divisia growth rate second moments is Barnett's (1979a, 1981b) aggregated version of Theil and Barten's Rotterdam model. This model has both advantages and disadvantages. For our application, the advantages are of more importance than its disadvantages. In particular, the model is explicitly derived in terms of Divisia indexes, so that the generalization to inclusion of Divisia second moments is immediate and obvious. In addition, the absolute price version of the Rotterdam model is linear in its parameters, which again facilitates incorporation of Divisia second moments in a unique and transparent fashion. Finally Barnett (1979a, 1981b) has derived the form of the remainder term in that model when aggregation over consumers is produced under weaker assumptions than those needed for the existence of a representative consumer.[19] As he has proven, the remainder term is linearly

---

[19] It perhaps should be observed that these results apply only to the absolute price version of the Rotterdam model. Very little is known about aggregation properties of the relative price version of the Rotterdam model, except under very strong assumptions. As a result,

added to the simpler exact aggregation form of the model and is stated in terms of second moments. Hence incorporation of an additional linear term in the Divisia total expenditure second moment has a direct connection with available economic theory. Finally the use of equations that are linear in the parameters is in accordance with common conventions in demand for money function modeling.[20]

The newer competing flexible functional forms are nonlinear in their parameters and are not specified in a manner that inherently reveals the nature of the remainder term that would be produced without Gorman's aggregation conditions. In fact, the complexity introduced into such models without Gorman's conditions has been revealed clearly by Berndt, Diewert, and Darrough (1977). Typically in aggregation theory the advantage of such newer flexible functional forms over the Rotterdam model arises when we need to estimate the aggregator function itself econometrically. In such cases, we need Gorman's conditions, since we need integrability to a community aggregator function. But the aggregated Rotterdam model is not globally integrable under reasonable assumptions. If it were our intention to estimate quantity aggregator functions directly, rather than to explore aggregation over consumers through the use of statistical index numbers, we should use the minflex Laurent model or the AIM model, since those are the only currently known consumer demand models that are integrable and neoclassical over large regions.[21] In fact the AIM model is globally regular at all orders of approximation as well as in the limit when estimated semiparametrically.

However, we here explicitly are permitting aggregate demand to be not integrable, perhaps as a result of potential violation of Gorman's conditions. Hence, we have no need for aggregate integrability. Furthermore, without aggregate integrability, it has been shown by Barnett (1979a, 1981b) that a reparameterized variation of the aggregated absolute price version of the Rotterdam model produces the same order of approximation as the newer flexible functional forms and therefore belongs to the same class of flexible functional forms.[22] As a result, Barnett's (1979a, 1981b) version of the Rotterdam model is better suited to our current purposes than either the AIM or minflex Laurent models.

The application of diagnostic DDT to the minflex Laurent or AIM models could be complex, as a result of those models' nonlinearity. However the Rotterdam model is not the only demand system that can easily benefit from

---

we do not use the relative price version of the model.

[20] An exception is Barnett (1983a).

[21] Regarding the minflex Laurent model, see Barnett (1983a), Barnett and Lee (1985), and Barnett, Lee, and Wolfe (1987). Regarding the AIM model, see Barnett and Jonas (1983), Barnett and Yue (1988), and Barnett, Geweke, and Yue (1991).

[22] Mountain (1988) acquired the same result prior to aggregation.

DDT diagnostic testing. For example, Deaton and Muellbauer's AIDS model is linear in its parameters and variables and hence can easily be treated with DDT. Furthermore, DDT can easily be applied to the linear versions of the translog model, such as the translog factor demand system and the homothetic translog consumer demand system. In fact, the linear translog application is equally as natural as the Rotterdam model application, since the Törnqvist-Divisia index is exact for the translog aggregator function [see Diewert (1976)]. Hence that index exactly measures real income within the translog model.[23]

The specification for Theil (1975, 1976, 1980) and Barten's absolute price version of the Rotterdam model, extended under Barnett's (1979a, 1981b) weaker assumptions, is

$$\bar{s}_{it} Dm_{it} = \mu_i DQ_t + \sum_{j=1}^{n} \beta_{ij} D\pi_{jt} + R_{it} + \varepsilon_{it}, \qquad (15)$$
$$i = 1, \ldots, n, \quad t = 1, \ldots, T,$$

where the expenditure shares averaged over the time interval again are $\bar{s}_{it} = \frac{1}{2}(s_{it} + s_{i,t-1})$, the log changes of the prices (user costs) are $D\pi_{jt} = \log \pi_{jt} - \log \pi_{j,t-1}$, and R_{it} is the remainder term characterized theoretically by Barnett (1979a, 1981b) under assumptions much weaker than Gorman's.[24] The assumption of white noise additive disturbances, ε_{it}, often is remarkably close to the truth with this model.[25]

If Gorman's assumptions were true, the remainder term, R_{it}, would be exactly zero for all t. However, Barnett (1979a, 1981b) has proven that the terms R_{it} in this model can remain zero under assumptions substantially weaker than Gorman's conditions for a representative consumer. Hence zero values for R_{it} are necessary but not sufficient for Gorman's conditions. When we test for zero values for R_{it}, we therefore are testing aggregation conditions

---

[23] With the AIM, minflex Laurent, or nonlinear (nonhomothetic) translog models, DDT could be introduced into the indirect utility function in the usual manner by which additional variables are introduced into such models. The resulting additional parameters would appear in the demand system nonlinearly through Roy's theorem. Although that approach is entirely feasible, we felt that the use of such nonlinear models diverges unnecessarily from the current linearity convention in demand for money modeling. For an exception, see Barnett (1983a).

[24] It should be observed that the interpretation of the parameters under Barnett's assumption structure differs from the interpretation under Theil and Barten's derivation, even if the remainder terms, R_{it}, are always zero. In particular, Barnett's derivation produces income weighted macroparameters, while Theil and Barten's stronger assumptions produce unweighted aggregation over the macroparameters.

[25] For systematic tests regarding the error structure of this model with goods and leisure consumption data, see Barnett (1981b, ch. 5).

that are weaker than Gorman's, although stronger than those needed to derive (15) with the terms R_{it} left in the equations.

Exploiting Barnett's (1979a, 1981b) derivation of the remainder terms as second moments, we consider the following more explicit 'augmented' empirical specification for system (15):

$$\bar{s}_{it} Dm_{it} = \mu_i DQ_t + \sum_{j=1}^{n} \beta_{ij} D\pi_{jt} + \gamma_i DK_t + \alpha_i + \varepsilon_{it}, \quad (16)$$

$$i = 1, \ldots, n, \quad t = 1, \ldots, T,$$

where K_t is the Divisia second moment over the growth rates of the components of Q_t and where α_i is an intercept. We have applied DDT for aggregation error by the inclusion of the term $\gamma_i DK_t$ in each equation.

For our purposes, the appeal of this model is evident from the appearance of the Divisia quantity index, DQ_t, on the right-hand side as an integral part of the model's derived specification. However, that index plays a different role from the one imputed to it in the earlier sections of this paper, when the index was used as a quantity index. In the Rotterdam model, DQ_t is the log change of real income. Since real income in the theoretical sense is utility and since the Divisia index under exact aggregation tracks the level of utility of its arguments, the Divisia index is indeed a direct measure of the real value of total expenditure on its components. In consumer demand system models, total expenditure on all goods in the budget constraint is the definition of 'income', and hence DQ_t is indeed the log change in real 'income'. Also observe that the budget constraint is necessarily satisfied by the model, since DQ_t is by definition equal to the sum of the variables on the left-hand side of each equation in the system. It is easily shown that the identity is necessary and sufficient for satisfaction of the budget constraint.

Under Barnett's (1979a, 1981b) very weak assumptions, the following constraints exactly hold after aggregation over consumers:

$$\sum_{i=1}^{n} \mu_i = 1, \quad (17)$$

$$\sum_{j=1}^{n} \beta_{ij} = 0, \quad (18)$$

$[\beta_{ij}]$ is a symmetric matrix, (19)

$[\beta_{ij}]$ is negative semidefinite. (20)

The augmented version of the model, (16), is subject to the additional restrictions

$$\sum_{i=1}^{n} \gamma_i = 1. \qquad (21)$$

5.3 The Results

Our data consists of quarterly time series of quantities and user costs from 1970:1 through 1984:4 of the 27 assets that the Federal Reserve Board currently recognizes as potential sources of monetary services in the U.S. economy. Those assets comprise the components of the Federal Reserve Board's official broadest aggregate, L. In Barnett's (1979a, 1981b) derivation of the aggregated Rotterdam model, all quantities after aggregation are per capita. Hence we divided all of the 27 component asset quantities by population. Furthermore, since the quantities of goods and assets in demand systems always are in real terms, we further divide all of the 27 component quantities by the geometric mean of the BLS's consumer price index and the Commerce Department's implicit price deflator. That geometric mean is an approximation to the Fisher ideal price index, which is an unbiased estimate of the true cost of living index.[26]

FIML estimation of a highly disaggregated demand system encompassing the full range of 27 assets is not possible in practice with available sample sizes and computing technology. As a result, we group the 27 assets into three categories, henceforth called monetary subaggregates.[27] Our first subaggregate contains all of the components of the Federal Reserve's M1 aggregate. Our second subaggregate contains all of the components of the Federal Reserve's M2 aggregate, but with the components of M1 deleted. Our third subaggregate contains all of the components of the Federal Reserve's L aggregate, but with the components of M2 deleted. Clearly our three groups of components are disjoint and exhaust all of the components of L. We therefore accept a priori the Federal Reserve's implicit assumption that those three groups of components are blockwise weakly separable from each other. Under

---

[26] By contrast, the CPI is a Laspeyres index and therefore is upward biased, while the implicit price deflator is a Paasche index and hence is downward biased. Each of these observations about price indexes requires the assumption that tastes are not price- or income-dependent [see, e.g., Basmann and Slottje (1987)].

[27] This a priori categorization of the assets is subjective and implies a blockwise weak separability assumption. Ideally the sample should be exploited to permit formal statistical testing for separability as a means of optimally clustering components. See Serletis (1987a, 1987b, 1988a, 1988b), Swofford and Whitney (1987, 1988), Belongia and Chalfant (1989), and Hancock (1987) for work along those lines and Barnett and Choi (1987) for Monte Carlo experiments revealing the limitations of currently available methods for testing for blockwise weak separability.

the utility tree implication of that assumption, the Federal Reserve's simple sum aggregation procedure is not appropriate, and hence we use the Divisia (Törnqvist) quantity index to aggregate over the components of each of the three groups. Also following Barnett (1983a), the corresponding dual user cost price indices are constructed from Fisher's weak factor reversal test.

When estimating the augmented model, (16), we impose restrictions (17), (18), (19), and (21). We do not impose the complicated restrictions in (20), but we do verify that our point estimates satisfy those restrictions in each case. In the simpler version of the model, the remainder terms are forced to be identically zero for all t. We shall refer to that version of the model as the 'original' version, as opposed to the augmented version, (16). In the original version, we impose restrictions (17), (18), and (19), and we verify that (20) holds for our point estimates. In all cases, we use FIML (joint maximum likelihood) estimation.

In testing for the simpler form of aggregation that produces the original model, we estimate three versions of the absolute price version of the Rotterdam model. First we estimate the full augmented model (16). In the second case, we estimate (16) subject to the restrictions that all intercepts, α_i, are zero. In the third case, we estimate (16) subject to the restrictions that the coefficients of the Divisia growth rate second moments, γ_i, are zero for all i. In the final case, we estimate the most restrictive case (the 'original model'), which is (16) subject to the restrictions that both α_i and γ_i are zero for all i. The results are displayed in Table 10.

In Table 10, the test statistics are the values of the asymptotic likelihood ratio statistic, $-2\log\lambda$, where λ is the likelihood ratio for the hypothesis in that row of the table relative to the full augmented model (16) as the maintained model. In other words, the denominator of λ is always the value of the optimized likelihood function for the full augmented model (16). The test statistic $-2\log\lambda$ is distributed asymptotically as the χ^2 with number of degrees of freedom equal to the number of restrictions on parameters imposed under the null. In each case, the tabulated area is acquired from the test statistic in that row of Table 10. The restrictions in that row are rejected if the tail area is small, perhaps less than 0.05. Clearly in all cases there is no support for rejecting the restrictions. Hence the evidence favors the original form of the model.

TABLE 10

Restrictions	Optimized log likelihood	Test statistic	Degrees of freedom of χ^2	Tail area of test
Unrestricted	570.61			
$\alpha_i = 0$, $\forall i$	567.80	5.62	2	0.06
$\gamma_i = 0$, $\forall i$	569.05	3.12	2	0.20
$\alpha_i = 0$, $\gamma_i = 0$, $\forall i$	566.76	7.69	4	0.11

Our conclusion then is that there is no significant gain acquired from incorporating distribution effects through the Divisia growth rate variances into the Rotterdam model under Barnett's (1979a, 1981b) aggregation assumptions. Again it should be observed that this conclusion is not equivalent to accepting Gorman's much stronger assumptions, since Barnett's assumptions are not sufficiently strong to produce existence of a representative consumer. We therefore have not accepted the existence of a representative consumer, but rather have accepted Barnett's aggregation assumptions under the further restrictions that the remainder terms are zero. The resulting assumptions, although stronger than those producing the extended model with remainder term, are the weakest available assumptions permitting retrieval of some of the microeconomic theory, namely restrictions (17) through (21), without the need explicitly to incorporate second or higher-order moments of the income distribution. Clearly in this case, DDT needs to be handled with suitable caution.

6 Conclusions

As is well known in economic aggregation theory, the primary role of exact aggregation over economic agents or over goods is to remove dependency of market behavior upon distribution effects, i.e., upon second or higher-order moments of the distribution of income or of second or higher-order moments of the distribution of component growth rates about their means. In this paper, we explore the empirical usefulness of some of the weakest available assumptions permitting exact aggregation over monetary assets and over consumers by explicitly introducing the Divisia second moments into various common tests, including Granger-causality tests, reduced form estimation and forecasting, and consumer demand function estimation. In these cases, the exact aggregate, if it existed, would be measured by the Divisia mean.

We demonstrate that the Divisia variance can measure the remainder term produced from aggregation error, when the assumptions necessary for exact aggregation are not satisfied. However, in all of our results the empirical gains acquired from introducing that measured remainder term is either modest or negligible. Perhaps the most noteworthy gains are in reduced form equation modeling, when broad monetary aggregates, such as M3 or L, are used and in Granger-causality testing at the M3 level of aggregation. In modeling a system of demand for money functions, however, our Divisia variance diagnostic test detected no evidence of aggregation error.

We feel that testing for the significance of Divisia second moments in econometric models provides a useful and easily applied *diagnostic test* for the existence of aggregation error. Such aggregation error can be produced by even the best index numbers, when the conditions for exact aggregation over goods or over economic agents are violated. Without running that test, one has no way of knowing whether important distribution effects within the models are being overlooked. We find that our diagnostic test procedure is most useful at high levels of aggregation. This result is not surprising, since the risks from aggregation error are greatest at high levels of aggregation.

A logical direction for future research on our test would be research on the power of the test. One would expect that the power of the test would be high if dependency upon moments higher than the second moment were not great and if the variability of the Divisia variance within the data sample were high. Depending upon the structure of the model and behavior of the data, limiting our consideration to Divisia first and second moments may not be adequate. Divisia third or higher-order moments may be needed, or Stoker's (1986) quantile test might be used along with our DDT test. In addition, there exist Divisia second moments other than the Divisia variance. Although we display the formulas for those moments, including the Divisia covariances, we have not applied them empirically in the current research.

The basic innovation provided by this paper is the observation that aggregation error produces within models an additive remainder term consisting of higher-order moments, just as specification error in a model's equations produces an additive remainder term consisting of higher-order terms. Since the Divisia first moment ('Divisia index') is — for many good reasons — the most respected index in the literature on index number theory, we believe for similar reasons that the Divisia variance is the most natural choice for a test statistic for the induced dispersion dependency in imperfectly aggregated models. As a result, we recommend application of DDT in econometrics, as an effective diagnostic treatment for aggregation error.[28]

Appendix A: Data Appendix

The Federal Reserve data on the component quantities and interest rates, as well as the derived user cost data and Divisia first-moment (Divisia monetary aggregates) data, is available from many official and unofficial sources. However, a convenient and extensive source of all of that data, not only in monthly but also weekly form, is Fayyad (1986), which is available from University Microfilm. Salam Fayyad currently is located at the International Monetary Fund in Washington, D.C. Regarding updated current data, see the appendix to this book.

---

[28] DDT stands for dispersion-dependency testing.

Section 3.3:
Extensions to Risk

3.3.1: Monetary Aggregation Theory under Risk

Chapter 10

Exact Aggregation Under Risk

*William A. Barnett**

1 Introduction

Virtually the entire literature on exact aggregation over goods and on duality theory requires perfect certainty or risk neutrality. It is widely believed that these theorems do not hold under risk aversion. This paper proves that much of the existing perfect certainty theory is immediately applicable when risk aversion applies only to future variables and not to any contemporaneous variables. Although the perfect certainty theory does not apply when there

---

*Originally published in *Social Choice, Welfare and Ethics*, W.A. Barnett, M. Salles, H. Moulin, and N. Schofield (eds.), Proceedings of the Eighth International Symposium in Economic Theory and Econometrics, Cambridge University Press, 1995, pp. 353–374. Reprinted with the permission of Cambridge University Press. Research on this project was partially supported by NSF grand SES 9223557.

is risk aversion relative to current variables, an exact aggregation theorem is proved that is applicable under those conditions.

2 Microfoundations of Consumer Demand for Money

2.1 Introduction

To illustrate our results, we use a model of a consumer who consumes goods and the services of monetary assets. In this section we formulate the consumer's stochastic decision problem over consumer goods and monetary assets. The consumer's decisions are made in discrete time over a finite planning horizon for the time intervals $t, t+1, \ldots, s, \ldots, t+T$, where t is the current time period and $t+T$ is the terminal planning period. The variables used in defining the consumer's decision are as follows:

$\mathbf{x}_s$ = n-dimensional vector of planned real consumption of goods and services during period s;
$\mathbf{p}_s$ = n-dimensional vector of goods and services' expected prices and of durable goods' expected rental prices during period s;
$\mathbf{a}_s$ = k-dimensional vector of planned real balances of monetary assets during period s;
$\boldsymbol{\rho}_s$ = k-dimensional vector of expected nominal holding-period yields of monetary assets;
A_s = planned holdings of the benchmark asset during period s;
R_s = expected one-period holding yield on the benchmark asset during period s;
$\mathbf{I}_s$ = sum of all other sources of income during period s;
$p_s^* = p_s^*(\mathbf{p}_s)$ = true cost-of-living index.

Define Y to be a compact subset of the $(n+k+2)$-dimensional nonnegative orthant. The consumer's consumption possibility set $S(s)$ for $s \in \{t, \ldots, t+T\}$ is:

$$S(s) = \{(\mathbf{a}_s, \mathbf{x}_s, A_s) \in Y :$$
$$\sum_{i=1}^{n} p_{is} x_{is} = \sum_{i=1}^{k}[(1+\rho_{i,s-1})p_{s-1}^* a_{i,s-1} - p_s^* a_{is}]$$
$$+ (1+R_{s-1})p_{s-1}^* A_{s-1} - p_s^* A_s + \mathbf{I}_s\}. \tag{1}$$

Under the assumption of rational expectations, the distribution of random variables is known to the consumer. Since current-period interest rates are not paid until the end of the period, they may be contemporaneously unknown to the consumer. Nevertheless, observe that during period t the only interest rates that enter into $S(t)$ are those paid during period $t-1$, which are known at the start of period t. Similarly, $\mathbf{p}_t$ and p_t^* are determined and known to the consumer at the start of period t. Hence $(\mathbf{a}_t, \mathbf{x}_t, A_t)$ can be chosen deterministically in a manner that assures that $(\mathbf{a}_t, \mathbf{x}_t, A_t) \in S(t)$ with certainty. However, this is not possible for $s > t$ because — at the beginning of time period t, when the intertemporal decision is solved — the constraint sets $S(s)$ for $s > t$ are random sets. Hence, for $s > t$ the values of $(\mathbf{a}_s, \mathbf{x}_s, A_s)$ must be selected as a stochastic process.

The benchmark asset A_s provides no services other than its yield R_s. As a result, the benchmark asset does not enter the consumer's intertemporal utility function except in the last instant of the planning horizon.[1] The asset is held only as a means of accumulating wealth to endow subsequent planning horizons. The consumer's intertemporal utility function is

$$U = U(\mathbf{a}_t, \ldots, \mathbf{a}_s, \ldots, \mathbf{a}_{t+T}; \mathbf{x}_t, \ldots, \mathbf{x}_s, \ldots, \mathbf{x}_{t+T}; A_{t+T}),$$

where U is assumed to be intertemporally additively (strongly) separable, such that

$$\begin{aligned} U &= u(\mathbf{a}_t, \mathbf{x}_t) + \left(\frac{1}{1+\xi}\right) u(\mathbf{a}_{t+1}, \mathbf{x}_{t+1}) + \cdots \\ &+ \left(\frac{1}{1+\xi}\right)^{T-1} u(\mathbf{a}_{t+T-1}, \mathbf{x}_{t+T-1}) + \left(\frac{1}{1+\xi}\right)^T u_T(\mathbf{a}_{t+T}, \mathbf{x}_{t+T}, A_{t+T}) \\ &= \sum_{s=t}^{t+T-1} \left(\frac{1}{1+\xi}\right)^{s-t} u(\mathbf{a}_s, \mathbf{x}_s) + \left(\frac{1}{1+\xi}\right)^T u_T(\mathbf{a}_{t+T}, \mathbf{x}_{t+T}, A_{t+T}), \end{aligned} \quad (2)$$

and the consumer's subjective rate of time preference, ξ, is assumed to be constant.[2] The single-period utility functions, u and u_T, are assumed to be increasing and strictly quasiconcave.

Given the price and interest-rate processes, the consumer selects the deterministic point $(\mathbf{a}_t, \mathbf{x}_t, A_t)$ and the stochastic processes $(\mathbf{a}_s, \mathbf{x}_s, A_s)$, $s = t+1, \ldots, t+T$, to maximize the expected value of U over the planning

---

[1] A nonzero probability must exist that R_s, the holding-period return on the benchmark asset, will exceed that of any other asset during period s, since no other motivation for holding the benchmark asset exists within Problem 2 at any s. In fact, since the variance of the distribution of R_s is likely to be high relative to that of r_{is} for any i, we should expect the mean of R_s to exceed that of any element of $\mathbf{r}_s$.

[2] Although money may not exist in the elementary utility function, there does exist a derived utility function that contains money, so long as money has positive value in equilibrium. See e.g. Arrow and Hahn (1971), Phlips and Spinnewyn (1982), and Feenstra (1986). We implicitly are using that derived utility function.

horizon, subject to the sequence of choice-set constraints. Formally, the consumer's decision problem is as follows.

Problem 1. Choose the deterministic point $(\mathbf{a}_t, \mathbf{x}_t, A_t)$ and the stochastic process $(\mathbf{a}_s, \mathbf{x}_s, A_s)$, $s = t+1, \ldots, t+T$, to maximize

$$u(\mathbf{a}_t, \mathbf{x}_t) + E_t \left[\sum_{s=t+1}^{t+T-1} \left(\frac{1}{1+\xi} \right)^{s-t} u(\mathbf{a}_s, \mathbf{x}_s) \right.$$
$$\left. + \left(\frac{1}{1+\xi} \right)^T u_T(\mathbf{a}_{t+T}, \mathbf{x}_{t+T}, A_{t+T}) \right] \quad (3)$$

subject to $(\mathbf{a}_s, \mathbf{x}_s, A_s) \in S(s)$ for $s = t, \ldots, t+T$.

We use E_t to designate the expectations operator conditional upon the information that exists at time t.

In the case of an infinite planning horizon, the decision problem becomes the following.

Problem 2. Choose the deterministic point $(\mathbf{a}_t, \mathbf{x}_t, A_t)$ and the stochastic process $(\mathbf{a}_s, \mathbf{x}_s, A_s)$, $s = t+1, \ldots, \infty$, to maximize

$$u(\mathbf{a}_t, \mathbf{x}_t) + E_t \left[\sum_{s=t+1}^{\infty} \left(\frac{1}{1+\xi} \right)^{s-t} u(\mathbf{a}_s, \mathbf{x}_s) \right] \quad (4)$$

subject to $(\mathbf{a}_s, \mathbf{x}_s, A_s) \in S(s)$ for $s \geq t$, and also subject to

$$\lim_{s \to \infty} E_t \left(\frac{1}{1+\xi} \right)^{s-t} A_s = 0.$$

The latter constraint rules out perpetual borrowing at the benchmark rate of return, R_t.[3]

2.2 Existence of a Monetary Aggregate for the Consumer

In order to assure the existence of a monetary aggregate for the consumer, we partition the vector $\mathbf{a}_s$ of monetary asset quantities so that $\mathbf{a}'_s = (\mathbf{m}'_s, \bar{\mathbf{m}}'_s)$.

---

[3] This constraint is common in infinite-horizon stochastic control problems. See, e.g., Sargent (1987, pp. 31, 33).

We correspondingly partition the vector $\boldsymbol{\rho}_s$ of those assets' interest rates so that $\boldsymbol{\rho}'_s = (\mathbf{r}'_s, \bar{\mathbf{r}}'_s)$. We then assume that the utility function u is blockwise weakly separable in $\mathbf{m}_s$ and in $\mathbf{x}_s$ for some such partition of $\mathbf{a}_s$. Hence there exists a monetary aggregator ('category utility') function M, consumer-goods aggregator function X, and a utility function u^* such that

$$u(\mathbf{a}_s, \mathbf{x}_s) = u^*(M(\mathbf{m}_s), \bar{\mathbf{m}}_s, X(\mathbf{x}_s)). \tag{5}$$

We assume that the terminal-period utility function in the case of a finite planning horizon is correspondingly weakly separable, so that

$$u_T(\mathbf{a}_s, \mathbf{x}_s, A_s) = u_T^*(M(\mathbf{m}_s), \bar{\mathbf{m}}_s, X(\mathbf{x}_s), A_s).$$

Then it follows that the exact monetary aggregate, measuring the welfare acquired from consuming the services of $\mathbf{m}_s$, is

$$M_s = M(\mathbf{m}_s). \tag{6}$$

We define the dimension of $\mathbf{m}_s$ to be k_1 and the dimension of $\bar{\mathbf{m}}_s$ to be k_2, so that $k = k_1 + k_2$.

It is clear that equation (6) does define the exact monetary aggregate in the welfare sense, since M_s measures the consumer's subjective evaluation of the services received from holding $\mathbf{m}_s$. However, it also can be shown that (6) defines the exact monetary aggregate in the aggregation-theoretic sense. In particular, the stochastic process M_s, $s \geq t$, contains all the information about $\mathbf{m}_s$ needed by the consumer in order optimally to solve the rest of his or her decision problem. This conclusion is based upon the next theorem, which we will call the consumer's aggregation theorem.

Let

$$\mathbf{I}'_s = \mathbf{I}_s + \sum_{i=1}^{k_1}[(1 + r_{i,s-1})p^*_{s-1}m_{i,s-1} - p^*_s m_{is}],$$

and let

$$S'(s) = \{(\bar{\mathbf{m}}_s, \mathbf{x}_s, A_s) \in Y' :$$
$$\sum_{i=1}^{n} p_{is}x_{is} = \sum_{i=1}^{k_2}[(1 + \bar{r}_{i,s-1})p^*_{s-1}\bar{m}_{i,s-1} - p^*_s \bar{m}_{is}]$$
$$+ (1 + R_{s-1})p^*_{s-1}A_{s-1} - p^*_s A_s + \mathbf{I}'_s\}, \tag{7}$$

where Y' is the projection of Y onto the $(n + k_2 + 2)$-dimensional subspace having $(\bar{\mathbf{m}}_s, \mathbf{x}_s, A_s)$ as components. Let the determinisitc point $(\mathbf{a}^*_t, \mathbf{x}^*_t, A^*_t)$ and the stochastic process $(\mathbf{a}^*_s, \mathbf{x}^*_s, A^*_s)$, $s \geq t+1$, solve Problem 1 (or Problem

2, if $T = \infty$). Consider the following decision problems, which are conditional upon prior knowledge of the aggregate process $M_s^* = M(\mathbf{m}_s^*)$, although not upon the component processes $\mathbf{m}_s^*$.

Problem 1a. Choose the deterministic point $(\bar{\mathbf{m}}_t, \mathbf{x}_t, A_t)$ and the stochastic process $(\bar{\mathbf{m}}_s, \mathbf{x}_s, A_s)$, $s = t+1, \ldots, t+T$, to maximize

$$u^*(M_t^*, \bar{\mathbf{m}}_t, \mathbf{x}_t) + E_t \left[\sum_{s=t+1}^{t+T-1} \left(\frac{1}{1+\xi}\right)^{s-t} u^*(M_s^*, \bar{\mathbf{m}}_s, \mathbf{x}_s) \right.$$
$$\left. + \left(\frac{1}{1+\xi}\right)^T u_T^*(M_T^*, \bar{\mathbf{m}}_T, \mathbf{x}_T, A_T) \right] \quad (8)$$

subject to $(\bar{\mathbf{m}}_s, \mathbf{x}_s, A_s) \in S'(s)$ for $s = t, \ldots, t+T$, with the process M_s^* given for $s \geq t$.

Problem 2a. Choose the deterministic point $(\bar{\mathbf{m}}_t, \mathbf{x}_t, A_t)$ and the stochastic process $(\bar{\mathbf{m}}_s, \mathbf{x}_s, A_s)$, $s = t+1, \ldots, \infty$, to maximize

$$u^*(M_t^*, \bar{\mathbf{m}}_t, \mathbf{x}_t) + E_t \left[\sum_{s=t+1}^{\infty} \left(\frac{1}{1+\xi}\right)^{s-t} u^*(M_s^*, \bar{\mathbf{m}}_s, \mathbf{x}_s) \right] \quad (9)$$

subject to $(\bar{\mathbf{m}}_s, \mathbf{x}_s, A_s) \in S'(s)$ for $s \geq t$, and also subject to

$$\lim_{s \to \infty} E_t \left(\frac{1}{1+\xi}\right)^{s-t} A_s = 0,$$

with the process M_s^* given for $s \geq t$.

Theorem 1 (consumer's aggregation theorem). *Let the deterministic point $(\mathbf{m}_t, \bar{\mathbf{m}}_t, \mathbf{x}_t, A_t)$ and the stochastic process $(\mathbf{m}_s, \bar{\mathbf{m}}_s, \mathbf{x}_s, A_s)$, $s = t+1, \ldots, t+T$, solve Problem 1. Then the deterministic point $(\bar{\mathbf{m}}_t, \mathbf{x}_t, A_t)$ and the stochastic process $(\bar{\mathbf{m}}_s, \mathbf{x}_s, A_s)$, $s = t+1, \ldots, t+T$, will solve Problem 1a conditional upon $M_s^* = M(\mathbf{m}_s)$ for $s = t, \ldots, t+T$. Similarly, let the deterministic point $(\mathbf{m}_t, \bar{\mathbf{m}}_t, \mathbf{x}_t, A_t)$ and the stochastic process $(\mathbf{m}_s, \bar{\mathbf{m}}_s, \mathbf{x}_s, A_s)$, $s \geq t+1$, solve Problem 2. Then the deterministic point $(\bar{\mathbf{m}}_t, \mathbf{x}_t, A_t)$ and the stochastic process $(\bar{\mathbf{m}}_s, \mathbf{x}_s, A_s)$, $s \geq t+1$, will solve Problem 2a conditional upon $M_s^* = M(\mathbf{m}_s)$ for $s \geq t$.*

Clearly this aggregation theorem, proved in the appendix of this chapter, applies not only when M_s is produced by voluntary behavior but also when the M_s process is exogenously imposed upon the consumer, as through a perfectly inelastic supply function for M_s imposed by central-bank policy. In that case, Problems 1a and 2a describe optimal behavior by the consumer in the remaining variables. Since $(\bar{\mathbf{m}}_s, \mathbf{x}_s, A_s)$ are not assumed to be weakly separable from M_s, the information about M_s is needed in the solution of Problems 1a and 2a for the processes $(\bar{\mathbf{m}}_s, \mathbf{x}_s, A_s)$. For example, the marginal rate of substitution between labor and goods may depend upon the value of M_s. Alternatively, information about the simple-sum aggregate over the components of $\mathbf{m}_s$ is of no use in solving either Problem 1a or 2a unless the monetary aggregator function M happens to be a simple sum. In other words, the simple-sum aggregate contains useful information about behavior only if the components of $\mathbf{m}_s$ are perfect substitutes in identical ratios (linear aggregation with *equal* coefficients).

The implications of Theorem 1 for monetary policy are most clearly indicated by the recursive Bellman solution of Problem 2a. Since we introduce the Bellman solution in Section 2.3, we leave further discussion of policy to Section 2.4.

2.3 The Solution Procedure

Using Bellman's principle, we can derive the first-order conditions for solving Problems 1 and 2.

We concentrate on the infinite planning horizon Problem 2, rather than on the finite-planning horizon Problem 1, because the contingency-plan functions ('feedback rules') that solve Problem 1 are time-dependent, whereas — in the case of an infinite planning horizon — those solution functions are independent of time. Time enters only through the variables that enter those equations as arguments, rather than through time shifting of the functions themselves.

We begin by solving the budget constraint in equation (1) for the quantity of an arbitrary consumer good, x_{js}. We then use the resulting rearranged constraint to eliminate x_{js} from the intertemporal utility function in Problem 2 for all $s \geq t$. For notational simplicity, we let $j = 1$. Let $\mathbf{z}_{1s} = (\mathbf{a}_s, A_s)$. To apply Bellman's method, we must define the control and state variables. Define the control variables during period s to be $\mathbf{z}_s = (\mathbf{z}_{1s}, \hat{\mathbf{x}}_s)$, where $\hat{\mathbf{x}}_s = (x_{2s}, \ldots, x_{ns})$; similarly define $\hat{\mathbf{p}}_s = (p_{2s}, \ldots, p_{ns})$. We define the state variables during period s to be $\boldsymbol{\sigma}_s = (\boldsymbol{\sigma}_{1s}, \boldsymbol{\phi}_s)$, where the price and income state variables are $\boldsymbol{\phi}_s = (\hat{\mathbf{p}}_s, p_s^*, p_{s-1}^*, R_{s-1}, \boldsymbol{\rho}_{s-1}, \mathbf{I}_s)/p_{1s}$, and where $\boldsymbol{\sigma}_{1s} = (\mathbf{a}_{s-1}, A_{s-1})$.

Having eliminated the budget constraint by substitution as just described, Problem 2 can be rewritten as follows.

Problem 2b. Choose the deterministic point $\mathbf{z}_t$ and the stochastic process

$\mathbf{z}_s$, $s = t+1, \ldots, \infty$, to maximize

$$u(\mathbf{z}_t, \boldsymbol{\sigma}_t) + E_t \left[\sum_{s=t+1}^{\infty} \left(\frac{1}{1+\xi} \right)^{s-t} u(\mathbf{z}_s, \boldsymbol{\sigma}_s) \right], \tag{10}$$

subject to

$$\sigma_{1,s+1} = \mathbf{z}_{1s} \tag{11}$$

and

$$\lim_{s \to \infty} E_t \left[\left(\frac{1}{1+\xi} \right)^{s-t} A_s \right] = 0, \tag{12}$$

with $\boldsymbol{\sigma}_t$ given.

Equations (11) are the transition equations, $\boldsymbol{\sigma}_{s+1} = \mathbf{g}(\mathbf{z}_s, \boldsymbol{\sigma}_s)$, providing the evolution of future state variables as functions of the controls and the current state. That the current state $\boldsymbol{\sigma}_s$ does not appear on the right-hand side of the transition equations permits a simplification in the derivation of the Euler equations. The stochastic evolution of the remaining state variables is treated as given by the price-taking consumer. We assume that the $\boldsymbol{\phi}_s$ process is Markovian. We define $F(\boldsymbol{\phi}_{s+1} \mid \boldsymbol{\phi}_s)$ to be the transition function of the $\boldsymbol{\phi}_s$ process, where the transition function of a Markov process is the conditional distribution of the value of the process at t, conditional upon its lagged value at $t-1$.

The recursive Bellman structure of the problem is clear, and hence we can write down the Bellman equation directly. To that end, we define the value function $V(\boldsymbol{\sigma}_t)$ to be the maximized value of intertemporal utility, (10), subject to (11) and (12), with $\boldsymbol{\sigma}_t$ given; hence $V(\boldsymbol{\sigma}_t)$ is the optimized value of the objective function in decision Problem 2b. The Bellman recursion equation is then

$$\begin{aligned}
V(\boldsymbol{\sigma}_s) &= \max_{\mathbf{z}_s} \left\{ u(\mathbf{z}_s, \boldsymbol{\sigma}_s) + E_t \left[\left(\frac{1}{1+\xi} \right) V(\boldsymbol{\sigma}_{s+1}) \mid \boldsymbol{\sigma}_s \right] : \sigma_{1,s+1} = \mathbf{z}_{1s} \right\} \\
&= \max_{\mathbf{z}_s} \left\{ u(\mathbf{z}_s, \boldsymbol{\sigma}_s) + E_t \left[\left(\frac{1}{1+\xi} \right) V(\boldsymbol{\phi}_{s+1}, \sigma_{1,s+1}) \mid \boldsymbol{\sigma}_s \right] : \sigma_{1,s+1} = \mathbf{z}_{1s} \right\} \\
&= \max_{\mathbf{z}_s} \left\{ u(\mathbf{z}_s, \boldsymbol{\sigma}_s) + E_t \left[\left(\frac{1}{1+\xi} \right) V(\boldsymbol{\phi}_{s+1}, \mathbf{z}_{1s}) \mid \boldsymbol{\sigma}_s \right] \right\} \\
&= \max_{\mathbf{z}_s} \left\{ u(\mathbf{z}_s, \boldsymbol{\sigma}_s) + \int \left[\left(\frac{1}{1+\xi} \right) V(\boldsymbol{\phi}_{s+1}, \mathbf{z}_{1s}) \right] dF(\boldsymbol{\phi}_{s+1} \mid \boldsymbol{\phi}_s) \right\}
\end{aligned} \tag{13}$$

with $\boldsymbol{\sigma}_s$ given (see e.g. Sargent 1987, p. 30).

To solve Problem 2b by Bellman's method, equation (13) would be solved subject to (12) recursively starting at $s = t$ with $\boldsymbol{\sigma}_t$ given. The solution at each iteration determines the state for the next iteration. The result is the following system of contingency plans ('feedback rules') that solve Problem 2b for the control variables $(\mathbf{a}_s, A_s, \hat{\mathbf{x}}_s)$ for all $s \geq t$:

$$(\mathbf{a}_s, A_s, \hat{\mathbf{x}}_s) = \mathbf{h}(\mathbf{a}_{s-1}, A_{s-1}, \boldsymbol{\phi}_s). \tag{14}$$

That is, $\mathbf{z}_s = \mathbf{h}(\boldsymbol{\sigma}_s)$.

Since we do not know the form of the value function V, we cannot solve Bellman's recursion in closed form for the optimal contingency plans. Instead we use Bellman's equation to solve for the first-order conditions. The method is straightforward. Let

$$\tilde{V}(\mathbf{z}_s, \boldsymbol{\sigma}_s) = u(\mathbf{z}_s, \boldsymbol{\sigma}_s) + E_t\left[\left(\frac{1}{1+\xi}\right)V(\boldsymbol{\phi}_{s+1}, \mathbf{z}_{1s}) \mid \boldsymbol{\sigma}_s\right]. \tag{15}$$

Then the Bellman recursion equation (13) can be written as

$$V(\boldsymbol{\sigma}_s) = \max_{\mathbf{z}_s}\{\tilde{V}(\mathbf{z}_s, \boldsymbol{\sigma}_s) : \boldsymbol{\sigma}_s \text{ given}\}. \tag{16}$$

Hence it follows that, for interior solutions, the solution contingency plans (14) must satisfy the following first-order conditions

$$\frac{\partial \tilde{V}(\mathbf{z}_s, \boldsymbol{\sigma}_s)}{\partial \mathbf{z}_s} = \mathbf{0}. \tag{17}$$

From equations (15) and (17), it follows that

$$\frac{\partial u(\mathbf{z}_s, \boldsymbol{\sigma}_s)}{\partial \mathbf{z}_s} + E_t\left[\left(\frac{1}{1+\xi}\right)\frac{\partial V(\boldsymbol{\phi}_{s+1}, \mathbf{z}_{1s})}{\partial \mathbf{z}_{1s}} \mid \boldsymbol{\sigma}_s\right] = \mathbf{0}. \tag{18}$$

However, observe that the unknown function V is in equation (18). The following procedure can be used to eliminate that unknown function. First, observe from the transition equations (11) that $\boldsymbol{\sigma}_{1,s+1} = \mathbf{z}_{1s}$, so that

$$\frac{\partial V(\boldsymbol{\phi}_{s+1}, \mathbf{z}_{1s})}{\partial \mathbf{z}_{1s}} = \frac{\partial V(\boldsymbol{\phi}_{s+1}, \boldsymbol{\sigma}_{1,s+1})}{\partial \boldsymbol{\sigma}_{1,s+1}}. \tag{19}$$

To evaluate the right-hand side of equation (19), we substitute the solution contingency plans, $\mathbf{z}_s = \mathbf{h}(\boldsymbol{\sigma}_s)$, into equation (13) to eliminate the control variables, and then differentiate (13) with respect to $\boldsymbol{\sigma}_s$ to acquire the Benveniste and Scheinkman equations. As is well known, the Benveniste and Scheinkman equations do not contain the unknown function V when $\partial \mathbf{g}'/\partial \boldsymbol{\sigma}_s = \mathbf{0}$, as is the case with our very simple transition equations

$\sigma_{1,s+1} = \mathbf{z}_{1s}$.[4] Hence equations (19) can be substituted into (18) to acquire the Euler equations for the control variables.

The Euler equations that will be of most use to us are those for monetary assets. Replacing $X(\mathbf{x}_t)$ by c_t in u, those Euler equations become:

$$E_t \left[\frac{\partial u}{\partial m_{it}} - \rho \frac{p_t^*(R_t - r_{it})}{p_{t+1}^*} \frac{\partial u}{\partial c_{t+1}} \right] = 0 \qquad (20)$$

for $i = 1, \ldots, k_1$, where $c_t = X(\mathbf{x}_t)$ is the exact quantity aggregate over $\mathbf{x}_t$, and p_t^* is its dual exact price aggregate.[5] Similarly, we can acquire the Euler equation for the consumer goods aggregate c_t, rather than for each of its components. The resulting Euler equation for c_t is

$$E_t \left[\frac{\partial u}{\partial c_t} - \rho \frac{p_t^*(1 + R_t)}{p_{t+1}^*} \frac{\partial u}{\partial c_{t+1}} \right] = 0. \qquad (21)$$

2.4 Deceptive Simplifications

After inspection of the expected utility function in either Problem 1 or 2, one is tempted to conclude that an easy way may exist of dealing with the challenging quantity aggregation problems posed by the model. In particular, the fact that the level of current-period utility, $u(\mathbf{a}_t, \mathbf{x}_t) = u^*(M(\mathbf{m}_s), \bar{\mathbf{m}}_s, \mathbf{x}_s)$, is known with certainty suggests that a method may exist for using perfect certainty methods for tracking $M = M(\mathbf{m}_s)$ without any approximation error at all, as perhaps by a Divisia index line integral in continuous time. But that appearance is deceiving.

There would appear to be two easy ways out of the risk-aversion complication. The first would be the approach derived by Barnett (1980a) in the perfect certainty case. By that means, the sequence of constraints in Problem 1 is collapsed into a single intertemporal wealth constraint containing discounted prices and user costs. The intertemporal decision is then solved in two stages. The second stage is maximization of $u(\mathbf{a}_t, \mathbf{x}_t)$ subject to a current-period expenditure constraint, in which monetary services flows are valued by their current-period user costs. That second-stage decision is in the standard form used in the literature on index number theory. Hence it would appear that we have access to the existing literature on index number theory under perfect certainty.

---

[4]See Sargent (1987, pp. 21, 31) regarding the Benveniste and Scheinkman equations when $\partial \mathbf{g}'/\partial \boldsymbol{\sigma}_s = \mathbf{0}$. See Sargent (1987, p.31) for the general form of the resulting Euler equations. Alternatively, the Euler equations could be derived by variational methods; see e.g. Stokey and Lucas (1989, sec. 4.5).

[5]Assuming that X is linearly homogeneous, the exact-price aggregator function is the unit cost function.

While this procedure works in the perfect certainty case, it is not applicable under risk aversion. The reason is that the current-period user costs derived by Barnett (1978) for the services of monetary asset a_{it} are $p_t^*(R_t - \rho_{it})/(1 + R_t)$. In Problem 1, however, R_t and ρ_{it} are not known during period i because interest is paid at the end of the period. Hence the second-stage budget constraints are random constraints containing random user costs. But the objective function in the second-stage decision is utility, not expected utility. Since it is impossible for binding deterministic choices of current monetary asset and goods purchases to satisfy a random constraint, Barnett's (1980a) method of decomposing the intertemporal decision into a two-stage budgeting procedure does not apply to our current model.

Another particularly enticing simplification is as follows. Recall that constraint (1) is entirely deterministic when $s = t$. Hence it may appear that we can maximize $u(\mathbf{a}_t, \mathbf{x}_t)$ subject to (1) with $s = t$, conditional upon optimal values of any variables not selected within that decision. In this manner, all aspects of the decision are deterministic. The utility function is deterministic and the constraint is deterministic. Again it may appear that we could find a means of producing a Divisia index that will track $M = M(\mathbf{m}_s)$ without any error due to risk aversion.

To see that this will not work, consider the last stage of a Bellman recursive solution to the decision problem. That final stage will indeed contain equation (1) with $s = t$ as its sole constraint. However, the objective function will not be $u(\mathbf{a}_t, \mathbf{x}_t)$ alone but rather the sum of $u(\mathbf{a}_t, \mathbf{x}_t)$ and the Bellman recursion function. In the final stage of the Bellman solution, that recursion function will include $(\mathbf{a}_t, A_t)$ as arguments. Hence the choice of $\mathbf{a}_t$ will affect both terms of the objective function, and not just the initial $u(\mathbf{a}_t, \mathbf{x}_t)$ term. As a result, blockwise weak separability of $\mathbf{a}_t$ within $u(\mathbf{a}_t, \mathbf{x}_t)$ would not be sufficient to permit us to use the conventional derivation of the Divisia index as a means of tracking the economic monetary aggregate.

2.5 Monetary Policy

With the Bellman solution at hand, we are in a position to give further consideration to the policy implications of monetary aggregation in light of $M(\mathbf{m}_s)$, the *Theoretical aggregate*. Hence we now return to Theorem 1 and Problem 2a. Clearly, the Bellman equation can be written in a manner analogous to that done for Problem 2. The only changes are that the controls now are $(\bar{\mathbf{m}}_s, \hat{\mathbf{x}}_s, A_s)$, $s = t, \ldots, \infty$, and the state variables are $(\bar{\mathbf{m}}_{s-1}, A_{s-1}, \boldsymbol{\phi}_s, M_s^*)$, where $\boldsymbol{\phi}_s = (\hat{\mathbf{p}}_s, p_s^*, p_{s-1}^*, R_{s-1}, \bar{\mathbf{r}}_{s-1}, \mathbf{I}_s')/p_{1s}$. Hence the solution contingency plans solving Problem 2a are of the form

$$(\bar{\mathbf{m}}_s, \hat{\mathbf{x}}_s, A_s) = \mathbf{h}(\bar{\mathbf{m}}_{s-1}, A_{s-1}, \boldsymbol{\phi}_s, M_s^*), \tag{22}$$

where all controls and state variables are deterministic for $s = t$.

The appearance of M_s^* as a state variable has interesting policy implications. If M_s^* is used as an indicator in the conduct of monetary policy then clearly the monetary aggregate will indeed contain information about $(\bar{\mathbf{m}}_s, \hat{\mathbf{x}}_s, A_s)$, and thereby about the final targets of monetary policy both in goods and labor markets. Alternatively, suppose that such policy instruments as the monetary base are used to target the equilibrium path of M_s^* as an intermediate target of policy. Assuming that the instruments are used in a manner not subject to the Lucas critique or time inconsistency, as for example through an open loop policy, the equilibrium stochastic process of M_s^* can be influenced by policy. Under our assumption of rational expectations, economic agents will know about the policy rule and hence about the targeted equilibrium process for M_s^*. The consumer then can solve Problem 2a to acquire the optimal solution for the remaining variables conditional upon the targeted process for M_s^*.

We see that only M_s^* can play these roles if policy operates through a monetary target or indicator. The simple-sum aggregate, which does not appear as a control in $\mathbf{h}$, can serve neither role. In fact the only information from the portfolio $\mathbf{m}_s^*$ that is useful in solving Problem 2a is $M_s^* = M(\mathbf{m}_s^*)$, since $\mathbf{m}_s^*$ enters the contingency plans $\mathbf{h}$ only through M. Analogous results for firm demand for monetary services are derived in the appendix.

3 The Risk-Neutral Case

Under risk neutrality, the decision of each of the agents modeled in this section can be solved in two stages. In the first stage, expenditure is budgeted to aggregates. In the second stage, the budgeted expenditure on each aggregate is allocated over its components. For details of the two-stage budgeting solutions, see Barnett (1987). Only the contemporaneous second-stage decision is relevant to our purposes. For each of our economic agents, the contemporaneous second-stage decision is to maximize the current-period service flow produced from the components of the aggregate, subject to the budgeted constraint on current-period expenditure on those components. The service-flow objective function is the agent's separable aggregator function over the components. Because that second-stage decision has the same form for firms and consumers (aside from a change in notation for variables and functions), we present it only for one economic agent, the consumer.

In the perfect certainty case, Barnett (1978, 1980a) proved that the nominal user cost of the services of m_{it} is π_{it}, where

$$\pi_{it} = p^* \frac{R_t - r_{it}}{1 + R_t}. \tag{23}$$

A Generalization

The correspondingly real user cost is $\pi_{it}^* = \pi_{it}/p^*$. In the risk-neutral case, the user cost formulas are the same as in the perfect certainty case, but with the interest rates replaced by their expected values. The second-stage decision may be summarized as follows.

Problem 3. Choose $\mathbf{m}_t \geq 0$ to maximize $M(\mathbf{m}_t)$ subject to $\mathbf{m}_t'\boldsymbol{\pi}_t = E_t$, where E_t is total expenditure budgeted to $\mathbf{m}_t$ in the first stage.

It can be shown that the solution value of the exact monetary aggregate $M(\mathbf{m}_t)$ can be tracked without error (see e.g. Barnett 1983a) by the Divisia index:

$$d \log M_t = \sum_{i=1}^{k_1} s_{it} d \log m_{it}, \tag{24}$$

where the flawless tracking ability of the index in the risk-neutral case holds regardless of the form of the unknown aggregator function M. However, under risk aversion the ability of equation (24) to track $M(\mathbf{m}_t)$ is compromised, and the rate at which that tracking ability deteriorates is unknown, as the degree of risk aversion increases above zero. We can investigate the magnitude of that error by econometrically estimating $M(\mathbf{m}_t)$.

4 A Generalization

That the Divisia index tracks exactly under perfect certainty is well known. However, we show in this section that neither perfect certainty nor risk neutrality are needed for exact tracking of the Divisia index; only contemporaneous prices and interest rates need be known. Future interest rates and prices need not be known, and risk-averse behavior need not be excluded. The proof is as follows.

Assume that R_t, p_t^*, and $\mathbf{r}_t$ are known at time t, although their future values are stochastic. Then the Euler equations (20) for $\mathbf{m}_t$ are

$$\frac{\partial u}{\partial m_{it}} - \rho p_t^*(R_t - r_{it})E_t\left[\frac{1}{p_{t+1}^*}\frac{\partial u}{\partial c_{t+1}}\right] = 0 \tag{25}$$

for $i = 1, \ldots, k_1$. Similarly, the Euler equation (21) for aggregate consumption c_t of goods becomes

$$\frac{\partial u}{\partial c_t} - \rho p_t^*(1 + R_t)E_t\left[\frac{1}{p_{t+1}^*}\frac{\partial u}{\partial c_{t+1}}\right] = 0. \tag{26}$$

Eliminating $E_t[(1/p_{t+1}^*)(\partial u/\partial c_{t+1})]$ between (25) and (26), we acquire

$$\frac{\partial u}{\partial m_{it}} = \frac{(R_t - r_{it})}{1 + R_t} \frac{\partial u}{\partial c_t}. \tag{27}$$

However, by the assumption of weak separability of u in $\mathbf{m}_t$ we have

$$\frac{\partial u}{\partial m_{it}} = \frac{\partial u}{\partial M_t} \frac{\partial M}{\partial m_{it}}, \tag{28}$$

where $M_t = M(\mathbf{m}_t)$ is the exact monetary aggregate that we seek to track. Substituting (27) into (28) and using (23), we find that

$$\frac{\partial M}{\partial m_{it}} = \pi_{it}^* \frac{\partial u/\partial c_t}{\partial u/\partial M_t}. \tag{29}$$

Now substitute (29) into the total differential of M to acquire

$$dM(\mathbf{m}_t) = \frac{\partial u/\partial c_t}{\partial u/\partial M_t} \sum_{i=1}^{k_1} \pi_{it}^* dm_{it}. \tag{30}$$

But since M is assumed to be linearly homogeneous, we have Euler's equation for linearly homogeneous functions. Substituting (29) into Euler's equation yields

$$M(\mathbf{m}_t) = \frac{\partial u/\partial c_t}{\partial u/\partial M_t} \sum_{j=1}^{k_1} \pi_{jt}^* m_{jt}. \tag{31}$$

Dividing (30) by (31) we acquire (24), which is the Divisia index. Hence the exact tracking property of the Divisia index is compromised neither by uncertainty regarding future interest rates and prices nor by risk aversion. Nevertheless, this assumption is not trivial, since current-period interest rates are not paid until the *end* of the current period.

Furthermore, all of the usual theorems regarding the Divisia index remain valid under uncertainty with respect to future interest rates and prices. This can be seen by dividing (29) by itself for two different values of i to acquire the marginal rate of substitution between m_{it} and m_{jt}:

$$\frac{\partial M/\partial m_{it}}{\partial M/\partial m_{jt}} = \frac{\pi_{it}^*}{\pi_{jt}^*}.$$

It immediately follows that the first-order conditions for solving Problem 3 are satisfied, and hence the usual properties and theorems regarding the Divisia index are relevant.

5 Strong Separability in Currency

Strong separability in currency produces an interesting special case of the Divisia index. In particular, that special case produces the CE ('currency equivalence') index advocated by Hutt (1963, p. 92, footnote), Rotemberg (1991), and Rotemberg, Driscoll, and Poterba (1995). In this section, we prove that the CE index is a fully nested special case of the Divisia index.

As demonstrated in Section 2.2, the derivation of the Divisia monetary index requires the assumption of blockwise weak separability of monetary assets from other goods and assets in the utility function, so that an exact monetary aggregate exists. In addition to that fundamental existence condition, we also need perfect certainty (or risk neutrality) with respect to contemporaneous current-period prices and interest rates, but not necessarily with respect to future prices and interest rates. Although for convenience we have assumed linear homogeneity of the monetary asset category utility function M, that assumption is not required. If M is not lineary homogeneous, then M is not the monetary asset aggregator function; rather, the distance function is, and the Divisia index then tracks the distance function. See Barnett (1987, sects. 7, 8).[6]

As we now show, the derivation of the CE index requires the category utility function M to be linearly homogeneous itself and also to be strongly separable in currency. Both of those assumptions are empirically implausible, but the CE index does produce a potentially useful special case under certain circumstances. In particular, the CE index is completely linear and hence can be aggregated over economic agents more easily that the Divisia index. The CE index also can be used to measure the stock of money, rather than the flow of monetary services, as has been shown by Barnett (1991).[7]

Under these assumptions of linear homogeneity and strong separability, the monetary asset category utility function over $\mathbf{m}_t$ can be written $M(\mathbf{m}_t) = \phi m_{1t} + h(m_{2t}, \ldots, m_{k_1 t})$, where ϕ is an unknown constant positive parameter and h is the aggregator function over noncurrency monetary assets. Setting $\phi = 1$ is a harmless positive linear transformation of the category utility function M, and hence we shall follow Rotemberg et al. (1995) by normalizing ϕ at 1 so that $M(\mathbf{m}_t) = m_{1t} + h(m_{2t}, \ldots, m_{k_1 t})$. Observe that the marginal utility $\partial M/\partial m_{jt}$ is independent of currency holding m_{1t}, and that $\partial M/\partial m_{1t} = 1$ independent of the holding of other assets $m_{2t}, \ldots, m_{k_1 t}$. These implications of the CE assumptions are empirically most unappealing, but the implied form of $M(\mathbf{m}_t)$ — as a simple sum of m_{1t} and of the exact aggregate over other monetary assets $h(m_{2t}, \ldots, m_{k_1 t})$ — clearly produces the currency equivalent interpretation. In particular, the exact aggregate

---
[6] That paper is reproduced as chapter 3 of this book.
[7] That paper is reproduced as chapter 14 of this book.

over other monetary assets is required by the assumed form of M to be a perfect substitute for currency, so that $M(\mathbf{m}_t)$ is the sum of currency and a perfect substitute for currency.

We now further explore the implications of the condition $\partial M/\partial m_{1t} = 1$. In particular, we multiply through by $m_{1t}/M(\mathbf{m}_t)$ to derive

$$\frac{\partial \log M_t}{\partial \log m_{1t}} = \frac{m_{1t}}{M_t}. \tag{32}$$

We shall now see what happens to the Divisia monetary index under the CE restriction (32). From the Divisia index formula (24), we know that

$$\frac{\partial \log M_t}{\partial \log m_{1t}} = s_{1t}. \tag{33}$$

From (32) and (33) we have that $M_t = m_{1t}/s_{1t} = (\mathbf{m}'_t \pi_t / m_{1t} \pi_{1t}) m_{1t}$, so that

$$M_t = \sum_{i=1}^{k_1} \frac{(R_t - r_{it})}{R_t} m_{it}, \tag{34}$$

which is the CE index.

Clearly, the CE index is acquired as a special case by imposing two very strong and entirely unnecessary assumptions upon the Divisia index. Furthermore, the CE index possesses a very undesirable property, which to my knowledge is not possessed by any reputable index number: it is not locally linearly homogeneous. In other words, even if all components are growing at exactly the same rate, the CE index itself may not be growing at that rate. In fact, the growth rate of this index could even have a different sign from the sign of the growth rate of all its components!

This can be seen by taking the total differential of (34) and dividing through by (34) to obtain

$$d\log M_t = \sum_{i=1}^{k_1} s_{it} d\log m_{it} + \sum_{i=1}^{k_1} s_{it} d\log \pi_{it}. \tag{35}$$

The problem is evident by comparing (35) with the Divisia index (24). In the Divisia index, if $d\log m_{it} = \lambda$ for all i, then $d\log M_t = \lambda$, since

$$\sum_{i=1}^{k_1} s_{it} = 1.$$

Hence the Divisia index gets the right answer in the one case in which everyone would agree on the right answer. In contrast, the CE index will get the wrong answer in that case, unless the second term of (35) is exactly equal to zero, where that second term is the Divisia user cost growth rate aggregate for monetary services. It is small consolation that (35) would exactly track linearly homogeneous $M(\mathbf{m}_t) = m_{1t} + h(m_{2t}, \ldots, m_{k_1 t})$, if that were exactly the utility function over $\mathbf{m}_t$ and if the Euler equations were exactly satisfied by the data.

Nevertheless, the CE index — unlike the Divisia index — is linear in the levels of the component monetary assets. Hence aggregation over economic agents is simple.[8] In addition, Barnett (1991) has shown that the CE index is the discounted present value of expenditure on the services of the Divisia aggregate under stationary expectations. This result permits the CE index to be interpreted as the stock aggregate implied by the Divisia flow aggregate under stationary expectations. In fact, such an interpretation provides a resolution of the troublesome issue raised by the non-homogeneity of equation (35), since (35) can be written as

$$d\log Q_t = d\log[M(\mathbf{m}_t)\Pi(\boldsymbol{\pi}_t)],$$

where Q_t is the CE index, $M(\mathbf{m}_t)$ is the Divisia quantity index, and $\Pi(\boldsymbol{\pi}_t)$ is the Divisia user cost index. The result is Barnett's (1991) interpretation as user cost-evaluated expenditure on the services $\mathbf{m}_t$. Under stationary expectations, the same result is evaluated after discounting the future stream of such expenditures over an infinite horizon to produce a stock aggregate.

If the CE aggregate is thereby interpreted as $M(\mathbf{m}_t)\Pi(\boldsymbol{\pi}_t)$ then we should not expect the aggregate to have the same properties that we require for an index measuring $M(\mathbf{m}_t)$, and hence (35) should not bother us. Furthermore, the ease of aggregation over consumers should not surprise us, since CE index values are given in units of expenditure, rather than units of quantity demanded.

6 Conclusions

In recent years, there has been much progress in the development of aggregation and index number theory. The two theories have become unified by the availability of theorems proving the order of approximation of certain index numbers to the exact aggregator functions of economic aggregation theory. In addition, the relevance of that literature to monetary aggregation

---

[8] With the Divisia index, formal aggregation usually requires subaggregation over similar demographic groups followed by Divisia aggregation over the groups. See Barnett (1987, section 9) and Barnett and Serletis (1990). Hence data is required for asset holdings by those demographic groups, unless the assumptions of Gorman or Muellbauer (see Barnett 1981a, appendix B1.2) for the existence of a representative economic agent are satisfied.

has been established since the derivation of the user cost formula for monetary services has been available. However, virtually the entire literature on index number theory and most of the theory on aggregation over goods were produced under the assumption of perfect certainty. Much research is needed on duality theory and functional structure and on nonparametric statistical approximations to aggregator functions under risk. We provide one such new aggregation theorem for consumers and for firms under risk. Our theorem demonstrates the role in aggregation theory of the Theoretical aggregate, and hence captures the potential usefulness of the Theoretical aggregate in modeling and in policy. We produce the theorem in a form that is immediately applicable to monetary aggregation.

The aggregation theory developed in this paper demonstrates that under rational expectations the Theoretical aggregate can be used either as an indicator or as an intermediate target. If used as an intermediate target, the Theoretical monetary aggregate becomes a state variable in the contingency plans ('feedback rules') solving the economic agent's decision problem, which we formulate as a recursive Bellman iteration. Hence if the Theoretical monetary aggregate is used as an intermediate target, its solution process will predictably influence behavior in other markets through the role of the intermediate target as a state variable in economic agents' contingency plans. The simple-sum aggregate, on the other hand, cannot be used as an intermediate target or as an indicator, since it plays no role in the behavior of any economic agent regardless of whether or not the aggregate is targeted. Without information on the Theoretical monetary aggregate, economic behavior remains conditional upon information regarding every disaggregated monetary asset's market. That dependency is not altered by the availability of information on any simple-sum monetary aggregate.

Having proved those theorems, we investigate nonparametric statistical index numbers as approximations to the exact Theoretical aggregate. We prove that the Divisia index tracks the exact aggregate without error when the only risk is relative to future prices and interest rates. However, if there is uncertainty and non-risk neutrality relative to contemporaneous interest rates, the Divisia index's exact tracking property is compromised.

Appendix A: Proof of Consumer's Aggregation Theorem

Proof of Theorem 1: Let the deterministic point $(\mathbf{m}_t, \bar{\mathbf{m}}_t, \mathbf{x}_t, A_t)$ and the stochastic process $(\mathbf{m}_s, \bar{\mathbf{m}}_s, \mathbf{x}_s, A_s)$, $s = t+1, \ldots, t+T$, solve Problem 1; but let the deterministic point $(\bar{\mathbf{m}}_t, \mathbf{x}_t, A_t)$ and the stochastic process

$(\bar{\mathbf{m}}_s, \mathbf{x}_s, A_s)$, $s = t+1, \ldots, t+T$, *not* solve Problem 1a conditionally upon the process $M_s^* = M(\mathbf{m}_s)$ given for $s = t, \ldots, t+T$. Then there exists $(\tilde{\bar{\mathbf{m}}}_s, \tilde{\mathbf{x}}_s, \tilde{A}_s) \in S'(s)$, $s = t, \ldots, t+T$, such that (8) evaluated at $(\tilde{\bar{\mathbf{m}}}_t, \ldots, \tilde{\bar{\mathbf{m}}}_{t+T}; \tilde{\mathbf{x}}_t, \ldots, \tilde{\mathbf{x}}_{t+T}; \tilde{A}_{t+T})$ is strictly greater than (8) evaluated at $(\bar{\mathbf{m}}_t, \ldots, \bar{\mathbf{m}}_{t+T}; \mathbf{x}_t, \ldots, \mathbf{x}_{t+T}; A_{t+T})$ conditionally upon $M_s^* = M(\mathbf{m}_s)$.

Hence (3) evaluated at $(\mathbf{m}_t, \ldots, \mathbf{m}_{t+T}; \tilde{\bar{\mathbf{m}}}_t, \ldots, \tilde{\bar{\mathbf{m}}}_{t+T}; \tilde{\mathbf{x}}_t, \ldots, \tilde{\mathbf{x}}_{t+T}; \tilde{A}_{t+T})$ is strictly greater than (3) evaluated at $(\mathbf{m}_t, \ldots, \mathbf{m}_{t+T}; \bar{\mathbf{m}}_t, \ldots, \bar{\mathbf{m}}_{t+T}; \mathbf{x}_t, \ldots, \mathbf{x}_{t+T}; A_{t+T})$. But since $(\tilde{\bar{\mathbf{m}}}_s, \tilde{\mathbf{x}}_s, \tilde{A}_s)$, $s = t+1, \ldots, t+T$, is feasible for Problem 1a conditionally upon $M_s = M(\mathbf{m}_s)$, it follows that $(\mathbf{m}_s, \tilde{\bar{\mathbf{m}}}_s, \tilde{\mathbf{x}}_s, \tilde{A}_s)$ is feasible for Problem 1; hence our assumption that $(\mathbf{m}_s, \bar{\mathbf{m}}_s, \mathbf{x}_s, A_s)$, $s = t, \ldots, t+T$, solves Problem 1 is contradicted. The analogous proof by contradiction applies to Problem 2a. □

Appendix B: Demand for Monetary Assets by Manufacturing Firms

B.1 The Model

Manufacturing firms also hold portfolios of monetary assets. The firm is assumed to maximize the expected present value of its profit flow subject to its technology. Although monetary services may enter the elementary decision only through constraints, there does exist a derived production function that contains monetary assets; see Barnett (1987) and Fischer (1974). We begin with that derived technology. The firm's intertemporal technology over the T-period planning horizon can be described by the transformation function

$$W(\boldsymbol{\delta}_t, \ldots, \boldsymbol{\delta}_{t+T}; \boldsymbol{\varepsilon}_t, \ldots, \boldsymbol{\varepsilon}_{t+T}; \boldsymbol{\kappa}_t, \ldots, \boldsymbol{\kappa}_{t+T}; \boldsymbol{\lambda}_t, \ldots, \boldsymbol{\lambda}_{t+T}) = 0,$$

where

$\boldsymbol{\delta}_s$ = vector of planned production of n outputs during period s;
$\boldsymbol{\varepsilon}_s$ = vector of planned real balances of k monetary assets held during period s;
$\boldsymbol{\kappa}_s$ = vector of planned use of $\bar{k}$ other factors during period s.

The transformation function W is assumed to be strictly quasiconvex in $\boldsymbol{\delta}_t, \ldots, \boldsymbol{\delta}_{t+T}; \boldsymbol{\varepsilon}_t, \ldots, \boldsymbol{\varepsilon}_{t+T}; \boldsymbol{\kappa}_t, \ldots, \boldsymbol{\kappa}_{t+T}$, increasing in $\boldsymbol{\delta}_s$, and decreasing in $\boldsymbol{\varepsilon}_s$ and in $\boldsymbol{\kappa}_s$. As indicated, we can incorporate $(\boldsymbol{\lambda}_t, \ldots, \boldsymbol{\lambda}_{t+T})$ as stochastic Markov shocks. As with the consumer, we assume that current interest rates and future prices are random.

The production possibility set of the firm is the closed random set

$$Y = \{(\boldsymbol{\delta}_t, \ldots, \boldsymbol{\delta}_{t+T}; \boldsymbol{\varepsilon}_t, \ldots, \boldsymbol{\varepsilon}_{t+T}; \boldsymbol{\kappa}_t, \ldots, \boldsymbol{\kappa}_{t+T}) \in \mathbf{Z} : \\ W(\boldsymbol{\delta}_t, \ldots, \boldsymbol{\delta}_{t+T}; \boldsymbol{\varepsilon}_t, \ldots, \boldsymbol{\varepsilon}_{t+T}; \boldsymbol{\kappa}_t, \ldots, \boldsymbol{\kappa}_{t+T}; \boldsymbol{\lambda}_t, \ldots, \boldsymbol{\lambda}_{t+T}) = 0\} \quad \text{(B.1)}$$

where Z is a compact subset of the $(n + k + \bar{k})T$-dimensional nonnegative orthant. The decision problem for the firm is to select the sequences of factor inputs and produced outputs over the planning horizon to maximize the expected present value of profits subject to the firm's technology constraint Y.

The firm's single-period profits during period s are

$$\psi_s = \delta'_s \nu_s - \kappa'_s \zeta_s + \sum_{i=1}^{k}[(1 + r_{i,s-1})p^*_{s-1}\varepsilon_{i,s-1} - p^*_s \varepsilon_{is}], \qquad (B.2)$$

where

$$\begin{aligned} \nu_s &= \text{vector of output prices, and} \\ \zeta_s &= \text{vector of prices of the factors } \kappa_s. \end{aligned}$$

The discounted present value of the firm's profit flow during the $T+1$ periods, plus the discounted present value of the firm's monetary asset portfolio at the end of the planning horizon, is

$$\psi^* = \sum_{s=t}^{t+T} \frac{\psi_s}{\theta_s} + \frac{1}{\theta_{t+T+1}} \sum_{i=1}^{k} p^*_{t+T}\varepsilon_{i,t+T}(1 + r_{i,t+T}),$$

where the discount factor $\theta_s = 1.0$ for $s = t$ and

$$\theta_s = \prod_{a=t}^{s-1}(1 + R_a) \quad \text{for} \quad t+1 \leq s \leq t+T+1$$

Hence the firm's decision problem is as follows.

Problem B1. Choose $(\delta_t, \ldots, \delta_{t+T}; \varepsilon_t, \ldots, \varepsilon_{t+T}; \kappa_t, \ldots, \kappa_{t+T})$ to maximize the expectation $E_t(\psi^*)$ subject to $(\delta_t, \ldots, \delta_{t+T}; \varepsilon_t, \ldots, \varepsilon_{t+T}; \kappa_t, \ldots, \kappa_{t+T}) \in Y$.

In this solution, $(\delta_t, \varepsilon_t, \kappa_t)$ are deterministic, since current purchases are binding. The firm's solution to (B.2) for optimized current profits also is deterministic, since it contains only lagged interest rates along with current and lagged prices, each of which is known with certainty during period t. However, the choices of $(\delta_{t+1}, \ldots, \delta_{t+T}; \varepsilon_{t+1}, \ldots, \varepsilon_{t+T}; \kappa_{t+1}, \ldots, \kappa_{t+T})$ are random. As a result, ψ_s for $s \geq t+1$ are random. We see that

$$E_t(\psi^*) = \psi_t + E_t \left[\sum_{s=t+1}^{t+T} \frac{\psi_s}{\theta_s} + \frac{1}{\theta_{t+T+1}} \sum_{i=1}^{k} p^*_{t+T}\varepsilon_{i,t+T}(1 + r_{i,t+T}) \right]. \qquad (B.3)$$

B.2 Existence of a Monetary Aggregate for the Firm

To assure the existence of a monetary aggregate for the firm, we partition the vector ε_s of monetary asset quantities so that $\varepsilon_s = (\varepsilon_{1s}, \bar{\varepsilon}_s)$, where ε_{1s} has k_1 elements and $\bar{\varepsilon}_s$ has $k_2 = k - k_1$ elements. We then assume that the transformation function W is blockwise weakly separable in ε_{1s}. Hence there exists a monetary aggregator function M^f and a transformation function W^* such that

$$W(\delta_t, \ldots, \delta_{t+T}; \varepsilon_t, \ldots, \varepsilon_{t+T}; \kappa_t, \ldots, \kappa_{t+T}; \lambda_t, \ldots, \lambda_{t+T})$$
$$= W^*(\delta_t, \ldots, \delta_{t+T}; M^f(\varepsilon_{1t}), \ldots, M^f(\varepsilon_{1,t+T});$$
$$\bar{\varepsilon}_t, \ldots, \bar{\varepsilon}_{t+T}; \kappa_t, \ldots, \kappa_{t+T}; \lambda_t, \ldots, \lambda_{t+T}). \quad (B.4)$$

It follows that the firm's exact monetary aggregate, measuring the service flow received by the firm from the monetary asset portfolio ε_{1s}, is

$$M_t^f = M^f(\varepsilon_{1s}). \quad (B.5)$$

Note that we assume only that there exists some partition, $\varepsilon_s = (\varepsilon_{1s}, \bar{\varepsilon}_s)$, such that (B.4) holds. Testing for which partition satisfies the weak separability assumption (B.4) is the subject of a growing literature.

As in the consumer case, the fact that equation (B.4) defines the monetary aggregate in the welfare sense is clear. By its definition, M_t^f is the productive service flow perceived to be received by the firm from the portfolio ε_{1s}. The following theorem demonstrates that M_t^f is the monetary aggregate in the aggregation-theoretic sense also — that is, in the sense of containing the information needed to permit conditional solution of the rest of the firm's decision problem.

Let $(\delta_t^*, \ldots, \delta_{t+T}^*; \varepsilon_t^*, \ldots, \varepsilon_{t+T}^*; \kappa_t^*, \ldots, \kappa_{t+T}^*)$ solve Problem B1, and let $M_s^{f*} = M^f(\varepsilon_{1s}^*)$. Define

$$Y'(M_t^{f*}, \ldots, M_{t+T}^{f*}) = \{(\delta_t, \ldots, \delta_{t+T}; \bar{\varepsilon}_t, \ldots, \bar{\varepsilon}_{t+T}; \kappa_t, \ldots, \kappa_{t+T}) \in \mathbf{Z}' :$$
$$W^*(\delta_t, \ldots, \delta_{t+T}; M_t^{f*}, \ldots, M_{t+T}^{f*}; \bar{\varepsilon}_t, \ldots, \bar{\varepsilon}_{t+T};$$
$$\kappa_t, \ldots, \kappa_{t+T}; \lambda_t, \ldots, \lambda_{t+T}) = 0\},$$

where Z' is the projection of Z onto the $(n + k_2 + \bar{k})T$-dimensional subspace having $(\delta_t, \ldots, \delta_{t+T}; \bar{\varepsilon}_t, \ldots, \bar{\varepsilon}_{t+T}; \kappa_t, \ldots, \kappa_{t+T})$ as components. Let

$$\bar{\psi}_s = \delta'_s \nu_s - \kappa'_s \zeta_s + \sum_{i=1}^{k_2} [(1 + r_{i,s-1}) p^*_{s-1} \bar{\varepsilon}_{i,s-1} - p^*_s \bar{\varepsilon}_{is}],$$

and let

$$\bar{\psi}^* = \sum_{s=t}^{t+T} \frac{\psi_s}{\theta_s} + \frac{1}{\theta_{t+T+1}} \sum_{i=1}^{k} p^*_{t+T} \bar{\varepsilon}_{i,t+T}(1 + r_{i,t+T}).$$

Consider the following decision problem, which is conditional upon knowledge of the stochastic process M_s^{f*} for $s = t, \ldots, t+T$.

Problem B2. Choose $(\delta_t, \ldots, \delta_{t+T}; \varepsilon_{2t}, \ldots, \varepsilon_{2,t+T}; \kappa_t, \ldots, \kappa_{t+T})$ to maximize the expectation $E_t(\bar{\psi}^*)$ subject to $(\delta_t, \ldots, \delta_{t+T}; \varepsilon_{2t}, \ldots, \varepsilon_{2,t+T}; \kappa_t, \ldots, \kappa_{t+T}) \in Y'(M_t^{f*}, \ldots, M_{t+T}^{f*})$.

Our aggregation theorem for the manufacturing firm can now be written as follows.

Theorem B1 (manufacturing firm's aggregation theorem). *Let the process* $(\delta_t, \ldots, \delta_{t+T}; \varepsilon_t, \ldots, \varepsilon_{t+T}; \kappa_t, \ldots, \kappa_{t+T})$ *solve Problem B1. Then* $(\delta_t, \ldots, \delta_{t+T}; \bar{\varepsilon}_t, \ldots, \bar{\varepsilon}_{t+T}; \kappa_t, \ldots, \kappa_{t+T})$ *solves Problem B2 conditional upon the process* $M_s^{f*} = M^f(\varepsilon_{1s})$ *given for* $s = t, \ldots, t+T$.

Proof: Let the process $(\delta_t, \ldots, \delta_{t+T}; \varepsilon_{1t}, \ldots, \varepsilon_{1,t+T}; \bar{\varepsilon}_t, \ldots, \bar{\varepsilon}_{t+T}; \kappa_t, \ldots, \kappa_{t+T})$ solve Problem B1; but let $(\delta_t, \ldots, \delta_{t+T}; \bar{\varepsilon}_t, \ldots, \bar{\varepsilon}_{t+T}; \kappa_t, \ldots, \kappa_{t+T})$ not solve Problem B2 conditional upon the given process $M_s^{f*} = M^f(\varepsilon_{1s})$ for $s = t, \ldots, t+T$. Then there exists $(\tilde{\delta}_t, \ldots, \tilde{\delta}_{t+T}; \tilde{\bar{\varepsilon}}_t, \ldots, \tilde{\bar{\varepsilon}}_{t+T}; \tilde{\kappa}_t, \ldots, \tilde{\kappa}_{t+T}) \in Y'(M_t^{f*}, \ldots, M_{t+T}^{f*})$ such that $E_t(\bar{\psi}^*)$ evaluated at $(\tilde{\delta}_t, \ldots, \tilde{\delta}_{t+T}; \tilde{\bar{\varepsilon}}_t, \ldots, \tilde{\bar{\varepsilon}}_{t+T}; \tilde{\kappa}_t, \ldots, \tilde{\kappa}_{t+T})$ is strictly greater than $E_t(\bar{\psi}^*)$ evaluated at $(\delta_t, \ldots, \delta_{t+T}; \bar{\varepsilon}_t, \ldots, \bar{\varepsilon}_{t+T}; \kappa_t, \ldots, \kappa_{t+T})$.

Hence $E_t(\psi^*)$ evaluated at $(\tilde{\delta}_t, \ldots, \tilde{\delta}_{t+T}; \varepsilon_{1t}, \ldots, \varepsilon_{1,t+T}; \tilde{\bar{\varepsilon}}_t, \ldots, \tilde{\bar{\varepsilon}}_{t+T}; \tilde{\kappa}_t, \ldots, \tilde{\kappa}_{t+T})$ is strictly greater than $E_t(\psi^*)$ evaluated at $(\delta_t, \ldots, \delta_{t+T}; \varepsilon_{1t}, \ldots, \varepsilon_{1,t+T}; \bar{\varepsilon}_t, \ldots, \bar{\varepsilon}_{t+T}; \kappa_t, \ldots, \kappa_{t+T})$. But since $(\tilde{\delta}_t, \ldots, \tilde{\delta}_{t+T}; \tilde{\bar{\varepsilon}}_t, \ldots, \tilde{\bar{\varepsilon}}_{t+T}; \tilde{\kappa}_t, \ldots, \tilde{\kappa}_{t+T})$ is feasible for Problem B2 conditional upon $M_s^{f*} = M^f(\varepsilon_{1s})$, it follows that $(\tilde{\delta}_t, \ldots, \tilde{\delta}_{t+T}; \varepsilon_{1t}, \ldots, \varepsilon_{1,t+T}; \tilde{\bar{\varepsilon}}_t, \ldots, \tilde{\bar{\varepsilon}}_{t+T}; \tilde{\kappa}_t, \ldots, \tilde{\kappa}_{t+T})$ is feasible for Problem B1. Thus our assumption that $(\delta_t, \ldots, \delta_{t+T}; \varepsilon_{1t}, \ldots, \varepsilon_{1,t+T}; \bar{\varepsilon}_t, \ldots, \bar{\varepsilon}_{t+T}; \kappa_t, \ldots, \kappa_{t+T})$ solves Problem B1 is contradicted, proving the theorem. □

Hence, as with the consumer, knowledge of the monetary aggregate M_s^{f*} process is sufficient for optimal solution for the remaining variables in the economic agent's decision. Knowedge of the component process ε_{1s} is not needed. The same cannot be said for the simple-sum aggregate over the components of ε_{1s} unless the aggregator function M_f happens to be a simple sum. In other words, the components of ε_{1s} must be indistinguishable perfect substitutes in order for the simple-sum aggregate to have information relevant to the firm's behavior in other markets.

Chapter 11

Monitoring Monetary Aggregates Under Risk Aversion

William A. Barnett, Melvin Hinich, and Piyu Yue[*]

1 Introduction

1.1 Objectives

This article advocates a particular view regarding modeling aggregation methodology. That view is perhaps best represented within the federal government by the activities of the research staff at the Bureau of Labor Statistics (BLS). Within academic research circles, the view is maintained by aggregation and index number theorists as well as by a growing number of microfoundations and rational expectations theorists. The intent of the approach is to assure that the construction of data and its use within models are all internally consistent with rational optimizing behavior by economic agents. We advocate the application of this modern approach to data construction, model specification, and model estimation in monetary economics.

Since the BLS has adhered to this approach both internally and externally for years, the approach perhaps is best described in terms of BLS practice. The BLS, like most other governmental agencies, regularly publishes data produced from statistical (i.e., nonparametric) index numbers. For example, the BLS publishes the well-known and very important Consumer Price Index (CPI), which is a Laspeyres price index. In fact, most price and quantity indexes produced in Washington are Laspeyres-Paasche dual pairs. By their definition, statistical index numbers, such as the CPI, are nonparametric, and their construction requires no econometric estimation. Statistical index numbers are functions only of measurable variables. But the exact quantity and price indexes of economic theory are parametric. For example, the aggregator function that produces the true cost of living index is the cost function. To use that aggregator directly, one must specify the cost function and estimate its parameters.

---

[*]Originally published in Michael T. Belongia (ed.), *Monetary Policy on the 75th Anniversary of the Federal Reserve System* (1991), 189-222. Proceedings of the 14th Annual conomic Policy Conference of the Federal Reserve Bank of St. Louis, Kluwer 1991, pp. 189-222.

Statistical index numbers, such as the Laspeyres and Paasche, are produced from approximation theorems to track the unknown aggregator function nonparametrically to within some specified order of approximation. For example, index numbers such as the Fisher Ideal or Törnqvist-Divisia are elements of Diewert's (1976) superlative class, defined to produce second order approximations to any unknown aggregator function. The Laspeyres and Paasche indexes are known to provide first order approximations. Rather than econometrically estimating the true cost of living index by specifying a cost function and estimating its parameters, the BLS publishes the CPI.

However, the research staff at the BLS is well aware of the second order remainder term in the CPI's Laspeyres approximation to the true cost of living index. That staff also is aware of the known upward bias in the Laspeyres index and the cumulative error produced by the failure to chain the index's weights continuously. Clearly some means are needed to assure that the convenient computation, interpretation, and use of the CPI statistical index number does not result in large errors relative to the underlying unknown true cost of living index. The BLS research staff historically has monitored this situation periodically by estimating the true cost of living index econometrically and publishing the resulting comparison between the CPI and the best available estimate of the true cost of living index. As new and more flexible specifications for the cost function become available and as improved econometric estimators become available, the BLS staff update its earlier research by adopting the latest methodology to estimate the true cost of living index.

This method is the best available one for walking the fine line between the convenience of statistical index numbers and the theoretical purity of estimated neoclassical aggregator functions. Even the third order remainder terms in superlative index numbers can become large, if the changes in component quantities or prices are large during a period. Only through the periodic estimation of the underlying aggregator function can the quality of a statistical index number be monitored. If the adequacy of the approximation is found to be deteriorating to an unacceptable degree, then the need arises for the adoption of a more sophisticated statistical index, or more frequent chaining, or more frequent collection of component data. To the end just described, there is a need for the existence of an economics research staff within data-generating government agencies to monitor the quality of the data and to publish papers containing estimated aggregator functions, so that the public can be kept informed of the prevailing quality of the available published statistical index numbers relative to the best available specification and estimation methodology.

We feel that the BLS over the years has admirably fulfilled this objective through the publications of its research staff in the Department of Labor's

Introduction

Monthly Labor Review and in various economics journals, such as the *Journal of Business and Economic Statistics*.[1] By doing so, the BLS has assured that data published by that agency not only adequately track the underlying economic aggregator functions but also are usable within economic models. Unless data track the relevant economic aggregator functions, the properties of the data are in conflict with the properties of the models within which they are used. An internal inconsistency arises.

In order for this method to be applied to monetary aggregation and to monetary modeling, there is a need for research in two related areas. One area is the specification and estimation of theoretical economic monetary aggregator functions. The other area is the derivation and computation of nonparametric monetary statistical index numbers. Ongoing research in the first area is needed to assure that monetary statistical index numbers being computed and published remain of adequate quality relative to the best available methods for specifying and estimating monetary aggregator functions. Observe that this is an ongoing process of continuous research, monitoring, and improvement. A procedure for adoption of this methodology within monetary economics was outlined by Barnett (1982a) and was used by Barnett (1980a, 1983a) in deriving and estimating monetary aggregator functions and in deriving and computing nonparametric monetary statistical index numbers, including both Divisia and Fisher Ideal monetary quantity and user cost index numbers. A large and growing empirical literature in monetary economics has been motivated by that approach. Much of that literature is surveyed in Barnett, Fisher, and Serletis (1992), and an especially interesting application recently was published by Belongia and Chalfant (1989). For a U.K. application, see Belongia and Chrystal (1991).

The state of the art in monetary aggregation and index number theory is synthesized in detail in Barnett (1987, 1990), both in terms of the demand for monetary services by consumers and manufacturing firms and the production of monetary services by financial intermediaries. However, the approach to the derivation and specification of aggregator functions in that article implicitly assumes either perfect certainty or risk neutrality, as is the case in virtually all of the literature on economic aggregation and index number theory. The needed theorems on duality, two-stage budgeting, and nonparametric approximation to aggregator functions do not yet exist to extend that literature to the case of risk aversion.[2] Poterba and Rotemberg (1987) have

---

[1] In fact, there recently has even been some research within the BLS on monetary aggregation. See, for example, Fixler (1988) and Fixler and Zieschang (1989a, 1989b, 1989c).

[2] While this was true at the time that this paper was originally published, the extension of index number theory to the case of risk aversion was subsequently accomplished by Barnett, Liu, and Jensen (1997) and further extended by Barnett and Xu (1998), which

demonstrated that estimation of theoretical economic monetary aggregator functions is presently possible under risk aversion.

1.2 Methodology

We therefore now advocate that the approach outlined by Barnett (1982a) be updated in the following manner to make use of the Poterba and Rotemberg extension:

1.2.1. Step 1 (Admissibility). As originally proposed by Barnett (1982a), the choice of component clusterings should be based upon testing for blockwise weak separability. But the testing should be conducted using models with intertemporal expected utility maximization or expected profit maximization, rather than utility or profit maximization. Such inference would have to be conducted from within Euler equations rather than from within money demand functions, since a closed form solution for demand functions typically is not available in the risk averse case. To our knowledge, no one has ever tested for weak separability from within Euler equations.[3] A literature on conducting such tests needs to be developed and then applied with monetary data.[4]

1.2.2. Step 2 (Approximation). Once admissible separable component groupings are acquired, the best available statistical index number should be applied to aggregate over those components. The resulting monetary aggregates should be made publicly available. At present, the best available index numbers are those within Diewert's class of superlative index numbers, with prices measured by user costs. However, the approximation theorems used to derive the remainder terms of those index numbers assume perfect certainty or risk neutrality. Nothing is known about the rate at which the quality of the approximation is degraded as the degree of risk aversion is increased.[5] Hence a literature needs to be produced on nonparametric approximations to

---

are reprinted in this book as chapters 12 and 13 respectively.

[3] While this was true at the time that this paper was originally published, tests for weak separability within Euler equations, based upon Hansen's test for overidentifying restrictions, were subsequently conducted by Barnett and Zhou (1994b) and Barnett, Kirova, and Pasupathy (1995), which are reprinted in this book as chapters 21 and 22 respectively.

[4] This is despite the fact that even in the perfect certainty case, testing for weak separability is very difficult. See Barnett and Choi (1989a, 1989b) for the results of a Monte Carlo study investigating the relative merits of various available weak separability tests in the perfect certainty case. For relevant theory, see Russell (1975) and Blackorby, Primont, and Russell (1977).

[5] While this was true at the time that this paper was originally published, experiments on that dependency were subsequently conducted by Barnett, Liu, and Jensen (1997), which is reprinted in this book as chapter 12.

Introduction

aggregator functions under risk aversion. This direction of research is certain to be challenging and slow to appear. But clearly research in that direction would produce major advances in this literature. In fact, the entire literature on duality and functional structure, surveyed by Blackorby, Primont, and Russell (1978), would benefit from extension to the case of risk aversion. Two initial theorems have been proven in this new research in Barnett, Hinich, and Yue (2000).

1.2.3. Step 3 (Monitoring). Ongoing research is needed on the comparison of the quality of the monetary index numbers produced from step 2 versus estimated economic aggregator functions. To this end, the most flexible available specifications for tastes and technology should be used along with the best available estimators of the parameters of the Euler equations. As in the case of the monitoring of the CPI by the BLS through estimation of the true cost of living index, step 3 is a continuous process which should advance by adoption of the best modeling and estimation methods, as they become available.[6] However, we advocate the use of the most recent developments in econometric estimation and modeling to permit this monitoring function to be conducted in a manner consistent with risk aversion by economic agents. As has been pointed out by Poterba and Rotemberg (1987) and as we shall see below, the fact that interest rates are paid at the end of periods renders risk aversion especially important in money demand modeling and monetary asset aggregation.

1.2.4. Step 4 (Application). For policy purposes, monetary aggregates are introduced into demand for money functions, which in turn are introduced into macroeconometric models, such as the Federal Reserve's quarterly model. Those models then are used to run simulations made available to the Open Market Committee and Federal Reserve Board members. The simulations contain information regarding the response of final policy targets to various hypothesized paths for policy instruments. The approach to monetary aggregation advocated by Barnett (1980a, 1982a) assures that the resulting aggregates would be internally consistent with the theory used to produce demand for money functions, when the demand for money functions are derived under the assumption of risk neutrality.

At present, all of the widely known macroeconometric models, such as the Federal Reserve's MPS (MIT-Penn-SSRC) model, use demand for money functions produced under the assumption of risk neutrality. Those models typically are versions of the linear Goldfeld demand for money function. The

---

[6]The need for monitoring increases as the Divisia variance increases. Hence monitoring the Divisia variance is useful for that purpose. See Barnett and Serletis (1990), which is reprinted in this book as chapter 9.

use of integrable demand for money function systems in this context was introduced by Barnett (1980a, 1983a) under risk neutrality. However, with the adoption of the modernized monitoring function in step 3, the generated aggregate data would be rendered consistent with risk aversion as well as integrability.

We therefore advocate that demand for money function modeling and estimation be conducted through the estimation of Euler equations under the assumption of risk aversion. Research is needed on the best means of introducing such estimated demand for money functions into macroeconometric models, given the difficulties in solving for demand for money functions in closed form in a rational expectations framework.

Although we shall maintain rational expectations in the research that follows, the four-step approach just outlined would be equally applicable under any other expectations formation hypothesis that is consistent with risk aversion.

1.3 A Moral of the Story

It is important to observe that each of the above four steps has its own appropriate purpose. Step 1 selects the clustering of components prior to aggregation. Step 2 produces the aggregation over the clustered components. Step 3 monitors the quality of the results from steps 1 and 2. Hence step 3 is relevant to the choice of method of aggregation, both in terms of the choice of clustering in step 1 and the choice of index number in step 2. In short, step 3 continually evaluates the results from steps 1 and 2. Step 4 assures that the data and their use are internally consistent and make the best use of available theoretical and econometric tools. If steps 1 and 2 produce aggregates at more than one level of aggregation, through acceptance of a recursively nested weakly separable blocking of components, such as M1, M2, M3, and so on, then the relative usefulness of the monetary aggregates at the different levels of aggregation in step 4 is relevant to the choice between those aggregates for any such use in step 4.

However, it is *very important* to observe that strict conformity with the principles just outlined would not permit step 4 to be used to evaluate different possible methods of aggregation over the same components, as, for example, simple sum versus Divisia aggregation over the components of M2. In valid statistical methodology, one is not permitted to select one's means of constructing data in a manner that considers its success in a possible application. Such a feedback from use to data construction method is among the most serious abuses of statistics. Unfortunately, that abuse is evident in many publications in monetary economics.

1.4 Illustration

Barnett, Hinich, and Yue (2000) illustrate the above four-step procedure by carrying out steps 2 and 3 with the monthly component data in Fayyad (1986). The economic theory on which that application is based is motivated by Poterba and Rotemberg (1987). In particular, Barnett, Hinich, and Yue (2000) estimated the economic aggregator function using generalized method of moments estimation and then used the resulting exact theoretical rational expectations monetary aggregate to monitor the tracking capabilities of two statistical index numbers — the simple sum and the Divisia — both in the time domain and in the frequency domain. We usually call the exact theoretical rational expectations aggregate simply the Theoretical aggregate.

In the frequency domain the approach used by Barnett, Hinich, and Yue (2000) to compare the dynamic properties of the three sets of aggregates is to test whether either of the statistical index numbers successfully extracts the nonlinearity from the path of the estimated theoretical aggregate. They conduct the comparisons at the M1 and M2 levels of aggregation. Although Barnett, Hinich, and Yue (2000) do not supply results relevant to step 4 in this article, results from cointegration tests between each monetary quantity index and Humphrey-Hawkins final targets are reported in Barnett and Serletis (1989).

In much of the following, we discuss the implications of the results in Barnett, Hinich, and Yue (2000).

2 Microfoundations for Consumer Demand for Money

2.1 Introduction

The model that Barnett, Hinich, and Yue (2000) estimate to acquire the exact theoretical rational expectations monetary aggregates is from Barnett and Yue (1989, 1991), which in turn is motivated by Poterba and Rotemberg (1987). The demand for money in Barnett and Yue's model is both by manufacturing firms and consumers. The supply of money is partially produced by financial intermediaries, which create the economy's inside money. Barnett and Yue model the stochastic decision problems of consumers, manufacturing firms, and financial intermediaries within a stochastic optimal control framework with Markov shocks to technology.[7] Barnett and Yue's model produces

---

[7]While the consumer model in the working papers by Barnett and Yue (1989, 1991) were absorbed into Barnett, Hinich,, and Yue (2000), the manufacturing firm and financial intermediary models in those working papers were absorbed into Barnett and Zhou (1994b).

a rational expectations equilibrium solution, which is recursive in the sense of Prescott and Mehra (1980). Using the first order conditions, Barnett and Yue prove the existence of a rational expectations equilibrium. Because of the model's recursive structure, the conditions for the use of Bellman's optimality principle are satisfied, and hence that principle is used in the solution procedure.

Barnett and Yue's model is functionally structured in a manner that produces the existence of an exact monetary aggregate for each economic agent.[8] In the current article, we provide results based only on the consumer's decision. In future research we plan similarly to operationalize Barnett and Yue's models of financial firms and of manufacturing firms to produce exact rational expectations aggregates for monetary services demanded by manufacturing firms and for monetary services supplied by financial intermediaries.

Unlike Barnett and Yue (1989), Poterba and Rotemberg (1987) did not model decisions by manufacturing firms or by financial intermediaries. Their paper contains only a consumer model, and they did not produce the implied monetary aggregate data. However, in the current article we also use only a consumer model, and our expected utility function is exactly the same as Poterba and Rotemberg's. We use the more explicit stochastic optimal control modeling and solution procedure applied by Barnett and Yue (1989) along with their more explicit assumption structure. However, the first order conditions (Euler equations) derived by Barnett and Yue reduce to those produced in another manner by Poterba and Rotemberg, when Poterba and Rotemberg's choice of utility function specification is applied. Hence the exact theoretical rational expectations aggregates produced below could equivalently be viewed as Poterba and Rotemberg's — or, at the very least, strongly motivated by their work.

Aside from the more explicit theorizing involved in our work, our approach differs from Poterba and Rotemberg's only in our use of Hansen and Singleton's (1982) full generalized method of moments (GMM) estimator with iteration to convergence on the weight matrix. Poterba and Rotemberg used three stage least squares, sometimes called the 'poor man's GMM estimator.' However, the literature on GMM estimation is still evolving. The modeling approaches used by us and by Poterba and Rotemberg are not inherently dependent upon any particular estimator. Any other researchers who may work in this area in the future surely will wish to use whatever may be the best available estimator at the time.

---

and Barnett, Kirova, and Pasupathy (1995), which are reprinted in this book as chapters 21 and 22 respectively.

[8]That is, the relevant blockwise weak separability conditions are satisfied.

2.2 The Shocks

In accordance with Barnett, Hinich, and Yue (2000), we assume that all stochastic shocks are Markovian. Hence, at each time period economic agents make decisions regarding current and subsequent actions, given the current state of the economy and relevant information about the future. The past contains no information about the future.

As in Barnett, Hinich, and Yue (2000), the uncertainty in the economy is produced by a random vector of shocks $\boldsymbol{\lambda}_t$. We assume that the vector of random shocks, $\boldsymbol{\lambda}_t$ follows a stationary Markov process with the bounded ergodic realization set Λ defined by

$$\Lambda = \{\boldsymbol{\lambda}_t \in R^K : P[\sup \|\boldsymbol{\lambda}_t\| \leq D] \geq \beta\},$$

where D is a finite number, P is probability measure, R^K is K-dimensional Euclidean space, $\|\cdot\|$ is the Euclidean norm, and β is a positive number less than one. Since $\boldsymbol{\lambda}_t$ follows a Markov process, the distribution of $\boldsymbol{\lambda}_t$ depends only upon the value of $\boldsymbol{\lambda}_{t-1}$. The dynamic properties of the random shocks are described by the transition function, $F(\boldsymbol{\lambda}_{t+1} \mid \boldsymbol{\lambda}_t)$, which is the conditional distribution of the random shocks. Since the shocks are stationary, the conditional distribution, F, is invariant to time, t. We assume that $F(\boldsymbol{\lambda}_{t+1} \mid \boldsymbol{\lambda}_t)$ is continuous in both of its arguments. As in Barnett, Hinich, and Yue (2000), the Markov stochastic shocks are assumed to be to technology, not to tastes. As a result, the shocks will not explicitly appear again in the following discussion, which will relate solely to consumer demand. However, the above assumptions have implications for the equilibrium stochastic behavior of the prices and interest rates that will be given to the consumer below.

2.3 Consumer Demand for Monetary Assets

In this section we describe the representative consumer's stochastic decision problem as formulated by Barnett, Hinich, and Yue (2000).[9] The consumer's decisions are made in discrete time over a finite planning horizon for the time intervals, $t, t+1, \ldots, s, \ldots, t+T$, where t is the current time period and $t+T$ is the terminal planning period. Hence the time interval s satisfies $s \in \{t, t+1, \ldots, t+T\}$. The variables used in defining the consumer's decision are as follows:

---

[9] In later research we plan to delete the representative consumer assumption and aggregate over consumers by weaker means. See Barnett (1981, appendix B1.2), Barnett (1987, section 9), and Barnett and Serletis (1990).

$\mathbf{x}_s = n$ dimensional vector of planned real consumption of goods and services during period s,

$\mathbf{p}_s = n$ dimensional vector of goods and services expected prices and of durable goods expected rental prices during period s,

$\mathbf{a}_s = k$ dimensional vector of planned real balances of monetary assets during period s,

$\boldsymbol{\rho}_s = k$ dimensional vector of expected nominal holding period yields of monetary assets,

$A_s = $ planned holdings of the benchmark asset during period s,

$R_s = $ the expected one-period holding yield on the benchmark asset during period s,

$L_s = $ planned labor supply during period s,

$w_s = $ the expected wage rate during period s,

$I_s = $ the sum of all other sources of income during period s,

$p_s^* = p_s^*(\mathbf{p}_s) = $ the true cost of living index.

Under the assumption of rational expectations, $F(\boldsymbol{\lambda}_{t+1} \mid \boldsymbol{\lambda}_t)$ is known to the consumer. Since current period interest rates are not paid until the end of the period, they may be contemporaneously unknown to the consumer. Barnett, Hinich, and Yue (2000) assume that the consumer maximizes the expected value of intertemporal utility subject to a sequence of flow of funds constraints (one for each period of the planning horizon). The benchmark asset A_s provides no services other than its yield R_s. As a result, the benchmark asset does not enter the consumer's intertemporal utility function except in the last instant of the planning horizon. The asset is held only as a means of accumulating wealth to endow the next planning horizons. The consumer's intertemporal utility function is

$$U = U(\mathbf{a}_t, \ldots, \mathbf{a}_s, \ldots, \mathbf{a}_{t+T}; L_t, \ldots, L_s, \ldots, L_{t+T};$$
$$\mathbf{x}_t, \ldots, \mathbf{x}_s, \ldots, \mathbf{x}_{t+T}; A_{t+T}),$$

where U is assumed to be intertemporally additively (strongly) separable, such that

$$\begin{aligned} U & = u(\mathbf{a}_t, L_t, \mathbf{x}_t) + \left(\frac{1}{1+\xi}\right) u(\mathbf{a}_{t+1}, L_{t+1}, \mathbf{x}_{t+1}) + \cdots \\ & \quad \cdots + \left(\frac{1}{1+\xi}\right)^{T-1} u(\mathbf{a}_{t+T-1}, L_{t+T-1}, \mathbf{x}_{t+T-1}) \\ & \quad + \left(\frac{1}{1+\xi}\right)^T u_T(\mathbf{a}_{t+T}, L_{t+T}, \mathbf{x}_{t+T}, A_{t+T}) \\ & = \sum_{s=t}^{t+T-1} \left(\frac{1}{1+\xi}\right)^{s-t} u(\mathbf{a}_s, L_s, \mathbf{x}_s) + \end{aligned}$$

$$\left(\frac{1}{1+\xi}\right)^T u_T(\mathbf{a}_{t+T}, L_{t+T}, \mathbf{x}_{t+T}, A_{t+T}), \tag{1}$$

and the consumer's subjective rate of time preference, ξ, is assumed to be constant.[10]

Given the price, wage, and interest rate processes, the consumer selects the deterministic point $(\mathbf{a}_t, L_t, \mathbf{x}_t, A_t)$ and the stochastic process $(\mathbf{a}_s, L_s, \mathbf{x}_s, A_s)$, $s = t+1, \ldots, t+T$ to maximize the expected value of U over the planning horizon, subject to the sequence of constraints.

2.4 Existence of a Monetary Aggregate for the Consumer

In order to assure the existence of a monetary aggregate for the consumer, Barnett, Hinich, and Yue (2000) partition the vector of monetary asset quantities, $\mathbf{a}_s$, such that $\mathbf{a}_s = (\mathbf{m}_s, \bar{\mathbf{m}}_s)$. They correspondingly partition the vector of interest rates of those assets, $\boldsymbol{\rho}_s$, such that $\boldsymbol{\rho}_s = (r_s, \bar{r}_s)$. They then assume that the utility function, u, is blockwise weakly separable in $\mathbf{m}_s$. Hence there exists a monetary aggregator ('category utility') function, M, and a utility function, u^*, such that

$$u(\mathbf{a}_s, L_s, \mathbf{x}_s) = u^*(M(\mathbf{m}_s), \bar{\mathbf{m}}_s, L_s, \mathbf{x}_s), \tag{2}$$

where u is the current period category utility function within the separable function U. Then it follows that the exact monetary aggregate, measuring the welfare acquired from consuming the services of $\mathbf{m}_s$, is

$$M_s = M(\mathbf{m}_s). \tag{3}$$

Note that Barnett, Hinich, and Yue (2000) assume only that there exists a partition, $\mathbf{a}_s = (\mathbf{m}_s, \bar{\mathbf{m}}_s)$, such that equation (2) holds. Testing for which partition satisfies the weak separability assumption (2) is the role of step 1 (Admissibility) in our advocated methodological approach. We define the dimension of $\mathbf{m}_s$ to be k_1, and the dimension of $\bar{\mathbf{m}}_s$ to be k_2, so that $k = k_1 + k_2$.

It is clear that equation (3) does define the exact monetary aggregate in the welfare sense, since M_s measures the consumer's subjective evaluation of the services that he receives from holding $\mathbf{m}_s$. However Barnett (1995) and Barnett, Liu, and Jensen (1997, appendix), which are reprinted as chapters

---

[10] Although money may not exist in the elementary utility function, there exists a derived utility function that contains money, so long as money has positive value in equilibrium. See, for example, Arrow and Hahn (1971), Phlips and Spinnewyn (1982), and Feenstra (1986). We implicitly are using that derived utility function.

10 and 12 of this book, respectively, also show that equation (3) defines the exact monetary aggregate in the aggregation theoretic sense.

Using Bellman's principle Barnett and Yue (2000) derived the first order conditions for solving problems 1 and 2.[11] Under the more restrictive conditions assumed by Poterba and Rotemberg (1987), the first order conditions derived by Barnett and Yue reduce to those acquired by Poterba and Rotemberg without the use of Bellman's method. Hence for their model, their Euler equations are confirmed.

3 The Risk Neutral Case

Under risk neutrality, the decision of each of the agents modeled in this section can be solved in two stages. In the first stage, expenditure is budgeted to aggregates. In the second stage, the budgeted expenditure on each aggregate is allocated over its components. For details of the two stage budgeting solutions, see Barnett (1987). For our purposes, only the contemporaneous second stage decision is relevant. For each of our economic agents, the contemporaneous second stage decision is to maximize the current period service flow produced from the components of the aggregate subject to the budgeted constraint on current period expenditure on those components. The service flow objective function is the agent's separable aggregator function over the components. Since that second stage decision has the same form for the various economic agents, (aside from a change in notation for variables and functions), we present the second stage decision only for one economic agent, the consumer.

In the perfect certainty case, Barnett (1978, 1980a) proved that the nominal user cost of the services of m_{it} is π_{it}, where

$$\pi_{it} = p_t^* \frac{R_t - r_{it}}{1 + R_t}. \tag{4}$$

The corresponding real user cost is π_{it}/p^*. In the risk neutral case, the user cost formulas are the same as in the perfect certainty case, but with the interest rates replaced by their expected values. The second stage decision is to choose $\mathbf{m}_t \geq 0$ to maximize $M(\mathbf{m}_t)$ subject to $\mathbf{m}_t' \pi_t = E_t$ where E_t is total expenditure budgeted to $\mathbf{m}_t$ in the first stage.

It can be shown that the solution value of the exact monetary aggregate $M_t = M(\mathbf{m}_t)$ can be tracked without error (see, e.g., Barnett (1983b)) by

---

[11]The derivation was reproduced in Barnett (1995), which is reprinted as chapter 10 of this book. Also see equation 4a in Barnett, Liu, and Jensen (1997), which is reprinted as chapter 12 of this book.

The Risk Neutral Case

the Divisia index:[12]

$$d\log M_t = \sum_{i=1}^{k_1} s_{it} d\log m_{it}, \qquad (5)$$

where the expenditure share of monetary asset i is $s_{it} = m_{it}\pi_{it}/E_t$. The flawless tracking ability of the index in the risk neutral case holds regardless of the form of the unknown aggregator function, M. However, under risk aversion the ability of equation (5) to track $M(\mathbf{m}_t)$ is compromised, and the rate at which that tracking ability deteriorates is unknown, as the degree of risk aversion increases above zero. Barnett, Hinich, and Yue (2000) investigate the magnitude of that error by econometrically estimating $M(\mathbf{m}_t)$.

It should be observed that the monetary aggregate $M(\mathbf{m}_t)$ measures the flow of monetary services rather than the stock of monetary wealth. However, one can acquire the stock of monetary wealth by discounting to present value the monetary service flow expenditure stream. First observe that by Fisher's factor reversal test, we know that there must exist a user cost aggregate $\Pi(\boldsymbol{\pi}_t)$ dual to $M(\mathbf{m}_t)$ such that $M(\mathbf{m}_t)\Pi(\boldsymbol{\pi}_t) = \mathbf{m}'_t \boldsymbol{\pi}_t$. Hence expenditure on aggregate services $M(\mathbf{m}_t)$ must equal the sum of the user-cost evaluated expenditures on the components $\mathbf{m}_t$. As a result, we can derive monetary wealth by discounting to present value either the expenditure flow $\mathbf{m}'_s \boldsymbol{\pi}_s$ or the equal expenditure flow $M(\mathbf{m}_s)\Pi(\boldsymbol{\pi}_s)$ for $s \geq t$.

Barnett (1991, reprinted as chapter 14 in this book) has derived that monetary capital stock by discounting to present value expenditure on the component flows $\mathbf{m}'_s \boldsymbol{\pi}_s$ for $s \geq t$. The resulting formula for the monetary stock, V_t, is:

$$V_t = \sum_{s=t}^{\infty} \sum_{i=1}^{n} \left[\frac{p_s^*}{\rho_s} - \frac{p_s^*(1+r_{is})}{\rho_s+1} \right] m_{is}. \qquad (6)$$

The discount factors in that formula are:

$$\rho_s = \begin{cases} 1 & \text{for } s = t \\ \prod_{u=t}^{s-1}(1+R_u) & \text{for } s > t. \end{cases}$$

In economics, variables in the structure of the economy usually are flows. The exceptions are the wealth variables that enter through intertemporal Fisherine wealth constraints, as appear on the right-hand-side of life-cycle consumption functions and in the monetary transmission mechanism, when it operates through a Pigou or real balance effect within the consumption function. In such cases, equation (6) can be used to measure monetary wealth

---

[12] In discrete time, the index's Törnqvist approximation is used by replacing s_{it} by its average s_{it}^* over the discrete time interval, where $s_{it}^* = (1/2)(s_{it}+s_{i,t-1})$, and by replacing the differential log changes by discrete log changes.

conditionally upon assumptions regarding expectations formation. In principle one could use econometric methods to incorporate adaptive expectations or rational expectations into (6).

It would clearly be more convenient to have a nonparametric statistical means of computing (6) without the need to use parametric econometric estimators. But at present there are only two available nonparametric statistical means of computing (6).

1. One is to assume stationary expectations, so that $R_s = R_t$ and $r_s = r_t$ for all $s \geq t$. The result is the measure proposed by Rotemberg (1991). See Barnett (1991, reprinted as chapter 14 in this book) for the proof that Rotemberg's money stock measure is correct under stationary expectations.

2. The other nonparametric method results from the implicit assumption made by the Federal Reserve in the production of its monetary aggregates: $r_s = 0$ for all $s \geq t$. Rotemberg's implicit assumption obviously is the one to be preferred. The days of noninterest-bearing money are long gone.

See Barnett (1991) for more discussion of money stock measures. In the general case of risk aversion and rational expectations, measurement of the economic stock of money is a complex capital asset pricing problem (see Merton, 1990).

4 Data and Specification

As in Barnett, Hinich, and Yue (2000), we first set $\mathbf{m}_s$ equal to those components of M1 found by Belongia and Chalfant (1989) to be weakly separable. We then repeat our analysis with $\mathbf{m}_s$ set equal to the components of M2, but with those components clustered into three groups with prior aggregation within groups, so that $\mathbf{m}_s$ contains three aggregated elements. Hence we implicitly assume that $\mathbf{a}_s$ is partitioned in accordance with a recursively nested two level separable blocking, such that the components of our M1 aggregate are separable within the components of our M2 aggregate, which in turn are separable within $\mathbf{a}_s$. Considering the little that is known about testing for separability in the risk averse case, the chosen clustering is hardly the last word on that subject. In short, we are not here seeking to advance the state of the art in step 1 Admissibility Testing, which nevertheless is an important part of proper aggregation.

Barnett, Hinich, and Yue (2000) assume that the monetary aggregator function, $M(\mathbf{m}_s)$, has the CES (constant elasticity of substitution) form, which then is nested into a Cobb-Douglas function of money and goods.[13] That utility tree then is embedded in an expected utility function having constant degree of relative risk aversion.

5 Estimation

Barnett, Hinich, and Yue (2000) use Hansen and Singleton's (1982) generalized method of moments estimator to estimate the parameters of the Euler equations. Poterba and Rotemberg used three-stage least squares. In accordance with Hansen and Singleton's estimator, the weighting matrix is iterated on until convergence.

TABLE 1
M2 COMPONENTS OF MONETARY ASSETS

Component	Mnemonic	Asset Description
1	CUR	currency and traveler checks
2	DDCON	demand deposits held by households
3	DDBUS	demand deposits held by business firms
4	OCD	other checkable deposits less Super NOW accounts
5	SNOWC	Super NOW accounts at commercial banks
6	SNOWT	Super NOW accounts at thrifts
7	ONRP	overnight repurchase agreements
8	ONED	overnight Eurodollars
9	MMMF	money market mutual fund shares
10	MMDAC	money market demand deposit accounts at commercial banks
11	MMDAT	money market demand deposit accounts at thrifts
12	SDCB	savings deposits at commercial banks less MMDAs
13	SDSL	savings deposits at savings and loans less MMDAs
14	SDMSB	savings deposits at mutual savings banks less MMDAs
15	SDCU	savings deposits at credit unions less MMDAs
16	STDCB	small-time deposits and retail repurchase agreements at commercial banks
17	STDTH	small-time deposits and retail repurchase agreements at thrifts
18	STDCU	small-time deposits at credit unions

Using the parameter estimates and the components data, the estimated theoretical M1 monetary aggregate, $M_S = M(\mathbf{m}_s)$, was computed at each observation. The Divisia quantity index and the simple sum index over the

---

[13]In later research, we plan to extend the model to the case of AIM preferences and technology, in accordance with Barnett, Geweke, and Wolfe (1989) and Barnett, Geweke, and Yue (1989).

same components also were computed. The resulting nominal per capita time paths of these three M1 index numbers are supplied in Table 2.

This procedure then was repeated with the M2 data. The components of M2 were clustered into three groups, and asset quantities within groups were aggregated by simple summation to produce three aggregated components over which we aggregate by the three methods. To identify the prior clustering of components, we list the components of M2 in Table 1. The definition of the three aggregated monetary components, in terms of the numbered lines in Table 1, is:

$m_{1s} = (1)+(2)+(3)+(4)$ (real per capita during time period s),

$m_{2s} = (5)+(6)+(7)+(8)+(9)+(10)+(11)+(12)+(13)+(14)+(15)$
(real per capita during the time period s)

$m_{3s} = (16)+(17)+(18)$ (real per capita during time period s).

Using these parameter estimates and the component data, the estimated theoretical M2 monetary aggregate, $M_s = M(\mathbf{m}_s)$, was computed at each observation. The Divisia quantity index and the simple sum index over the same components also were computed. The nominal per capita time paths of these three M2 index numbers are supplied in Table 2. See Barnett, Hinich, and Yue (2000) for the resulting parameter estimates and for the plots of the resulting estimated Theoretical aggregates.[14] Central to the analysis of their data is the Hinich bispectrum test for nonlinearity. That test was used by Barnett, Hinich, and Yue (2000) to determine whether either of the statistical monetary indices (simple sum or Divisia) successfully extracts the nonlinear structure from the estimated Theoretical aggregate.

The Hinich test is a powerful and very general method for testing for nonlinear structure in a time series, and hence can be useful for comparing the dynamic structures of any two time series. As a result, we present the relevant theory required for the use of the Hinich test in the Appendix. We present the background and methodology in a self-contained form to make the use of the test available to others in any relevant applications. For a related survey and application of methods of testing for chaos (a form of deep nonlinearity), see Barnett and Chen (1988).

---

[14] One of those plots also appears in Barnett, Kirova, and Pasupathy (1995), which is reprinted in this book as chapter 22. In that chapter, see figure 3.

TABLE 2
MONTHLY GROWTH RATES OF NOMINAL MONETARY AGGREGATE INDICES OF M1 AND M2 (PERCENT PER MONTH, PER CAPITA, NOT ANNUALIZED)

Year	Month	$M1_{THEO}$	$M1_{SS}$	$M1_{DIV}$	$M2_{THEO}$	$M2_{SS}$	$M2_{DIV}$
1969	2	0.29	0.27	0.30	0.32	0.36	0.33
1969	3	0.25	0.27	0.25	0.11	0.16	0.15
1969	4	0.03	−0.03	0.02	0.00	0.06	0.03
1969	5	0.21	0.14	0.20	0.21	0.25	0.23
1969	6	0.14	0.10	0.14	−0.03	0.08	0.30
1969	7	0.02	−0.05	0.02	−0.09	0.01	−0.02
1969	8	0.11	0.07	0.11	0.16	0.24	0.21
1969	9	0.32	0.28	0.32	0.09	0.13	0.13
1969	10	0.28	0.23	0.28	0.48	0.56	0.53
1969	11	0.09	0.05	0.09	0.28	0.39	0.35
1969	12	0.98	1.05	0.97	0.22	0.10	0.16
1970	2	0.32	0.31	0.33	−0.04	0.07	0.01
1970	3	0.30	0.31	0.30	0.06	0.18	0.12
1970	4	0.25	0.17	0.26	0.22	0.40	0.31
1970	5	0.13	0.06	0.13	0.27	0.43	0.35
1970	6	0.14	0.09	0.15	0.30	0.44	0.37
1970	7	0.76	0.82	0.75	0.74	0.82	0.79
1970	8	0.74	0.79	0.74	0.87	0.93	0.90
1970	9	0.32	0.32	0.32	0.65	0.73	0.68
1970	10	0.31	0.30	0.31	0.53	0.65	0.58
1970	11	0.31	0.27	0.31	0.72	0.83	0.73
1970	12	0.38	0.36	0.37	0.66	0.85	0.73
1970	1	−0.50	−0.62	−0.49	−0.76	−0.56	−0.64
1971	1	0.79	0.82	0.80	1.04	1.21	1.31
1971	2	0.53	0.56	0.54	1.11	1.28	1.10
1971	3	0.44	0.42	0.43	1.19	1.41	1.17
1971	4	0.77	0.84	0.80	1.04	1.12	1.06
1971	5	0.59	0.56	0.58	0.70	0.75	0.70
1971	6	0.56	0.50	0.54	0.76	0.86	0.78
1971	7	0.29	0.25	0.28	0.63	0.79	0.67
1971	8	0.31	0.28	0.30	0.74	0.90	0.77
1971	9	0.15	0.13	0.14	0.62	0.75	0.62
1971	10	0.21	0.21	0.21	0.64	0.83	0.68
1971	11	0.17	0.16	0.17	0.61	0.73	0.60
1971	12	0.64	0.65	0.64	0.74	0.90	0.82
1972	1	0.84	0.91	0.87	0.96	1.07	1.02
1972	2	0.74	0.79	0.77	0.95	1.00	0.94
1972	3	0.34	0.38	0.36	0.67	0.73	0.65
1972	4	0.18	0.11	0.15	0.42	0.55	0.44
1972	5	0.28	0.25	0.27	0.65	0.76	0.64
1972	6	0.71	0.76	0.73	1.05	1.20	1.09
1972	7	0.83	0.86	0.84	1.03	1.15	1.07
1972	8	0.82	0.83	0.82	0.96	1.08	1.01
1972	9	0.64	0.62	0.63	0.89	1.01	0.90
1972	10	0.56	0.52	0.55	0.73	0.82	0.74
1972	11	1.01	1.06	1.02	0.98	0.99	1.00
1972	12	0.84	0.87	0.84	0.81	0.99	0.90

TABLE 2 cont'd

Year	Month	$M1_{THEO}$	$M1_{SS}$	$M1_{DIV}$	$M2_{THEO}$	$M2_{SS}$	$M2_{DIV}$
1973	1	0.21	0.16	0.20	0.30	0.43	0.34
1973	2	−0.15	−0.27	−0.17	0.03	0.06	0.01
1973	3	0.39	0.30	0.39	0.44	0.52	0.45
1973	4	0.76	0.80	0.76	0.72	0.78	0.74
1973	5	0.71	0.69	0.71	0.71	0.73	0.71
1973	6	0.18	0.17	0.19	0.33	0.38	0.33
1973	7	0.12	0.05	0.13	0.02	0.20	−0.03
1973	8	0.06	−0.05	0.07	−0.04	0.02	−0.07
1973	9	0.31	0.30	0.32	0.36	0.37	0.36
1973	10	0.71	0.72	0.70	0.56	0.64	0.47
1973	11	0.68	0.64	0.68	0.64	0.69	0.60
1973	12	0.39	0.33	0.39	0.32	0.47	0.19
1974	1	0.52	0.45	0.53	0.40	0.48	0.31
1974	2	0.53	0.48	0.54	0.62	0.65	0.62
1974	3	0.14	0.04	0.16	0.21	0.24	0.22
1974	4	0.22	0.13	0.24	0.17	0.19	0.16
1974	5	0.33	0.30	0.34	0.31	0.29	0.32
1974	6	0.20	0.17	0.20	0.28	0.31	0.29
1974	7	0.33	0.21	0.33	0.16	0.23	0.16
1974	8	0.34	0.29	0.35	0.29	0.36	0.31
1974	9	0.40	0.32	0.41	0.43	0.46	0.44
1974	10	0.53	0.46	0.54	0.50	0.51	0.51
1974	11	0.17	0.10	0.18	0.27	0.26	0.28
1974	12	−0.09	−0.21	−0.09	0.19	0.36	0.22
1975	1	0.27	0.22	0.26	0.67	0.79	0.69
1975	2	0.66	0.63	0.65	1.11	1.16	1.10
1975	3	−0.26	−0.30	−0.28	0.80	0.01	0.82
1975	4	0.95	0.03	0.94	1.24	1.30	1.25
1975	5	1.25	1.25	1.25	1.46	1.46	1.43
1975	6	0.13	0.07	0.11	0.89	1.13	0.95
1975	7	0.48	0.44	0.47	0.64	0.76	0.69
1975	8	0.19	0.20	0.19	0.66	0.78	0.69
1975	9	−0.14	−0.28	−0.18	0.37	0.53	0.41
1975	10	0.84	0.84	0.84	0.90	0.93	0.91
1975	11	−0.12	−0.22	−0.16	0.55	0.74	0.60
1975	12	0.38	0.32	0.36	0.82	0.99	0.88
1976	1	0.72	0.70	0.71	1.25	1.26	1.19
1976	2	0.40	0.33	0.37	0.86	0.80	0.76
1976	3	0.59	0.51	0.56	1.00	1.02	0.95
1976	4	0.61	0.56	0.59	1.09	1.21	1.10
1976	5	−0.07	−0.16	−0.10	0.21	0.31	0.23
1976	6	0.28	0.21	0.26	0.65	0.77	0.68
1976	7	0.52	0.52	0.52	0.99	1.11	1.01
1976	8	0.14	0.06	0.11	0.75	0.97	0.79
1976	9	0.92	0.95	0.93	1.21	1.27	1.21
1976	10	0.10	0.07	0.09	0.88	1.03	0.85
1976	11	0.78	0.81	0.79	1.19	1.24	1.17
1976	12	0.78	0.77	0.78	0.94	1.08	0.99

Estimation

TABLE 2 cont'd

Year	Month	$M1_{\text{THEO}}$	$M1_{\text{SS}}$	$M1_{\text{DIV}}$	$M2_{\text{THEO}}$	$M2_{\text{SS}}$	$M2_{\text{DIV}}$
1977	1	0.67	0.67	0.67	0.83	0.88	0.83
1977	2	0.52	0.52	0.52	0.84	0.86	0.81
1977	3	0.76	0.73	0.75	0.87	0.90	0.87
1977	4	0.13	0.08	0.11	0.64	0.79	0.63
1977	5	0.44	0.41	0.43	0.55	0.62	0.57
1977	6	0.66	0.60	0.64	0.74	0.79	0.75
1977	7	0.36	0.36	0.36	0.55	0.60	0.55
1977	8	0.59	0.55	0.58	0.64	0.69	0.65
1977	9	0.78	0.78	0.78	0.68	0.67	0.69
1977	10	0.43	0.40	0.42	0.52	0.57	0.52
1977	11	0.60	0.54	0.59	0.56	0.59	0.57
1977	12	0.85	0.91	0.86	0.62	0.66	0.65
1978	1	0.21	0.11	0.21	0.27	0.33	0.27
1978	2	0.42	0.37	0.41	0.52	0.48	0.50
1978	3	0.83	0.85	0.83	0.60	0.54	0.61
1978	4	0.84	0.87	0.84	0.63	0.61	0.65
1978	5	0.60	0.57	0.61	0.40	0.48	0.42
1978	6	0.43	0.41	0.43	0.36	0.54	0.35
1978	7	0.40	0.38	0.41	0.33	0.45	0.31
1978	8	0.98	0.98	0.98	0.77	0.87	0.72
1978	9	0.21	0.12	1.23	0.37	0.57	0.25
1978	10	0.13	0.03	0.16	0.20	0.44	−0.01
1978	11	0.23	0.12	0.26	0.42	0.63	0.20
1978	12	−0.38	−0.53	−0.33	−0.06	0.36	−0.46
1979	1	0.10	0.01	0.14	0.18	0.40	−0.09
1979	2	0.43	0.39	0.44	0.58	0.64	0.49
1979	3	1.00	1.04	0.98	0.79	0.85	0.64
1979	4	−0.13	−0.23	−0.08	0.29	0.48	0.12
1979	5	1.04	1.08	1.03	0.99	0.94	0.99
1979	6	0.71	0.72	0.70	0.75	0.74	0.75
1979	7	0.48	0.41	0.51	0.48	0.55	0.40
1979	8	0.45	0.38	0.48	0.50	0.69	0.36
1979	9	0.11	0.03	0.15	−0.08	0.27	−0.38
1979	10	0.03	−0.01	0.05	−0.38	0.10	−0.88
1979	11	0.16	0.12	0.18	0.24	0.41	0.06
1979	12	0.53	0.48	0.56	0.40	0.56	0.21
1980	1	0.85	0.87	0.85	0.68	0.79	0.54
1980	2	−0.18	−0.30	−0.11	−0.01	0.31	−0.29
1980	3	−1.58	−1.85	−1.45	−1.18	−0.42	−1.72
1980	4	−0.04	−0.16	−0.01	0.32	0.55	0.24
1980	5	0.93	0.97	0.93	1.55	1.20	1.61
1980	6	0.71	0.70	0.71	1.60	1.23	1.63
1980	7	1.54	1.62	1.54	1.35	0.95	1.35
1980	8	0.88	0.96	0.87	0.94	0.82	0.95
1980	9	0.80	0.78	0.80	0.68	0.69	0.64
1980	10	0.17	0.02	0.24	0.41	0.74	0.15
1980	11	−1.04	−1.27	−0.92	−0.66	0.00	−1.06
1980	12	−3.09	−3.57	−2.84	−0.01	0.49	−0.42
1981	1	−1.43	−1.76	−1.21	0.53	0.66	0.41
1981	2	−0.29	−0.42	−0.19	1.14	0.99	1.29
1981	3	0.25	0.17	0.31	1.45	1.11	1.73

TABLE 2 cont'd

Year	Month	$M1_{THEO}$	$M1_{SS}$	$M1_{DIV}$	$M2_{THEO}$	$M2_{SS}$	$M2_{DIV}$
1981	4	−0.65	−0.80	−0.52	0.05	0.30	−0.06
1981	5	−0.48	−0.56	−0.41	0.27	0.46	0.21
1981	6	0.02	−0.07	0.10	0.70	0.61	0.77
1981	7	0.15	0.13	0.17	0.72	0.86	0.64
1981	8	−0.49	−0.56	−0.41	0.33	0.56	0.13
1981	9	−0.04	−0.09	0.01	0.43	0.70	0.09
1981	10	0.18	0.12	0.22	0.92	0.90	0.96
1981	11	0.42	0.34	0.46	1.06	0.89	1.18
1981	12	0.78	0.83	0.76	1.25	1.00	1.36
1982	1	−0.64	−0.80	−0.53	−0.15	0.10	−0.30
1982	2	−0.21	−0.30	−0.15	0.40	0.48	0.37
1982	3	0.28	0.19	0.35	0.53	0.52	0.53
1982	4	0.16	0.05	0.24	0.47	0.60	0.43
1982	5	−0.07	−0.15	−0.01	0.47	0.52	0.47
1982	6	−0.09	−0.17	−0.03	0.43	0.60	0.39
1982	7	0.53	0.53	0.53	1.05	0.93	1.06
1982	8	0.57	0.58	0.57	0.91	0.79	0.89
1982	9	0.83	0.83	0.83	1.05	0.65	0.95
1982	10	0.52	0.56	0.51	0.97	0.68	0.88
1982	11	0.39	0.35	0.41	1.28	0.72	1.00
1982	12	0.04	−0.02	0.05	3.90	2.71	2.84
1983	1	0.41	0.31	0.43	2.54	1.76	1.78
1983	2	0.72	0.68	0.74	1.27	0.75	0.94
1983	3	0.29	0.21	0.32	0.81	0.63	0.70
1983	4	0.86	0.87	0.85	0.93	0.70	0.86
1983	5	0.55	0.55	0.56	0.68	0.60	0.66
1983	6	0.49	0.47	0.50	0.45	0.53	0.47
1983	7	0.28	0.25	0.29	0.30	0.43	0.31
1983	8	0.21	0.12	0.27	0.37	0.53	0.38
1983	9	0.41	0.33	0.45	0.63	0.80	0.63
1983	10	0.20	0.12	0.25	0.38	0.56	0.39
1983	11	0.26	0.20	0.30	0.34	0.42	0.34
1983	12	0.33	0.31	0.35	0.46	0.54	0.47
1984	1	0.44	0.42	0.45	0.59	0.59	0.58
1984	2	0.33	0.29	0.37	0.54	0.48	0.53
1984	3	0.29	0.26	0.32	0.47	0.47	0.46
1984	4	0.23	0.21	0.25	0.48	0.56	0.49
1984	5	0.94	0.95	0.93	0.48	0.55	0.50
1984	6	−0.21	−0.28	−0.15	0.13	0.40	0.14
1984	7	0.12	0.06	0.17	0.19	0.46	0.17
1984	8	0.23	0.21	0.25	0.38	0.58	0.34
1984	9	−0.71	−0.80	−0.62	0.12	0.36	0.06
1984	10	0.69	0.71	0.67	1.12	1.08	1.10
1984	11	0.61	0.62	0.60	1.08	1.02	1.05
1984	12	0.09	0.09	0.10	1.17	1.08	1.09
1985	1	0.89	0.91	0.89	1.09	0.85	1.01
1985	2	0.24	0.21	0.26	0.42	0.28	0.38

THEO — Growth rate of estimated theoretic index.
SS — Growth rate of simple sum index.
DIV — Growth rate of Divisia index.

6 Results

Barnett, Hinich, and Yue (2000) found at both the M1 and M2 levels of aggregation that the Divisia monetary aggregate tracks the estimated Theoretical aggregate well, while the simple sum aggregate does not. The few exceptional cases were during periods of unusually high economic uncertainty within the economy, so that the Theoretical index's ability to incorporate risk aversion became particularly important.[15] In general, the risk neutrality assumption implied by the Divisia index was found to be an adequate approximation for purposes of monetary aggregation. Their conclusions were largely based upon comparisons of the plots of the series tabulated in Table 2 of this article.[16]

7 Another Example

In this article we have emphasized one application of monitoring in monetary economics. However, it should be observed that another exists. Since monitoring is by definition a means of verifying robustness of the tracking ability of an index to variations in the underlying economic model's specification, the monitoring role can be applied to check robustness to any aspect of that specification. Barnett, Hinich, and Weber (1986) have checked for robustness to the rate of taxation on interest. In particular, they observed that many financial intermediaries are subject to required reserves, which pay no interest. The result is an implicit tax on financial intermediaries. That tax is seen on the supply side of money markets, since financial intermediaries supply monetary services. However, that implicit tax is not seen on the demand side of money markets by the consumers and firms that demand monetary services.

As a result of this regulatory wedge, the user cost of produced monetary services by financial intermediaries is not equal to the user cost of demanded monetary services. The reason is that the interest rates that appear in the user cost formula, (4), are holding period yields and hence are after-tax yields. Hence the supply side Divisia index may be different from the demand side Divisia index. This conclusion should not be viewed as a defect of the Divisia index, since the exact economic aggregate produces the same paradox. Even if all component markets are cleared, the exact demand side aggregate may not be equal to the exact supply side aggregate, when a regulatory wedge exists. See Barnett, Hinich, and Weber (1986, Figure 2) for a demonstration of that fact in terms of exact economic aggregator functions in economic equilibrium.

---

[15] In particular, uncertainty was high immediately following the three years of the "monetarist experiment" in the United States (October 1979-October 1982).

[16] For one of those plots, see figure 3 in chapter 22 of this book.

In effect, when a regulatory wedge exists, the suppliers of services believe that the total quantity of services that they are producing is different from the quantity of services that demanders perceive themselves to be receiving. As a result, the demand side and supply side aggregates *should not* be equal.

Although it is perhaps comforting to know that the difference between the demand side and supply side Divisia index is no error, in practice we usually must choose between the demand and supply side aggregate, since joint use of both defeats the informational simplification that is the primary justification for the use of aggregates. As a result, Barnett, Hinich, and Weber (1986) used a Hilbert transform method and a spectral method to test the significance of the difference in growth rates between the demand and supply side Divisia monetary aggregates. The conclusion is that no statistical significance exists, except perhaps at very high frequency (i.e., in the very short run). Hence the choice between the demand side and supply side Divisia aggregate is of no consequence.[17]

8 Conclusions

The Bureau of Labor Statistics has adopted data construction procedures and data quality monitoring methods which use the available literature on index number and aggregation theory extensively. We advocate analogous procedures in the production and monitoring of monetary data. However, the fact that interest rates are not paid until the end of the period increases the importance of risk in estimating money demand and supply functions and in aggregating over component monetary assets. With many nonmonetary goods, prices are paid at the start of the period, so that the assumption of perfect certainty need not be a serious issue in applying index number theory. But as pointed out by Poterba and Rotemberg (1987), the lack of perfect certainty regarding contemporaneous interest rates raises a serious complication for index number theory when applied to monetary data.

We advocate modeling, estimation, testing, and monitoring procedures that are analogous to those used by the Bureau of Labor Statistics, but which are rendered necessarily more complex in monetary economics as a result of the problems raised by risk. We believe that these procedures not only could produce immediate improvement in the quality of existing monetary data but also would encourage and promote much deep new research in the area. For example, much research is needed on duality theory and functional structure and on nonparametric statistical approximations to aggregator functions under risk. Barnett (1995) provided two such theorems.[18]

---

[17]That paper is reprinted as chapter 19 of this book.
[18]Barnett (1995) is reprinted as chapter 10 of this book. Also see the appendix to

Conclusions

Those theorems demonstrate the role in aggregation theory of the Theoretical aggregate, and hence capture the potential usefulness of the Theoretical aggregate in modeling and in policy. Much more research in that direction is needed.

The two existing theorems in Barnett (1995) demonstrate that under rational expectations the Theoretical aggregate can be used either as an indicator or as an intermediate target. The simple sum monetary aggregates, on the other hand, do not enter into the economy's structure and hence cannot be used either as an indicator or as an intermediate target. We see no useful role for the simple sum monetary aggregates in modeling or in policy.

In conclusion, it should be observed that the particular results discussed in this article are of less importance that the methodology. In the monitoring function that is emphasized in this article, an estimated aggregator function is used to monitor the tracking ability of a statistical index, in a manner analogous to the periodic use by BLS staff of estimated cost functions to monitor the tracking ability of the CPI, which is a Laspeyres price index. However, it should be observed that the estimation of only one aggregator function cannot adequately serve that role. Hence the results in Barnett, Hinich, and Yue (2000), which we emphasize, should be viewed only as an illustration. Fully adequate monitoring of a statistical index can be accomplished only by continuous research demonstrating its *robustness* as a tracking tool relative to many specifications for the aggregator function and many estimators of the parameters of the aggregate.

In fact, if one were faced with a choice between any one estimated parametric aggregator function and a high quality 'superlative' statistical index, such as the Törnqvist-Divisia, one should prefer the index. The reason is that a superlative index, at least under risk neutrality, will track any aggregator function up to a third order remainder term *in the changes*. The fact that the order of the remainder is in the changes, rather than in the levels, results from the chaining of the index. However, estimated aggregator functions, including those produced from flexible function forms, produce approximations that are no better than those of fixed base indexes, since the parameters of an estimated aggregator function are not re-estimated at each observation. Hence it is hardly reasonable to view a single estimated aggregator function as a standard against which to compare a chained superlative index number, when in fact the index should be viewed as preferable to any such single estimated aggregator function.

The monitoring role can only be accomplished in a satisfactory manner when viewed as a check on robustness. At present, we have two such studies: Barnett, Hinich, and Weber's (1986) study of robustness to taxation, and

---

Barnett, Liu, and Jensen (1997), which is reprinted as chapter 12 of this book.

Barnett, Hinich, and Yue's (2000) test of robustness to one specification of tastes under risk aversion. In this article we report only upon those two illustrations of monitoring. Many more such studies are needed.

Appendix A: The Hinich Bispectral Approach

A.1 Definitions and Background

If $\{x(t)\}$ is a zero mean third order stationary time series, then the mean $\mu_x = E[x(t)] = 0$, the covariance $c_{xx}(m) = E[x(t+m)x(t)]$, and the general third order moments $c_{xxx}(s,r) = E[x(t+r)x(t+s)x(t)]$ are independent of t. If $c_{xx}(m) = 0$ for all non-zero m, the series is white noise. Priestley (1981) and Hinich and Patterson (1985) stress that, although a series may be white noise, $x(n)$ and $x(m)$ may be stochastically dependent unless $\{x(t)\}$ is multivariate Gaussian. Only under multivariate Gaussianity are lack of correlation (whiteness) and stochastic independence the same. If the distribution of $x(n_1), \ldots, x(n_N)$ is multivariate normal for all $n_1, \ldots, n_N$, then the series is defined to be Gaussian, where N is the sample size.[19] Hinich and Patterson (1985, p. 70) fault Box and Jenkins (1970, p. 8 vs. p. 46) and Jenkins and Watts (1968, p. 149 vs. p. 157) for blurring the definitions of whiteness and independence.

We define a pure white noise series as one in which $x(n_1), \ldots, x(n_N)$ are independent random variables for all values of $n_1, \ldots, n_N$. All pure white noise series are white. All white noise series are not pure white noise unless, in addition, they are Gaussian.

In addition to stationarity, whiteness, and pure whiteness, another often assumed property of a time series is linearity. Many researchers implicitly assume the errors of their models are Gaussian, and test for pure white noise by using the covariance function $c_{xx}(m)$, but ignore the information regarding possible nonlinear relationships which are found in the third order moments $c_{xxx}(s,r)$.

The above discussion suggests the need to test for both nonlinearity and Gaussianity, in addition to testing in the usual manners for whiteness.

A.2 The Test Method

Hinich (1985) argues that the bispectrum in the frequency domain is easier to interpret than the multiplicity of third order moments $\{c_{xxx}(r,s) : s \leq r,$

---

[19] In accordance with time series conventions, we equate Gaussianity of the process with multivariate Gaussianity.

Appendix A: The Hinich Bispectral Approach 241

$r = 0, 1, 2, \ldots\}$ in the time domain. For frequencies f_1 and f_2 in the principal domain

$$\Omega = \{(f_1, f_2) : 0 < f_1 < .5,\ f_2 < f_1,\ 2f_1 + f_2 < 1\},$$

the bispectrum, $B_{xxx}(f_1, f_2)$, is defined by

$$B_{xxx}(f_1, f_2) = \sum_{r=-\infty}^{\infty} \sum_{s=-\infty}^{\infty} c_{xxx}(r, s) \exp[-i2\pi(f_1 r + f_2 s)]. \quad (A.1)$$

The bispectrum is the double Fourier transformation of the third order moments function.[20]

The statistical tests based on the sample bispectrum that we briefly discuss in this section were applied with success to the study of acoustic signals and noise by Brockett, Hinich, and Wilson (1987) and to stock prices and exchange rates by Hinich and Patterson (1985, 1989) and Brockett, Hinich, and Patterson (1988).

The skewness function $\Gamma(f_1, f_2)$ is defined in terms of the bispectrum as follows:

$$\Gamma^2(f_1, f_2) = |B_{xxx}(f_1, f_2)|^2 / S_{xx}(f_1) S_{xx}(f_2) S_{xx}(f_1 + f_2), \quad (A.2)$$

where $S_{xx}(f)$ is the (ordinary power) spectrum of $x(t)$ at frequency f. Since the bispectrum is complex valued, the absolute value (vertical) lines in equation (A.2) designate modulus. Brillinger (1965) proves that the skewness function $\Gamma(f_1, f_2)$ is constant over all frequency pairs $(f_1, f_2) \in \Omega$, if $\{x(t)\}$ is linear, while $\Gamma(f_1, f_2)$ is zero over all frequencies, if $\{x(t)\}$ is Gaussian. Linearity and Gaussianity can be tested using a sample estimator of the skewness function $\Gamma(f_1, f_2)$. We now outline the procedure we use to obtain the bispectrum.

A.3 Computation of the Test Statistics

Let $f_k = k/N$ for each integer k. For the sample $\{x(0), x(1), ..., x(N-1)\}$, define $F_{xxx}(f_j, f_k)$ to be an estimate of the bispectrum of $\{x(t)\}$ at the

---

[20] The bispectrum is the third order polyspectrum, while the ordinary power spectrum is the second order polyspectrum. Strictly speaking, the polyspectrum of order k is the Fourier transform of the cumulant function (not the moment function) of order k.

Cumulants are defined to be the coefficients of the terms in the power series expansion of the *logarithm* of the characteristic function of a distribution, while the moments are the coefficients of the terms in the power series expansion of the *level* of the characteristic function of the distribution. Unlike the moments, the cumulants have the merit of being semi-invariants. However, for a stationary time series with zero mean, the second and third order cumulant functions are identical to the second and third order moment functions. Only at the fourth and higher orders do the cumulant functions differ from the moment functions. But since we here use only the second and third orders under the assumption of stationarity and zero mean, we need draw no distinction between moments and cumulants.

frequency pair (f_j, f_k) such that:

$$F_{xxx}(f_j, f_k) = Z(f_j)Z(f_k)Z^*(f_j + f_k)/N, \qquad (A.3)$$

where

$$Z(f_j) = \sum_{t=0}^{N-1} x(t)\exp(-i2\pi f_j t).$$

The asterisk in equation (A.3) designates complex conjugate.

The function $F_{xxx}(f_j, f_k)$ must be smoothed as follows to form a consistent estimator. Let $\langle B_{xxx}(f_m, f_n)\rangle$ denote a smoothed estimate of $B_{xxx}(f_m, f_n)$, which is obtained by averaging over values of $F_{xxx}(f_j, f_k)$ at adjacent frequency pairs such that

$$\langle B_{xxx}(f_m, f_n)\rangle = M^{-2} \sum_{j=(m-1)M}^{mM-1} \sum_{k=(m-1)M}^{nM-1} F_{xxx}(f_j, f_k). \qquad (A.4)$$

This estimator, $\langle B_{xxx}(f_m, f_n)\rangle$, is the average of the $F_{xxx}(f_j, f_k)$ over a square on M^2 points. It is a consistent and asymptotically complex normal estimator of the bispectrum, $B_{xxx}(f_1, f_2)$, if the sequence (f_m, f_n) converges to (f_1, f_2) (see Hinich, 1982).

As discussed earlier, the estimated skewness function, $\Gamma(f_m, f_n)$, will not be significantly different from a constant at any frequency pair in Ω under the null hypothesis of linearity. If the null hypothesis is Gaussianity as well as linearity, then that constant will be zero. The skewness function can be used to motivate construction of the normalized test statistics, $2|\delta(f_m, f_n)|^2$, where

$$\delta(f_m, f_n) = \langle B_{xxx}(f_m, f_n)\rangle / [(N/M^2)\langle S_{xx}(f_m)\rangle$$
$$\langle S_{xx}(f_n)\rangle\langle S_{xx}(f_m + f_n)\rangle]^{1/2}. \qquad (A.5)$$

In this formula, $\langle S_{xx}(\cdot)\rangle$ is defined to be a consistent and asymptotically normal estimator of the power spectrum $S_{xx}(\cdot)$, and f_m is defined by $f_m = (2m-1)M/2N$ for each integer m. Hinich has shown that $2[\delta(f_m, f_n)]^2$ is approximately distributed as an independent noncentral chi-squared variate with two degrees of freedom at frequency pair (f_m, f_n).

The larger M, the less the finite sample variance and the larger the sample bias. Because of this tradeoff, there is no one unique M that is appropriate to use for performing nonlinearity and Gaussianity tests based upon the estimated statistics given by equation (A.5). When M is large, the bandwidth is large, the variance is reduced, and the resolution of the tests is small, since there are too few terms for the linearity test. If M is small, there is a large

Appendix A: The Hinich Bispectral Approach

number of terms to sort for the linearity tests, the variance may be too large, and the chi-square approximation used for the linearity test may not be good. Hinich (1982) has suggested that M should be selected to be approximately the square root of the number of observations, N.

Let P denote the number of frequency pairs in the principal domain, Ω, and let

$$D = \{(m,n) : (f_m, f_n) \in \Omega\},$$

so that P is the cardinal number of the set D. Hinich (1982) has shown that the P values of $2|\delta(f_m, f_n)|^2$ for $(m,n) \in D$ are approximately distributed as independent, noncentral chi-square variates with noncentrality parameter $\lambda(f_m, f_n)$, where

$$\begin{aligned}\lambda(f_m, f_n) &= (2M^2/N)|B_{xxx}(f_m, f_n)|^2 / S_{xx}(f_m) S_{xx}(f_n) S_{xx}(f_m + f_n) \\ &= (2M^2/N)\Gamma^2(f_m, f_n).\end{aligned} \quad (A.6)$$

Define the test statistic

$$CHISUM = 2 \sum\sum_{(m,n) \in D} |\delta(f_m, f_n)|^2. \quad (A.7)$$

The distribution of $CHISUM$ is approximately a noncentral chi-square with $2P$ degrees of freedom with a noncentrality parameter that is the sum of the $\lambda(f_m, f_n)$ over all $(m,n) \in D$.

Under the null hypothesis that $\{x(t)\}$ is Gaussian and thus the skewness function, $\Gamma(f_m, f_n)$, is identically zero over all $(m,n) \in D$, $CHISUM$ is approximately a central chi-square $2P$ variate. Equation (A.7) gives us an asymptotic chi-square test of the Gaussianity hypothesis. If the time series is linear but not necessarily Gaussian, then the skewness function is constant, which implies from (A.6) that the noncentrality parameters are constant. The Hinich linearity test uses the empirical distribution function of $\{2|\delta(f_m, f_n)|\}$ in the principal domain to test the null hypothesis that the $\lambda(f_m, f_n)$'s are all the same. A robust single test statistic for this dispersion is the 80th quantile of these statistics.

For details of the test, see Hinich (1982), Hinich and Patterson (1985, 1989), and Ashley, Patterson, and Hinich (1986). In particular, the final transformed test statistics are distributed as standard normal random variates under the respective null hypotheses. When the null is Gaussianity, the resulting test statistic is denoted by H. When the null is linearity, the test statistic is denoted by Z. In both cases, the distribution of the standard normal is used to produce a one-sided test, in which the null is rejected if the test statistic is large.

Ashley, Patterson, and Hinich (1986, p. 174) presented an equivalence theorem which proves that the Hinich bispectral linearity test statistic is invariant to linear filtering of the data. This important result proves that *the linearity test can be applied either to the raw series or to the residuals of a linear model fitted to the data.* Hence there is no need to choose between possible linear methods of detrending or prefiltering the data. An additional important implication of the theorem is that if $x(t)$ is found to be nonlinear, then the residuals of a linear model of the form $y(t) = f(x(t))$ will also be nonlinear, since the nonlinearity in $x(t)$ will pass through any linear filter, f. The above article further reported tables on the power of the Hinich linearity test for detecting violations of the linearity and Gaussianity hypotheses for a number of sample sizes and M values. The table indicates substantial power for both tests, even when N is as small as 256, if the value of M used is between 12 and 17. For this sample size, the power of the test falls off as M increases above 17.

Introduction

3.3.2: Monetary Index Number Theory under Risk

Chapter 12

CAPM Risk Adjustment

William A. Barnett, Yi Liu, and Mark Jensen[*]

> "The economic statistics that the government issues every week should come with a warning sticker: User beware. In the midst of the greatest information explosion in history, the government is pumping out a stream of statistics that are nothing but myths and misinformation."
>
> (Source: Michael J. Mandel, "The Real Truth About the Economy: Are Government Statistics So Much Pulp Fiction? Take a Look," *Business Week*, cover story, November 7, 1994, pp. 110–118.)

Barnett originated the Divisia monetary aggregates, which in continuous time exactly track any monetary aggregator function under perfect certainty. With user costs measuring the prices of the services of components, Barnett's aggregates are based on Francois Divisia's derivation of the Divisia line integral from the first-order conditions for optimizing behavior by economic agents under perfect certainty. We derive an extended Divisia index from the first-order conditions (Euler equations) that apply under risk. Our extended Divisia index is the first extension of index number theory into the domain of decision making under risk and thereby

---

[*]Originally published in *Macroeconomic Dynamics* 1 (1997), 485–512. Reprinted with the permission of Cambridge University Press. Barnett's research was partially supported by NSF grant SES 9223557; Jensen's research was supported under that grant as research assistant. Address correspondence to: William A. Barnett, Department of Economics, Washington University, Campus Box 1208, One Brookings Drive, St. Louis, MO 63130-4899, USA; e-mail: barnett@wuecon.wustl.edu.

produces a route for the extension of all index number theory to permit non-risk-neutrality. We generate simulated data from a modeled rational consumer and investigate the tracking accuracy of the extended Divisia index to the consumer's exact aggregator function.

1 Introduction

In the case of perfect certainty, the Divisia index exactly tracks any aggregator function. This follows from the fact that the Divisia line integral is directly derivable from the first-order conditions for optimizing behavior. This result is especially well known in the case of consumer behavior, in which the Divisia index is derived directly from the total differential of the demand function, after substitution of the first-order conditions for maximizing utility subject to a budget constraint. However, the exact tracking property of the Divisia index also applies to the demand for monetary services by firms and the supply of produced monetary services by financial intermediaries. See Barnett (1987).

Risk aversion is another story. The first-order conditions in the case of risk aversion are Euler equations. Because those are not the first-order conditions used in deriving the Divisia index under perfect certainty, the tracking ability of the unadjusted Divisia index is compromised. The degree to which the tracking ability degrades is a function of the degree of risk aversion and the amount of risk. In principle, this problem could be solved by estimating the Euler equations by generalized method of moments and producing the estimated exact rational expectations monetary aggregator function. This inference procedure is in accordance with the one widely advocated as the solution to the Lucas critique and, more recently, also advocated as the solution to what Chrystal and MacDonald (1994, p. 76) have called the Barnett critique.[1] However, estimation of aggregator functions, although in strict accordance with the principles of microeconomic aggregation theory, produces results that depend on the parametric specification of the aggregator function and the choice of econometric estimator for estimating the parameters of the aggregator.

Index number theory exists precisely for the purpose of permitting specifi-

---

[1] According to the Barnett critique, the appearance of structural shift can be produced from an inconsistency between the aggregator function tracked by the index number used to produce the data and the aggregator function that is implied by the structural model within which the index number is used. The use of simple sum monetary aggregates as variables within models is an extreme example. See Barnett, Fisher, and Serletis (1992), Chrystal and MacDonald (1994), and Belongia (1996).

Introduction

cation-free, nonparametric tracking ability. The Divisia index is such a parameter-free index number and hence depends only on data. Although the Divisia index number is known to permit exact tracking for any economic aggregator function under perfect certainty [see Hulten (1973)], that index has never been extended to a statistical index number that will track exactly under risk aversion. In fact, to our knowledge, no nonparametric, statistical index numbers have ever previously been derived directly from Euler equations in a manner that retains tracking ability under risk. In this paper, we derive a statistical index number directly from the Euler equations.[2] The resulting index number turns out to be an extension of the original Divisia index derived by Francois Divisia (1925) under perfect certainty, such that our extended Divisia index remains exact under risk aversion and reduces to the usual Divisia index in the special case of perfect certainty. The derivation is analogous to that for the usual Divisia index, but our extended Divisia index is derived from the Euler equations that are the correct first-order conditions produced from rational behavior of economic agents under risk.

If additional assumptions are imposed, we find that the resulting generalized Divisia index has a direct connection with the capital asset pricing model (CAPM) in finance. In a sense, our theory is a simultaneous generalization of both the CAPM and economic index number theory, because our theory contains both as nested special cases. In particular, CAPM deals with a two-dimensional trade-off between expected return and risk, whereas the Divisia index deals with the two-dimensional trade-off between investment return and liquidity. Our generalized theory includes the three-dimensional trade-off among mean return, risk, and liquidity. The two well-known special cases are based on two-dimensional sections, which are orthogonal to each other, through the relevant three-dimensional space.

A particularly productive area of possible application of this new index number is monetary aggregation, because money-market assets are characterized by substantially different degrees of each of the three characteristics: mean rate of return, risk, and liquidity, especially when the collection of money-market assets includes those subject to prepayment penalties, such as Series EE bonds and nonnegotiable certificates of deposit, and those subject to regulated low rates of return, such as currency. When central banks first produced monetary aggregates, all of the components over which they aggregated yielded no interest. Hence, there was perfect certainty about the rate of return on each component. In addition, because that rate of return was exactly zero for each component, the user costs were known to be the same for each component. Under those circumstances, it is well known in aggre-

---

[2] Many of the results in this paper are based on those in the working paper by Barnett, Liu, and Jensen (1997).

gation theory that the correct method of aggregation is simple summation; but monetary assets no longer yield the same rates of return and cannot be viewed as perfect substitutes. In addition, the interest yield is not a monetary service, so that the interest yield's capitalized value, although embedded in the value of the stock of such assets, is not part of the economic monetary stock. The capitalized value of the monetary service flow, net of that interest yield, is the economy's economic monetary stock. Furthermore, because interest is not paid in advance, there is some degree of uncertainty about that rate of return, which is needed to compute the foregone interest (user cost) of any interest-yielding monetary asset. These observations indicate that the ability to track a nonlinear aggregator function under risk is needed to be able to measure the economy's monetary service flow.

In the case of the current monetary aggregates, the component assets yield rates of return having low variance and low correlation with consumption. As a result, the ordinary Divisia index produced from perfect-certainty first-order conditions may be adequate to track the service flows of those collections of assets, but there is growing research interest in the possibility of incorporating into monetary aggregates some assets that have substantial risk, such as common stock and bond funds. See, e.g., Barnett and Zhou (1994) and Feldstein and Stock (1996). With such potential component assets, the perfect-certainty first-order conditions are not suitable and hence the ordinary Divisia monetary aggregates may not track well.

In its most general interpretation, the objective of this paper is to extend index number theory to apply to aggregation over goods for which contemporaneous prices are not known with certainty. Because the user cost prices of financial assets depend upon risky contemporaneous rates of return, aggregation over financial assets seems like an especially suitable area for application of risk-extended index number theory.

1.1 Money in the Utility Function

A large and growing literature seeks to explain why rate-of-return-dominated money exists (i.e., has positive value) in equilibrium. This issue is important and merits much research. Nevertheless, it is well known in general equilibrium theory that if money has positive value in equilibrium, then a derived utility function containing money exists such that behavior can be described by maximizing that derived utility subject to a budget constraint. See, e.g., Samuelson (1947), Quirk and Saposnik (1968), Arrow and Hahn (1971), Phlips and Spinnewyn (1982), Feenstra (1986), Poterba and Rotemberg (1987), and Croushore (1993). The same result is available for firms. See, e.g., Fischer (1974). In fact, the resulting derived utility or production function has indeed been derived for many of the explicit mechanisms producing positive value for money in equilibrium.

The converse of the theorem is especially challenging in its implications. If a model containing an explicit motive for holding money cannot generate a derived utility function from its original utility function and constraints, then money cannot have positive value in equilibrium. Only two possible conclusions then can be reached. Either the model fails to produce a positive-equilibrium quantity of money, and money is driven out of existence in equilibrium as a result of its rate dominance, or the asset being modeled as 'money' is in fact not money and need not exist in equilibrium.

Empirically, that well-known theorem and its converse imply that behavior under explicit motives for holding money induces rational (transitive, consistent) behavior within the space of goods and monetary assets, and indeed many tests of the axioms of revealed preference have accepted those axioms in that space. However, knowledge of the induced preference preordering over that Cartesian product space is not sufficient to produce a unique inverse mapping back to the original decision. Hence, the properties of the derived utility function do not uniquely reveal the explicit motive for holding money. The nonuniqueness of the inverse mapping is a constructive reason for interest in models containing an explicit motive for holding money, but, for some purposes, we do not need to know that motive.

Macroeconomists, monetary economists, and central bankers have many reasons for wanting an explanation of the fact that positive quantities of money are held in equililbrium, despite the fact that many monetary assets are rate dominated as investments. However, in aggregation theory we have no need for such an explanation. Monetary assets are indeed held in positive quantities, and not all monetary assets yield the same investment rate of return. Within the derived utility function over the Cartesian product space of goods and monetary assets, we know that monetary assets having different own rates of return are most certainly not perfect substitutes. That fact alone is sufficient to permit us to deduce that simple sum aggregation over currency and any interest-yielding monetary asset makes no sense whatsoever, and any empirical research using such a simple sum aggregate over such assets is contaminated by those data. We need no further information about the explicit motive for holding money to deduce that result in microeconomic aggregation theory.

In this paper, we display the derivation of the CAPM-extended Divisia monetary index based upon the derived utility function containing money. However, it should be observed that exactly the same result would be produced from any explicit motive for holding money, such as a model having transactions technology constraint. Even the case of perfect substitution between components is a nested special case of the index derived below.

2 Consumer Demand for Monetary Assets

2.1 The Decision

In this section we formulate a representative consumer's stochastic decision problem over consumer goods and monetary assets. The consumer's decisions are made in discrete time over an infinite planning horizon for the time intervals, $t, t+1, \ldots, s, \ldots$, where t is the current time period. The variables used in defining the consumer's decision are as follows: $\mathbf{x}_s = n$-dimensional vector of real consumptions of goods and services during period s, $\mathbf{p}_s = n$-dimensional vector of goods and services prices and of durable-goods rental prices during period s, $\mathbf{a}_s = k$-dimensional vector of real balances of monetary assets during period s, $\boldsymbol{\rho}_\mathbf{s} = k$-dimensional vector of nominal holding-period yields of monetary assets, $A_s =$ holdings of the benchmark asset during period s, $R_s =$ the one-period holding yield on the benchmark asset during period s, $I_s =$ the sum of all other sources of income during period s, and $p_s^* = p_s^*(\mathbf{p}_s) =$ the true cost-of-living index.

Define Y to be the consumer's survival set, assumed to be a compact subset of the $n + k + 2$ dimensional nonnegative orthant. The consumer's consumption possibility set, $S(s)$ for period s, is

$$S(s) = \left\{ (\mathbf{a}_s, \mathbf{x}_s, A_s) \in Y : \sum_{i=1}^{n} p_{is} x_{is} \right.$$

$$= \sum_{i=1}^{k} \left[(1 + \rho_{i,s-1}) p_u^* {}_{1} a_{i,s}{}_{1} - p_s^* a_{i,s} \right]$$

$$\left. + (1 + R_{s-1}) p_{s-1}^* A_{s-1} - p_s^* A_s + I_s \right\}.$$

The benchmark asset A_s provides no services other than its yield R_s. As a result, the benchmark asset does not enter the consumer's contemporaneous utility function. The asset is held only as a means of accumulating wealth. The consumer's subjective rate of time preference, ξ, is assumed to be constant.[3] The single-period utility function, $u(\mathbf{a}_t, \mathbf{x}_t)$, is assumed to be increasing and strictly quasi-concave.

The consumer's decision problem is the following.

Problem 1. Choose the deterministic point $(\mathbf{a}_t, \mathbf{x}_t, A_t)$ and the stochastic

---

[3] Although money may not exist in the elementary utility function, there exists a derived utility function that contains money, so long as money has positive value in equilibrium. See, e.g., Quirk and Saposnik (1968), Arrow and Hahn (1971), Phlips and Spinnewyn (1982), Samuelson (1947), and Feenstra (1986). We implicitly are using that derived utility function.

process $(\mathbf{a}_s, \mathbf{x}_s, A_s), s = t+1, \ldots, \infty$, to maximize

$$u(\mathbf{a}_t, \mathbf{x}_t) + E_t \left[\sum_{s=t+1}^{\infty} \left(\frac{1}{1+\xi} \right)^{s-t} u(\mathbf{a}_s, \mathbf{x}_s) \right] \qquad (1)$$

subject to $(\mathbf{a}_s, \mathbf{x}_s, A_s) \in S(s)$ for s, t, and also subject to the transversality condition

$$\lim_{s \to \infty} E_t \left(\frac{1}{1+\xi} \right)^{s-t} A_s = 0.$$

The transversality condition rules out perpetual borrowing at the benchmark rate, R_t.

2.2 Existence of a Monetary Aggregate for the Consumer

To ensure the existence of a monetary aggregate for the consumer, we partition the vector of monetary asset quantities, $\mathbf{a}_s$, such that $\mathbf{a}_s = (\mathbf{m}_s, \mathbf{h}_s)$. We correspondingly partition the vector of interest rates of those assets, $\boldsymbol{\rho}_s$, such that $\boldsymbol{\rho}_s = (\mathbf{r}_s, \mathbf{i}_s)$. We then assume that the utility function, u, is blockwise weakly separable in $\mathbf{m}_s$ and in $\mathbf{x}_s$ for some such partition of $\mathbf{a}_s$ and blockwise strongly separable in $\mathbf{h}_s$.[4] Hence, there exists a monetary aggregator ("category utility") function, M, a consumer goods aggregator function, X, and utility functions, F and H, such that

$$u(\mathbf{m}_s, \mathbf{h}_s, \mathbf{x}_s) = F[M(\mathbf{m}_s), X(\mathbf{x}_s)] + H(\mathbf{h}_s), \qquad (2)$$

and we define the implied utility function V by $V(\mathbf{m}_s, c_s) = F[M(\mathbf{m}_s), c_s]$, where aggregate consumption of goods is defined by $c_s = X(\mathbf{x}_s)$. Then, it follows that the exact monetary aggregate is

$$M_s = M(\mathbf{m}_s). \qquad (3)$$

We define the dimension of $\mathbf{m}_s$ to be k_1, and the dimension of $\mathbf{h}_s$ to be k_2, so that $k = k_1 + k_2$. The fact that blockwise weak separability is a necessary condition for exact aggregation is well known in the perfect-certainty case. In fact, if the resulting aggregator function also is linearly homogeneous, the theory of two-stage budgeting can be used to prove that the consumer behaves as if the exact aggregate were an elementary good. Because two-stage budgeting theory is not applicable under risk, we provide in the Appendix to

---
[4] The strong separability assumption is largely for expository convenience. Weak separability would be sufficient.

this chapter an aggregation theorem proving that $M(\mathbf{m}_s)$ can be treated as a quantity aggregate, in a well-defined sense, even under risk.

The Euler equations that will be of the most use to us below are those for monetary assets. Those Euler equations are

$$E_s\left[\frac{\partial V}{\partial m_{is}} - \rho\frac{p_s^*(R_s - r_{is})}{p_{s+1}^*}\frac{\partial V}{\partial c_{s+1}}\right] = 0 \quad (4a)$$

for s, t, and $i = 1, \ldots, k_1$, where $\rho = 1/(1+\xi)$ and where p_s^* is the exact price aggregate that is dual to the consumer goods quantity aggregate c_s.[5] Similarly, we can acquire the Euler equation for the consumer goods aggregate c_s, rather than for each of its components. The resulting Euler equation for c_s is

$$E_s\left[\frac{\partial V}{\partial c_s} - \rho\frac{p_s^*(1+R_s)}{p_{s+1}^*}\frac{\partial V}{\partial c_{s+1}}\right] = 0. \quad (4b)$$

For the formal derivation of (4a) and (4b), using Bellman's method, see Barnett (1995, Sec. 2.3), which is reprinted as chapter 10 of this book.

3 The Perfect-Certainty Case

In the perfect-certainty case, nonparametric index number theory is highly developed and is applicable to monetary aggregation. In the perfect-certainty case, Barnett (1978, 1980a) proved that the contemporaneous real user cost of the services of m_{it} is π_{it}, where

$$\pi_{it} = \frac{R_t - r_{it}}{1 + R_t}. \quad (5)$$

The corresponding nominal user cost is $p_t^*\pi_{it}$. It can be shown that the solution value of the exact monetary aggregate $M(\mathbf{m}_t)$ can be tracked without error in continuous time [see, e.g., Barnett (1980a)] by the Divisia index:

$$d\log M_t = \sum_{i=1}^{k_1} s_{it}\, d\log m_{it}, \quad (6)$$

where the user-cost-evaluated expenditure shares are

$$s_{it} = \pi_{it}m_{it}\Big/\sum_{j=1}^{k_1}\pi_{jt}m_{jt}.$$

---

[5] Assuming that X is linearly homogeneous, the exact price aggregator function is the unit cost function.

The flawless tracking ability of the index in the perfect-certainty case holds regardless of the form of the unknown aggregator function, M. In discrete time, the Simpson's rule discrete time approximation to the Divisia index is called the Törnqvist index and is exact for any aggregator function up to a third-order remainder term in the changes. That remainder term usually is less than the roundoff error in the component data and typically is negligible for data that are available with at least annual frequency. However, under risk, the ability of equation (6) to track $M(\mathbf{m}_t)$ is compromised in continuous time and hence also in discrete time at all data sampling frequencies.

4 New Generalized Divisia Index

4.1 User Cost of Money Under Risk Aversion

We now return to the Euler equations for optimal behavior of consumers under risk. Those Euler equations are displayed in equation (4a) for monetary assets and equation (4b) for consumer goods. Our objective is to find the formula for the user cost of monetary services in a form that is applicable to our model of decision under risk. The following definition for the contemporaneous user cost simply states that the real user cost price of a monetary asset is the marginal rate of substitution between those assets and consumer goods.

Definition 1 *The contemporaneous risk-adjusted real user cost price of the services of monetary asset i is Π_{it}, defined such that*

$$\Pi_{it} = \frac{\partial V}{\partial m_{it}} \Big/ \frac{\partial V}{\partial c_t}.$$

No expectations operators appear in that definition, because the marginal utilities at t are known with certainty in period t. Nevertheless, formula (5), which applies under perfect certainty, cannot be correct under risk because the interest rates in equation (5) are not known contemporaneously, and so, the right-hand side of equation (5) is stochastic, whereas Definition 1 defines Π_{it} to be deterministic. In this section, we derive the correct deterministic formula for the user cost defined by Definition 1.

For notational convenience, we sometimes convert the nominal rates of return, r_{it} and R_t, to real total rates of return, $1 + r_{it}^*$ and $1 + R_t^*$, such that

$$1 + r_{it}^* = \frac{p_t^*(1 + r_{it})}{p_{t+1}^*} \quad \text{and} \quad 1 + R_t^* = \frac{p_t^*(1 + R_t)}{p_{t+1}^*}, \tag{7}$$

where r_{it}^* and R_t^* defined in that manner are called the real rates of excess return. Under this change of variables and observing that current-period marginal utilities are known with certainty, Euler equations (4a) and (4b) become

$$\frac{\partial V}{\partial m_{it}} - \rho E_t \left[(R_t^* - r_{it}^*) \frac{\partial V}{\partial c_{t+1}} \right] = 0 \tag{8}$$

and

$$\frac{\partial V}{\partial c_t} - \rho E_t \left[(1 + R_t^*) \frac{\partial V}{\partial c_{t+1}} \right] = 0. \tag{9}$$

We now can prove our user cost theorem under risk.

Theorem 1. *The risk adjusted user cost of the services of monetary asset i under risk is $\Pi_{it} = \pi_{it} + \psi_{it}$, where*

$$\pi_{it} = \frac{E_t R_t - E_t r_{it}}{1 + E_t R_t} \tag{10}$$

and

$$\psi_{it} = \rho(1 - \pi_{it}) \frac{\mathrm{Cov}\left(R_t^*, \frac{\partial V}{\partial c_{t+1}}\right)}{\frac{\partial V}{\partial c_t}} - \rho \frac{\mathrm{Cov}\left(r_{it}^*, \frac{\partial V}{\partial c_{t+1}}\right)}{\frac{\partial V}{\partial c_t}}. \tag{11}$$

Proof. Equation (8) can be rewritten for current period t to be

$$\frac{\partial V}{\partial m_{it}} = \rho E_t \left[(R_t^* - r_{it}^*) \frac{\partial V}{\partial c_{t+1}} \right]. \tag{12}$$

If the marginal utility and the interest rates in the expectation on the right-hand side of (12) were uncorrelated, we could write the expectation of the product as the product of the expectations. However, under our assumption of weak separability in monetary assets, $\mathbf{m}_t$, the utility function V can be written in the form $V(\mathbf{m}_t, c_t) = F[M(\mathbf{m}_t), c_t]$, where the consumer is risk neutral if and only if F is linear in $M_t = M(\mathbf{m}_t)$ and in c_t. Hence, under risk neutrality, V must be linear in c_t, so that the marginal utility of consumption must be a constant. Without risk neutrality and the resulting constancy of the marginal utility of consumption, we have no reason to expect the interest rates and marginal utility on the right-hand side of (27) to be uncorrelated. The result is that (12) becomes

$$\begin{aligned}\frac{\partial V}{\partial m_{it}} &= \rho E_t \left[\frac{\partial V}{\partial c_{t+1}} \right] (E_t R_t^* - E_t r_{it}^*) \\ &\quad + \rho \,\mathrm{Cov}\left(R_t^*, \frac{\partial V}{\partial c_{t+1}}\right) - \rho \,\mathrm{Cov}\left(r_{it}^*, \frac{\partial V}{\partial c_{t+1}}\right), \end{aligned} \tag{13}$$

where the covariances would become zero if we were to assume risk neutrality. Similarly, without risk neutrality, equation (9) becomes

$$\frac{\partial V}{\partial c_t} = \rho E_t \left[\frac{\partial V}{\partial c_{t+1}} \right] + \rho E_t \left[R_t^* \right] E_t \left[\frac{\partial V}{\partial c_{t+1}} \right] + \rho \operatorname{Cov}\left(R_t^*, \frac{\partial V}{\partial c_{t+1}} \right). \quad (14)$$

By eliminating $\rho E_t[\partial V/\partial c_{t+1}]$ between equations (13) and (14), we get

$$\frac{\partial V}{\partial m_{it}} = (\pi_{it} + \psi_{it}) \frac{\partial V}{\partial c_t}, \quad (15)$$

where

$$\pi_{it} = \frac{E_t R_t^* - E_t r_{it}^*}{1 + E_t R_t^*} \quad (16)$$

and

$$\psi_{it} = \rho(1 - \pi_{it}) \frac{\operatorname{Cov}\left(R_t^*, \dfrac{\partial V}{\partial c_{t+1}} \right)}{\dfrac{\partial V}{\partial c_t}} - \rho \frac{\operatorname{Cov}\left(r_{it}^*, \dfrac{\partial V}{\partial c_{t+1}} \right)}{\dfrac{\partial V}{\partial c_t}}. \quad (17)$$

Using equation (7) to convert the real rates in equation (16) back to nominal rates, equation (16) becomes (10), whereas equation (17) is immediately identical to equation (11). Solving equation (15) for $\Pi_{it} = \pi_{it} + \psi_{it}$, Theorem 1 follows from Definition 1. □

Under risk neutrality, the covariances in (17) would all be zero because the utility function would be linear in consumption. Hence, the user cost would reduce to π_{it}, as defined in equation (10). The following corollary is immediate.

Corollary 1 to Theorem 1. *Under risk neutrality, the user cost formula is the same as equation (5) in the perfect-certainty case, but with all interest rates replaced by their expectations.*

However, under risk aversion the utility function is strictly concave in consumption, so that marginal utility is inversely related to consumption. In principle, it is possible for the interest rate on a slightly risky investment to reduce the risk in the consumer's consumption stream if that interest rate and consumption are negatively correlated. Because of the inverse relationship between consumption and marginal utility, we conclude that risk is decreased by an investment if the rate of return is positively correlated with marginal utility. For monetary assets, with little or no principle risk and low volatility, the riskiness of the asset is likely to contribute relatively little to the riskiness of the household's consumption stream, and hence the sign of the covariance between the asset's rate of return and of the consumption stream is not easy to predict a priori. But with a very risky asset, such as common stock, it is far more likely that holding such a risky investment will increase risk rather than decrease it. That occurs if the rate of return on the asset is positively correlated with consumption and thereby negatively correlated with marginal utility. This phenomenon is central to the consumption-based capital asset pricing model (CCAPM).

Consider the interpretation of equation (11), which defines the adjustment for risk under risk aversion. Suppose we normalize relative to $\partial V/\partial c_t$, so that we need not consider the denominator of equation (11). Now consider first the second term on the right-hand side of equation (11). Suppose that the own rate of return on monetary asset i is positively correlated with the marginal utility of consumption of goods, so that holding that monetary asset decreases risk. Because holding the asset decreases the consumer's consumption risk, we should expect that the risk-adjusted user cost price $\Pi_{it} = \pi_{it} + \psi_{it}$ that the consumer would have to 'pay' to hold that asset would be decreased as that positive covariance increases; and that is precisely what the second term of equation (11) would do in that case. Conversely, if the covariance between the own rate and the marginal utility of consumption of goods is negative, so that holding the asset increases the risk of the consumer's consumption stream, the second term in equation (11) introduces a positive term into the risk-adjusted user cost $\Pi_{it} = \pi_{it} + \psi_{it}$ to reflect the increased cost of holding the asset as that covariance increases the consumer's risk. If the central bank were to introduce common stock or bond funds into monetary aggregates or other assets having substantial principal risk, we should expect to find the latter case would apply to those assets.

Now consider the first term on the right-hand side of equation (11). The benchmark rate is the interest rate foregone by not holding the benchmark asset. If the benchmark rate decreases consumption risk through a positive covariance between the benchmark rate and the marginal utility of consumption of goods, then the opportunity cost of foregoing the benchmark asset by instead holding monetary asset i is increased. Hence, we should expect that such a positive covariance should increase the risk-adjusted user cost Π_{it}, as indeed is the effect of the first term of equation (11). Conversely, if that covariance is negative, so that holding the benchmark asset increases the consumer's risk, then foregoing the benchmark asset in favor of monetary asset i decreases risk and hence results in a subtraction from the risk-adjusted user cost, Π_{it}, of holding asset i.

4.2 Generalized Divisia Index Under Risk Aversion

The ordinary Divisia index was derived by Francois Divisia from the first-order conditons for rational consumer behavior under perfect certainty. In the case of risk aversion, the first-order conditions are Euler equations, and we have found that those Euler equations for monetary assets demanded by consumers can be put into the form (8), which we now use to derive a generalized Divisia index, as follows.

Theorem 2. *In the share equations $s_{it} = \pi_{it} m_{it} / \sum_{j=1}^{k_1} \pi_{jt} m_{jt}$ replace the unadjusted user costs π_{it}, defined by (5), by the risk-adjusted user costs Π_{it}, defined by Definition 1, to produce the adjusted shares $S_{it} = \Pi_{it} m_{it} / \sum_{j=1}^{k_1} \Pi_{jt} m_{jt}$. Under our weak-separability assumption, $V(\mathbf{m}_t, c_t) = F[M(\mathbf{m}_t), c_t]$, and our assumption that the monetary aggregator function M is linearly homogeneous, the following generalized Divisia index is true under risk:*

$$d \log M_t = \sum S_{it} \, d \log m_{it}. \tag{18}$$

Proof. Under our weak-separability assumption, $V(\mathbf{m}_t, c_t) = F[M(\mathbf{m}_t), c_t]$, we have that

$$\frac{\partial V}{\partial m_{it}} = \frac{\partial F}{\partial M_t} \frac{\partial M_t}{\partial m_{it}}. \tag{19}$$

Substituting (15) into (19), we acquire

$$\frac{\partial M_t}{\partial m_{it}} = (\pi_{it} + \psi_{it}) \left(\frac{\partial V}{\partial c_t} \bigg/ \frac{\partial F}{\partial M_t} \right). \tag{20}$$

Because the total differential of $M_t = M(\mathbf{m}_t)$ is

$$dM_t = \sum_i \frac{\partial M}{\partial m_{it}} \, dm_{it}, \tag{21}$$

we can substitute (20) into (21) to get

$$dM_t = \left(\frac{\partial V}{\partial c_t} \bigg/ \frac{\partial F}{\partial M_t} \right) \sum (\pi_{it} + \psi_{it}) \, dm_{it}. \tag{22}$$

Using the linear homogeneity of M, we have from Euler's theorem for homogeneous functions that

$$M_t = \sum_i \frac{\partial M}{\partial m_{it}} m_{it}. \tag{23}$$

Substituting (20) into (23), we acquire

$$M_t = \left(\frac{\partial V}{\partial c_t} \bigg/ \frac{\partial F}{\partial M_t} \right) \sum (\pi_{it} + \psi_{it}) m_{it}. \tag{24}$$

Dividing (22) by (24), we get equation (18). □

Hence, we see that the exact tracking of the Divisia monetary index is not compromised by risk aversion, as long as the adjusted user costs $\pi_{it} + \psi_{it}$ are used in computing the index. As we have observed, the adjusted user costs reduce to the usual user costs in the case of perfect certainty and our generalized Divisia index (18) reduces to the usual Divisia index (6). Similarly, the risk-neutral case is acquired as the special case with $\psi_{it} = 0$, so that equation (16) serves as the user cost. In short, our generalized Divisia index (18) is a true generalization in the sense that the risk-neutral and perfect-certainty cases are strictly nested special cases. Formally, that conclusion is the following.

Corollary 1 to Theorem 2. *Under risk neutrality, the generalized Divisia index (18) reduces to (6), where the user costs in the formula are defined by (16). Under perfect certainty, the user costs reduce to (5).*

The need for the generalization can be explained as follows. The consumer has a three-dimensional decision, in terms of asset characteristics. The monetary assets having nonzero own rates of return produce investment returns, contribute to risk, and provide liquidity services. Our objective is to track the nested utility function, $M(\mathbf{m}_t)$, which measures only liquidity and is the true economic monetary aggregate. To do so, we must remove the other two motives: investment yield and risk aversion. Although those two motives are relevant to savings and intertemporal substitution, we seek to track the liquidity flow alone. The ordinary Divisia monetary aggregate removes the investment motive and would track the liquidity services if there were no risk. The generalized Divisia index removes both the investment motive and the aversion-to-risk motive to extract the liquidity service flow, when the data are produced by consumers who in fact are making decisions that involve a three-way trade-off among mean investment return, risk aversion, and liquidity service consumption.

5 CCAPM Special Case

As a means of illustrating the nature of the risk adjustment ψ_{it}, we consider a special case, based on the usual assumptions in CAPM theory of either quadratic utility or Gaussian stochastic processes. Direct empirical use of Theorems 1 and 2, without any CAPM simplifications, would require availability of prior econometric estimates of the parameters of the utility function V and of the subjective rate of time discount. Under the usual CAPM assumptions, we show in this section that empirical use of Theorems 1 and 2 would require prior estimation of only one property of the utility function: the degree of risk aversion, on which a large body of published information is available. Consider first the following case of utility that is quadratic in consumption of goods, conditionally on the level of monetary asset service consumption.

Assumption 1. Let V have the form

$$V(\mathbf{m}_t, c_t) = F[M(\mathbf{m}_t), c_t] = A[M(\mathbf{m}_t)]c_t - \frac{1}{2}B[M(\mathbf{m}_t)]c_t^2, \qquad (25)$$

where A is a positive, increasing, concave function and B is a nonnegative, decreasing, convex function.

The alternative assumption is Guassianity, as follows:

Assumption 2. Let (r_{it}^*, c_{t+1}) be a bivariate Gaussian process for each asset $i = 1, \ldots, k_1$.

We also make the following conventional CAPM assumption[6]:

Assumption 3. The benchmark rate process is deterministic or already risk-adjusted, so that R_t^* is a risk-free rate.

Under this assumption, it follows that

$$\mathrm{Cov}\left(R_t^*, \frac{\partial V}{\partial c_{t+1}}\right) = 0.$$

We define $H_{t+1} = H(M_{t+1}, c_{t+1})$ to be the well-known Arrow–Pratt measure of absolute risk aversion,

$$H(M_{t+1}, c_{t+1}) = \frac{-E_t[V'']}{E_t[V']}, \qquad (26)$$

where $V' = \partial V(\mathbf{m}_{t+1}, c_{t+1})/\partial c_{t+1}$ and $V'' = \partial^2 V(\mathbf{m}_{t+1}, c_{t+1})/\partial c_{t+1}^2$. In this definition, risk aversion is measured relative to consumption risk, conditionally upon the level of monetary services produced by $M_{t+1} = M(\mathbf{m}_t)$. Under risk aversion, H_{t+1} is positive and increases as the degree of absolute risk aversion increases. The following lemma is central to our Theorem 3.

---

[6] It amounts to the assumption that the risk premium already has been extracted from the benchmark rate. In practice, this assumption is harmless because the risk premia adjustments below are applied to all component assets before the benchmark rate is computed — usually as an upper envelope of the component rates. If other asset paths also are included among those used to produce the upper envelope, then this assumption requires that the same risk premia adjustments also be applied to those paths before the upper envelope is generated. Because the risk premia already have been extracted at the time that the envelope is produced, the benchmark rate automatically is risk adjusted.

Lemma 1. *Under Assumption 3 and either Assumption 1 or Assumption 2, the user-cost risk adjustment, ψ_{it}, defined by equation (11) reduces to*

$$\psi_{it} = \frac{1}{1+R_t^*} H_{t+1} \operatorname{Cov}(r_{it}^*, c_{t+1}). \tag{27}$$

Proof: Assuming that R_s^* is a risk-free rate, equation (9) simplifies to

$$\frac{\partial V}{\partial c_t} = \rho(1+R_t^*) E_t \left[\frac{\partial V}{\partial c_{t+1}}\right], \tag{28}$$

and the risk-adjustment term (11) simplifies to

$$\psi_{it} = -\rho \left[\operatorname{Cov}\left(r_{it}^*, \frac{\partial V}{\partial c_{t+1}}\right) \bigg/ \frac{\partial V}{\partial c_t}\right]. \tag{29}$$

Substituting (28) into (29), we acquire

$$\psi_{it} = -\frac{1}{1+R_t^*} \left[\operatorname{Cov}\left(r_{it}^*, \frac{\partial V}{\partial c_{t+1}}\right) \bigg/ E_t\left[\frac{\partial V}{\partial c_{t+1}}\right]\right]. \tag{30}$$

Consider first the case in which we accept Assumption 1. Substituting the quadratic specification (25) into (30), we get

$$\psi_{it} = \frac{1}{1+R_t^*} \left[\frac{-EV''}{EV'}\right] \operatorname{Cov}(r_{it}^*, c_{t+1}), \tag{31}$$

which, under our definition of H_{t+1}, is identical to (27).

Now, consider the alternative possibility of accepting Assumption 2 instead of Assumption 1. Applying Stein's lemma for bivariate normal distributions to equation (30), we again acquire (31) and thereby (27).[7] □

Observe that equation (27) provides a CCAPM-type result, because the risk adjustment term, ψ_{it}, is very much like the risk premium on a risky asset in CCAPM. In CCAPM, as in our model, compensation for risk is proportional to the covariance of the asset's return with consumption through the factor $\operatorname{Cov}(r_{it}, c_{t+1})$ in (27) and also to the degree of risk aversion H_{t+1} in (27).[8]

---

[7] For Stein's lemma, see Rubinstein (1976).
[8] If own interest rates are positively correlated with consumption, equation (27) is positive because H_{t+1} would be positive under risk aversion. Alternatively, if the asset's return is not sufficiently risky to dominate the direction of the net shocks to consumption from risk, the opposite could happen. The asset's rate of return could correlate negatively with the consumption stream in a manner tending to decrease the household's consumption risk,

CCAPM Special Case

In effect, what the adjustment does for very risky rates is to remove the risk premium from $E_t r_{it}$ so that the adjusted user cost becomes positive. To see this more clearly, define $Z_t = H_{t+1} c_t$, where Z_t is a modified (time shifted) Arrow–Pratt relative risk aversion measure. Our theorem now follows immediately.

Theorem 3. *Under the assumptions of Lemma 1, we have*

$$\Pi_{it} = \frac{E_t R_t^* - (E_t r_{it}^* - \phi_{it})}{1 + E_t R_t^*}, \qquad (32)$$

where

$$\phi_{it} = Z_t \operatorname{Cov}\left(r_{it}^*, \frac{c_{t+1}}{c_t}\right). \qquad (33)$$

Proof. Substitute (27) and (10) into $\Pi_{it} = \pi_{it} + \psi_{it}$ and substitute $Z_t = H_{t+1} c_t$. □

As is evident from this theorem, the risk-premium adjustment is ϕ_{it}, where c_{t+1}/c_t is a measure of the consumption growth rate. Hence, the risk adjustment depends on relative risk aversion and the covariance between the consumption growth path c_{t+1}/c_t and the real rates of excess return r_{it}^*. We see that the adjusted user cost $\Pi_{it} = \pi_{it} + \psi_{it}$ can be written in the same form as the unadjusted user cost (10), if the benchmark rate is defined to be risk free and if the risk-premium adjustment ϕ_{it} is subtracted out of the expected value of the real rates of excess return r_{it}^*. As we have observed, that adjustment should be expected to decrease the expected own rate of return, if the asset is very risky and thereby contibutes positively to consumption risk.

---

and hence (27) would be negative. In the CCAPM theory of finance, beta of a very risky asset is usually positive, where beta is defined to be $\beta_{ic} = \operatorname{Cov}(r_{it}^*, c_{t+1})/\operatorname{Var}(c_{t+1})$. The subscript c in β_{ic} designates 'consumption based' beta, and the lack of a time subscript in the notation β_{ic} results from the assumption of stationarity of the interest rate and consumption bivariate process. Clearly, the usual finance view of positive β_{ic} can hold if and only if $\operatorname{Cov}(r_{it}, c_{t+1})$ is positive. This conclusion about the sign of the adjustment term, ψ_{it}, in the adjusted user cost $\pi_{it} + \psi_{it}$ of very risky assets is especially revealing, when the benchmark rate is defined to be riskless, as we have just done. Consider the definition of the unadjusted user cost in equation (10). Because we now are assuming that the benchmark rate is defined to be the maximum available rate of return on a risk-free asset, we can conclude that the benchmark asset has no embedded liquidity premium and cannot be less than the own rate of return on any risk free monetary asset i. Hence, (10) is nonnegative if monetary asset i is risk free. But suppose that consumers are risk averse and that monetary asset i is not risk free. Then, $E_t r_{it}$ will contain a risk premium, despite the fact that R_t does not (or its risk premium has been removed). Hence, the unadjusted user cost (10) could be negative. But as we have just observed, ψ_{it} in this case will be positive, and we would expect that, in fact, it will be sufficiently positive to offset the possible negativity of the unadjusted user cost to produce positive value of the adjusted user cost $\pi_{it} + \psi_{it}$.

6 Magnitude of the Adjustment

In accordance with the large and growing literature on the equity premium puzzle, we should expect that ϕ_{it} is small for most i. In fact, our initial computations of that risk-premium adjustment term for the components of the existing monetary aggregates produces very small correction terms, such that the usual Divisia monetary aggregate and the extended Divisia monetary aggregate are nearly identical to within the roundoff error of the data. There recently has been growing interest in the inclusion of common stock and bond mutual funds in monetary aggregates, but no such change has yet been made officially by the Federal Reserve. In addition, our confidence in the available data on those additional potential components is limited at the present time. Because the rates of return on those assets are subject to much more risk than the rates of return on the existing components of the monetary aggregates, the gain in moving from the usual Divisia index to the extended Divisia index could be greater, if those assets are incorporated into monetary aggregates. Nevertheless, our initial computations with data including those risky assets produce small, although no longer trivial, differences between the extended and unextended Divisia monetary aggregates. The equity premium puzzle issues with CCAPM do not go away with the incorporation of assets with substantial rate-of-return risk.

One possible explanation of the surprisingly small risk adjustment terms, even with risky assets, may be aggregation over economic agents. In some sense, the risk adjustments may tend to cancel each other out across economic agents, and our initial computations, mentioned above, are produced from data aggregated over economic agents. To explore this possibility further, we now turn to the use of simulated data generated from a single modeled economic agent. Generation of those data requires numerical solution of that consumer's Euler equations. Having generated the simulated data, we compare the exact aggregator function implied by the weakly separable structure of the utility function with the unextended Divisia monetary aggregate to isolate the effect of the needed risk adjustment, because the correctly computed adjusted Divisia aggregate should track the exact aggregator function accurately.

The loss in tracking ability of the unextended Divisia index under risk has been investigated previously by Barnett, Kirova, and Pasupathy (1995), but with an aggregator function that was estimated using actual data aggregated over consumers.[9] Hence there was no control in that study for the possible decrease in the risk adjustment that may have been produced by aggregation over consumers or for possible specification error in the estimated paramet-

---

[9]That paper is reprinted in this book as chapter 22.

ric model. In particular, there is no way to know the degree to which the tracking error of the unadjusted Divisia index was produced by the missing risk adjustment or alternatively by the specification error in the estimated utility function of the representative consumer. By the use of simulated data below, we know the exact aggregator function for the simulated single consumer and hence we control for the possible downward bias that may have been produced by earlier studies using macroeconomic data and we eliminate any possible specification error effect, because our simulated data are exactly consistent with rational behavior of our modeled consumer.

7 Generation of Simulated Data

7.1 Introduction

To show how well the unadjusted Divisia monetary aggregate tracks the 'true' theoretical aggregate for one consumer, we numerically solve for the individual monetary assets from the Euler equations associated with a dynamic optimization problem. We use the calculated rational-expectation equilibrium to determine both the Divisia and the theoretical monetary aggregate, and we compare how well the unadjusted Divisia index tracks the movement of the theoretical aggregate. The magnitude of the effect of the missing risk adjustment in the unadjusted Divisia index is measured by the gap between our two simulated aggregates.

Although there are a number of numerical methods that solve for the rational expectation equilibrium of such problems, for this paper we have selected the approach advocated by Den Haan and Marcet (1990).[10] The Den Haan and Marcet approach has been shown to provide good results for a number of complex optimization problems.[11] Furthermore, the complexity of the dynamic programming problem found in this paper is an important factor in choosing the Den Haan and Marcet algorithm, because this solution method does not require discretizing the state space — a formidable task for any computer, when the number of state variables is as plentiful as in our model.

7.2 Parameterized Model of Preferences

In this section we formulate a parameterized special case of the model presented in Section 2. The decision problem again is a discrete-time-period

---

[10] See Taylor and Uhlig (1990) for a list and comparison of the known methodologies for solving dynamic optimization problems.

[11] See Den Haan and Marcet (1989), Marshall (1992), and Bansal et.al. (1992).

optimization problem for a consumer, under the assumption that monetary assets are weakly separable from consumer goods, so that an exact aggregate exists over consumer goods and another exact aggregate exists over monetary assets. Because our model of tastes will be parameterized, the model now is a special case of the model that was used above to derive the extended Divisia index, which therefore can be assumed to track the exact aggregate over monetary assets accurately. In our model, there are three component monetary assets within the exact monetary aggregate. We make that choice so that we can use the empirical results found by Barnett, Hinich,, and Yue (2000) to set the unknown parameters of the model. In addition, we have tried to use the same notation that Barnett, Hinich,, and Yue (2000) used in an attempt to keep some consistency in that literature.

We assume that the consumer's intertemporal utility, (1), has the form

$$F[M(\mathbf{m}_t), c_t] + E_t \left[\sum_{s=t+1}^{\infty} \rho^{s-t} F[M(\mathbf{m}_s), c_s] \right], \quad (34)$$

where F is the constant relative-risk-aversion utility function

$$F(M_s, c_s) = \frac{1}{\sigma} \left[c_s^{\beta} M_s^{1-\beta} \right]^{\sigma}$$

with $\sigma \in (-\infty, 0) \cup (0, 1)$, $\rho \in (0, 1)$, and $\beta \in (0, 1)$, and where c_s and $M_s = M(\mathbf{m}_s)$ are, respectively, the consumption good and the monetary asset quantity aggregates.[12] The three-dimensional vector $\mathbf{m}_s$ contains the three component assets. As $\sigma \to 0$, the consumer's utility function becomes $F(M_s, c_s) = \log(c_s^{\beta} M_s^{1-\beta})$. This is the risk-neutral case, because the degree of relative risk aversion is equal to $1 - \sigma$.

We assume that the exact monetary aggregator function, $M(\mathbf{m}_s)$, is the CES function

$$M(\mathbf{m}_s) = \left(\sum_{i=1}^{3} \delta_i m_{is}^{\alpha} \right)^{1/\alpha} \quad \text{with} \quad \sum_{i=1}^{3} \delta_i = 1 \quad \text{and} \quad \alpha \in (0, 1].$$

The simple-sum and Cobb–Douglas aggregates are nested special cases, because the monetary aggregator function becomes Cobb–Douglas if $\alpha \to 0$ and simple sum if $\alpha = 1$. Substitutability among components declines as α declines below 1.

---

[12] In much of this literature, a finite-period planning horizon is assumed, as in Jensen (1997), but the resulting exact aggregate is the same in the finite and infinite planning cases. See Barnett (1995) regarding the equivalency. That paper is reprinted in this book as chapter 10.

7.3 Euler Equations

Following Barnett, Hinich, and Yue (2000) and Poterba and Rotemberg (1987), the Euler equations from the consumer's decision in Problem 1 with the above specification for the objective function are

$$c_s^{\sigma\beta-1} M_s^{\sigma(\beta-1)} = E_s \left\{ \left[\rho \frac{p_s^*}{p_{s+1}^*}(1+R_s) \right]^{-1} c_{s+1}^{1-\sigma\beta} M_{s+1}^{\sigma(\beta-1)} \right\},$$

$$c_s^{-\sigma\beta} M_s^{\sigma(\beta-1)+\alpha} m_{1s}^{1-\alpha} = E_s \left[\left(\frac{1}{\delta_1} \frac{\beta\rho}{1-\beta} \frac{p_s^* R_s}{p_{s+1}^*} \right)^{-1} c_{s+1}^{1-\sigma\beta} M_{s+1}^{\sigma(\beta-1)} \right],$$

$$c_s^{-\sigma\beta} M_s^{\sigma(\beta-1)+\alpha} m_{2s}^{1-\alpha} = E_s \left\{ \left[\frac{1}{\delta_2} \frac{\beta\rho}{1-\beta} \frac{p_s^*(R_s - r_{2s})}{p_{s+1}^*} \right]^{-1} c_{s+1}^{1-\sigma\beta} M_{s+1}^{\sigma(\beta-1)} \right\},$$

$$c_s^{-\sigma\beta} M_s^{\sigma(\beta-1)+\alpha} m_{3s}^{1-\alpha} = E_s \left\{ \left[\frac{1}{\delta_3} \frac{\beta\rho}{1-\beta} \frac{p_s^*(R_s - r_{3s})}{p_{s+1}^*} \right]^{-1} c_{s+1}^{1-\sigma\beta} M_{s+1}^{\sigma(\beta-1)} \right\}.$$

In the dynamic programming Problem 1, the consumer faces the exogenous stochastic state vector

$$\phi_s = \left(R_{s-1}, r_{2,s-1}, r_{3,s-1}, \frac{p_s^*}{p_{s-1}^*}, \frac{I_s}{I_{s-1}} \right),$$

along with the endogenously evolving state vector $\mathbf{m}_{s-1}$. Together, they define the state vector $\boldsymbol{\sigma}_s' = (\mathbf{m}_{s-1}', \boldsymbol{\phi}_s')$, whereas the consumer's control vector for the optimization problem is $\mathbf{z}_s' = (\mathbf{m}_s', c_s)$.

We assume that the stochastic process $\{\phi_s\}$ behaves as two independent Markovian processes such that

$$\phi_{1s} = \mathbf{a}_1 + \Lambda_1 \phi_{1,s-1} + \mathbf{u}_{1s}$$

and

$$\ln(\phi_{2s}) = \mathbf{a}_2 + \Lambda_2 \ln(\phi_{2,s-1}) + \mathbf{u}_{2s},$$

where $\phi_{1s} = (R_{s-1}, r_{2,s-1}, r_{3,s-1})'$ and $\phi_{2s} = (p_s^*/p_{s-1}^*, I_s/I_{s-1})'$.[13] The disturbances $\mathbf{u}_{1s}$ and $\mathbf{u}_{2s}$ are both distributed i.i.d. $N(\mathbf{0}, \Omega_i)$ for $i = 1, 2$, with Λ_1 and Ω_1 being 3×3 matrices, whereas Λ_2 and Ω_2 are 2×2 matrices. The processes' intercept terms $\mathbf{a}_1$ and $\mathbf{a}_2$ are 3×1 and 2×1 vectors, respectively.

---

[13] More complex stochastic processes for the exogenous state process could be used if the economist so desires. We here define the log of a vector to be the vector of the logarithms.

Each Markovian process is a first-order vector autoregressive process. The natural logarithmic transformation of ϕ_{2s} ensures that the process is stationary. Because ϕ_{1s} is comprised only of interest rates, there is no reason to transform this process. Regarding the method of computing the benchmark asset's rate of return, the sources of exogenous data, and the algorithms used in solving the system, see Jensen (1997).

If we define the economy's parameter vector as $\lambda = (\rho, \sigma, \alpha, \beta, \delta_1, \delta_2, \delta_3, \mathbf{a}'_1, \mathbf{a}'_2, \text{vec}(\mathbf{\Omega_1})', \text{vec}(\mathbf{\Omega_2})')$, then for each value of λ, the above optimization problem defines a nonlinear mapping from the exogenous state process $\{\phi_s\}$ to $\{\mathbf{z}_s\}$. The theoretical monetary aggregate, $\{M_s\}$, and the Divisia monetary aggregate

$$Q_s = Q_{s-1} \prod_{i=1}^{3} \left(\frac{m_{is}}{m_{i,s-1}} \right)^{s^*_{is}}$$

then can be calculated from $\{\phi_s\}$ and $\{\mathbf{z}_s\}$, where

$$s^*_{is} = \frac{1}{2}(s_{is} + s_{i,s-1}),$$

$$s_{is} = \frac{\pi_{is} m_{is}}{\sum_{j=1}^{3} \pi_{js} m_{js}},$$

and the user costs π_{is} are as in equation (5).

7.4 Solving the Euler Equations

To explore the implications of risk aversion and of substitutability among component assets for the tracking ability of the unadjusted Divisia index, we use the solution for $\{\mathbf{z}_s\}$ provided by Jensen (1997) for various settings of the degree of risk aversion and of substitutability. On the basis of the simulation results in his paper, we generate the plots of the unadjusted Divisia index and of the exact parametric aggregate. Because the procedures used by Jensen (1997) are provided in detail in his paper, we outline the approach only briefly.

A rapidly growing literature exists on numerical methods for solving dynamic optimization problems.[14] Of those algorithms currently available, the Parameterized Expectation Approach (PEA) of Den Haan and Marcet (1990) has performed well in head-to-head tests with other algorithms. In addition, the PEA has been applied to a number of different economic areas, including

---

[14] See Taylor and Uhlig (1990) for an excellent source on the available methods and a comparison of their performance record.

growth models [Den Haan and Marcet (1990)], asset markets with heterogenous agents [Marcet and Singleton (1990)], and monetary economies [Den Haan (1990a,b), Marshall (1992), Bansal et al. (1994, 1995)].

The PEA approximates the expectation operators found in the Euler equations by parameterizing them with a basis function that spans the set of expectation operators in Hilbert space. The basis function is a globally flexible functional form having arguments that are the state variables $\sigma_\mathbf{s}$.[15] We have chosen the first-order polynomial function, as in Jensen (1997). One then iterates over the parameters of these flexible functional forms until a convergence criterion is met.

Intuitively, each iteration of the PEA can be viewed as nonlinear least-squares learning behavior by the consumer.[16] Once learning is no longer occurring, the agent selects that stochastic solution $\{z_s\}$ that satisfies the Euler equations, given the learned prediction of the expectation operators. Hence, it can be argued that the numerical solution found with the PEA is an equilibrium for an agent restricted to the learning associated with a specific globally flexible functional form.

In applying the PEA, Jensen (1997) used the convergence criterion recommended by Bansal et al. (1994, 1995), except for cases in which the degree of risk aversion was set at high levels. In those cases, Jensen (1997) used the convergence criterion advocated by Marshall (1992) to determine the stopping point for the PEA algorithm.[17] Marshall argues that the PEA algorithm converges to an approximate equilibrium, if the coefficient vectors, $\mathbf{v}_i$ for $i = 1, 2, 3, 4$, are the optimal prediction vectors.

To determine whether the numerical solution is close to the true solution, Jensen (1997) employed the Den Haan and Marcet test statistic (DHM-stat) [see Den Haan and Marcet (1994) and Taylor and Uhlig (1990)]. The DHM-stat provides a test of the theoretical martingale property $E[\boldsymbol{\nu}_s \otimes \mathbf{h}_{sij}] = 0$, where $\boldsymbol{\nu}_s$ is the 4×1 residual vector from the Euler equations and $\mathbf{h}_{sij} = \sigma^i_{s-j}$. If Hansen's (1982) regularity conditions hold and the approximation is an exact solution satisfying the above martingale property, then the DHM-stat $TBA^{-1}B$ will be distributed as χ^2 with 20 degrees of freedom, where

$$B = (1/T) \sum_{s=t}^{t+T} [\boldsymbol{\nu}_s \otimes \mathbf{h}_{sij}] \quad \text{and} \quad A = (1/T) \sum_{s=t}^{t+T} [\boldsymbol{\nu}_s \otimes \mathbf{h}_{sij}][\boldsymbol{\nu}_s \otimes \mathbf{h}_{sij}]'.$$

To ensure that our solution reflects the empirical world, Jensen (1997)

---

[15] See Gallant (1982), Barnett and Jonas (1983), and Barnett and Yue (1988) for the properties and examples of globally flexible functions.

[16] See Marcet and Sargent (1989a,b) for examples of linear least-squares learning models that have a locally stable equilibrium.

[17] We initially used the convergence criterion of Bansal et al. (1994,1995) but the PEA algorithm failed to converge within 40,000 iterations.

set the parameters in the Euler equations equal to the generalized method of moment estimates of those parameters found by Barnett, Hinich. and Yue (2000). The other parameters associated with the two Markovian processes were set equal to the estimated parameters for the two VAR(1), using monthly data from January 1960 to December 1990.

The size of the simulation is equal to 500, i.e., $T = 500$. We know from Corollary 1 to Theorem 1 that the unadjusted Divisia index will track well under risk neutrality. Hence our interest is in other cases. Conditionally basing Jensen's (1997) solutions of the Euler equations on Barnett, Hinich, and Yue's (2000) parameter estimates, we computed the mean squared errors of the fit of the Divisia growth rates to the numerically solved exact aggregate's growth rates. The mean squared errors are supplied in Table 1 for each of the settings used in the numerical solutions.

TABLE 1
DIVISIA INDEX GROWTH-RATE TRACKING OF THE SIMULATED EXACT AGGREGATE, MEAN SQUARED ERRORS

α	σ	MSE
0	0	0.000070
0.1	0	0.000097
0.2	0	0.000137
0.3	0	0.000208
0.4	0	0.000336
0.5	0	0.000570
0.6	0	0.001063
0	−0.1	0.011939
0	−0.2	0.011961
0	−0.3	0.012425
0	−0.4	0.012917
0	−0.5	0.013413
0	−0.6	0.013881

For our constant relative-risk-aversion specification, the degree of relative risk aversion is equal to $1 - \sigma$. Clearly, the tracking ability of the unadjusted Divisia index is not independent of the degree of risk aversion, and tracking accuracy declines as relative risk aversion increases. In addition, at any setting of the degree of risk aversion, the tracking ability depends on substitutability among the components of the aggregator function. In our CES specification of the aggregator function, component assets are perfectly substitutable at $\alpha = 1$, and substitutability among components declines as α declines below 1. As is evident from Table 1, tracking error grows as substitutability increases, but as can be expected from the theory, the dependency

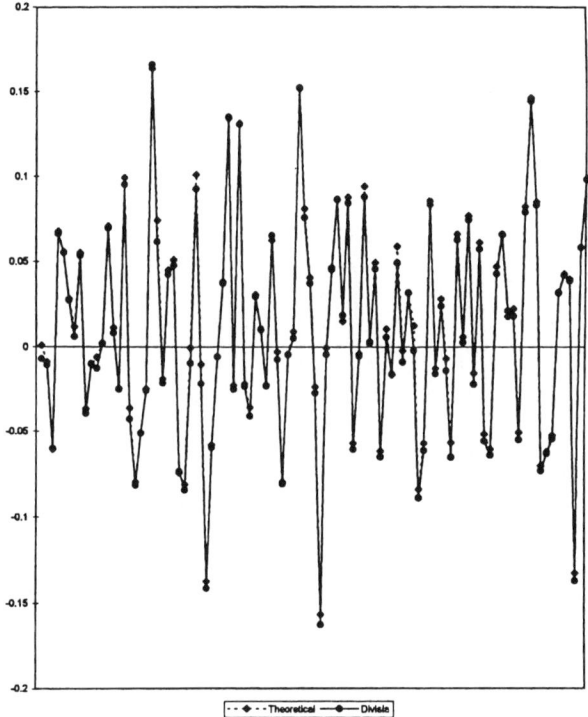

Figure 1: Divisia and theoretical growth: $\alpha \to 0$ and $\sigma \to 0$ (centered moving average over 5 observations).

of tracking error upon substitutability is small relative to the dependency upon relative risk aversion. In fact, just how small is graphically displayed in two cases in Figures 1 and 2 for two of the risk-neutral cases summarized in Table 1. Because 500 points produce a dense and unclear plot for the growth rates, we produced Figures 1 and 2 from centered moving averages with window of size 5.

Hence the risk-adjusted Divisia index and the associated risk-adjusted user costs are likely to be useful, in some non-risk-neutral cases, although in many cases with moderate risk aversion, the gain may be slight. It also appears that aggregation over economic agents is a relevant factor, because we find greater loss in tracking ability with simulated data from one consumer than with the economy's aggregate per-capita data.[18]

---

[18] Regarding the results with aggregate per-capita data, see Barnett and Liu (2000) and

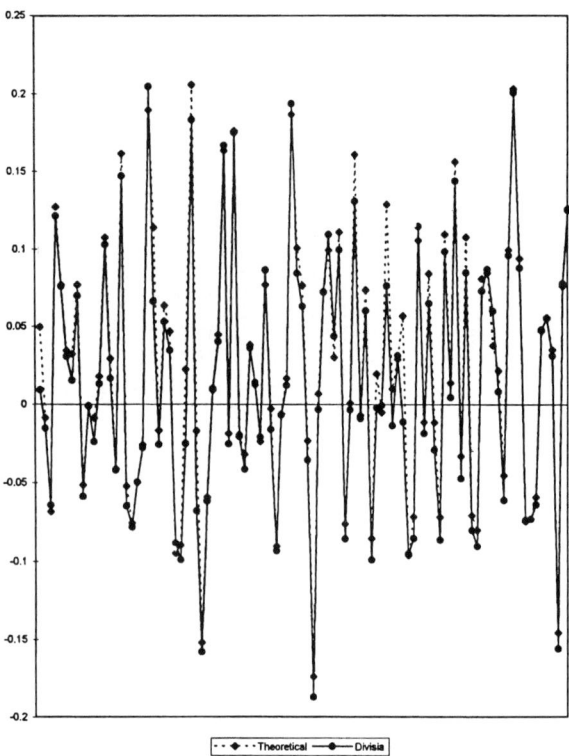

Figure 2: Divisia and theoretical growth: $\alpha = 0.6$ and $\sigma \to 0$ (centered moving average over 5 observations).

For details about the parameter estimation and data, see Barnett, Hinich, and Yue (2000), and for details of the solution for the endogenous variables conditionally upon the exogenous processes, see Jensen (1997). At this point, we are not comfortable about reaching stronger conclusions in this regard, because competing approaches to solving rational-expectations models may be preferable in some of the cases considered above, and hence we cannot be certain of the degree to which our conclusions have been affected by inaccuracies in the solution method used. It would be useful to repeat these experiments with the alternative solution methods proposed by Baxter *et al.* (1990), Coleman (1990, 1991), or Baxter (1991).

Barnett, Kirova, and Pasupathy (1995).

8 Conclusion

In earlier research on aggregation theoretic foundations for monetary modeling, the primary issue has been to explore the degree of the tracking error of the unadjusted Divisia monetary index, derived from the first-order conditions under perfect certainty, to the degree of risk aversion. In this paper, we develop a CCAPM adjustment to user costs that permits the Divisia index to be derived directly from the Euler equations under risk, so that the tracking error produced from risk aversion disappears, because the risk is internalized within the resulting extended Divisia index. Further details regarding that derivation can be found in the closely related working paper by Barnett, Liu, and Jensen (1997).

Using the components of the usual monetary aggregates, we find that the CCAPM adjustment to user costs is very small, and the gain from moving from the unadjusted Divisia index to the extended index seems slight, at least with those relatively low-risk components. These results are very similar to related results on the equity premium puzzle, because the small adjustments in both cases result from the very low covariance between rates of return and the consumption stream. We then explore the possibility that aggregation over economic agents may have smoothed that covariance, or the possibility that earlier results on the tracking error of the unadjusted Divisia index may have been produced by specification error in the parametric model of the utility function. We do so by producing simulated data from a modeled rational consumer. The procedure used to solve the Euler equations is that of Jensen (1997). We find that the tracking error of the unadjusted index is nontrivial under risk aversion, and depends upon the degree of risk aversion. Hence, the CCAPM adjustment to user costs and the risk-adjusted Divisia index can be expected to be needed, when modeling the behavior of one economic agent under risk aversion. How to progress further in the direction of aggregation over economic agents is not explored in this paper.

Although the CCAPM approach to risk adjustment is a natural extension of the Divisia index, we hasten to add that as better approaches to risk adjustment become available, they should be used in this literature. Because economic index number theory and aggregation theory are directly derived from microeconomic theory, the Divisia index always can be extended to incorporate new developments. Considering the established empirical problems of CCAPM, especially in the equity-premium-puzzle literature, we have no doubt that better or perhaps generalized methods will become available in the future.[19] We no more advocate unwavering commitment to the CCAPM risk adjustment than unwavering commitment to perfect-certainty modeling.

---

[19] Regarding the equity premium puzzle, see Mehra and Prescott (1985).

We do wish to indicate the relevancy to financial aggregation theory of developments in finance and decision making under risk — including future developments not yet in existence.

Appendix A: Consumer's Aggregation Theorem

It is clear that equation (3) does define the exact monetary aggregate in the welfare sense, because M_s measures the consumer's subjective evaluation of the services that he or she receives from holding $\mathbf{m}_s$. However, it also can be shown that equation (6) defines the exact monetary aggregate in the aggregation theoretic sense. In particular, the stochastic process M_s contains all of the information about $\mathbf{m}_s$ that is needed by the consumer to solve the rest of his or her decision problem. This conclusion is based on the following theorem, which we call the consumer's aggregation theorem:

Let
$$D_s = I_s + \sum_{i=1}^{k_1} \left[(1 + r_{i,s-1})p_{s-1}^* m_{i,s-1} - p_s^* m_{is}\right],$$

and let

$$D(s) = \{(\mathbf{h}_s, \mathbf{x}_s, A_s) \in Y : \sum_{i=1}^n p_{is} x_{is} \quad (A.1)$$

$$= \sum_{i=1}^{k_2}[(1 + i_{i,s-1})p_{s-1}^* h_{i,s-1} - p_s^* h_{is}] + (1 + R_{s-1})\nu_{s-1}^* A_{s-1} - p_s^* A_s + D_s\}.$$

Let $(\mathbf{a}_s^*, \mathbf{x}_s^*, A_s^*)$ solve Problem 1, and assume that the utility function $u(\mathbf{m}_s, \mathbf{h}_s, \mathbf{x}_s)$ is weakly separable in $\mathbf{m}_s$, so that there exist aggregator function M and utility function U such that $U(M(\mathbf{m}_s), \mathbf{h}_s, \mathbf{x}_s) = u(\mathbf{m}_s, \mathbf{h}_s, \mathbf{x}_s)$. Consider the following decision problem, which is conditional upon prior knowledge of the aggregate process $M_s^* = M(m_s^*)$, although not upon the component processes $\mathbf{m}_s^*$.

Problem A.1. Choose the deterministic point $(\mathbf{h}_t, \mathbf{x}_t, A_t)$ and the stochastic process $(\mathbf{h}_s, \mathbf{x}_s, A_s)$, $s = t+1, \ldots, \infty$, to maximize

$$U(M_t^*, \mathbf{h}_t, \mathbf{x}_t) + E_t \left[\sum_{s=t+1}^{\infty} \left(\frac{1}{1+\xi}\right)^{s-t} U(M_s^*, \mathbf{h}_s, \mathbf{x}_s) \right] \quad (A.2)$$

subject to $(\mathbf{h}_s, \mathbf{x}_s, A_s) \in D(s)$ for $s - t$, and also subject to

$$\lim_{s \to \infty} E_t \left(\frac{1}{1+\xi}\right)^{s-t} A_s = 0,$$

Appendix A: Consumer's Aggregation Theorem 273

with the process M_s^* given for $s - t$.

Theorem A.1 (Consumer's Aggregation Theorem). *Let the deterministic point* $(\mathbf{m}_t, \mathbf{h}_t, \mathbf{x}_t, A_t)$ *and the stochastic process* $(\mathbf{m}_s, \mathbf{h}_s, \mathbf{x}_s, A_s)$, $s = t + 1, \ldots, t + T$ *solve Problem 1. Then, the deterministic point* $(\mathbf{h}_t, \mathbf{x}_t, A_t)$ *and the stochastic process* $(\mathbf{h}_s, \mathbf{x}_s, A_s)$, $s = t+1, \ldots, t+T$, *will solve Problem A.1 conditionally upon* $M_s^* = M(\mathbf{m}_s)$ *for* $s = t, \ldots, t+T$.

Proof. Let $(\mathbf{m}_s, \mathbf{h}_s, \mathbf{x}_s, A_s)$ solve Problem 1, but let $(\mathbf{h}_s, \mathbf{x}_s, A_s)$ not solve Problem A.1 conditionally upon the process $M_s^* = M(\mathbf{m}_s)$ given for $s = t, \ldots, t + T$. Then there exist $(\tilde{\mathbf{h}}_s, \tilde{\mathbf{x}}_s, \tilde{A}_s) \in D(s)$ satisfying the transversality condition, such that equation (A.2) evaluated at $(\tilde{\mathbf{h}}_s, \tilde{\mathbf{x}}_s, \tilde{A}_s)$ is strictly greater than equation (A.2) evaluated at $(\mathbf{h}_s, \mathbf{x}_s, A_s)$ conditionally upon $M_s^* = M(\mathbf{m}_s)$.

Hence, equation (1) evaluated at $(\mathbf{m}_s, \tilde{\mathbf{h}}_s, \tilde{\mathbf{x}}_s, \tilde{A}_s)$ is strictly greater than (1) evaluated at $(\mathbf{m}_s, \mathbf{h}_s, \mathbf{x}_s, A_s)$. However, because $(\tilde{\mathbf{h}}_s, \tilde{\mathbf{x}}_s, \tilde{A}_s)$ is feasible for Problem A.1 conditionally upon $M_s = M(\mathbf{m}_s)$, it follows that $(\mathbf{m}_s, \tilde{\mathbf{h}}_s, \tilde{\mathbf{x}}_s, \tilde{A}_s)$ is feasible for Problem 1. Our assumption that $(\mathbf{m}_s, \mathbf{h}_s, \mathbf{x}_s, A_s)$ solves Problem 1 is contradicted. □

Clearly, this proof by contradiction applies not only when M_s is produced by voluntary behavior, but also when the M_s process is exogenously imposed upon the consumer, as through a perfectly inelastic supply function for M_s imposed by central bank policy. In that case, Problem A.1 describes optimal behavior by the consumer in the remaining variables. Clearly, the information about M_s is needed in the solution of Problem A.1 for the processes $(\mathbf{h}_s, \mathbf{x}_s, A_s)$. Alternatively, information about the usual simple-sum monetary aggregate over the components of $\mathbf{m}_s$ is of no use in solving either Problem 1 or A.1 unless the monetary aggregator function M happens to be a simple sum. In other words, the simple-sum aggregate contains useful information about behavior only if the components of $\mathbf{m}_s$ are perfect substitutes in identical ratios (linear aggregation with *equal* coefficients).

Chapter 13

Stochastic Volatility in Interest Rates and Nonlinearity in Velocity

William A. Barnett and Haiyang Xu[*]

> In this study, it is shown that money velocity in a monetary general equilibrium model is deterministically nonlinear, when there is no exogenous uncertainty. When interest rates are stochastic and money and income growth are uncertain, the dynamics of money velocity are nonlinear and its coefficients are stochastic. We simulate the slope coefficient of the money velocity function and find that it exhibits stochastic volatility. The Swamy and Tinsley (1980) random coefficient model is then estimated to compare the results with those from model simulation. It is found that the estimated stochastic slope coefficient has important similarities with the simulation results. The findings of this paper provide some useful information regarding the source of the appearance of instability of money velocity functions in many studies that overlook the stochastic nonlinearity that is central to this paper.

1 Introduction

Some economists continue to insist that linearity is a good assumption for all economic time series, despite the fact that economic theory provides virtually no support for the assumption of linearity. See, e.g., Barnett and Chen (1986, 1988). The controversy is partly due to the fact that the currently available tests do not test for the existence of chaos or nonlinearity produced from within the structure of the economy. As recently pointed out by Day (1992), the tests have no way of determining the source of the chaos or nonlinearity. Even if the economy is totally linear and stable, the current tests, such as the BDS (Brock et al. (1996)), could still find evidence of nonlinearity or even chaos in economic data if the economy is affected by a chaotic and unstable surrounding weather system. Therefore it is interesting if we can

---

[*]Originally published in the *International Journal of Systems Science*, 29, (1998), pp. 1189–1201. This research was partially supported by NSF grant SES 9223557.

identify some sources of potential nonlinearity and instability from within the economic system. In this paper, we theoretically show that money velocity is nonlinear. We use the comparison between model simulation and estimation to examine the relevance of our theoretical results.

Traditionally money velocity is viewed as a constant or at least a stable function of its few determinants. The unusual behavior of money velocity and the instability of the traditional money demand function since the late 1970's in the U.S. have called for reexamination of the traditional views. See, e.g., Stone and Thornton (1987). Several lines of research have been pursued in the recent monetary economics literature. One line of research focuses on the correct measurement of money and challenges the traditional practice of ignoring the aggregation problem in monetary economics research and policy design.[1] Some research focuses on the effects of institutional change on money velocity. See, e.g., Bordo and Jonung (1981, 1987, and 1989). Another hypothesis, proposed by Friedman (1983), attributes the several substantial declines of M1 velocity in the U.S. since 1981 to the increased money growth variability following the change of Federal Reserve operating procedures in October 1979. However, empirical tests of this variability hypothesis have not provided uniform evidence.[2] Time-varying coefficient models have been employed in econometric modeling of money velocity. See Dueker (1993 and 1995).

In this paper we find that money velocity is nonlinear when there is no uncertainty in nominal interest rates. When interest rates are stochastic and money and income growth are uncertain, we find that money velocity is nonlinear and coefficients of traditional money velocity functions are stochastic. That is, the dynamics of money velocity are unstable. More specifically, if covariances change between interest rates and the consumption growth rate, or between interest rates and the real money growth rate, the model shows that in addition to the nonlinearity in money velocity, the coefficients of the money velocity process will shift stochastically. In fact, anything that causes the covariances to change will contribute to a random shift of the coefficients of the money velocity process. The causes could include financial innovations or money growth variability, as previously investigated in the literature.[3] In this sense, our study provides a general and coherent theoretical explanation for the instability of money velocity and nests many earlier explanations as special cases.

---

[1] For the measurement of money, see Barnett (1980a, 1987), Barnett et al. (1992), Belongia (1996), and Serletis and Krause (1996).

[2] See Belongia (1985), Fisher and Serletis (1989), Hall and Noble (1987), and Thornton (1995) for empirical evidence of the variability hypothesis.

[3] For the effect of financial innovation on the economy, see recent work by Thornton (1994).

We simulate the process of the slope coefficient of a simple traditional money velocity function based on U.S. quarterly data from 1960.1 to 1992.4, and find that the theoretical model generates a volatile slope coefficient when the degree of risk aversion in the model is moderately high, especially during the 1973-1976 and 1979-1982 periods. The Swamy and Tinsley (1980) random coefficients model for money velocity is estimated to compare the behavior of the estimated stochastic coefficients with the simulated coefficients from the theoretical model. The estimated stochastic slope coefficient has important similarities with the simulation results. Since the sample size for the data on money velocity is very small for testing nonlinearity, we do not attempt to test for nonlinearity in money velocity data. For recent developments in testing nonlinearity and chaos in economics, see Barnett et al (1995, 1997).

The remainder of this paper is organized as follows. Section 2 develops a monetary general equilibrium model in which monetary assets provide monetary services as well as interest income. Section 3 derives the theoretical results for money velocity under the assumption that nominal interest rates are known. It is shown that Latane's equation (Latane (1954)) is a special case of the model developed in this paper. Section 4 generalizes the result when the assumption of certain nominal interest rates is relaxed. The effect of risk aversion and interest rate uncertainty is investigated. Section 5 presents the results from model simulation and from estimation of a random coefficient model. The last section provides concluding remarks.

2 Assumptions and Theoretical Specifications

In this section we outline an infinite-horizon, representative-agent model with a set of monetary assets which pay interest. Suppose that there exist k monetary assets. Monetary asset i pays nominal return rate R_{it} at the end of time period t. Money supply is assumed to be exogenous and serves as a moving endowment point in the consumer's budget constraint. There exists one nominal bond with holding period yield R_t, which is also paid at the end of period t. We assume that

$$R_t \geq \max\{R_{it},\ i=1,\ldots,k\} \quad \text{for all} \quad t.$$

This assumption says that monetary assets are dominated in holding period returns by the nominal bond, which is assumed to yield no monetary services. The price for the bond in period t is P_{bt}. There exists one equity asset, which is the exogenous endowment asset and yields resource flow $d_t > 0$. The price of one unit of the equity is P_{st}, and dividend d_t per unit is paid before the share is sold. The only consumption good is the resource flow d_t which is perishable. The price of that consumption good is P_t in period t. There are finitely many identical consumers with utility function $U(c_t, \mathbf{m}_t)$, which is continuous, increasing, and concave in all of its arguments, where c_t is the demand for consumption goods, and $\mathbf{m}'_t = (m_{1t}, m_{2t}, \ldots, m_{kt})$ is a vector of real monetary assets held during period t.

The exogenous supply of monetary asset i in period t is X_{it}, and let $\sum_{i=1}^{k} X_{it} = X_t$ be the simple sum aggregate of money supply. The representative consumer is assumed to maximize the infinite lifetime expected utility:

$$E_t \sum_{t=0}^{\infty} \beta^t U(c_t, m_t) \tag{1}$$

where $\beta \in (0,1)$ is the subjective rate of time discount and E_t is the expectation operator, conditional on information at time period t. The budget constraint in each period is:

$$P_t c_t + P_{st} s_t + P_{bt} b_t + P_t \sum m_{it} \leq s_{t-1}(d_t P_t + P_{st})$$
$$+ P_{b,t-1} b_{t-1}(1 + R_{t-1}) + \sum m_{i,t-1}(1 + R_{i,t-1}) P_{t-1}$$
$$+ \sum [X_{it} - (1 + R_{it-1}) X_{i,t-1}], \tag{2}$$

where s_t is the quantity of equity, b_t is the quantity of bonds held during time period t, and $\sum$ is the summation from $i = 1$ to k. The last term of the budget constraint is different from that in a traditional model.[4] Since we assume that monetary assets pay interest, the supply of money must be adjusted for it.

Money is introduced through the money-in-utility-function approach in this model. In this approach, the utility function must be viewed as the derived utility function that exists if money has positive value in equilibrium.[5] Alternatively, in a cash-in-advance model, it is difficult to justify the existence of a variety of monetary assets which pay different interest rates. In all the cash-in-advance models in the literature, there can exist only one monetary asset in the equilibrium of an economy.

Since monetary assets are dominated or stochastically dominated in returns by the nominal bond, a rational economic agent will not hold monetary assets if monetary assets do not yield monetary services. However, we cannot nest the simple sum monetary aggregator function in the utility function unless all the monetary assets are perfect substitutes for each other (see Barnett,

---

[4] Regarding the traditional budget constraint, which here is only slightly modified, see Giovannini and Labadie (1991, eqs. (3) and (12)) and Hodrick, Lakota, and Lucas (1991, eq. (4)).

[5] See Blanchard and Fischer (1989, p. 192), Arrow and Hahn (1971), and Feenstra (1986).

1987). To reduce the dimension of the vector of monetary assets to an aggregate index of 'money,' we need to assume that the utility function $U(c_t, \mathbf{m}_t)$ is weakly separable in monetary assets and can be written as $F(c_t, f(\mathbf{m}_t))$, where $f(\mathbf{m}_t)$ is a linearly homogenous subutility function.[6] Under this assumption, it can be proved that the Divisia monetary aggregate can track the theoretical function $f(\mathbf{m}_t)$ exactly in continuous time or up to a third order remainder term in discrete time, if nominal yields R_t and R_{it} are known at the beginning of the time period.[7] If the agent is risk averse and nominal yields R_t and R_{it} are not known exactly to the agent at the beginning of time interval t, the Divisia aggregate's tracking ability is somewhat compromised. For the purpose of this paper, we first assume that R_t and R_{it} are known to consumers at the beginning of time interval t, and in Section 4 we will relax this assumption.

Let m_t be the value of the exact monetary aggregate over its components $m_{it}, i = 1, 2, \ldots, k$, so that $m_t = f(\mathbf{m}_t)$. The utility function $U(c_t, \mathbf{m}_t)$ consequently can be written as $F(c_t, m_t)$. In order to deal with the first order conditions in terms of the quantity aggregate rather than each individual monetary assets, we have to transform the budget constraint to replace the vector of monetary assets $\mathbf{m}_t$ with the exact monetary aggregate m_t. To do this, let π_t be the exact money price aggregate (or user cost aggregate) dual to m_t, and let π_{it} be the user cost of monetary asset $i = 1, 2, \ldots, k$ in period t. It can be shown that the exact aggregation-theoretic price aggregator function is the unit cost function. See Barnett (1987). According to Fisher's factor reversal test, expenditure on the aggregate must equal expenditure on the components, so that π_t must satisfy

$$\sum_{i=1}^{k} \pi_{it} m_{it} = \pi_t m_t \qquad (3)$$

where

$$\pi_{it} = \frac{R_t - R_{it}}{1 + R_t} \qquad (4)$$

as derived in Barnett (1978). We define R_{mt} such that

$$\sum_{i=1}^{k} (1 + R_{it}) m_{it} = (1 + R_{mt}) m_t. \qquad (5)$$

Note that R_{mt} can be interpreted as the aggregate rate of return dual to the exact monetary aggregate. Dividing equation (5) by $(1 + R_t)$ and adding the

---

[6] For a discussion of macroeconomic dimension reduction, see Barnett (1994), which is reprinted as chapter 25 of this book.

[7] For the microeconomic theory of monetary aggregation, see Barnett (1987), which is reprinted as chapter 3 of this book.

Assumptions and Specifications

resulting equation to equation (3), we have

$$\sum_{i=1}^{k} m_{it} = \left(\pi_t + \frac{1+R_{mt}}{1+R_t}\right) m_t. \qquad (6)$$

Let M_t^n be the nominal supply-side exact monetary aggregate. We assume that the monetary asset markets are in equilibrium when $M_t^n = m_t P_t$, where $m_t P_t$ is the nominal demand side exact monetary aggregate.[8] Under these assumptions the budget constraint can be written as

$$P_t c_t + P_{st} s_t + b_t P_{bt} \left(\pi_t + \frac{1+R_{mt}}{1+R_t}\right) \leq s_{t-1}(d_t P_t + P_{st})$$
$$+ P_{t-1}(1+R_{m,t-1})m_{t-1} + b_{t-1}(1+R_{t-1})P_{b,t-1}$$
$$+ M_t^n \left(\pi_t + \frac{1+R_{mt}}{1+R_t}\right) - M_{t-1}^n (1+R_{m,t-1}) \qquad (7)$$

The representative agent chooses controls $u_t = (c_t, m_t, s_t, b_t)$ for $t \geq 1$ to maximize expected lifetime utility

$$E_t \sum_{t=0}^{\infty} \beta^t F(c_t, m_t)$$

subject to constraint (7) with given m_0 and d_0. We have the exact monetary aggregate in both the utility function and budget constraint, and the macroeconomic 'dimension reduction' is completely consistent with the microeconomic theory of monetary aggregation.

Let $\mathbf{z}_t' = (m_{t-1}, s_{t-1}, b_{t-1}, c_{t-1}, P_t, P_{st}, P_{bt}, R_t, M_t^n)$ be the set of state variables, and let

$$T(\mathbf{z}_t) = \sum_{t=0}^{\infty} \beta^t F(c_t, m_t).$$

In equilibrium, $T(\mathbf{z}_t)$ must satisfy the following Bellman's equation

$$T(\mathbf{z}_t) = \max_{u_t} \{F(c_t, m_t) + \beta E_t T(\mathbf{z}_{t+1})\} \qquad (8)$$

when the following market clearing conditions are satisfied:

$$c_t = d_t,$$
$$s_t = 1,$$
$$b_t = 0,$$

---

[8] Actually there is a possible regulatory wedge between the supply and demand side aggregator functions, when required reserves pay no interest and thereby produce an implicit tax on the supply side. For more discussion on this issue, see Barnett (1987), who provides the formulas for both the demand and supply side exact monetary aggregator functions.

and
$$m_t = M_t^n/P_t.$$
The equilibrium condition on equities is a normalization, while the equilibrium condition on bonds states that bonds are privately issued by some consumers and bought by others, and the net demand for bonds is zero in equilibrium. Recall that the representative agent is aggregated over consumers under Gorman's conditions for the existence of a representative consumer. Hence b_t is net per capita borrowing among consumers, where lending is negative borrowing. If interest rates are out of equilibrium, net borrowing need not be zero.[9]

3 Money Velocity With No Nominal Risk

In this section we derive the necessary first order conditions and the equations for money velocity, under the assumption that the nominal interest rates are known. The first order conditions of the maximization problem are

$$F_{ct} = \lambda_t P_t, \tag{9}$$

$$F_{mt} = \lambda_t P_t \left(\pi_t + \frac{1 + R_{mt}}{1 + R_t} \right) - \beta E_t[\lambda_{t+1}](1 + R_{mt})P_t, \tag{10}$$

$$\lambda_t P_{st} = \beta E_t[\lambda_{t+1}(d_{t+1}P_{t+1} + P_{s,t+1})], \tag{11}$$

$$\lambda_t = \beta E_t[\lambda_{t+1}](1 + R_t), \tag{12}$$

where F_{ct} and F_{mt} are the marginal utilities of consumption goods and monetary services, respectively, and λ_t is the Lagrange multiplier of the budget constraint (7). Equation (10) is the first order condition for monetary services. Equations (11) and (12) are standard Euler equations for stocks and bonds.

From equations (9), (10), and (12), we have:

$$\pi_t = \frac{F_{mt}}{F_{ct}}. \tag{13}$$

That is, the marginal rate of substitution between consumption goods and monetary services equals the aggregate user cost of the monetary services.[10] Assume that the utility function takes the constant relative risk aversion form

$$F(c_t, m_t) = \frac{1}{1-\phi}(c_t^s m_t^{1-s})^{1-\phi} \quad \text{if } \phi \neq 1$$
$$= \ln(c_t^s m_t^{1-s}), \quad \text{if } \phi = 1$$

---
[9]Similarly, see Marshall (1992, p. 1321) and Boyle (1990, p. 1042).
[10]We can get the same result if we start with the maximization problem in terms of the original disaggregated individual monetary assets. See appendix B of this chapter.

where m_t is the real exact monetary aggregate, $s \in (0,1)$ is a constant, and $\phi \in (0, \infty)$ is the coefficient of relative risk aversion. We get the following relationship:

$$\pi_t = \frac{(1-s)}{s} \frac{c_t}{m_t}. \tag{14}$$

When solved for m_t, equation (14) is the equation of demand for the exact monetary aggregate. Given $c_t = d_t$ and the parameter s, the only determinant of the demand for monetary services in equilibrium is the user cost π_t. Although other factors, such as the inflation rate, are not in this equation directly, they may affect the demand for money through the user cost π_t, which is a function of the nominal interest rates R_t and R_{it}. Given these equilibrium conditions, we can examine the behaviour of money velocity.

Traditional money velocity is usually defined as the ratio of nominal income to the simple sum monetary aggregate

$$V_t = \frac{P_t d_t}{X_t}.$$

We define the aggregation theoretic exact money velocity by replacing the simple sum monetary aggregate with the exact monetary aggregate to get

$$v_t = \frac{d_t}{m_t}.$$

Using the definition $\pi_{it} = (R_t - R_{it})/(1+R_t)$, the identity $\pi_t m_t = \sum_{i=1}^{k} \pi_{it} m_{it}$, and the equilibrium condition $X_{it} = P_t m_{it}$, we have the following results from equation (14):

$$v_t = \frac{s}{1-s} \pi_t \tag{15}$$

$$V_t = \frac{s}{1-s} \Pi_t \tag{16}$$

where

$$\Pi_t = \sum_{i=1}^{k} \frac{\pi_{it} X_{it}}{\left(\sum_{i=1}^{k} X_{it}\right)}$$

$$= (R_t - R_{smt})(1 + R_t)^{-1}$$

with

$$R_{smt} = \sum_{i=1}^{k} \theta_{it} R_{it}, \quad \text{and} \quad \theta_{it} = \frac{X_{it}}{\left(\sum_{i=1}^{k} X_{it}\right)}$$

Observe that Π_t is a weighted average of the user costs π_{it}, which are the opportunity costs of holding monetary assets instead of the bond. The results of equations (15) and (16) both say that money velocity is a function of the user costs $\{\pi_{it},\ i = 1, 2, \ldots, k\}$. If we define velocity in the traditional way (V_t), then the corresponding determinant should be a weighted average of the user costs π_{it}, with the weights being ratios of the X_{it} to the simple sum aggregate $X_t = \sum_{i=1}^{k} X_{it}$. If alternatively we define money velocity relative to the theoretic exact monetary aggregate, then the relevant determinant is the user cost aggregate π_t dual to the exact monetary quantity aggregate. Both velocity functions have the same form with the key elements being the user costs of monetary assets. The equivalence of the forms of the two velocity functions (15) and (16) depends upon our specification of the utility function.

Note that if all monetary assets yield no interest so that $R_{it} = 0$ for all i, then $\pi_t = \Pi_t = R_t/(1 + R_t)$, as in Boyle (1990) and LeRoy (1984). In this special case, the inverse of money velocity is a linear function of the inverse of interest rates:

$$\frac{1}{v_t} = \frac{s}{1-s} + \frac{s}{1-s}\frac{1}{R_t}.$$

This equation was first estimated by Latane (1954) without rigorous derivation and reestimated by Christ (1993) for M1 velocity.[11] According to this equation, variations in velocity are caused solely by fluctuations in the benchmark interest rates R_t. But when monetary assets themselves yield positive interest rates R_{it}, velocity could fluctuate even when the benchmark rate does not vary.

In short, money velocity is a variable rather than a constant in the model developed in this section. The opportunity cost and the taste parameters determine the stochastic behaviour of money velocity. Observe that, equations (15) or (16) have no intercepts and have constant slopes. These implications conflict with many published results. In the next section when interest rates uncertainty is introduced, we show that the intercept becomes nonzero, and the slope may be time-varying, if time-varying risk is present.

4 Money Velocity With Nominal Interest Risk

In this section the assumption that nominal interest rates are known is relaxed, and we keep the assumption that the economic agents are risk averse. We focus on the question of whether the model can explain the instability of money velocity reported in the literature through interest rate uncertainty.

---

[11] Also see Dickey (1993) and Laidler (1993) for a discussion.

We start with the monetary aggregation problem. In the previous section, the exact monetary quantity aggregator function $m_t = f(\mathbf{m}_t)$ can be tracked very accurately by the Divisia monetary aggregate, m_t^d, since that tracking ability is known under perfect certainty. However, when nominal interest rates are uncertain, the Divisia monetary aggregate's tracking ability is somewhat compromised. That compromise is eliminated by using the extended Divisia monetary aggregate derived by Barnett, Liu, and Jensen (1997) under risk. Let m_t^G denote the extended Divisia monetary aggregate over the monetary assets. The only difference between m_t^G and m_t^d is the user cost formula used to compute the prices in the Divisia index formula.

Let π_{it}^G denote the generalized user cost of monetary asset i. Barnett, Liu, and Jensen (1997, theorem 1) prove that

$$\pi_{it}^G = \pi_{it}^e + \varphi_{it}$$

where

$$\pi_{it}^e = \frac{E_t(R_t - R_{it})}{E_t(1 + R_t)}$$

and

$$\varphi_{it} = \frac{E_t(1 + R_{it})}{E_t(1 + R_t)} \frac{\operatorname{Cov}\left(R_t, \frac{\partial T}{\partial C_{t+1}}\right)}{\partial T / \partial C_T} - \frac{\operatorname{Cov}\left(R_{it}, \frac{\partial T}{\partial C_{t+1}}\right)}{\partial T / \partial C_t},$$

and where

$$T = E_t \sum_{t=0}^{\infty} \beta^t F(c_t, m_t^G).$$

Barnett, Liu, and Jensen (1997) show that the φ_{it} for each i determine the risk premia in interest rates. Note that π_{it}^G reduces to equation (4) under perfect certainty.

We define the aggregate generalized user cost π_t^G dual to m_t^G by Fisher's factor reversal test:

$$\sum_{i=1}^{k} \pi_{it}^G m_{it} = \pi_t^G m_t^G,$$

and let

$$\Pi_t^G = \sum_{i=1}^{k} \frac{\pi_{it}^G X_{it}^G}{\left(\sum_{i=1}^{k} X_{it}\right)}$$

be the weighted average of the individual generalized user costs of monetary assets. We have the following proposition:

Proposition: *When nominal interest rates (R_t, R_{it}) are not known with certainty at the beginning of period t, an equation analogous to equation (13) still holds, and money velocity is a function of the aggregate generalized user cost, which equals the marginal rate of substitution between consumption goods and monetary services, so that*

$$\frac{F_{mt}}{F_{ct}} = \pi_t^G \qquad (17)$$

$$v_t = \frac{s}{1-s}\pi_t^G \qquad (18)$$

$$V_t = \frac{s}{1-s}\Pi_t^G \qquad (19)$$

Proof: see Appendix A of this chapter. □

Equation (17) can also be proved from the maximization problem without prior aggregation over monetary assets. See Appendix B of this chapter. Equations (18) and (19) are analogous to equations (15) and (16) respectively, although in equations (18) and (19), the generalized user cost becomes the determinant of money velocity.

We can simplify the generalized user cost π_{it}^G to get a more intuitive equation for money velocity V_t. Dropping the remainder term of a second order Taylor series approximation to T, we have the approximation:

$$\frac{\partial T}{\partial c_{t+1}} = \left.\frac{\partial T}{\partial c_{t+1}}\right|_t + (c_{t+1} - c_t)\left(\left.\frac{\partial^2 T}{\partial c_{t+1}^2}\right|_t\right) + (m_{t+1}^G - m_t^G)\left(\left.\frac{\partial^2 T}{\partial c_{t+1}\partial m_{t+1}^e}\right|_t\right)$$

where $|_t$ denotes function values evaluated at the point (c_t, m_t^G). Taking the covariance of the left hand side with R_t, we get from the right hand side that

$$\text{Cov}\left(R_t, \frac{\partial T}{\partial c_{t+1}}\right)$$
$$= \left(\left.\frac{\partial^2 T}{\partial c_{t+1}^2}\right|_t\right)\text{Cov}(R_t, c_{t+1}) + \left(\left.\frac{\partial^2 T}{\partial c_{t+1}\partial m_{t+1}^e}\right|_t\right)\text{Cov}(R_t, m_{t+1}^G).$$

Let k_1 be defined such that

$$k_1 = \frac{\left(-c_t\left.\frac{\partial^2 T}{\partial c_{t+1}^2}\right|_t\right)}{(\partial T/\partial c_t)} = \beta(1-s-s\phi).$$

Then k_1 is the discounted relative risk aversion parameter, which in our specification is a constant. Similarly, define k_2 such that

$$k_2 = \frac{\left(m_t^e \frac{\partial^2 T}{\partial c_{t+1} \partial M_{t+1}^e}\big|_t\right)}{(\partial T/\partial c_t)} = \beta(1-s)(1-\phi).$$

Now assume that

$$\sigma_{rc} = \text{Cov}\left(R_t, \frac{c_{t+1}}{c_t}\right) \quad \text{and} \quad \sigma_{rm} = \text{Cov}\left(R_t, \frac{m_{t+1}^G}{m_t^G}\right)$$

are constants, so that the effect of R_t risk on the consumption of goods and monetary services is time-invariant. Let

$$\theta_1 = \frac{\text{Cov}\left(R_t, \frac{\partial T}{\partial c_{t+1}}\right)}{\partial T/\partial c_t} \quad \text{and} \quad \theta_{2i} = \frac{\text{Cov}\left(R_{it}, \frac{\partial T}{\partial c_{t+1}}\right)}{\partial T/\partial c_t}$$

Then it follows that

$$\theta_1 = k_2 \sigma_{rm} - k_1 \sigma_{rc} \quad \text{and} \quad \theta_{2i} = k_2 \sigma_{im} - k_1 \sigma_{ic},$$

where

$$\sigma_{im} = \text{cov}\left(R_{it}, \frac{m_{t+1}^G}{m_t^G}\right) \quad \text{and} \quad \sigma_{ic} = \text{cov}\left(R_{it}, \frac{c_{t+1}}{c_t}\right)$$

are assumed to be time-invariant. It follows that

$$\begin{aligned} \pi_{it}^G &= \pi_{it}^e + (1-\pi_{it}^e)\theta_1 - \theta_{2i} \\ &= (1-\theta_1)\pi_{it}^e + (\theta_1 - \theta_{2i}). \end{aligned}$$

Let θ_2 be the weighted average of the θ_{2i} such that

$$\theta_2 = \sum_{i=1}^{k} \frac{\theta_{2i} X_{it}}{\left(\sum_{i=1}^{k} X_{it}\right)}.$$

We find that

$$V_t = a_0 + a_1 \Pi_t^e, \tag{20}$$

where

$$a_0 = \frac{s}{1-s}(\theta_1 - \theta_2), \quad a_1 = \frac{s}{1-s}(1-\theta_1), \quad \text{and} \quad \Pi_t^e = \sum_{i=1}^{k} \frac{\pi_{it}^e X_{it}}{\left(\sum_{i=1}^{k} X_{it}\right)}.$$

Note that if the covariances σ_{ic}, σ_{im}, and σ_{rm} are time-varying, then a_0 and a_1 are also time-varying, and equation (20) is a time-varying or random coefficient model. Hence, a time-varying coefficient model of money velocity can be justified by the fact that interest rate uncertainty may change over time, as for example from an ARCH process.

It is worthwhile to look at the effect of risk aversion and interest rate uncertainty on money velocity in more detail. Note that under our assumptions about the parameters of the model, we have $k_1 > 0$. Also note that $k_2 > 0$, if $\phi < 1$, and $k_2 < 0$, if $\phi > 1$. For expositional purpose, we call $\phi < 1$ low risk aversion and $\phi > 1$ high risk aversion.

In the low risk aversion case, if $\sigma_{rm} < 0$, then the larger the value of $|\sigma_{rm}|$, the larger the value of a_1, and the smaller the value of a_0. The net effect of an increase of $|\sigma_{rm}|$ in this case is to reduce the money velocity, since $\Pi_t^e < 1$ and the magnitude of the decrease of the intercept is larger than that of the increase of $a_1 \Pi_t^e$. Therefore, if increased money growth variability raises the value of $|\sigma_{rm}|$, and if the $|\sigma_{im}|$ are not affected, then money velocity will decline. In the high risk aversion case, the results are just the opposite. An increase of $|\sigma_{rm}|$ will lead to higher money velocity. It follows that Friedman's (1983) hypothesis that the increased money growth variability causes money velocity to decline can be justified in our model by either (1) $\phi < 1$ and $\sigma_{rm} < 0$ or (2) $\phi > 1$ and $\sigma_{rm} > 0$. Also note that the magnitude of the effect of money growth variability on money velocity depends upon other parameters of the model, such as s.

But there remains the effect of uncertainty of the individual monetary assets' own rates of return. Note that the covariances σ_{im} are not important in determining the magnitude of slope a_1, though those covariances are important in determining the value of the velocity function's intercept. Therefore, a shift in the values of the $|\sigma_{im}|$ will lead to a shift in the intercept of a money velocity function. If increased money growth variability raises both $|\sigma_{rm}|$ and $|\sigma_{im}|$, and if σ_{rm} and σ_{im} have the same sign, then the effect of the money growth variability on money velocity through σ_{rm} will be partially offset. The complicated nature of the effect of money growth variability on money velocity may partially explain the controversies in the empirical literature.

In short, if $\phi \neq 1$, the money growth variability will affect money velocity, but the direction and magnitude of the effect depends upon the degree of risk aversion and the correlation between interest rates and real money growth. If all the covariances are zero, as would be the case under perfect certainty, then (20) reduces to (16), as we would expect.

To further explore the economic interpretation of the coefficients in the money velocity function, note that using the first order condition on the bond price,

$$\lambda_t = \beta E_t[\lambda_{t+1}(1 + R_t)],$$

the parameter θ_1 can be written as

$$\theta_1 = 1 - E_t(1+R_t)E_t\left(\frac{T_{c,t+1}}{T_{ct}}\right),$$

where $E_t(T_{c,t+1}/T_{ct})$ is the expected growth rate of the marginal utility of consumption goods. Therefore, the slope coefficient of the money velocity function is

$$a_1 = \frac{s}{1-s}E_t(1+R_t)E_t\left(\frac{T_{c,t+1}}{T_{ct}}\right).$$

If we use $E(R_t - R_{smt})$ as the independent variable in the money velocity function, rather than the user cost Π_t^e, we have

$$V_t = a_{0t} + b_t E(R_t - R_{smt}) \tag{21}$$

where

$$b_t = \frac{s}{1-s}E_t\left(\frac{T_{c,t+1}}{T_{ct}}\right)$$

The subscript t in b_t and a_{0t} is used to indicate that the values of b_t and a_{0t} may not be time constant. In our model, given the specification of the utility function, we have

$$b_t = \frac{\beta_s}{1-s}E_t\left[\left(\frac{c_{t+1}}{c_t}\right)^{s(1-\phi)-1}\left(\frac{m^G_{t+1}}{m^G_t}\right)^{(1-s)(1-\phi)}\right]. \tag{22}$$

From equation (22), it can be seen that the slope coefficient b_t depends upon both the growth rate of consumption and the growth rate of real money stock. If the conditional expectation operator depends upon the second or higher moments of the growth rate processes, the slope process b_t will depend on the variabilities of both the consumption growth rate and the real money growth rate. If $\phi = 1$, the expected growth rate of the real money stock will not affect the coefficient b_t, since in that case, the marginal utility of consumption goods does not depend on the real money stock. This section provides a theoretical avenue to examine the effects of money growth rate and consumption growth rate and their variability on the stochastic behaviour of money velocity. It is shown in this section that the expected real money growth rate or its variability will affect money velocity by shifting the coefficients of the traditional money velocity function. The magnitude of this effect is also determined by other parameters in the representative agent's preferences, such as risk aversion. If the representative agent in this model is risk neutral, the changes in money growth rate and its variability will not affect the stability of the money velocity function in equilibrium. On the other side, the higher the degree of risk aversion, the larger the effect of real money growth rate and consumption growth rate and their variabilities on the stability of the money velocity function.

5 Empirical Results

In this section, we first simulate the model using quarterly data over the period of 1960.1 to 1992.4 for some specifications of parameters to examine the stability of the coefficients in the traditional money velocity function implied by our theoretical model. We then estimate a random coefficient model of money velocity to examine the stability of the coefficients empirically. In the random coefficient model approach, we follow Swamy and Tinsley (1980). The results from both the empirical estimation and the theoretical simulation are compared to see whether the empirical behaviour of the money velocity can be explained by the model developed in this paper.

The data on monetary assets and their corresponding holding period yields were provided by the Federal Reserve Bank of St. Louis. Output data are GNP. The inflation rate is the growth rate of the price deflator for GNP. The benchmark asset return path is approximated by the upper envelope of the three month Treasury bill rate path and the time paths of each individual monetary asset's own rate of return.[12] The growth rate of consumption is replaced by the real GNP growth rate. With M1, which includes no assets having highly risky rates of return, the regular Divisia monetary aggregate closely tracks the generalized Divisia monetary aggregate Hence we use ordinary Divisia M1 to measure the theoretical monetary quantity aggregate.

To simulate the process b_t in equation (21), we first set $\beta = 0.99$, $s = 0.972$, and $\phi \in \{0.5, 2, 5\}$. The three different values of ϕ are chosen to capture the influence of different degrees of risk aversion on the stability of the coefficient b_t. The parameter s mainly affects the sample mean of b_t. We estimate a VAR (vector autoregressive) model of real money and GNP growth rates using quarterly data from 1960.1 to 1992.4. The estimated VAR model is then used to estimate the conditional expectation

$$E_t \left[\left(\frac{c_{t+1}}{c_t} \right)^{s(1-\phi)-1} \left(\frac{m_{t+1}}{m_t} \right)^{(1-\phi)(1-s)} \right].$$

---

[12] Even the upper envelope is too low, since the theoretical benchmark asset is completely illiquid and therefore must have higher expected yield than the upper envelope over any expected yield-curve-adjusted rates of return on monetary assets providing any monetary services.

Empirical Results

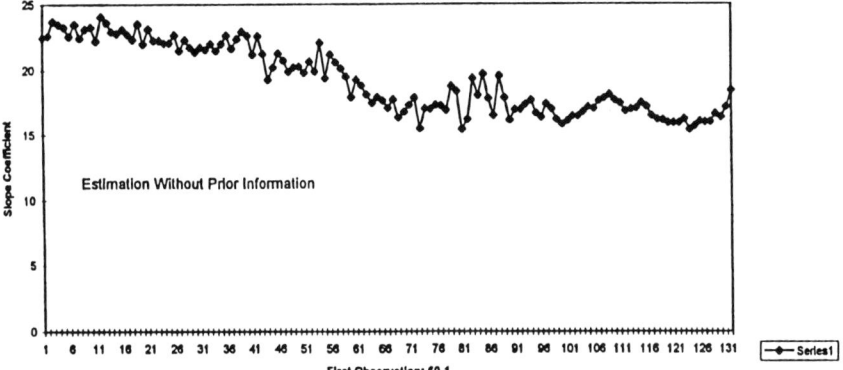

Figure 1: Slope coefficient of money velocity function, by random coefficient estimation.

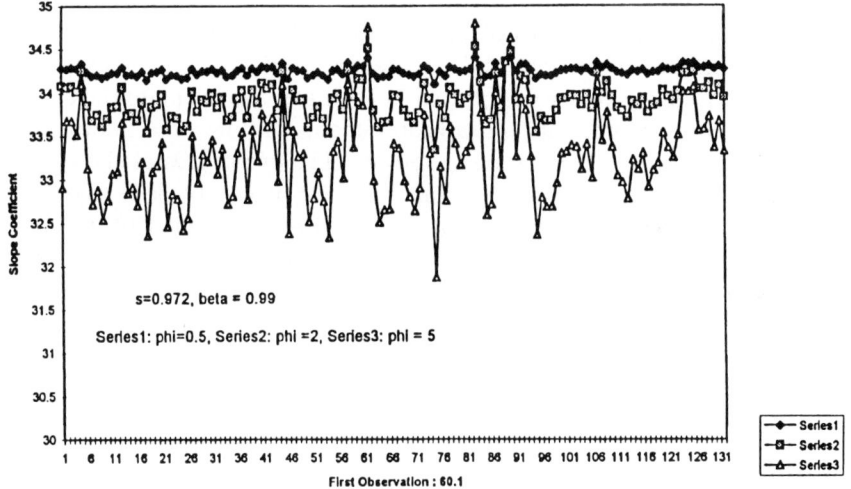

Figure 2: Simulated slope coefficient of velocity function.

The simulated b_t process is plotted in Figure 1. From Figure 1, it can be seen that when $\phi = 0.5$ (low risk aversion case), the simulated slope process b_t is almost constant. When the value of ϕ increases, the variability in b_t also increases. When $\phi = 5$, the process b_t shows a lot of variability. There are two periods during which b_t is extremely volatile. One is from 1972 to 1976 and the other is from 1979-1982. The latter period approximately corresponds with the episode of the 'monetarist experiment' of the Federal Reserve System. The b_t process also shows some variability in the recent years of 1991-1992. These simulation results confirm the theoretical prediction that if the degree of risk aversion is higher, the traditional money velocity function will be less stable.

These theoretical results from model simulation can be compared with empirical estimation. We estimate equation (21) with stochastically varying coefficients. We use the Swamy and Tinsley (1980) asymptotically efficient estimation procedure. Letting $\alpha'_t = (a_{0t}, b_t)$, we assume, as in Swamy and Tinsley (1980):

$$\alpha_t = \alpha^0 + \mathbf{e}_t$$

where α^0 is a vector of constants, and

$$\mathbf{e}_t = \Phi_1 \mathbf{e}_{t-1} + \Phi_2 \mathbf{e}_{t-2} + \mathbf{u}_t,$$

where Φ_1 and Φ_2 are matrices of parameters to be estimated, and $\mathbf{u}_t$ is a random vector with mean zero and covariance matrix Ω. The estimated b_t process for M1 money velocity is plotted in Figure 2. We estimate the b_t process with both prior information incorporated and with no prior information (i.e., with diffuse prior information) about b_t. The two processes show some significant important similarities. From Figure 2, it can be seen that b_t is very volatile during the periods from 1972 to 1974 and from 1979 to 1982. This is approximately coincident with the simulation result with moderate risk aversion.

Overall, the results from model simulation and from model estimation of a random coefficient model show that our model can capture the main features of the coefficient process b_t in the traditional money velocity equation.

6 Conclusion

In this paper we have theoretically explored the determinants of money velocity. The effects of risk aversion and interest rate uncertainty on money velocity are examined within a monetary general equilibrium model. This paper indicates that if covariances between interest rates and consumption growth or between interest rates and money growth are generated by an

ARCH type process, the traditional money velocity function will become unstable. Both model simulation and estimation produce significant variability in the slope of the traditional money velocity function, especially during the 1972-1974 and 1979-1982 periods. This study sheds some new light on the nature of the instability of traditional money velocity functions.

Appendix A: Proof of Proposition 1

We define Δ_t by setting

$$\sum_{i=1}^{k}(1-\pi_{it}^G)m_{it} = \Delta_t m_t^G,$$

so that

$$\sum_{i=1}^{k} m_{it} = (\pi_t^G + \Delta_t)m_t^G$$

and we define R_{mt}^G such that

$$\sum_{i=1}^{k}(1+R_{it})m_{it} = (1+R_{mt}^G)m_t^G.$$

If we write the budget constraint in real terms, the first order conditions (9), (10), and (12), become

$$F_{ct} = \lambda_t \tag{23}$$

$$F_{mt} = \lambda_t(\pi_t^G + \Delta_t) - \beta E_t[\lambda_{t+1}(1+R_{mt}^G)] \tag{24}$$

$$\lambda_t = \beta E_t[\lambda_{t+1}(1+R_t)], \tag{25}$$

From equation (25), we have

$$E_t \lambda_{t+1} = \frac{(\lambda_t/\beta) - \text{Cov}\,(\lambda_{t+1}, R_t)}{E_t(1+R_t)}$$

Substituting this equation into (24), we have

$$F_{mt} = \lambda_t(\pi_t^G + \Delta_t) - [\lambda_t - \beta_t \text{Cov}\,(\lambda_{t+1}, R_t)]\frac{E_t(1+R_{mt}^G)}{E_t(1+R_t)} - \beta\text{Cov}\,(\lambda_{t+1}, R_{mt}^G).$$

Note that $\lambda_t = F_{ct} = T_{ct}$ and $\beta\lambda_{t+1} = \beta F_{c,t+1} = T_{c,t+1}$. Therefore

$$F_{mt} = F_{ct}(\pi_t^G + \Delta_t) - [F_{ct} - \text{Cov}\,(T_{c,t+1}, R_t)]\frac{E_t(1+R_{mt}^G)}{E_t(1+R_t)} - \text{Cov}\,(T_{c,t+1}, R_{mt}^G)$$

and hence

$$\frac{F_{mt}}{F_{ct}} = \pi_t^G + \Delta_t - \left[1 - \frac{\text{Cov}(T_{c,t+1}, R_t)}{T_{ct}}\right] \frac{E_t(1+R_{mt}^G)}{E_t(1+R_t)} - \frac{\text{Cov}(T_{c,t+1}, R_{mt}^G)}{T_{ct}}.$$

Recall that

$$\pi_{it}^G = \frac{E_t(R_t - R_{it})}{E_t(1+R_t)} + \frac{E_t(1+R_{it})}{E_t(1+R_t)} \frac{\text{Cov}(R_t, T_{c,t+1})}{T_{ct}} - \frac{\text{Cov}(R_{it}, T_{c,t+1})}{T_{ct}},$$

and therefore

$$\sum_{i=1}^{k} (1 - \pi_{it}^G) m_{it}$$

$$= \sum_{i=1}^{k} \left[\frac{E_t(1+R_{it})}{E_t(1+R_t)} \left(1 - \frac{\text{Cov}(R_t, T_{c,t+1})}{T_{ct}}\right) + \frac{\text{Cov}(R_{it}, T_{c,t+1})}{T_{ct}}\right] m_{it}$$

$$= \left[\frac{E_t(1+R_{mt}^G)}{E_t(1+R_t)} \left(1 - \frac{\text{Cov}(R_t, T_{c,t+1})}{T_{ct}} + \frac{\text{Cov}(R_{mt}^G, T_{c,t+1})}{T_{ct}}\right)\right] m_t^G,$$

and

$$\Delta_t = \frac{E_t(1+R_{mt}^G)}{E_t(1+R_t)} \left(1 - \frac{\text{Cov}(R_t, T_{c,t+1})}{T_{ct}}\right) + \frac{\text{Cov}(R_{mt}^G, T_{c,t+1})}{T_{ct}}.$$

Hence

$$\frac{F_{mt}}{F_{ct}} = \pi_t^G.$$

Appendix B: Aggregation over First Order Conditions

The results in sections 3 and 4 are in terms of monetary quantity aggregates and their dual user cost price aggregates. In this appendix, we show that if we aggregate over the first order conditions of each individual disaggregated monetary asset, we can get the same result.

To see this, let us first consider the case of riskless interest rates. The decision problem is to maximize

$$E_t \sum_{t=0}^{\infty} \beta^t U(c_t, m_t) \tag{26}$$

Appendix B: Aggregation over First Order Conditions

subject to

$$P_t c_t + P_{st} s_t + P_{bt} b_t + P_t \Sigma m_{it} \leq s_{t-1}(d_t P_t + P_{st}) + P_{b,t-1} b_{t-1}(1 + R_{t-1})$$
$$+ \Sigma m_{i,t-1}(1 + R_{i,t-1}) P_{t-1} + \Sigma [X_{it} - (1 + R_{i,t-1}) X_{i,t-1}], \qquad (27)$$

where the summation is from $i = 1$ to k.

The first order conditions are

$$U_{ct} = \lambda_t P_t, \qquad (28)$$

$$U_{it} = \lambda_t P_t - \beta E_t[\lambda_{t+1}](1 + R_{it}) P_t, \qquad (29)$$

$$\lambda_t P_{st} = \beta E_t[\lambda_{t+1}(d_{t+1} P_{t+1} + P_{s,t+1})], \qquad (30)$$

$$\lambda_t = \beta E_t[\lambda_{t+1}](1 + R_t), \qquad (31)$$

where U_{it} is the partial derivative of U with respect to m_{it}.

From equations (28), (29), and (31), we have

$$\begin{aligned} U_{it} &= U_{ct} - \frac{\lambda_t P_t}{1 + R_t}(1 + R_{it}) \\ &= \frac{R_t - R_{it}}{1 + R_t} U_{ct} = \pi_{it} U_{ct}. \end{aligned} \qquad (32)$$

Recall that we have defined $m_t = f(\mathbf{m}_t)$. The utility function $U(c_t, \mathbf{m}_t) = F(c_t, f(\mathbf{m}_t))$ consequently can be written as $F(c_t, m_t)$. From Fisher's factor reversal test, we have

$$\sum_{i=1}^{k} \pi_{it} m_{it} = \pi_t m_t$$

and hence

$$\pi_t \frac{\partial m_t}{\partial m_{it}} = \pi_{it}. \qquad (33)$$

Taking the summation of equation (32) over $i = 1, 2, \ldots, k$, we have

$$\sum_{i=1}^{k} U_{it} = U_{ct} \sum_{i=1}^{k} \pi_{it}$$

or

$$\sum_{i=1}^{k} \left(\frac{\partial F_t}{\partial m_t} \frac{\partial m_t}{\partial m_{it}} \right) = F_{ct} \sum_{i=1}^{k} \pi_{it},$$

so that

$$F_{mt} \sum_{i=1}^{k} \frac{\partial m_t}{\partial m_{it}} = F_{ct} \sum_{i=1}^{k} \pi_{it}.$$

Substituting equation (33) into the above equation, we have

$$F_{mt} \frac{1}{\pi_t} \sum_{i=1}^{k} \pi_{it} = F_{ct} \sum_{i=1}^{k} \pi_{it},$$

so that

$$\frac{F_{mt}}{F_{ct}} = \pi_t.$$

We have the same result as that in Section 3.

Now consider uncertain interest rates. In this case equation (29) becomes

$$U_{it} = \lambda_t P_t - \beta E_t[\lambda_{t+1}(1 + R_{it})]P_t \qquad (34)$$

and equation (31) becomes

$$\lambda_t = \beta E_t[\lambda_{t+1}(1 + R_t)], \qquad (35)$$

while equation (28) remains unchanged.

From equations (34) and (28), we have

$$U_{it} = U_{ct} - \beta P_t E_t[\lambda_{t+1}(1 + R_t)]. \qquad (36)$$

From equations (36) and (28), we have

$$U_{ct} = \beta E_t[U_{c,t+1}(1 + r_t)]$$

$$\neg \quad \beta E_t[U_{c,t+1}]E_t[(1 + r_t)] + \beta \text{Cov}\,(U_{c,t+1}, (1 + r_t)],$$

where r_t is the real interest rate corresponding to R_t. So we have

$$E_t U_{c,t+1} = \frac{U_{ct} - \beta \text{Cov}\,[U_{c,t+1}, (1 + r_t)]}{\beta E_t(1 + r_t)}. \qquad (37)$$

Equation (36) can be written as

$$U_{it} = U_{ct} - \beta E_t[U_{c,t+1}]E_t[(1 + r_{it})] - \beta \text{Cov}\,[U_{c,t+1}, (1 + r_{it})], \qquad (38)$$

where r_{it} is the real interest rate corresponding to R_{it}. Substituting equation (37) into (38), we have

$$U_{it} = U_{ct} - \beta \frac{U_{ct} - \beta \text{Cov}\,(U_{c,t+1}, r_t)}{\beta E_t(1 + r_t)} E_t[(1 + r_{it})] - \beta \text{Cov}\,[U_{c,t+1}, (1 + r_{it})],$$

or

$$U_{it} = U_{ct}\left[\frac{E_t(r_t - r_{it})}{E_t(1 + r_t)} + \frac{\beta \text{Cov}\,(U_{c,t+1}, r_t)}{U_{ct}} \frac{E_t(1 + r_{it})}{E_t(1 + r_t)} - \frac{\beta \text{Cov}\,(U_{c,t+1}, r_{it})}{U_{ct}}\right].$$

Appendix B: Aggregation over First Order Conditions

Hence we have
$$U_{it} = U_{ct}\pi^G_{it}, \qquad (39)$$

where π^G_{it} is the generalized user cost of monetary asset i.

Note that we use π^G_t as the aggregate monetary price index dual to the generalized Divisia quantity aggregate m^G_t. By taking derivatives with respect to m_{it} on both sides of Fisher's factor reversal test condition,
$$\sum_{i=1}^{k} \pi^G_{it} m_{it} = \pi^G_t m^G_t,$$

we have
$$\pi^G_{it} = \pi^G_t \frac{\partial m^G_t}{\partial m_{it}}. \qquad (40)$$

Taking the summation of (39) over $i = 1, 2, \ldots, k$ and using equation (40), we have
$$U_{it} = U_{ct} \sum_{i=1}^{k} \pi^G_{it} = U_{ct}\pi^G_t \sum_{i=1}^{k} \frac{\partial m^G_t}{\partial m_{it}}, \qquad (41)$$

since in this case
$$U_{it} = \frac{\partial F}{\partial m^G_t} \frac{\partial m^G_t}{\partial m_{it}},$$

and equation (41) becomes
$$\frac{\partial F}{\partial m^G_t} \sum_{i=1}^{k} \frac{\partial m^G_t}{\partial m_{it}} = F_{ct}\pi^G_t \sum_{i=1}^{k} \frac{\partial m^G_t}{\partial m_{it}}.$$

Therefore
$$\frac{F_{mt}}{F_{ct}} = \pi^G_t.$$

This is the same result as in section 4.

Section 3.4: Extension to Capitalized Money Stock Aggregation Monetary Services

Chapter 14

A Reply to Julio J. Rotemberg

William A. Barnett[*]

1 Introduction

Among the many excellent ideas contained in Rotemberg's comments is a proposed new monetary aggregate, which Rotemberg calls the CE (currency equivalent) index. My reply consists primarily of the proof of a theorem regarding that index. The theorem supports Rotemberg's index by providing a derivation of his index directly from economic theory, when the index is treated as a measure of the economic stock of money under stationary expectations.

Rotemberg argues for his index largely on the basis of the intuitive appeal of its 'weights.' However, I feel that the greatest contribution of that index can be found in Rotemberg's observation that the index is measured in units

---

[*]Originally published in Michael T. Belongia (ed.), *Monetary Policy on the 75th Anniversary of the Federal Reserve System* (1991). Proceedings of the 14th Annual Economic Policy Conference of the Federal Reserve Bank of St. Louis, Kluwer 1991, pp. 232–243.

of *stock* and therefore seems to measure the monetary capital stock, while the Divisia monetary aggregates and estimated Theoretical aggregates considered in chapters 2 and 11 of this book are measures of service *flow*. As a result, I shall refer to the CE index as the 'Rotemberg Money Stock.' I prove that Rotemberg is indeed correct in viewing his index as a measure of the economic stock of money. The Rotemberg Money Stock is a special case of the money stock measure derived in Barnett (1978, eq. 2, p. 148; 1980a, eq. 3.3, p. 19; 1981b, eq. 7.3, p. 196). In particular, my measure of the stock of money reduces to the Rotemberg Money Stock under the assumption of stationary expectations.

As a result, the indexes considered in chapters 2 and 11 of this book and in Rotemberg are tied together through discounting. The indexes in chapters 2 and 11 of this book measure the service flow, while the Rotemberg Money Stock discounts that service flow to present value, if expectations are stationary. The Rotemberg Money Stock is produced from a particularly useful special case, since stationary expectations require no parametric modeling of expectations formation, and hence the Rotemberg Money Stock can be constructed directly from current period data.

2 The Economic Stock of Money

Barnett (1987, sec. 12, p. 160; 1990) defined the economic stock of money to be the discounted present value of expenditure on the services of monetary assets. Barnett (1978, eq. 2, p. 148; 1980a, eq. 3.3, p. 19; 1981b, eq. 7.3, p. 196) derived that discounted present value in the form that we display below. Also see Barnett, Hinich, and Yue (1991, section 3) reprinted in chapter 11 of this book for the same result, but with less discussion. During period s, let p_s^* be the true cost of living index, let M_{is} be nominal balances of monetary asset i, let r_{is} be the nominal expected holding period yield on monetary asset i, and define $m_{is} = M_{is}/p_s^*$ to be real balances of monetary asset i. The current period is defined to be period t, so that $s \geq t$. Define the discount rate for period s to be

$$p_s = \begin{cases} 1 & \text{for } s = t \\ \prod_{u=t}^{s-1}(1+R_u) & \text{for } s > t. \end{cases} \quad (1)$$

By letting the planning horizon, T, go to infinity in the second term of Barnett (1978, eq. 2, p. 148; 1980a, eq. 3.3, p. 19; 1981b, eq. 7.3, p. 196), we immediately acquire the following definition for the Economic Stock of Money.

Definition 1: Under risk neutrality, The Economic Stock of Money during period t is

$$V_t = \sum_{s=t}^{\infty} \sum_{i=1}^{n} \left[\frac{p_s^*}{p_s} - \frac{p_s^*(1+r_{is})}{p_{s+1}} \right] m_{is}. \tag{2}$$

Also see Barnett, Hinich, and Yue (1991), reprinted in chapter 11 of this book for the same result. The concept of economic stock used to produce definition 1 is the user-cost evaluated expediture on the services of the n component monetary assets. It should be observed that the procedure used in Barnett (1978, eq. 2, p. 148; 1980a, eq. 3.3, p. 19; 1981b, eq. 7.3, p. 196) to acquire that discounted present value was just back substitution and algebraic manipulation of the sequence of flow of funds identities to collapse the sequence of flow of funds identities into a single Fisherine discounted wealth constraint. Hence our conclusion is produced entirely from accounting identities.

If we now substitute (1) and $m_{is} = M_{is}/p_s^*$ into equation (2), we acquire the following result:

$$V_t = \sum_{s=t}^{\infty} \sum_{i=1}^{n} \left[\frac{R_s - r_{is}}{\prod_{u=t}^{s}(1+R_u)} \right] M_{is}. \tag{3}$$

Our problem is to determine the conditions under which (3) reduces to the Rotemberg Money Stock, which is the following.

Definition 2: The Rotemberg Money Stock is

$$V_t = \sum_{i=1}^{n} \frac{R_t - r_{it}}{R_t} M_{it}. \tag{4}$$

We seek to find conditions under which equation (4) will equal (3). To that end, suppose that expectations are stationary in the sense that $r_{is} = r_{it}$ and $R_{is} = R_{it}$ for all $s \geq t$, and consider the static portfolio, $(M_{1s}, M_{2s}, \ldots, M_{ns}) = (M_{1t}, M_{2t}, \ldots, M_{nt})$ for all $s \geq t$. Equation (3) reduces to

$$V_t = \sum_{i=1}^{n} \sum_{s=t}^{\infty} \left[\frac{R_t - r_{it}}{(1+R_t)^{s-t+1}} \right] M_{it}. \tag{5}$$

However, observe that

$$\sum_{s=t}^{\infty} \frac{R_t - r_{it}}{(1+R_t)^{s-t+1}} = \frac{R_t - r_{it}}{R_t}, \tag{6}$$

since the left-hand side of equation (6) is a convergent geometric series (minus the first term in the series). Substituting (6) into (5), we acquire our result:

Theorem 1: *Under stationary expectations, the Rotemberg Money Stock is equal to the Economic Money Stock.*

3 Implications for Simple Sum Aggregation

Theorem 1 is especially interesting as a means of illustrating the source of confusion that has existed in recent years regarding the role of the official simple sum monetary aggregates. In particular, it is sometimes argued that the simple sum monetary aggregates measure the stock of money, while the Divisia monetary aggregates measure the service flow. Hence the use of the simple sum aggregates sometimes is defended on the grounds that stock measures are needed in some uses of monetary data. For example, monetary wealth is relevant to modeling the real balance effect, which is intended to explain the monetary transmission mechanism through a wealth effect.

However, it is evident both from the Rotemberg Money Stock and from the more general money stock formula in definition 1 that the simple sum aggregates do not measure the economic stock of money. In this section I consider why it is that the accounting stock does not equal the economic stock.

It is perhaps worth observing that at one time the use of the simple sum aggregates as measures of the money stock may have been justified. The reason is that up until recent decades, the only assets that were viewed as candidates for inclusion in monetary assets were assets yielding zero own rates of return.[1] Consideration of broad monetary assets has been a relatively recent phenomenon within the central banks of the world and has largely resulted from the expanded role of financial intermediation along with the increased nominal yield on money substitutes in the inflationary environment of recent decades. Inspection of the Rotemberg Money Stock reveals immediately that simple sum aggregation is correct when $r_{it} = 0$ for all i.[2]

While this observation may provide a comforting explanation for the historical use of simple sum monetary aggregation by central banks, we still are left with a paradox. In order to acquire the services of the nominal portfo-

---

[1] Some economists believe that demand deposits have always yielded a positive implicit rate of return. If so, then the simple sum aggregates have never measured the economic stock of money.

[2] Actually the same is true for the Divisia index of monetary services, when own rates are all zero, although the demonstration is less transparent than with the Rotemberg Money Stock index.

lio $(M_{1t}, M_{2t}, \ldots, M_{nt})$, we must pay $\sum_{i=1}^{n} M_{it}$, although under stationary expectations the economic value of the money stock is (4). How can that be?

The answer is acquired by discounting to present value the portfolio's investment yield as well as expenditure on the service flow. In particular, under the stationary expectations assumption, we easily can discount to present value the expected investment yield flows, $r_{is}M_{is} = r_{it}M_{it}$ for $s \geq t$ to get the following capitalized value:

$$V_t^* = \sum_{s=t}^{\infty} \sum_{i=1}^{n} \left[\frac{r_{it}M_{it}}{(1+R_t)^{s-t+1}} \right]. \qquad (7)$$

Again we have a convergent geometric series in the summation over s at any given i, so that we find:

$$V_t^* = \sum_{i=1}^{n} \frac{r_{it}}{R_t} M_{it}. \qquad (8)$$

Adding equation (8) to (4), we find that

$$V_t + V_t^* = \sum_{i=1}^{n} M_{it}. \qquad (9)$$

The conclusion is clear. The simple sum monetary aggregates measure the stock of money only if the investment (interest) yield of the monetary components is treated as a monetary service. Yet it is difficult to think of any macroeconomic school of thought which has *ever* viewed the interest yield on monetary assets to be a monetary service. In fact, that possibility was considered carefully and rejected unequivocally in Pesek and Saving (1967).

4 The Economic Stock of Money and the Divisia Monetary Aggregate

Expenditure on the monetary service flow was evaluated in definition 1 by summing the user-cost evaluated expenditures over individual monetary assets. We now shall ask whether there exists a connection between that monetary stock aggregate and the aggregation-theoretic aggregator function, $M(\mathbf{m}_t)$, which measures the service flow. I have long advocated the use of the Divisia monetary aggregate or any other element of Diewert's superlative index number class (with user costs as prices), since such index numbers track the aggregator function $M(\mathbf{m}_t)$ to within a third order remainder term, regardless of the form of the unknown aggregator function, M. See Diewert (1976).

But by Fisher's factor reversal test, we know that there must exist a user-cost price aggregate $\Pi(\boldsymbol{\pi}_t)$ dual to the exact service quantity aggregate $M(\mathbf{m}_t)$, such that $M(\mathbf{m}_t)\Pi(\boldsymbol{\pi}_t) = \mathbf{m}'_t\boldsymbol{\pi}_t$. Hence expenditure on aggregate monetary services $M(\mathbf{m}_t)$ must equal the sum of the user-cost evaluated expenditures on the components $\mathbf{m}_t$. As a result, we can derive monetary wealth by discounting to present value either the expenditure flow $\mathbf{m}'_s\boldsymbol{\pi}_s$ for $s \geq t$ or the exactly equal aggregate expenditure flow $M(\mathbf{m}_s)\Pi(\boldsymbol{\pi}_s)$ for $s \geq t$. In fact, if the user costs are themselves already computed as discounted present values, we need only sum the expenditure flow to get:

$$V_t = \sum_{s=t}^{\infty} \Pi(\boldsymbol{\pi}_s) M(\mathbf{m}_s). \tag{10}$$

It is clear from equation (3) above that the discounted user costs π_s in (10) must be

$$\pi_{is} = \frac{R_s - r_{is}}{\prod_{u=t}^{s}(1+R_u)},$$

as has explicitly been derived by Barnett (1978, p. 148; 1980a, eq. 3.4; 1981b, eq. 7.4, p. 196).

If we impose the stationarity assumption used to acquire the Rotemberg Money Stock in definition 2 above, we find that

$$V_t = M(\mathbf{m}_t) \sum_{s=t}^{\infty} \Pi(\boldsymbol{\pi}_s),$$

where

$$\pi_{is} = \frac{R_t - r_{it}}{(1+R_t)^{s-t+1}}.$$

Hence we see that under the implicit stationary expectations assumption, the Rotemberg Money Stock is proportional to the monetary service flow $M(\mathbf{m}_t)$, which is measured by the Divisia monetary index. But the proportionality factor $\sum_{s=t}^{\infty} \Pi(\boldsymbol{\pi}_s)$ need not be a constant over time, when actual ex post data on the interest rates is used. In any case, it is clear from (10) that the Economic Stock of Money equals the discounted present value of expenditure on the aggregate service flow $M(\mathbf{m}_s)$, $s \geq t$, regardless of whether or not expectations are stationary; and the Divisia index tracks that aggregate flow $M(\mathbf{m}_s)$, $s \geq t$, very accurately (to within a third order remainder term in the changes).

5 Uses of the Stock and the Flow Monetary Aggregates

As we have seen, a clear economic connection exists between the stock and flow monetary aggregates. Rotemberg has emphasized some practical matters regarding the choice between them. I would like to emphasize that in theory the service flow and the stock are not substitute methods of measuring the same variable. On the contrary, they are separate variables, and both may exist within the structure of the economy simultaneously. Hence I am inclined to suggest that both be used, but only for the purposes that are relevant in theory.

Most variables appearing in structural economic theory are flows. However, stocks do appear through Fisherine discounted intertemporal wealth constraints. For example, demand and supply functions are demands and supplies for flows. Flow index numbers (such as Divisia, Laspeyres, etc.) with user-cost prices should be used to measure such flows. On the other hand, life-cycle consumption functions typically have wealth variables as explanatory variables. Hence consumption functions containing Pigou or real balance effects should contain stock measures as explanatory variables.

My position on this subject seems to be somewhat different from Rotemberg's. He appears to argue that there is a greater need to monitor the tracking ability of the Divisia index than the Rotemberg Money Stock. I do not agree. That which is tracked by the Rotemberg Money Stock is the capital value of the stock of money. Under risk aversion and rational expectations, measuring that stock is a complex capital asset pricing problem.[3] The tracking error produced by the Rotemberg Money Stock's implicit stationary expectations assumption is undoubtedly formidable. On the other hand, the tracking error of the Divisia index (actually we use its Törnqvist discrete time approximation) is third order in the changes, as has been proven by Diewert (1976). Furthermore, Barnett, Hinich, and Yue (1991, 2000) have shown that tracking ability is usually not badly compromised by risk aversion. In fact investigation of robustness to the degree of relative risk aversion is the primary purpose of Barnett, Hinich, and Yue (1991, 2000).

The chaining property that Rotemberg criticizes is necessary for the third order remainder to be in changes (rather than in levels). Unchained indexes have remainder terms defined in differences from the fixed base. Those changes are far greater than the discrete time changes between succeeding periods. Hence fixed base indexes are very much inferior to chained indexes in measuring flows.[4] Again, see Diewert (1976). However, Rotemberg is cor-

---

[3] See, for example, Merton (1990).

[4] In that regard, it perhaps should be observed that the Laspeyres index displayed in

rect in observing that there is no need to choose between chaining or fixed base with the Rotemberg Money Stock, since his stock index has no 'base' to chain, as also is true of my more general Economic Stock of Money in definition 1.

Although the tracking problems of the Rotemberg Money Stock are undoubtedly many orders of magnitude greater than those of the Divisia index, I do not view that as being a reason to prefer the Divisia index over the Rotemberg Money Stock (and certainly not vice versa). As I already have pointed out, the two indexes measure different variables, and therefore neither is a substitute for the other. Each can serve its own purpose. I agree with Rotemberg that his stock index 'deserves further study.' In fact as a measure of the stock of money, the Rotemberg Money Stock would surely be a major advance over the official simple sum aggregates.

Under no circumstances should the simple sum monetary aggregates be used to measure either the flow or stock, except perhaps in investigating the distant economic past, when money maybe did not yield interest. The simple sum monetary aggregates are an anachronism.

6 Other Comments

Rotemberg offers a number of other comments, on which I have little to offer, other than the following brief observations — largely because I agree with nearly all of those comments.

6.1 Nested Hierarchies of Aggregates

Rotemberg feels that the use of a recursively nested tree of aggregates, such as M1, M2, M3, and L, should be abandoned, and only the broadest of aggregates should be used. His point is that a properly weighted index captures the contribution of each component to the total service flow, so that there remains no reason to impute zero weights to some components. In fact I tend to lean in that same direction, as is evident from the conclusion in Barnett (1982a), in which I find that Divisia L should be favored both on theoretical and empirical grounds.

However, I am probably somewhat less militant about that conclusion than Rotemberg appears to be. For example, Rotemberg states that Barnett,

---

Barnett (1983) was a chained index, rather than the fixed base Laspeyres index defined in Rotemberg's (1989) equation 2. I did try the fixed base Laspeyres index in that research, but did not supply the fixed base plot in the article, since I found that the well-known substitution bias of the unchained Laspeyres index accumulated alarmingly rapidly. In short, fixing the base — far from being a means of solving the problem of biased drift — is its cause. Chaining is the remedy.

Hinich, and Yue (1991) include and exclude components 'arbitrarily.' Actually there is a rigorous criterion for including components in an aggregate: blockwise weak separability. As made clear in Barnett (1982a), blockwise weakly separable nesting is the uniquely correct method of clustering components in aggregation theory. Hence, I do not oppose in principle the use of multiple clusterings in producing aggregates, so long as each is blockwise weakly separable and so long as aggregation over the components is accomplished by the use of a competent index number, such as the Laspeyres, Divisia, or Rotemberg Money Stock indexes mentioned by Rotemberg. Such multiple levels of aggregation are admissible in aggregation theory. The clustering used in Barnett, Hinich, and Yue (1991) were the ones that resulted from weak separability testing in Belongia and Chalfant (1989), and hence were hardly arbitrary.

Nevertheless, I do share Rotemberg's preference for the broadest weakly separable component clustering. In addition, the reliability of the available tests for weak separability is currently in question, as a result of Barnett and Choi's (1989a) published Monte Carlo results. Under risk aversion, the state of the art in separability testing is even more unsettled.

6.2 Benchmark Rate

Rotemberg observes that Poterba and Rotemberg (1987) use the return on common stock as the benchmark rate, while Barnett, Hinich, and Yue (1991, 2000) use the maximum ex post yield-curve-adjusted rate of return among all assets in the aggregate. In fact, the rate of return on common stocks cannot be used in the computation of any of the monetary indexes, (1), (2), (3), or (4), in Rotemberg. The reason is that the ex post rate of return on common stock is not always greater than the rate of return on all monetary components. As a result, the weights on some of the monetary components in each of those aggregates would sometimes be negative. However, it should be observed that while such indexes (in particular the Divisia) were used in Barnett, Hinich, and Yue (1991, 2000), no such indexes were used in Poterba and Rotemberg (1987), so the problem of negative weights did not arise in their article.

The subject of measurement of the benchmark rate merits more research. In theory, the benchmark asset is the rate of return on human capital, which is the least liquid of all assets (in a world without slavery). Without frequent direct measurements on that rate of return, one can only construct proxy measures, which need not be acquired from the rate of return on only one other asset. We believe that the procedure used in Barnett, Hinich, and Yue (1991, 2000) provides the best currently available proxy, although we have no doubt that better proxies could be generated. In any case, since the benchmark yield enters symmetrically in all of the index numbers under consideration here, the conclusions reached in Barnett, Hinich, and Yue (1991, 2000) and in Poterba and Rotemberg (1987) can be shown to be robust to variations in the benchmark yield within plausible limits, as has been shown in some of my earlier research on robustness to the benchmark yield.

6.3 Long-Run versus Short-Run Applications

Rotemberg argues very convincingly that a broad monetary index should be able to do well both in long-run and short-run applications (especially forecasting), while each simple sum aggregate is applicable to only one time horizon. As a result, he argues that the hierarchy of increasingly broad aggregates could be replaced by one aggregate, if it were constructed as a proper index number.

There is, in fact, now a large literature demonstrating that the Divisia monetary index does better in applications than the simple sum index in monetary aggregation. For a survey of those empirical results, see Barnett, Fisher, and Serletis (1992). Rotemberg's intriguing observation may go a long way toward explaining that growing body of empirical results.

6.4 Aggregation over Economic Agents

Rotemberg observes correctly that distributional effects could become important, if Gorman's conditions for the existence of a representative consumer are not satisfied. Barnett and Serletis (1989) have, in fact, extended Divisia monetary aggregation to include a Divisia second moment capturing such potential distribution effects. At present, we do not find much evidence for important distribution effects, since the Divisia second moments usually are far less statistically significant in applications than the Divisia first moments (i.e., the Divisia index, which itself is a first moment). However, in any applications in which such distribution effects might become important, Barnett and Serletis's (1989) procedure for including Divisia second moments would permit inclusion and use of those distribution effects.

6.5 The Use of Coherent Demand Systems

Rotemberg concludes by observing that the coherent approach to money demand modeling based upon integrable models should be used in policy. I agree. The approach to generating and applying money demand models in Poterba and Rotemberg (1987) and Barnett (1983) is far preferable to the incoherent linear modeling procedure that is so common in monetary economics. However, the use of well-structured models is not a substitute for aggregation (as seems to be implied in Rotemberg's concluding paragraph). It is inconceivable that every disaggregated component of the broadest monetary aggregate, L, could be included as a separate good in the model developed by Poterba and Rotemberg (1987) or the model developed by Barnett (1983). In fact, a primary objective of aggregation theoretic indexes is to permit the construction of aggregated data that are internally consistent with the assumptions on which coherent models are based, so that the data construction is not in conflict with the models within which the data are used.

In other words, the aggregator functions tracked by the aggregated data and the model in which the data are used should be jointly coherent. For further discussion of that connection between model and data and the critical role of robustness, see the conclusion in Barnett, Hinich, and Yue (1991, section 7), reprinted as chapter 11 of this book.

7 Conclusion

As perhaps is evident from the length of this reply, I found Rotemberg's (1991) comments to be filled with interesting and often important ideas, as also was the case with Poterba and Rotemberg's (1987) earlier article.

Chapter 15

Partition of M2+ as a Joint Product: Commentary

*William A. Barnett and Ge Zhou**

1 Introduction

We were very pleased to be invited to comment on the new M2+ index, recently proposed in interesting papers by some Federal Reserve Board staff members (Collins and Edwards, 1994; and Orphanides, Reid and Small, 1994). The two papers presented at this conference by those Board staff members raise important and challenging questions that we believe should motivate much research in future years. In addition, we wish to commend those Board staff economists for their courage and integrity in pushing past barriers that have intimidated prior researchers and thereby precluded prior research on these difficult matters.

The basic issue is whether riskiness of the investment rate of return on an asset is a characteristic that rules out the possibility of an asset's contribution to the economy's liquidity. Oddly, that issue has largely precluded prior consideration of risky assets as components of central bank monetary aggregates. Yet clearly the position is groundless. While it is clear that risky assets are not good candidates for legal means of payment, monetary aggregates now contain many assets that are not legal means of payment. It has long been recognized that currency and demand deposits provide much, but by no means all, of the economy's monetary service flow.

No one has suggested that bond or stock mutual funds should be made legal means of payment. In addition, stock and bond mutual funds currently are bundled into packages of funds by companies that include money market funds within the bundle. Hence, it often is as easy as a telephone call to transfer funds from stock and bond funds into checkable money market funds. Although stock and bond funds certainly should not be made legal means of payment, it simply makes no sense to exclude bond and stock mutual funds from consideration as assets contributing monetary liquidity to the economy.

---

*Originally published in the Federal Reserve Bank of St. Louis *Review* 76 (1994), 53-62. We benefited from a useful discussion with Athanasios Orphanides about some of these issues. Research on this project was partially supported by NSF grant SES 9223557.

There is no necessary conflict between the existence of risky return and the contribution of liquidity to the economy. The two are not mutually exclusive.[1] Yet prior researchers have excluded assets having substantial principle risk from consideration as components of monetary aggregates. It indeed is odd that such an obviously groundless prejudice has precluded research by the entire economics profession on an important topic. The authors of the two Board staff papers are right. The authors have provided a service to the profession by exploring the topic for the first time.

2 Challenges Presented to Economic Theory

Riskiness of the rate of return simply does not preclude the production of monetary services by an asset. Riskiness of the rate of return, however, certainly does make life more difficult for index number theorists and aggregation theorists. Most of the literature in those fields is produced under the assumption of perfect certainty or risk neutrality. Extensions of that literature to risk aversion were begun recently by Poterba and Rotemberg (1987), Barnett and Yue (1991), Barnett, Hinich, and Yue (2000), and Barnett and Zhou (1994b). We believe that the important issues raised by Collins and Edwards (1994) and Orphanides, Reid, and Small (1994) at this conference should serve as motivation for further research on index number theory and aggregation theory under risk aversion. We do indeed welcome the increased motivation in that area provided by the work of those Board staff researchers.

But there is an even more fundamental problem. The existence of an investment rate of return, even a perfectly certain one, raises questions about how an asset should be incorporated into an aggregate. While the existence of such a rate of return does not prevent an asset from producing monetary services, the share of the asset's services that can be viewed as 'monetary' is strongly affected. This comment is directed towards an investigation of that share.

3 Historical Background

At one time, money was cash plus demand deposits. No controversy existed on that topic. But a sequence of technological changes and innovations

---

[1] Formally, the correct method used to determine the clustering of components within an aggregation-theoretic monetary aggregate is testing for blockwise weak separability. An innovative new approach to testing for weak separability recently was proposed by Swofford and Whitney (1994). Although risky return complicates testing for weak separabilty, risk in no way precludes acceptance of that hypothesis. In fact a successful test of weak separability with random rates of return is included in Barnett and Zhou (1994).

occurred and continued to occur, such that an increasingly large number of substitutes for money produced an increasingly large share of the economy's monetary services. The result was the Bach Commission, the Gurley and Shaw (1960) book, the Pesek and Saving (1967) book, and many other important contributions that influenced the growing movement towards the construction of increasingly broad monetary aggregates. The response of most central banks, however, has been to accept one aspect of that research while conveniently overlooking another closely related aspect.

In particular, the researchers who first worked in that area were very clear on one simple, elementary fact: *Investment yield is not a monetary service.* There was a reason that all monetary economists once agreed that money included only cash and non-interest-bearing demand deposits. If investment yield were a monetary service, then coal mines would be money. Land would be money. The entire capital stock of the United States would be money.

This is not to deny that assets that produce an investment rate of return, whether or not risky, can produce monetary services. However, interest yielding monetary assets are joint products. Some of their services are monetary. Some are not. This fact seems to have escaped many of the world's central banks. To the degree that the economy equates marginal utilities per dollar across assets, the marginal utility of monetary services produced by an asset must decrease as its marginal non-monetary services increase — and investment return is very clearly not a monetary service.

To underscore our point, we bring up the famous diamonds-versus-water paradox. The total utility of water exceeds that of diamonds, even though the marginal utility of diamonds exceeds that of water. In fact, as one moves along a concave utility function, marginal utility varies inversely with total utility. Hence, the statements made above about marginal utilities should not be confused with the total or average monetary service flow produced by any asset. But it is the marginal utilities that are relevant to measuring the prices in index numbers, such as the Divisia, Fisher ideal, Paasche, or Laspeyres quantity indexes. We hope that we also do not have to remind this audience that the prices (user costs) in such indexes are not the weights. We nevertheless find that this literature contains many misunderstandings of monetary index number theory, and most of those misunderstandings are produced by confusing prices with weights and marginal utilities with total or average utilities.

4 Ferrari Sports Cars

It has been asked at this conference whether stock funds or bond funds are 'money,' or are they not money. We would like to ask a different question.

Are Ferrari sports cars transportation machines or recreational machines? We can imagine a Ferrari owner responding that a Ferrari is strictly a transportation machine, and that the high price is produced by the Ferrari's superior performance on highways and on winding roads. Hence, the price of a Ferrari is the discounted present value solely of the transportation services. But I expect that most of the rest of us would view the price of a Ferrari as being the sum of the discounted present values of two different flows: transportation services and recreational services.

Ferraris are joint products, in terms of the services produced. Interest-bearing monetary assets similarly are joint products. Such assets produce both monetary and non-monetary services, whereby the interest yield unquestionably is in the latter category. Hence the correct answer to the question asked by the Board's staff economists at this conference is that such assets, including stock and bond mutual funds, are partially money and partially not money.

5 What to Do Next

We see that we are presented with a paradox. More and more assets are contributing to the economy's monetary service flow. As made clear by the authors of the two Board staff papers, stock and bond funds now are among those assets. However the investment yields of that growing collection of assets are not monetary services. If we do not add such assets into the monetary aggregates, we overlook some of the economy's monetary service flow. If we do add those assets into the aggregates, we contaminate the aggregates with non-monetary services.

The answer should be obvious. We must untangle the two discounted present values: the discounted present value of the monetary service flow and the discounted present value of the investment yield. Indeed, it can be done.

6 The Theory

Barnett (1987) defined the economic stock of money to be the discounted present value of expenditure on the services of monetary assets. Barnett (1991) derived that discounted present value in the form that we display below. During period s, let p_s^* = the true cost of living index, let M_{is} be nominal balances of monetary asset i, let r_{is} be the nominal expected holding period yield on monetary asset i, and define $m_{is} = M_{is}/p_s^*$ to be real balances of monetary asset i. The current period is defined to be period t so that $s \geq t$.

The Theory

Define the discount rate for period s to be

$$\rho_s = \begin{cases} 1 & \text{for } s = 1 \\ \prod_{u=t}^{s-1}(1+R_u) & \text{for } s > t. \end{cases} \quad (1)$$

By letting the planning horizon, T, go to infinity in the second term of Barnett (1978, eq. 2; 1980a, eq. 3.3; 1981b, eq. 7.3), we immediately acquire the following definition for the Economic Stock of Money, first derived as definition 1 and equation 2.2 in Barnett (1991), which has been reprinted in this book as chapter 10.

Definition 1: *Under risk neutrality, the economic stock of money during period t is*

$$V_t = \sum_{s=t}^{\infty} \sum_{i=1}^{n} \left[\frac{p_s^*}{\rho_s} - \frac{p_s^*(1+r_{is})}{\rho_{s+1}} \right] m_{is}. \quad (2)$$

The concept of economic stock used to produce Definition 1 is the user-cost-evaluated expenditure on the services of the n monetary assets that are its components. It should be observed that the procedure used in Barnett (1978, eq. 2; 1980a, eq. 3.3; 1981b, eq. 7.3) to acquire that discounted present value for finite T was just back substitution and algebraic manipulation of the sequence of flow-of-funds identities. Hence our conclusion is produced entirely from accounting identities.

If we now substitute (1) and $m_{is} = M_{is}/p_s^*$ into equation (2), we acquire the following result:

$$V_t = \sum_{s=t}^{\infty} \sum_{i=1}^{n} \left[\frac{R_s - r_{is}}{\prod_{u=t}^{s}(1+R_u)} \right] M_{is}. \quad (3)$$

Unfortunately, this equation includes expected future values of interest rates and of monetary asset holdings. While it may be reasonable to assume that interest rates are stationary, no such easy simplification is available for the stochastic process of future monetary asset holdings. We believe that a useful way to proceed would be to use VAR forecasts of the monetary asset holdings and rates of return. We plan to produce results using that approach. But considering the time constraint that we faced with this conference, we had no choice but to make strongly simplifying assumptions. In particular, we make the assumption which causes (3) to collapse into the Rotemberg, Driscoll, and Poterba (1995) CE index, first interpreted to be a stock index in Barnett (1991).

Definition 2: *The CE index is*

$$V_t = \sum_{i=1}^{n} \frac{R_t - r_{it}}{R_t} M_{it} \tag{4}$$

We seek to find conditions under which (4) will equal (3). To that end, suppose that expectations are stationary in the sense that $r_{is} = r_{it}$ and $R_{is} = R_{it}$ for all $s \geq t$, and consider the static portfolio, $(M_{1s}, M_{2s}, \ldots, M_{ns}) = (M_{1t}, M_{2t}, \ldots, M_{nt})$, for all $s \geq t$. Equation (3) reduces to

$$V_t = \sum_{i=1}^{n} \sum_{s=t}^{\infty} \left[\frac{R_t - r_{it}}{(1+R_t)^{s-t+1}} \right] M_{it}. \tag{5}$$

Observe, however, that

$$\sum_{s=t}^{\infty} \frac{R_t - r_{it}}{(1+R_t)^{s-t+1}} = \frac{R_t - r_{it}}{R_t}, \tag{6}$$

since the left hand side of (6) is a convergent geometric series (minus the first term in the series). Substituting (6) into (5), we acquire our result:

Theorem 1: *Under stationary expectations, the CE index is equal to the Economic Money Stock.*

Under the stationary expectations assumption, we easily can discount to present value the expected investment yield flows, $r_{is}M_{is} - r_{it}M_{it}$ for $s \geq t$ to get the following capitalized value:

$$V_t^* = \sum_{s=t}^{\infty} \sum_{i=1}^{n} \left[\frac{r_{it} M_{it}}{(1+R_t)^{s-t+1}} \right]. \tag{7}$$

Again we have a convergent geometric series in the summation over s at any given i, so that we find:

$$V_t^* = \sum_{i=1}^{n} \frac{r_{it}}{R_t} M_{it} \tag{8}$$

Adding (8) to (4), we find that

$$V_t + V_t^* = \sum_{i=1}^{n} M_{it}. \tag{9}$$

The conclusion is clear. The simple sum monetary aggregates measure the stock of money only if the investment (interest) yield of the monetary components is treated as a monetary service. Yet it is difficult to think of any macroeconomic school of thought which has ever viewed the interest yield on monetary assets to be a monetary service. In fact, that possibility was considered carefully and rejected unequivocally in Pesek and Saving (1967).

In the discussion that follows, we shall use this result to decompose the simple-sum aggregates into their investment share and their monetary services share. In each case, the share is produced by discounting the flow to present value, the interest yield in one and the service flow in the other. The decomposition then is into V_t and V_t^*, which partition

$$\sum_{i=1}^{n} M_{it}$$

into its two parts, in accordance with equation (9).

7 'Ancient' History

There was a time — long, long ago — when money was currency and demand deposits, and demand deposits did not yield interest. In those days, we see that

$$V_t^* = 0, \text{ so that } V_t = \sum_{i=1}^{n} M_{it}.$$

Those were the days when the simple-sum monetary aggregates were created, and we see that the people who created them knew what they were doing. But that simpler world is long gone. Many assets that contribute to the economy's monetary services also yield an investment rate of return.

8 The Data

We computed the decomposition into V_t and V_t^* of the official simple-sum M1 and M2 indexes along with the corresponding decomposition into V_t and V_t^* of the newly proposed simple-sum M2+ index. We also computed the decomposition into V_t and V_t^* of bond mutual funds and stock mutual funds as a means of further investigating the source of the difference in behavior of M2 versus M2+. The attached figures provide the results.

The decomposition depends upon the measurement of the benchmark rate of return R_t. Clearly, V_t increases as R_t increases, and V_t^* decreases as R_t increases. Hence, the monetary service share (versus the investment share) of the simple-sum aggregate 'joint product' increases as R_t increases. The results can be biased in the direction favoring the inclusion of stock and bond funds by choosing an artificially high setting for R_t. For the purpose of biasing the results in that direction intentionally, we chose the highest possible setting for R_t that could be connected in any way with the available data.

As shown by Rotemberg, Driscoll and Poterba (1995), V_t has a very volatile growth rate and, hence, they advocate smoothing the interest rates to produce smoother growth of the aggregates. This is not surprising, since V_t and V_t^* are stock aggregates which tend to have volatile growth rates. We use the same smoothing method advocated by Rotemberg, Driscoll and Poterba (1995). In particular, we replaced all of the interest rates in the index by 13-quarter centered moving averages. Since the moving averages are centered, they are not defined for the first six quarters or the last six quarters. We used the method advocated by Rotemberg, Driscoll and Poterba and phased in the centered moving average from asymmetric averages computed during the first six and last six observations.

Once the smoothed interest data had been constructed, we searched over those series for the highest smoothed interest rate ever attained by any component asset during our sample. That ex post rate of return was 24.2 percent, which we selected to be the value of R_t for all t. In general there is no reason for the benchmark rate to be a constant or to equal any ex post rate of return, since ex post rates of return tend to be much more volatile than ex ante expected rates of return. Our selection for the benchmark rate, however, produces the largest value that we could connect with the data, and we wanted to produce results that would be biased in favor of the Board staff members' proposal. In interpreting our results, the division of the simple sum into the components V_t and V_t^* should be understood to be biased very strongly towards V_t and away from V_t^*. Hence, the monetary services share in the joint product should be viewed as intentionally exaggerated.

9 The Results

Figure 1 contains the partition of simple-sum M1 into its investment share and its monetary services share. The solid line is the monetary services share produced from the computed value of V_t. The vertical gap between the solid line and the dotted line is the investment-motivated share, V_t^*, which could be interpreted as the 'error-in-the variable' embedded in the simple-sum index, M1. The height of the dotted line from the horizontal axis is the simple-sum index, equaling the sum of V_t and V_t^*. As is evident from Figure 1, the error-in-the-variable gap is relatively small and does not vary much over the sample. With a relatively constant vertical gap, the rate of

The Results

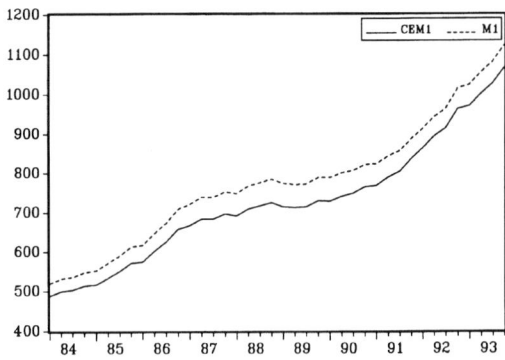

Figure 1: M1 Joint Product and Economic Capital Stock. (M1=simple sum joint product; CEM1=economic capital stock part of the joint product.)

growth of M1 is not greatly affected by the error-in-the-variable gap. For most statistical inferences and for policy, the growth rate of money is what matters. Hence, we see that the existence of the V_t^* error gap produces little difficulty for M1.

Figure 2 contains the analogous plot and decomposition for the official simple-sum M2 aggregate. Observe that the error-in-the-variable gap is large (and would be much larger for a more realistic choice of R_t). In addition, that gap is variable and trends downward, especially recently. Hence, the existence of the error gap not only effects the short run growth rate dynamics of the aggregate, but also biases downward the long term growth rate. Inferences and policy are not invariant to the existence of this gap.

Figure 3 contains the decomposition for the M2+ aggregate that has been proposed at this conference by Collins and Edwards (1994) and Orphanides, Reid, and Small (1994). Observe that while the error gap is even larger than for M2, the size of the gap is less variable and no longer trends downward. Hence, the growth rate of the error-shifted dotted line approximately tracks the growth rate of the 'correct' solid line.

To see why M2+ stabilizes the size of the gap and thereby improves on the aggregate's growth rate performance, see Figures 4 and 5, which display the decomposition of the stock mutual funds data and the bond mutual funds data into their economic capital stock share and their error-in-the-variable shift. Observe that in each of those two cases, the size of the gap grows rapidly during the past two years. This growing error gap offsets the declining error gap in M2, when the stock and bond fund data are added into M2. In short, we conclude that the authors of the two papers presented at this conference are correct in concluding that the growth rate behavior of M2 is improved by

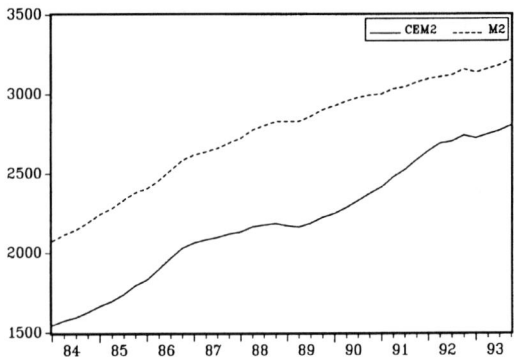

Figure 2: M2 Joint Product and Economic Capital Stock. (M2=simple sum joint product; CEM2=economic capital stock part of the joint product.)

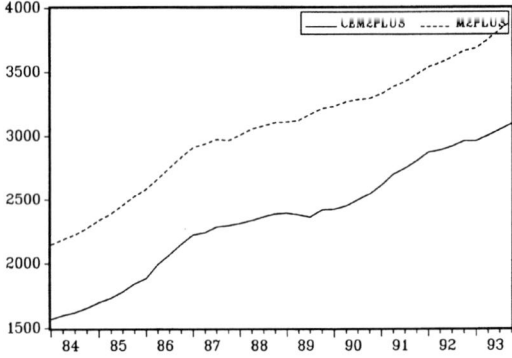

Figure 3: M2+ Joint Product and Economic Capital Stock. (M2+=simple sum joint product; CEM2+=economic capital stock part of the joint product.)

The Results   317

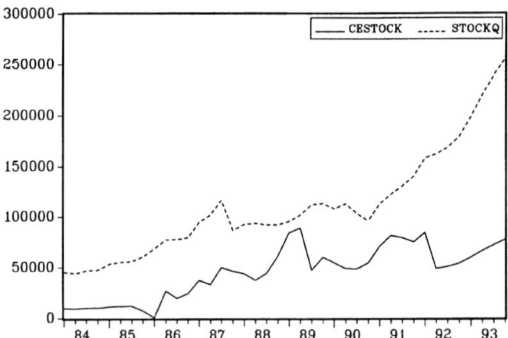

Figure 4: Common Stock Mutual Funds Joint Product and Their Economic Capital Stock. (StockQ=simple sum joint product; CEstock=economic capital stock part of the joint product.)

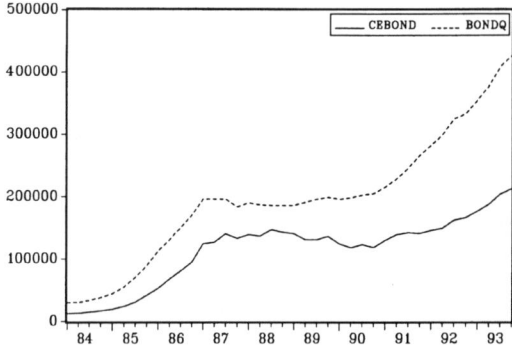

Figure 5: Bond Mutual Funds Joint Product and Their Economic Capital Stock. (BondQ=simple sum joint product; CEbond=economic capital stock part of the joint product.)

incorporating the stock and bond mutual fund data into M2. Indeed, it does appear that substitution from M2 components into stock and bond mutual funds has become important.

10 Where is All of This Going?

There is an underlying dynamic to this trend in monetary theory. Stabilizing the size of the error gap requires continually incorporating more assets into the monetary aggregates. The size of the gap keeps growing. The share of the monetary aggregate representing discounted monetary services continues to decrease, and the monetary aggregates look increasingly like pure investment capital rather than money. Even if stabilizing the size of the gap offsets long-run errors in growth rate paths, the short-run dynamics of the aggregates are likely to become increasingly disjoint from monetary services growth.

In this paper, we use the CE index, equation (4), to permit easy decomposition of the simple-sum aggregate 'joint product' into its monetary service and investment shares. Using the formula (4) with forecasted variables, perhaps by a VAR, would be better. But generating data that depends upon forecasts is unpleasant for data-producing governmental agencies. Smoothing interest rates to decrease the volatility of the resulting aggregate is also unpleasant for governmental agencies. For this conference, decomposition of the stocks in that manner was revealing. But as a means to produce data for a central bank, there is a better way. It is the Divisia monetary aggregates long advocated by Barnett (1980a). See Barnett, Fisher and Serletis (1992) and Belongia and Chalfant (1989) for an overview and some of the relevant empirical results.

The Divisia monetary aggregates directly measure monetary service flows, not the discounted stock levels. The Divisia monetary aggregates do not require smoothing of interest rates to smooth the index's growth rate, and the Divisia monetary aggregates contain no variables that need forecasting.[2] In addition, Barnett (1991) proved that if we could do the forecasting needed to

---

[2]It is necessary to measure the benchmark rate, R_t, to construct the Divisia monetary aggregates, and we advocate the use of the upper envelope of the yield-curve-adjusted, holding-period yields on all of the components in the broadest aggregate. Obviously we do not advocate the use of the extreme, constant setting of 24.4 percent, chosen for an illustrative purpose in this paper. However, it should be observed that the behavior of the Divisia monetary aggregate is much more robust to variations in the method of measuring the benchmark rate than is the CE index, which is very sensitive to that rate's selection. The reason is that the benchmark rate appears symmetrically in both the numerator and denominator of the share weights of the Divisia index, which in turn is a growth-rate index. Since the CE index is a level index, variations in any interest rate, including the benchmark rate, produce jumps in the level of the unsmoothed index. Jumps in levels produce spikes in growth rates.

compute the monetary capital stock (equation 3), the result would be identical to that produced by discounting to present value the future stochastic process of the Divisia monetary aggregate.

PART 4:
CONSUMER MONETARY AGGREGATION UNDER PERFECT CERTAINTY

Section 4.1: Editors' Overview of Part 4

William A. Barnett and Apostolos Serletis

The following table contains a brief summary of the contents of each chapter in Part 4 of this book.

Part 4 Section Contents
Consumer Monetary Aggregation under Perfect Certainty

Chapter Number	Chapter Title	Contents
16	New Indices of Money Supply and the Flexible Laurent Demand System	Originates the Laurent series class of flexible functional forms and applies them to modeling systems of money demand equations in a manner that is consistent with aggregation theory.
17	The New Divisia Monetary Aggregates	Empirically compares the simple sum and Divisia monetary aggregates relative to the conventional comparison methods, and demonstrates that many of the instability paradoxes in the literature disappear if money supply is correctly measured.
18	Consumer Theory and the Demand for Money	A *Journal of Economic Literature* survey of the state of the art, with particular emphasis on the empirical results internationally.

Chapter 16:

Since index number and aggregation theory are based upon microeconomic theory, the gains from their use are greatest when the resulting aggregated data are used within a model that also is based upon microeconomic theory. The result is an internally consistent approach to economic inference. Although Chapter 2 does so, that chapter nests the aggregation-theoretic monetary aggregates within a nested CES ("S-Branch") utility tree, which no longer represents the state of the art in system-wide modeling. Chapter 16 develops a sophisticated demand system model based upon the Laurent series expansion. That model has better regional properties than the popular Taylor series based models, such as the translog.

While the Laurent series approach remains very much at the state of the art in specification selection, there has recently been growing research interest in a more difficult approach using seminonparametric inference in infinite dimensional parameter space. The series expansion being used in that research is the Müntz-Szatz series, which was generalized to the multivariate case by Barnett and Jonas (1983). The resulting demand and supply functions are called the AIM model (Asymptotically Ideal Model). For applications with monetary data, see Barnett and Yue (1988), Barnett, Geweke and Wolfe (1991a, 1991b), and Barnett, Geweke and Yue (1991).

Chapter 17:

Chapter 17 is from an older tradition. It was produced while Barnett was on the staff of the Special Studies Section of the Board of Governors of the Federal Reserve System. The chapter compares the simple sum with the Divisia monetary aggregates relative to the conventional tests that were used by the Federal Reserve System at that time. Those tests include reduced form tests, Goldfeld money demand functions, indicator and information tests, stochastic coefficient tests, and Granger causality tests.

Of particular interest are the results finding superior information content for the Divisia monetary aggregates within the Federal Reserve Board's own quarterly econometric model. Also of particular interest are the stochastic coefficient demand for money function results. Those results find that instability of the coefficients of the Goldfeld demand for money function disappear when estimated with Divisia monetary aggregates data instead of simple sum monetary aggregates data.

Chapter 18:

Chapter 18 is a survey paper on the subject matter of this book. The chapter consists of a paper originally published in the *Journal of Economic Literature*. Of particular interest is the emphasis upon the vast accumulated quantity of international research using the approach advocated by this book. References to published sources of those results are contained in the chapter. The international research has been produced both by academic researchers and central bank economists from throughout the world.

Section 4.2: Consumer Money Demand

Chapter 16

New Indices of Money Supply and the Flexible Laurent Demand System

William A. Barnett[*]

> The article begins by surveying the existing results on the new Divisia monetary aggregates. Charts display the differences in behavior between the Divisia aggregates and the Federal Reserve's official simple-sum monetary aggregates. The article then compares system-wide fit for the simple-sum and Divisia monetary aggregates when used as data in the joint estimation of a system of demand equations. The demand system is derived from a new Laurent expansion approximation to the reciprocal indirect utility function. The Laurent expansion provides a better-behaved remainder term than that of the more commonly used Taylor series.

[*]Reprinted with permission from the *Journal of Business and Economic Statistics*. Copyright (1983) by the American Statistical Association. Much of this research was completed while the author was at the Board of Governors of the Federal Reserve System. The views expressed herein are solely those of the author and do not necessarily represent the views of the Board of Governors of the Federal Reserve System. The author has benefited substantially from many hours of discussion with Andrew Jonas about the theoretical properties of Laurent expansions and from the comments of R. P. Byron, Carl Christ, Erwin Diewert, Ronald Gallant, John Geweke, and Arnold Zellner.

1 Introduction

1.1 Overview

In this paper, the new Divisia monetary aggregates are discussed. Some of the existing graphical comparisons between the Divisia aggregates and the official simple-sum aggregates are surveyed. System-wide modeling methods are then applied to comparisons of the use of Divisia and simple-sum monetary aggregates as data in estimated demand systems. For this purpose, a new demand system is introduced. The demand system is derived from a Laurent series expansion, rather than from the usual Taylor series expansions. The Laurent series model is shown to possess a better behaved remainder term than the remainder terms in the Taylor series models. Since the Divisia monetary aggregates and the Laurent demand model are of independent interest, they each are now introduced separately.

1.2 The Divisia Monetary Aggregates

In recent years, the Federal Reserve System has experienced considerable difficulty in controlling its monetary aggregates. During those years of unsteady monetary control, numerous innovations evolved in the money markets. The result was the introduction of many new liquid assets, which were not included in the then existing monetary aggregates. As a result, the Federal Reserve System embarked on a large-scale research effort aimed at redefinition of its monetary aggregates. The official result was publication of new monetary aggregates (see Barnett et al. 1979). However, Barnett (1979b, 1980a,b, 1981b, 1982), during his research on that project at the Federal Reserve Board, found that both the old and the new aggregates, which are simple sums of component quantities, are constructed in a manner that is not consistent with aggregation or index number theory. As a result, another set of monetary aggregates was constructed, based on Barnett's (1980a, 1981b) aggregation theoretic proposal. The historical values of the resulting theoretically based aggregates recently were released officially by the Federal Reserve Board in Barnett and Spindt (1982).

Simple-sum aggregation implies perfect substitutability between components, but monetary assets are not perfect substitutes. The fact that simple-sum monetary aggregation is unsatisfactory has long been recognized, and there has been a steady stream of attempts at weakening the perfect substitutability assumption by constructing weighted average monetary aggregates (see, e.g., Hawtrey 1930; Gurley 1960, pp. 7–8; Friedman and Meiselman 1963, p. 185; Kane 1964; Ford and Stark 1967; Chetty 1969, 1972; Friedman and Schwartz 1970, pp. 151–152; Steinhauer and Chang 1972; Lee 1972;

Bisignano 1974; Moroney and Wilbratte 1976; Barth, Kraft, and Kraft 1977). But those attempts possessed no uniqueness properties, since the weighted averages were not directly based on aggregation and index number theory. Without theory, a continuum of possible weighting schemes exists. Nevertheless, as quoted from Bob Dylan by Bisignano (1974), "You don't need a weatherman to know which way the wind blows." The direct applicability of economic aggregation and index number theory to monetary aggregation has only recently been recognized. These results were developed by Barnett (1981b). Also see Donovan (1978), Offenbacher (1979), and Cockerline and Murray (1981a) for related results. Determination of the properties of the theoretically based aggregates has been a subject of Federal Reserve Board staff research for four years. Relative to *all* of the conventional criteria, the theoretically based aggregates were found to outperform the simple-sum aggregates. The theoretical derivation of those aggregates is contained in Barnett (1979b, 1980a,b, 1981b). Empirical comparisons against the currently targeted simple-sum aggregates are provided in Barnett (1980a, 1981b), who used aggregation theoretic tests. Empirical comparisons of the two sets of aggregates relative to policy criteria are provided in Barnett and Spindt (1979) and Barnett, and Offenbacher, and Spindt (1984). Controllability of the two sets of aggregates is considered in Barnett and Spindt (1982) and Barnett, Offenbacher, and Spindt (1984). Selection between aggregates at different levels of aggregation is investigated in Barnett (1982a). An overview of much of that research can be found in Barnett (1982a) and Barnett, Offenbacher, and Spindt (1981).

One of the most important of the policy criteria for selection of monetary aggregates is the behavior of estimated demand-for-money (or velocity) functions. The demand-for-money functions estimated in Barnett, Offenbacher, and Spindt (1984) are all based on conventional single-equation demand-for-money function specifications. Those specifications have the merit of providing direct comparability with the literature on simple-sum aggregates. However, estimation of a single equation does not permit imposition of the constraints that result from microeconomic demand theory. For this reason, demand modeling for other goods has moved towards the system-wide approach, by which systems of demand functions are jointly estimated subject to the constraints of microeconomic theory. In this article we use the system-wide approach to compare the fit of a joint monetary sector demand model estimated separately with each of the two sets of aggregates.

1.3 The Laurent Demand System

In testing hypotheses in the system-wide approach, demand systems usually are derived (through duality theory) from a generating-function specification for tastes or technology, and the specification usually is a locally 'flexible functional form.' An exception is the Rotterdam model, which uses an approximation that is inherently linked with the convergence approach to aggregation over consumers. See Barnett (1979a,b, 1981b). The class of locally flexible functional forms was defined by Diewert (1973, 1974) to be the class of functions that can attain, at an arbitrary point, arbitrary values of the function and of its first and second derivatives. (We do not adopt the common practice of dropping the important qualifier 'locally' from before the characterization 'flexible functional form.') Equivalently those functions can attain arbitrary elasticities of substitution at a point.

Although Diewert's important class of functions is large, almost all of the currently available elements of that class were derived as second-order Taylor series approximations. An exception is Diewert's generalized Cobb-Douglas model. Also Gallant (1981) constructed a model from a Fourier series expansion; the model may be a locally flexible functional form, although that result has not been proved. However, recent evidence suggests that the small Taylor series subclass may be poorly behaved over the finite region of the data. See, e.g., Barnett (1977a, 1979a, 1981b); Gallant (1981); Wales (1977); Blackorby, Primont, and Russell (1977); Guilkey and Lovell (1980); Christensen and Caves (1980); and White (1980). In other words, the remainder term of the approximation may be poorly behaved away from the point of the approximations. In addition, we shall see later that no justification exists in the theory of analytic functions for preferring second-order Taylor series approximations over all other elements of the class of locally flexible functional forms.

The Laurent expansion is known to have a remainder term that varies less severely over the region of the approximation than does the remainder term of the Taylor series approximation. This global regularity property is acquired at the expense of a remainder term that need not attain zero within the region of approximation. Nevertheless, the remainder term of a Laurent expansion typically will be small throughout that region. In addition, while the region of convergence of a Taylor series approximation is a sphere, the region of approximation of a Laurent expansion is a torus or annulus. In this article we derive our system of demand functions from a locally flexible functional form based on a second-order Laurent expansion.

2 The New Monetary Quantity Index Numbers

2.1 Aggregation Theory

In economic aggregation theory, an economic quantity aggregate, Q, is a function of component quantities, $\mathbf{q}$. The function, f, is called the aggregator function. Then $Q = f(\mathbf{q})$. Substitutability among the components, $\mathbf{q}$, in the function, f, is equal to substitutability among those components in the preferences or technologies of the economic agents who use the components. In particular, to a consumer the function f is his (category) utility function over $\mathbf{q}$; to a firm, f is the firm's (category) production function. Tastes and technology are assumed to be weakly separable in $\mathbf{q}$, so that an aggregator function exists over $\mathbf{q}$ alone. In aggregation theory, the distinction between utility and production functions is of little importance, since both have the same properties. The term aggregator function is used without regard to whether its components are purchased by consumers or by firms. In either case, f is assumed to be linearly homogeneous; hence if all components grow at rate λ, then the aggregate will also grow at rate λ.

Even if monetary assets are not in consumers' elementary utility functions or in firms' elementary production functions, it has been proved in general equilibrium theory that each consumer has a *derived* utility function containing monetary assets along with consumer goods, and analogously each firm possesses a derived production function containing monetary assets along with other factors of production. See Arrow and Hahn (1971, p. 350) and Quirk and Saposnik (1968, p. 97). Assuming that the derived utility and production functions are weakly separable in monetary assets, aggregator functions and therefore economic aggregates exist over monetary components alone.

Under Gorman's (1953) and Muellbauer's (1975, 1976) aggregation conditions, we can aggregate over the aggregator functions of the firms and consumers to acquire an aggregator function for the economy. A particularly interesting special case of the above result arises if the derived utility and production functions are the Lagrangians from decision problems containing a transactions constraint. In that case, the economy's monetary aggregator function is its transactions technology (see Phlips and Spinnewyn 1979).

The above results are derived formally in Barnett (1980a, 1981b), who tested and rejected the conditions for simple-sum monetary aggregation. This result is consistent with over a decade of empirical evidence on substitutability among monetary assets. If the aggregator function, f, is a simple sum, then the monetary components, $\mathbf{q}$, are perfect substitutes. Yet the components of the existing simple-sum monetary aggregates are far from perfect substitutes.

2.2 Index Number Theory

Since the aggregator function, f, is not a simple sum, aggregation theory leaves us with the need to specify and estimate the nonlinear function, f, which then permits imperfect substitution between components. However, economic aggregates, $F(\mathbf{q})$, depending on estimated unknown parameters, are not usually acceptable as data to be supplied by governmental agencies. The solution to this problem is the objective of index number theory, which provides parameter-free approximations to economic aggregates. While quantity index numbers contain no unknown parameters, quantity index numbers depend on prices as well as on quantities. For overviews of index number theory, see Barnett (1981a; 1981b, ch. 7).

Diewert (1976) recently showed that a class of index numbers with particularly good properties exists. He named the class the superlative class. Superlative index numbers are defined to be exact for aggregator functions that are flexible functional forms, which can provide second-order local approximations to any arbitrary aggregator functions. Two particularly well-known index numbers in the superlative class are the Fisher ideal index and the Törnqvist-Theil discrete time approximation to the Divisia index. The latter index is usually called the Törnqvist-Theil index or just the Divisia index (in discrete time). We shall follow Theil's (1967) convention by calling the index the Divisia index. (Strictly speaking, the Divisia index is a continuous-time line integral approximated in discrete time by the Törnqvist-Theil approximation.)

The selection between the index numbers in the superlative class is of little importance, since all of those index numbers move closely together. However, the Divisia index has a form that is particularly easy to interpret in policy applications. Hence we follow Barnett's (1980a,b) proposal to use the Divisia quantity index (with user cost prices) in monetary aggregation. That proposal was also recently adopted by the Bank of Canada in its research on monetary aggregation. See Cockerline and Murray (1981a).

The Divisia index is defined as follows. Let q_{it} be the quantity of good i during period t. Let π_{it} be the price of good i during period t. Let $s_{it} = \pi_{it} q_{it} / \sum_{k=1}^{N} \pi_{kt} q_{kt}$, and let $s_{it}^* = (1/2)(s_{it} + s_{i,t-1})$. Then the Divisia quantity index, Q_t, over the components q_{it} ($i = 1, \ldots, N$) during period t is defined such that

$$\log Q_t - \log Q_{t-1} = \sum_{i=1}^{N} s_{it}^* (\log q_{it} - \log q_{i,t-1}). \tag{1}$$

Clearly the growth rate (log changes) of the Divisia quantity index equals the weighted average of the growth rates (log changes) of the components. The weights are the shares, s_{it}^* $(i = 1, \ldots, N)$.

2.3 The User Cost of Money

In order to apply (1) to monetary quantity aggregation, we must define the price and quantity variables for monetary assets. The component quantity, q_{it}, can be real or nominal, total or per capita balances of monetary asset i. In constructing a monetary target or indicator, q_{it} would be nominal balances (either total or per capita). However, in estimating demand for money functions, q_{it} would be per capita real balances, as used in the estimation below.

If the prices of the component assets were all equal to one, then relative prices would never change. In the case of all equal prices, the Divisia index can be shown to reduce (approximately) to the simple-sum index. However, money is a durable good, and the one dollar 'price' of a unit of its *stock* is applicable only for an infinite holding period. Our concern is with the flow of monetary *services* generated by that stock during a finite holding period. At the end of the finite holding period, the monetary asset remains in existence, and therefore the asset's lifetime services (valued at the price of the stock) have not yet been fully consumed. It is the service flow of a durable, and not its stock, that enters the economy's structure as a variable. Hence, we need the price of the service flow generated by a monetary asset.

The price of a durable good's service flow is called its user cost (or rental price). When a perfect rental market exists for a durable, the user cost equals the market rental price. Until recently the form of the user cost function for monetary assets was not known. This fact had hindered the application of aggregation and index number theory to monetary aggregation. The way to application of index number theory to monetary aggregation was opened by Barnett (1978, 1980a) in his formal mathematical derivation of the user cost of monetary assets. The same result, also was deduced by Donovan (1978) through analogy with the consumer durables case.

The monetary asset user cost formula is constructed as follows. Let p_t^* be the true cost-of-living index during period t; let R_t be the maximum available expected one-period holding yield during period t; let r_{it} be the own rate of return on asset i during period t; and let τ_t be the marginal tax rate during period t. Then the user cost of the services of monetary asset i during period t is

$$\pi_{it} = \frac{p_t^*(R_t - r_{it})(1 - \tau_t)}{1 + R_t(1 - \tau_t)}. \tag{2}$$

When (1) is computed with π_{it} as in (2), we have found that the aggregate is robust to errors in the weights, s_{it}^*. The variations in the weights in the experiments were induced by varying the variables in (2) within the limits of plausible data error.

3 Behavior of the Divisia Monetary Aggregates

Barnett's (1980a) Divisia monetary aggregates were constructed from (1) with the user costs computed from (2). After the data used in those aggregates were refined, the Divisia aggregates were extensively compared with the simple-sum aggregates. The results of the empirical comparisons were summarized and discussed in Barnett (1982a). However, the available graphical comparisons have remained scattered over various sources. In this section, some of the more interesting graphical comparisons from those sources are collected together and discussed jointly.

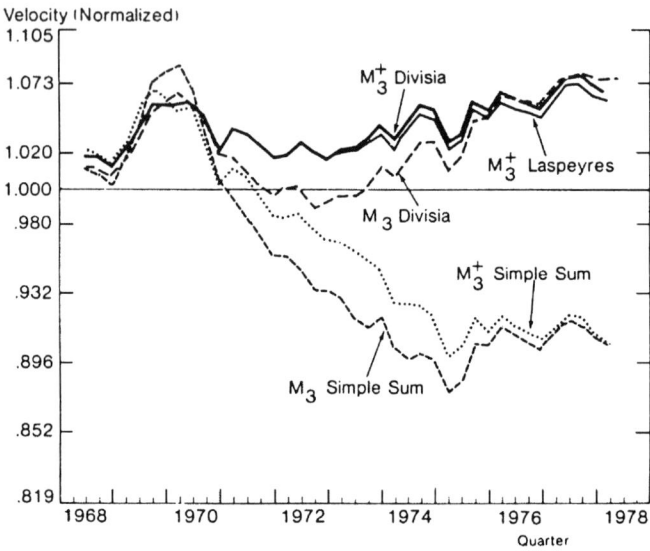

Figure 1: Income velocity of monetary aggregate, quarterly, 1968.II–1978.I, normalized in 1968.I.

The first charts of the behavior of the Divisia aggregates appeared in Barnett (1980a) and Barnett and Spindt (1979). The most interesting of those charts is reproduced as Figure 1. That figure contains plots of the

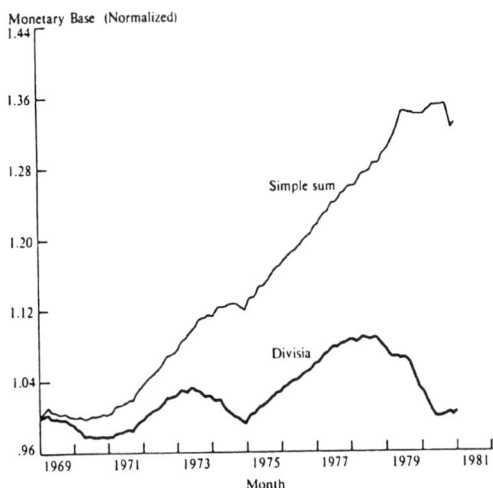

Figure 2: Base multiplier for monetary aggregate L, 1969.I–1980.XII, monthly, normalized in 1969.I.

velocity of M3 and of M3$^+$, which roughly corresponds to the aggregate now called L. Velocity is plotted in each of those cases with the monetary aggregate alternatively computed as a simple sum or as a Divisia quantity index. With M3$^+$ the Laspeyres quantity index also is used.

The velocity of the Divisia aggregates can be seen to follow a path that closely resembles that of the interest-rate cycle from 1968 to 1978. Hence velocity appears to be a stable function of the interest rate. In addition the Laspeyres quantity index moves much more closely to the Divisia index than to the simple-sum index. By contrast, the velocity of the simple-sum aggregates can be seen to trend downwards in a manner that violates prior theoretical views regarding the behavior of velocity during periods of rising interest rates and inflationary expectations. Substitution (disintermediation) appears to go in the wrong direction.

Similar time series plots for the multiplier between the monetary base and the monetary aggregates were presented in Barnett and Spindt (1982). The most interesting of those graphs is reproduced in Figure 2, which contains the monetary base multiplier for both simple-sum and Divisia L. As is evident from Figure 2, the base multiplier for Divisia L is relatively stable over the long run, and the cycles in the multiplier negatively correlate with the interest rate cycle. The long-run multiplier for the simple-sum aggregate is far from stable. These results with the high-level aggregates are particularly important, since the high-level Divisia aggregate is designed to capture the total contributions of all monetary assets to the economy's monetary service flow. The high-level Divisia aggregates in theory perfectly internalized pure substitution effects.

Since an interest rate is not a dimension of either Figure 1 or 2, the precise nature of the functional relationship with interest rates is not entirely clear from those graphs. In addition, Figure 1 terminates in 1978, and it would be interesting to see whether the relationship to the interest-rate cycle continued through 1981. We can explore those questions from the cross plots against interest rates that were present in Barnett, Offenbacher, and Spindt (1984). The most interesting of those plots are reproduced in Figures 3 through 6.

Figures 3 and 4 contain cross plots of the velocity of M3 against a bond rate. Three plotting symbols are used to differentiate between three time periods. Since function shifts in money markets are widely reported to have occurred in mid-1974, comparison of the results before and after mid-1974 are particularly interesting. Figure 3 contains the results when M3 is computed as a simple sum. The expected shift is very evident. Figure 4 contains the analogous plot when M3 is computed as a Divisia aggregate. No significant function shift is evident. A stable nearly linear function of only one explanatory variable is revealed by the plot. The demand appears to be stable and easily modeled.

Figures 5 and 6 contain analogous plots for the base multiplier of M3, although each axis now measures the deviation from a linear time trend. Figure 5 contains the cross plot for the base multiplier against a bond rate when M3 is computed as a simple sum. A very dramatic shift occurred in the functional relationship in mid-1974. Before mid-1974, the function is parabolic. After mid-1974 an intersecting linear function appears. Figure 6 contains the same plot when M3 is computed as a Divisia aggregate. A stable linear relationship is revealed. Hence Divisia M3 is evidently controllable through the use of the base.

The literature using the simple-sum monetary aggregates has identified many substantial shifts in important structural functions, including the velocity function, the demand-for-money function, and the monetary base multiplier function. These troublesome shifts have posed formidable problems for monetary policy makers. Figures 1–6 illustrate the conclusions reached from various recently published hypothesis tests and simulations: the shifts disappear when the simple-sum aggregates are replaced by the corresponding Divisia monetary aggregates.

In the rest of this article we develop and apply a more formal comparison criterion: the fit of a joint monetary sector demand system.

Behavior of the Divisia Monetary Aggregates

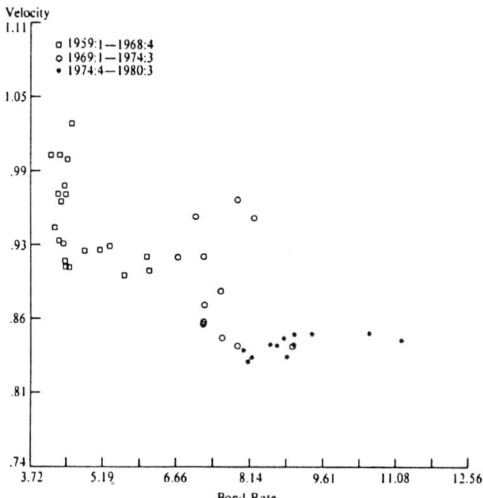

Figure 3: Simple sum M3 velocity versus Moody's AAA corporate bond rate, quarterly, 1959.I–1980.III.

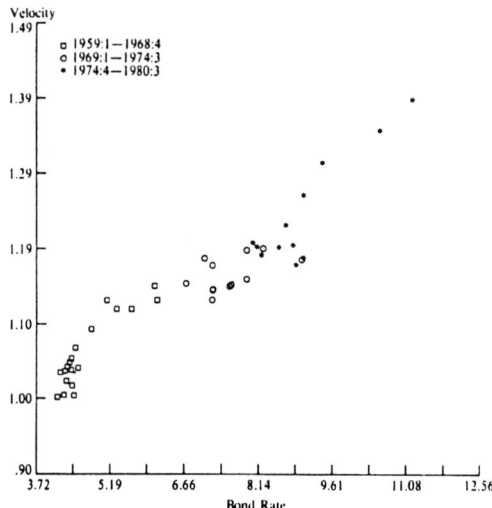

Figure 4: Divisia M3 velocity versus Moody's AAA corporate bond rate, quarterly, 1959.I–1980.III.

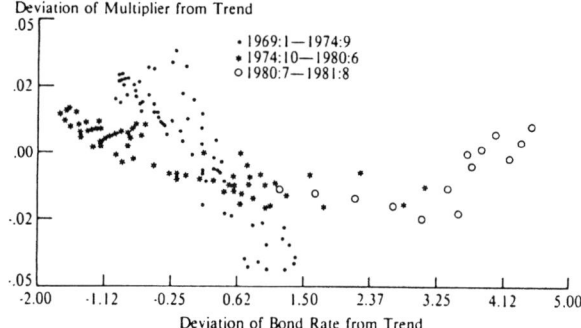

Figure 5: Deviation from time trend of simple sum M3 base money multiplier versus deviation from time trend of Moody's Baa corporate bond rate, monthly, 1969.I–1981.VIII.

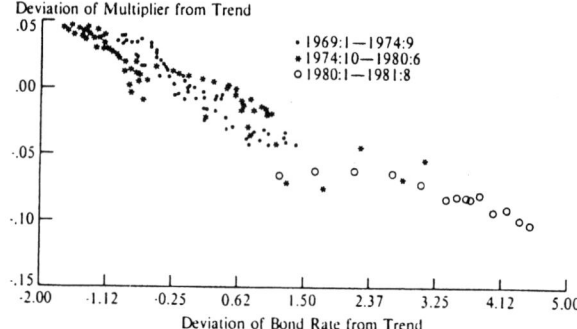

Figure 6: Deviation from time trend of Divisia M3 base money multiplier versus deviation from time trend of Moody's Baa corporate bond rate, monthly, 1969.I–1981.VIII.

4 The Demand System

We partition the goods into three groups with N_i ($i = 1, 2, 3$) goods in the ith group. Correspondingly, $\mathbf{q}_t$ and $\boldsymbol{\pi}_t$ are partitioned such that $\mathbf{q}_t = (\mathbf{q}'_{1t}, \mathbf{q}'_{2t}, \mathbf{q}'_{3t})'$ and $\boldsymbol{\pi}_t = (\boldsymbol{\pi}'_{1t}, \boldsymbol{\pi}'_{2t}, \boldsymbol{\pi}'_{3t})'$. We assume that the conditions for existence of consistent aggregates over the three groups are satisfied. The conditions are blockwise homogeneous separability of f (see Barnett 1980a). There then exist functions f_i and g_i ($i = 1, 2, 3$) such that $Q_{it} = f_i(\mathbf{q}_{it})$ and $\Pi_{it} = g_i(\boldsymbol{\pi}_{it})$, where ($Q_{it}, \Pi_{it}$) are the quantity and user cost aggregates over group i. Let $\mathbf{Q}_t = (Q_{1t}, Q_{2t}, Q_{3t})'$ and $\boldsymbol{\Pi}_t = (\Pi_{1t}, \Pi_{2t}, \Pi_{3t})'$.

We define the components of each group as follows. Group 1 contains deflated per capita consumption of consumer goods, group 2 contains per capita real balances of the components of M1B, and group 3 contains per capita real balances of the components that are in L (the Federal Reserve's highest-level monetary aggregate) but are not in M1B. We assume that the conditions for the existence of a community utility (or production) function, $u(\mathbf{Q}_t)$, over $\mathbf{Q}$ are satisfied. Regarding aggregation over economic agents, see Gorman (1953), Muellbauer (1975, 1976), and Barnett (1979a,b).

Let $\mathbf{v}_t = (v_{1t}, v_{2t}, v_{3t})'$ such that $\mathbf{v}_t = \boldsymbol{\Pi}_t / m_t$, where $m_t = \mathbf{Q}'_t \boldsymbol{\Pi}_t$. Then there exists a community indirect utility function, $U(\mathbf{v}_t)$. If $S = \{\mathbf{Q}_t : \mathbf{v}'_t \mathbf{Q}_t = 1\}$, then $U(\mathbf{v}_t) = \max\{u(\mathbf{Q}_t) : \mathbf{Q}_t \in S\}$. Let

$$V(\mathbf{v}_t) = 1/U(\mathbf{v}_t) \tag{3}$$

be the community reciprocal indirect utility function. Both $u(\mathbf{Q}_t)$ and $V(\mathbf{v}_t)$ are monotonically increasing, strictly quasiconcave functions.

Let

$$\mathbf{Q}_t = \mathbf{Q}(\mathbf{v}_t) \tag{4}$$

be the system of three demand equations that solves the consumer's decision problem of maximizing $u(\mathbf{Q}_t)$ subject to $\mathbf{Q}'_t \mathbf{v}_t = 1$. Then by the modified Roy's identity we have that

$$\mathbf{Q}(\mathbf{v}_t) = \frac{\nabla V(\mathbf{v}_t)}{\mathbf{v}'_t \nabla V(\mathbf{v}_t)}, \tag{5}$$

where $\nabla = \partial/\partial \mathbf{v}_t$ is the gradient operator. The above results are equally applicable to a firm's cost-constrained output-maximization decision.

We seek to estimate the demand system (4) using both simple-sum and Divisia quantity aggregation over $\mathbf{q}_{it}$ to get Q_{it} for each $i = 1, 2, 3$. In order to specify the system of functions, $\mathbf{Q}(\mathbf{v}_t)$, it suffices, from (5), to specify the single function V. We shall use a second-order Laurent expansion to derive a flexible functional form specification for V. But before defining that specification, we explore the currently popular specification selection methods.

5 Functional Approximation Methods

5.1 Definition of Second-Order Approximation

Most of the currently used demand system specifications are intended to permit a second-order approximation to the direct, indirect, or inverse indirect utility function from which the system was derived. While two concepts of 'second-order approximation' are used in the demand literature, it appears that the definition used in the mathematics literature has not appeared in the demand system literature. However, we shall show that one of the definitions used in the demand literature is equivalent to the usual mathematical definition. We also shall show that the other definition from the demand literature is equivalent to a related but stronger condition in mathematics.

We first present the usual mathematical definition. Let V^* be an approximation to the function V, and let $\|\cdot\|$ designate the Euclidean norm. The definition of a second-order local approximation is the following:

Definition 1: V^* *is a second-order local approximation to V at the point $\mathbf{v}_0$, if*

$$\frac{V^*(\mathbf{v}) - V(\mathbf{v})}{\|\mathbf{v} - \mathbf{v}_0\|^2} \to 0 \quad \text{as} \quad \mathbf{v} \to \mathbf{v}_0. \tag{6}$$

If V^* were a series expansion of V, then $V^*(\mathbf{v}) - V(\mathbf{v})$ would be the remainder term. Equation (6) is commonly interpreted to imply that $V^*(\mathbf{v}) - V(\mathbf{v})$ converges to zero faster than $\|\mathbf{v} - \mathbf{v}_0\|^2$. Equation (6) is sometimes equivalently written as $V^*(\mathbf{v}) - V(\mathbf{v}) = o(\|\mathbf{v} - \mathbf{v}_0\|^2)$, which commonly is read as '$V^*(\mathbf{v}) - V(\mathbf{v})$ is of little o order $\|\mathbf{v} - \mathbf{v}_0\|^2$' or as '$V^*(\mathbf{v}) - V(\mathbf{v})$ is of smaller order than $\|\mathbf{v} - \mathbf{v}_0\|^2$' (see, e.g., Theil 1971, p. 358).

The two definitions used in the demand system literature are those proposed by Diewert (1971) and by Christensen, Jorgenson, and Lau (1973, 1975). Diewert defines V^* to be a second-order approximation to V at $\mathbf{v}_0$, if

$$V^*(\mathbf{v}_0) = V(\mathbf{v}_0), \tag{7}$$

$$\left.\frac{\partial V^*}{\partial \mathbf{v}}\right|_{\mathbf{v}=\mathbf{v}_0} = \left.\frac{\partial V}{\partial \mathbf{v}}\right|_{\mathbf{v}=\mathbf{v}_0}, \tag{8}$$

$$\left.\frac{\partial^2 V^*}{\partial \mathbf{v} \partial \mathbf{v}'}\right|_{\mathbf{v}=\mathbf{v}_0} = \left.\frac{\partial^2 V}{\partial \mathbf{v} \partial \mathbf{v}'}\right|_{\mathbf{v}=\mathbf{v}_0}. \tag{9}$$

If V^* possesses that capability at $\mathbf{v}_0$ for any V (that is, for any values on the right sides of (7), (8), and (9)), then Diewert calls V^* a locally flexible functional form. (Diewert deletes the word 'locally,' which we insert, since Diewert's flexibility property is defined to apply only at the one point, $\mathbf{v}_0$.)

Functional Approximation Methods

In Appendix A of this chapter we prove that if V^* and V are twice continuously differentiable, then (7), (8), and (9) are necessary and sufficient for (6). Hence, Diewert's definition is *equivalent* to Definition 1 and therefore is in agreement with the usual definition in mathematics.

According to Lau (1974, p. 183), the definition of 'second-order approximation' used by Christensen, Jorgenson, and Lau (1973, 1975) can be stated to be the existence of some neighborhood, J, of $\mathbf{v}_0$ and some constant, K, such that

$$|V^*(\mathbf{v}) - V(\mathbf{v})| \leq \frac{K\|\mathbf{v} - \mathbf{v}_0\|^3}{\|\mathbf{v}_0\|^3} \qquad (10)$$

for all $\mathbf{v} \in J$. To see the relationship of (10) to the mathematics literature, we must introduce the concept of a 'big O' order remainder term. (In the discussion following Definition 5.1, we discussed the concept of a 'little o' order remainder term.)

Definition 2: $V^*(\mathbf{v}) - V(\mathbf{v}) = O(\|\mathbf{v} - \mathbf{v}_0\|^k)$ *if there exists a punctured (at $\mathbf{v}_0$) neighborhood of $\mathbf{v}_0$ such that*

$$\frac{|V^*(\mathbf{v}) - V(\mathbf{v})|}{\|\mathbf{v} - \mathbf{v}_0\|^k} \quad \textit{is bounded} \qquad (11)$$

for every $\mathbf{v}$ in that punctured neighborhood. (A neighborhood punctured at $\mathbf{v}_0$ is a neighborhood with $\mathbf{v}_0$ removed from it.)

The equality $V^*(\mathbf{v}) - V(\mathbf{v}) = O(\|\mathbf{v} - \mathbf{v}_0\|^k)$ commonly is read as '$V^*(\mathbf{v}) - V(\mathbf{v})$ is of big O order $\|\mathbf{v} - \mathbf{v}_0\|^k$' or as '$V^*(\mathbf{v}) - V(\mathbf{v})$ is at most of order $\|\mathbf{v} - \mathbf{v}_0\|^k$' (see, e.g., Theil 1971, p. 358). It is easily shown that Lau's definition of second-order approximation is equivalent to

$$V^*(\mathbf{v}) - V(\mathbf{v}) = O(\|\mathbf{v} - \mathbf{v}_0\|^3). \qquad (12)$$

It can be shown that $V^*(\mathbf{v}) - V(\mathbf{v}) = O(\|\mathbf{v} - \mathbf{v}_0\|^3)$ implies $V^*(\mathbf{v}) - V(\mathbf{v}) = o(\|\mathbf{v} - \mathbf{v}_0\|^2)$, but the converse is not necessarily true. Hence (12) imposes a stronger condition on the approximation than does Definition 1, and thus Lau imposes a stronger, if somewhat less conventional, condition on second-order approximations than does Diewert.

In specification selection, the significance of (12) results from the fact that second-order Taylor series expansions satisfy (12), although not every other approximation satisfying Definition 1 need satisfy (12). However, the added control over the remainder term in going from Definition 1 to (12) should not be overemphasized. Equation (12) does not bound the remainder term at any fixed $\mathbf{v}$. For fixed $\mathbf{v}$, (12) only requires that the remainder be finite. All that Definition 2 provides is a stronger condition than Definition 1 on the *rate of convergence* of $V^*(\mathbf{v})$ to $V(\mathbf{v})$ as $\mathbf{v}$ approaches $\mathbf{v}_0$.

In fact there need be no prior bound to the size of the remainder term of the Taylor series for *fixed* $\mathbf{v} - \mathbf{v}_0$ and for *fixed* order of approximation. (In the demand systems literature, it is sometimes argued that the approximation error is bounded by the remainder term, or that the error of the approximation is bounded by the size of the higher-order terms. However the higher-order terms *are* the remainder, which in turn *is* the approximation error. An equivalent statement would be that the error can be no larger than itself.) We have only two results on the remainder term of the Taylor series approximation. Let $R_n(\mathbf{v})$ be the remainder term at $\mathbf{v}$ of the nth-order Taylor series approximation about $\mathbf{v}_0$. Then the two available results are the following.

Property 1: Let δ be the distance from $\mathbf{v}_0$ to the nearest singular point, and let $B_\delta(\mathbf{v}_0)$ be the open ball with center $\mathbf{v}_0$ and radius δ. (The open ball, $B_\delta(\mathbf{v}_0) = \{\mathbf{v} : |\mathbf{v} - \mathbf{v}_0| < \delta\}$, is also called a spherical neighborhood or δ-neighborhood. The concept of singular point is discussed in Appendix B of this chapter.) Then $R_n(\mathbf{v}) \to 0$ uniformly in $\mathbf{v} \in B_\delta(\mathbf{v}_0)$ as $n \to \infty$. If $\mathbf{v}$ is not in the closure of $B_\delta(\mathbf{v}_0)$, then the sequence $\{R_n(\mathbf{v}) : n = 1, 2, \ldots\}$ diverges.

Property 2: For any fixed n, $R_n(\mathbf{v}) = O(\|\mathbf{v} - \mathbf{v}_0\|^{n+1})$.

There are circumstances under which the Taylor series can be very useful. That usefulness is a result of Property 1, which permits us to acquire an approximation of arbitrarily good quality within the region of convergence, if we are able to incorporate as many terms as may be necessary. Since a fixed second-order Taylor series approximation provides us with no such freedom, it is not clear that we need consider Property 1 further at all. Nevertheless, in the interest of completeness, we shall further consider Property 1 and the general behavior of the remainder term in the next section.

6 The Taylor Series Approximation

6.1 Analytic Function Theory

In mathematics, the usefulness of the Taylor series approximation results largely from Property 1. By that property we know that within the region of convergence, $B_\delta(\mathbf{v}_0)$, of the Taylor series expansion, a Taylor series approximation of *some* order can always attain a uniformly smaller remainder term than that of any approximation satisfying Definition 1, which defines the entire class of possible second-order approximations in the usual sense. However, the Taylor series approximation that would accomplish that objective may be of much higher order than the second order. Since existing demand systems use a fixed-order approximation, Property 1 does not apply. However, *even* if we could consider an iterative step-wise estimation procedure with no prior upper limit to the converged order of the approximation, the necessity of restricting the approximation to points within $B_\delta(\mathbf{v}_0)$ is a stronger restriction than one might expect; and if $\mathbf{v}$ is not within $B_\delta(\mathbf{v}_0)$, then the remainder term will *diverge*. In that case, increasing the order of the expansion could *increase* the remainder term. We further consider the restrictiveness of $B_\delta(\mathbf{v}_0)$ in Appendix B of this chapter. In short, the capabilities of the Taylor series in generating numerical approximations are irrelevant to the existing flexible functional form demand models, and no reason exists in theory to prefer second-order Taylor series approximations to any other elements of Diewert's class of flexible functional forms.

In fact we could lose a great deal by restricting consideration solely to second-order Taylor series approximations, since the Taylor series approximation is frequently not among the best approximating functions. Other approximations of the same order can have uniformly smaller remainders within the region of convergence of the Taylor series. As explained by Buck (1965, p. 128–129),

> "... while the Taylor polynomials have the advantage that they are easily defined and computed, they need not be the best approximation to use. For example, the Taylor polynomial of degree 2 at the origin for e^x is $1 + x + x^2/2$ which approximates it uniformly on $[-1, 1]$ within .22; however, there are other polynomials of degree 2 which are better approximations; $.99 + 1.175x + .543x^2$ approximates e^x uniformly on $[-1, 1]$ within .04."

Another example given by Buck (1965, p. 128) is the function $f(x)$ defined such that $f(0) = 0$ and $f(x) = \exp(-1/x^2)$ for $x \neq 0$. The resulting function has continuous derivatives of all orders everywhere. It follows from the Weierstrass approximation theorem that it is possible, on any bounded interval, to approximate f uniformly with arbitrary accuracy with some polynomial. Yet the Taylor polynomial of any order about the origin is zero everywhere. The remainder is f itself!

6.2 Behavior of the Remainder Term

The quality of a single local Taylor series approximation of fixed order declines increasingly rapidly as the distance from the point of expansion increases. This systematic behavior can be very troublesome when a Taylor series approximation of *fixed order* is used to specify a function to be *empirically estimated*. In that case, we would estimate the parameters of the specification and use the estimated function as a function-valued estimator of the underlying approximated function. The properties of that function valued estimator depend upon the convolution of the parameter estimators, conditionally upon the Taylor series approximation being exact, and upon the values of the actual (nonzero) remainder term at each data point. As has been observed by Gallant (1981), the properties of the convolution are not known for the Taylor series remainder term, and that convolution results in biased predictions.

In addition, it is very difficult to interpret parameter estimates based upon that procedure. The parameter estimators (whether FIML or otherwise) do not know where the point of approximation is or what the radius of convergence is or how the remainder term behaves within that region. It might be expected that the estimated parameters could be usable, if the remainder term (which the estimator assumes is uniformly zero) does not greatly vary in magnitude within the region of the data. That condition clearly is not satisfied for the remainder term of a Taylor series approximation.

We believe that the possibility of large values of the remainder term is less serious than the systematic nature of the variation of the remainder term over the region of convergence. It is quite possible that more reliable empirical inferences could be acquired with an approximation having a remainder term that tends to be larger but less variable than the Taylor series remainder term.

6.3 Conclusion

We find nothing to criticize in Diewert's definition of 'second-order approximation,' since his definition is equivalent to Definition 1. Furthermore, we agree with Diewert that the class of second-order approximations can be used to define the class of locally flexible functional forms, since the class of functions capable of attaining arbitrary elasticities of substitution at a point is the same as the class of functions satisfying Definition 1. However, we do not agree with the currently fashionable practice of further limiting the *definition* of the class of second-order approximations to include only second-order *Taylor series* expansions.

The approach used in this article generates a specification that satisfies Definition 1 and hence is a local second-order approximation. But the specification is not a Taylor series expansion. Instead we use a different series expansion that possesses a potentially better behaved remainder term and that contains the Taylor series as a special case.

7 The Laurent Series Expansion

When we seek an approximation within a region containing one or more singular points, we cannot use the Taylor series expansion. However, a generalization of the Taylor series, called the Laurent series, can handle these cases. (The series is named after the famous French mathematician, Hermann Laurent (1841–1908).) The Laurent expansion of a function, f, in one variable, z, about the point z_0 is of the form

$$f(z) = \sum_{n=-\infty}^{+\infty} a_n(z-z_0)^n. \tag{13}$$

The variable, z, can be complex. Clearly (13) can be written as $f(z) = g_1(z) + g_2(z)$, where

$$g_1(z) = \sum_{n=0}^{\infty} a_n(z-z_0)^n$$

and

$$g_2(z) = \sum_{n=-\infty}^{-1} a_n(z-z_0)^n.$$

Then $g_1(z)$ is called the analytic part, and $g_2(z)$ is called the principal part.

The analytic part has the same form as the Taylor expansion, and the principal part has the analogous form with negative powers. An example of a Laurent expansion is the series $e^{1/z} = \sum_{n=0}^{\infty}(1/n!)z^{-n}$. In this case the order of the analytic part is zero. For our purposes, the behavior of the remainder term of (13) is of particular importance. If we use only a finite number of terms from $g_1(z)$ and $g_2(z)$ in the expansion (13), then a remainder term can exist in the approximation to both the analytic and principal parts. Let $R^{(1)}(z)$ be the remainder term in the finite-order approximation to $g_1(z)$, and let $R^{(2)}(z)$ be the remainder term in the finite-order approximation to $g_2(z)$. The remainder term for the complete Laurent expansion is the sum $R(z) = R^{(1)}(z) + R^{(2)}(z)$. The terms $R^{(1)}$ and $R^{(2)}$ vary in opposite directions, with $R^{(1)}$ rising and $R^{(2)}$ falling as $|z-z_0|$ increases. Hence $R(z)$ varies considerably less severely than does $R^{(1)}$ alone within the expansion's region of convergence. This fact accounts for our earlier observation that the Laurent expansion possesses a better-behaved remainder term than does the Taylor series approximation within the region of convergence.

Furthermore, the correlations between the regressors and the disturbances are lower for specifications based on Laurent expansions than on the corresponding Taylor series expansions. This result follows from the fact that those correlations depend on the derivatives of the remainders with respect to the regressors, and those derivatives are lower for the Laurent than the Taylor remainders. Also observe that the Laurent expansion is not a 'local' approximation, since $R(z)$ need not attain zero anywhere within the region of convergence. In addition, the remainder term of the principal part is small over a huge region. In particular, $R^{(2)}(z) \to 0$ as $z \to \infty$, which implies that for any $\varepsilon > 0$ there exists $\delta > 0$ such that $R^{(2)}(z) < \epsilon$ for $|z| > \delta$. In terms of Euclidean distance, the region $|z| > \delta$ is infinitely large for any δ. By contrast, the remainder term of the Taylor series approximation can be kept small only within a ball of finite, and frequently very small, diameter.

The formulas for finding the coefficients of (13) can be found in Apostol (1957, p. 520) or Ahlfors (1966, p. 183). The coefficients are line integrals, not derivatives. In the multivariate case, the form of the analytic part is the same as the form of the multivariate Taylor series approximation. However, again the coefficients are integrals rather than derivatives. The form of the principal part again is acquired by replacing positive with corresponding negative powers in the analytic part. Appendix C of this chapter contains discussion of the theoretical foundations of the Laurent expansion.

It should be observed that our motivation for basing the specification on a Laurent expansion is not acquisition of the ability to approximate $V(\mathbf{v})$ near particularly difficult kinds of singularities. Our motivation is to attain a better-*behaved* approximation. The smoother variation of the Laurent expansion's remainder term can be understood, in a rather simplified fashion, by comparing the bases used to span a function space in the Taylor series and Laurent cases. The Taylor series seeks to span the space with the basis $\Gamma_1 = \{x^m : m = 0, 1, \ldots\}$. If we used only the principal part of the Laurent expansion, we would be using the basis $\Gamma_2 = \{x^{-m} : m = 1, 2, \ldots\}$. With a full Laurent expansion, the basis is the union $\Gamma = \Gamma_1 \cup \Gamma_2$.

If $|x| < 1$, then x^m decreases as m increases. Hence increasing m results in increasing refinement of the approximation. So Γ_1 appears to be a reasonable basis, when $|x| < 1$. The same observation applies to Γ_2 when $|x| > 1$. Hence Γ_2 appears to be a reasonable basis when $|x| > 1$. To acquire a basis applicable over a larger region, we need the Laurent basis, Γ.

8 The Specifications

8.1 The Generalized Leontief Model

We now return to the selection of a specification for $V(\mathbf{v})$ to be used in deriving the demand system from (5). We first discuss Diewert's (1973) generalized Leontief approximation to $V(\mathbf{v})$.

Let $\mathbf{w} = (w_1, w_2, w_3)'$, where $w_i = v_i^{1/2}$ for $i = 1, 2, 3$. Define the function

The Specifications

W such that $W(\mathbf{w}) = V(\mathbf{v})$. Expanding $W(\mathbf{w})$ in a second-order Taylor series approximation about $\mathbf{w} = \mathbf{0}$, we get

$$V(\mathbf{v}) = a_0 + 2\mathbf{a}'\mathbf{w} + \mathbf{w}'\mathbf{A}\mathbf{w} + R^{(1)}(\mathbf{v}), \tag{14}$$

where $\mathbf{A} = [a_{ij}]$ is a 3×3 symmetric matrix of fixed coefficients, $\mathbf{a}$ is a three-dimensional vector of fixed coefficients, a_0 is a scalar constant, and $R^{(1)}(\mathbf{v})$ is a remainder term. The same functional form results, after some algebraic manipulation, if V is expanded about $\mathbf{v} = \mathbf{1}$. See Blackorby, Primont, and Russell (1978, p. 293).

If we drop the remainder term, we get the generalized Leontief reciprocal indirect utility function. The demand system derived by applying (5) to that specification for $V(\mathbf{v})$ is called the generalized Leontief demand system. The generalized Leontief specification for $V(\mathbf{v})$ is an element of Diewert's class of locally flexible functional forms and in many cases can be very useful. However, problems with the global behavior of second-order Taylor series models have arisen in both theoretical and Monte Carlo studies. See, e.g., Wales (1977). For an overview of those studies, see Barnett (1981b, pp. 319–321). The problems result from absorption of the remainder term into the model's stochastic disturbance. The properties of $R^{(1)}(\mathbf{v})$ are not at all conducive to its absorption into a white-noise disturbance term and would not be, even if we were to add that disturbance directly onto (14).

8.2 The Full Laurent Model

To permit us to acquire the better behavior of the Laurent expansion's remainder term, we now expand $W(\mathbf{w})$ into a Laurent expansion of the second order in both its principal and analytic parts about $\mathbf{w} = \mathbf{0}$ to acquire

$$V(\mathbf{v}) = \alpha_0 + 2\mathbf{a}'\mathbf{w} + \mathbf{w}'\mathbf{A}\mathbf{w} - 2\mathbf{b}'\mathbf{w} - \mathbf{w}'\mathbf{B}\mathbf{w} + R(\mathbf{v}), \tag{15}$$

where $\mathbf{w} = (w_1^{-1}, w_2^{-1}, w_3^{-1})'$ and $R(\mathbf{v})$ is the remainder term. The coefficient matrices $\mathbf{A} = [a_{ij}]$ and $\mathbf{B} = [b_{ij}]$ are 3×3 and symmetric, while $\mathbf{a} = (a_i)$ and $\mathbf{b} = (b_i)$ are three-dimensional vectors of coefficients, and a_0 is a scalar constant. We set $R(\mathbf{v}) = 0$ for all $\mathbf{v}$, and we call (15) the full Laurent reciprocal indirect utility function. Strictly speaking, we should use the more awkward name 'full Leontief-Laurent,' since other 'full Laurent' models could be acquired by redefining $\mathbf{w}$. Any locally flexible functional form of the analytic part can be used to generate a corresponding principal part and thereby another full Laurent model.

Applying (5) and converting to value shares, $s_i = v_i Q_i$ ($i = 1, \ldots, n$), we acquire the full Laurent demand system (in value share form):

$$s_i = \frac{a_i w_i + \sum_{j=1}^{n} a_{ij} w_j w_i + b_i \bar{w}_i + \sum_{j=1}^{n} b_{ij} \bar{w}_j \bar{w}_i}{\mathbf{a'w} + \mathbf{w'Aw} + \mathbf{b'\bar{w}} + \mathbf{\bar{w}'B\bar{w}}} \qquad (16)$$

($i = 1, \ldots, n$), where $n = 3$ is the number of goods in the demand system. Observe that the full Laurent model is an extension of the generalized Leontief, as the Laurent expansion is an extension of the Taylor series. Hence the generalized Leontief cannot have capabilities not also possessed by the full Laurent. The same cannot be said for Gallant's (1981) Fourier model. Taylor series expansions are not nested within Fourier expansions, and vice versa. Hence Gallant's important model provides fundamentally new capabilities, rather than an extension of the existing capabilities of the class of flexible functional forms. In addition, as seen in Section 8.3, the Laurent approach provides easier control over the regularity properties of the approximating function than does the Fourier approach. Furthermore, Gallant's model has not been shown to satisfy Diewert's definition of a locally flexible functional form.

Since (16) is homogeneous of degree zero in its parameters, a normalizing restriction is needed. Any one of the parameters (or sum of parameters) could be set equal to one.

8.3 The Minflex Laurent Model

The full Laurent reciprocal indirect utility function has far more free parameters than are needed to acquire a specification that is locally flexible in the Diewert sense. In fact either the principal or the analytic part alone is locally flexible. To conveniently restrict the model further, we could set some parameters equal to zero, or we could restrict their signs. We can force the sign of a coefficient to be nonnegative by replacing it by its square. For example, we could let $a_{11} = \phi^2$ and estimate ϕ. Then a_{11} is always nonnegative. For notational convenience in such cases, we shall not change symbols. So instead of letting a_{11} become ϕ^2, we would let a_{11} become a_{11}^2.

The ability to restrict the signs of parameters without the loss of the specification's flexibility property is particularly valuable. The generalized Leontief specification for $V(\mathbf{v})$ satisfies the theoretical restrictions of monotonicity and quasiconcavity if all of its coefficients are nonnegative. However, prior imposition of any of those restrictions results in loss of the generalized Leontief's flexibility property. In addition if those restrictions are imposed, the probability of satisfying all of them with unrestricted estimates is extremely low. With the richer full Laurent specification, we have the ability

The Specifications

to impose many sign restrictions before the flexibility property is lost.

A particularly useful special case of the full Laurent model is acquired by letting $\mathbf{b} = \mathbf{0}$, letting the diagonal elements of $\mathbf{B}$ be zero, and forcing the off diagonal elements of both $\mathbf{A}$ and $\mathbf{B}$ to be nonnegative. We now impose those restrictions. Define the set of subscript pairs $S = \{(i,j) : i \neq j; i, j = 1, \ldots, n\}$, where n is the number of goods. Setting $R(\mathbf{v}) = 0$, (15) becomes

$$V(\mathbf{v}) = a_0 + 2\mathbf{a}'\mathbf{w} + \sum_i a_{ii} v_i + \sum\sum_{(i,j)\in S} a_{ij}^2 w_i w_j - \sum\sum_{(i,j)\in S} b_{ij}^2 \bar{w}_i \bar{w}_j, \quad (17)$$

which we call the minflex Laurent reciprocal indirect utility function. The value share equations, (16), become

$$s_i = \frac{a_i w_i + a_{ii} v_i + \sum_{j: j \neq i} a_{ij}^2 w_i w_j + \sum_{j: j \neq i} b_{ij}^2 \bar{w}_j \bar{w}_i}{\mathbf{a}'\mathbf{w} + \sum_k a_{kk} v_k + \sum\sum_{(j,k)\in S} a_{jk}^2 w_j w_k + \sum\sum_{(j,k)\in S} b_{jk}^2 \bar{w}_j \bar{w}_k} \quad (18)$$

($i = 1, \ldots, n$). The minflex Laurent model possess a number of very interesting properties. As proved in Appendix D of this chapter, (17) satisfies Diewert's definition of a locally flexible functional form. In addition, the model is minimal in the sense that imposition of any further prior restrictions eliminates the flexibility property. The specification possesses just enough parametric freedom to be a locally flexible functional form. This may appear to be surprising, since the generalized Leontief is also locally flexible and minimal but has fewer parameters. However, none of the generalized Leontief's coefficients are sign-constrained.

If n is the number of goods, then (17) contains only $2n + 1$ coefficients having unconstrained signs, while the generalized Leontief reciprocal indirect utility function, (14) has all $(1/2)(n^2+3n+2)$ of its coefficients unconstrained in sign (in our application $n = 3$ assets). The generalized Leontief globally satisfies the restrictions of microeconomic theory if all of its coefficients are nonnegative. (An exception is the sign of the unidentified intercept, a_0, which can be negative.) In Appendix E of this chapter, we prove the same for the full Laurent and therefore for minflex Laurent. But observe that the number of coefficients that would have to be forced to be nonnegative to acquire the theoretically globally regular case for the generalized Leontief is much higher than for the minflex Laurent, despite the fact that the total number of parameters in the minflex Laurent model exceeds that in the generalized Leontief. Hence in terms of the change in degrees of freedom, imposition of global theoretical regularity on the minflex Laurent model is a considerably less severe restriction than imposition of global theoretical regularity on the generalized Leontief.

The full Laurent model possesses the ability to approximate $V(\mathbf{v})$ over large regions, even when the region of convergence of a Taylor series approximation is small or even empty. However, the number of parameters poses substantial estimation problems. As a result, in practice the minflex Laurent model has greater appeal than the full Laurent. Furthermore, we believe that the minflex Laurent model possesses sufficient elements of the Laurent basis, Γ, to permit a well behaved approximation over a large region.

However, if the minflex Laurent is treated *explicitly* as a Laurent expansion, and if the point of the expansion is itself a singularity, then the model is restrictive, since minflex Laurent can handle only certain kinds of singularities appearing at the precise point of the approximation. For example, if the model is treated as a Laurent expansion about an isolated singularity, then the residue of $V(\mathbf{v})$ at the point of the approximation is $\mathbf{b}$, which we have set equal to zero in the minflex case. Although a zero residue restriction does not exclude singularities, nonzero residues are not uncommon for isolated singularities. If the singularity is not isolated, then the concept of a residue is not defined.

9 Estimation

9.1 Data and Restrictions

In this section we apply our model to the comparison of simple sum and Divisia monetary aggregation. We estimate both the full Laurent model, (16), and the minflex Laurent model, (18), using the three aggregated goods defined at the beginning of Section 3. The three aggregated goods can be characterized as Q_1 = consumer goods, Q_2 = transactions balances, and Q_3 = substitutes for transaction balances. The data are quarterly from the first quarter of 1961 to the fourth quarter of 1980. With each model, we estimate the system with Q_2 and Q_3 computed as simple-sum aggregates and again with those two goods computed as Divisia quantity indexes. In both cases, Q_1 is the Commerce Department's deflated consumption expenditure, and its corresponding price index, Π_1, is its price deflator, which is also used to convert nominal to real balances in Q_2 and Q_3. The Commerce Department's deflated consumption expenditure values are Laspeyres quantity indexes. In principle, there would be a gain in converting them to Divisia aggregates. However, the gain in converting from Laspeyres to Divisia is small by comparison with the gain in converting from simple-sum to either Laspeyres or to Divisia. Hence we do not believe that the need to convert consumption to a Divisia index is anywhere near as great as the need to convert the simple-sum monetary aggregates to Divisia indexes. For such comparisons, involving Laspeyres as well as Divisia, see Barnett and Spindt (1979) and Barnett (1981b, ch. 7). We then compare the fits of the estimated systems.

In the minflex Laurent case, we estimate the model in its 'free' form defined in (18) and also in a constrained form. In the constrained form we apply the result in Appendix E of this chapter to permit us to impose global theoretical regularity by replacing each unsquared parameter by a squared parameter. In that manner, we assure that every coefficient of $V(\mathbf{v})$ is nonnegative, and hence, by Theorem 3 in Appendix E of this chapter, we assure that $V(\mathbf{v})$ is globally nondecreasing and concave.

Since an identifying normalization is required, we set an arbitrary parameter equal to 1.0. In some cases, nonnegativity constraints imposed by squaring a parameter are binding. Since all parameters are squared in the globally regular case, the risk exists of normalizing on such a parameter that is at zero. In that case, the other parameters begin to become explosively large during estimation. We then renormalize on another parameter. When global regularity is not imposed, we normalize on an arbitrary unsquared parameter to avoid this problem.

When a corner solution at zero occurs on a parameter that we have not normalized to equal 1.0, another estimation difficulty can arise. As the parameter approaches zero during estimation, the parameter can become so small that estimation may be terminated by a zero-divide or $\log(0)$ internal to the algorithm. In such cases estimation is restarted with the initial condition for the parameter at zero reset to .1 and with the initial conditions for the other parameters reset to their values at the last iteration of the previous run. In rare cases this procedure may have to be performed twice before convergence. At convergence, parameters at corner solutions will be very small, but not small enough to be treated as zero by the computer.

All of these complications could be avoided by using a computer program that permits inequality side constraints. In that case, no parameters would have to be squared to impose nonnegativity, and the identifying normalization could be unitary value for the sum of all parameters. We used the Eisenpress program, which does not possess that capability.

Observe that our selection of goods permits us to treat consumption of consumer goods jointly with consumption of monetary services. Hence we do not require an assumption of weak separability between consumer goods and monetary assets. Earlier systemwide studies of monetary asset demand usually have required that separability assumption. (See, e.g., Chetty 1969; Donovan 1978; Offenbacher 1979; and Barnett 1980a.)

Corresponding to each of the two monetary quantity aggregates, (Q_{2t}, Q_{3t}), we need a (user-cost) price index. (Details regarding the interest rate data used in computing the component user-costs, (2), are in Barnett and Spindt

1982 and Barnett 1981b, ch. 7.) When those quantity aggregates are computed as Divisia indexes, the corresponding price indexes, (Π_{2t}, Π_{3t}), are computed from Fisher's factor reversal test. Fisher's factor reversal test states that $Q_{it}\Pi_{it} = \mathbf{q}'_{it}\boldsymbol{\pi}_{it}$, so that $\Pi_{it} = \mathbf{q}'_{it}\boldsymbol{\pi}_{it}/Q_{it}$. When the quantity aggregates, (Q_2, Q_3), are simple-sum aggregates, the dual user cost indexes are the Leontief indexes, so that Π_{it} ($i = 2, 3$) is the smallest element of the vector of component user costs, $\boldsymbol{\pi}_{it}$. Simple-sum quantity aggregation implies perfect substitutability of components and hence consumption only of the least expensive good. We then computed the value shares, in either case, from $s_{it} = \boldsymbol{\pi}'_{it}\mathbf{q}_{it}/\boldsymbol{\pi}'_t\mathbf{q}_t$. Since user costs are used as prices for monetary assets, the entire model is stated in flow terms.

Formula (2) for the component user costs requires knowledge of the representative marginal tax rate. Since we did not have those data available, we used the average rate. More recently we have become aware of the existence of marginal tax rate data. See 'Background and Issues Relating to Individual Income Tax Reduction,' Joint Committee on Taxation, U.S. Government Printing Office, April 27, 1981, pp. 22. To explore robustness to the measurement, we repeated all of our estimation with $\tau = 0$.

Finally, arbitrary data normalizations are selected. We select the first quarter of 1961 as the base period for the chained Divisia index for Q_{2t} and Q_{3t}. We normalized v_{it} for each $i = 1, 2, 3$ to equal 1.0 in the median quarter. Since we do not alter the shares, $\mathbf{s} = (s_1, s_2, s_3)'$, our rescaling of $\mathbf{v}_t$ induces a rescaling of $\mathbf{Q}_t$, so that $\Pi_{it}Q_{it}$ remains unchanged for each $i = 1, 2, 3$.

9.2 Results

In Table 1 we display the maximized value of the log-likelihood function resulting from joint maximum likelihood estimation of the full Laurent and minflex Laurent models. Those values can be used as measures of fit, since the maximized value of the log-likelihood function for models in explicit form is inversely proportional to the generalized variance of the fit. (See Barnett 1976, Property 4.9, p. 86. Regarding the use of a normally distributed additive error structure with share equations, see Woodland 1979.)

In every case, the fit is better with Divisia indexes for (Q_2, Q_3) than with simple-sum indexes. Hence our conclusion supports all of the other theoretical and empirical work favoring the new Divisia monetary aggregates over the simple-sum aggregates. In general, it appears that the numerous problems that have arisen with the use of the simple-sum monetary aggregates disappear when Divisia aggregation is used. In this case we find a dramatic gain in system fit.

Estimation

TABLE 1
Values of Log-Likelihood Function for Estimated Demand System
(comparison of simple-sum vs. Divisia monetary aggregation)

Model	Parameter Restrictions	Tax Rate[a]	Value of Log Likelihood Simple-Sum	Divisia
Full Laurent	Free	Average	692.96	903.19
Full Laurent	Free	Zero	668.01	887.40
Minflex Laurent	Free	Average	663.90	895.24
Minflex Laurent	Free	Zero	636.11	881.70
Minflex Laurent	Global regularity[b]	Average	548.18	815.97
Minflex Laurent	Global regularity[b]	Zero	557.21	796.50

[a] Marginal tax rate assumption: marginal tax rate equals average tax rate or marginal tax rate equals zero.
[b] To impose global theoretical regularity (monotonicity and concavity of $V(\mathbf{v})$), all unsquared parameters are squared. See Appendix E of this chapter.

The results in Table 1 are also useful in considering the merits of the new Laurent expansion approach to demand modeling. The loss in fit in restricting the full Laurent model to the minflex Laurent special case is small by comparison with the much larger loss in fit in further restricting the full Laurent model to its globally theoretically regular special case. In terms of complexity of estimation, we found estimation of the free minflex Laurent model, (18), to be straightforward. Convergence was generally rapid and inexpensive. The globally theoretically regular special case was somewhat more expensive to estimate, since corner solutions (discussed in Section 9.1) become more troublesome in this case and frequently required an additional renormalized run. Estimation of the full Laurent model was found to be both very difficult and very expensive. In that case, the problem of 'almost local nonidentification' (see Rothenberg 1971) occurred frequently.

We conclude that the gain in fit in going from the (free) minflex Laurent model to the full Laurent model is not sufficient to justify the formidable increase in estimation complexity and expense. Furthermore the loss in fit in going from the (free) minflex Laurent model to its globally theoretically regular special case is substantial in this application. In future applications of the Laurent expansion approach, it is therefore our belief that estimation of the full Laurent model need not be attempted, and the (free) minflex Laurent model should be used as the maintained model. The globally regular special case of minflex Laurent could be viewed as a nested null hypothesis to be considered empirically in each application, but not maintained *a priori*. This result is as might be expected from the fact that the (free) minflex Laurent model possesses just enough parametric freedom to permit satisfaction of the conditions for local flexibility under Diewert's definition. (Barnett and Jonas's 1983 Müntz-Szatz demand system could be used in cases in which a globally regular series expansion must be maintained. However, the approximating properties of that demand system are not yet fully known.)

The results can be seen to be robust to the selection of the measure for the marginal tax rate, τ. In principle, many of our conclusions above could have been explored through formal nested hypothesis tests. However, the sample size in our case is so large as to make empirical acceptance of any simple hypothesis virtually impossible. As is well known, all simple equality hypotheses are asymptotically rejected, since consistency of the estimators assures the ability to discriminate against virtually any equality hypothesis with a sufficiently large sample size. Hence we limited our investigation to comparisons of fit.

10 Conclusions

10.1 Conclusions Regarding Monetary Aggregation

We have compared the current simple-sum monetary aggregates with the new Divisia monetary quantity index numbers. The new index numbers are based on the discrete time Divisia quantity index, (1), with the prices π_t, in the index computed to be the user costs, (2), of the component assets. The component assets thereby are viewed as being durable goods having useful lifetimes exceeding one period. Any other quantity index in Diewert's (1976) superlative class would do equally well, if its component prices were computed as the user costs, (2); all elements of the superlative index number class move very closely together, although they all jointly diverge from the simple-sum index.

Our earlier research favored Divisia monetary aggregation over simple-sum aggregation on theoretical grounds and on each of the empirical grounds that are widely used in such comparisons in the monetary literature. In this article we use the joint demand system approach to comparing the simple-sum and the Divisia monetary aggregates in terms of the fit of a joint sectorwide demand system. Our findings again support the use of Divisia monetary aggregation over simple-sum aggregation. In all cases our demand system models fit dramatically better when we use Divisia monetary aggregation to generate the data than when we use simple-sum aggregation. Furthermore the graphs displayed in Section 3 illustrate the fact that the shifts in the velocity, demand, and base-multiplier functions that have plagued policy and research using the simple-sum aggregates disappear when the Divisia monetary aggregates are used.

10.2 Conclusions Regarding the Laurent Expansion Approach to Modeling

In exploring the Laurent expansion approach to generating demand systems, we find the minflex Laurent specification, (18), without imposition of global theoretical regularity, to be the most promising. The model possesses Diewert's local flexibility property, is relatively easily estimated, and performed almost as well as the full Laurent model, (16). The latter result provides particularly strong support for the minflex Laurent's approximation.

10.3 Areas for Further Research

Our results are suggestive of a number of areas for potentially useful further research. While we have investigated minflex Laurent's globally regular special case, we have not explored the regions of the model within which it satisfies monotonicity and concavity restrictions only locally. Theoretical and empirical research into that subject is clearly warranted. In addition we have not conducted any formal hypothesis tests. Hypotheses that can be tested with other locally flexible functional forms can also be tested with minflex Laurent in the analogous manner. With Gallant's (1981) unfavorable results on the power of tests using the translog model, comparable experiments with the minflex Laurent model could prove fruitful.

Our utility function, u, is actually an aggregate over households' utility functions and firms' production functions, each of which is maximized by economic agents subject to a constraint on previously optimized aggregate expenditure. Although the aggregation problems in that formulation are not insurmountable in theory (in aggregation theory, utility and production functions are indistinguishable when firms' decisions are cost-constrained output-maximizations), they could be lessened by subtracting out firm holdings and modeling the demand for firm holdings separately from household holdings. In addition, potential problems of simultaneity bias could be lessened by simultaneously estimating supply functions. However, a high degree of professional tolerance for simultaneity bias problems presently exists in the demand system literature, since the estimation difficulties in simultaneous nonlinear estimation are formidable. An exception is Barnett (1977b).

Appendix A: Diewert's Definition of Second-Order Approximation

In this Appendix we prove that Diewert's conditions for a local second-order approximation, (7), (8), and (9), are both necessary and sufficient for the usual definition of a local second-order approximation, stated in Definition 1.

Let $\mathbf{v}$ follow the time path $\mathbf{v}(t)$ as $t \to t_0$ from below, and let $\mathbf{v}(t)$ be a continuous function of t such that $0 < d\mathbf{v}/dt < \infty$ for all $t \leq t_0$. Then $\mathbf{v}(t) \to \mathbf{v}(t_0)$ as $t \to t_0$. Let V^* and V both be twice continuously differentiable functions of $\mathbf{v}$. We now prove the following theorem.

Theorem A.1: *Let $\mathbf{v}_0 = \mathbf{v}(t_0)$. Then (7), (8), and (9) are necessary and sufficient for (6) as $t \to t_0$ from below.*

PROOF: We first prove sufficiency. Let (7), (8), and (9) hold, and let

$$F(t) = \frac{V^*(\mathbf{v}(t)) - V(\mathbf{v}(t))}{\|\mathbf{v}(t) - \mathbf{v}(t_0)\|^2} \qquad (A.1)$$

$$= \frac{V^*(\mathbf{v}(t)) - V(\mathbf{v}(t))}{\sum_i (v_i(t) - v_i(t_0))^2}.$$

Differentiating the numerator and denominator of (A.1), we get

$$G(t) = \frac{\sum_i \frac{\partial V^*}{\partial v_i} \frac{dv_i}{dt} - \sum_i \frac{\partial V}{\partial v_i} \frac{dv_i}{dt}}{\sum_i (v_i(t) - v_i(t_0))^2 \frac{dv_i}{dt}}. \qquad (A.2)$$

For $t = t_0$, both the numerator and denominator of $F(t)$ are zero by (7). Hence by L'Hospital's rule, it follows that

$$\lim_{t \to t_0} F(t) = \lim_{t \to t_0} G(t). \qquad (A.3)$$

Differentiating the numerator and denominator of (A.2), we get

$$H(t) = \frac{\sum_i \sum_j \left[\frac{\partial^2 V^*}{\partial v_i \partial v_j} \frac{dv_j}{dt} \frac{dv_i}{dt} + \frac{\partial V^*}{\partial v_i} \frac{d^2 v_i}{dt^2} \right]}{\sum_i \left(\frac{dv_i}{dt} \right)^2 + [v_i(t) - v_i(t_0)] \frac{d^2 v_i}{dt^2}}$$

$$- \frac{\sum_i \sum_j \left[\frac{\partial^2 V}{\partial v_i \partial v_j} \frac{dv_j}{dt} \frac{dv_i}{dt} + \frac{\partial V}{\partial v_i} \frac{d^2 v_i}{dt^2} \right]}{\sum_i \left(\frac{dv_i}{dt} \right)^2 + [v_i(t) - v_i(t_0)] \frac{d^2 v_i}{dt^2}}.$$

For $t = t_0$, both the numerator and denominator of $G(t)$ are zero by (8). Hence it follows that
$$\lim_{t \to t_0} G(t) = \lim_{t \to t_0} H(t). \qquad (A.4)$$

By (9) we find that
$$\lim_{t \to t_0} H(t) = H(t_0) = 0. \qquad (A.5)$$

Hence by (A.3), (A.4), and (A.5) we conclude that $F(t) \to 0$ as $t \to t_0$.

We now prove the converse. Let $F(t) \to 0$ as $t \to t_0$. Then (7) follows. In addition, (A.3) follows from L'Hospital's rule. So $G(t) \to 0$ as $t \to t_0$. Hence (8) follows, and also we then have (A.4). So $H(t) \to 0$ as $t \to t_0$. Thus (9) follows. □

We conclude that Diewert's definition of a local second-order approximation is correct.

Appendix B: Analytic Function Theory

If the Taylor series is expanded about a singular point, the remainder term will diverge everywhere. If the nearest singular point is close to the point of expansion, then the region of convergence will be very small with divergence everywhere else.

In Property 1, the radius of $B_\delta(\mathbf{v}_0)$ is the distance from $\mathbf{v}_0$ to the nearest singular point. A singular point of the function V is a point at which V is not analytic. Since economic theory can impose strong regularity conditions on V, we might suspect that we can exclude singular points. But this is not the case. Economic theory cannot exclude singular points, even through the strong assumptions that V is continuous, has continuous derivatives of all orders, is monotonically increasing, and is strictly concave.

In fact, if we consider only restrictions on V that can be defined in terms of real variables, then we cannot even *define* the word 'analytic,' except in circular fashion. The circular definition, often found in real variables texts, requires a point at which V is analytic to be a point about which the Taylor series expansion converges. See Buck (1965, p. 128) for details of that 'definition,' which clearly is of no value to a potential user of a Taylor series approximation. To define 'analytic' we must use complex analysis. Microeconomic theory uses real analysis, functional analysis, topology, group theory, and measure theory, but not complex analysis. This fact is no accident. Behavioral axioms cannot generate complex variables. Hence the behavioral theory on which microeconomics is based *cannot* generate restrictions excluding singularities.

The fact that the definition of 'analytic' uses complex variable theory does not exclude the possibility of the existence of a singularity at a real value of **v**, since in a complex space there are complex vectors in every neighborhood of a real vector. Suppose that **v** is a real vector with n dimensions. Since n-dimensional Euclidean space is imbedded in n-dimensional complex space, **v** also lies in n-dimensional complex space, and every neighborhood of **v** contains complex vectors. The function $V(\mathbf{v})$ is defined to be analytic at **v** (whether or not complex), if V possesses a first derivative, as defined in complex analysis, everywhere in some neighborhood of **v** within n-dimensional complex space. In addition, even if V is analytic at every real value of the vector, **v**, the radius of $B_\delta(\mathbf{v}_0)$ still may be small, since there may be a complex vector, $\mathbf{v}_c$, that is near $\mathbf{v}_0$. In that case, the radius of convergence, δ_c, about the real vector, $\mathbf{v}_0$, will be the distance from $\mathbf{v}_0$ to $\mathbf{v}_c$. Although $\mathbf{v}_c$ itself could never be attained in the 'real' world, the Taylor series expansion of V about $\mathbf{v}_0$ nevertheless would diverge at any *real* value, $\mathbf{v}_1$, which was more than the small distance, δ_c, from $\mathbf{v}_0$. It is important to recognize that in this case there is nothing pathological or identifiably unusual about V anywhere in the region of divergence (outside of $B_\delta(\mathbf{v}_0)$) or at any point in the real domain of V.

Unfortunately there is nothing at all unusual about the existence of singularities in otherwise well-behaved functions. An example of a very large class of functions containing singularities is provided by Liouville's theorem, which states that *every* nonconstant bounded function contains singularities. Included in that class are many strictly concave functions. However, the singularity can occur at infinity. The theorem is named after the French mathematician Joseph Liouville (1809–1882), but actually is due to Cauchy.

Examples of well-behaved functions with singularities include the function, f, defined in Section 5.1. That function has a singularity at the origin, although f has continuous derivatives everywhere along the real line. Another example is the function $g(x) = 1/(1 + x^2)$. The function g is defined everywhere on the real line and has continuous derivatives of every order everywhere on the real line. Nevertheless the Taylor series expansion about zero diverges for x outside of the open interval $(-1, 1)$. Outside of that interval, the Taylor series can never be a good approximation, no matter how high the order of the approximation, and can get worse as the order increases (see Buck 1965, p. 129). There is nothing in real variable theory that can explain that convergence problem. The explanation in complex variable theory is the existence of a singularity at $x = i = (-1)^{1/2}$, which is a distance of 1 from the origin.

Other examples would include a Taylor series approximation to $V(\mathbf{v}_t)$ about $\mathbf{v}_t = \mathbf{1}$, when $V(\mathbf{v}_t)$ is actually translog, but the Taylor series is not in the logarithms. For example, the expansion could be in the square roots, which would generate the generalized Leontief for a second-order expansion. Although we have not derived the radius of convergence in that case, the radius clearly is no greater than one, since an obvious singularity exists at the origin. So the expansion *must* diverge at least at every v_t such that $\|v_t - 1\| \geq 1$. In fact the points $v(0)$ and $V(0)$ are likely to be singular points in general, and the lower boundary of the consumer's survival set can be expected to produce a large singular region.

As a result of these problems, Taylor series approximations of functions in mathematics are computed through the procedure of analytic continuation, by which Taylor series expansions about different points are pieced together. See, for example, Ahlfors (1966, pp. 275–290). Through this procedure, all parts of the function can usually be kept within the radius of convergence of the applicable series. When estimating the parameters of a function with data, the spread of the data frequently is sufficient to require analytic continuation in order to remain within regions of convergence; however, the procedure of analytic continuation applies to converged series, not to fixed-order approximations.

Even if all of the data fall within the region of convergence, Property 1 gives little reason to have confidence in a Taylor series approximation of fixed predetermined order. Property 1 defines a convergent *algorithm* for attaining the approximated function. Use of Property 1 requires that the algorithm be iterated, by successively adding more terms, until the percentage change of the approximated value of the function between successive iterations is less than one's predetermined convergence criterion at every data point.

Appendix C: Properties of the Laurent Expansion

As is true with the Taylor series, the analytic part of the Laurent expansion converges on an open disk, $|z-z_0| < \rho_2$, centered at z_0. But the principal part itself can be viewed as an ordinary power series in $(z - z_0)^{-1}$. Hence $g_2(z)$ will converge *outside* of some circle, $|z - z_0| = \rho_1$, so that $g_2(z)$ converges for $|z - z_0| > \rho_1$. A common region of convergence exists only if $\rho_1 < \rho_2$ and if $f(z)$ is analytic in the annulus $\rho_1 < |z - z_0| < \rho_2$. In that case (13) converges uniformly on that annulus.

Furthermore, it can be shown conversely that if a function $f(z)$ is analytic within an annulus, $\rho_1 < |z - z_0| < \rho_2$, then $f(z)$ always can be developed in a general power series of the form (13), and the expansion is unique. That converse result, called Laurent's theorem, is the result of importance in applications.

By analogy to the Taylor series case, we know that $R^{(1)}(z) \to 0$ as $z \to z_0$ within the region $|z - z_0| < \rho_1$. But recall that $g_2(z)$ can be viewed as an ordinary power series in z^{-1}. Thus within $|z - z_0| > \rho_2$ we have that $R^{(2)}(z) \to 0$ as $(z - z_0)^{-1} \to 0$ or equivalently as $z \to \infty$. Hence $R^{(1)}$ and $R^{(2)}$ vary in opposite directions, with $R^{(1)}$ rising and $R^{(2)}$ falling as $|z - z_0|$ increases.

Appendix D: Local Flexibility of the Minflex Laurent Model

In this Appendix we show that the minflex Laurent specification satisfies Diewert's definition of a locally flexible functional form. We do so by proving the following theorem.

Theorem D.1: Let $V^*(\mathbf{v})$ be defined by (17). Let $V(\mathbf{v}_0)$ be an arbitrary scalar, let $(\partial V/\partial \mathbf{v})|_{\mathbf{v}=\mathbf{v}_0}$ be an arbitrary n-dimensional vector, and let $(\partial^2 V/\partial \mathbf{v} \partial \mathbf{v}')|_{\mathbf{v}=\mathbf{v}_0}$ be an arbitrary $n \times n$ matrix. Then for any one value of the vector, $\mathbf{v}$, there exist values of the parameters of (17) such that (7), (8), and (9) are jointly satisfied.

PROOF: By (17), we have that

$$V^*(\mathbf{v}) = a_0 + 2\sum_i a_i v_i^{1/2} + \sum_i a_{ii} v_i + \sum\sum_{(i,j)\in S} a_{ij}^2 v_i^{1/2} v_j^{1/2} \\ - \sum\sum_{(i,j)\in S} b_{ij}^2 v_i^{-1/2} v_j^{-1/2} \quad \text{(D.1)}$$

Differentiating twice, we get the following first and second partial derivatives for $k, m = 1, \ldots, n$.

$$\frac{\partial V^*}{\partial v_k} = a_k v_k^{-1/2} + a_{kk} + \sum_{j:j\neq k} a_{kj}^2 v_k^{-1/2} v_j^{1/2} + \sum_{j:j\neq k} b_{kj}^2 x_k^{-3/2} x_j^{-1/2}; \quad \text{(D.2)}$$

$$\frac{\partial^2 V^*}{\partial v_k^2} = -\frac{1}{2} a_k v_k^{-3/2} - \frac{1}{2} \sum_{j:j\neq k} a_{kj}^2 v_k^{-3/2} v_j^{1/2} - \frac{3}{2} \sum_{j:j\neq k} b_{kj}^2 x_k^{-5/2} x_j^{-1/2}; \quad \text{(D.3)}$$

$$\frac{\partial^2 V^*}{\partial v_k \partial v_m} = \frac{1}{2} a_{km}^2 v_k^{-1/2} v_m^{-1/2} - \frac{1}{2} b_{km}^2 v_k^{-3/2} v_m^{-3/2} \quad (k \neq m). \quad \text{(D.4)}$$

Let $\mathbf{v} = \mathbf{v}_0$ in (D.1), (D.2), (D.3), and (D.4) and substitute into (7), (8), and (9) to replace their left sides. We now shall solve the resulting system of equations for the parameters.

If $(\partial^2 V^*/\partial v_k \partial v_m)|_{\mathbf{v}=\mathbf{v}_0}$ is nonnegative, set $b_{km} = 0$. Otherwise set $a_{km} = 0$. Then solve the off-diagonal equations of (9) for the rest of the off-diagonal elements of the matrices $[a_{km}]$ and $[b_{km}]$. The signs selected for those parameters are arbitrary, since each of them is always squared. Now solve the equations on the diagonal of the matrix of (9) for a_k ($k = 1, \ldots, n$). Next solve (8) for a_{kk} ($k = 1, \ldots, n$), and finally solve (7) for a_0. □

Observe that in the proof we have uniquely set the absolute value of every parameter in (D.1). In addition we required the ability to set the sign of every parameter that is not already squared in (D.1). Hence we would lose the local flexibility property of the minflex Laurent specification, (D.1), if we were to impose any further restrictions on the magnitudes of any of its parameters or if we were to restrict the signs (as by squaring) of any of the unsquared parameters. Thus minflex Laurent possesses the minimality property discussed in Section 7.3.

Appendix E: Global Theoretical Regularity Conditions for the Full Laurent Model

In this Appendix we show that if all of the coefficients of the full Laurent specification for $V(\mathbf{v})$ are nonnegative, then $V(\mathbf{v})$ satisfies the restrictions on that function implied by microeconomic theory. In particular, we prove the following theorem.

Theorem E.1: *If $V(\mathbf{v})$ takes the form of (15) with $R(\mathbf{v}) = 0$ for every $\mathbf{v} \geq 0$, and if $a_0 \geq 0$, $\mathbf{a} \geq 0$, $\mathbf{b} \geq 0$, $\mathbf{A} \geq 0$, and $\mathbf{B} \geq 0$, then $V(\mathbf{v})$ is nondecreasing and concave.*

PROOF: Let the coefficients of (15) all be nonnegative. Since $\bar{\mathbf{w}}$ is a decreasing function of $\mathbf{v}$ and $\mathbf{w}$ is an increasing function of $\mathbf{v}$, it follows that $V(\mathbf{v})$ is a nondecreasing function of $\mathbf{v}$.

The Hessian matrix of the function $v_i^{1/2} v_j^{1/2}$ with $i \neq j$ is negative semidefinite for all $v_i, v_j \geq 0$. Hence the function is concave. For the same reason, the funciton $-v_i^{-1/2} v_j^{-1/2}$ is concave for $i \neq j$. In both cases, concavity when $i = j$ is easily verified from the sign of the second derivative. Hence $\mathbf{w}'\mathbf{A}\mathbf{w}$ and $-\bar{\mathbf{w}}'\mathbf{B}\bar{\mathbf{w}}$ are concave, since they are sums of concave functions.

Both w_i and $-\bar{w}_i$ are concave functions of v_i. Hence $2\mathbf{a}'\mathbf{w}$ and $-2\mathbf{b}'\bar{\mathbf{w}}$ are concave, since they are sums of concave functions. Thus $V(\mathbf{v})$ is a sum of concave functions and thus is concave. □

Chapter 17

The New Divisia Monetary Aggregates

William A. Barnett, Edward K. Offenbacher, and Paul A. Spindt*

Barnett's Divisia monetary aggregates were derived to be elements of Diewert's class of superlative quantity index numbers. Relative to aggregation theory, Barnett's resulting monetary aggregates are strictly preferable to the official sum monetary aggregates, since the component monetary assets are not perfect substitutes. Formal empirical tests based on the relevant aggregation-theoretic criteria have likewise uniformly favored the Divisia monetary aggregates. The current article compares the Divisia with the sum monetary aggregates relative to numerous conventional policy-relevant criteria. The Divisia monetary aggregates, especially at high levels of aggregation, usually perform best in these tests.

1 Introduction

Recently a rapidly growing line of research has appeared concerning the rigorous use of aggregation and index number theory in the construction of monetary aggregates based on Diewert's (1976) 'superlative' class of quantity index numbers. Research on this application of the superlative class was motivated by and built on Barnett's (1980a) proposal and initial results.[1]

---

*Originally published in the *Journal of Political Economy* 92 (1984), 1049–1085. Reprinted with the permission of the University of Chicago Press. All rights reserved. We have benefited from the comments of Robert Barro. We also have benefited from comments on this research of participants at conferences at the N.B.E.R. (Cambridge, 1981), at the European Econometric Society meetings (Athens, Greece, 1979), at the North American Econometric Society meetings (Denver, 1980), at the Latin American Econometric Society meetings (Santiago, Chile, 1983), at the University of Aix-Marseille (Aix-en-Provence, France, 1980), and at the University of Chicago (1980, 1982). Some of the research on which this paper is based was conducted while we were at the Federal Reserve Board. The views expressed herein are solely ours and do not necessarily represent the views of the Board of Governors of the Federal Reserve System. The research on this paper was partially supported by National Science Foundation grant SOC 8305162 along with the Sam P. Woodson Memorial Centennial chair and the Janey Briscoe Centennial fellowship at the University of Texas at Austin.

[1] Some of the foundations of this research are contained in Barnett (1978, 1980a, 1981b, 1982a, 1983a) and Barnett and Spindt (1979), and an overview of that literature is contained in Barnett, Offenbacher, and Spindt (1981). The first official source of the historical data, supplied for 1969–81, is Barnett and Spindt (1982), which is available on request at

Barnett (1980a, p. 38; 1981b, p. 221) proposed use of either the Divisia or Fisher ideal index for monetary quantity aggregation. Since all such index numbers in the superlative class move very closely together (and are in fact usually identical, to within round-off error, for monetary asset data), the choice among elements of the class is little more than arbitrary. The purpose of this article is to provide a quantitative asessment of the relative merits of the official (summation) versus Divisia monetary quantity indexes, constructed with the same components and component groupings. The sample for the comparisons consists of quarterly data from 1959 through the end of 1982.[2]

2 History and Objectives

Although many types of financial intermediaries and monetary substitutes have evolved over the past 30 years, most economists have placed little faith in broad monetary aggregates, since summation aggregation has long seemed inappropriate at high levels of aggregation over imperfect substitutes. Friedman and Schwartz (1970, pp. 151–52) clearly described the problem with the high-level official aggregates:

> "This [summation] procedure is a very special case of the more general approach. In brief, the general approach consists of regarding each asset as a joint product having different degrees of 'moneyness,' and defining the quantity of money as the weighted sum of the aggregate value of all assets, the weights for individual assets varying from zero to unity with a weight of unity assigned to that asset or assets regarded as having the largest quantity of 'moneyness' per dollar of aggregate value. The procedure we have followed implies that all weights are either zero or unity. The more general approach has been suggested frequently but

---

no cost from the Publications Services Department at the Federal Reserve Board in Washington. Data for 1979–83 are supplied in the app. of Barnett (1984). The complete data series, continually updated to the latest month, are available to subscribers to the services of Data Resources Incorporated (DRI). Those series are located in DRI data bank USEMS/DATA under the series names JM1D, JM2D, and JM3D for Divisia M1, M2, and M3, respectively. Related research includes Hawtrey (1930); Chetty (1969, 1972); Friedman and Schwartz (1970); Bisignano (1974); Moroney and Wilbratte (1976); Barth, Kraft, and Kraft (1977); Donovan (1978); Offenbacher (1979, 1980c); and Barnett (1980b). For a unified overview of all that literature, see Barnett (1990). For a discussion of the recent behavior of the Divisia monetary aggregates, see Dorfman (1983).

[2] The original results in Barnett, Offenbacher, and Spindt (1984) used quarterly data ending in 1980. In the present paper we have updated all of the results except those in Table 2 and Sec. 6.2. The computer programs needed to update those results were unavailable to us when we updated our other results.

experimented with only occasionally. We conjecture that this approach deserves and will get much more attention than it has so far received."

By equally weighting components, aggregation by summation can badly distort an aggregate. For example, if one wished to obtain an aggregate of transportation vehicles, one would never aggregate by summation over the physical units of, say, subway trains and roller skates. Instead one would construct a quantity index (such as the Department of Commerce's many Laspeyres quantity indexes) using weights based on the *values* of the different modes of transportation. As another example, suppose the money supply were measured by the Federal Reserve's current highest level official aggregate, L, which contains most of the national debt of short and intermediate maturity. All of that portion of the national debt could be monetized without increasing either taxes or the 'money supply,' L, since the public would simply have exchanged securities for currency. However, the new Divisia index over the components of L would not treat this transfer as an exchange of 'pure money' for 'pure money.' Instead Divisia L would rise at about the same rate as the hyperinflation in prices that we would expect would result from this action.[3]

The traditionally constructed high-level aggregates (such as M2 or M3) implicitly view distant substitutes for money as perfect substitutes for currency. Rather than capture only part of the economy's monetary services, as M1 does, the broad aggregates swamp the included monetary services with heavily weighted nonmonetary services. The result no longer resembles economists' concept of 'money.' Nevertheless, the need remains for aggregates that capture the contributions of all monetary assets to the economy's flow of monetary services.

Regarding the simple sum (arithmetic average) index, Irving Fisher wrote over a half century ago that "the simple arithmetic average produces one of the very worst of index numbers, and if this book has no other effect than to lead to the total abandonment of the simple arithmetic type of index number, it will have served a useful purpose. ... The simple arithmetic [index] should not be used under any circumstances" (1922, pp. 29, 36).

---

[3]On the other hand, the problems associated with policies that target very low-level aggregates result from the inability of such aggregates to internalize pure substitution effects occurring within the economy's transactions technology, since low-level aggregates aggregate over a small subset of the factors of production in that transactions technology.

3 The Divisia Monetary Quantity Index

Let m_{jt} and π_{jt} be the quantity and price, respectively, of the jth component of an aggregate during period t. Törnqvist (1936), and subsequently Theil (1967), advocated the following discrete-time approximation to the continuous-time Divisia quantity index:

$$Q_t^* = Q_{t-1}^* \prod_j \left(\frac{m_{jt}}{m_{j,t-1}}\right)^{(1/2)(s_{jt}+s_{j,t-1})}$$

where $s_{jt} = \pi_{jt} m_{jt} / \sum_k \pi_{kt} m_{kt}$ is the expenditure share on component j during period j.[4] We shall refer to Q_t^* as the Divisia index (in discrete time), although it also frequently is called the Törnqvist index. Taking logarithms of each side, observe that

$$\log Q_t^* - \log Q_{t-1}^* = \sum_j \bar{s}_{jt}(\log m_{jt} - \log m_{j,t-1}), \tag{1}$$

where $\bar{s}_{jt} = (1/2)(s_{jt} + s_{j,t-1})$. The same index number results regardless of whether the exact aggregation-theoretic aggregate being approximated is the output of a utility function or of a production function. The aggregation-theoretic procedure for selecting the component assets is described in Barnett (1982a).[5]

Diewert (1976) has proved that the Divisia index lies within his class of 'superlative' index numbers, which all are nearly identical numerically. In fact, as a quantity index, the Divisia index is by far the most widely used element of Diewert's superlative class, because of the index's numerous theoretical optimality properties. Those remarkable properties result from that index's simultaneous theoretical links with the Divisia line integral, the translog aggregator function, the Malmquist index, and the Konüs index (see, e.g., Diewert 1980a, 1981; and Caves, Christensen, and Diewert 1982b). Recently Caves, Christensen, and Diewert (1982a, p. 1411) have proved that the Divisia index is "superlative in a considerably more general sense than shown by Diewert. We are not aware of other indexes that can be shown to be superlative in this more general sense." Also observe that the growth rate of the index is a weighted average of the growth rates of the components. The

---

[4] For details regarding the Divisia index, see Barnett (1982b). Regarding aggregation over consumers, see Barnett (1981b, chap. 3).

[5] The procedure requires testing for blockwise weakly separable groupings of assets. Those tests require knowledge of both the quantity and the user-cost price of each asset that is to be considered as a possible element of a weakly separable group. The formula for the user-cost price of an asset is presented in the next section. A nonparametric approach to testing for blockwise weak separability is available from Pudney (1981).

weights are the share contributions of each component to the total expenditure on the services of all components. Because of the availability of such a natural interpretation and because of the index's optimality properties, we advocate use of the Divisia index to measure the quantity of money at all levels of aggregation, as first proposed by Barnett (1980a; 1981b, chap. 7).

In order to be able to use (1) for aggregation over monetary asset quantities, we need the price, π_{jt}, corresponding to each component quantity asset, m_{jt}. In economic quantity aggregation, the appropriate price of a component durable good is its user cost. Barnett (1978, 1980a) derived the user cost of a monetary asset and found that the current-period user cost, π_{it} of m_{it} is

$$\pi_{it} = \frac{p_t^*(R_t - r_{it})(1 - \tau_t)}{1 + R_t(1 - \tau_t)}, \qquad (2)$$

where p_t^* is the true cost-of-living index, r_{it} is the own current-period holding yield on component i, R_t is the maximum available expected holding-period yield in the economy, and τ_t is the marginal tax rate. The corresponding real user cost is

$$\pi_{it}^* = \frac{\pi_{it}}{p_t^*}. \qquad (3)$$

The holding period used in defining R_t must be the same as that of r_{it}, which is a short rate. Details of our procedure for measuring R_t are defined in Barnett and Spindt (1982), which also describes the data used for the r_{it}'s. A few of the more noteworthy details follow. The return on demand deposits is a version of Klein's (1974) competitive rate on demand deposits. The raw data on the other r_{it}'s are for various holding periods. Hence the unadjusted yield differentials, $R_t - r_{it}$, can reflect differences in term to maturity as well as differences in monetary services at the margin. However, Barnett's derivation of equation (2) requires all yields to be for the same holding period. As a result, all yields are converted to a 1-month holding-period basis by using the Treasury securities yield curve and the yield curve adjustment procedure developed for the Federal Reserve's FRB-Penn-MIT quarterly model (developed jointly by the Federal Reserve Board, University of Pennsylvania, and MIT). The certainty-equivalence theory on which (2) was based required that any risk premiums be left within the rate structure, if freedom from default risk ('store of value') is to be valued by the Divisia quantity index as a monetary service. We left any such risk premiums within the r_{it}'s, although the components of the existing monetary aggregates all possess very low default risk. If the components were to be selected properly by tests for blockwise weak separability (as described in chapter 7), then it is conceivable that assets such as gold or equity shares could appear in the nested aggregates at some level of aggregation. In such cases, the expected holding-period yields, r_{it}, would depend nontrivially on expected capital gains and losses and expected transactions costs.

Observe that the 'weights' are not the user costs, but rather the average shares, $\bar{s}_{jt}$, which depend jointly on all quantities and user costs. Those share weights were not acquired by an ad hoc weighting scheme (such as weighting by variances, bid-ask spreads, denominations, maturities, velocities, or turnover rates), but rather were derived directly from microeconomic aggregation and index number theory.[6] Also note that in equation (1) the user costs appear only in the share weights, $\bar{s}_{jt}$, and all factors in (2) except for $R_t - r_{it}$ cancel out of the numerator and denominator of each $\bar{s}_{jt}$. Hence in computing the Divisia monetary aggregates, we could view the user-cost price, π_{it}, as the opportunity cost, $R_t - r_{it}$, which measures the interest foregone by holding monetary asset i when R_t is available. However, an exception to that statement results from the fact that our implicit competitive rate of return on demand deposits is not taxed, while the other rates are. Hence it is not strictly true that all marginal tax rates cancel out of each $\bar{s}_{it}$. We expect that this problem is not of great empirical consequence, but in future work we plan to refine the Divisia monetary aggregates further by using results of work on average marginal tax rates, such as Barro and Sahasakul (1983).

4 Granger Causality and Prediction Risk Reduction

In this section, we report the results of applying several standard tests of the Granger causality relation between money and income, where money is measured first by an official summation aggregate and then by the corresponding Divisia aggregate. We use three different empirical test procedures.

The first procedure is advocated by Pierce and Haugh (1977). In the first two columns of Table 1, we display the tail areas for Haugh's (1972) small-sample test against the hypothesis of independence. The results are provided for both 8- and 12-quarter symmetric lags.[7] In every instance, the hypothesis of independence between GNP and money, as measured by either the official or the Divisia aggregate, would be rejected by a test at the 5 percent significance level. However, each Divisia aggregate produced a smaller test tail area than the corresponding official aggregate. As a result,

---

[6] See Barnett (1981a, 1982b). For a general nontechnical discussion of the properties and interpretation of the Divisia monetary aggregates, see Barnett (1983b). See Barnett (1990) for a discussion of the various ad hoc weighting schemes (such as the linear regression index, the latent variables index, the so-called Fisher money stock index, M_Q, etc.).

[7] For details of the estimated ARIMA models, see Barnett, Offenbacher, and Spindt (1984).

the tail area comparisons favor the Divisia aggregates.

The second approach is due to Sims (1972). The tail areas of the Sims test are presented in the third and fourth columns of Table 1 for both directions of causality. We find that in all cases the hypothesis that money does not Granger-cause GNP would be rejected at the 5 percent significance level. However, the tail area for the official (sum) aggregate was less than that for the corresponding Divisia aggregate at each level of aggregation except at the highest level, L. The hypothesis that GNP does not Granger-cause money would be accepted at the 5 percent level with each of the monetary aggregates except for the official M1 aggregate. The tail area for the sum aggregate exceeded that for the corresponding Divisia aggregate at the two highest levels of aggregation, M3 and L.[8]

In the third procedure, we compute an approximate likelihood ratio test of the hypothesis that $C(L) = 0$ in the bivariate autoregression

$$\begin{pmatrix} Z_t \\ Y_t \end{pmatrix} = \begin{bmatrix} A(L) & B(L) \\ C(L) & D(L) \end{bmatrix} \begin{pmatrix} Z_t \\ Y_t \end{pmatrix} + \begin{pmatrix} \epsilon_{1t} \\ \epsilon_{2t} \end{pmatrix}.$$

It is immediate from Granger's definition (without contemporaneous causality) that Z_t does not cause Y_t if $C(L) = 0$.[9] We assume that the orders of A, B, C, and D are each no more than eight. The tail areas of the test of the hypothesis that $C(L) = 0$ are presented in the fifth column of Table 1.[10] The hypothesis that money does not Granger-cause GNP would be rejected at the 5 percent level with the Divisia aggregates at all levels of aggregation except at the lowest, M1, level, at which the tail area was a marginal .056. The same hypothesis would be accepted at the .05 level with the official summation aggregates at all levels of aggregation except M2. In addition, the tail area of the test for the Divisia aggregates was lower than that for the corresponding sum aggregate at all levels of aggregation. These tail area comparisons favor the Divisia aggregates.

Table 1 does not reveal a single uniformly best aggregate. In terms of 5 percent significance levels, sum M2, Divisia M2, Divisia M3, and Divisia L

---

[8]It is crucial to the Sims procedure to account for autocorrelation of the untransformed disturbances properly. We correct for serial correlation in those disturbances by using a general fifth-order autoregressive transformation. As a test of the assumed lack of autocorrelation of the resulting transformed disturbances, we computed the tail area of the test that the first eight autocorrelations of the transformed disturbance terms are zero. As seen from the tail areas displayed in Table A1 in App. A, the hypothesis was accepted at the .05 level in all cases.

[9]This result follows from Feige and Pearce (1979). Simplifying along the same lines as Feige and Pearce (1979) to avoid the problems discussed by Pierce and Haugh (1977), we rule out instantaneous causality by assuming $b_0 = c_0 = 0$. The model is normalized by taking $a_0 = d_0 = 0$. Using common time-series notation (see, e.g., Granger and Newbold 1977, p. 6). A, B, C, and D are polynomials and L is the backshift (lag) operator.

[10]See Wall (1974) for a discussion of the test procedure.

produce successful test results in all cases. In terms of the test tail areas, none of those three aggregates uniformly dominates, although Divisia L is most frequently best. While Divisia M1 was unsuccessful in one causality test at the .05 level, the failure was only marginal with a tail area of .056. Otherwise Divisia M1 also did well in these tests.

TABLE 1
Tail Areas of Tests of Granger Causality from Money Measures to GNP

Monetary Measures	Haugh-Pierce Test		Sims Test*		Direct Test†
	8-Quarters Lag	12-Quarters Lag	GNP to Money	Money to GNP	
M1	.0000	.0000	.0130	.0038	.074
M1^D	.0000	.0000	.1277	.0171	.056
M2	.0222	.0113	.1143	.0014	.005
M2^D	.0105	.0082	.1959	.0040	.001
M3	.0303	.0251	.6950	.0058	.090
M3^D	.0267	.0243	.4023	.0088	.021
L	.0152	.0175	.0901	.0047	.079
L^D	.0016	.0080	.0870	.0029	.002

NOTE: Sample period, quarterly observations: 1959:1–1982:4. The superscript D designates a Divisia aggregate. The other aggregates are sums.
* Degrees of F-statistic = 8, 90.
† Df of χ^2 statistic = 8.

Because Granger-causality tests are tests of 'incremental information content' (Schwert 1979, p. 82), causality results have an important bearing on the usefulness of monetary aggregates as indicators. When a monetary aggregate Granger-causes some variable of policy interest, such as income, the prediction variance of that variable can be reduced by conditioning on measurements of the monetary aggregate. Barnett and Spindt (1979) and Barnett, Offenbacher, and Spindt (1984) have found that the Divisia monetary aggregates are usually better than the corresponding official sum aggregates as indicators of a variety of policy target variables. Direct estimates of the proportionate reduction in prediction risk achievable by using Divisia and sum M2 as indicators in the context of the FRB-Penn-MIT quarterly model are presented in Table 2. Prediction risk is measured by the generalized variance of the model forecast errors for the target variables. In the indicator use of the monetary aggregates, the unconditional model forecast is revised to a conditional forecast given the indicator measurement along the lines detailed in Tinsley, Spindt, and Friar (1980, p. 67). It can be seen from Table 2 that considerable reductions in prediction risk are achievable by policymakers using Divisia M2 as an indicator.

5 Velocity

A substantial controversy has arisen in the literature regarding a 'shift' in the demand-for-money function that frequently is purported to have occurred in the middle of 1974.[11] Over the past decade, interest rates have generally been rising. Hence the opportunity cost (user cost) of holding money has been rising. Under those circumstances, tests of functional stability can be deceptive. Conventional tests of functional stability are most useful when explanatory variable values are replicated or at least lie within the same region both before and after the potential shift period. When explanatory variables are continually moving into new regions, it can be very difficult to separate function shift from specification error.

TABLE 2
Proportionate Reduction of Prediction Risk with Respect to Income, Prices, and Unemployment: FRB-Penn-MIT Quarterly Model Forecasting

Monetary Aggregate	$I_{\mathbf{Y}_t | \mathbf{Z}_t}$ by Definition of $\mathbf{Y}_t$			
	Univariate			
	$\dot{x}^*$	$\dot{p}^*$	$\dot{u}^*$	Multivariate
M2	.120	.049	.000	.156
M2^D	.349	.163	.020	.389

NOTE: The superscript D designates a Divisia aggregates. M1^D, M3^D, and L^D are not yet available on the FRB-Penn-MIT quarterly model. Also $\dot{x}^*$ here is the growth rate of nominal GNP, $\dot{p}^*$ is the rate of change in the GNP deflator, and $\dot{u}^*$ is the total unemployment rate. Sample period, quarterly observations: 1969:1–1979:4.

Suppose, for example, that the true demand-for-money function is nonlinear in its variables and parameters but has never shifted. Then the parameters of the best linear approximation will differ over different regions of the space of explanatory variables. If the explanatory variables move into new regions of that space as time passes, then tests of functional stability of a linear approximation are likely to reject stability. Similarly, if the parameters of the function are estimated over one period of time and the estimated function is then used in a dynamic simulation over another time period, the function is likely to track poorly. Fortunately, however, the existence of interest-rate cycles over the past decade has resulted in approximate replication regions that

---

[11] See Enzler, Johnson, and Paulus (1976); Goldfeld (1976); Tinsley and Garrett, with Friar (1980); and Simpson and Porter (1981). This problem has been most heavily investigated at low levels of monetary aggregation, but it appears to arise also at higher levels of aggregation. This feature of the problem is most troublesome, since it suggests that the 'shift' is a result not of explainable substitution within the money market, but rather of a true shift in the economy's transactions technology.

Velocity

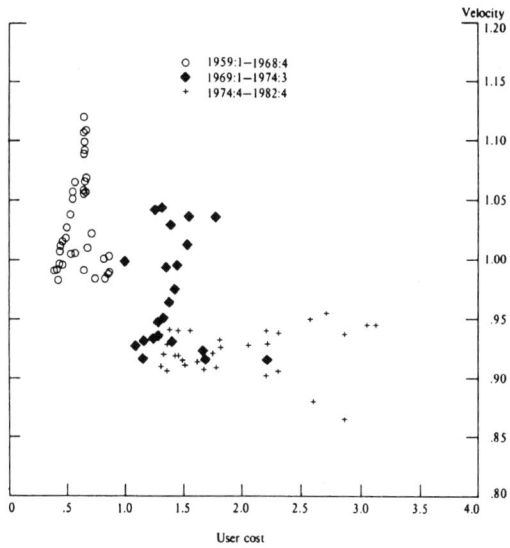

Figure 1: Sum M3 velocity versus Divisia user-cost aggregate, quarterly, 1959:1–1982:4.

can be explored. In this section we present velocity cross plots permitting investigation of the ability of the economy's true demand-for-money function to replicate. If the true function that generated the data over one time period cannot replicate the data over another time period with similar explanatory variables values, then we can validly conclude that the demand-for-money function has shifted.

The following exploratory data analysis relates velocity to various commonly used opportunity-cost variables. Three different plotting symbols are used to differentiate between data from three different time periods: (1) data after the purported shift, (2) data from the 5 years preceding the purported shift, and (3) data from the prior decade. We seek to determine whether velocity data acquired from different time periods tend to replicate when the potential explanatory variable retraces the same region during the different time periods. The explanatory variables we consider are the Divisia user cost and Moody's AAA corporate bond rate.

Figures 1 and 2 plot sum M3 against the two potential explanatory variables. Strong evidence exists of a shift in the relationship between velocity and either of the two opportunity-cost measures. Of course the reason could be additional omitted variables. But a stable relationship between velocity and any one of the opportunity-cost variables taken alone does not appear to

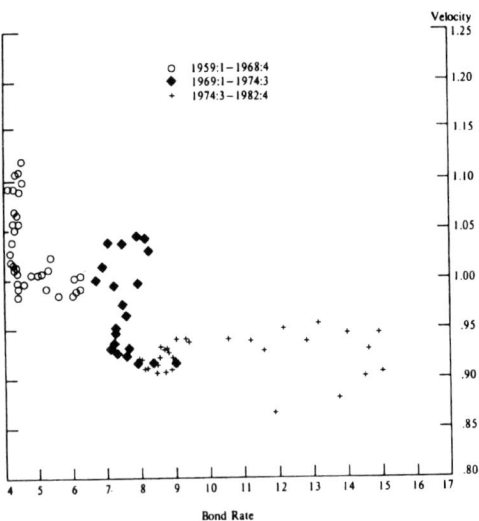

Figure 2: Sum M3 velocity versus Moody's AAA corporate bond rate, quarterly, 1959:1–1982:4.

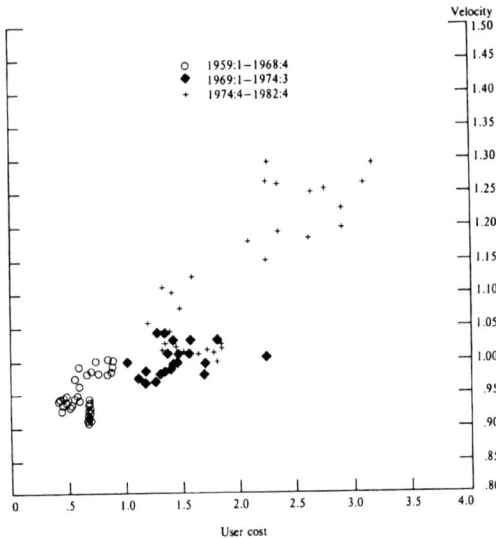

Figure 3: Divisia M3 velocity versus Divisia user-cost aggregate, quarterly, 1959:1–1982:4.

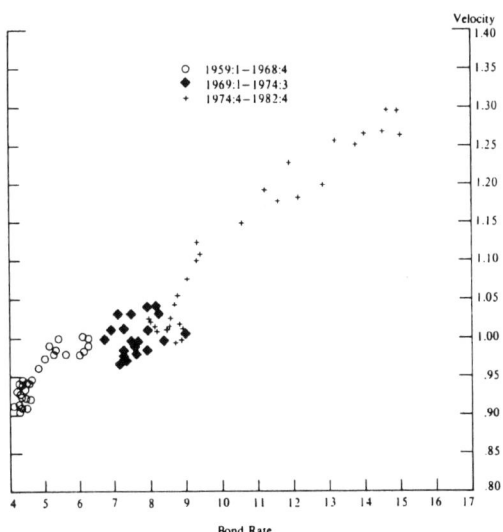

Figure 4: Divisia M3 velocity versus Moody's AAA corporate bond rate, quarterly, 1959:1–1982:4.

exist, since the function that generated the data after 1974 does not appear to be able to replicate the earlier data in the middle region of overlapping opportunity-cost values.

Figures 3 and 4 plot Divisia M3 against the same two potential explanatory variables. No clear evidence of function shift remains. For example, with ordinary-least-squares linear regression of Divisia M3 on Moody's AAA corporate bond rate, the tail area of the Chow test of the hypothesis of no parameter shift in the middle of 1974 is .1337. The tail area of the corresponding test with sum M3 is .0027. The result is substantially more favorable for the Divisia than for the official aggregate.[12]

Although not reported here, analogous results were found with the 6-month Treasury bill rate and the 5-year government note rate (see Barnett, Offenbacher and Spindt 1984). As space is limited, we display only M3 plots in this section and in Section 9 below, although the results acquired with M2 and L are similar. The available empirical evidence, including the causality tests in the last section, suggests that Divisia L is the potentially most interesting aggregate. In addition, Divisia L is the aggregate that comes closest to capturing the contributions of all elements of the money market to the economy's monetary service flow. However, updates for Divisia L are

---

[12] A first-order autoregressive error structure was used.

not currently available with the same frequency as for Divisia M3, and hence Divisia L is of less potential policy usefulness than Divisia M3 at present. In any case, the plots for L are very similar to those displayed here for M3, as demonstrated in Barnett, Offenbacher, and Spindt (1984). At the M1 level, as might be expected, the plots for the Divisia aggregate do not differ from those of the sum aggregate by as much as at the higher levels of aggregation.[13]

6 Money Demand Functions

6.1 Specification

In this section we compare the official monetary aggregates with the Divisia monetary aggregates in terms of the resulting properties of estimated demand-for-money equations. When using the official aggregates, we use the conventional specifications that were used in the literature on demand-for-money function shifts. When using the Divisia aggregates, we use the analogous specifications appropriate to Divisia aggregation. We explore plausibility of the estimates, parametric stability, and simulated forecasting accuracy.

We use the double log specification that has appeared widely in the literature on 'shifting' demand-for-money functions:[14]

$$\log\left(\frac{M_t}{p_t^*}\right) = \alpha_0 + \alpha_1 \log\left(\frac{M_{t-1}}{p_t^*}\right) + \alpha_2 \log\left(\frac{Y_t}{p_t^*}\right) + \sum_{k=1}^{K} \alpha_{2+k} \log(OC)_k, \quad (4)$$

where M_t = a given per capita Divisia or simple sum monetary aggregate, p_t^* = GNP price deflator, Y_t = nominal per capita GNP, K = total number of opportunity-cost variables (one or two), and $(OC)_k$ = kth opportunity-cost variable (interest-rate or Divisia user-cost aggregate). The opportunity-cost variables differ among the different equations. When M_t is a summation aggregate, the opportunity-cost variables are interest rates: the commercial paper rate (as a representative market interest rate) and, with M1, the commercial bank passbook rate. When M_t is a Divisia index, all opportunity-cost

---

[13] Plots at all levels of aggregation, for both this section and Section 9, are available from the authors on request.

[14] All variables are quarterly averages, and all variables except interest rates are seasonally adjusted. Similarly, the Divisia aggregates are constructed from seasonally adjusted quantitites and unadjusted interest rates. While this functional form is well known, two aspects of the precise specification require clarification. First, the lagged value of money, which appears as a predetermined variable, is deflated by the current value of the price level to allow for partial adjustment of nominal balances to price-level shocks in the short run, while maintaining long-run linear homogeneity of M_t in (Y_t, p_t). Regarding such double log inventory models, see Baumol (1952), Tobin (1956), and Fisher (1978).

variables are Divisia user-cost indexes acquired from Divisia price aggregation over the real user costs, π_{it}^*, of equation (3). The Divisia user-cost index is computed for the own price of M_t and, with M1, for a competing aggregated good. The competing opportunity-cost variable is the Divisia user-cost aggregate for those assets that are in L but not in M3.

6.2 Empirical Results

The first section below describes the results of estimation with fixed coefficient methods. In the following section, we use stochastic coefficient methods to explore parametric stability.

Forecasting

The parameter estimates for equation (4) for both the Divisia and sum aggregates are found in Appendix A.[15] The estimates seem reasonable by conventional standards. Usually the coefficients on real GNP and on the opportunity-cost variables are statistically significant, have the correct sign, and are of reasonable magnitude. Two exceptions are the wrong signs acquired for the coefficient of real GNP with Divisia M2 and Divisia L during 1974:3–1982:4.[16] No such exceptions occurred during 1959:3–1974:2. In the literature on money demand, the most troublesome parameter to interpret has always been the coefficient on the lagged dependent variable (LDV), which has almost always implied unreasonably slow speeds of adjustment. While Divisia aggregation has not totally resolved this problem, the coefficient on the LDV is lower for the Divisia aggregates than for their official sum counterparts in eight of the 12 cases. The eight cases include all four levels of aggregation during the 1959:3–1974:2 sample period. The coefficient on the LDV exceeds 1.0 in three cases, all using the official sum aggregates. With both the Divisia and sum aggregates, the coefficient estimates were most plausible during the 1959:3–1974:2 sample period.

The predictive performance of each equation with its parameters estimated using the 1959:3–1974:2 sample period is summarized by the results that appear in the first two columns of Table 3. The first of the columns reports the root mean squared error (RMSE) for the predicted growth rates implied by each estimated equation over the period 1974:3–1980:4. The second column reports the mean error of the same growth-rate predictions.[17]

---

[15] A first-order autoregressive error structure was used.

[16] Also note that the own-price elasticity of the demand for Divisia M3 has the wrong sign during 1959:3–1982:4, and the coefficient of $(OC)_2$ is statistically insignificant for both Divisia and sum M1.

[17] Growth-rate forecast errors are obtained by simulating each equation dynamically.

The simulation results uniformly favor the Divisia aggregates. At all levels of aggregation, both the RMSE and the absolute value of the mean error for the Divisia forecasts are lower than for their sum counterparts.

TABLE 3
Forecasting Properties of Fixed Coefficient Demand Functions

Monetary Aggregate	Forecasting*	
	RMSE†	Mean Error
M1	5.739	−.319
$M1^D$	3.924	−.058
M2	5.141	2.678
$M2^D$	4.966	−.213
M3	5.296	3.015
$M3^D$	4.472	−.150
L	5.617	3.493
L^D	4.109	−.085

NOTE: All data are quarterly. The results use parameters estimated for the 1959:3–1974:2 sample period in forecasting from 1974:3 through 1982:4. The D superscript on the monetary aggregates designates Divisia aggregates; the others are sums.
* Based on growth-rate forecast errors in percentage points per year.
† Root mean squared errors of forecasts.

Parametric Stability

In order to explore parametric stability, we estimate equation (4) with stochastically varying coefficients. We permit the coefficients to be stationary stochastic processes and use the Swamy and Tinsley (1980) asymptotically efficient estimation procedure. With this technique, it is necessary to use the same specification for equation (4) with both the Divisia and official sum aggregates, in order to assure comparability of the coefficient time paths (and test statistics) between results with both sets of aggregates.[18] To avoid prejudicing the results in favor of the Divisia aggregates, we do not use Divisia user-cost aggregates as explanatory variables, but rather the conventional demand-for-money equation adopted with the official sum M1 aggregate in

---

Starting in 1974:3, we obtain predicted levels of the relevant aggregate and then compute the predicted growth rates. The estimation sample period was ended and the forecasts begun in mid-1974, since the widely reported shift in the demand for money function is professed to have occurred at that time.

[18] Otherwise it would be impossible to separate the effect of the different aggregation procedure from the effect of the different equation specification. In fact, if different specifications were used, there would be no formal procedure for determining which coefficient path from one equation to compare with any given coefficient path from the other equation.

the last section. In this section, we use that one specification at all levels of aggregation and with both the Divisia and sum aggregates.

The coefficients of equation (4) now are viewed as stochastic processes and hence are written with time subscripts as $\boldsymbol{\alpha}_t = (\alpha_{0t}, \alpha_{1t}, \alpha_{2t}, \alpha_{3t}, \alpha_{4t})$. In accordance with the Swamy and Tinsley (1980) procedure, we further specify that $\boldsymbol{\alpha}_t = \bar{\boldsymbol{\alpha}} + \mathbf{e}_t$ and $\mathbf{e}_t = \Phi \mathbf{e}_{t-1} + \mathbf{u}_t$, where $\mathbf{u}_t$ is a random vector with mean zero and covariance matrix, Δ, and where $\bar{\boldsymbol{\alpha}}$ is a vector of parameters (the mean coefficient vector) and Φ is a matrix of parameters.[19] The Swamy and Tinsley estimates of the mean coefficient vector, $\bar{\boldsymbol{\alpha}}$, are tabulated in the first five columns of Table 4. The estimates appear to be plausible at all three levels of aggregation with both the sum and Divisia aggregates, although the common problem of slow speed of adjustment is evident in all cases.

In Figures 5, 6, and 7, we have plotted for M3 the time path of $(\alpha_{2t}, \alpha_{3t}, \alpha_{4t})$, which are the coefficients of the three exogenous variables.[20] Each of the three coefficient paths is substantially more stable with the Divisia aggregate than with the sum aggregate. Furthermore, the cyclical drift evident in the results with the sum aggregate is absent from the Divisia results.

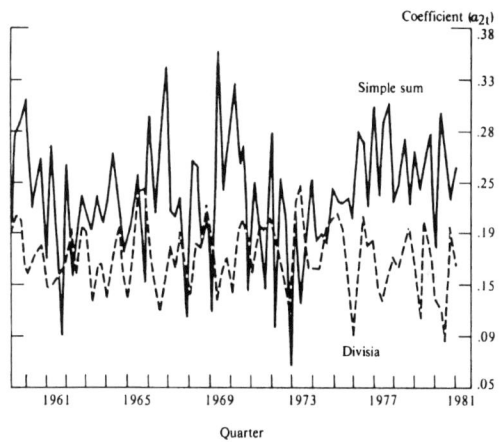

Figure 5: Time path of the income coefficient, α_{2t}, 1959:2–1980:4.

---

[19] Estimates of Φ and Δ are reported in an earlier draft of this paper, which is available from the authors on request.

[20] The coefficient path realizations charted in Figures 5–7 were computed as $\boldsymbol{\alpha}_t = \bar{\boldsymbol{\alpha}} + \mathbf{e}_t$, following the precedures outlined by Swamy and Tinsley (1980). The estimator $\bar{\boldsymbol{\alpha}}$ is consistent for the mean of the stochastic process $\boldsymbol{\alpha}_t$. Our predictions, $\mathbf{e}_t$, of the coefficient innovation process are based on the minimum norm generalized inverse solution given by Swamy and Tinsley (1980, p. 116, eq. [4.10]).

TABLE 4
Mean Parameter Estimates and Stability Tests

Monetary Aggregate	Mean Parameter Estimates					F-statistic*	Chow[†]	Df[‡]
	Intercept ($\bar{\alpha}_0$)	Lagged Money ($\bar{\alpha}_1$)	Income ($\bar{\alpha}_2$)	Commercial Paper ($\bar{\alpha}_3$)	Passbook Rate ($\bar{\alpha}_4$)			
M1	...	...	...	...	...	...	3.89 [.002]	6,74
M1^D	...	...	...	...	...	...	3.86 [.002]	6,74
M2	.008 (2.12)	.860 (11.46)	.212 (3.21)	−.032 (−4.67)	.020 (1.66)	7.348 [.000]	2.36 [.048]	5,76
M2^D	.008 (1.59)	.896 (7.36)	.135 (1.62)	−.037 (−2.00)	.002 (.08)	3.085 [.000]	2.32 [.051]	5,76
M3	.008 (.19)	.844 (6.56)	.222 (1.94)	−.015 (−.36)	.033 (.20)	47.449 [.000]	1.82 [.119]	5,76
M3^D	.005 (1.61)	.868 (10.24)	.167 (2.98)	−.035 (−3.95)	.003 (.21)	1.418 [.137]	1.40 [.234]	5,76
L	.010 (3.92)	.901 (24.99)	.150 (3.75)	−.014 (−3.45)	.012 (1.15)	8.859 [.000]	1.62 [.164]	5,76
L^D	.002 (.17)	.797 (7.92)	.128 (2.55)	−.023 (−3.22)	.020 (.88)	1.938 [.019]	.95 [.452]	5,76

NOTE: Sample period, quarterly data: 1959:3-1980:4. Numbers in parentheses are t-ratios. Numbers in brackets are tail areas of tests. The D superscripts after the monetary aggregates designate Divisia aggregates; the others are sums. The Swamy and Tinsley estimation algorithm failed to converge with the M1 data, so no results could be presented for those data.
* $Df = 24, 62$.
[†] The Chow test statistic, for a shift at the end of 1974:2, is an F-statistic.
[‡] Df for the Chow test F-statistic.

The observations above on coefficient path behavior are formally verified by the F-statistics in the sixth column of Table 4. Those F-statistics are for the test of the hypothesis that equation (4) has constant coefficients and an additive first-order autoregressive error structure. At every level of aggregation, the F-statistic with the Divisia aggregate is lower than with the simple sum aggregate. Since the tail area of the test is inversely related to the level of the F-statistic, the hypothesis of parametric stability was more acceptable with the Divisia than with the sum aggregates. The result is most striking at the M3 level. At the .05 level of significance, stability of the demand function for the sum aggregate would be decisively rejected, while stability would be decisively accepted for the corresponding Divisia aggregate. Nevertheless, at all other levels of aggregation, stability would be rejected at the .05 significance level with either the sum or Divisia aggregate.

The seventh column of Table 4 contains the F-statistic for a Chow test of the hypothesis of no break in regimes after 1974:2. Since we do not pro-

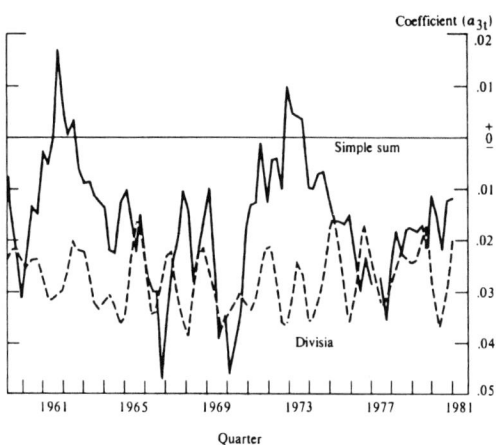

Figure 6: Time path of commercial paper rate coefficient, α_{3t}, 1959:2–1980:4.

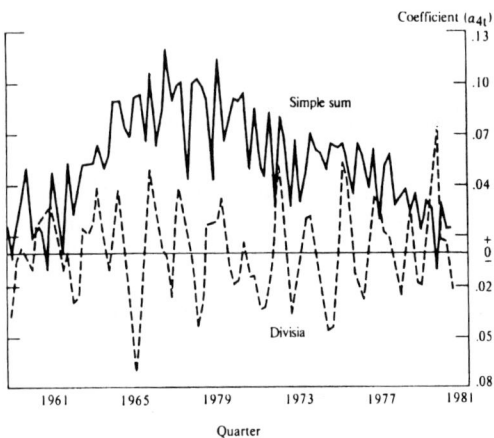

Figure 7: Time path of passbook rate coefficient, α_{4t}, 1959:2–1980:4.

duce stochastic coefficient paths in this test, the problem of comparability with different specifications is less severe than with the stochastic coefficient results.[21] As a result, we use the same equation specifications as in the last section for each aggregate. The F-statistic is larger for the Divisia aggregate than for the sum aggregate at each level of aggregation. These results are uniformly favorable to the Divisia aggregates. However, at a fixed .05 level of significance, the hypothesis of no shift would be accepted for both the Divisia and sum aggregates at the M3 and L levels of aggregation. The hypothesis would be rejected for both Divisia and sum M1. The hypothesis would be marginally accepted for Divisia M2 and marginally rejected for sum M2.

Searching over Tables 3 and 4 for a uniformly best aggregate, we find none. In terms of forecasting, Divisia M1 and Divisia L were most successful. In terms of stability, Divisia L was most successful with the Chow test, but Divisia M3 was most successful with the stochastic coefficient F-test.

7 Reduced-Form Equations

7.1 The Equations

Another basis for comparing various monetary aggregates is a comparison of their performance in reduced-form equations.[22] These equations relate the growth rate of GNP to current and lagged money growth rates and to current and lagged values of a fiscal policy variable. Such an equation is interpreted as a reduced-form equation from an unspecified structural econometric model.

The specification adopted here is from Carlson (1980) and has the form

$$\dot{Y}_t = \beta_0 + \sum_{i=1}^{14} \beta_{1i} \dot{M}_{t-i} + \sum_{k=1}^{14} \beta_{2k} \dot{F}_{t-k},$$

where $\dot{Y}_t$ = annualized percentage rate of growth of GNP, $\dot{M}_t$ = annualized percentage rate of growth of a given Divisia or sum monetary aggregate during quarter t, and $\dot{F}_t$ = annualized percentage rate of growth of high employment federal expenditures. The parameters are estimated both with and without the constraint, $\sum_{i=1}^{14} \beta_{1i} = 1.0$, which is necessary for steady-state (long-run) superneutrality.[23]

---

[21] In addition, using different specifications decreases the degree of partial redundancy of this test with the stochastic coefficients F-test.

[22] The interpretation of such reduced-form equations is subject to a number of well-known difficulties (see e.g., Lucas 1976).

[23] Strictly speaking, superneutrality refers to the lack of any effect of inflation on the level of real output; here the term refers to the lack of any effect of inflation on real output growth. The distributed lags are third-order Almon polynomial distributed lags. All the equations were estimated by the Cochrane-Orcutt technique.

TABLE 5
Fit, Forecasting, and Stability Properties of Estimated Reduced-Form Equations

Specification	Monetary Aggregate	R^2	Forecasting*		Stability	
			RMSE†	Mean Error	Chow‡	LR§
Unconstrained	M1	.2872	4.795	−.092	.96 [.466]	7.72 [.461]
Constrained	M1	.2937	4.813	−.267	1.15 [.341]	8.89 [.261]
Unconstrained	$M1^D$	.2527	3.417	−.276	1.17 [.326]	9.03 [.251]
Constrained	$M1^D$	.2528	3.527	−.710	1.46 [.194]	10.14 [.181]
Unconstrained	M2	.2458	4.829	−.222	2.08 [.048]	16.38 [.037]
Constrained	M2	.2531	4.829	−.233	.69 [.682]	4.83 [.680]
Unconstrained	$M2^D$	.3155	4.811	.954	.47 [.871]	4.49 [.810]
Constrained	$M2^D$	.3154	4.845	1.044	.53 [.813]	4.09 [.769]
Unconstrained	M3	.2111	5.032	.396	1.82 [.086]	13.89 [.080]
Constrained	M3	.2171	5.024	−.206	1.10 [.370]	8.83 [.265]
Unconstrained	$M3^D$	.3002	4.833	1.335	.58 [.789]	4.84 [.775]
Constrained	$M3^D$	.3019	3.028	1.239	.43 [.880]	4.66 [.701]
Unconstrained	L	.2178	5.540	−2.033	.84 [.557]	8.19 [.415]
Constrained	L	.2152	5.412	−1.699	1.06 [.394]	8.79 [.357]
Unconstrained	L^D	.3376	2.814	−.282	.77 [.627]	6.38 [.603]
Constrained	L^D	.3294	4.635	.301	.52 [.818]	4.49 [.722]

NOTE: Sample period, quarterly data: 1959:3–1982:4. Numbers in brackets are tail areas of tests. The D superscript on the monetary aggregates designates Divisia aggregates; the others are sums. The stability results test for a shift at the end of 1974:2. The forecasting results use parameters estimated for the 1959:3–1974:2 sample period in forecasting from 1974:3 through 1982:4.
* Based on growth-rate forecasting errors in percentage points per year.
† Root mean squared errors of forecasting errors.
‡ The Chow test statistic is an F-statistic. Df of the constrained test are 7,80; df of the unconstrained test are 8,78.
§ The LR test statistic is the asymptotic likelihood ratio test statistic, $-2\log\lambda$, which has a limiting χ^2 distribution. The number of df is the same as the numerator df for the Chow F-statistic.

7.2 Results

Table 5 summarizes the results. The criteria for comparing the findings are essentially the same as for the money demand equations: forecasting performance and stability tests. We again split the sample after 1974:2 in acquiring the forecasting and stability results. Further details for the estimation results can be found in Barnett, Offenbacher, and Spindt (1984). Table 5 contains all of the results on forecasting performance and stability behavior.

The results in Table 5 are mixed, although certain patterns are evident. The performance of the Divisia aggregates judged relative to the corresponding sum aggregates gradually improves as the level of aggregation increases. At the highest level of aggregation, Divisia L outperforms sum L relative to all of the criteria in Table 5. At lower levels of aggregation, the forecasting results depend heavily on the criterion used. Relative to RMSE, the Divisia aggregates usually outperform the sum aggregates, but the reverse conclusion is acquired relative to mean error. In terms of both stability (test tail area) and fit (R^2), the sum aggregate outperforms the Divisia aggregate at the M1 level of aggregation, but that conclusion is reversed relative to both criteria at all other levels of aggregation.

Comparisons across levels of aggregation do not reveal any single best aggregate, although Divisia L generaly did very well in Table 5.

7.3 Divisia Second Moments

The right-hand side of equation (1) is in the form of a statistical expectation or first moment. This result follows from the fact that $\Sigma_j \bar{s}_{jt} = 1$, and $\bar{s}_{jt} \geq 0$, so that each $\bar{s}_{jt}$ can be viewed as a probability from a discrete probability distribution. Hence we can define corresponding Divisia second moments in the obvious manner.[24] In Appendix B we show how those Divisia second moments can be used to complement the Divisia quantity index (or Divisia quantity mean) by providing a dispersion measure of 'potential aggregation error.' We find that the potential aggregation error of the Divisia monetary aggregates has not been subject to appreciable cyclical variation over our sample period of 1969:1–1982:4, and any slight cyclical variation decreases as the level of aggregation increases.

7.4 Controllability

Since this paper primarily explores the relationship between monetary (intermediate) targets and final targets, we do not here extensively investigate con-

---

[24]See Barnett, Offenbacher, and Spindt's (1984) equations (12.1)–(12.7) for formal definitions.

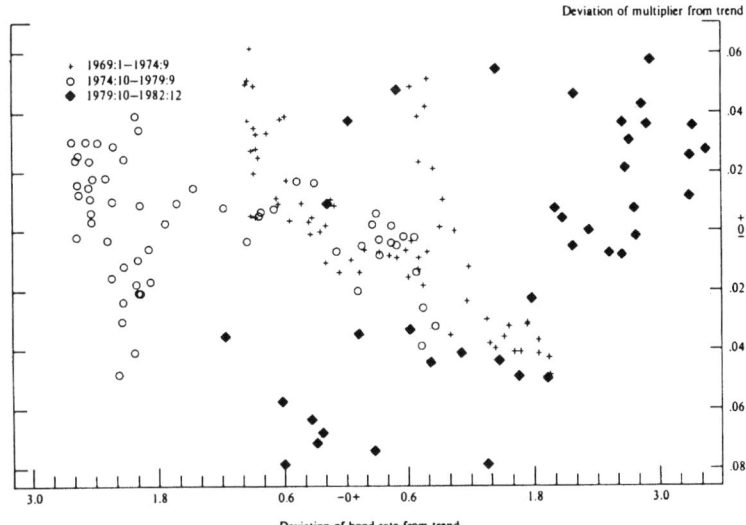

Figure 8: Deviation from time trend of sum M3 base money multiplier versus deviation from time trend of Moody's Baa corporate bond rate, monthly, 1969:1–1982:12.

trollability, which is defined in terms of the relationship between instruments and intermediate targets. Nevertheless we have explored the stability of multipliers between instruments and intermediate targets. The instruments we considered were the monetary base, total reserves, and nonborrowed reserves. The intermediate targets we considered were Divisia and sum M1, M2, M3, and L. All of the multipliers were erratic over time except for the ratio of the Divisia aggregates to the base. Those ratios exhibited stable long-run trends. The slope of the trend decreased as the level of aggregation increased, the ratio becoming approximately constant in the long run for Divisia L (with a short-run cycle correlating with interest rates).

Most of these results are available in Barnett and Spindt (1982).[25] Their results with sum and Divisia M3 are updated and displayed below. Using monthly data, we cross plot in Figures 8 and 9 the base money multiplier (monetary aggregate divided by monetary base) against Moody's Baa (average quality debt) corporate bond rate for both sum and Divisia M3. As in Figures 1–4, we use three plotting symbols for three different time periods.[26]

---

[25] For further consideration of the predictability of the base multipliers of the Divisia monetary aggregates, see Spindt (1984).

[26] In order to detrend the series, we measure each variable (whether base multiplier or interest rate) as its residual in a linear regression of the variable on time.

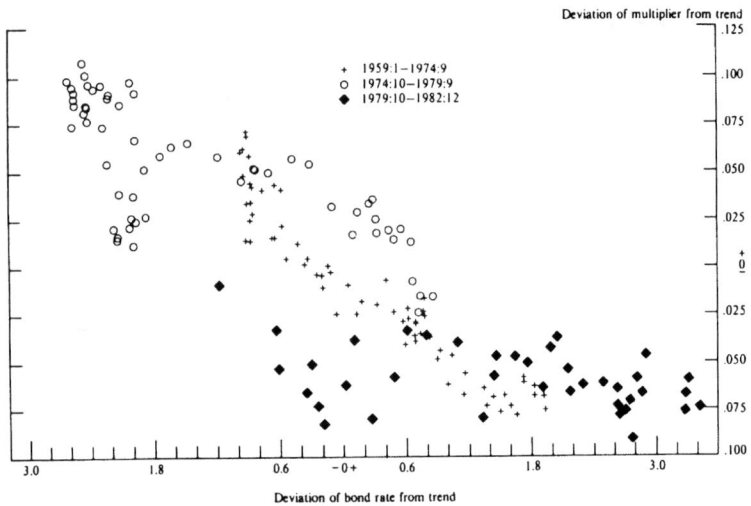

Figure 9: Deviation from time trend of Divisia M3 base money multiplier versus deviation from time trend of Moody's Baa corporate bond rate, monthly, 1969:1–1982:12.

As is evident from Figure 9, an interest rate has high explanatory power relative to the base multiplier of Divisia M3. The same cannot be said for sum M3, as is evident from the broad dispersion in Figure 8.

Since relevant microeconomic foundations for the supply-of-money function have only recently been developed, theoretical interpretation at this time of the results above would be speculative.[27] One might, for example, view the monetary base as both the output of the Federal Reserve System and a wealth constraint on the private sector. In this interpretation, a change in the base would cause the economy to re-equilibrate itself and thereby produce a new equilibrium monetary service flow. Since the broad Divisia monetary aggregates measure that service flow, a stable relationship could be expected to exist, at any given level of interest rates, between the monetary base and Divisia M3 or L. Figure 9 tends to support that view.

---

[27] Barnett, Hinich, and Weber (1986) have derived the supply functions for the Divisia monetary aggregates and have estimated those functions through the application of Hilbert transform methods. The results provide a direct test of controllability. Also see Hancock (1985) for further relevant theory.

8 Conclusion

Aggregation theory favors the Divisia quantity index over the sum index as a measure of the quantity of an aggregated economic good, when the components are not perfect substitutes. Barnett's (1980a, 1981b) tests using monetary data resulted in rejection of the necessary and sufficient conditions in aggregation theory for sum aggregation (see also Feige and Pearce 1977; Offenbacher 1979; Ewis and Fisher 1984, 1985; Serletis 1984, 1987a). The present paper systematically compares the empirical performance of the Divisia and the sum monetary aggregates relative to various criteria relevant to policymaking. Neither the Divisia aggregates nor the sum aggregates uniformly dominated the others relative to all of the criteria considered, and no one aggregate, whether Divisia or sum, was uniformly best. However, some general tendencies are evident from these results, as can be seen from the following summary of results.

In the causality tests, the Divisia aggregates generally performed better than the corresponding sum aggregates, although sum M2 did rather well. Divisia L was perhaps the best aggregate in those tests. In terms of the demand-for-money functions, the best forecasting results were acquired with Divisia M1 and Divisia L. The most stable demand-for-money functions were acquired with Divisia M3 and Divisia L. In addition, the velocity function for Divisia M3 was found to be stable. In the reduced-form comparisons, sum M1 performed better than Divisia M1, but at higher levels of aggregation the Divisia aggregates became increasingly superior to the corresponding sum aggregates, with Divisia L usually providing the best reduced-form results.

In earlier work, using information theory, we found that the Divisia aggregates tend to perform better than the sum aggregates as indicators, especially at high levels of aggretation. Using that criterion with the FRB-Penn-MIT quarterly model, we further confirm that result with M2. In addition, using the Divisia second moments, we find that the Divisia monetary aggregates are not subject to cyclical variation in potential aggregation error. Relative to that criterion, Divisia L was best. In addition, we provide updated results further supporting our earlier results on the superior controllability of the broad Divisia aggregates.

In short, at the lowest (M1) level of aggregation we acquire conflicting results in our comparisons between the sum and the Divisia aggregate. However, at higher levels of aggregation, the Divisia aggregates generally tend to perform better than the sum aggregates, with that degree of superiority tending to increase at increasing levels of aggregation.[28] Since the divergence between the time paths of the Divisia and the sum aggregates increases as the

---

[28] Preliminary results suggest that these conclusions also apply to Canadian data (see Cockerline and Murray 1981a).

level of aggregation increases (and the discrepancies between the two weighting methods increases), the power of any tests comparing the two aggregation methods should be expected to increase as the aggregation level increases. With so many criteria being considered, the selection of a 'best' aggregate is a hazardous matter. Cagan's (1982) results, based on fewer criteria and an earlier sample period, generally favored Divisia M1. While no aggregate was uniformly best relative to all of our criteria, our results reflect most favorably on Divisia L.

Appendix A: Error Structure Analysis and Demand for Money Function

The results of the error structure analysis for the Sims test are displayed in Table A1. The parameter esimates for the fixed coefficients demand-for-money functions are displayed in Tables A2–A5.

TABLE A1
Tail Areas of the Test that the First Eight Autocorrelations of the Sims Disturbance Terms are All Zero

Monetary Measure	GNP to Money	Money to GNP
M1	.459	.619
$M1^D$	.621	.520
M2	.091	.735
$M2^D$	.368	.420
M3	.127	.280
$M3^D$	.483	.652
L	.197	.363
L^D	.533	.212

NOTE: Sample period, quarterly observations: 1959:1–1982:4. The superscript D designates a Divisia aggregate. The other aggregates are sums.

Appendix A: Error Structure Analysis

TABLE A2
Money Demand Estimates for Divisia and Sum M1, Double Logarithmic Specification

Aggregate and Period of Fit	Constant	Real GNP	OC1*	OC2†	Lagged Dependent	ρ	SEE	R^2	D-W	Box-Pierce‡
Divisia M1:										
1959:3–1974:2	−1.243 (.437)	.1065 (.0216)	−.0070 (.0067)	−.0022 (.0011)	.7919 (.0796)	.538 (.1088)	.0054	.976	1.689	13.321
1974:3–1982:4	−.953 (.360)	.0140 (.0217)	−.0244 (.0089)	−.0013 (.0028)	.8177 (.0734)	−.2150 (.1675)	.0062	.956	2.071	7.835
1959:3–1982:4	−.255 (.148)	.0640 (.0108)	−.0129 (.0043)	.0000 (.0011)	.9691 (.0274)	.2458 (.1000)	.0065	.967	1.895	10.929
Sum M1:										
1959:3–1974:2	−1.059 (.440)	.1094 (.0220)	−.0184 (.0043)	−.0219 (.0139)	.8165 (.0841)	.4364 (.1162)	.0042	.909	1.900	11.141
1974:3–1982:4	−.401 (.214)	.0625 (.0283)	−.0083 (.0044)	−.0930 (.1167)	.9170 (.0674)	−.3557 (.1603)	.0018	.970	2.140	11.138
1959:3–1982:4	−.059 (.073)	.0584 (.0145)	−.0111 (.0027)	.0000 (.0089)	1.0018 (.0148)	−.0427 (.1031)	.0063	.990	1.957	8.124

NOTE: Standard errors are in parentheses.
* Divisia: $OC1$ = Divisia user cost for M1; sum: $OC1$ = commercial paper rate.
† Divisia: $OC2$ = Divisia user cost for the assets in L but not in M3 ($RLL3$); sum: $OC2$ = passbook rate.
‡ Box-Pierce χ^2 statistic for first 12 sample autocorrelations.

TABLE A3
Money Demand Estimates for Divisia and Sum M2, Double Logarithmic Specification

Aggregate and Period of Fit	Constant	Real GNP	OC*	Lagged Dependent	ρ	SEE	R^2	D-W	Box-Pierce†
Divisia M2:									
1959:3–1974:2	−1.006 (.537)	.1421 (.0570)	−.0102 (.0050)	.8484 (.0870)	.7110 (.0908)	.0053	.996	1.656	10.983
1974:3–1982:4	−.119 (.231)	−.1019 (.0381)	−.0248 (.0111)	.9347 (.0416)	.1173 (.1703)	.0095	.987	1.984	6.222
1959:3–1982:4	−.098 (.220)	.0409 (.0281)	−.0088 (.0054)	.9916 (.0357)	.5877 (.0835)	.0080	.992	2.034	5.508
Sum M2:									
1959:3–1974:2	−.383 (.300)	.1409 (.0498)	−.0304 (.0040)	.9573 (.0428)	.4133 (.1176)	.0039	.999	1.935	7.927
1974:3–1982:4	−1.014 (.455)	.1705 (.0696)	−.0170 (.0049)	.8479 (.0687)	−.1874 (.1685)	.0054	.985	1.960	4.294
1959:3–1982:4	−.721 (.275)	.1764 (.0455)	−.0238 (.0035)	.9057 (.0394)	.4644 (.0913)	.0046	.999	2.048	4.910

NOTE: Standard errors are in parentheses.
* Divisia: OC = Divisia user cost for M2; sum: OC = commercial paper rate.
† Box-Pierce χ^2 statistic for first 12 sample autocorrelations.

TABLE A4
Money Demand Estimates for Divisia and Sum M3, Double Logarithmic Specification

Aggregate and Period of Fit	Constant	Real GNP	OC*	Lagged Dependent	ρ	SEE	R^2	D-W	Box-Pierce†
Divisia M3:									
1959:3–1974:2	−.855 (.522)	.1499 (.0661)	−.0129 (.0055)	.8799 (.0817)	.7615 (.0837)	.0056	.997	1.646	12.039
1974:3–1982:4	−.196 (.257)	−.0671 (.0383)	−.0219 (.0108)	.9319 (.0484)	−.2296 (.1669)	.0086	.985	1.998	5.933
1959:3–1982:4	−.098 (.220)	.0409 (.0280)	−.0088 (.0053)	.9916 (.0357)	.5876 (.0835)	.0080	.992	2.035	5.019
Sum M3:									
1959:3–1974:2	−.028 (.382)	.0862 (.0711)	−.0287 (.0055)	1.0086 (.0519)	.5951 (.1038)	.0049	.999	1.749	10.947
1974:3–1982:4	−.349 (.289)	.1018 (.0438)	−.0087 (.0032)	.9588 (.0446)	.2671 (.1653)	.0041	.994	1.943	6.898
1959:3–1982:4	−.506 (.269)	.1487 (.0508)	−.0196 (.0039)	.9394 (.0366)	.6566 (.0777)	.0048	.999	1.863	7.002

NOTE: Standard errors are in parentheses.
* Divisia: OC = Divisia user cost for M3; sum: OC = commercial paper rate.
† Box-Pierce χ^2 statistic for first 12 sample autocorrelations.

TABLE A5
Money Demand Estimates for Divisia and Sum L,
Double Logarithmic Specification

Aggregate and Period of Fit	Constant	Real GNP	OC^*	Lagged Dependent	ρ	SEE	R^2	D-W	Box-Pierce[†]
Divisia L:									
1959:3–1974:2	−1.152 (.519)	.1502 (.0502)	−.0100 (.0043)	.8229 (.0852)	.6820 (.0944)	.0046	.996	1.739	5.081
1974:3–1982:4	−.131 (.258)	−.0750 (.0417)	−.0187 (.0099)	.9426 (.0481)	.3756 (.1589)	.0079	.988	2.082	4.912
1959:3–1982:4	−.200 (.231)	.0501 (.0252)	−.0085 (.0045)	.9749 (.0386)	.6729 (.0764)	.0063	.993	2.059	5.013
Sum L:									
1959:3–1974:2	.156 (.338)	.0442 (.0519)	−.0184 (.0036)	1.0345 (.0490)	.4380 (.1160)	.0036	.999	1.968	6.789
1974:3–1982:4	−.463 (.210)	.1240 (.0363)	−.0065 (.0029)	.9450 (.0310)	−.3530 (.1605)	.0034	.997	1.888	11.676
1959:3–1982:4	−.456 (.191)	.1238 (.0321)	−.0110 (.0027)	.9442 (.0270)	.5607 (.0854)	.0037	.999	1.995	3.090

NOTE: Standard errors are in parentheses.
* Divisia: OC = Divisia user cost for L; sum: OC = commercial paper rate.
[†] Box-Pierce χ^2 statistic for first 12 sample autocorrelations.

Appendix B: Divisia Second Moments

Let K_{it} be the Divisia quantity growth rate variance for component group i, and let J_{it} be the Divisia user-cost price growth rate variance. Also let Γ_{it} be the Divisia price-quantity growth rate covariance, and let Ψ_{it} be the Divisia growth rate variance of the shares, $\bar{s}_{it}$, within group i. Theil (1967, p. 155) has shown that the Divisia second moments are related by the following equality:

$$K_{it} = \Psi_{it} - J_{it} - 2\Gamma_{it}. \tag{B.1}$$

Equation (B.1) permits us to decompose K_{it}, which is the Divisia second moment of primary interest in monetary policy.

If the aggregation conditions described in Section 3 are exactly satisfied, then the continuous-time Divisia index always exactly equals the economic aggregate, and then the aggregation error of the Divisia index, (1), is very small. However, if the aggregation conditions from Section 3 are only approximately satisfied, the aggregation error (difference from the exact economic aggregate) of the index (1) could be nonnegligible. The Divisia quantity growth rate variance, K_{it} (or the corresponding coefficient of variation), can be used as a measure of potential aggregation error. That interpretation of K_{it} can be seen from the fact that K_{it} measures the dispersion of growth rates between the components of the Divisia monetary quantity index. Clearly, if $K_{it} = 0$, then any index number or aggregator function that is linearly homogeneous in the components is as good as any other, since all aggregates grow at the common rate at which each component grows. As K_{it} increases, the quality of the index number formula becomes increasingly important and the risks of aggregation error and information loss increase.

The Divisia share growth rate variance, Ψ_{it}, is a measure of the change in the dispersion of the Divisia weights. We might expect that as interest rates increase, Ψ_{it} would rise, since relative prices (user costs) between rate-regulated and rate-unregulated monetary assets move away from 1.0. It might then further be thought that the Divisia quantity growth rate variance, K_{it}, would also increase with increasing interest rates, as a result of the increasing dispersion of its weights. However, (B.1) shows that this conclusion need not be true, since the increase in J_{it} resulting from the increasing dispersion of component user-cost growth rates could offset the increasing value of Ψ_{it}.

TABLE B1
Correlations of Divisia Second Moments with the Federal Funds Rate

Monetary Aggregate	Divisia Second Moment			
	K	Ψ	J	Γ
M2	.19	.61	.49	.10
M3	.13	.39	.47	.08
L	.10	.37	.36	.00

NOTE: Sample period, quarterly observations: 1969:1–1982:4.

To explore this possibility, we computed the Divisia second moments and their correlation with the interest rate on federal funds. We display the correlation coefficients between the Divisia second moments and the funds rate in Table B1. Neither K_{it} nor Γ_{it} correlates appreciably with the funds rate, but both Ψ_{it} and J_{it} do, with nearly equal correlation coefficients. Hence, as hypothesized in the previous paragraph, variations in Ψ_{it} and J_{it} over the business cycle tend to cancel each other out continuously, so that K_{it} remains largely independent of the business and interest rate cycles.

Hence our degree of confidence in the quality of the Divisia monetary quantity index, equation (1), should not be altered by variations in interest rates. Variations in the potential aggregation error, K_{it}, of the Divisia monetary aggregates bear little relationship to the business cycle. In addition, the correlation decreases as the level of aggregation increases.

Chapter 18

Consumer Theory and the Demand for Money

*William A. Barnett, Douglas Fisher, and Apostolos Serletis**

1 Introduction

The demand for money has been at the center of the macro-policy debate ever since Keynes's *General Theory* set down the initial version of what has become the standard macroeconomic version of the theory. Over the years it has become almost a dictum that a necessary condition for money to exert a predictable influence on the economy is a stable demand function for money, as often emphasized by Milton Friedman. While 'stability' hardly means 'simplicity,' it has also become believed, rather optimistically in our view, that this self-same demand function should be linear (or linear in the logs) and should have as arguments a *small* number of variables, themselves representing significant links to spending and economic activity in the other sectors of the economy. This complete argument appears in numerous places in the literature, from basic textbooks to research monographs (see, for example, the statement in John Judd and John Scadding (1982, p. 993)).

The theoretical literature on money demand does not contain the result that a linear function of a few key variables would be expected to serve as the demand for money. In particular, there exist a large number of potential alternatives to money, the prices of which might reasonably be expected to influence the decision to hold money. Furthermore, microeconomic theory rarely produces linear demand functions for rational economic agents. Even so, linear single-equation estimates of money demand with only a few variables continue to be produced, in spite of serious doubts in the literature about their predictive performance. Stephen Goldfeld (1976) brought wide attention to the poor predictive performance of the standard function. The result was a large literature that introduced new variables and/or transformations of the old; this largely inconclusive literature is surveyed in Judd and Scadding.[1]

---

*Originally published in the *Journal of Economic Literature* 30 (1992), 2086-2119.
[1] Separately, Thomas Cooley and Stephen LeRoy (1981) question the econometric methodology common in the literature. A key concern is whether classical statistical prop-

There is another problem with this literature, and this is that the studies of the demand for money — and the many studies of the influence of money on the economy — are based on official monetary aggregates (currently M1, M2, M3, and L) constructed by a method (simple-sum aggregation over arbitrary financial components) that does not take advantage of the results either of existing aggregation theory or of recent developments in the application of demand theory to the study of financial institutions. Part of the problem is certainly perceived in the literature: the possible influences of financial innovation and regulatory changes. How this is usually handled is that money is frequently redefined — in the sense of composing new arrangements of the component assets — in order to capture the appearance of changing characteristics of the representative monetary product. This largely unstructured approach appears not to have produced an agreed-upon monetary measure. Instead, what we have seen over time is a considerable array of what actually turn out to be temporary monetary aggregates whose existence creates both unnecessary baggage in empirical studies as well as obvious problems for monetary-policy decision makers.

More central to the objectives of this survey are problems arising from the simple-sum method of aggregation itself. There are conditions under which this approach is appropriate, as we will explain, but if the relative prices of the monetary components fluctuate over time, then neither this method nor the Hicksian approach to aggregation will produce theoretically satisfactory definitions of money. The problem is the incorrect accounting for substitution effects that these methods entail, and the result is a set of monetary aggregates that do not accurately measure the actual quantities of the monetary services that optimizing economic agents select (in the aggregate). To underscore this issue we note that the empirical work discussed and illustrated below suggests that actual fluctuations in the relative prices of the monetary products of the U.S. financial system definitely are sufficient to generate concern about the method of aggregation.

Until recently the existing attempts to structure the search for a stable money demand — and a satisfactory measure of moneyness — using traditional macroeconomic paradigms (e.g., Keynesian, monetarist) do not seem to have provided any very firm assistance for empirical purposes. In contrast, as this survey will make clear, there is in place a steadily growing literature that does offer a solution; this is the integrated literature on monetary aggregation and the demand-systems approach to money demand. What we propose to do here is to lay out the theory and main empirical results of this important 'microfoundations' approach to money demand. Microfoundations

---

erties can be attributed to estimators obtained by the "grid search" approach common to many of these studies.

approaches to macro topics usually imply either disaggregated general equilibrium modelling or the use of simple forms of aggregation over goods and over economic agents, but the literature we have in mind uses aggregation theory in a way that enables the researcher to test for the existence of both the postulated aggregate good and the aggregate economic agent while estimating the demand for (aggregate) financial services. Success here could well provide significant gains in both the study of monetary phenomena and in the application of monetary policy.

This new literature is actually an ongoing one that has only just begun to produce empirical results worthy of the effort required to understand it. The main research lies in two areas: the construction of *monetary aggregates* that conform to the specifications of demand theory and the estimation of systems of financial asset-demand equations in which the restrictions of demand theory are incorporated in such a manner as to assure consistency with the optimizing behavior of economic agents. Of course, there are useful paradigms in existence that employ a simultaneous-equations structure — notably the asset and transactions approaches to money demand — as typified by the mean-variance model of James Tobin (1958) or the transactions model as explained by Jürg Niehans (1978). But these approaches do not integrate the choice of monetary aggregate with the consumer choice problem and, depending on the version, often do not take full advantage of the simultaneous-equations structure inherent in the choice of a portfolio of monetary assets.[2]

We have four tasks before us. First, we discuss the problem of the definition (aggregation) of money; after a consideration of the theoretical problems, we will propose the use of the Divisia method of aggregation for the construction of monetary aggregates. Second, we show how a simultaneous-equations financial assets structure both fits neatly into the definitional approach we are recommending and also provides a structure that can be used to measure income and interest rate elasticities as well as the important elasticities of substitution among financial entities. An econometric digression here will emphasize the contribution that can be made by employing one of the flexible functional forms at the estimation stage. Third, in our discussion of the empirical literature, we will emphasize how the theory might be implemented (and briefly show some of the results); the purpose of this discussion will be to illustrate the theory rather than to survey what is a rapidly changing empirical record. Finally, we briefly discuss ongoing research and extensions of the literature. The work discussed here includes the use of formal methods of

---

[2]The two general approaches mentioned can be shown to be special cases of the approach we are surveying once risk is introduced into decisions; see James Poterba and Julio Rotemberg (1987); Barnett, Melvin Hinich, and Piyu Yue (1991a); Barnett and Apostolos Serletis (1990); and Barnett, Hinich, and Yue (2000).

aggregating over economic agents as well as the incorporation into the general framework of risk aversion and rational expectations (both for consumers and firms).

2 The Definition of Money

The natural place to begin is with the definition of money. Currently, the common practice among central banks is to construct monetary aggregates from a list of entities by adding together those that are considered to be the likely sources of monetary services. That is, commercial banks and other financial intermediaries provide demand deposits, certificates of deposit and the like, and it is from this list that the (usually simple-sum) monetary aggregates are composed. At the Federal Reserve, for example, there are currently 27 components in the entire collection of liquid financial assets — as shown in Table 1 — and, as also shown, the four popular aggregates of M1, M2, M3, and L are constructed directly from this list by means of a recursive form of accounting that starts with M1 (the inside block) and adds blocks of items to M1 until all 27 entities are included (in L, for 'liquid assets').

What is important about these components for what follows in this paper is that the quantities of each vary at different rates over time (and so do their 'prices').[3] To see the behavior of the quantities, consider the collection in Figure 1 of monthly Federal Reserve data.[4]

Here Figure 1a shows the behavior of the components of M1 in recent years, while Figures 1b and 1c show that behavior for the items added to M1 to construct M2. Not only are the fluctuations of the quantities different for different assets, especially since 1979, but also new assets appear in the list from time to time. These sorts of changes potentially complicate the calculation of a unique measure of moneyness, although broader measures might well perform better than narrower ones simply because the new assets, e.g., are likely to draw funds from other entities within the broader collection of potential substitutes.

As noted, the monetary aggregates currently in use by the Federal Reserve are simple-sum indices in which all monetary components are assigned a constant and equal (unitary) weight. This index is M in

---

[3] As we will describe below, from the point of view of this survey, the appropriate price for each entity in Table 1 is the *user cost* of the asset. These are based partly on the nominal interest rate just mentioned. Some of the more liquid items (such as currency) do not possess an "own" interest rate and so a zero rate is usually assumed. We illustrate the behavior of user costs in Figure 3, below.

[4] These numbers were supplied by the Federal Reserve and are available from the authors.

TABLE 1
Official Monetary Aggregates/Components
U.S. Federal Reserve

L
- **M3**
  - **M2**
    - **M1**
      - Currency and travelers' checks
      - Demand deposits held by consumers
      - Demand deposits held by businesses
      - Other checkable deposits
      - Super NOW accounts held at commercial banks
      - Super NOW accounts held at thrifts
    - Overnight RPs
    - Overnight Eurodollars
    - Money market mutual fund shares
    - Money market deposit accounts at commercial banks
    - Money market deposit accounts at thrifts
    - Savings deposits at commercial banks
    - Savings deposits at savings and loans (S&Ls)
    - Savings deposits at mutual savings banks (MSBs)
    - Savings deposits at credit unions
    - Small time deposits and retail RPs at commercial banks
    - Small time deposits at S&Ls and MSBs and retail RPs at thrifts
    - Small time deposits at credit unions
  - Large time deposits at commercial banks
  - Large time deposits at thrifts
  - Institutional money market funds
  - Term RPs at commercial banks and thrifts
  - Term Eurodollars
- Savings bonds
- Short-term Treasury securities
- Bankers' acceptances
- Commercial paper

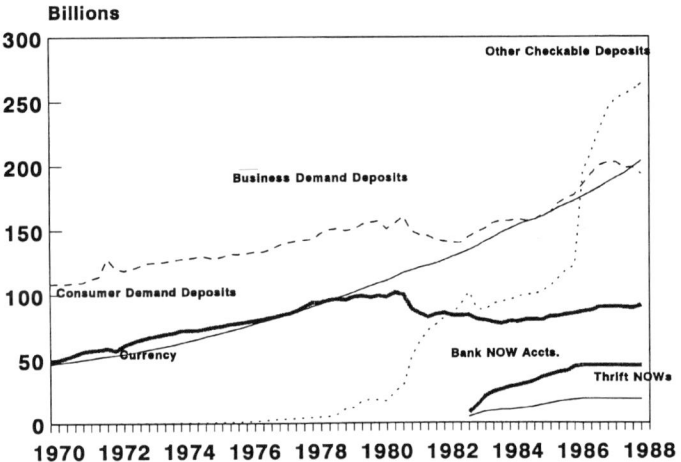

Figure 1a: Components of M1 in the United States.

$$M = \sum_{i=1}^{n} x_i, \tag{1}$$

where x_i is the ith monetary component of, say, the subaggregate M1; it clearly implies that all monetary components are weighted linearly and equally in the final total. This sort of index has some use as an accounting measure of the stock of nominal monetary wealth, of course, and this is an important advantage. More tellingly, this form of aggregation implies that all components are dollar-for-dollar perfect substitutes, since all indifference curves and isoquants over those components must be linear with slopes of minus 1.0 if this aggregate is to represent the monetary service flow selected by the economic agents. This is the source of its potential weakness.

The main problem with the simple-sum index arises from the fact that in aggregation theory a quantity index should measure the income effects (i.e., welfare or service flow changes) of a relative price change but should be unresponsive to pure substitution effects (at constant utility), which the index should internalize. The simple-sum index cannot untangle income from substitution effects if its components are not perfect substitutes.[5] In the face

---

[5]What is required for a consistent aggregation is an *aggregator function*, which the simple sum is. The problem is that the natural choice for an aggregator function is a utility or production function; only if the components are perfect substitutes is the simple-sum the appropriate utility or production function.

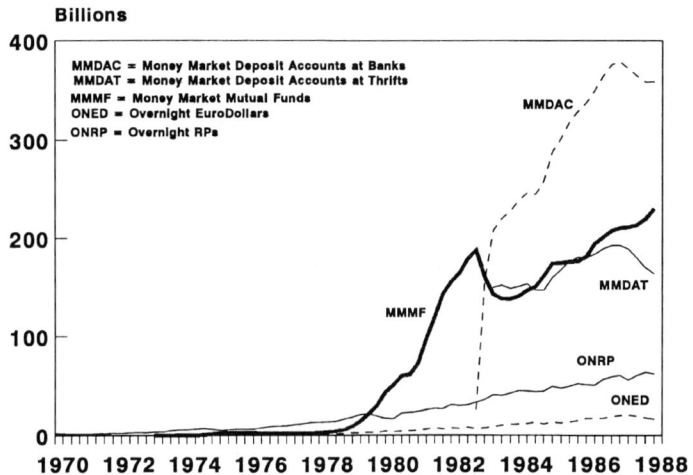

Figure 1b: Liquid instruments in the United States.

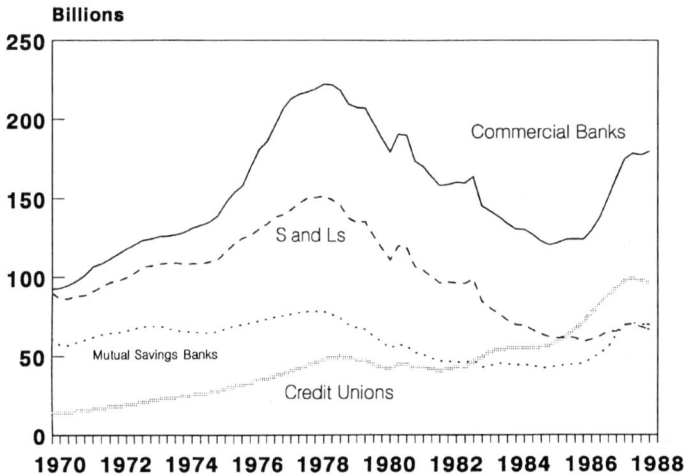

Figure 1c: Savings deposits in the United States.

of what appear to be significant changes in the relative prices of financial assets and with increasing numbers of apparently imperfect substitutes among the relevant short-term financial assets, it is not surprising that attempts are now common to arrive at a definitional procedure that will accommodate this volatility. Milton Friedman and Anna Schwartz, in their monumental survey of the literature on the definition of money, when discussing the simple-sum approach, discuss the basic issue in the following terms:

> "This (summation) procedure is a very special case of the more general approach. In brief, the general approach consists of regarding each asset as a joint product having different degrees of 'moneyness,' and defining the quantity of money as the weighted sum of the aggregate value of all assets, the weights for individual assets varying from zero to unity with a weight of unity assigned to that asset or assets regarded as having the largest quantity of 'moneyness' per dollar of aggregate value. The procedure we have followed implies that all weights are either zero or unity. The more general approach has been suggested frequently but experimented with only occasionally. We conjecture that this approach deserves and will get much more attention than it has so far received." (Friedman and Schwartz 1970, pp. 151-152)

Their observation is deficient only in failing to point out that even weighted aggregation implies perfect (but not dollar-for-dollar) substitutability unless the aggregation procedure is nonlinear.[6]

Over the years, there have been a series of attempts to achieve a rule for aggregating monetary components without abandoning the simple-sum structure. There is, indeed, a theory that might seem to back this up: that of Hicksian aggregation (John Hicks 1946; Don Patinkin 1965). The main difficulty is that for Hicksian aggregation to be possible it is required that the relative prices (user costs) of the financial commodities not change over the sample period. Even if that assumption were true, Hicksian aggregation alone is not sufficient for simple-sum aggregation; it also is necessary that the constant user cost between any two assets be equal to 1.0. Once again, this condition can be expected to hold only if the component assets are indistinguishable perfect substitutes; this is unlikely if only because all financial assets one can think of provide different services and hence have different 'own rates' of return — and these change over time. The user costs depend upon those yields.

---

[6]For example, introduction of estimated multiplicative coefficients into Equation (1) would retain the linearity of the aggregation and hence the implication of perfect substitutability.

An attractive alternative to the simple-sum approach is to use microeconomic aggregation theory to define money. This theory has two branches, one leading to the construction of index numbers using methods derived from economic theory and one leading to the construction of money-demand functions in the context of a system of equations modelling the wealthholder's allocation of funds among money and non-money assets. The two branches are supported by the same structure, in that the supporting theory in both cases is that of the constrained maximization of the aggregate consumer's intertemporal utility function. The following section, in spelling out the theory, emphasizes this theoretical coherence.

3   The Microeconomic Theory of a Monetary Economy

Consider an economy with identical individuals, having three types of goods: consumption goods, leisure, and the services of monetary assets. Assuming that the services of these three entities enter as arguments in the individual's utility function, the utility function can be written as[7]

$$u = U(\mathbf{c}, L, \mathbf{x}) \qquad (2)$$

where **c** is a vector of the services of consumption goods, L is leisure time, and **x** is a vector of the services of monetary assets. For money, the services could be convenience, liquidity, and information (as in Karl Brunner and Allan Meltzer 1971).

---

[7] Putting money into the utility function, for some utility functions, is observationally equivalent to putting money (solely) into the constraints. This result is established by Robert Feenstra (1986), whose demonstration applies for a broad class of utility functions and a broad class of transactions cost models (including the inventory-theoretic model and the Robert Clower (1967) cash-in-advance constraint formulation). Much of this is also discussed in Patinkin (1965). Feenstra notes

> "We demonstrate a functional equivalent between using real balances as an argument of the utility function and entering money into liquidity costs which appear in the budget constraints." (p. 271)

This should dispose of the issue for purposes of this survey, since the utility-maximizing models discussed here are of the very general sort that Feenstra discusses. In a general equilibrium context, the same result also has been proved by Kenneth Arrow and Frank Hahn (1971); a parallel proof in a production context is due to Stanley Fischer (1974). See also Louis Philips and Frank Spinnewyn (1982) and Poterba and Rotemberg (1987). Once money has been put into the utility function, the inverse mapping to the motivating transactions constraint is not unique, so that the reason for holding money is lost. But we do not seek to explain the reason for holding money. We simply observe that money does have a positive value in equilibrium so that we can appeal to the Arrow and Hahn proof.

The utility function in Equation (2) can be assumed to be maximized subject to the full income constraint

$$\mathbf{q}'\mathbf{c} + \boldsymbol{\pi}'\mathbf{x} + wL = y \qquad (3)$$

where y is full income (i.e., income reflecting expenditures on time as well as on goods and services); $\mathbf{q}$ is a vector of the prices of $\mathbf{c}$; $\boldsymbol{\pi}$ is a vector of monetary asset *user costs* (or rental prices); and w is the shadow price of leisure (see Barnett 1981b). The ith component of $\boldsymbol{\pi}$ is given by (see Barnett 1978 and Donal Donovan 1978),

$$\pi_i = p^* \left(\frac{R - r_i}{1 + R} \right) \qquad (4)$$

This formula measures the opportunity cost — at the margin — of the monetary services provided by asset i. It is calculated as the discounted value of the interest foregone by holding a dollar's worth of that asset. Here r_i is the expected nominal holding-period yield on the ith asset, R is the maximum expected holding-period yield available on an alternative asset (the 'benchmark' asset) and p^* is the true cost-of-living index.[8] Note, especially, that this formula is not arbitrary but can be derived from an intertemporal optimization problem of a standard sort (see Barnett 1981b).[9]

In order to focus on the details of the demand for monetary services, a good starting point is the theory of two-stage optimization investigated initially in the context of consumer theory by Robert Strotz (1957, 1959) and

---

[8] The benchmark asset is specifically assumed to provide no liquidity or other monetary services and is held solely to transfer wealth intertemporally. In theory, R is the maximum expected holding period yield in the economy. It is usually defined in practice in such a way that the user costs for the monetary assets are positive. The true cost of living index, p^*, is defined for the consumer goods, $\mathbf{c}$; we use the term "true" merely to warn the reader that this is an *exact* price index, as this concept is described below. Note that if p^* is deleted from the user cost formula, the formula produces real rather than nominal user cost. The interest rates are nominal so that inflationary expectations appear here (in the denominator, since the effects in the two rates in the numerator of the formula may well cancel out).

[9] For example, suppose that the representative consumer (under continuous replanning) maximizes utility over three periods $(1, 2, 3)$, subject to a budget constraint. For simplicity, we can fix the time path of leisure and consider only one monetary asset and one consumption good. The one-period budget constraint for period 2 is

$$p_2^* c_2 = (1 + r_1) p_1^* x_1 - p_2^* x_2 + [(1 + R_1) A_1 - A_2]$$

where A denotes per capita holdings of an alternative asset (say, a bond), while R is the expected nominal yield on A and r is that on x. The other variables are defined the same way as in the text, above.

Solve the period 2 budget constraint for A_2 and write the resulting equation for each of the three periods. Then by back substituting for A, starting from A_3 and working down to A_1, we obtain (after some manipulation) the consumer's budget constraint in present value form:

William Gorman (1959). The theory describes a sequential expenditure allocation in which in the first stage (that of budgeting or 'price aggregation') the consumer allocates his expenditure *among* broad categories (consumption goods, leisure, and monetary services in the context of the model used here) and then in the second stage (that of 'decentralization') allocates expenditures *within* each category. In the first stage his decision is guided by price indices among the three categories, while in the monetary part of the decentralized decision, he responds to changes in the relative prices of the monetary assets (π_i/π_j as defined above).

Decomposition of the consumer choice problem along these lines is possible only if the individual's utility function (2) is *weakly separable* in the services of monetary assets. That is, it must be possible to write the utility function as

$$u = U[\mathbf{c}, L, f(\mathbf{x})] \tag{5}$$

in which f defines the monetary subutility function. As laid out originally by Masaza Sono (1961) and Wassily Leontief (1947a), the condition of weak separability described in (5) is equivalent to

$$\frac{\partial}{\partial \phi}\left(\frac{\partial U/\partial x_i}{\partial U/\partial x_j}\right) = 0 \tag{6}$$

for $i \neq j$, where ϕ is any component of $\{\mathbf{c}, L\}$. This condition asserts that under weak separability the marginal rate of substitution between any two monetary assets is independent of the values of $\mathbf{c}$ and L.[10]

If we have established a separable subset of assets, whether by separability test or by assumption, we then can continue in the framework of the following neoclassical consumer problem,

$$\text{Max } f(\mathbf{x}) \quad \text{subject to } \boldsymbol{\pi}'\mathbf{x} = m \tag{7}$$

where m is the total expenditures on monetary services, a total that is determined in the first stage of the two-level optimizing problem. It is this simple structure that we will need to recall in the work in the following sections.

$$(1+R_0)A_0 + (1+r_0)p_0^* m_0 = \frac{A_3}{\rho_3} + \sum_{s=1}^{3} \frac{p_s^*}{\rho_s} c_s$$
$$+ \sum_{s=1}^{3} \left[\frac{p_s^*}{\rho_s} - p_s^* \frac{(1+r_s)}{\rho_{s+1}}\right] x_s + \frac{p_3^*(1+r_3)}{\rho_4} x_3$$

where the discount factor, ρ_s, equals 1 for $s = 1$, $(1 + R_1)$ for $s = 2$, etc. .... In the equation just given, the term in the bracket is the user cost of x. Writing the user cost for $s = 1$ (the current period), we obtain Equation (4).

[10] Note that the separability structure is asymmetric. That is, $\mathbf{c}$ is not separable from $\mathbf{x}$ and L in U unless there exists a function $g(\mathbf{c})$ such that $u = U(\mathbf{c}, L, \mathbf{x}) = U[g(\mathbf{c}), L, f(\mathbf{x})]$. For an extensive discussion of separability, see Charles Blackorby, Daniel Primont, and Robert Russell (1978).

Whether or not the utility function (2) is weakly separable in monetary services is, ultimately, an empirical question. Ideally, instead of treating Equation (5) as a maintained (and therefore untested) hypothesis as so much of the money-demand literature implicitly does, one could test whether the utility function (2) is appropriately separable in monetary services — the assumption implicit in the traditional 'money-nonmoney' dichotomization. The existing methods of conducting such tests are not, however, very effective tools of analysis, as discussed below.

3.1 The Aggregation-Theoretic Approach to Money Demand

In the preceding discussion we have shown the steps that are normally taken to reduce a very general consumer choice problem to an asset choice problem. At this point, we are prepared to proceed to results in the 'aggregation-theoretic' literature on money demand. This literature ties up the theory just sketched with that on the macroeconomic demand for money in an obvious and logical way. What we are after here are monetary aggregates that are consistent with the optimizing behavior of rational economic agents.

We begin with the *aggregator function*. In the aggregation-theoretic literature for the consumer choice problem, the quantity aggregator function has been shown to be the subutility function defined solely over the individual monetary components (as listed in Table 1). This function, for the monetary services problem defined in Equation (7), is $f(\mathbf{x})$.[11] Using a specific and differentiable form for the monetary services aggregator function $f(\mathbf{x})$, and solving decision (7), we can derive the inverse and/or the direct demand-function system. Using these derived solution functions and specific monetary data, we then could estimate the parameters and replace the unknown parameters of $f(\mathbf{x})$ by their estimates. The resulting estimated function is called an *economic* (or functional) monetary *index*, and its calculated value at any point is an economic monetary-quantity index number.

We have noted that the researcher would choose a specific and differentiable functional form if he were to follow this approach. The problem is that the use of a specific function necessarily implies a set of implicit assumptions about the underlying preference structure of the economic agent. For example, as we have already emphasized, the use of a weighted-linear function for $f(\mathbf{x})$ implies perfect substitutability among the monetary assets. If the

---

[11]The argument just given requires that $f(\cdot)$ be homothetic. In the nonhomothetic utility case, the aggregator function is the distance function (see Barnett 1987). However, since the resulting index is the same in either case, the conclusions of this section are unaffected by this assumption. This topic is considered further, below.

weights are all unity so that we get the widely used simple-summation functions, the consumer will specialize in the consumption of the highest yielding asset. The use of the more general Cobb-Douglas function imposes an elasticity of substitution equal to unity between every pair of assets. To continue, the constant elasticity of substitution function, although relaxing the unitary elasticity of substitution restriction imposed by the Cobb-Douglas, nevertheless imposes the restriction that the elasticity of substitution is the same between any pair of assets. The list of specific functional forms is, of course, boundless, but the defining property of the more popular of these entities is that they imply strong limitations on the behavior of the consumer. While the issue of their usefulness is ultimately an empirical question — and we shall treat the issue that way below — we feel that most members of this class of functions should be rejected for estimation of money demand, partly in view of the restrictive nature of their implicit assumptions, and partly because of the existence of attractive alternatives.

Among the alternatives is a member of the class of quadratic utility functions. With a member of the quadratic class, we would be using a *flexible functional form* to approximate the unknown monetary-services aggregator function. Flexible functional forms — such as the translog — can locally approximate to the second order any unknown functional form for the monetary services aggregator function, and even higher quality approximations are available.[12] We will consider the details of this method below.

If one is to do away with the simple-sum method of aggregating money and replace it with a nonlinear aggregator function as suggested, one will be able to deal with less than perfect substitutability and, for that matter, with variations over time in the elasticities of substitution among the components of the monetary aggregates. There is a problem, however, and this is that the functions must be estimated over specific data sets (and re-estimated periodically) with the attendant result that the index becomes dependent upon the specification. This dependence is particularly troublesome to government agencies that have to justify their procedures to persons untrained in econometrics. This is a reasonable concern — and it is exacerbated by the fact that there are many possible nonlinear models from which to choose. Under these circumstances, government agencies around the world have taken a more direct approach and use index number formulas from statistical index number theory for most of their calculations. We will explain how this approach can be implemented in a way that simultaneously deals with the theoretical and the practical issues. We will not, however, be able to explain

---

[12] Such as the Minflex Laurent (see Barnett 1983a, 1985; Barnett and Yul Lee 1985), the Fourier (see Ronald Gallant 1981), and the Asymptotically Ideal Models (see Barnett and Andrew Jonas 1983; Barnett and Yue 1988; Yue 1991; and Barnett, John Geweke, and Michael Wolfe 1991a).

why there is not more use of the approach by the monetary authorities of these same governments.

3.2 Index Number Theory and Monetary Aggregation

Statistical index-number theory provides a variety of quantity and price indices that treat prices and quantities as jointly independent variables. Indeed, whether they are price or quantity indices, they are widely used, since they can be computed from price and quantity data alone, thus eliminating the need to estimate an underlying structure. In fact, since the appearance of Irving Fisher's (1922) early and now classic study on statistical index number theory, nearly all national government data series have been based upon aggregation formulas from that literature. Well-known examples are the Consumer Price Index (a Laspeyres price index), the Implicit GNP Deflator (a Paasche price index), and real GNP (a Laspeyres quantity index). The simple-sum index often used for monetary quantities is a member of the broad class. But the simple sum is a degenerative measure, since it contains no prices.

Statistical indices are distinguished by their known statistical properties. These properties are described in detail by Irving Fisher (1922), and in that work he provides a set of tests (known as Fisher's System of Tests) useful for assessing the quality of a particular statistical index.[13] The index that he believes often to be the best in the sense of possessing the largest number of satisfactory statistical properties, has now become known as the Fisher Ideal Index. Another index found to possess a very large number of these properties is the Törnqvist discrete-time approximation to the Divisia Index.[14] We note that Fisher found the simple-sum index and to be the worst of the literally hundreds of possible indices that he studied.

Let x_{it} be the quantity of the ith asset during period t, and let π_{it} be the rental price (that is, user cost) for that good during period t. Then, the *Fisher ideal index* (Q_t^F) during period t is the geometric average of the Laspeyres and Paasche indices:

$$\frac{Q_t^F}{Q_{t-1}^F} = \left[\frac{\sum_{i=1}^n s_{i,t-1}\left(\frac{x_{it}}{x_{i,t-1}}\right)}{\sum_{i=1}^n s_{it}\left(\frac{x_{i,t-1}}{x_{it}}\right)}\right]^{1/2} \tag{8}$$

---

[13] Fisher's tests for statistical indices are proportionality, circularity, determinateness, commensurability, and factor reversal. For recent discussions, see Eichhorn (1976, 1978), Diewert (1992), and Balk (1995).

[14] The Divisia index was originated by the French economist Francois Divisia (1925).

where
$$s_{it} = \frac{\pi_{it} x_{it}}{\sum_{k=1}^{n} \pi_{kt} x_{kt}}.$$

On the other hand, the discrete time (Törnqvist) *Divisia index* during period t is Q_t^D, where

$$\frac{Q_t^D}{Q_{t-1}^D} = \prod_{i=1}^{n} \left(\frac{x_{it}}{x_{i,t-1}}\right)^{(1/2)(s_{it}+s_{i,t-1})} \qquad (9)$$

It is informative to take the logarithms of each side of (9), so that

$$\log Q_t^D - \log Q_{t-1}^D = \sum_{i=1}^{n} s_{it}^* (\log x_{it} - \log x_{i,t-1}) \qquad (10)$$

where $s_{it}^* = (1/2)(s_{it} + s_{i,t-1})$. In this form, it is easy to see that for the Divisia index the growth rate (log change) of the aggregate is the share-weighted average of the growth rates of the component quantities.

A characteristic of the Fisher Ideal Index is that the Fisher Index is 'self dual.' In such a case, if the quantity index is the Fisher *quantity* index, then the implied price index — defined by dividing total expenditure on the components by the quantity index — is the Fisher *price* index. Hence, the Fisher price and quantity indices comprise a dual pair in the sense that their product equals total expenditure on their components; this is known as Fisher's *factor reversal test*. In contrast, the price index that is dual to the Divisia quantity index is actually not a Divisia price index. Nevertheless, even if the Divisia price index were used to measure the price of the Divisia quantity index, the size of the error produced as a result of the violation of the factor reversal test would be very small (third order in the changes). Indeed, the failure to be self-dual is common among the most popular index numbers.[15] In view of the fact that the Divisia quantity index has the very considerable advantage of possessing an easily interpreted functional form, as in Equation (10), it is now often employed in the emerging literature on monetary aggregation. It has another desirable property, as we shall see in a moment.

3.3 The Links Between Aggregation Theory, Index Number Theory, and Monetary Theory

Until relatively recently, the fields of aggregation theory and statistical index number theory developed independently. Erwin Diewert (1976, 1978),

---

[15] For example, neither the Paasche nor the Laspeyres index is self-dual, although the Paasche and the Laspeyres are a dual pair. Hence it is common to use Laspeyres (not Paasche) quantity indexes with Paasche (not Laspeyres) price indexes.

however, provided the link between aggregation theory and statistical index number theory by attaching economic properties to statistical indices. These properties are defined in terms of the statistical indices' effectiveness in tracking a particular functional form for the unknown aggregator function. Recall in thinking about this that the utility function is itself the appropriate aggregator function. What Diewert shows is that using a number of well-known statistical indices is equivalent to using a particular functional form to describe the unknown economic aggregator function. Such statistical indices are termed *exact* in this literature. Exactness, briefly, occurs when the specific aggregator function (e.g., the linear-homogeneous translog) is exactly tracked by a particular statistical index (e.g., the discrete-time Divisia); the parentheses illustrate one such case.[16]

Having the property of exactness for *some* aggregator function, however, is not sufficient for acceptability of a particular statistical index when the true functional form for the aggregator function is not known, *a priori*. What can be done in these circumstances is to choose a statistical index that is exact for a *flexible* functional form — a functional form that can provide a second-order approximation to any arbitrary unknown aggregator function. Taking this approach cuts through the problem of not knowing the underlying structure. Diewert terms such a statistical index *superlative*. As it turns out, the Divisia Index is exact for the linearly homogeneous (*and flexible*) translog and is, therefore, superlative; that is, it approximates an arbitrary unknown exact aggregator function up to a third-order remainder term.[17] What one gains from this is the ability to do precise work even when the form of the underlying function is not known.

With Diewert's successful merging of index number theory and economic aggregation theory and the rigorous derivation of the appropriate price of monetary services in the form of the user cost of these services (Donovan 1978; Barnett 1978), the loose link between monetary theory and economic aggregation theory has been turned into a firm one and the scene has been set for the construction of theoretically inspired monetary aggregates. In our discussion, we have pointed out that either the Divisia Index or the Fisher-Ideal Index of monetary services would be superlative. Actually, it has been demonstrated (Barnett 1980a) that the difference between the two is typically less than the roundoff error in the monetary data. The Federal Reserve, indeed, has employed both procedures as alternatives to the much more widely-known simple-sum aggregates.[18]

---

[16] Diewert also shows that the Fisher-Ideal Index is exact for the square root of a homogeneous quadratic function.

[17] In fact, even if the aggregator is not homogenous, the Divisia Index remains exact — but for the distance function, which is the economic aggregator function in that case.

[18] However, the Federal Reserve does not publish these numbers.

There is one other aggregate in at least limited use in the monetary literature, and that is MQ, the monetary quantities index. In the particular form computed by Paul Spindt (1985a), MQ is measured as in Equation (8), but with the user costs replaced by monetary-asset turnover rates. The problem with this procedure is that the MQ index, unlike the Divisia, is inconsistent both with existing aggregation and index number theories. The relevant foundations (both index-number theoretic and aggregation theoretic) for the Fisher-Ideal Index *require* the use of prices and quantities and not turnover rates and quantities.[19] An attempt to define money in yet another way is due to Don Roper and Stephen Turnovsky (1980). In their paper the object is to determine the optimal monetary aggregate for stabilization policy assuming a one-goal objective function — which is the minimization of the variance of income. This, too, is an atheoretical approach from the point of view of this survey. It has the added difficulty that there are significant theoretical and empirical problems associated with expanding the objective function to incorporate multiple goals (and with dealing with a large number of monetary assets and other policy tools).

There has recently been some interest in measuring wealth effects produced from changes in expected monetary service flows. The formula for the monetary capital stock was derived by Barnett (1991, eq. 2.2), who proved that it equals the discounted present value of the expected future Divisia monetary service flow. Under the assumption of stationary expectations, this expected discounted present value simplifies to an index called the CE index (see Barnett 1991, theorem 1).[20] Rotemberg (1991) and Rotemberg, Driscoll, and Poterba (1995) present some interesting empirical results with the CE index. While the implicit stationary expectations assumption is troubling, the CE index, unlike the MQ and the Roper-Turnovsky indexes, is not atheoretical. We anticipate that future applications of Barnett's capital stock formula, with less restrictive assumptions on expectations than used in generating the CE special case, will produce further advances in measuring monetary wealth effects.

At this point we might pause to consider the composition of these new indices and what their recent behavior has been. The indices are constructed from the same components as the traditional measures (e.g., Divisia M1 is constructed from the components list used for M1, as described in Table

---

[19] For a proof, see Barnett (1987, 1990). If nothing else, MQ can be said to be no less arbitrary than the official simple-sum aggregates. But the number of such atheoretical aggregates is infinite, as is the number of possible nonlinear functions of quantities and turnover rates.

[20] There is also a considerably less attractive interpretation of the CE index as a flow index. See Barnett (1995, section 5) regarding the flow interpretation, which requires stronger assumptions than those needed to derive the Divisia flow index. Barnett (1995) is reprinted in this book as chapter 10.

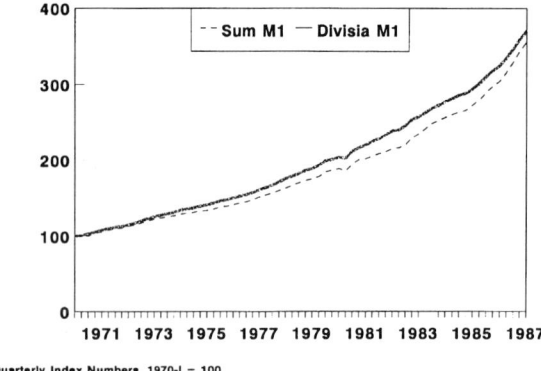

Figure 2a: Sum M1 versus Divisia M1 in the United States.

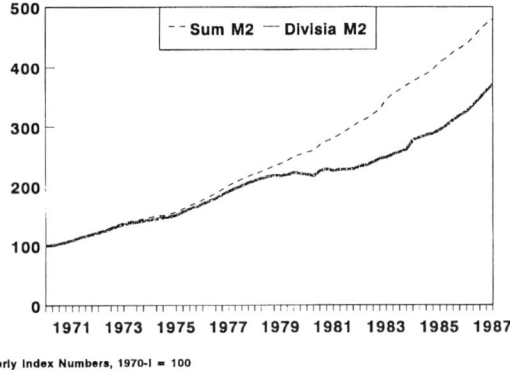

Figure 2b: Sum M2 versus Divisia M2 in the United States.

1); they employ user costs, as defined above, in their calculations. As the graphs in Figure 2 indicate, these numbers differ, sometimes considerably, from the summation indices. This difference is especially large for the broader measures and for the years since 1978.

The simple correlations that go with these figures are

	Level	Differenced
Sum/Divisia M1	.998	.964
Sum/Divisia M2	.986	.542
Sum/Divisia M3	.982	.407
Sum/Divisia L	.985	.487

Microeconomics of a Monetary Economy

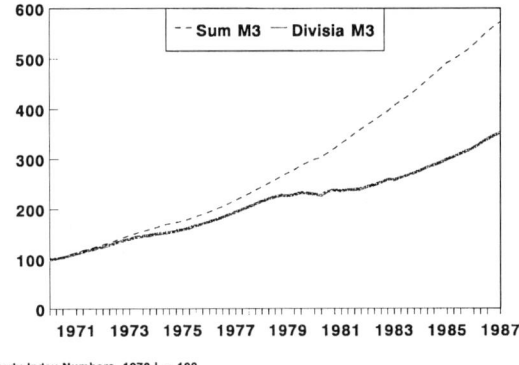

Figure 2c: Sum M3 versus Divisia M3 in the United States.

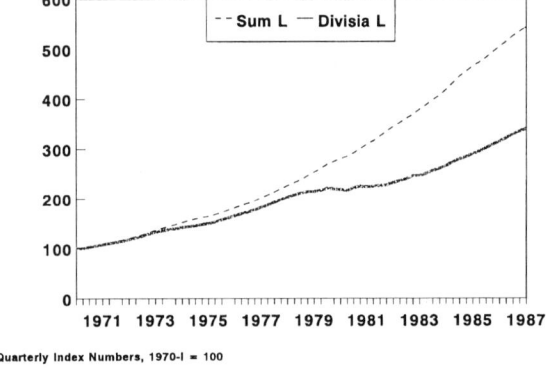

Figure 2d: Sum L versus Divisia L in the United States.

While these correlations are quite high in the trend-dominated level figures, when differenced, the broader series show considerably smaller correlations. Because it is in differenced form that the monetary data are usually studied, there is sufficient reason in these figures to dig further into their relative performances. Note also that the user costs (of the components of these aggregates) are often not highly correlated (see Figure 3 below).

3.4 Understanding the New Divisia Monetary Aggregates

To understand the new Divisia aggregates, we must consider the underlying microeconomic theory behind the Divisia Index. Let us return to the consumer's utility function over monetary assets as defined above (this was $f(\mathbf{x})$). Writing out the total differential of $f(\mathbf{x})$, we obtain

$$df(\mathbf{x}) = \sum_{i=1}^{n} \left(\frac{\partial f}{\partial x_i}\right) dx_i \qquad (11)$$

where the partial derivatives are marginal utilities (which are functions themselves containing the unknown parameters of the function $f(\mathbf{x})$). From the first-order conditions for the expenditure-constrained maximization of $f(\mathbf{x})$, we can write the marginal utilities as

$$\lambda \pi_i = \frac{\partial f}{\partial x_i} \qquad i = 1, \ldots, n \qquad (12)$$

Here λ is the Lagrange multiplier, and π_i is the user-cost (i.e., the rental price) of asset i. This expression can then be substituted into Equation (11) to yield

$$df(\mathbf{x}) = \sum_{i=1}^{n} \lambda \pi_i \, dx_i \qquad (13)$$

which is written not in unknown marginal utilities but in the unknown Lagrange multiplier, user costs, and changes in quantities.

In Equation (13) the Lagrange multiplier is itself a function of unknown tastes and thereby a function of the parameters of the unknown utility function. Hence, we have one more step to go; we must eliminate the Lagrange multiplier. This involves the assumption that the economic quantity aggregate, $f(\mathbf{x})$, is linearly homogeneous in its components. This is, indeed, a reasonable assertion, since it would be very curious indeed if linear homogeneity of $f(\mathbf{x})$ failed. It is reasonable because if it does not hold, the growth rate of the aggregate differs from the growth rates of its components, even if all components are growing at the same rate.[21]

Let us now define $P(\boldsymbol{\pi})$ to be the dual price index satisfying Fisher's factor-reversal test as this was described above.

$$P(\boldsymbol{\pi})f(\mathbf{x}) = \sum_{i=1}^{n} \pi_i x_i \quad [= m]. \qquad (14)$$

---

[21] In fact, the linear homogeneity assumption not only is necessary, but also is harmless. In the general case of nonhomothetic tastes and technology, the aggregator function is the distance function — which *always* is linearly homogeneous.

It can then be shown that[22] $\lambda = 1/P(\pi)$, in which case Equation (13) can be written as

$$df(\mathbf{x}) = \sum_{i=1}^{n} \frac{1}{P(\pi)} \pi_i \, dx_i. \qquad (15)$$

Manipulating Equation (15) algebraically to convert to growth rate (log change) form, we find that

$$d \log f(\mathbf{x}) = \sum_{i=1}^{n} s_i \, d \log x_i \qquad (16)$$

where

$$s_i = \frac{\pi_i x_i}{\sum_{k=1}^{n} \pi_k x_k}$$

is the ith asset's value share in the total expenditures on monetary services. The result is the Divisia index, as defined in Equation (10), where the log change in the utility level (and therefore in the level of the aggregate) is the weighted average of the log changes of the component levels, with expenditure shares providing the weights. This exercise demonstrates the solid microfoundations of the Divisia index. It is, indeed, the logical choice for an index from a theoretical point of view, being exactly the transformed first-order conditions for constrained optimization. In addition, the derivation just completed demonstrates that the prices appearing in index numbers cannot be replaced by any other variables, such as turnover rates, bid-ask spreads, brokerage fees, etc. To do so would be to violate the first-order conditions, (12). In particular, for the case of monetary assets, it is user costs that preserve (12) and therefore permit (13).

3.5 The Optimal Level of Monetary Subaggregation

Even if the utility function, $U(\cdot)$, is weakly separable in its monetary assets group, there remains the problem of selecting monetary asset subgroups for inclusion in monetary *subaggregates*. In particular, the use of any monetary sub-aggregate (such as M1, M2, M3, or L) implies that the components of

---

[22] Let $\mathbf{x} = D(m, \pi)$ to be the solution to the maximization of $f(\mathbf{x})$ subject to $\pi'\mathbf{x} = m$. The linear homogeneity of $f(\mathbf{x})$ implies that there must exist a vector of functions $\mathbf{h}(\pi)$ such that $\mathbf{x} = m\mathbf{h}(\pi)$. Substituting for $\mathbf{x}$ into $f(\mathbf{x})$, we find that

$$f(\mathbf{x}) = f[m\mathbf{h}(\pi)] = mf[\mathbf{h}(\pi)].$$

As $\lambda = \partial f/\partial m$, we have from the last equation that $\lambda = f[\mathbf{h}(\pi)]$. In addition, from Equation (14), $P(\pi)f(\mathbf{x}) = m$. Hence from $f(\mathbf{x}) = mf[\mathbf{h}(\pi)]$ we have that $f[\mathbf{h}(\pi)] = 1/P(\pi)$. Hence, $\lambda = 1/P(\pi)$.

the subaggregate are themselves weakly separable within **x**. This additional nested separability condition is required, regardless of the type of index used *within* the subaggregate. Weak separability over the component assets is both necessary and sufficient for the existence of stable preferences (or technology) over those components of the subaggregate. This implies that without separability such a subaggregate has no meaning in theory, since the subaggregate fails the existence condition.

Even so, weak separability establishes only a necessary condition for subaggregation in its simplest form. In particular, if we wish to measure the subaggregate using the most elementary method, we would require the additional assumption that the separable subfunction within f be homothetic. Then f is said to be homothetically weakly separable. Indeed, homothetic weak separability is necessary and sufficient for the simplified form of subaggregation.[23]

For illustration, let us describe the Federal Reserve Board's *a priori* assignment of assets to monetary subaggregates. As illustrated in Table 1, their method is based on the implicit assumption that the monetary services aggregator function, $f(\mathbf{x})$, has the recursive weakly separable form of

$$f(\mathbf{x}) = f_4(\mathbf{x}^4, f_3(\mathbf{x}^3, f_2(\mathbf{x}^2, f_1(\mathbf{x}^1)))). \qquad (17)$$

This clearly implies that the marginal rate of substitution between, say, an asset in $\mathbf{x}^1$ and an asset in $\mathbf{x}^2$ is independent of the values of assets in $\mathbf{x}^3$ and $\mathbf{x}^4$.

In Equation (17), the components of $\mathbf{x}^1$ are those included in the Federal Reserve Board's M1 monetary aggregate, the components of $\{\mathbf{x}^1, \mathbf{x}^2\}$ are those of the M2 aggregate, the components of $\{\mathbf{x}^1, \mathbf{x}^2, \mathbf{x}^3\}$ are those of the M3 aggregate, and the components of $\mathbf{x}$ are those of the L aggregate. The aggregator functions f_i, for $i = 1, \ldots, 4$, would rationalize the Federal Reserve's component groupings, M1, M2, M3, and L. Of course, the actual numbers produced for the official monetary aggregates further require the assumptions that f_1, f_2, f_3, f_4 (and hence f itself) are all simple summations.

4 Econometric Considerations

In recent years there have been a number of related developments that have increased the usefulness of the 'demand systems' modeling approach for monetary studies. The following discussion attempts to clarify just what these

---

[23] In its most general form, however, aggregation is possible without homotheticity but with only the minimal existence condition of weak separability. That generalization uses the distance function for the aggregator function and produces the Malmquist index (see Barnett 1987); see below for more on the distance function. Hence we currently are presenting a special case, to which the Malmquist index reduces if and only if f is linearly homogeneous.

developments are and how they are tending to reorganize a very traditional literature on an important topic.

The first problem is involved with the definition of money: what assets should be selected and how should they be grouped? As a first pass, one might aggregate (by a Divisia index) those assets that have highly collinear rates of return; examples would be savings deposits held by consumers at various types of financial institutions or negotiable large-scale CDs and commercial paper. Similarly, small time deposits at various financial institutions would probably qualify for this sort of preaggregation. One is still left with a considerable number of other disaggregated assets when this is done, however. If a demand system is the object of the exercise, the problem becomes that of an excessive number of equations and thereby also of parameters to estimate (for the sample size available).

Instead of the *a priori* assignment of assets to monetary groups, the structure of preferences over monetary assets could be discovered by actually testing for weakly separable sub-groupings. There are problems, however, with the available tests for separability. For example, consider the most common separability pretest in this literature: Hal Varian's (1982, 1983) nonparametric (NONPAR) revealed preference procedure. This test examines the results of (what are assumed to be) actual consumer choices to see if there are any violations of consistency.[24] However, the NONPAR procedure possesses a number of undesirable features, possibly the most serious being its inherently nonstatistical nature.[25] Even so, there do exist studies in the monetary literature that employ this methodology, with a frequent result being that the traditional monetary subgroupings are not those that appear to be separable within wealth holders' choices.[26] This is clearly a very preliminary

---

[24] A violation would occur if consumers actually choose new market baskets that make them worse off than their original choice (evaluated at the original prices).

[25] The NONPAR procedure produces a total rejection if there is a single violation; in this case, the data having been rejected, it is also impossible to test for separable groupings, even though the rejection could have been produced from purely white noise in the data. See Barnett and Seungmook Choi (1989a) for some rather pessimistic results drawn from Monte Carlo experiments on various methods used (including NONPAR) in testing for weak separability.

[26] James Swofford and Gerald Whitney (1988) *on annual data*, conclude that there exist relatively liquid sets of assets — one group being M1, other checkable deposits, and savings deposits at each institution type (taken separately) — that are separable from consumption expenditures and leisure. *On quarterly data*, they find that no interesting collection of financial assets passes both of Varian's necessary and sufficient conditions for weak separability. This is discouraging, although the NONPAR procedure is definitely biased toward rejection (since one violation of consistency produces a rejection). Michael Belongia and James Chalfant (1989) also test for what they call "admissible" monetary groupings on quarterly U.S. data; the groupings that pass the necessary conditions are M1A (currency plus demand deposits), M1 (as currently defined), and M1+ (M1 plus interest-bearing checkable deposits currently included in M2).

observation, however.

There is a further problem, already discussed in a theoretical context, that concerns the separability of the monetary asset decision from the consumption/leisure decision. Most money-demand studies simply ignore the possible difficulties, but recent empirical tests, either utilizing the NONPAR procedure or embedding the hypothesis parametrically in a set of simultaneous equations, generally do not support this separability.[27] We should note, somewhat parenthetically, that tests that employ the wage rate in the money demand function — usually as a proxy for the 'value of time' — also could be interpreted as providing evidence of the lack of separability of the money-holding decision from the leisure (and hence consumption) decision.[28]

Moving on to the main issues of this section, the next topic concerns the relationship between the direct monetary services aggregator function and the indirect user cost aggregator function. Since the structural properties of the two are not necessarily the same, and since one generally theorizes about the direct function but estimates the indirect function, a correspondence between the two must be established. In the case at hand, the indirect utility function corresponding to the direct utility function in Equation (2) would be weakly separable in expenditure-normalized monetary-asset user costs if there exists an indirect aggregator function $H(\mathbf{v})$ such that we can write

$$g = G(\mathbf{q}, w, H(\mathbf{v})) \qquad (18)$$

where $\mathbf{q}$ and $\mathbf{v}$ are the expenditure-normalized price vectors for $\mathbf{c}$ and $\mathbf{x}$, respectively, and w is the expenditure-normalized wage rate.[29] The weak separability condition in Equation (18) holds if and only if the marginal rate of substitution between any two user costs in the monetary index is independent of changes in prices outside the monetary group.[30]

---

[27] The Swofford and Whitney paper just mentioned provides the nonparametric results as does Salam Fayyad (1986). For a system study that rejects the separability of consumption goods from monetary assets, also see Fayyad, who employs the Rotterdam model in his calculations.

[28] The rationale (see Edi Karni 1974; Thomas Saving 1971; or Dean Dutton and William Gramm 1973) is often that of saving time in transactions by employing money; time is then valued at the wage rate. A recent paper by Kevin Dowd (1990) continues this tradition. Note that the lack of separability between money holding and consumption is explicit in the Dutton and Gramm paper just referred to.

[29] In particular, if $(\mathbf{q}, w, \boldsymbol{\pi})$ are the corresponding nonnormalized prices and if y is total expenditure on $(\mathbf{c}, L, \mathbf{x})$, then the expenditure-normalized prices are $(\mathbf{q}, w, \boldsymbol{\pi})/y$.

[30] Lawrence Lau (1969, Theorem VI) shows that a homothetic direct aggregator function is weakly separable if and only if the indirect aggregator function is weakly separable in the same partition. Hence, if one wishes to test for homothetic separability of the direct aggregator function, one equivalently can test for homothetic separability of the more easily approached indirect aggregator function. This survey deals with the homothetic case, which has self-duality of separability between the direct and indirect utility function.

4.1 Approximating the Monetary Services Subutility Function

In recent years a number of empirical studies have made use of the *flexible functional form* method to approximate unknown utility functions. The advantage of this method is that the corresponding demand system can approximate systems of demand equations (for liquid assets in this case) that arise from a broad class of utility functions. Flexible functional forms have the defining property that they can attain arbitrary level and both first- and second-order derivatives at a predetermined single point (see Diewert 1974); they are, in the terminology of the literature, 'locally' flexible, and they provide second-order local approximations to the desired function.

The two most commonly used flexible functional forms are the Generalized Leontief, introduced by Diewert (1971), and the translog, introduced by Laurits Christensen, Dale Jorgenson, and Lau (1975). These have been especially appealing in econometric work because they have close links to economic theory and because their strengths and weaknesses are generally understood. Below we will use the translog as an example that reveals the characteristics of this approach in modeling the demand for money.

The decision problem with which we are working is the maximization of 'second-stage' utility subject to the second-stage monetary expenditures constraint. That is, in the second stage of a two-stage maximization problem with weak separability between monetary assets and consumer goods, the consumer maximizes a direct utility function of the general form

$$f(x_{1t}, x_{2t}, \ldots, x_{nt})$$

subject to

$$\sum_{i=1}^{n} \pi_{it}^* x_{it} - m_t^* = 0$$

with $m^* = m/p^*$ being real expenditure on the services of monetary assets (determined in the first stage and hence given at this point), and where $\pi_{it}^* = \pi_{it}/p^*$ is the real user cost of asset i, so that,

$$\pi_{it}^* = \left(\frac{R_t - r_{it}}{1 + R_t}\right).$$

The user cost here would be calculated from the own rate of return and the return (R_t) on the benchmark asset. The latter would normally be the highest available rate in the set of monetary assets.[31]

---

[31]The role of the benchmark asset is to establish a nonmonetary alternative. It is acceptable for this to be a different asset in each period, since the maximization is repeated each period. In theory, any measurement of R_t could be viewed as a proxy for the unknown rate of return on human capital.

Let the indirect utility function be

$$H(v_1, v_2, \ldots, v_n)$$

with v_i defining the expenditure-normalized user costs, as in

$$v_i = \frac{\pi_i}{m} \qquad i = 1, \ldots, n.$$

Then, by application of Roy's Theorem, we will be able to move directly from the estimates of the parameters of the indirect utility function to calculations of income and price elasticities and the elasticities of substitution among the various assets.[32]

The demand-systems approach provides the ability to impose, and for that matter to test, the set of neoclassical restrictions on individual behavior; here we are referring specifically to monotonicity and curvature restrictions.[33] In addition, the approach provides an infinite range of possible parametric functional forms, thereby affording a rich supply of alternative models for actual estimation. Indeed, in the monetary literature a number of such models have been employed in the attempt to represent consumer preferences. These alternative models transform the behavioral postulates of the theory into restrictions on parameters; they differ in the specific parameterization and approximation properties of the model.

In many studies of money demand, the restrictions of theory are *implicit* at best — as in the standard Goldfeld (1973) money-demand specification — but because the connection with optimization theory is either unclear or nonexistent in such cases, we are often not in a position to test or impose those restrictions. A simultaneous-equations demand system is an effective alternative, because in this case the restrictions of theory become *explicit* in the context of a particular functional form. In addition, flexible functional forms, because they permit a wide range of interactions among the commodities being tested, are especially useful in this respect.[34]

---

[32] Once the form of the indirect utility function is specified (and under the assumption that this function is differentiable), Roy's Theorem allows one to derive the system of ordinary demand functions by straightforward differentiation, as follows:

$$-x_i(\pi_1, \pi_2, \ldots, \pi_n, m) = \frac{\partial H}{\partial \pi_i} \Big/ \frac{\partial H}{\partial m} \qquad (i = 1, \ldots, n).$$

[33] The monotonicity restriction requires that, given the estimated parameter values and given prices v_i, the values of fitted demand be nonnegative. It can easily be checked by direct computation of the values of the fitted budget shares. The curvature condition requires quasi-convexity of the indirect utility function.

[34] But note that the application of a separability restriction in this context will generally alter the flexibility characteristics of a flexible functional form (toward less flexibility); see Blackorby, Primont, and Russell (1977).

4.2 An Example

Consider the popular basic translog model. The logarithm of the indirect utility function $\log h = H(\log v_1, \log v_2, \ldots, \log v_n)$ can be approximated by a function that is quadratic in the logarithms as in Equation (19).

$$\log h = \log \alpha_0 + \sum_i \alpha_i (\log v_i) \tag{19}$$

$$+ \frac{1}{2} \sum_i \sum_j \gamma_{ij} (\log v_i)(\log v_j).$$

In fact, the function just exhibited can be derived as a second-order Taylor-series expansion to an arbitrary indirect utility function at the point $v_i^* = 1$ ($i = 1, \ldots, n$). The translog actually is likely to be an adequate approximation at that point, although away from the point its effectiveness decreases rapidly (see Barnett and Lee 1985).

One normally does not estimate the translog model in the form of Equation (19). Rather, starting with the indirect utility function of

$$\log h = \log H(v_1, v_2, \ldots, v_n) \tag{20}$$

and applying Roy's Theorem (see Varian 1984), the budget share for the jth asset for translog tastes becomes

$$S_j = \frac{\alpha_j + \sum_i \delta_{ij} \log v_i}{\alpha + \sum_i \delta_i \log v_i} \tag{21}$$

with $j = 1, \ldots, n$ where, for simplicity, $S_j = \pi_j x_j / m$, $\alpha = \sum_j \alpha_j$ and $\delta_i = \sum_j \delta_{ij}$. The equation system given in (21) is what is typically estimated.

There is, however, a significant weakness to the translog model just described, in that as a *locally* flexible functional form it is capable of an effective approximation of an arbitrary function only at or near a single point ($\mathbf{v}^*$). This has inspired research on approximating the unknown monetary services aggregator function based on the use of flexible functional forms possessing *global* properties (in the limit implying an approximation at *all* points). Three such forms in use with U.S. monetary data are the Fourier, the Minflex Laurent generalized Leontief, and the Minflex Laurent translog. The Fourier form uses the Fourier series expansion as the approximating mechanism (see Gallant 1981, and footnote 40), while the Minflex Laurent models make use of the Laurent series expansion — a generalization of the Taylor series expansion — as the approximating mechanism (see Barnett 1985; Barnett and Lee 1985; and Barnett, Lee and Wolfe 1985, 1987).[35] We shall discuss their brief empirical record in the next section.

---

[35] An especially promising global approximation not yet applied to monetary data is the

5 Empirical Dimensions

There are two major observations in what has gone before in this survey. These are (1) that ideal index numbers represent a theoretically attractive alternative to fixed weight or simple sum aggregation and (2) that a systems approach to studying the demand for money is consistent with the same theory that generates the ideal index numbers, and clearly provides a promising alternative strategy for locating the apparently elusive demand for money. These topics will be the theme of the following discussion.

5.1 Empirical Comparisons of Index Numbers

Divisia indices will be more effective — and simple-sum (and fixed weight) indices less, ceteris paribus — if user costs of the different component monetary assets are unequal and fluctuate to any degree over the sample period, whether one needs the aggregate for direct policy purposes or as an input into a money demand study. In Figures 3a and 3b, we graph the behavior of the user costs of some of the components of the monetary aggregates M1, M2, M3, as defined in Table 1. There are two collections, one with user costs picked from three simple-sum categories, and one with three user costs taken from among the components of M1.[36]

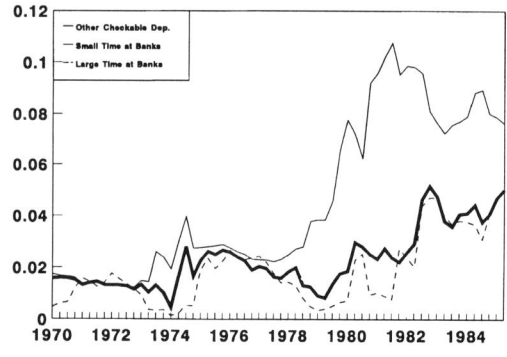

Figure 3a: Sample user costs, items from M1, M2, M3.

AIM ("asymptotically ideal model"), generated from the Müntz-Szatz series expansion (Barnett and Jonas 1983; Barnett and Yue 1988; and Barnett, Geweke, and Wolfe 1991a).

[36] These user costs were obtained from Gerald Whitney of the University of New Orleans; their method of construction is described by Swofford and Whitney (1987, 1988) but is, in any case, carried out by the method of calculation recommended in this survey.

Empirical Dimensions

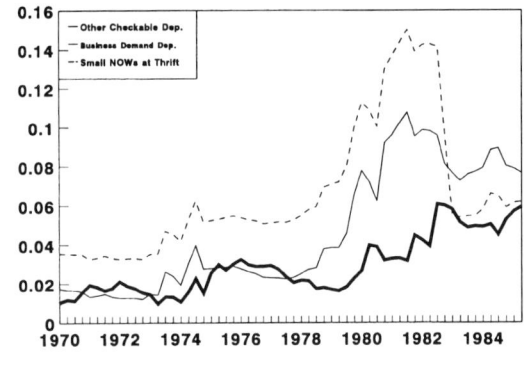

Quarterly Data, 1970.1 - 1985.2

Figure 3b: Sample user costs, items from M1.

In Figure 3a, three series are graphed, one from M1, one from the additional set of assets that makes up M2, and one, similarly, from M3. They are not very highly correlated (a significant fact for the construction of M3) and, what is particularly noticeable, they often go in different directions during periods of general economic disturbance (1970, 1973-5, 1977-85). Similar results hold for the three items selected from the six that make up M1 in the official aggregates.[37]

Because the user costs (as estimated) are neither equal to each other nor constant, an interesting question is opened up about the relative performance of the monetary aggregates over this period. The safest generalization at which we could arrive at is that the different aggregates behave differently (as we illustrated in Figure 2) and, when compared for particular money demand models, often perform differently there, too. For example, the Divisia numbers usually provide a better fit than the simple-sum measures, but the nature of the differences among the aggregates appears to depend on the particular specification at hand and upon the choice of components over which the aggregation occurs. Under these circumstances it would be premature to

[37] The correlation matrix for the level figures of the three entities in Figure 3a is:

	OCD	STDCB	LTDCB
Other Checkable Deposits	1.00		
Small Time Deposits at Banks	.71	1.00	
Large Time Deposits at Banks	.50	.90	1.00

The matrix for the items in Figure 3b is:

	BUSDD	OCD	SNOWT
Business Demand Deposits	1.00		
Other Checkable Deposits	.78	1.00	
Small NOW Accounts at Thrifts	.44	.82	100

assert that one component grouping is best for all purposes and, in fact, that simply may not be the case.

For example, Barnett, Edward Offenbacher, and Spindt (1984) provide a comparison in the context of a Granger-causality test of money on income (and prices) — where simple sums sometimes show up well — while Serletis (1988a) employs the Akaike Information Criterion (as defined in H. Akaike 1969b) to effect statistical comparisons. In another study, Belongia and Chalfant test the St. Louis Equation and find evidence in favor of Divisia M1A; this measure is currency plus demand deposits. Cagan (1982) finds the velocity of money series more stable when Divisia M1 is employed, while Douglas Fisher and Serletis (1989) find that Divisia measures built from short-term assets work better than those constructed from longer-term assets in a framework that attempts to explain recent velocity behavior in terms of monetary variability (see Friedman 1983). Finally, Lawrence Christiano (1986), attempting to explain the alleged structural shift in the U.S. monetary data in 1979, finds that a differenced Divisia measure does just that.

5.2 Empirical Results for the Demand System Approach

The second major issue raised above concerns the advantages one might gain by employing the demand-systems approach to the study of money demand (and monetary interaction). The fluctuations in the user costs just referred to provide one possible reason for taking this route, since the same economic theory that recommends using the Divisia technique also supports the use of the demand systems approach coupled with a flexible functional form. Before beginning, however, the reader should be warned that the best of the models put a lot of strain on the data in terms of their need for large sample size (generally, the more flexible models have more parameters to estimate).[38]

The demand-system approach produces interest-rate and income elasticities — as well as the elasticities of substitution among monetary assets. The underlying question for the income elasticities is whether they are less than 1.0, particularly for the narrowest measures. On the whole, across this entire literature, the answer is 'yes.' With respect to the elasticities of substitution, one of the most curious — *and consistent* — results in all of monetary economics is the evidence in such studies of very low substitution or even (sometimes) complementarity among the liquid financial assets; this is a general result that occurs in all but the very earliest studies.[39] These results

---

[38] Most seriously, when the simple-sum aggregates are included, tests for model failure (e.g., symmetry, monotonicity, and quasi-convexity) generally show such failures (sometimes even quite a few failures); see Donovan (1978), Nabil Ewis and Douglas Fisher (1984, 1985), and Douglas Fisher (1989, 1992).

[39] The early study by Karuppan Chetty (1969), which employed a constant elasticity of

are robust across definitions of the money stock and across *flexible* functional forms. We should note that the reason for referring to this as a 'curious result' is that there is a traditional view in the monetary literature that most of these assets are very close substitutes, as is, in fact, necessary for simple-sum aggregation. The policy importance of this result, should it continue to stand up, can hardly be exaggerated in view of the dependence of existing policies on aggregation procedures that require very high (really infinite) elasticities of substitution.

A second equally important finding concerns the temporal behavior of these same elasticities. We noted in Figure 3 that user costs appear to have fluctuated considerably in recent years; the next question concerns the behavior of the various elasticities over the same period. One can certainly generate a time series of elasticities of substitution for models such as the translog, but a far more attractive approach is to use a model like Gallant's (1981) Fourier flexible form because it provides a global approximation (at each data point) rather than a local one.[40] A few of these results have been published; we reproduce one set of these (Douglas Fisher 1989) for the same U.S. data that figured in the calculations in Figure 3. At stake is the reputation of single equation money demand studies that (implicitly) rely on linearity of the demand equation in its parameters. The results, which appear in Figure 4, are drawn from a four-equation system (three financial assets and one set of con-

---

substitution format, found relatively high elasticities of substitution. Since then, Donovan (1978), Ewis and Douglas Fisher (1984, 1985), Fayyad (1986), Serletis and Leslie Robb (1986), Serletis (1988b), and Douglas Fisher (1992), have found the lower elasticities. These studies have in common their employment of one or another of the popular flexible functional forms.

Another controversial finding is that in several studies it is suggested that currency might be a closer substitute for time deposits than it is for demand deposits (Offenbacher 1979, Ewis and Douglas Fisher 1984).

[40]The Fourier model that is equivalent to Equation (19) for the translog is

$$h_k(\mathbf{v}) = u_0 + \mathbf{b}'\mathbf{v} + \frac{1}{2}\mathbf{v}'\mathbf{C}\mathbf{v}$$
$$+ \sum_{\alpha=1}^{A} \left(u_{0\alpha} + 2 \sum_{j=1}^{J} [u_{j\alpha} \cos(j\mathbf{k}'_\alpha \mathbf{v}) - w_{j\alpha} \sin(j\mathbf{k}'_\alpha \mathbf{v})] \right)$$

in which

$$\mathbf{C} = -\sum_{\alpha=1}^{A} u_{0\alpha} \mathbf{k}_\alpha \mathbf{k}'_\alpha.$$

This is a set of equations (which would be estimated in budget share form after application of Roy's identity) in which the parameters are the b_i, u_{ij}, and w_{ji}. The researcher picks the degree of the approximation (by picking j) and the particular form and number of the so-called multi-indices, (the **k** vectors). The latter are generally taken as 0, 1 vectors of length $n-1$ (n is the number of assets in the problem) whose purpose is to form simple indices of the normalized user costs. These decisions are made on goodness-of-fit criteria. See Gallant (1981) or Douglas Fisher (1989).

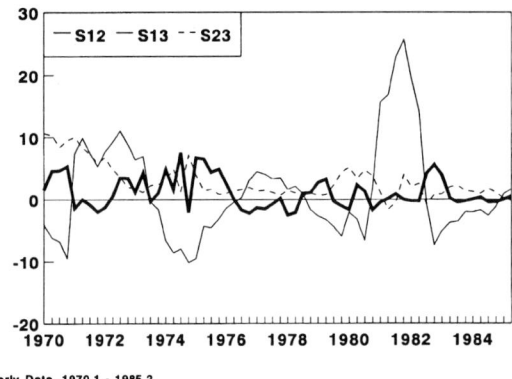

Figure 4a: Substitution elasticities.

sumption expenditures) for quarterly U.S. data.[41] S12 refers to the elasticity of substitution between cash assets and savings deposits (and money market accounts), S13 refers to the elasticity of substitution between cash assets and small time deposits, while Y_i is the income elasticity of the ith category.[42]

It is readily apparent that none of the elasticities are constant for the comparisons made, and that, in particular, the elasticities of substitution change considerably over approximately the same subperiods of the data as did the user costs. This is no coincidence, of course, since the elasticities often change in response to changes in relative prices for plausible *fixed* tastes. What it does provide — and the differences were often statistically significant in the study from which they were taken — is a possible explanation of why approaches involving simple-sum aggregation and single-equation linear money demand functions might not perform particularly well, as indeed they often have not.[43]

---

[41] The financial categores are:

Group 1: currency, consumer demand deposits, other checkable deposits
Group 2: small NOW accounts, money market deposit accounts, and savings deposits
Group 3: small time deposits

The fourth category, total consumption expenditures, was included in the system because of the failure to establish separability between financial asset holding and consumption for these data. See the discussion in Douglas Fisher (1989). There is another, similar, study by Douglas Fisher (1992).

[42] The model estimates a set of parameters employing the iterative seemingly unrelated equation approach. The elasticities and their standard errors are generated from these estimated parameters and the data at each point.

[43] For similar results with other series expansion models, see Barnett (1983a) and Yue (1991). Briefly, the evidence of instability of money demand from the old linear models results from the fact that in general the slopes of local linear approximations to nonlinear

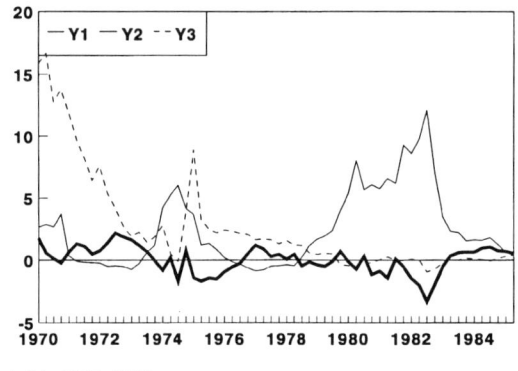

Figure 4b: Income elasticities.

We should note that most of the early studies of demand systems — such as that in Equation (19) — have tended to be cast in static terms, although the issue of dynamic adjustment has been addressed frequently in the traditional money-demand literature.[44] Recently, though, attention has been focused on the development of dynamic generalizations of the traditional static systems models in such a way as to enable tests of the model and its theoretical restrictions and simplifications. Gordon Anderson and Richard Blundell (1982), for instance, develop an unrestricted dynamic formulation in order to accommodate short-run disequilibrium; this is effected through the use of lagged endogenous and exogenous regressors. In the same spirit, Serletis (1991a) applies the Anderson and Blundell approach to various demand-systems models and demonstrates that the dynamic generalizations of the traditional static models (e.g., the dynamic translog) provide more convincing overall fits as well as empirically credible estimates of the various elasticities.

6 Extensions

The purpose of this paper is to survey and assess the mainstream of the recent literature on neoclassical system-wide modeling and testing in monetary economics. Because of the complexity of that topic — and the limitations

---

functions vary over time as the tangency moves along the nonlinear function.

[44] For example, there is a "real adjustment" specification in Gregory Chow (1966), a "price adjustment" specification in Robert Gordon (1984), and the "nominal adjustment" specification in Goldfeld (1976). For a recent approach, see Choi and Sosin (1992).

of space — the discussion to this point has been limited to the most central and fundamental of the research in this area. Extensions including such important topics as uncertainty, rational expectations, nonhomotheticity, intertemporal optimization, and the possibility of extending the framework to study the supply of money function, have not been presented. Nevertheless, the reader should not thereby conclude that the literature has not in fact been extended in those directions.

In Section 3, we stated the consumer's decision problem to be the maximization of contemporaneous single-period utility, in Equation (2), subject to the current period expenditures constraint, Equation (3). In fact, it can be shown that this decision is consistent with rational *intertemporal optimization* by the consumer if the consumer's intertemporal utility function is intertemporally blockwise weakly separable, so that $U(\mathbf{c}, L, \mathbf{x})$ is a weakly separable block within the intertemporal utility function. The current period decision that we use in Section 3 then can be shown to be the second-stage decision in the two-stage decision of maximizing intertemporal utility subject to a sequence of single-period constraints (Barnett 1980a, 1987). Hence, all of the results surveyed above are consistent with rational intertemporal optimization by the consumer if the relevant weak separability assumption holds. As nearly all intertemporal decision models currently in use in economics are in fact intertemporally *strongly* separable, the assumption of intertemporal *weak* separability does not seem excessive.

The first stage of the two-stage decomposition of the intertemporal decision allocates total wealth over periods. In the second stage, the total expenditure allocated in the first stage to the current period is then allocated over current period consumption of individual goods, asset services, and leisure. The two-stage decomposition can be produced under intertemporal weak separability of tastes, if there is perfect certainty or risk aversion. However, the two-stage solution, producing the current period conditional second-stage decision, is not possible under risk aversion. With risk aversion, the intertemporal decision becomes a problem in stochastic optimal control, which can be solved by dynamic programming methods.

This implies that another productive direction for future research in this area is likely to be the search for nonparametric statistical index numbers that will track the exact *rational expectations aggregator function* in the risk-averse case as effectively as the Divisia can track the exact aggregator function in the risk-neutral case.[45] The existing literature on index number theory,

---

[45] In the work referred to in earlier sections, there is the assumption of risk neutrality, so that the decision can be stated in certainty-equivalent form, with random variables replaced by their expectations. A means for extending this literature to include risk aversion and rational expectations has been proposed by Poterba and Rotemberg (1987). Subsequent work by Barnett, Hinich, and Yue (1991) and Barnett, Hinich, and Yue (2000) has produced

which has never before been extended to the risk-averse case, provides no guidance here. This is in striking contrast to the risk-neutral case, in which the existing literature on index numbers and aggregation theory has provided all of the tools that have been found necessary.

In the discussion so far, we have assumed that the aggregator function is linearly homogeneous. We also have assumed that the aggregator function is a utility function. There is a paradox in this. On the one hand, it is clear that the aggregator function does indeed have to be linearly homogeneous. Otherwise the aggregate will grow at a different rate than the components in the case of identical growth rates for all components. That, of course, would make no sense. On the other hand, linear homogeneity of a utility function is a strong assumption empirically. The solution to the paradox is that the aggregator function is a utility function only if the utility function is linearly homogeneous. If the utility function over component quantities is not linearly homogeneous, then it is known from aggregation theory that the aggregator function is the distance function.

The quantity aggregate defined by the distance function is called the Malmquist index.[46] The distance function is always linearly homogeneous in **x**, regardless of whether or not the utility function, U, is itself linearly homogeneous. We concentrate above on the special case of linear homogeneous utility in this paper for expositional reasons, but the generalization to the nonhomothetic utility case presents no problems at all. If we seek to estimate the aggregator function, then the literature described in the earlier sections is directly applicable to estimating the parameters of the utility function. Once the estimation is complete, the parameter estimates are substituted into the distance function rather than into the utility function to produce the estimated aggregator function. The situation is even simpler if we seek a nonparametric statistical index number. Diewert (1976, pp. 123-4) has proved that under an appropriate method for selecting the base level of utility, U_0, the Divisia index provides a superlative approximation to the distance function, just as it did to the utility function in the special case of linearly

---

a solution to the intertemporal stochastic optimal control problem characterizing a rational consumer, when current period consumption of monetary services is weakly separable within the consumer's intertemporal expected utility function. Those papers also contain an empirical implementation that produces the "exact" rational expectations monetary aggregates for M1. This does not appear to differ materially from Divisia M1 (but does differ from the simple-sum version of M1).

[46] For the definition of the distance function, see Barnett (1987, Equations (7.1) and (7.2), pp. 146-47). For the Malmquist index, see Barnett (1987, Equation (7.7), p. 148). The distance function $d(u_0, \mathbf{x})$ relative to base utility level u_0 can be acquired by solving the equation $f(\mathbf{x}/d(u_0, \mathbf{x})) = u_0$ for $d(u_0, \mathbf{x})$ where f is the utility function. Hence, the distance function measures the amount by which the monetary asset vector **x** must be deflated to reduce the utility vector to its base level u_0.

homogeneous utility. Hence, the second-order approximation property of the Divisia index to the exact aggregator holds true, regardless of whether or not utility is homothetic (Barnett 1987).

Since we see that homotheticity of utility is not needed at all — and was used in our earlier discussion only to simplify the presentation — we are left with the weak separability condition as the key indispensable assumption. Here it is important to observe that weak separability is not an additional assumption imposed to permit use of one particular approach to modeling or aggregation, but rather is the fundamental *existence* condition, without which aggregates and sectors do not exist. It should be observed that we do not require that weak separability hold for some particular prior clustering, but rather that there exists at least one clustering of goods or assets that satisfies weak separability. Empirically, when one is free in that way to consider all possible clusterings, weak separability is indeed a weak assumption.[47]

Another important extension that is just beginning to appear in this literature is the application of the available theorems on aggregation over economic agents. It should be observed that the theory of aggregation over economic agents is independent of the theory of aggregation over goods, and hence the theory discussed above on aggregation over goods for one economic agent remains valid for any means of aggregation over economic agents. However, the existing theory on aggregation over economic agents is much more complicated than that for aggregation over goods. While a unique solution exists to the problem of aggregation over goods, and the necessary and sufficient conditions are known, the same cannot be said for aggregation over economic agents. The solution to the latter problem is dependent upon the modeler's views regarding the importance of distribution effects.

In particular, an array of solutions exists to the problem of aggregation over economic agents, depending upon the model's dependence on distribution effects. At one extreme is Gorman's (1953) solution by means of the 'representative agent' who can be proved to exist if all Engel curves are linear and are parallel across economic agents. At the other extreme is Pareto's perfectly general stratification approach, which integrates utility functions over the distribution functions of all variables that can produce distribution effects; these would be such as the distribution of income or wealth and the distribution of demographic characteristics of the population. Between these two extremes are such approaches as John Muellbauer's, which introduces dependency upon the second moments as well as on the first moments of distributions but does so in a manner that preserves the existence of a rep-

---

[47] If the procedure is reversed, and a clustering is chosen by some other means prior to separability testing — and one clustering then is subjected to a test for weak separability — the assumption of weak separability becomes a strong one that is not likely to be satisfied empirically!

resentative consumer.[48] Somewhat closer to the general Pareto approach is Barnett's (1981b, pp. 58-68) stochastic convergence method, which requires fewer assumptions than Muellbauer's method while, at the same time, not preserving the existence of the representative consumer.[49]

The importance of distribution effects is central to the choice between methods of aggregating over economic agents. The Gorman method assumes away all distribution effects and leaves only dependence upon means (i.e., per capita variables). The further away one moves from Gorman's assumptions, the further one must move along the route to the Pareto method, which requires estimation of all of the moments of the distribution functions.[50] At present, the empirical research on this subject seeks to test for the depth of dependence upon distribution effects. Barnett and Serletis (1990) have done so with monetary data by explicitly introducing Divisia second moments into models and testing for their statistical significance. The importance of the induced distribution effects was found to be low.[51]

In short, the empirical evidence does not yet suggest the need to move away from Gorman's representative consumer approach towards any of the generalizations. However, should the need arise, these generalizations do exist for any applications in which complex distribution effects might be suspected. There are surveys of many of these approaches in Barnett (1981b, pp. 306–07 and 1987, pp. 153–54) and Barnett and Serletis (1990).

Finally, we consider some results that come from the application of the neoclassical theory of the firm to the financial sector. For the supply of money problem there exists system-wide modeling that employs aggregation and index number theory that is analogous to that for the demand side. An especially interesting development from this literature is the proof that the exact supply-side monetary aggregate may not equal the exact demand-side monetary aggregate, even if all component markets are cleared. This situation is produced by the existence of a regulatory wedge created by the nonpayment of interest on the reserves required of financial intermediaries. The wedge is reflected in different user costs on each side of the market.

---

[48] In particular, Muellbauer preserves the representative consumer by retaining the dependence of the decision upon only one income index, although that income index, in turn, depends jointly upon the mean and variance of the income distribution.

[49] In this case some of the properties of the Slutsky equation are retained after aggregation over consumers.

[50] Another highly general approach, requiring extensive data availability, is the Henri Theil (1967) and Barnett (1987, p. 154) approach to Divisia aggregation over economic agents. By this method, a single Divisia index can aggregate jointly over goods and economic agents, although detailed data on the distribution of asset holdings over economic agents is required.

[51] Similarly, Ernst Berndt, W. Erwin Diewert, and Masako Darrough (1977) use the Pareto appproach by integrating over the entire income distribution with Canadian consumption data and similarly find little significance to the distribution effects.

The relevant theory is available in Diana Hancock (1985, 1991) and Barnett (1987), and the statistical significance of the wedge is investigated empirically by Barnett, Hinich, and Weber (1986). They find that the size of the wedge is astonishingly large when measured in terms of the dollar value of the implicit tax on financial firms but nevertheless produces only insignificant divergence between the demand-side and supply-side exact monetary aggregates. In that study, the wedge was found to have potentially important effects in the dynamics of the monetary transmission mechanism only at very high frequency (i.e., in the very short run).

It is perhaps worth observing that analogous wedges are produced by differences in explicit marginal tax rates among demanders and suppliers of monetary services through differences in capital gains taxation, in local and federal income taxation, and in sales and corporate income taxation. The resulting divergence in user costs between the demand and supply side of the market can create the analogous paradox to the one produced by the implicit taxation of financial firms through the nonpayment of interest on required reserves. The empirical importance of these explicit wedges for the monetary transmission mechanism has not yet been investigated systematically.

7 Conclusions

In the history of economic thought, economic paradigms rise and fall based upon how well they actually work in the eyes of the public. The acid test usually is the connection between the paradigm and the performance of economies that adopt the paradigm for policy purposes. The approach that we survey in this paper has been used in research in many countries, both in academia and in central banks.[52] While these data along with some of the modeling principles described in this paper are available and are being used internally within some central banks, the methods we have just surveyed have not yet, to our knowledge, been adopted publicly as formally announced targeting methods by any country's central bank or government. Hence, the ultimate acid test cannot yet be applied.

A way to visualize how this new work affects the traditional money-demand literature is to think — as we have occasionally done in this survey — in terms of the well-known 'missing money' puzzle (Goldfeld 1976). What is being suggested here is that a good part of the problem may be in the way money is measured — both in the choice of component groupings

---

[52] For example, Divisia monetary aggregates have been produced for Britain (Roy Batchelor 1989, Leigh Drake 1992, and Belongia and Alec Chrystal 1991), Japan (Kazuhiko Ishida 1984), Holland (Martin Fase 1985), Canada (Jon Cockerline and John Murray 1981b), Australia (Tran Van Hoa 1985), and Switzerland (Yue and Fluri 1991).

Conclusions

and in the method of aggregating over those groups — and in the way that the demand model's capabilities relate to the generally nonlinear optimizing behavior of economic agents. Unlike conventional linear money demand equations, a system of demand equations derived from a flexible functional form with data produced from the Divisia index can be expected to capture those movements in money holding that are due to changes in the relative prices among assets. In the increasingly unregulated and volatile financial markets that have followed the collapse of the Bretton-Woods system, this would seem to be useful. In addition, the approach offers a solution to the long-running money-demand puzzle: the observed variability of elasticities is actually consistent with the variability occurring naturally along stable, nonlinear, integrable demand systems. Linear approximations to nonlinear functions are useful only locally.

In sum, the successful use in recent years of the simple representative consumer paradigm in monetary economics has opened the door to the succeeding introduction into monetary economics of the entire microfoundations, aggregation theory, and microeconometrics literatures. The moral of the story is that the nonlinearity produced by economic theory is important.[53] We have surveyed a growing literature on the importance of the use of nonlinear economic theory in modeling the demand for money. We also have surveyed the recent literature on the use of aggregation theoretic nonlinear quantity aggregation in producing monetary data. Finally, we agree with Irving Fisher (1922) that the simple-sum index should be abandoned both as a source of research data and as an intermediate target or indicator for monetary policy.

---

[53] In fact there recently has been an explosion of interest in the dynamic implications of nonlinearity in economics, and the relationship with chaotic dynamics. It is possibly not surprising that the only successful detection of chaos with economic data has been with the Divisia monetary aggregates. See Barnett and Ping Chen (1988).

PART 5: DEMAND AND SUPPLY SIDE MONETARY AGGREGATION BY FIRMS AND FINANCIAL INTERMEDIARIES

Section 5.1: Editors' Overview of Part 5

William A. Barnett and Apostolos Serletis

The following table contains a brief summary of the contents of each chapter in Part 5 of this book.

Part 5 Section Contents
Demand and Supply Side Monetary Aggregation by Firms and Financial Intermediaries

Chapter Number	Chapter Title	Contents
19	The Regulatory Wedge between the Demand-side and Supply-side Aggregation Theoretic Monetary Aggregates	Explores the regulatory wedge between the demand and supply for monetary services, when required reserves exist and are paid no interest. The gap between the demand side and supply side monetary aggregates is analyzed.
20	Financial Firm Production of Monetary Services: A Generalized Symmetric Barnett Variable Profit Function Approach	Estimates a theoretically coherent model of financial intermediation and financial output aggregation under perfect certainty using the Generalized Symmetric Barnett Variable Profit Function.
21	Financial Firm's Production and Supply Side Monetary Aggregation under Dynamic Uncertainty	Extends supply side monetary aggregation over financial intermediary output to the case of risk, such that the first order conditions are Euler equations.
22	Estimating Policy-Invariant Deep Parameters in the Financial Sector, when Risk and Growth Matter	Extends the model of financial intermediation under risk to the case of dynamics.

Chapter 19:

Although the origins of much of this research are on the demand side, as emphasized by the survey in Chapter 18, an analogous literature, based upon the same aggregation theoretic foundations, exists on the supply side. Much of that literature relates to the production of financial services and inside money by financial intermediaries. Those produced services comprise output value added. When no regulatory wedge exists between the demand and supply side, the equality of the demand and supply side Divisia monetary aggregates is necessary for clearing of component money markets. But when the demand and supply side are taxed differently, a regulatory wedge can be produced. The result is an equilibrium that is not consistent with the existence of a separating hyperplane between the demand and supply side.

Chapter 19 explores the implications of nonpayment of interest on required reserves in the United States. Although the resulting regulatory wedge can produce a divergence between the Divisia demand and supply side monetary aggregates in equilibrium, the chapter finds that the gap is statistically insignificant, except during very short periods of time after shocks.

Chapter 20:

Chapter 20 is the supply side analogue to Chapter 16. Chapter 20 nests aggregation theoretic output monetary aggregates into a microeconometric model of bank behavior. Although the model is based upon the Laurent series expansion, the model is not directly analogous to the model originated by Barnett (1983), since the indirect utility function specification used in Chapter 16 is not in a form that is immediately usable to model technology. Instead Chapter 20 uses the related Generalized-Symmetric-Barnett variable-profit-function specification originated by Diewert and Wales (1987).

Researchers interested in the alternative seminonparametric AIM approach using the Müntz-Szatz series expansion could see Barnett, Geweke, and Wolfe (1991a). Recent work on that approach has emphasized the advantages of less restrictive methods of imposing neoclassical regularity on the AIM model than the relatively simple method used by Barnett, Geweke, and Wolfe.

Chapters 21 and 22:

Chapters 21 and 22 extend Chapter 20 to the case of risk. The first order conditions then become Euler equations, which are estimated by generalized method of moments. Diewert and Wales' (1987) Generalized Symmetric McFadden model produces more easily estimated Euler equations than their Generalized Symmetric Barnett model, so Chapters 21 and 22 use the Generalized Symmetric McFadden specification to model technology.

Section 5.2: Production and Supply Side

Chapter 19

The Regulatory Wedge Between the Demand-Side and Supply-Side Aggregation-Theoretic Monetary Aggregates

*William A. Barnett, Melvin J. Hinich, and Warren E. Weber**

> Barnett introduced the use of neoclassical demand-side aggregation theory into monetary economics. More recently he has introduced supply-side aggregation theory into monetary economics. We show that the demand-side and supply-side exact monetary aggregates need not be equal, even if aggregation is over the same component assets on both sides of the market and if all component-asset markets are cleared. The non-payment of interest on required reserves produces a classical regulatory wedge between the two sides of the aggregate market. We use time-series

---

*Reprinted from the *Journal of Econometrics*, 33, William A. Barnett, Melvin J. Hinich, and Warren E. Weber, "The Regulatory Wedge Between the Demand-Side and Supply-Side Aggregation-Theoretic Monetary Aggregates," pp. 165-185, Copyright (1986), with permission from Elsevier Science. The views expressed herein are those of the authors and not necessarily those of the Federal Reserve Bank of Minneapolis or of the Federal Reserve System. We have benefited substantially from the research assistance of Salam Fayyad. This research was partially supported by National Science Foundation Grant SOC89305162.

methods, including a new Hilbert transform method, to investigate the empirical importance of this aggregate gap.

1 Introduction

1.1 The issue

Barnett (1980a; 1981b, ch. 7) introduced the use of neoclassical aggregation and index number theory into monetary economics. His Divisia aggregates, based upon Diewert's (1976) superlative class of index numbers, measure the economy's flow of monetary services, as perceived by the users of those monetary services. As a result, the relevant aggregation theory is that produced by neoclassical consumer and factor demand theory. Much empirical research now exists on that subject; and, as would be expected from the theory, the empirical research is mostly related to demand-side empirical tests.[1] More recently Barnett (1987) has introduced the Divisia supply monetary aggregates, which are based upon supply-side aggregation theory with a conventional neoclassical model of financial intermediary monetary asset supply.[2]

Unfortunately, as shown both theoretically and empirically in this paper, the aggregation-theoretic exact money demand aggregate need not always equal the aggregation-theoretic exact money supply aggregate. This potential complication can arise, even if both aggregates are produced from Divisia aggregation over the same components, and even if the markets in all monetary components are continually cleared. This paradox is caused by the existence of required reserves having regulated zero rates of return. That regulatory constraint produces an implicit tax on financial intermediation, in terms of foregone investment interest. Financial intermediaries receive zero return on part of their deposits and a market return on the rest. However, depositors receive the same marginal return on every dollar deposited in a given account.

Both the Divisia demand and Divisia supply monetary aggregates depend jointly upon component quantities and user-cost prices, which are functions of after-tax component yields. As a result, even if all component markets are continually cleared, the demand and supply aggregates can differ, since the 'after (implicit) tax' component yields seen by financial intermediaries and depositors are not the same. The implicit tax produced by required reserves

---

[1]See, e.g., Barnett (1982a, 1983a, 1984) and Barnett, Offenbacher, and Spindt (1981, 1984). The Federal Reserve Board calls Barnett's monetary aggregates the Monetary Services Indexes.

[2]A very small model of a financial firm, originated by Hancock (1985, 1986), has been employed by Hancock (1987) empirically to investigate supply-side monetary aggregation.

creates a regulatory wedge between the user cost paid by the demander of the asset and the user cost received by the supplier of the asset. In brief, a classical regulatory wedge appears between the two sides of the aggregated money market, as a result of the asymmetric taxation on the two sides of the market.[3]

If the difference between a Divisia demand monetary aggregate and the corresponding Divisia supply monetary aggregate were small, we could use only one of them. The result would be a substantial simplification in modeling, since we then could use an aggregate money demand and aggregate-money supply function to produce a market that can be cleared in the monetary aggregate. For that to be the case, the difference between the Divisia demand monetary aggregate and the Divisia supply monetary aggregate would have to be statistically insignificant, so that we could treat each as a drawing from the same distribution. We investigate that possibility empirically. We use simple time domain methods to investigate the instantaneous size of the regulatory wedge. But to investigate the dynamic effects of the wedge, we use frequency domain methods, including spectral analysis, inferences based upon coherencies between processes, and Hinich and Weber's (1986) new Hilbert transform estimator. We consider the frequency domain analysis to be important, since regulation, especially of the banking system, can be expected to have substantial effects on the dynamic behavior and flexibility of the economy.

Alternative monetary aggregates, such as the so-called MQ index, recently have been proposed using turnover rate 'weights' and other such *ad hoc* weighting schemes. The issues addressed in this paper cannot be considered using such arbitrary 'indices', which are not based validly upon aggregation or index number theory and therefore do not possess microfoundations. For discussion of that literature, see Barnett (1985, 1987).

2 Demand-Side Monetary Aggregation and Index Number Theory

2.1 Aggregation theory

Demanders of monetary assets are treated as either maximizing intertemporal utility subject to a sequence of budget constraints or as maximizing

---

[3] Complications of the same sort are produced in many goods markets, including money markets, by the differences in the direct taxation rates on the two sides of the market. However, we do not consider that phenomenon, which is well known in welfare economics. In this paper, we consider the empirical effects and importance of the regulatory wedge and implicit taxation produced by the existence of required reserves.

the discounted present value of profits subject to given technology, expressed as an intertemporal transformation function. Real balances of each monetary asset appear in the utility or transformation function. That utility or transformation function is the derived function shown in general equilibrium theory always to exist if money has positive value in equilibrium.[4] In short, we begin with conventional neoclassical theory applicable both to consumer demand for monetary assets and to firm demand for monetary assets. We further assume that the utility or transformation function for each economic agent is blockwise weakly separable in the current-period portfolio of monetary assets.[5]

Barnett (1980a, 1987) has proved that the economic agent, whether a consumer or firm, then can be viewed as solving a simple conditional current-period decision problem. That current-period conditional decision is of the form

$$\text{maximize } u(\mathbf{m}_t) \text{ subject to } \mathbf{m}_t' \boldsymbol{\pi}_t = y_t, \qquad (1)$$

where $\mathbf{m}_t = (m_{1t}, \ldots, m_{nt})'$ is the economic agent's current-period real balance's of the n monetary assets, $\boldsymbol{\pi}_t = (\pi_{1t}, \ldots, \pi_{nt})'$ is the vector of real user-cost prices of those assets, and y_t is current-period real expenditure on the services of monetary assets. The function u is the weakly separable subfunction that is nested within the full intertemporal transformation function or utility function. Hence, in the case of a firm, u is a subproduction function, and in the case of a consumer, u is a subutility function. The function u is monotonically increasing and strictly quasiconcave.

Barnett (1978, 1980a) has proved that the real user-cost price of monetary asset i, for either a firm or a consumer, is

$$\pi_{it} = \frac{R_t - r_{it}}{1 + R_t}, \qquad (2)$$

where R_t is the 'benchmark' rate measuring the maximum expected rate of return available in the economy and r_{it} is the own rate of return on monetary asset i. In the general case, the exact economic quantity aggregate produced by decision (1) is the distance function treated as a function of $\mathbf{m}_t$ at fixed reference level, u_0.[6]

---

[4] E.g., Arrow and Hahn (1971), Fischer (1974), Phlips and Spinnewyn (1982), and Samuelson and Sato (1984).

[5] For tests of that assumption, see Serletis (1987) and Barnett and Fayyad (1986).

[6] The distance function $d(u_0, \mathbf{m}_t)$ is defined in implicit form by $u(\mathbf{m}_t/d(u_0, \mathbf{m}_t)) = u_0$, which has an interesting geometric interpretation. We see that $d(u_0, \mathbf{m}_t)$ is the factor by which $\mathbf{m}_t$ must be deflated to reduce (or increase) the level of u to the fixed reference level, u_0. When deflated by its value in a base period, the distance function becomes the Malmquist quantity index, which is dual to the famous Konüs true cost of living index. In the special case of homotheticity of the function u, the Malmquist index becomes the

2.2 Index number theory

At this point we see that we can estimate the exact monetary quantity index for a consumer or firm by estimating the function u. If u is linearly homogeneous, then u is itself the quantity aggregator function. If u is not linearly homogeneous, then the distance function, which is derivable from u, is the exact quantity aggregator function. However, estimation of u produces an aggregate which depends both upon the empirical specification of u and the estimator of its parameters. In practice, index numbers that are specification and estimator dependent, are rarely used by data-producing governmental agencies.

The solution to that practical problem is to use non-parametric methods to estimate the unknown exact aggregator function of aggregation theory. The field of statistical index number theory exists precisely for that purpose. Statistical index numbers are defined to be functions only of the data and not of any unknown parameters, although statistical quantity index numbers do depend jointly upon prices as well as quantities. On the other hand, the aggregation-theoretic exact quantity aggregator function, which does contain unknown parameters, depends only upon quantity data.

In recent years it has become increasingly clear from new theoretical results that the best statistical quantity index in continuous time is the Divisia index, and the best quantity index in discrete time is the Törnqvist (Simpson's rule) discrete time approximation to the Divisia index, which we call simply the Divisia index in discrete time.[7] The Divisia index, whether in discrete or continuous time, computes the growth rate of the quantity aggregate as a weighted average of the growth rates of the component quantities. The weights are the expenditure shares. In continuous time, the weight applied to the growth rate of component i at instant t is the ith good's instantaneous share $s_{it} = m_{it}\pi_{it}/\mathbf{m}'_t\boldsymbol{\pi}_t$. In discrete time, the weight applied to the growth rate of component i during period t is the ith good's average share $s_{it} = 1/2(s_{it}+s_{i,t-1})$, where s_{it} is this period's share and $s_{i,t-1}$ is last period's share.[8]

---

function u, deflated by its value in the base period. Hence in that elementary case the function u is itself the quantity aggregator function.

[7] See, e.g., Caves, Christensen, and Diewert (1982a, b) and Diewert (1980a,c).

[8] The microeconomic theory used in this section is available in detail in Barnett (1987). Relevant index number theory can be found in Barnett (1980b, 1981b, 1982a, 1983b, 1985), Denny and Pinto (1978), and Diewert (1976, 1980a). Results relevant to the economic aggregation theory used in section 2.1 can be found in Berndt and Christensen (1973) and Fuss (1977).

3 Supply-Side Monetary Aggregation and Index Number Theory

3.1 Aggregation theory

Financial intermediaries are suppliers of monetary assets. Such firms will be treated as maximizing the discounted present value of profits subject to given technology, expressed as an intertemporal transformation function. Real balances of produced monetary assets are outputs in the transformation function. We assume that the transformation function is blockwise weakly separable in the current-period vector of monetary assets produced.[9]

Barnett (1987) has proved that the financial intermediary then can be viewed as solving a simple current-period decision problem since solution to that conditional decision is necessary for solution to the firm's full intertemporal decision. That current-period conditional decision is to select the value of the monetary asset output quantity vector, $\boldsymbol{\mu}_t$, to

$$\text{maximize } \boldsymbol{\mu}_t'\boldsymbol{\gamma}_t \text{ subject to } f(\boldsymbol{\mu}_t; \mathbf{k}_t) = M_t, \qquad (3)$$

where $\boldsymbol{\mu}_t = (\mu_{1t}, \ldots, \mu_{nt})'$ is the current-period produced real balances of the financial intermediary's n outputs, $\boldsymbol{\gamma}_t = (\gamma_{1t}, \ldots, \gamma_{nt})'$ is the vector of real user-cost prices of those assets, $\mathbf{k}_t$ is the vector of reserve requirement ratios applying to the n assets, and M_t is total aggregate production of monetary services. In short, the financial intermediary maximizes revenue conditionally upon given (from a prior-stage decision in aggregates) production of monetary services, which, in turn, is a function of factor quantities employed. The function f is the weakly separable subfunction that is nested within the transformation function. The function f is called the factor requirement function, and is monotonically increasing and strictly *convex*. The constraint in decision (3) defines the production possibility surface at given level of factor usage, since M_t is a function of factor quantities. The production possibility surface is concave to the origin.

It can be proved [see Barnett (1987)] that the real user-cost price of monetary asset i produced by the financial intermediary is

$$\gamma_{it} = \frac{(1 - k_{it})R_t - r_{it}}{1 + R_t}. \qquad (4)$$

where R_t is the maximum yield that the financial intermediary can earn on an additional dollar of loans, and r_{it} is the yield paid by the financial

---
[9] For empirical tests of that assumption, see Hancock (1986).

intermediary on monetary asset (deposit account type) i.[10]

Clearly the user cost in (4) would equal the user cost in (2), if k_{it} were zero. We find that under some fairly common simplifying assumptions about the equality of interest rates seen on both sides of the markets, the user cost of monetary asset i would be the same for every firm demanding that asset, every consumer demanding that asset, and every financial intermediary producing that asset, if there were no required reserves for that asset.[11]

Observe that revenue can be written in the form

$$\mu'_t \gamma_t = \mu'_t \pi_t - \frac{R_t k'_t \mu_t}{1 + R_t}, \tag{5}$$

where π_t is the monetary asset demanders' user costs from (2). It therefore is clear that the second term on the right-hand side of (5) is the discounted (to the beginning of the time interval) present value of the implicit tax 'paid' by the financial intermediary as a result of the existence of the reserve requirements. If we do not discount by dividing by the denominator, then we acquire the end-of-period tax, which is the foregone interest on required reserves. The discounted or end-of-period tax could be evaluated in nominal, rather than real, dollars by measuring μ_t in nominal dollars.

In the general case, the exact economic quantity aggregate produced by decision (3) is the output distance function, treated as a function of μ_t at fixed reference level of factor quantities.[12]

---

[10] For a nearly identical result (except for a puzzling difference in the discount rate in the denominator), see Hancock (1985, 1986). Hancock's user-cost formulation also includes explicit transactions costs, which we do not incorporate, although our yields could be viewed as net of transactions costs. The issue raised and approach used below would not be affected, although the data would be altered. Incorporation of Hancock's transactions-costs adjustments could produce a worthwhile extension of our empirical work.

[11] Those simplifying assumptions eliminate other differences in taxation between demanders and suppliers of monetary assets. Further research would be useful to investigate those other differences in implicit and explicit taxation, which can further drive the wedge that we are exploring. For example, differences exist in income tax rates paid by consumers, firms, and financial institutions. Also financial intermediaries pay deposit insurance on their demand liabilities. Furthermore, the maximum yield, R_t, available to financial intermediaries may differ from that available to depositors. The effects of these ignored sources of the wedge may not be negligible.

[12] The output distance function has definition and interpretation analogous to those for the input distance function defined in section 2.1. See Barnett (1987). When deflated by its value in a base period, the output distance function becomes the Malmquist output quantity index. In the special case of linear homogeneity of the function f, the Malmquist output quantity index becomes the function f, deflated by its value in the base period. Hence in that elementary case, f is itself the output quantity aggregator function.

3.2 Index number theory

The problem of acquiring a non-parametric approximation to the exact output quantity aggregate again arises, although we now are dealing with an output quantity aggregate, and again the best known statistical index is the Divisia index in continuous time or its Törnqvist (Simpson's rule) approximation in discrete time. The formula is the same as that described in section 2.2 above, but with quantities demanded, $\mathbf{m}_t$, replaced by quantities supplied, $\boldsymbol{\mu}_t$, and with paid user costs, $\boldsymbol{\pi}_t$, replaced by received user costs, $\boldsymbol{\gamma}_t$.[13]

4 The Regulatory Wedge

The nature of the regulatory wedge and its associated shadow price is most easily seen by considering the simple case of an economy with one consumer, who consumes all of the economy's monetary services, one financial intermediary, which produces all of the economy's monetary services, and two monetary assets.[14] Equilibrium in the monetary sector of the economy is illustrated in Figure 1, when no reserve requirements exist. Money market equilibrium, when one or both of the monetary assets is subject to reserve requirements, is illustrated in Figure 2.

In Figure 1, equilibrium is produced by the familiar separating hyperplane. The separating hyperplane simultaneously supports an indifference curve from below and a production possibility curve from above. The axes represent quantities of each of the two monetary assets demanded and supplied. Equilibrium in the two markets exists at the mutual tangency of the separating hyperplane, the indifference curve, and the production possibility curve. In equilibrium, the quantities demanded, $\mathbf{m}_t$, equal the quantities supplied, $\boldsymbol{\mu}_t$. In addition, the gradient vector to the separating hyperplane produces the equilibrium user-cost prices. The user-cost prices paid by the consumer, $\boldsymbol{\pi}_t$, are equal, in equilibrium, to the user-cost prices received by the financial intermediary, $\boldsymbol{\gamma}_t$.[15]

Clearly in this case it makes no difference whether we apply the Divisia index (discrete or continuous) to the demand side of the market or the supply side of the market. The same value for the monetary quantity aggregate will

---

[13] For a detailed presentation of the microeconomic theory relevant to section 3, see Barnett (1987). For results relevant to microeconometric modeling of this economic theory, see Berndt and Khaled (1979), Brown, Caves and Christensen (1979), Denny and Pinto (1978), and Lau (1978b).

[14] Relevant approaches to aggregation over economic agents are considered in Barnett (1987, sec. 9).

[15] We previously acquired the same result regarding those user-cost prices by setting the reserve requirement ratios equal to zero in the formula for $\boldsymbol{\gamma}_t$ and showing that we then acquired the formulas for $\boldsymbol{\pi}_t$.

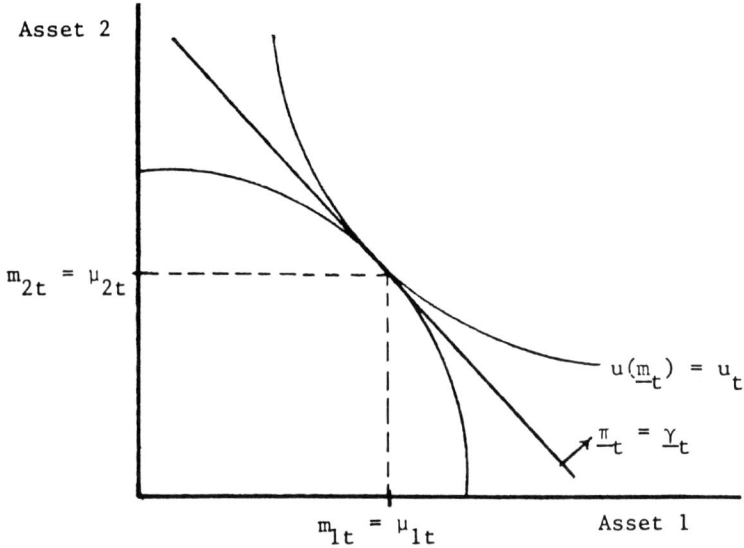

Figure 1: Money market equilibrium with zero required reserves.

be acquired from either side of the market at every t. This result follows from the fact that we would acquire the same quantity and price data from either side of the market, and the Divisia index depends upon only those quantities and prices. Hence the Divisia demand aggregate always exactly equals the Divisia supply aggregate.[16]

However, the situation is very much different, when required reserves exist. In that case, two different supporting hyperplanes exist *in equilibrium*. One supporting hyperplane exists for the financial intermediary, and another exists for the consumer. In Figure 2, the line with gradient equal to the

---

[16]The result also follows from direct comparison of (2) and (4), since if we set the reserve requirement ratios equal to zero in the supply-side user-cost formulas, then monetary-asset component user-cost price data will always be exactly the same on both sides of the market. Hence, in this case, the equality of the Divisia demand and supply aggregates is an identity. It is also possible to acquire the same result from the underlying aggregation theory, rather than directly from the Divisia index. However, the result does not follow as an identity from the aggregation theory, despite the fact that the result is an identity in index number theory. To acquire continuous equality of the supply-side and demand-side economic aggregator functions, we need not only continuous market clearing, but also linear homogeneity of both the utility function and the factor requirements function. Also for the real demand side and real supply side indexes to be the same over time, the price deflator used to deflate nominal to real balances must be the same on both sides of the market.

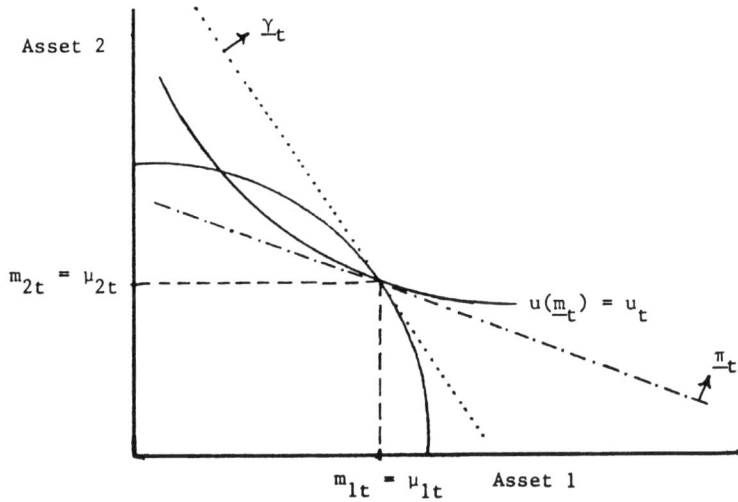

Figure 2: Money market equilibrium with positive required reserves.

consumer's monetary-asset user-cost prices, π_t, is the consumer's supporting hyperplane, and it is his budget constraint in equilibrium. That line is represented by alternate dots and dashes, and is tangent to the displayed indifference curve in equilibrium. The financial intermediary's supporting hyperplane has gradient equal to the financial intermediary's user-cost prices, γ_t. That hyperplane is the financial intermediary's iso-revenue line, which is tangent to the firm's production possibility curve at the equilibrium point. The equilibrium point is the point at which the two supporting hyperplanes intersect, and the angle between them is the regulatory wedge produced by the implicit reserve-requirement tax 'paid' by the financial intermediary in the form of foregone interest on required reserves. At the equilibrium point both markets are cleared, and the consumer is maximizing utility subject to the displayed budget constraint, and the financial intermediary is maximizing revenue subject to the displayed production possibility curve.

It no longer is true that the Divisia demand monetary aggregate need identically and mechanically always equal the Divisia supply monetary aggregate. Since the component markets are cleared, the component quantities are still the same on both sides of the market. However, the statistical Divisia quantity index also depends upon the user-cost prices, which are not equal on the two sides of the market when a regulatory wedge exists. Our conclusion regarding the Divisia demand and Divisia supply aggregates would also follow directly from the underlying economic aggregation theory.[17]

The difference between the Divisia demand and supply aggregates is related to the size of the regulatory wedge, since we know that the difference between the two indexes must equal zero, when no regulatory wedge exists. Hence the degree to which the two Divisia quantity indexes tend to differ over time is an indirect measure of the size of the regulatory wedge.

5 Dynamic Behavior

5.1 Data

The data consists of seasonally adjusted monthly observations from 1/69 through 2/84 of simple sum, supply Divisia, and demand Divisia quantity indices for the $M1$, $M2$ and $M3$ aggregation levels. There are similar curvilinear upward trends in the data. A least squares analysis of the Divisia and simple sum indices shows that the quadratic terms are significant. We therefore use second differencing to remove the trend.[18]

---

[17] The aggregation-theoretic Malmquist demand and supply quantity aggregates are produced from the distance function. In the case of the Malmquist demand quantity aggregate, the distance is that from a base level indifference curve. In the case of the Malmquist supply quantity aggregate, the distance is that from a base-level production possibility curve. Since the curvature properties of indifference curves and production possibility curves are different, the base level indifference curve and production possibility curve will not lie on top of each other (although they may be tangent at one point). As a result, even if all component markets are always cleared, the distance from the equilibrium-point to the base-level indifference curve will not always equal the distance from the equilibrium-point to the base-level production possibility curve. The exception would be the case in which the economy always moves along a single ray through the origin. That exceptional case, which would produce continuous market clearing in the quantity aggregate as well as in the component quantities, would be produced if both the factor requirements function and the utility function were linearly homogeneous and the size of the wedge (angle between the two supporting hyperplanes) remained constant over time. In that case, we would not only get continuous equality of the Malmquist demand and supply aggregates, but also of the Divisia demand and supply quantity indexes, since the growth rates of all component quantities are always equal along a ray through the origin. These observations also could be used to produce our results regarding Figure 1 as a special case, since in Figure 1 the size of the wedge always is constant over time — at zero. However, that route to our conclusions regarding Figure 1 would also require the assumptions of linear homogeneity of the utility function and the factor requirements function. By using the Divisia index, we only need a zero wedge, but not necessarily linear homogeneity of any function.

[18] A convenient source of the data is Fayyad (1986). We did not use data for the highest level of aggregation, called L by the Federal Reserve, since there are no reserve requirements, and hence no implicit taxes, on those assets that are contained in L, but not in $M3$. As a result, for our purposes $M3$ is the highest relevant level of aggregation. We used identical components for both the Divisia demand and Divisia supply aggregate at each level of aggregation to produce direct comparability between the corresponding demand and supply aggregate. As a result we assume blockwise weak separability of tastes and

5.2 Estimating spectra

The spectrum of each series analyzed was estimated using simple spectral methods. The periodogram was smoothed by using a moving average of $M = 33$ periodogram terms.[19] Details of our approach to spectral and cross-spectral estimation are given in Hinich and Weber (1984). The spectra were estimated using a sample size of 180 months. This sample size is sufficiently large to permit us to employ the large-sample statistical properties of spectral estimators derived in the literature.

If the true spectrum is a smooth function, the bias can be reduced somewhat by spline smoothing on the output of the moving average. We spline smoothed the moving-average-smoothed periodogram with the IMSL spline smoothing routine. The log of the sample spectrum is an estimate of the spectral density function. The spectral density, which has total area of one, indicates the distribution of the random process's variance over the frequency spectrum.

To designate the three types of aggregation, Divisia demand, Divisia supply, and simple sum, we use the following notational conventions. At the three levels of aggregation, we use the conventional notation, $M1$, $M2$, and $M3$, to designate the three simple sum aggregates (quantity indices). We designate the corresponding supply Divisia quantity indices by $SDM1$, $SDM2$, and $SDM3$, and the demand Divisia indices by $DDM1$, $DDM2$, and $DDM3$. We also use $M1$, $M2$, and $M3$ to designate the three common component groupings; so, for example, the demand Divisia $M1$ aggregate is $DDM1$.

In Figure 3, the log estimated spectrum of $DDM1$, the demand Divisia $M1$ quantity index, is superimposed on the 95% confidence band of the spectrum of $SDM1$, the supply Divisia $M1$ quantity index. The demand Divisia spectrum everywhere lies well within the confidence band, lending support to the hypothesis that the small differences between the spectra are indistinguishable from sampling variability in the indices. Figure 4 provides the corresponding results at the $M2$ level of aggregation, and Figure 5 provides the results at the $M3$ level of aggregation. The figures at the $M2$ and $M3$

---

technology, on both sides of the money markets, in identical blocks.

[19] The value of M determines the trade-off between bias and variance for a fixed sample size. The larger the value of M, the smaller the variance of the estimated spectrum at a given frequency, but the larger the bias. The bias results from the smearing of the true spectrum by the moving average used in the estimation. The greater the variation of the true spectrum in the moving average 'window', the greater the bias. Since we do not know the shape of the true spectrum when we estimate it, we have no way of quantifying the bias for a given data set. We tried $M = 11$ and $M = 33$. Since the spectrum was smooth at $M = 11$, the bias will remain low for higher M. So variance can be decreased without much increase in bias by increasing M. We selected $M = 33$ which is as large a value as seemed feasible at the given sample size. Degrees of freedom would have become too low at higher M.

Dynamic Behavior

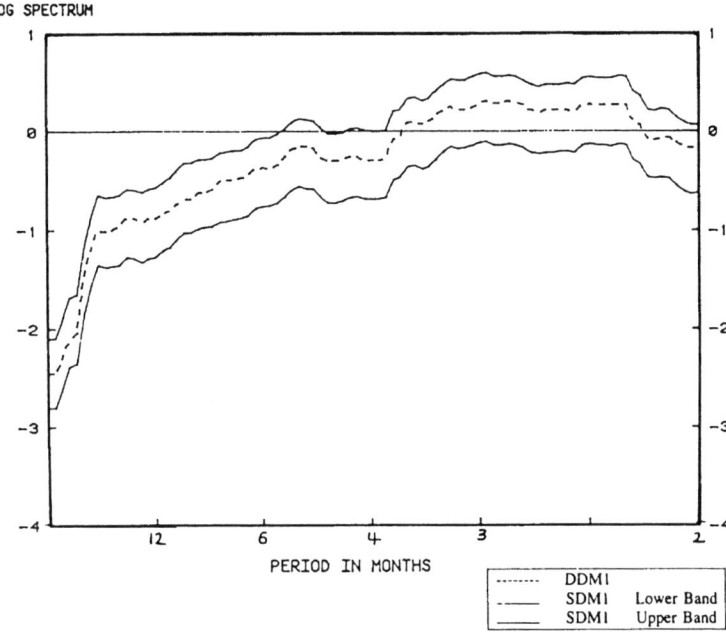

Figure 3: Log spectrum of DDM1 and confidence band for spectrum of SDM1.

levels of aggregation produce the same conclusions as those at the $M1$ level of aggregation. Overall, these results indicate that the covariance functions of the second differenced supply and demand Divisia quantity indices are very similar at each level of aggregation.

5.3 Cross-spectral Estimation

Consider two correlated time series, $a(t)$ and $b(t)$, whose spectra are denoted $S(f_a)$ and $S(f_b)$. Let $CS(f_{ab})$ denote the cross-spectrum between $a(t)$ and $b(t)$.[20] An important function of the spectra of $a(t)$ and $b(t)$ and of the cross-spectra is the coherence, here denoted by $\gamma(f_{ab})$. It is defined in terms of squared coherence by $\gamma^2(f_{ab}) = [CS(f_{ab})]^2/S(f_a)S(f_b)$. It can be shown that the coherence for each frequency is between zero and one. It is the correlation

---

[20]We smooth the cross-periodogram using a moving average of $M = 33$ terms. Once again we assume that the bias in the estimate of $CS((k/N)_{ab})$ is small for this smoothing window. In order to reduce the bias under the assumption that the true cross-spectrum has slowly varying real and imaginary parts, we spline smooth the output of the moving average.

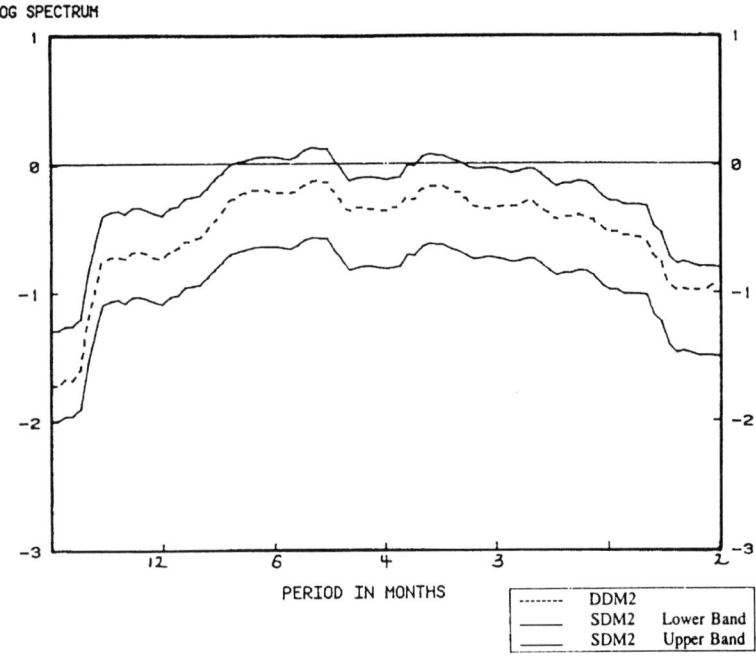

Figure 4: Log spectrum of DDM2 and confidence band for spectrum of SDM2.

of the fth frequency components of the two processes. An approximately unbiased estimator of the squared coherence is obtained by substituting the estimators of the cross-spectrum and of the spectra of $a(t)$ and $b(t)$ into the above expression.

The estimated squared coherence between the supply and demand Divisia indices is plotted in Figure 6. At the $M1$ level of aggregation, the squared coherence between the series is high for all frequencies. The generally high coherence indicates that the two indices remain highly correlated at all frequencies after differencing. The estimated squared coherence between $SDM2$ and $DDM2$ drops somewhat to around 0.9 for periods shorter than three months, indicating that the series differ more for high frequency moves than did the $M1$ level aggregates. The coherence between $SDM3$ and $DDM3$ is slightly higher at the high frequencies than is the case for the $M2$ level aggregates. Overall, the squared coherence plots in Figure 6 indicate that the supply and demand indices are nearly, but not completely, the same. The differences in dynamic behavior, although always small, are most evident at the $M2$ level of aggregation.

Dynamic Behavior

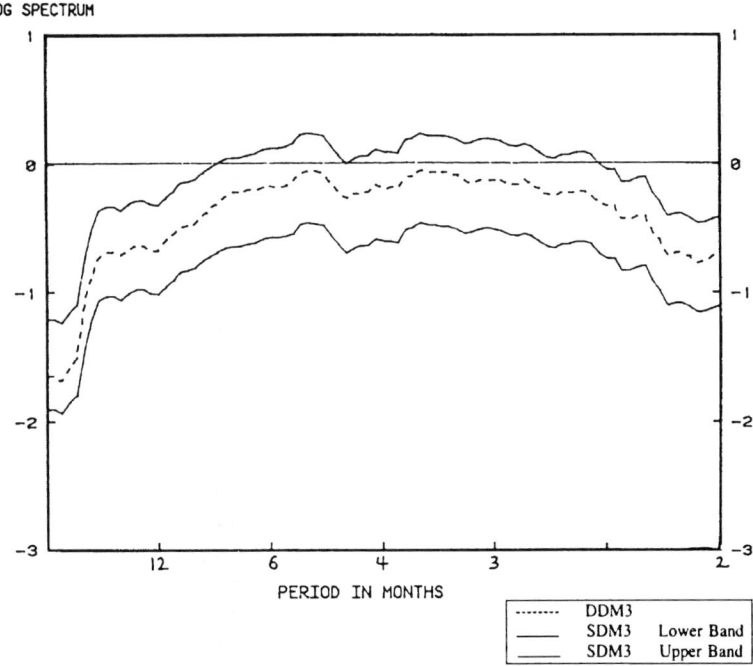

Figure 5: Log spectrum of DDM3 and confidence band for spectrum of SDM3.

5.4 The Hilbert Transform Estimator

Suppose that we wish to estimate a causal distributed lag model for the unobserved time series $x(t)$ and $y(t)$. Suppose that we observe the series $a(t) = x(t) + ex(t)$ and $b(t) = y(t) + ey(t)$, where $ex(t)$ and $ey(t)$ are random noise processes. Now assume that $x(t)$ and $y(t)$ are related by the causal distributed lag model $y(t) = \sum_{n=0}^{\infty} h(n)x(t-n)$, where the $h(n)$ sequence is assumed to be absolutely summable. In each application of this model, we shall be using alternative measures of monetary services, at a common level of aggregation, as $a(t)$ and $b(t)$. Hence it is appropriate to incorporate the noise processes, $ex(t)$ and $ey(t)$, into the observations. In effect, our specification introduces errors-in-the-variables into all variables, both dependent and independent.

Suppose that the filter (distributed lag) is invertible. Then the Hilbert transform relates the log gain with phase function. Details of the use of the Hilbert transform to estimate the gain, and then, combined with the phase, to estimate the $h(n)$ weights, are presented in Hinich and Weber (1986) along

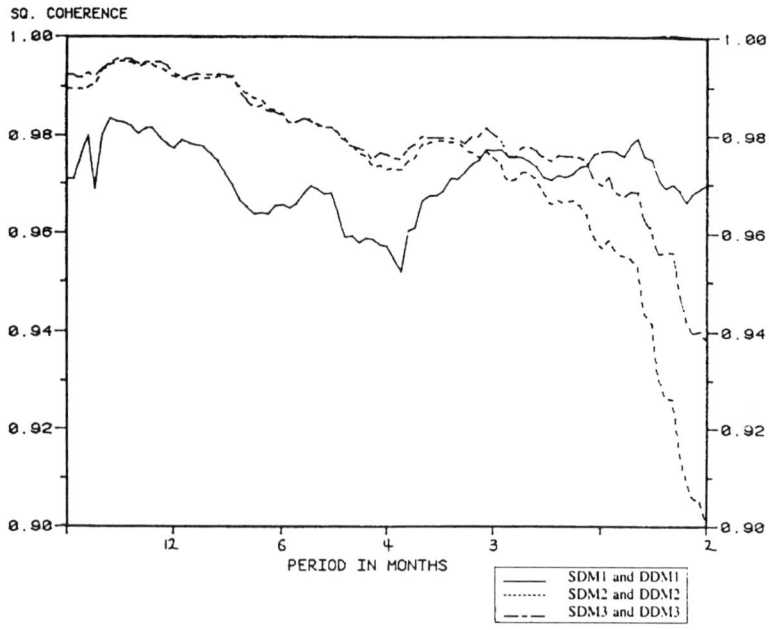

Figure 6: Squared coherence between the Divisia demand and Divisia supply aggregates.

with the formula for the large sample standard errors for the estimates of the $h(n)$ weights. It is shown that the large sample standard errors are the same for all the n.

The Hinich-Weber method was applied to the data. Ordinary least squares was also used for comparison. The results are displayed in Table 1. If the errors in the variables problem were small, then the results from OLS and from the Hilbert transform approach would be similar. The first two columns of Table 1 contain the two sets of results using demand Divisia $DDM1$ as the dependent variable. The independent variable is supply Divisia $SDM1$. The estimates for lag coefficients higher than lag 7 are so small that we display only the first eight coefficient estimates plus the zero lag coefficient. There is little difference between the OLS and Hilbert estimates. This is not surprising, since the high coherence between $DDM1$ and $SDM1$ implies that there is little additive error in the series and thus the OLS estimates are unbiased (as are the Hilbert estimates). The standard error of the Hilbert estimates is smaller than all the standard errors of the OLS estimates; and, in fact, the standard error of the Hilbert estimates is sufficiently small to make the estimates at lags 2, 4 and 6 statistically significant. Thus these estimates suggest that there is a small distributed lag effect between the two Divisia indices. Perhaps the distributed lag could be imputed to the transmission mechanism through the aggregated money market from one side of the market to the other.

TABLE 1
HILBERT TRANSFORM AND OLS RESULTS WITH THE CORRESPONDING DEMAND DIVISIA AGGREGATE AS THE DEPENDENT VARIABLE.[a]

Coefficient	SDM1 Hilbert	SDM1 OLS	SDM2 Hilbert	SDM2 OLS	SDM3 Hilbert	SDM3 OLS
$h(0)$	1.00^b (0.011)	1.02^b (0.017)	1.00^b (0.013)	1.039^b (0.014)	1.00^b (0.011)	1.01^b (0.013)
$h(1)$	−0.000 (0.001)	−0.005 (0.019)	-0.068^b (0.013)	-0.049^b (0.014)	-0.047^b (0.011)	-0.032^b (0.012)
$h(2)$	0.026^b (0.011)	0.015 (0.021)	0.036^b (0.013)	0.023 (0.014)	0.035^b (0.011)	0.010 (0.013)
$h(3)$	0.001 (0.011)	0.005 (0.021)	-0.012 (0.013)	-0.026^b (0.014)	-0.015 (0.011)	-0.018^b (0.012)
$h(4)$	-0.035^b (0.011)	−0.021 (0.022)	0.003 (0.013)	−0.007 (0.014)	0.007 (0.011)	−0.004 (0.013)
$h(5)$	0.011 (0.011)	0.009 (0.021)				
$h(6)$	0.027^b (0.011)	0.010 (0.21)				
$h(7)$	0.014 (0.011)	0.012 (0.020)				
$h(8)$	−0.007 (0.011)	−0.023 (0.018)				

[a] Standard errors are in parentheses. The Hilbert method necessarily produces identical standard errors at all lags.
[b] t-ratios exceeding 2.0.

The third and fourth columns present comparisons for the $M2$ level aggregates. Demand Divisia $DDM2$ is the dependent variable for both the OLS and Hilbert results. The OLS and Hilbert estimated models are basically the same with the supply Divisia independent variable, and they suggest, as was the case at the $M1$ level of aggregation, that a small distributed lag effect exists between the demand and supply Divisia quantity indices. In the fifth and sixth columns, the results using the Divisia $M3$ level aggregates are qualitatively similar to those acquired at the $M1$ and $M2$ levels of aggregation.

These results suggest that there are subtle structural differences of the supply and demand Divisia indices. That conclusion follows from joint consideration of the three parts of our data analysis: the spectra, the squared coherencies, and especially the Hilbert estimated distributed lags.

6 Steady State Behavior

In the previous section, we used frequency domain methods to explore the dynamic behavior of the Divisia demand and Divisia supply monetary aggregates. Since regulatory constraints have important effects upon the dynamic behavior and flexibility of the economy, our findings regarding the relationship between the dynamic behavior of the Divisia demand and Divisia supply aggregates provide information about the economic effects of the regulatory wedge between aggregate monetary services demand and supply. However, the deadweight welfare loss and shadow price associated with such regulatory constraints are most easily understood in terms of steady state or comparative statics analysis. As a result, in this section we use more elementary time domain methods to explore the effects of the regulatory wedge.

There are two direct methods of investigating the size of the wedge and its stationary effect on monetary markets. One method is simply to observe the size of the gap that develops over time between the Divisia demand and corresponding Divisia supply aggregate. In Figure 7 we display, without any form of detrending, the time paths of the $M3$ level Divisia demand and Divisia supply monetary aggregates, along with the time paths of the corresponding simple sum aggregates, provided for comparison. Clearly the gap between the Divisia demand and corresponding Divisia supply aggregate is small relative to the gap between either Divisia aggregate and the corresponding simple sum aggregate. Inspection of that figure tends further to confirm the impressions previously acquired in the frequency domain with detrended data. We display those results only at the $M3$ level of aggregation, since the implicit tax, and hence the wedge, is greatest at the highest level of aggregation.

However, a more direct measure exists of the stationary effect of regulation. We can compute the dollar value of the implicit tax paid by financial intermediaries as a result of the existence of required reserves with regulated zero rate of return. The formula for computing that shadow tax was provided in section 3, both for the end-of period foregone interest and for its discounted value. In Table 2, we display those computed taxes, for each of the three groupings of components. The implicit tax reaches its maximum

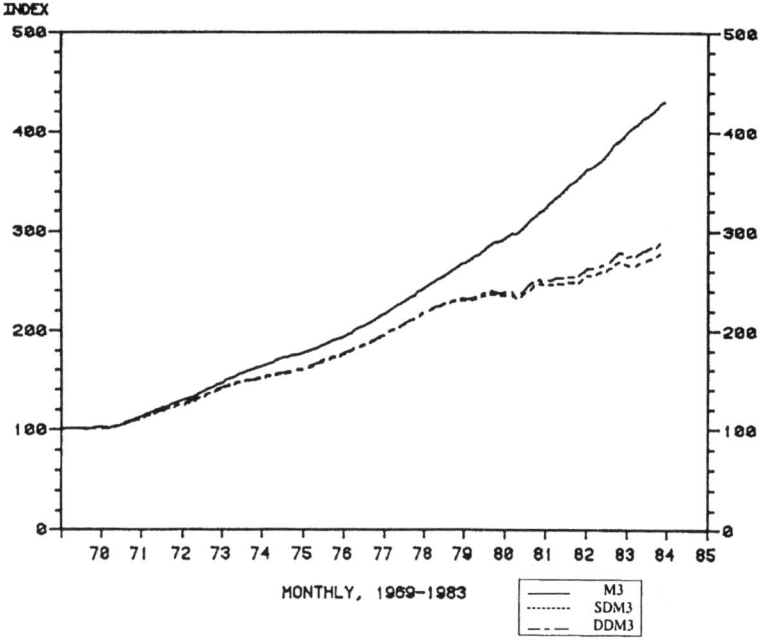

Figure 7: M3 level aggregates.

when all of the components in $M3$ are included, since $M3$ includes all of the reservable monetary assets in the economy. That tax has reached levels as high as 9 percent of GNP (in 12/80). The implicit tax is formidable indeed. If the constraint were removed entirely, or if interest were paid on reserves as occasionally has been seriously proposed, the effect on the economy would certainly be non-negligible. Nevertheless, as has been shown in the previous section, the taxation wedge between Divisia monetary demand and Divisia supply may not pose much of a problem for modeling, except perhaps relative to very short-term transitory phenomena.

While the empirically subtle results acquired with the Divisia aggregates may appear to contrast greatly with the very large computed implicit tax, the issues considered in the two cases are entirely different. Our static and dynamic analyses with the Divisia demand and supply aggregates investigate the effects on modeling of the wedge between aggregate monetary services demand and supply — given that the regulatory constraints exist. The results with the computed implicit tax explore the comparative statics effect of the regulatory constraint — relative to the alternative of no constraint at all (or of payment of the market interest rate on required reserves).

TABLE 2
ANNUAL IMPLICIT RESERVE REQUIREMENTS TAX IN MILLIONS OF DOLLARS, (ANNUAL TAX AND DISCOUNTED BEGINNING-OF-PERIOD TAX).

	Annual tax			Discounted tax		
	M1	M2	M3	M1	M2	M3
Date	components	components	components	components	components	components
1969	41,741.27	64,360.66	66,970.18	38,154.72	58,830.58	61,215.89
1970	39,913.12	62,464.31	65,105.87	37,069.53	57,998.43	60,451.13
1971	38,297.80	60,366.63	63,809.95	35,559.70	56,050.70	59,247.86
1972	37,344.64	60,870.98	64,840.62	34,482.59	56,205.89	59,871.30
1973	45,134.86	74,988.57	81,663.11	41,143.90	68,357.86	74,422.23
1974	50,557.10	84,676.57	94,224.44	45,670.37	76,491.93	85,116.92
1975	41,091.36	66,616.56	71,750.29	38,047.56	61,682.00	66,435.45
1976	37,247.42	61,326.58	64,817.57	35,541.43	58,517.73	61,848.83
1977	34,095.26	58,292.35	61,521.98	30,855.43	52,753.25	55,676.00
1978	37,515.62	64,693.54	69,225.77	33,199.66	57,250.92	61,261.74
1979	45,613.84	79,620.50	85,948.00	39,907.12	69,659.23	75,195.10
1980	55,150.74	97,247.90	105,501.50	45,541.48	80,370.17	87,191.32
1981	63,758.17	114,729.80	125,465.00	54,078.18	97,311.11	106,416.45
1982	54,886.94	101,242.70	125,465.00	47,562.34	87,731.98	108,721.84

7 Conclusion

The existence of reserve requirements on some monetary assets has effects on the behavior of the economy. The computed value of the implicit tax paid by financial intermediaries is very large, so payment of interest on required reserves or the removal of the reserve requirement constraints would produce substantial redistribution of income within the economy.

In addition, with the reserve requirements in place, the resulting constraint produces a regulatory wedge between perceived aggregate monetary services received by demanders of monetary assets and aggregate monetary services produced by financial intermediaries. We acquire that result both empirically and in theory. The regulatory wedge produces some divergence over time between the Divisia demand and corresponding Divisia supply monetary aggregates. However, that divergence looks small, especially at high levels of aggregation, when compared with the divergence between the simple sum aggregate and either of the two corresponding Divisia aggregates.

With the reserve requirements in place, the regulatory wedge also produces dynamic effects, which appear to be related to the transmission mechanism through the money markets. We find that the dynamic effects are small at all frequencies, but are most noticeable at high frequencies. The spectra alone do not display any significant differences between the Divisia demand and supply aggregates at any frequencies. However, a small short-run (high-frequency) effect is evident from the existence of a small but statistically significant distributed lag between Divisia demand and Divisia supply; that phenomenon was captured through the use of the Hilbert estimator. The high frequency effect also appears in the lowered coherency between the $M2$ level Divisia demand and corresponding Divisia supply monetary aggregate at high frequencies.

In all aspects of this analysis, we use a certainty equivalence approach to modeling and do not include transactions costs in computing user costs. One potentially useful extension to this research would be to incorporate measured transactions costs and explicit treatment of uncertainty.

Chapter 20

Financial-Firm Production of Monetary Services: A Generalized Symmetric Barnett Variable-Profit-Function Approach

William A. Barnett and Jeong Ho Hahm*

An alternative monetary-production model of financial firms is employed to investigate supply-side monetary aggregation. Financial firms are conceived to produce monetary services as outputs through financial intermediation. A new method for testing the existence of consistent monetary-output aggregates in financial firms' production technology is developed in terms of a multiproduct firm's variable profit function, and the method does not require homotheticity of the aggregator function. We use a generalized symmetric Barnett flexible functional form. That specification satisfies global curvature conditions and retains its flexibility under the null hypothesis of weak separability. Neither of those properties is possessed by other flexible functional forms.

Monetary policy is transmitted to the economy through banking firms and other financial intermediaries. Financial firms supply monetary assets through their financial intermediation between borrowers and lenders. These monetary assets play a central role in providing transaction services in the economy. In this context, rigorous microeconomic analysis of the optimal behavior of financial firms is essential to a clear understanding of the monetary transmission mechanism and of the reason for existence of those financial institutions.

The main objective of this study is to employ an alternative monetary-production model of financial firms that produce monetary services as outputs through financial intermediation and empirically to investigate supply-side monetary aggregation. Specifically, this article examines financial firms'

---

*Reprinted with permission from the *Journal of Business and Economic Statistics*. Copyright (1994) by the American Statistical Association. Barnett is from the Department of Economics, Washington University in St. Louis, St. Louis, MO 63130 U.S.A.; Hahm is from the Institute for Monetary and Economic Research, Bank of Korea, Seoul 100-794, Korea.

optimal behavior and tests the hypothesis of functional weak separability and hence the existence of consistent monetary aggregates in financial firms' monetary-production technology. That is, the admissibility of the supply-side monetary aggregation for a subset of monetary components in the producer context is investigated empirically.

In this context, we use the generalized symmetric Barnett flexible functional form, which satisfies global curvature conditions. Although previous studies with the generalized symmetric Barnett model have used a cost-function approach with a single output, this study employs a multiproduct firm's variable-profit-function approach with multiple outputs. A new framework for testing separability and the existence of consistent monetary aggregates is developed in terms of a multiproduct firm's variable profit function, and this testing framework does not require homotheticity of the aggregator function. Unlike other available flexible functional forms, the generalized Barnett model retains flexibility under the null hypothesis of weak separability. In particular, the generalized Barnett model is globally regular and quasi-flexible and remains quasiflexible under the null. Other models are severely biased against the null, since those models lose all relevant forms of flexibility under the null.

The theoretical foundations of the monetary-production model are based on Barnett's monetary aggregation-theoretic approach (Barnett 1980, 1987). Financial firms are modeled as maximizing the discounted present value of variable profits, subject to given technology, expressed as an intertemporal transformation function, while producing monetary assets through financial intermediation. With the derivation of user-cost prices for monetary assets, the monetary-production model can be formulated into the conventional neoclassical form of production by multiproduct firms. As a result, a neoclassical aggregate money-supply function on the production side can be constructed, under some separability conditions in financial firms' monetary-production technology, using the existing literature on output aggregation.

Section 1 provides a general discussion of our model of the monetary production of financial firms, based on Barnett's aggregation-theoretic approach, and describes the derivation of the user-cost prices for monetary assets on the production side. The section also provides a discussion of aggregation theory relevant to our model formulation. Section 2 proposes a new framework for testing separability without imposing homothetic separability and without losing the flexibility of the estimating function under the null. Our approach is produced in terms of a multiproduct firm's variable-profit function. Section 3 describes the data employed in the study and some measurement problems. Section 4 discusses empirical results. Specifically, in that section we examine the admissibility conditions for the construction of theoretically meaningful monetary aggregates on the supply side. Section 5 presents concluding remarks.

For a survey of the analogous empirical results on the consumer-demand side, see Barnett, Fisher, and Serletis (1992). Although that article surveys the available results on demand for monetary assets and exact aggregation over those demands, this article produces results dealing with the supply of monetary services produced by financial intermediaries and the aggregation over those supplies.

1 The Model

The issue concerning the nature and definition of financial firms' outputs is still unsettled. As Santomero (1984) pointed out, there has been little solid work on the nature of financial firms' product, particularly with regard to their role in providing payments services in the economy. In this context, Barnett's (1987) model, based on aggregation-theoretic formulation, shed new light on the modeling of financial firms because the use of neoclassical aggregation and index-number theory provided a direct linkage from the analysis of the individual financial firm's optimal behavior to monetary economics in general and the money-supply mechanism in particular.

Barnett developed a model of monetary production by financial firms based on a conventional neoclassical form of production by multiproduct firms and supply-side aggregation theory. Financial firms are conceived of as producing monetary assets (deposit-account type) that provide monetary services in the economy and marketing these in the form of various loans and securities. Outputs of financial firms are real balances of produced monetary assets such as demand and time deposits. Monetary-asset user-cost prices on the supply side have been derived. Therefore, the model can be formulated into the conventional neoclassical form of production by multiproduct firms and the neoclassical money-supply function for aggregated money on the supply side can be constructed using the existing literature on aggregation and index-number theory. Barnett's approach is in agreement in many ways with that of Hancock (1985, 1987, 1991).

1.1 A Brief Overview of the Literature

Over the past decade, there has been growing acceptance of the view that the supply of money by financial firms should be viewed not as a mechanical process reflecting a fixed reserve multiplier, which relates the supply of money to the monetary base, but as a behavioral decision that financial firms would solve in attempting to perform financial intermediation in an optimal manner.

The Model

Although a substantial body of literature has been developed that attempts to model and explain financial firms' optimal behavior, the literature is still not sufficiently advanced to form a unified and generally accepted theory of financial firms' behavior. In a sense this may reflect the difficult nature of this area, as well as the different objectives pursued in various studies. The review in this section relies primarily on Baltensperger (1980) and Santomero (1984).

The methodology most often applied to the analysis of the behavior of financial firms has been portfolio theory — a category into which a large portion of the existing literature on financial-firm theory falls. The inadequacy of this approach stems primarily from the fact that total firm size, as well as the structure of liabilities, is exogenously determined, and the problem to be solved is simply the optimal allocation of given funds among various assets. One characteristic of this approach is that it completely neglects the aspect of real resource cost in banking operations; thus it cannot explain anything about production cost and other supply characteristics of outputs offered by financial firms. Moreover, solid empirical work has not kept up with the theoretical literature.

Even though various studies have attempted to explain the behavior of financial firms by using the concepts of the theory of the firm — thus correcting the deficiencies of portfolio analysis — they have not been completely successful in developing an adequate model of banking firms and other financial intermediaries, especially under the important null hypothesis of blockwise weak separability of outputs.

One strand of the literature represents *production-cost* or *real-resource* models of financial firms. Such models explain firm size and the structure of bank assets and liabilities in terms of the real-resource cost of generating and maintaining stocks of assets and liabilities. This approach has generated various empirical studies, most of which, however, are cost (or economies-of-scale) studies. These studies have been conducted primarily to provide regulatory authorities with an empirical basis for evaluating the influence of bank mergers on competition and on the cost structure of financial firms.

A noteworthy aspect of this approach is that no general consensus has been reached regarding the appropriate nature and definition of *outputs* of financial firms. This may have very important implications for the analysis of financial firms' optimal behavior because the different definition of financial firms' outputs directly affects the estimation of their production technology, thus affecting estimates of elasticities of substitution and transformation, price elasticities of demand and supply, measurements of economies of scale, and bank profitability. This lack of consensus is reflected in a diversity of measures of outputs employed in the economies-of-scale literature. *Total loans plus investments and total deposits* have often been used, as has *total revenue of banks. Number of accounts* was used by Benston (1965), Bell and Murphy (1968), Benston, Hanweck, and Humphrey (1982), Benston, Berger, Hanweck, and Humphrey (1983), and Gilligan, Smirlock, and Marshall (1984). *Loans in dollar amounts* were used by Murray and White (1983). *Total earning assets in dollar amounts* were used by Clark (1984). *Dollar volume of loans, securities, and deposits* was used by Hunter and Timme (1986). For more details, see Gilbert (1984) and Clark (1984).

The definition of outputs of financial firms has long been a controversial issue. Accordingly a large variety of measures of bank outputs has been employed in theoretical and empirical studies. It is surprising, however, that few studies have actually attempted to define the nature of outputs of financial firms, particularly with regard to their role in providing payment or transaction services. It would be instructive to cite Taggart (1984, p. 612):

> "It is very interesting to observe that although some notion of standing at the center of the payments mechanism is part of most people's intuitive view of the function of commercial banks, this notion has not been a major element in formal models of financial intermediation."

Clearly, outputs or services offered by financial firms in conjunction with their role in the transactions technology underlying the payments mechanism within the economy required considerably more attention than they are currently receiving in the banking literature.

Hancock (1985, 1987, 1991) developed a path-breaking model of bank production based on a rigorous neoclassical formulation, unlike most earlier studies in this area. Her work is an important contribution to the field and shares many characteristics with ours. Her model, however, has some of the same difficulties as the previous studies as far as the definition of banks' outputs is concerned: Hancock stated that it is not clear ex-ante whether monetary goods are inputs or outputs in production. According to her classification rule, demand deposits are classified as outputs, whereas time deposits are classified as inputs. We do not agree with that classification, and we develop and apply an approach to testing weak separability having many advantages over the earlier approach used by Hancock.

1.2 An Alternative Approach to the Modeling of Financial Firms

The model of monetary production by financial firms will be derived under perfect certainty (Barnett 1987). We assume that a financial firm is a competitive profit maximizer. Thus it is assumed that the firm takes input and

The Model

output prices as given in markets and that the objective of the firm is to maximize its variable profit. For simplicity, we also assume that the financial firm makes only one kind of loan, yielding R_t, and produces a vector $\boldsymbol{\mu}_t$ of real balances of monetary assets through financial intermediation. The firm uses real units of excess reserves c_t in the form of currency, a vector $\mathbf{L}_t$ of labor quantities, and a vector $\mathbf{z}_t$ of other factor quantities as factors of production in producing $\boldsymbol{\mu}_t$ during period t. Monetary assets produced by financial intermediation are treated as outputs of financial firms, and thereby the user costs of such assets are implicitly assumed to be positive.

Hancock (1985, 1987) postulated that some such assets can be inputs to financial firms if the corresponding user costs are negative. That possibility is not excluded by the formulation presented here, although we shall not explicitly discuss the probably unusual case of negative user costs. In that rather rare case, the corresponding assets could be removed from $\boldsymbol{\mu}_t$ and treated as a component of $\mathbf{z}_t$. Real balances of $\boldsymbol{\mu}_t$ and c_t are defined to equal nominal balances divided by p_t^*, which is the true cost-of-living index. The Fisher Ideal price index, which is defined as the geometric mean of the Laspeyres and Paasche indexes, can be used operationally for the true cost-of-living index p_t^*. For a detailed discussion of the Fisher Ideal statistical index, see Barnett (1981b, p. 204).

Let a vector of reserve requirement be $\mathbf{k}_t$, where k_{it} is the reserve requirement ratio applicable to μ_{it} and $0 \leq k_{it} \leq 1$ for all i. Then the financial firm's efficient production technology is defined by the following transformation function F:

$$F(\boldsymbol{\mu}_t, \mathbf{z}_t, \mathbf{L}_t, c_t; \mathbf{k}_t) = 0. \tag{1}$$

If $(\mathbf{z}_t, \mathbf{L}_t) = 0$, then no financial intermediation takes place, no value added exists, and no loans are made. In this case, the financial firm is acting as a vault so that all of $\sum_i p_t^* \mu_{it}$ are reserves, and excess reserves are $p_t^* c_t = \sum_i \mu_{it}(1 - k_{it})p_t^*$. See Barnett (1987, p. 121).

The transformation function F satisfies the appropriate regularity conditions. That is, F is strictly quasiconvex in $(\boldsymbol{\mu}_t, \mathbf{z}_t, \mathbf{L}_t, c_t)$ and $\partial F/\partial L_{it} < 0$, $\partial F/\partial z_{it} < 0$, $\partial F/\partial c_t < 0$, and $\partial F/\partial \mu_{it} > 0$, since $\mathbf{L}_t, \mathbf{z}_t$, and c_t are inputs and $\boldsymbol{\mu}_t$ are outputs. The firm's technology can equivalently be represented by its efficient production possibility set S or its production correspondence G defined such that $S(\mathbf{k}_t) = \{(\boldsymbol{\mu}_t, \mathbf{z}_t, \mathbf{L}_t, c_t) \geq 0 : F(\boldsymbol{\mu}_t, \mathbf{z}_t, \mathbf{L}_t, c_t; \mathbf{k}_t) = 0\}$ or $G(\mathbf{z}_t, \mathbf{L}_t, c_t; \mathbf{k}_t) = \{\boldsymbol{\mu}_t \geq 0 : (\boldsymbol{\mu}_t, \mathbf{z}_t, \mathbf{L}_t, c_t) \in S(\mathbf{k}_t)\}$.

Now we proceed to derive the firm's variable-profit function. First, the firm's variable revenue from loans can be expressed by

$$\left[\sum_i (1 - k_{it})\mu_{it} p_t^* - c_t p_t^* - \mathbf{q}_t' \mathbf{z}_t\right] R_t + c_t p_t^* (R_t - R_t^*), \tag{2}$$

where $R_t^* = \min\{R_t, R_t^d\}$, R_t^d is the discount rate during period t, and $\mathbf{q}_t$ is a vector of prices of the factors $\mathbf{z}_t$. Suppose that $R_t \leq R_t^d$ so that $R_t^* = R_t$; then the firm's variable revenue is $(\sum_i \mu_{it} p_t^* - \sum_i k_{it}\mu_{it} p_t^* - c_t p_t^* - \mathbf{q}_t' \mathbf{z}_t) R_t$. If $R_t > R_t^d$, however, so that $R_t^* = R_t^d$, then the variable revenue is $(\sum_i \mu_{it} p_t^* - \sum_i k_{it}\mu_{it} p_t^* - \mathbf{q}_t' \mathbf{z}_t) R_t - c_t p_t^* R_t^d$. For a more detailed discussion of the interrelationship between R_t and R_t^d, see Barnett (1987, p. 122).

The next variable cost that must be paid out of variable revenue is defined by

$$\sum_i \mu_{it} p_t^* \rho_{it} + \mathbf{q}_t' \mathbf{z}_t + \mathbf{w}_t' \mathbf{L}_t, \tag{3}$$

where $\mathbf{w}_t$ is a vector of wage rates corresponding to labor quantities $\mathbf{L}_t$, and $\boldsymbol{\rho}_t$ is a vector of yields paid by the firm on produced monetary assets $\boldsymbol{\mu}_t$. Observe that $\mathbf{w}_t' \mathbf{L}_t$ appears in (3), but not in (2), because $\mathbf{w}_t' \mathbf{L}_t$ is not paid until the end of the period and therefore is not subtracted out of loan quantities placed at the beginning of the period. All other factors, $\mathbf{z}_t$, are purchased at the beginning of period t for use during period t, and the firm must pay for those factors at the beginning of the period t. The exception is labor $\mathbf{L}_t$, which receives its wages at the end of period t for labor quantities supplied to the firm during the period. Interest on produced monetary assets $\boldsymbol{\mu}_t$ is paid at the end of the period, and interest on loans outstanding during the period is received at the end of the period.

Hence variable profits at the end of period t, total revenue less variable cost, is obtained by subtracting (3) from (2). Observe that fixed factors are not relevant to the determination of variable profit. For example, stockholders' equity capital (net worth) is a fixed factor during period t and hence does not enter the variable-profit function. Since stockholder capital is not reservable, all stockholder capital will go into loans at yield R_t. If capital is paid the competitive rate of return, then all of the yield on the investment of stockholder capital will be paid to stockholders as dividends and hence will not affect either total or variable profits. In this context, the profit function can be referred to as an implicit variable-profit function. See Barnett (1987). We divide by $1+R_t$ to discount the variable profits to the beginning of period t. Then the present value of period t variable profits is defined as

$$\Pi_t(\boldsymbol{\mu}_t, \mathbf{z}_t, \mathbf{L}_t, c_t; \mathbf{p}_t^*, \mathbf{q}_t, R_t, \boldsymbol{\rho}_t, \mathbf{w}_t; \mathbf{k}_t) \tag{4}$$
$$= \boldsymbol{\mu}_t' \boldsymbol{\gamma}_t - \mathbf{q}_t' \mathbf{z}_t - \mathbf{w}_t' \mathbf{L}_t/(1 + R_t) - \gamma_{0t} c_t,$$

where γ_{it} is nominal user-cost price of ith produced monetary asset μ_{it} and is derived by

$$\gamma_{it} = \frac{p_t^*[(1 - k_{it})R_t - \rho_{it}]}{1 + R_t}. \tag{5}$$

The Model

And γ_{0t} is nominal user-cost price of excess reserves c_t and is derived by

$$\gamma_{0t} = \frac{p_t^* R_t^*}{1 + R_t}. \tag{6}$$

The user-cost price formula defined by (5) can be rewritten as $\gamma_{it} = \delta_{it} - p_t^* R_t k_{it}/(1 + R_t)$, where $\delta_{it} = p_t^*(R_t - \rho_{it})/(1 + R_t)$, which has the same form as the monetary-asset user-cost formula for the consumer. The user cost of a monetary asset in demand theory was rigorously derived from microeconomic theory by Barnett (1978). Observe that δ_{it} would be equal to γ_{it} if $k_{it} = 0$. As we see, $p_t^* R_t k_{it} \mu_{it}/(1 + R_t)$ is the present value, at the beginning of the period t, of the *implicit reserve tax* $p_t^* R_t k_{it} \mu_{it}$ paid by the financial firm at the end of the period due to the existence of reserve requirements. The Federal Reserve's reserve requirement is a *tax*, because it requires member banks to hold deposits that do not bear interest with the Federal Reserve. The tax is the foregone interest on uninvested required reserves. For example, suppose that k_{it} is the required reserve ratio on deposit i. Then $(1 - k_{it})$ is available for each dollar deposited and can be used for loans and investments. Thus $R_t k_{it}$ is the implicit tax rate imposed by the reserve requirement.

In the user-cost price formula defined by (5) and (6), the own yields paid by the firm $\boldsymbol{\rho}_t$ may include various transactions costs such as service and handling charges and Federal Deposit Insurance Corporation (FDIC) insurance premia. One approach employed to derive the user cost of a monetary asset can be found in the work of Hancock (1985, 1987). The user-cost formulas defined by (5) and (6), after some manipulation, become equivalent to those formulas used by Hancock, although her method of measuring the discount rate is not consistent with the preceding theory that produced the results of (5) and (6). She also incorporated explicit transactions costs into the formulas.

If we write the vector of all variable factor quantities as $\boldsymbol{\alpha} = (\mathbf{z}_t', \mathbf{L}_t', c_t)'$ and the vector of corresponding factor prices $\boldsymbol{\beta}_t = (\mathbf{q}_t', \mathbf{w}_t'/(1 + R_t), \gamma_{0t})'$, variable profits can be defined as

$$\Pi_t = \boldsymbol{\mu}_t' \boldsymbol{\gamma}_t - \boldsymbol{\alpha}_t' \boldsymbol{\beta}_t. \tag{7}$$

Hence the firm's variable-profit-maximization problem takes the conventional form of selecting $(\boldsymbol{\mu}_t, \boldsymbol{\alpha}_t) \in S(\mathbf{k}_t)$ to maximize (7) such that

$$\pi_t(\boldsymbol{\gamma}_t, \boldsymbol{\beta}_t; \mathbf{k}_t) = \max_{(\boldsymbol{\mu}_t, \boldsymbol{\alpha}_t)} \{\boldsymbol{\mu}_t' \boldsymbol{\gamma}_t - \boldsymbol{\alpha}_t' \boldsymbol{\beta}_t : \boldsymbol{\mu}_t, \boldsymbol{\alpha}_t \in S(\mathbf{k}_t)\}. \tag{8}$$

The preceding variable-profit function simply denotes the maximum revenue minus variable cost that the firm can obtain, given that it faces strictly positive prices $\boldsymbol{\gamma}_t, \boldsymbol{\beta}_t$ for variable outputs and inputs.

Using Hotelling's lemma, supplies of outputs and demands for inputs are defined by

$$\mu_{it}(\boldsymbol{\gamma}_t, \boldsymbol{\beta}_t; \mathbf{k}_t) = \frac{\partial \pi_t(\boldsymbol{\gamma}_t, \boldsymbol{\beta}_t; \mathbf{k}_t)}{\partial \gamma_{it}}, \quad \text{for } i = 1, 2, ..., n, \qquad (9)$$

and

$$\alpha_{jt}(\boldsymbol{\gamma}_t, \boldsymbol{\beta}_t; \mathbf{k}_t) = \frac{\partial \pi_t(\boldsymbol{\gamma}_t, \boldsymbol{\beta}_t; \mathbf{k}_t)}{\partial \beta_{jt}}, \quad \text{for } j = 1, 2, ..., m, \qquad (10)$$

where $\mu_{it}(\boldsymbol{\gamma}_t, \boldsymbol{\beta}_k; \mathbf{k}_t)$ and $\alpha_{jt}(\boldsymbol{\gamma}_t, \boldsymbol{\beta}_t; \mathbf{k}_t)$ are the profit-maximizing amounts of outputs i and inputs j, given $\boldsymbol{\gamma}_t$, $\boldsymbol{\beta}_t$, and $\mathbf{k}_t$.

Thus when we postulate a functional form for the variable-profit function $\pi_t(\boldsymbol{\gamma}_t, \boldsymbol{\beta}_t; \mathbf{k}_t)$ of the financial firm, we can obtain functional forms for output supply and input demand functions. And if we assume that the variable profit function $\pi_t(\boldsymbol{\gamma}_t, \boldsymbol{\beta}_t; \mathbf{k}_t)$ is twice differentiable, then unknown parameters that occur in the system of equations defined by (8), (9), and (10) can be jointly estimated, given an appropriate stochastic specification. Furthermore, the existing literature on output aggregation for multiproduct firms becomes immediately applicable to aggregating over the produced monetary assets $\boldsymbol{\mu}_t$ and to measuring value added and technological change in financial intermediation.

1.3 Separability of Technology and Supply-Side Monetary Aggregation

Monetary aggregation theory requires weak separability of the production or transformation function in the block of monetary components over which aggregation is to be performed. In our model of monetary production defined by (1), aggregation over all monetary assets produced as outputs is possible only when the block of monetary outputs is separable from inputs. For a detailed discussion of functional separability and its theoretical implications, see Goldman and Uzawa (1964), Shephard (1970), Berndt and Christensen (1973, 1974), Denny and Fuss (1977), Blackorby, Primont, and Russell (1977), and Denny and Pinto (1978).

Although this separability assumption is empirically testable and will be tested later in this article, we shall at this stage assume that an output aggregate exists in the financial firm's production technology to permit us to investigate the implications of monetary aggregation theory on the supply side of the money market. The transformation function defined by (1), is assumed to be weakly separable in the block of monetary assets produced as

The Model

outputs from inputs. The existence of an output aggregate implies that there exist functions f and H such that

$$F(\boldsymbol{\mu}_t, \mathbf{z}_t, \mathbf{L}_t, c_t; \mathbf{k}_t) = H[f(\boldsymbol{\mu}_t; \mathbf{k}_t), \mathbf{z}_t, \mathbf{L}_t, c_t] = 0, \qquad (11)$$

with $\partial H/\partial f > 0$. For a more detailed explanation of this efficiency condition, see Brown, Caves, and Christensen (1979, pp. 257–258). The implicit function theorem ensures the existence of a function g such that

$$f(\boldsymbol{\mu}_t; \mathbf{k}_t) = g(\mathbf{z}_t, \mathbf{L}_t, c_t). \qquad (12)$$

The function $f(\boldsymbol{\mu}_t; \mathbf{k}_t)$ is called the factor-requirements function because it equals $g(\mathbf{z}_t, \mathbf{L}_t, c_t)$, which is the minimum amount of the aggregate input required to produce the output vector $\boldsymbol{\mu}_t$. The function $g(\mathbf{z}_t, \mathbf{L}_t, c_t)$ is the production function because it equals $f(\boldsymbol{\mu}_t; \mathbf{k}_t)$, which is the maximum amount of the aggregate output that can be produced from the inputs $(\mathbf{z}_t, \mathbf{L}_t, c_t)$. Hence f is both the factor requirements function and the output aggregator function, and g is both the output production function and the input aggregator function.

The aggregation theory is consistent with decentralization in the decision-making process and makes two-stage optimization possible. We now proceed to consider the two-stage decentralized decision process within the firm. In the first stage, the financial firm solves for profit-maximizing factor demands $\boldsymbol{\alpha}_t$ and the profit-maximizing level of the aggregate monetary-asset quantity. In the second stage, the revenue-maximizing vector of individual monetary-asset quantities supplied is determined subject to the aggregate monetary-asset quantity selected from the first stage.

As defined in (8), a financial firm's decision problem is to select $(\boldsymbol{\mu}_t, \boldsymbol{\alpha}_t) \in S(\mathbf{k}_t)$ to

$$\begin{aligned} \text{maximize} \quad & \boldsymbol{\mu}_t' \boldsymbol{\gamma}_t - \boldsymbol{\alpha}_t' \boldsymbol{\beta}_t \\ \text{subject to} \quad & F(\boldsymbol{\mu}_t, \mathbf{z}_t, \mathbf{L}_t, c_t; \mathbf{k}_t) = 0. \end{aligned} \qquad (13)$$

We now decompose the firm's profit-maximization decision defined by (13) into two stages: In the first stage, it is assumed that, for some indexes of the aggregate monetary-asset quantity $M_t = f(\boldsymbol{\mu}_t; \mathbf{k}_t)$ and aggregate monetary-asset price $\Gamma_t = \Gamma(\boldsymbol{\gamma}_t)$, the firm selects factor demands $\boldsymbol{\alpha}_t^*$ to

$$\begin{aligned} \text{maximize} \quad & M_t \Gamma_t - \boldsymbol{\alpha}_t' \boldsymbol{\beta}_t \\ \text{subject to} \quad & f(\boldsymbol{\mu}_t; \mathbf{k}_t) = g(\boldsymbol{\alpha}_t). \end{aligned} \qquad (14)$$

With $\boldsymbol{\alpha}_t^*$ selected, the firm can obtain the optimum aggregate monetary quantity supplied, M_t^*. In stage 2 of the decentralized decision process, the firm chooses a vector of individual monetary assets quantities $\boldsymbol{\mu}_t^*$ to

$$\begin{aligned} \text{maximize} \quad & \boldsymbol{\mu}_t' \boldsymbol{\gamma}_t \\ \text{subject to} \quad & f(\boldsymbol{\mu}_t; \mathbf{k}_t) = M_t^*. \end{aligned} \qquad (15)$$

The financial firm's supply function for aggregated money M_t^* is obtained in the first stage. Observe that $M_t = f(\boldsymbol{\mu}_t^*; \mathbf{k}_t)$ is the exact economic monetary-output quantity aggregate, where $\boldsymbol{\mu}_t^*$ is the profit-maximizing vector of monetary assets produced and the corresponding monetary-output price aggregate is $\Gamma_t = \Gamma(\boldsymbol{\gamma}_t)$. Under the assumption of linear homogeneity of the aggregator function $f(\boldsymbol{\mu}_t; \mathbf{k}_t)$, Fisher's output reversal test states that $M_t \Gamma_t$ must equal actual revenue from production of $\boldsymbol{\mu}_t$ so that $M_t \Gamma_t = \boldsymbol{\mu}_t' \boldsymbol{\gamma}_t$. See Barnett (1987).

In the preceding discussion, if the solution $(\boldsymbol{\mu}_t, \boldsymbol{\alpha}_t) \in S(\mathbf{k}_t)$ to the two-stage decision by solving (14) and (15) is the same as that to the problem (13) for some indexes of aggregated money M_t and the aggregate monetary-output price Γ_t, then the two-stage decentralized decision process is said to be consistent. The economic aggregation theory provides necessary and sufficient conditions for the consistency of the two-stage decision process. See Green (1964, p. 25). The necessary and sufficient conditions are (a) the existence of a linearly homogeneous monetary-asset quantity aggregator function $f(\boldsymbol{\mu}_t; \mathbf{k}_t)$ in the component monetary assets produced and (b) blockwise weak separability of the production (or transformation) function in the blocks of monetary components over which aggregation is performed (often referred to as the admissibility or existence condition). Among the preceding two conditions, the weak separability (or admissibility) condition is of primary concern in this study, and hence we shall test the condition empirically.

2 Separability Testing

The separability specification substantially restricts the structure of production technology and therefore its possible functional form. Separability is consistent with decentralization in the decision-making process, however, and makes stagewise optimization possible. Thus separability (i.e., the existence of consistent aggregates) permits the use of aggregate data.

Separability tests of production structures can be found in the work of Berndt and Christensen (1973, 1974), Denny and Fuss (1977), Woodland (1978), Denny and Pinto (1978), Blackorby, Schworm, and Fisher (1986), and Hancock (1987). Most of the separability studies performed on the production side test for the existence of consistent input aggregates in the manufacturing firm's production technology. An exception is that of Hancock (1987). On the demand side, Serletis (1987a), Swofford and Whitney (1988), and Belongia and Chalfant (1989) investigated testing for blockwise weakly separable groupings of monetary assets. Barnett and Choi (1989a), however, found in a Monte Carlo study that previously available tests for blockwise weak separability perform poorly.

Blackorby, Primont, and Russell (1977) and Denny and Fuss (1977) showed that the restriction of global weak separability, when imposed on a flexible functional form, destroys the flexibility of the specification. This result is very damaging to the use of flexible functional forms in testing for weak separability. Nevertheless, Berndt and Christensen (1973, 1974) used a flexible functional form, the translog, to test for weak separability. The exact test with the translog flexible functional form becomes the joint test of weak separability and homotheticity of the aggregator function, where the homothetic aggregator function under the null is no longer capable of providing an arbitrary second-order approximation to the true aggregator function. This problem has long been recognized, and the most frequently suggested solution is to treat the specified function as a local approximation to the true underlying function rather than to treat the specification as part of the maintained hypothesis. Denny and Fuss (1977) used the approximate test with a translog flexible functional form. The translog function used is considered to be a second-order approximation to the true function, and the null hypothesis is imposed only at a point of approximation.

The approximate test has its own problems, however. First, the disturbances in the estimating equations represent both the usual errors in optimization and the approximation error. Thus it is not clear that the properties of these disturbances can be specified independently of the approximated functional form and the true function (Woodland 1978, p. 384). Second, the least squares estimates of the coefficients may not even approximately be Taylor-series coefficients. If this is the case, the estimated coefficients cannot represent second-order derivatives of the underlying true function. This is very problematic because the local test of separability is related to the properties of the second-order derivatives of the estimating functional forms used (Blackorby, Schworm, and Fisher 1986, p. 3).

An alternative test of separability, using a variable profit (cost) function, was applied by Burgess (1974), Denny and Pinto (1978), Woodland (1978), Hancock (1987), and Blackorby, Schworm, and Fisher (1986). Most relevantly, Hancock (1987) used a translog variable profit (cost) function to test for the existence of a monetary aggregator function for the financial firm.

Some difficulties are found in their studies, however: They used the translog functional form, which has only local approximation properties. The estimated translog profit (cost) functions frequently fail to satisfy the convexity (concavity) conditions that are implied by economic theory. Several researchers have imposed the neoclassical curvature properties globally or locally on the translog profit (cost) function, while also imposing constant returns to scale. See Lau (1978a), Wiley, Schmidt, and Bramble (1973), Jorgenson and Fraumeni (1981), Diewert and Wales (1987), Hall (1973), Woodland (1978), and Hancock (1987). Imposition of both the neoclassical curvature and monotonicity conditions on the translog function, however, results in the model's collapse to Cobb-Douglas regardless of whether or not constant returns to scale are also imposed.

Now we propose an alternative separability-testing method that does not have any of those problems. We use a generalized symmetric Barnett variable-profit-function approach, which is a generalized version of that of Blackorby, Schworm, and Fisher (1986). Although we use a generalized symmetric Barnett variable-profit function for testing for the existence of an output monetary aggregate in the multiproduct financial firm's production technology, Blackorby, Schworm, and Fisher used a generalized symmetric Barnett cost function with a single output to test the existence of input aggregates in an aggregate production model. For a detailed discussion of the generalized symmetric Barnett function, see Diewert and Wales (1987).

We discuss some advantages of using this method of testing for separability: First, we are able to test for separability in the multiproduct firm's production technology without requiring homotheticity of the aggregator function and without losing flexibility of the estimating function. Second, the functional form generated by using a generalized symmetric Barnett function has attractive global properties. The variable-profit function is globally convex in prices. Consequently it is not necessary to check convexity of the profit function once the parameters have been estimated. Third, this method does not require the assumption of a constant-returns-to-scale technology.

Suppose that a multiproduct firm's transformation function can be represented by

$$F(\mathbf{x}) = 0, \tag{16}$$

where $\mathbf{x}$ is a vector of net outputs. Following Debreu's convention, we index outputs as positive and inputs as negative. Then the firm's variable-profit function can be written as

$$\pi(\mathbf{p}) = \max_{\mathbf{x}}\{\mathbf{p}'\mathbf{x} \colon F(\mathbf{x}) = 0\}, \tag{17}$$

where $\mathbf{p}$ is a vector of prices of outputs and inputs. The variable-profit function denotes the maximum revenue minus variable cost that the firm can obtain, given positive input and output prices $\mathbf{p}$. The variable-profit function is a nonnegative continuous function, which is linearly homogeneous and convex in prices. Under certain regularity conditions, the variable-profit function $\pi(\mathbf{p})$ defined by (17) and the transformation function F defined by (16) are dual and thus equivalent representations of the firm's technology. See Diewert (1973) and McFadden (1978).

Let $I = \{1, \ldots, n\}$, and $I^0 = \{I^1, I^2\}$. Then let $\{I^1, I^2\}$ index a partition of the net output vector $\mathbf{x} = (\mathbf{x}^1, \mathbf{x}^2)$, whose corresponding price vector is $\mathbf{p} = (\mathbf{p}^1, \mathbf{p}^2)$. Suppose that there exists a monetary aggregate $M = f(\mathbf{x}^1)$. Then the firm's transformation function is separable in $\mathbf{x}^1$ and may be expressed as

$$F(f(\mathbf{x}^1), \mathbf{x}^2) = 0. \tag{18}$$

It has been shown that the structure of (18) for the transformation function is equivalent to that of the variable-profit function (see Brown et al. 1979; Diewert 1973; Lau 1972);

$$\pi(\mathbf{p}) = \pi^*(\pi^1(\mathbf{p}^1), \mathbf{p}^2). \tag{19}$$

For tests of separability in the multiproduct firm's production technology, we employ the variable-profit function defined by (19), which is a dual representation of (18). To construct the firm's variable-profit function, first define the maximum conditional profits of producing any given level of monetary aggregate $M = f(\mathbf{x}^1)$ as

$$\pi^1(\mathbf{p}^1, M) = \max_{\mathbf{x}^1}\{\mathbf{p}^{1'}\mathbf{x}^1 : f(\mathbf{x}^1) \leq M\}. \tag{20}$$

Next define the maximum conditional profit of producing outputs (which are not included in M), conditioned on a particular level of the monetary aggregate M as

$$\pi^2(\mathbf{p}^2, M) = \max_{\mathbf{x}^2}\{\mathbf{p}^{2'}\mathbf{x}^2 : F(M, \mathbf{x}^2) = 0\}. \tag{21}$$

Then the firm's *total variable-profit function* can be written as

$$\pi(\mathbf{p}) = \max_M\{\pi(\mathbf{p}, M)\} = \max_M\{\pi^1(\mathbf{p}^1, M) + \pi^2(\mathbf{p}^2, M)\}, \tag{22}$$

where $\pi(\mathbf{p}, M) = \pi^1(\mathbf{p}^1, M) + \pi^2(\mathbf{p}^2, M)$, and is called the *conditional variable-profit function*. Equation (22) implies that the firm's total variable profits are the maximum of the sum of two conditional profit functions, (20) and (21), with respect to a particular level of the monetary aggregate M. As a special case, if we suppose that the monetary aggregate M contains all outputs, then $\pi^1(\mathbf{p}^1, M)$ in (20) becomes a revenue function at a given level of monetary aggregate M. On the other hand, $\pi^2(\mathbf{p}^2, M)$ in (21) becomes a variable-cost function (i.e., minus of the variable-profit function) in producing the given level of output aggregate M.

It can be shown, in fact, that (18) holds if and only if (22) is true. A formal statement of this was given by Lau (1972), who attributed it to Gorman. See Blackorby, Schworm, and Fisher (1986, p. 5). As a result, separability of the transformation function F defined by (18) can be tested by testing additivity restrictions on the conditional variable-profit function $\pi(\mathbf{p}, M)$ defined by (22).

In actual separability testings, the estimating system constitutes input-demand and output-supply functions. The input-demand and output-supply functions are derived from the conditional variable-profit function defined by (22), using the duality and envelope theorems (Varian 1984, pp. 376–379):

$$x_i^*(\mathbf{p}, M^*) = \frac{\partial \pi(\mathbf{p})}{\partial p_i} = \frac{\partial \pi(\mathbf{p}, M^*)}{\partial p_i}, \qquad (23)$$

where $M^*(\mathbf{p})$ is the maximizer in (22) and $x_i^*(\mathbf{p}, M^*)$ is the profit-maximizing amount of output i [or input if $x_i^*(\mathbf{p}, M^*) < 0$] given prices $\mathbf{p}$ and the monetary aggregate M.

We specify the preceding conditional variable-profit function $\pi(\mathbf{p}, M)$ to be a quadratic in a particular level of the monetary aggregate M as follows:

$$\pi(\mathbf{p}, M) = A + B \cdot M + (1/2)\, D \cdot M^2. \qquad (24)$$

From the first-order condition for optimization [i.e., $\partial \pi(\mathbf{p}, M)/\partial M = 0$], we have

$$M^*(\mathbf{p}) = -B/D. \qquad (25)$$

Then the firm's total variable-profit function may be expressed as

$$\pi(\mathbf{p}) = A - (1/2)\, B^2/D, \qquad (26)$$

where A, B, and D are functions of prices $\mathbf{p}$. We specify A as a *generalized symmetric Barnett function* and B and D as linear functions of prices as follows:

$$\begin{aligned}
A &= \sum_i a_{ii} p_i - 2 \sum_{\{(i,j):j>i\}} a_{ij}(p_i p_j)^{1/2} \\
&\quad + \sum_{\{(i,j,k):j\neq i, k\neq i, k>j\}} a_{ijk}(p_i)^2 (p_j p_k)^{-1/2}, \qquad (27) \\
B &= \sum_i b_i p_i, \qquad (28) \\
D &= \sum_i d_i p_i, \qquad (29)
\end{aligned}$$

where $a_{ij} \geq 0$, $a_{ijk} \geq 0$, and $d_i \geq 0$.

Observe that the conditional variable-profit function $\pi(\mathbf{p}, M)$ specified in (24)–(29) is linearly homogeneous in prices $\mathbf{p}$. Observe also that $\pi(\mathbf{p}, M)$ is globally convex in prices $\mathbf{p}$, with nonnegativity restrictions on the parameters imposed ($a_{ij} \geq 0$ and $a_{ijk} \geq 0$). Thus the preceding specified profit function $\pi(\mathbf{p}, M)$ already satisfies all the regularity conditions to be a valid profit function.

The estimating system of input demands and output supplies may be obtained by applying (23) to the profit function $\pi(\mathbf{p}, M)$ specified in (24)–(29):

$$x_i^*(\mathbf{p}, M^*) = A_i + b_i M^* + (1/2) d_i M^{*2}, \qquad (30)$$

where

$$M^* = -\frac{(\sum_i b_i p_i)}{(\sum_i d_i p_i)}, \qquad (31)$$

and

$$\begin{aligned}
A_i &= \partial A/\partial p_i \\
&= a_{ii} - \sum_{\{(j,k):j>i\}} a_{ij}(p_j/p_i)^{1/2} + 2 \sum_{\{(j,k):j\neq i, k\neq i, k>j\}} a_{ijk} p_i (p_j p_k)^{-1/2} \\
&\quad - (1/2) \sum_{\{(j,k):j\neq i, k\neq j, k>i\}} a_{jik}(p_j)^2 (p_k)^{-1/2} (p_i)^{-3/2} \\
&\quad - (1/2) \sum_{\{(j,k):j\neq i, k\neq j, k<i\}} a_{jki}(p_j)^2 (p_k)^{-1/2} (p_i)^{-3/2} \qquad (32)
\end{aligned}$$

with $a_{ij} \geq 0$, $a_{ijk} \geq 0$, and $d_i \geq 0$.

It can be shown, from equations (18) and (22), that the firm's technology is separable in $\mathbf{x}^1$ iff $\pi(\mathbf{p}, M)$ is additive in $\mathbf{p}^1$ and $\mathbf{p}^2$, given the level of the monetary aggregate M. That is, separability of the transformation function F in (18) can be imposed by additivity restrictions on the conditional variable-profit function $\pi(\mathbf{p}, M)$ in (22). Notice that B and D are already additive in any partition of prices $\mathbf{p}$. Therefore the separability restrictions are as follows:

$$a_{ij} = 0 \quad \text{unless} \quad i, j \in I^1 \quad \text{or} \quad i, j \in I^2, \qquad (33)$$

and

$$a_{ijk} = 0 \quad \text{unless} \quad i, j, k \in I^1 \quad \text{or} \quad i, j, k \in I^2. \qquad (34)$$

The parameter restrictions of (33) and (34) can be used to test for separability or equivalently for the existence of a monetary output aggregate M in the financial firm's monetary-production technology. Under these separability restrictions, there exist two functions, that are flexible:

$$\pi^1(\mathbf{p}^1, M) = A^{(1)} + B^{(1)} \cdot M + (1/2) D^{(1)} \cdot M^2, \qquad (35)$$

and

$$\pi^2(\mathbf{p}^2, M) = A^{(2)} + B^{(2)} \cdot M + (1/2) D^{(2)} \cdot M^2, \qquad (36)$$

where $A^{(1)}$, $B^{(1)}$, and $D^{(1)}$ depend on $\mathbf{p}^1$, but $A^{(2)}$, $B^{(2)}$, and $D^{(2)}$ depend on $\mathbf{p}^2$. With the separability restrictions imposed, $x_i^*(\mathbf{p}, M)$ for $i \in I^2$ depends on $\mathbf{p}^1$ only through $M^*(\mathbf{p})$, while $x_i^*(\mathbf{p}, M)$ for $i \in I^1$ depend on $\mathbf{p}^2$ only through $M^*(\mathbf{p})$.

3   Data and Some Measurement Problems

The primary source of data used in this study is the Federal Reserve's Functional Cost Analysis (FCA). See Board of Governors of the Federal Reserve System (1979–1983). The sample data are longitudinal observations on 41 Chicago (Federal Reserve District 7) banks for 1979–1983. Hancock (1985, 1987) used longitudinal observations on 18 New York and New Jersey (District 1) banks for 1973–1978. A primary motivation of the use of District 7 data is that we want to concentrate on an individual district rather than national sample data, because many factors affecting operating expenses and income vary from area to area. Most of our sample banks from District 7 are unit banks. Mullineaux (1978) and Benston *et al.* (1983) emphasized that unit and branch banking firms have significantly different cost functions. Their results indicate that separate equations should be estimated for unit and branch banks. We believe that financial firms operating in a similar market environment should provide a more appropriate basis for microeconomic analysis of optimizing behavior.

In our model, financial firms are considered to produce monetary assets (deposit-account type), which play an essential role in providing transaction services in the economy. Demand and time deposits are outputs. Three input categories are identified as cash balances, labor, and materials.

Prior to describing the procedures used in constructing data on the quantities and prices of monetary and nonmonetary goods, an average balance sheet is briefly outlined. This balance sheet is from 292 banks with total deposits from $50 million to $200 million. See Board of Governors of the Federal Reserve System (1983). From Table 1, we see that balance sheet items are divided into two functions, fund-providing functions and fund-using functions. Fund-providing functions are primary sources of funds; among them are demand deposits, time deposits, and nondeposit funds. Fund-using functions represent primary users of funds; cash balances, loans, and investments belong to fund-using functions.

Let total available funds be total assets (or total liabilities and capital) less bank premises and other assets. Among fund-using functions on the asset side of the balance sheet, cash balances consist of 6.15%, and loans and investments constitute 93.59% of total available funds. Looking at the fund-providing functions on the other side of the balance sheet, total available funds are provided by demand deposits (26.74%), time deposits (52.61%), and nondeposit funds (20.64%). Nondeposit funds consist of equity capital, federal funds purchased, borrowed money, capital notes and debentures, time deposits of $100,000 and over, other money-market instruments, and other liabilities. Bank premises and other assets are subtracted from equity capital, which belongs to nondeposit funds. We believe that physical capital, such

TABLE 1
AVERAGE BALANCE SHEET (292 BANKS, TOTAL DEPOSITS $50M–$200M)

Assets			Liabilities and capital		
Items	Amounts ($)	Percent[a] (90)	Items	Amounts ($)	Percent[a] (90)
Cash total	8,018,491.0	6.15	Total deposits	103,399,395.0	79.35
Loans & Investments	121,939,821.0	93.59	Demand deposits	34,853,745.0	26.74
			Time deposits	68,545,649.0	52.61
Investments	56,101,306.0	43.06			
Loans	65,838,514.0	50.53	Other liabilities	21,083,714.0	16.18
Real estate	21,631,252.0	16.60	Borrowed & purchased	1,878,250.0	1.44
Installment	13,128,618.0	10.07	Money market[b]	17,202,231.0	13.20
Credit Card	677,911.0	.52	Other liabilities	2,003,233.0	1.53
Commercial					
& other	30,398,371.0	23.33			
International	339,678.0	.26			
Portfolio total	122,279,499.0	93.84			
Total available funds (=Total financial assets)	130,297,992.0	100.00	Total liabilities (=Total financial liabilities)	124,483,111.0	95.53
Bank premises & other	5,450,803.0	4.18	Total capital accounts	11,265,685.0	8.65
			Capital notes	216,558.0	0.16
			Equity capital	11,049,126.0	8.48
			Preferred stock	9,073.0	0.01
			Common stock	1,822,462.0	1.39
			Surplus, undivided		
			Profits and reserves	8,511,416.0	6.53
			Valuation reserves	706,175.0	.53
Total assets	135,748,796.0	104.18	Total liabilities and capital	135,748,796.0	104.18
			*Memorandum		
			Nondeposit funds[c]	26,898,597.0	20.64

[a] Percent of total available funds.
[b] Time deposits $100,000 and over are classified as money-market instruments and included in nondeposit funds.
[c] Nondeposit funds = equity capital + other liabilities + capital notes and debentures + borrowed and purchased
 + market instruments − bank premises and other assets.
[d] Source: Board of Governors of the Federal Reserve System (1983).

as bank buildings, equipment, and furniture, is usually associated with the shareholders' equity capital.

Several important points concerning balance-sheet management at financial firms should be noted. First, financial firms face balance sheet constraints. Total amounts of portfolio (loans and investments plus cash reserves) cannot exceed total available funds provided by deposits and nondeposit funds. Second, demand deposits and time deposits, which are outputs in our model, provide almost 80% of total available funds, whereas nondeposit funds provide only about 20%. Among nondeposit funds, other liabilities — including borrowed money, federal funds purchased, money-market instruments, and other liabilities — take only 16.18% of total available funds. Thus they can be subtracted from loans and investments on the asset side of the balance sheet. Third, equity capital is composed of preferred and common stock, surplus, undivided profits, and reserves and valuation reserves. Equity capital can be computed as the sum of physical capital, such as bank premises, furniture and equipment, and financial capital. Financial capital is total financial assets less total financial liabilities.

Note that equity capital may be treated as a fixed factor during the period and may not enter in the variable-profit function as mentioned previously. If equity capital less bank premises and other assets is entered in the variable-profit function, it may increase the total amount of loans and investments, hence increasing total amount of accounting profits. Thus all nondeposit funds (about 20% of total available funds) including equity capital are subtracted from the total amount of loans and investments on the asset side of the balance sheet. Finally, it can be seen that an average 83.03% of demand deposits are invested in loans and investments yielding R, whereas 16.97% are assigned as cash reserves. On the other hand, 97.5% of total time deposits are used for loans and investments, but only 2.5% are left as cash reserves.

One important observation from the preceding balance sheet analysis can be drawn: Demand and time deposit categories, which are outputs in our model, occupy almost 80% of total portfolio activities of the average financial firm, and therefore our monetary production model has a sufficient basis for analysis of the financial firm's optimal behavior. In our monetary-production model, demand and time deposits are outputs of financial firms, but cash balances are used as a factor of monetary production. Quantities of the two outputs are their dollar values deflated by the price index on the balance sheet. As a measure of quantity of cash balances, real excess reserves held above required reserves are used. Therefore, the nominal balance of excess reserves can be derived from $p_t^* c_t = C_t - \sum_i k_{it} \mu_{it} p_t^*$, where C_t is total cash and dues on the balance sheet, μ_{it} is the ith produced monetary asset, and k_{it} is the required reserve ratio.

Real balances of cash, demand deposits, and time deposits on the balance sheet are stock variables. They are commonly considered to be durable goods yielding continuous monetary-service flows. To convert these stock variables into flows of monetary services, user-cost prices for the monetary assets are derived from (5) and (6). Observe that as a first step we should derive the loan rate R, which is included in the user-cost price formulas. In our model, financial firms are assumed to make only one kind of primary market loan yielding R. Five types of fund-using functions of loans and investments are reported in the FCA data, however. They are investments, real-estate mortgage loans, installment loans, credit-card loans, and commercial and industrial loans. These five types of loans and investments reported in the FCA are aggregated to obtain an index of loan quantity and its dual interest rate index R.

Actually R should be the marginal cost of borrowing an additional dollar for one-period or the marginal return on an additional dollar of bank loans. It is, however, extremely difficult to obtain the true marginal cost. Thus a dual price index of the aggregate loan will be operationally used for R. The procedure to derive R is as follows: First, we construct an aggregate loan quantity using the Divisia multilateral index (or Törnqvist-Theil-translog index), which is also a member of the superlative class of index numbers as defined by Diewert (1976). The Divisia multilateral index is transitive, but a chained (or bilateral) Divisia index for time series is not transitive. See Caves, Christensen, and Diewert (1982b, pp. 75–82). See also Benston et al. (1982, pp. 439–442) for an excellent application of the Divisia multilateral index to measuring the numbers of bank accounts, which are bank outputs.

Then, the dual yield index (the aggregate loan rate) R has been derived from Fisher's factor-reversal test. The own yield ρ_i paid on produced monetary asset i by the firm includes interest paid and the FDIC premium paid less service charges earned. The interest paid on demand deposits includes only those for the interest-bearing demand deposits. Hence the interest rate on demand deposits is the explicit rate. For the implicit-interest-rate approach to demand deposits, see Klein (1974). All of these data are available from the FCA data.

Finally, required reserve ratios are computed using member bank reserve requirements reported in the *Federal Reserve Bulletin*. For demand deposits, reserve requirements for 1979–1980 are calculated according to the schedule of member bank requirements before implementation of the Monetary Control Act. Those for 1981–1983 are computed according to the schedule of depository institution requirements after implementation of the Monetary Control Act. For time deposits, since the information on maturity is not available from the FCA data, an average of 3% is used in computing reserve requirements (Board of Governors of the Federal Reserve System 1979–1983).

Data on the quantities and prices of nonmonetary goods such as labor and materials inputs are not available directly from the FCA data. They are constructed using various available information from the FCA income statement, the *Survey of Current Business*, and the *Federal Reserve Bulletin*.

In the FCA data, labor inputs are classified as two groups of employment — namely, managerial (officers) and nonmanagerial (employees) labor. A Divisia quantity index was acquired by aggregating these two categories of labor inputs. Since the labor-quantity aggregate is constructed as a Divisia index, the corresponding price index can be computed from Fisher's factor-reversal test. Thus the corresponding price index of labor aggregate quantity is the ratio of total labor expenditures to the Divisia aggregate-labor quantity.

Materials include (a) printing, stationary, and office supplies; (b) postage, freight, and delivery; and (c) telephone and telegraph. Total expenditures on these items are reported in the FCA data. Quantities for these are not available from the FCA data, but producer price indexes are available from the U.S. Departments of Labor and Commerce, as published in *Producer Prices and Price Indexes* and *Survey of Current Business*. A Divisia price index is constructed by aggregating producer price indexes for these three groups each year. Then the materials-quantity index is computed from Fisher's factor-reversal test. That is, the material-quantity index is the ratio of total material expenditures to the Divisia price index.

Prior to estimation of our monetary-production model, we deflate the nominal dollar balances of demand deposits, time deposits, and cash balances by the true cost-of-living index p_t^* to convert them into real balances. Moreover, each user-cost price is multiplied by p_t^* so that the user costs are in nominal terms. For the true cost-of-living index, we used the Fisher Ideal price index, which is defined as the geometric mean of the Laspeyres and Paasche indexes. In computing the Fisher Ideal price index, the Consumer Price Index of the Bureau of Labor Statistics was used as the Laspeyres index, and the Implicit Price Deflator of the Commerce Department was used as the Paasche index (Barnett 1981b, p. 205). Furthermore, we rescale the data to be closer to 1.0. We take 1981 as the base year. Then each price series for each bank is divided by the price in the base year. To ensure that total revenues or total expenditures remain unchanged by rescaling, we correspondingly multiply each bank's real quantity series by the original base-period price.

4 Empirical Results

In this section we estimate the unknown parameters of the generalized symmetric Barnett variable-profit function described previously and perform hypothesis tests. There are several important points concerning the estimation and hypothesis-testing procedures. First, a classical additive disturbance term is included in each of the estimating equations. The disturbance terms are assumed to have a multivariate normal distribution with mean zero and a nonzero contemporaneous variance-covariance matrix that is constant over time.

Second, the system of equations defined previously is nonlinear in both the variables and the unknown parameters, with nonnegativity restrictions imposed. The system is estimated by the method of nonlinear maximum likelihood. The maximum likelihood method of estimation is associated with costs and benefits. The method has been chosen primarily on the ground that this method has several important advantages associated with empirical econometric work: (a) Under some regularity conditions, the maximum likelihood estimators are consistent, asymptotically efficient, and asymptotically normally distributed; (b) the method is well established for dealing with nonlinear characteristics in both the variables and the parameters; (c) the method is linked with the likelihood ratio test; and (d) the computational difficulties can be reduced by using the concentrated likelihood function. In this study the maximum likelihood estimators are obtained by maximizing the concentrated version of the log-likelihood function, and the maximization is carried out by minimizing the negative of the original objective function. See Barten (1969, p. 20).

Third, the nonnegativity constraints on some of the parameters are imposed by reparameterizing the model: We maximize the likelihood function with respect to new parameters defined as the square roots of the squares of the original ones. For more detailed discussions of squaring techniques and asymptotic distribution theory for nonnegative parameters, see Barnett (1976, 1983a) and Blackorby, Schworm, and Fisher (1986). Fourth, we ignore the simultaneous-equation-bias problem by assuming that the explanatory variables are uncorrelated with the disturbances. It may not be an easy task to estimate the system of equations specified with a generalized symmetric Barnett functional form. Thus for empirical implementability we also ignore the possibility of autocorrelation. Finally, hypothesis tests are performed using the asymptotic likelihood ratio test.

Our objective is to investigate the existence of consistent monetary aggregates in the financial firm's monetary-production technology. For the financial firm, the technology contains both monetary and nonmonetary goods. In our monetary-production model, demand and time deposits are outputs, and cash balances, labor, and materials are inputs.

There exist three admissible (separable) groups of monetary assets that need to be considered. In the first group, the potential monetary aggregate contains cash balances and demand deposits. Nonmonetary goods are time deposits, labor, and materials. In the second group, the potential aggregate money index comprises demand and time deposits, which are all monetary outputs. In the third group, the potential money index includes cash balances and demand and time deposits. Thus we have the following three cases, where M is an aggregate money index, x_i is the quantity of net output i, p_i is the price of net output i, and the subscripts are C = cash balances, D = demand deposits, T = time deposits, L = labor, and M = materials:

Case 1: There exists a monetary aggregator function over cash balances and demand deposits; that is, $F(f(x_C, x_D), x_T, x_L, x_M) = 0$ or $\pi = \pi^1(p_C, p_D; M) + \pi^2(p_T, p_L, p_M; M)$.

Case 2: There exists a monetary aggregator function over demand and time deposits; that is, $F(f(x_D, x_T), x_C, x_L, x_M) = 0$ or $\pi = \pi^1(p_D, p_T; M) + \pi^2(p_C, p_L, p_M; M)$.

Case 3: There exists a monetary aggregator function over cash balances and demand and time deposits; that is, $F(f(x_C, x_D, x_T), x_L, x_M) = 0$ or $\pi = \pi^1(p_C, p_D, p_T; M) + \pi^2(p_L, p_M; M)$.

For each case, to make the firm's variable-profit function $\pi(\mathbf{p}, M)$, defined in (24)–(29), separable, we need to impose the parameter restrictions as defined by (33) and (34). If the parameter restrictions imposed cannot be rejected statistically, a monetary aggregate exists in the financial firm's monetary production.

In what follows, the estimation and hypothesis-testing results are presented. The convergence criterion was that total fractional change in the objective function from one iteration to the next be no greater than 1.0E–15 for 10 consecutive iterations. Thus if the total fractional change in the objective function is less than 1.0E–15 for 10 consecutive iterations, then the program will stop. The program will also stop if the Kuhn-Tucker optimality conditions are satisfied within 1.0E–15. During estimation, several initial values for parameters were tried to find the global maxima. There were no serious difficulties in obtaining convergence and finding global maxima. The system was estimated by nonlinear maximum likelihood, using Lasdon and Warren's GRG2 nonlinear programming package. The GRG2 nonlinear programming package is a FORTRAN program that solves nonlinear optimization problems using the generalized reduced gradient method.

Note that the variable-profit function itself is not estimated because it contains no additional information. Instead the system of input demands and output supplies defined by (30) through (32) was estimated. As expected, the direct parameter estimates may not provide an adequate source of information, because nonnegativity constraints are imposed on many parameters. Therefore we compute and report Allen-Uzawa partial elasticities of transformation (substitution), as well as Hicks-Allen price elasticities of input demands and output supplies.

The estimated average elasticities of transformation (substitution) are reported in Table 2. These elasticities measure the responsiveness in the production of outputs when relative prices are changed. We see from Table 2 that own elasticities of transformation (substitution) are all positive and that hence the necessary conditions on curvature are satisfied. The off-diagonal terms measure the degree of substitutability and complementarity among inputs and outputs. Between two inputs or two outputs, if $\sigma_{ij} > 0$, they are substitutes, but if $\sigma_{ij} < 0$, they are complements. For each input and output, if $\sigma_{ij} > 0$, they are complements, and if $\sigma_{ij} < 0$, they are substitutes. See Hancock (1985, p. 871). As can be seen from Table 2, two outputs appear to be complements, and all inputs are substitutes for one another. All of the combinations of output and input are complements, except for the combination of time deposits and materials, which appear to be substitutes. As for the elasticities of transformation between monetary assets, all elasticities are less than unity, except for the elasticity between cash and demand deposits. Thus there appears to be no evidence of strong substitutability among monetary assets. This result is consistent with most empirical studies on the demand side. See Barnett (1981b), Ewis and Fisher (1984, 1985), and Hancock (1985).

TABLE 2
ALLEN-UZAWA PARTIAL (AVERAGE) ELASTICITIES OF TRANSFORMATION AND SUBSTITUTION

σ_{ij}	Demand deposits	Time deposits	Cash balances	Labor	Materials
Demand deposits	.6932	−.0957	2.0356	.5597	.9788
Time deposits	−.0957	.8794	.0061	.6047	−.2210
Cash balances	2.0356	.0061	73.3636	.3247	.0079
Labor	.5597	.6047	.3247	1.5322	.0136
Materials	.9788	−.2210	.0079	.0136	10.3218

NOTE: Allen-Uzawa partial elasticities of transformation and substitution are computed from $\sigma_{ij} = \pi \pi_{ij}/\pi_i \pi_j = (\partial x_i/\partial p_j)(\pi/x_i x_j)$, $i, j = D, T, C, L.M$, where $\pi_i = \partial \pi/\partial p_i$ and $\pi_{ij} = \partial^2 \pi/\partial p_i \partial p_j$.

Table 3 contains estimated average price elasticities of input demands and output supplies. We do not require that $\xi_{ij} = \xi_{ji}$. Those elasticities may differ because their respective shares differ. The elasticities in Table 3 reveal a pattern consistent with production theory. All own-price elasticities for outputs (supply elasticities for the firm) are positive, whereas all own-price elasticities for inputs (demand elasticities for the firm) are negative. Cross-price elasticities vary between positive and negative: When the price of each output rises, the own quantity of the output is increased and quantities of all inputs are increased. When the price of each input rises, the quantities of outputs and inputs are decreased.

TABLE 3
Hicks-Allen (average) Price Elasticities of Supply of Outputs and of Demand for Inputs

Percentage change in prices	Demand deposits	Percentage change in quantities			
		Time deposits	Cash balances	Labor	Materials
Demand deposits	1.0662	−.1610	2.8241	.8419	1.5228
Time deposits	−.0675	.6219	.0046	.4273	−.1527
Cash balances	−.4103	−.0012	−2.5970	−.0822	−.0163
Labor	−.4538	−.4931	−.2307	−1.1857	−.0085
Materials	−.1333	.0333	−.0010	−.0014	−1.3725

NOTE: The Hicks-Allen (compensated) price elasticities of input demands and output supplies are computed from $\xi_{ij} = (\partial x_i/\partial p_j)(p_j/x_i) = \sigma_{ij}s_j$, $i,j = D,T,C,L.M$, where $s_j = p_j x_j/\pi$ and $\sigma_{ij} = \pi\pi_{ij}/\pi_i\pi_j = (\partial x_i/\partial p_j)(\pi/x_i x_j)$.

Observe that all inputs are relatively own-price elastic, but all outputs are relatively own-price inelastic: The own-price elasticity of supply for demand deposits is 1.0662, but that for time deposits is .6219. In Table 3, each row represents the percentage changes in quantities for each of four goods given a unit percentage price change of a given good. From the first and second rows, it can be seen that an increase in the price of demand deposits results in a decrease in time deposits and an increase in all inputs. Similarly, an increase in the price of time deposits results in a decrease in demand deposits and an increase in all inputs. From the third, fourth, and fifth rows, it can be seen that an increase in the prices of inputs results in a decrease in quantities of outputs and a decrease in all input quantities. The one exception is the response of time-deposit demand to a change in materials price. In that case, those two factors behave as substitutes in production.

Now we proceed to consider tests for the existence of consistent monetary aggregates in the financial firm's production technology. The three null hypotheses are tested using the asymptotic likelihood ratio test. The negative of twice the difference between the log of the likelihood function under the maintained hypothesis and under the null hypothesis is asymptotically distributed as a chi-square with degrees of freedom equal to the number of independent parameter restrictions imposed under the null hypothesis.

The calculated chi-squared statistics for the hypothesis tests and selected critical values are presented in Table 4. Recall that, for Case 1, the potential monetary aggregate comprises cash balances and demand deposits. As is clear from Table 4, the null hypothesis that there exists a monetary aggregator function for cash balances and demand deposits cannot be rejected statistically by the data at the .05 level of significance. If the null hypothesis is imposed, the log of the likelihood function is −282.72, and the unrestricted

Empirical Results

value of the likelihood function is -265.94. Thus the calculated chi-squared value for the likelihood ratio test of the null hypothesis is $\chi^2 = 33.56$. This is sufficiently below the critical chi-squared value with 33 df at the .05 significance level. That critical value is $\chi^2 = 47.34$. This result strongly supports the assertion that there exists a monetary aggregator function for cash balances and demand deposits in the financial firm's monetary-production technology.

TABLE 4
Test Statistics and Critical Values

	Log-likelihood	Test statistics[a]	Degrees of freedom	Critical values[b]		
				$\chi^2(.05)$	$\chi^2(.01)$	$\chi^2(.001)$
Unrestricted	-265.94	—	—	—	—	—
Case 1 (C,D)	-282.72	33.56^{*c}	33	47.34	54.78	63.81
Case 2 (D,T)	-289.50	47.12^{*c}	33	47.34	54.78	63.81
Case 3 (C,D,T)	-296.74	61.60^{**c}	33	47.34	54.78	63.81

[a] The test statistic is calculated as $-2\log(L_1/L_0)$ and distributed as χ^2, where L_1 and L_0 are the values of the unconstrained and constrained likelihood functions, respectively.
[b] Critical values were calculated by linear interpolation. See Wonnacott and Wonnacott (1977).
[c] * = significant at the .05 level. ** = significant at the .01 level.

As for Case 2, where the potential monetary aggregate comprises all monetary outputs — namely, demand and time deposits — it can be seen from Table 4 that the null hypothesis cannot be rejected statistically by the data at the .05 level of significance. If the null hypothesis is imposed, the log of the likelihood function is -289.50, but the unrestricted value of the likelihood function is -265.94. Thus the calculated chi-squared value for the likelihood ratio test of the null hypothesis is $\chi^2 = 47.12$. This is less than the critical chi-squared value with 33 df at the .05 significance level, which is $\chi^2 = 47.34$. That result statistically supports the assertion that there exists a monetary aggregator function for demand and time deposits in the financial firm's monetary-production technology. Hence monetary outputs are weakly separable from all inputs, and aggregation over all monetary outputs is possible. When all outputs are separable from inputs, there exists a single output aggregate, and thus the use of a single output aggregate can be justified in the formulation and estimation of the production technology. For our monetary production model, this means that monetary outputs of demand and time deposits can be aggregated to produce a monetary aggregate index M, which is just such an aggregate money-supply function as discussed in Section 1.

For Case 3, where the potential monetary aggregate contains cash balances, demand, and time deposits, the null hypothesis is rejected by the data with a test statistic of 61.60 against a critical value of 47.34 at the .05 significance level with 33 df. The null hypothesis cannot be rejected statistically by the data at the .001 level of significance, however. If the null hypothesis is imposed, the log of the likelihood function is -296.74, but the unrestricted value of the likelihood function is -265.94. Thus the calculated chi-squared value for the likelihood ratio test of the null hypothesis is $\chi^2 = 61.60$. This is barely below the critical chi-squared value with 33 df at the .001 significance level, which is $\chi^2 = 63.81$. Thus there appears to exist some mild statistical support for the existence of a consistent monetary aggregator function for cash balances, demand, and time deposits in the financial firm's monetary-production technology.

5 Concluding Remarks

In this article, a monetary-production model of financial firms is employed to investigate supply-side monetary aggregation. Financial firms are viewed as producing monetary goods (services) as outputs through financial intermediation and investing these in various loans and securities. The nature of financial firms' outputs is related to their role in the transaction technology underlying the payment mechanism in the economy. A new method for testing for the existence of consistent monetary aggregates in financial firms' production technology is developed in terms of a multiproduct firm's variable-profit function. The method does not require homotheticity of the aggregator function. We used a generalized symmetric Barnett flexible functional form, which satisfies global curvature conditions. The model, unlike other available models used in this literature, retains its flexibility under the tested null hypothesis of blockwise weak separability of outputs.

Although much work remains to be done, our empirical results indicate the following tentative conclusions. First, the degree of substitutability among monetary goods appears to be low and variable over time. This implies that simple summation is not an appropriate method of constructing monetary aggregates. Second, the monetary production of financial firms is relatively insensitive to changes in user-cost prices (hence interest rates). Third, we cannot rule out the admissibility of production-side monetary aggregation over some monetary components.

In particular, there is strong support for the existence of a monetary aggregate containing cash balances and demand deposits and some mild sta-

Concluding Remarks

tistical support for the existence of a monetary aggregate containing cash balances, demand deposits, and time deposits. Moreover, there exists strong statistical support for the existence of a monetary aggregate containing demand and time deposits. This implies that monetary outputs are weakly separable from all inputs, and aggregation over monetary outputs is possible. For our monetary-production model, monetary outputs of demand and time deposits can be aggregated to produce a monetary aggregate, which then enters an aggregate money-supply function, as discussed in Section 1. When all outputs are separable from inputs, there exists a single output aggregate, and hence the use of a single output aggregate can be justified in the formulation and estimation of the monetary-production technology.

In this article, we assume perfect certainty. For a discussion of the very complicated extension to generalized method-of-moments estimation, see Barnett and Zhou (1994b), which is reprinted in this book as chapter 21.

Acknowledgments:
Data were provided by the Federal Reserve Bank of New York with the assistance of Michael Hannaway and Kenneth H. Behrens of the Federal Reserve Bank of New York and Jerry Bramlett and James Pearce of the Federal Reserve Bank of Dallas.

Section 5.3:
Extensions to Risk

Chapter 21

Financial-Firms' Production and Supply-Side Monetary Aggregation Under Dynamic Uncertainty

*William A. Barnett and Ge Zhou**

This paper is focused on the production theory of the financial firm and supply-side monetary aggregation in the framework of dynamics and risk. On the demand side, there has been much progress in applying consumer demand theory to the generation of exact monetary aggregates and integrating them into consumer demand system modelling.[1] However, on the supply-side, monetary services are produced by financial firms through financial intermediation, and, hence, exact supply-side monetary aggregation must be based upon financial firm output aggregation. Most of the literature on exact aggregation theory is based upon perfect certainty, which often is a reasonable assumption regarding contemporaneous consumer goods allocation decisions. Risk, however, is an important consideration in modeling

---

*Originally published in the Federal Reserve Bank of St. Louis *Review* 76 (1994), 133–165. During this research, Ge Zhou was a graduate student at Washington University in St. Louis and subsequently received a doctorate in economics from that university. He is now at Caterpillar Inc. Research on this project was partially supported by NSF grant SES 9223557. We wish to thank William Brainard for his comments, which substantially influenced the final revision of this paper.

[1] See Barnett, Fisher and Serletis (1992).

the decisions of financial intermediaries. Furthermore, that risk not only applies to future prices and interest rates, but also to contemporaneous interest rates and thereby to the contemporaneous user costs of produced monetary services. In this paper we derive a model of financial firm behavior under dynamic risk, and we find the exact monetary services output aggregate. We estimate the Euler equations that comprise the first-order conditions for optimal behavior by financial firms.

Barnett (1978, 1980a) introduced economic aggregation and index number theory to demand-side monetary aggregation by applying Diewert's (1976) results on superlative index numbers. The proposed Divisia index in Barnett's work is an element of Diewert's superlative index number class. Analogous to demand-side monetary aggregation, Hancock (1985, 1987), Barnett (1987), and Barnett, Hinich, and Weber (1986) have provided results on supply-side monetary aggregation.[2] They use neoclassical economic theory to model financial firms' production, so the existing economic aggregation and index number theory are directly applicable. In fact, throughout the literature on applying economic aggregation and index number theory to monetary aggregation, researchers usually assume perfect certainty. Exceptions are Barnett, Hinich, and Yue (2000) and Poterba and Rotemberg (1987), who generalize to demand-side exact monetary aggregation under risk. Supply-side monetary aggregation under risk has not previously been the subject of research.

Introduction of dynamics and uncertainty into supply-side monetary aggregation requires extensions of earlier research in this area. A financial firm's portfolio is generally diversified across different investment instruments, and the portfolio's rate of return is unknown at the time that the investment decision is made. Hence, the assumption of perfect-certainty and single–period modeling is not appropriate. Furthermore, superlative index numbers, such as the discrete time Divisia index, have known tracking ability only under the assumption of perfect certainty. In this paper, we develop a dynamic approach to supply-side monetary aggregation under uncertainty.

Historically, the literature on financial intermediation has produced many diverse models, often linked only weakly with neoclassical economic theory and having various objectives. The early view of the creation of money by financial firms, primarily viewed to be banks, was the deposit multiplier

---

[2]'Demand-side' and 'supply-side' imply respectively the demand for monetary services by consumers and manufacturing firms, and the production of monetary services by financial intermediaries. Barnett (1987) has shown that consumer's demand for money and manufacturing firm's demand for money result in the identical aggregation problem, at least in the perfect certainty case. However, supply-side aggregation of produced monetary services creates uniquely different aggregation problems resulting from the existence of required reserves, which alter the user cost of produced monetary services. For further results regarding demand for monetary services by manufacturing firms, see Robles (1993) and Barnett, Hinich, and Yue (2000).

approach. By this theory in its original form, the process of creating money is simply determined by the reserve requirement ratio. Another approach is based upon the Miller-Modigliani theorem, which asserts the irrelevance of financial firms to the real economy in a setting of a perfect capital market. In recent years, many economists have questioned the appropriateness of either of those two very different propositions and attempts have been made to extend those theories by weakening the underlying assumptions.

Another approach is based upon the capital-asset pricing model (CAPM). Under the assumptions of that model, either the financial firm's portfolio rate of return is normally distributed or investors have a quadratic utility function defined over end-of-period wealth. Under either of those assumptions, the financial firm's optimal portfolio behavior can be represented by maximizing utility over the portfolio's expected rate of return and variance. This approach has been useful in modeling the optimal portfolio allocation decision conditionally upon the real resource inputs, which are not explained endogenously. Another important approach is represented by Diamond and Dybvig (1983). They apply traditional consumption-production theory and use an intertemporal model subject to privately observed preference shocks to examine the equilibrium between banks and depositors. The studies in this tradition have been successful in explaining bank runs. However, banks serving solely as a production technology to depositors, play only a passive role in that approach.

Another approach is represented by Hancock (1985, 1987), Barnett (1987), and Barnett, Hinich, and Weber (1986). They treat the financial intermediary in the same manner as a conventional production unit and use neoclassical firm theory to model a financial intermediary's production of output services and employment of inputs subject to the firm's technological feasibility constraint.[3] This approach fully models the role played by financial firms as producers of monetary services. Moreover, it provides the needed tools to apply existing economic aggregation theory to aggregation over financial firms' output monetary services, which comprise the economy's inside money. However, those studies have not developed a dynamic model of financial firms' production under uncertainty. This paper provides that difficult extension of financial firm modeling and output aggregation under neoclassical assumptions with dynamic risk. With the theoretical model of a financial firm's monetary services production and the derived exact theoretical output aggregate, we estimate the model's parameters and test for weak separability of output services from factor inputs. We then substitute the parameter estimates into the weakly separable output aggregator function to generate the

---

[3]The papers of Tobin (1961) and Brainard and Tobin (1963, 1968) were the first to argue forcefully for the use of microeconomics and equilibrium theory in modeling the financial firm.

estimated exact supply-side monetary aggregate.[4] To this end, we develop a procedure for testing weak separability and for estimating the parameters of a flexible functional form specification of bank technology. The estimation is accomplished through Hansen and Singleton's (1982) generalized method of moments approach to estimating Euler equations.

Our empirical results are based upon commercial banking data. Our evidence indicates that banks' outputs are weakly separable from factor inputs in the transformation function. Moreover, even under uncertainty, the Divisia index provides a better approximation to the estimated theoretical aggregate than does the simple-sum or CE index.[5] These findings support the existence of a supply-side monetary aggregate and the potential usefulness of the Divisia index to aggregate over the weakly separable monetary assets on the supply side of money markets. The result is a measure of inside money, in the sense of monetary services produced by private financial firms.

The paper proceeds as follows. In the next section, we construct our theoretical model of monetary service production by financial firms under dynamic uncertainty. The model reduces to a dynamic stochastic choice problem, for which we derive the Euler equations. In the third section, we present our approach to flexible parametric specification, weak separability testing and parameter estimation using Hansen and Singleton's (1982) generalized method of moments estimation. The fourth section formulates the empirical application using banking industry data. The fifth section contains the empirical results, including parameter estimates, weak separability test results, the estimated theoretical aggregate, and the comparison among index number approximations to the estimated exact aggregate, where the index numbers considered include the Divisia, simple-sum, and CE indexes. Section 6 brings together the demand side with the supply side to investigate the implications of our model in general equilibrium. Section 7 provides a graphical illustration of the errors-in-the-variables problem produced by the use of the simple-sum index as a measure of the monetary service flow. The final section presents a few concluding remarks.

---

[4] Diewert and Wales (1987) and Blackorby, Schworm and Fisher (1986) have illustrated the difficulty of maintaining flexibility, regularity and weak separability simultaneously.

[5] The formula for computing the Divisia index is in Barnett (1980a). Further details regarding the data sources used with the index are in Thornton and Yue (1992), who also provide instructions on downloading the data from the Federal Reserve Bank of St. Louis' public electronic bulletin board, called FRED. The formula for computing the CE ('currency equivalent') index is in Rotemberg, Driscoll and Poterba (1995). That data now is maintained and updated regularly by the St. Louis Federal Reserve Bank. See the appendix of this book regarding that source for the U.S. data and available sources of international Divisia monetary aggregate data.

1 Theoretical Model

In this section, we derive our theoretical model of monetary services production by financial firms under dynamic uncertainty. Consider a financial firm which issues its own liabilities and reinvests the borrowed funds in primary financial markets. In this process, real resources such as labor, materials and capital are used as factors of production in creating the services of the produced liabilities. Those produced liabilities are deposit accounts providing monetary service combinations that would not have existed in the economy without the financial firm. The liabilities of the financial firms include, for example, demand deposits and passbook accounts, and are assets to the depositors. The value added through the creation of those assets by a financial intermediary is that firm's contribution to the economy's inside money services. Without the existence of financial firms and the accounts that they create, investors in money markets would be limited to the use of primary money-market securities as the short maturity assets in their portfolios. While the produced liabilities of financial firms may not appear to be 'outputs' to an accountant looking at the firm's balance sheet, the produced liabilities of financial firms are the outputs of the firms' production technologies.[6]

The financial firm's profits are made from the interest rate spread between the financial firm's financial assets (loans) and the firm's produced liabilities. That spread must exceed the real resource costs, in order for the firm to profit from its operation. Let Y_t be the real balances of the financial firm's asset (loan) portfolio during period t.[7] Let R_t be the portfolio rate of return, which is unknown at the beginning of each period. Financial firms also hold excess reserves in the form of cash, which has a nominal return of zero. The real balance of cash holding is C_t. Let y_{it} be real balances in the firm's ith produced account type and h_{it} be holding cost per dollar for that liability, where $i = 1, \ldots, I$.[8] The amount of the jth real resource used is z_{jt}, and its price is w_{jt}, where $j = 1, \ldots, J$. Let P_t be the general price index, which is used to deflate nominal to real units. All financial transactions are contracted at the beginning of each period, but interest is paid or received at the end of the period. The cost of employing resource, z_{jt} is paid at the start of the

---

[6]See Barnett (1987).

[7]As used in this paper, portfolio is the sum of all investments.

[8]The holding cost h_{it} is defined as $h_{it} = r_{it} + R_t k_{it}$. In this formula, r_{it} is the account's net interest rate, which is defined such that all the benefits (for example, service charges) and costs (for example, deposit insurance) generated by the borrowed funds have been factored into the interest rate, and $R_t k_{it}$ is the implicit tax rate on the financial firm from the existence of a reserve requirement on that account type. Required reserves are assumed to yield no interest and hence produce an opportunity cost to the financial firm, since the firm otherwise could have invested the required reserves at a positive rate of return.

Theoretical Model

period.

The firm's variable profit at the beginning of period t in accordance with Hancock's (1991, equation 3.1) formula, is

$$\pi_t = (1 + R_{t-1})Y_{t-1}P_{t-1} - Y_t P_t + C_{t-1}P_{t-1} - C_t P_t \quad (1)$$
$$+ \sum_{i=1}^{I}[y_{it}P_t - (1 + h_{i,t-1})y_{i,t-1}P_{t-1}] - \sum_{j=1}^{J} w_{jt}z_{jt}.$$

The first two terms in equation (1) represent the net cash flow generated from rolling over the loan portfolio during period t. The third and fourth terms represent the change in the nominal value of excess reserves. The fifth term is the net cash flow from issuing produced financial liabilities. The last term is total payments for real resource inputs.

Portfolio Y_t investment, however, is constrained by total available funds, under the assumption that all earnings are paid out as dividends. The relationship is

$$Y_t P_t = \sum_{i=1}^{I}(1 - k_{it})y_{it}P_t - C_t P_t - \sum_{j=1}^{J} w_{jt}z_{jt}, \quad (2)$$

where k_{it} is the reserve requirement ratio for the ith produced account type, with $0 \leq k_{it} \leq 1$. Rearranging, equation (2) can be seen to state that total deposits $\sum_{i=1}^{I} y_{it}P_{it}$ are allocated to required reserves, excess reserves, investment in loans, and payments for all real resource inputs. Substituting (2) into (1) to eliminate Y_t, we obtain the firm's profit function subject to its balance sheet constraint:

$$\pi_t = \sum_{i=1}^{I}\{[(1 + R_{t-1})(1 - k_{i,t-1}) \quad (3)$$
$$- (1 + h_{i,t-1})]y_{i,t-1}P_{t-1} + k_{it}y_{it}P_t\}$$
$$- R_{t-1}C_{t-1}P_{t-1} - \sum_{j=1}^{J}(1 + R_{t-1})w_{j,t-1}z_{j,t-1}.$$

We assume the financial firm chooses the level of borrowed funds, excess reserves, and real resource inputs to maximize its expected discounted intertemporal utility of variable profits, subject to the firm's technology. We further assume the financial firm's intertemporal utility function is additively separable. Then, the firm's maximization problem can be expressed by the following dynamic choice problem:

$$\max E_t\left[\sum_{s=t}^{\infty}\left(\frac{1}{1+\mu}\right)^{s-t} U(\pi_s)\right] \quad (4)$$

s.t. $\Omega(y_{1s},\ldots,y_{Is},C_s,z_{1s},\ldots,z_{Js}) = 0 \quad \forall s \geq t,$

where E_t denotes expectation conditional on the information known at time t, μ is the subjective rate of time preference and is assumed to be constant, U is the utility function, π_s is the variable profit at period s given by equation (3), and Ω is the firm's transformation function, defining the firm's efficient production technology from

$$\Omega(y_{1s},\ldots,y_{Is},C_s,z_{1s},\ldots,z_{Js}) = 0 \quad \forall s \geq t. \tag{5}$$

In accordance with the usual properties of a neoclassical transformation function, Ω is convex in its arguments. In addition, the inputs are distinguished from the outputs by the inequality constraints:[9]

$$\frac{\partial \Omega}{\partial C_t} \leq 0, \quad \frac{\partial \Omega}{\partial z_{jt}} \leq 0 \quad \forall j = 1,\ldots,J \tag{6}$$

and

$$\frac{\partial \Omega}{\partial y_{it}} \geq 0 \quad \forall i = 1,\ldots,I. \tag{7}$$

We also assume that Ω is continuous and second-order differentiable.

Substituting equation (3) into (4), we have

$$\max E_t \left\{ \sum_{s=t}^{\infty} \left(\frac{1}{1+\mu}\right)^{s-t} U\left(\sum_{i=1}^{I} \{[(1+R_{t-1})(1-k_{i,t-1}) \right. \right. \tag{8}$$
$$- (1+h_{i,t-1})]y_{i,t-1}P_{t-1} + k_{it}y_{it}P_t\}$$
$$\left. \left. - R_{t-1}C_{t-1}P_{t-1} - \sum_{j=1}^{J}(1+R_{t-1})w_{j,t-1}z_{j,t-1} \right) \right\}$$

s.t. $\Omega(y_{1s},\ldots,y_{Is},C_s,z_{1s},\ldots,z_{Js}) = 0 \quad \forall s \geq t.$

We now proceed to derive the Euler equations, comprising the first-order conditions, for this stochastic optimal control problem. We use Bellman's method. To do so, we must put the decision into Bellman's form, which requires identifying the state and control variables and determining that the decision, stated in terms of those variables, is in the form providing known Euler equation structure.

We assume that the financial firm behaves competitively, so that the prices $h_{i,s-1}$ and $w_{j,s-1}$ are taken as given by the firm. In addition, $h_{i,s-1}$ and $w_{j,s-1}$ are nonstochastic, since they are lagged one period. From the

---

[9]See Barnett (1987), Hall (1973) and Diewert (1973).

same perfect-competition assumption, it follows that R_s, k_{is}, and P_s are random processes that are not controllable by the firm. We select as state variables during period s : $y_{i,s-1}$ $\forall i$, $z_{j,s-1}$ $\forall j$, $C_{s-1}, R_{s-1}, R_s, k_{is}, h_{i,s-1}$ $\forall i$, $w_{j,s-1}$ $\forall j$, P_{s-1}, and P_s. We choose y_{is} $\forall i$ and z_{js} $\forall j$ to be the control variables during period s.

Define $\mathbf{w}_s$ to be the vector of all of the state variables, and define $\mathbf{u}_s$ to be the vector of all control variables. Let $\mathbf{\Lambda}_s$ be the subset of state variables defined by $\mathbf{\Lambda}_s = (R_s, k_{is}, h_{i,s-1}\forall i, w_{j,s-1}\forall j, P_s)$. We assume that $\mathbf{\Lambda}_s$ follows a first-order Markov process, with transitions governed by the conditional distribution function $F(\mathbf{\Lambda}_{s+1} \mid \mathbf{\Lambda}_s)$. Hence, the transition equation for state variables $(R_{s-1}, R_s, k_{is}, h_{i,s-1}$ $\forall i$, $w_{j,s-1}$ $\forall j$, $P_{s-1}, P_s)$ is implicitly defined by $F(\mathbf{\Lambda}_{s+1} \mid \mathbf{\Lambda}_s)$. The transition equations for $y_{i,s-1}$ $\forall i$ and $z_{j,s-1}$ $\forall j$ are the trivial identities

$$y_{is} = y_{is}, \quad \forall s \tag{9}$$

and

$$z_{js} = z_{js}, \quad \forall s. \tag{10}$$

The role played by these two equations in our application of Bellman's method follows from the fact that each of the variables in equations (9) and (10) are included both among the control and state variables, although with a time shift distinguishing them in each of their roles.[10] Hence, with the appropriate time shift in the subscript, equations (9) and (10) can be viewed as connecting together some of the control and state variables. This connection accounts for the function of those equations as transition equations. In particular, the left-hand sides can be identified as next-period state variables, while the right-hand sides can be identified as current-period control variables. Hence, each of those equations can be interpreted as defining the evolution of a state variable conditionally on a control variable. The transition equation for C_{s-1} is implicitly determined by the transformation function (5).

The objective function in equation (8) is an infinite summation of discounted utilities of variable profits, starting at period t. Recalling the time shifts appearing in our definition of the state and control variables during period s, we see that the discounted utility of variable profit at period s depends only on that period's state variables and control variables. By examining the transition equations, it is evident that each state variable is a function of

---

[10] The use of such trivial identities as transition equations (laws of motion) in optimal control and dynamic programming is not unusual. For example, it is common in optimal growth models to define current capital stock to be a state variable, while next period's capital stock is defined to be a control, with those state and control variables tied together by a trivial identity. The nontrivial dynamics are found in the objective function of such models. See, for example, Sargent (1987, p. 24).

only previous controls and not of previous values of the states. In particular, if we let **g** represent the vector of all transition functions, we can rewrite the dynamic decision problem as

$$\max E_t \left\{ \sum_{s=t}^{\infty} \left(\frac{1}{1+\mu} \right)^{s-1} U[\pi_s(\mathbf{w_s}, \mathbf{u_s})] \right\}$$

s.t. $\mathbf{w}_{s+1} = \mathbf{g}(\mathbf{u}_s), \quad s \geq t.$

This dynamic problem meets all of the conditions to be a recursive problem in the Bellman form. Using Bellman's principle, we can derive the first-order conditions for solving the dynamic problem (8). The Bellman recursive equation is

$$v(\mathbf{w}_t) = \max_{\mathbf{u}_t} E_t \{ U[\pi_t(\mathbf{w}_t, \mathbf{u}_t)]$$
$$+ \frac{1}{1+\mu} v(\mathbf{w}_{t+1}) \mid \mathbf{w}_t, \text{ s.t. } \mathbf{w}_{t+1} = \mathbf{g}(\mathbf{u}_t) \},$$

where $v(\mathbf{w}_t)$ is the optimized value of the objective function.

The first-order conditions for the Bellman equation are

$$E_t \left[\frac{\partial U}{\partial \pi_t}(\pi_t) \frac{\partial \pi_t}{\partial \mathbf{u}_t}(\mathbf{w}_t, \mathbf{u}_t) + \frac{1}{1+\mu} \frac{\partial \mathbf{g}'}{\partial \mathbf{u}_t}(\mathbf{u}_t) \frac{\partial v}{\partial \mathbf{w}_t}(\mathbf{w}_{t+1}) \mid \mathbf{w}_t \right] = 0. \quad (11)$$

The functional form of v is unknown. However, since $\partial \mathbf{g}'/\partial \mathbf{w}_t = \mathbf{0}$ we can use the Benveniste and Scheinkman equations to eliminate $\partial v(\mathbf{w}_{t+1})/\partial \mathbf{w}_t$.[11]

The general form of the Benveniste and Scheinkman equations is

$$\frac{\partial v}{\partial \mathbf{w}_t}(\mathbf{w}_t) = \frac{\partial U}{\partial \pi_t}(\pi_t) \frac{\partial \pi_t}{\partial \mathbf{w}_t}(\mathbf{w}_t, \mathbf{u}_t) + \frac{1}{1+\mu} E_t \left[\frac{\partial \mathbf{g}'}{\partial \mathbf{w}_t}(\mathbf{w}_t, \mathbf{u}_t) \frac{\partial v}{\partial \mathbf{w}_t}(\mathbf{w}_{t+1}) \right].$$

Since $\partial \mathbf{g}'/\partial \mathbf{w}_t = \mathbf{0}$, the above equation implies

$$\frac{\partial v}{\partial \mathbf{w}_t}(\mathbf{w}_t) = \frac{\partial U}{\partial \pi_t}(\pi_t) \frac{\partial \pi_t}{\partial \mathbf{w}_t}(\mathbf{w}_t, \mathbf{u}_t). \quad (12)$$

Substituting (12) into (11), we get

$$E_t [\frac{\partial U}{\partial \pi_t}(\pi_t) \frac{\partial \pi_t}{\partial \mathbf{u}_t}(\mathbf{w_t}, \mathbf{u_t}) \quad (13)$$
$$+ \frac{1}{1+\mu} \frac{\partial \mathbf{g}'}{\partial \mathbf{u}_t}(\mathbf{u}_t) \frac{\partial U}{\partial \pi_t}(\pi_{t+1}) \frac{\partial \pi_t}{\partial \mathbf{w}_t}(\mathbf{w}_{t+1}, \mathbf{u}_{t+1}) \mid \mathbf{w}_t] = 0.$$

---

[11] See Sargent (1987) for an excellent presentation of dynamic programming.

Theoretical Model

A very general specification of utility to represent risk is the hyperbolic absolute risk aversion (HARA) class, defined by

$$U(\pi_t) = \frac{1-\rho}{\rho}\left(\frac{h}{1-\rho}\pi_t + d\right)^\rho, \qquad (14)$$

where ρ, h and d are three parameters to be estimated. The following useful utility functions are fully nested special cases of the HARA class:[12]

a. risk neutrality: $\rho = 1$, $U(\pi_t) = h\pi_t$,

b. quadratic: $\rho = 2$, $U(\pi_t) = -(1/2)(-h\pi_t + d)^2$,

c. negative exponential: $\rho = -\infty$ and $d = 1$, $U(\pi_t) = -e^{-h\pi_t}$,

d. power: $d = 0$ and $\rho < 1$, $U(\pi_t) = (\pi_t^\rho/\rho)$,

e. logarithmic: $d = \rho = 0$, $U(\pi_t) = \log \pi_t$.

The general HARA specification for $U(\pi_t)$ satisfies the relevant theoretical regularity conditions when the domain of $U(\pi_t)$ is constrained to $\{\pi_t : [h/(1-\rho)]\pi_t + d > 0\}$ with h constrained to satisfy $h > 0$. The power utility function special case is very widely used. Since that functional form exhibits constant relative risk aversion (CRRA), the power utility function often is called the CRRA or isoelastic case.[13]

Differentiating (14) with π_t, we get

$$\frac{\partial U}{\partial \pi_t} = h\left(\frac{h}{1-\rho}\pi_t + d\right)^{\rho-1}. \qquad (15)$$

Using equations (13) and (15) along with the defined state variables, control variables and transition equations, we obtain

$$E_t\left\{P_t k_{it}\left(\frac{h}{1-\rho}\pi_t + d\right)^{\rho-1}\right. \qquad (16)$$

$$+ P_t \frac{1}{1+\mu}\left[(1+R_t)(1-k_{it}) - (1+h_{it})\right.$$

$$\left.+ R_t \frac{\partial\Omega/\partial y_{it}}{\partial\Omega/\partial C_t}\right]\left(\frac{h}{1-\rho}\pi_{t+1} + d\right)^{\rho-1}\right\}$$

$$= 0 \quad \forall\; y_{it}, \quad i = 1, \ldots, I$$

---

[12] See Ingersoll (1987, pp. 37–40). In case (d) below, imposing the restriction $d = 0$ alone on equation 14 will not produce the exact form provided for the power function. However, the form acquired subject to that sole restriction is a positive affine transformation of the power function. Hence both forms represent the same risk behavior.

[13] See, for example, Barnett, Hinich and Yue (2000).

and

$$E_t \left[P_t R_t \frac{\partial \Omega / \partial z_{jt}}{\partial \Omega / \partial C_t} \left(\frac{h}{1-\rho} \pi_{t+1} + d \right)^{\rho-1} \right.$$
$$\left. - (1 + R_t) w_{jt} \left(\frac{h}{1-\rho} \pi_{t+1} + d \right)^{\rho-1} \right]$$
$$= 0 \quad \forall \ z_{jt}, \quad j = 1, \ldots, J. \tag{17}$$

Equations (16) and (17) are a system of $I + J$ nonlinear equations. Theoretically, from (16) and (17) plus the transformation function (5), we could solve for $(y_{1t}, \ldots, y_{It}, C_t, z_{1t}, \ldots, z_{Jt})$. However, in practice the solution could be produced only numerically, since a closed form algebraic solution rarely exists for such Euler equations.

In the following discussion, we extend the dynamic decision (8) into the more general case incorporating learning by doing technological change. In the econometric literature on estimating returns to scale in manufacturing, increasing returns to scale usually are found, despite the fact that increasing returns to scale violates the second-order conditions for profit maximization. We believe that a likely source of this paradox is the potential to confound technological change with returns to scale, when learning by doing technological change exists but is not incorporated within one's model.

Let $\mathbf{y}_t$ be the vector of $\mathbf{y}_{it}$ for all i and $\mathbf{z}_t$ be the vector of $\mathbf{z}_{jt}$ for all j. We then write the maximization problem as

$$\max E_t \left[\sum_{s=t}^{\infty} \left(\frac{1}{1+\mu} \right)^{s-t} U(\pi_s) \right] \tag{18}$$
$$\text{s.t.} \ \Omega(\mathbf{y}_s, C_s, \mathbf{z}_s, \mathbf{y}_{s-1}) = 0 \quad \forall \ s \geq t.$$

The appearance of $\mathbf{y}_{s-1}$ in the transformation function represents learning by doing. Firm technology improves through experience.

At the present stage of this research, we are not using the learning by doing extension of our model in our empirical work, so we only provide the Euler equations below, without supplying the details of the derivation. Those Euler equations under learning by doing are

$$E_t \left\{ \frac{\partial U}{\partial \pi_t}(\pi_t) \frac{\partial \pi_t}{\partial \mathbf{y_t}}(\mathbf{w_t}, \mathbf{u_t}) \right.$$
$$+ \frac{1}{1+\mu} \left[\frac{\partial U}{\partial \pi_t}(\pi_{t+1}) \frac{\partial \pi_t}{\partial \mathbf{y}_{t-1}}(\mathbf{w}_{t+1}, \mathbf{u}_{t+1}) \right]$$
$$- \frac{1}{1+\mu} \frac{\partial \Omega / \partial \mathbf{y}_{t-1}}{\partial \Omega / \partial C_t}(\mathbf{w}_{t+1}, \mathbf{u}_{t+1}) \tag{19}$$

$$\frac{\partial U}{\partial \pi_t}(\pi_{t+2})\frac{\partial \pi_t}{\partial C_{t-1}}(\mathbf{w}_{t+2}, \mathbf{u}_{t+2})$$
$$-\frac{\partial \Omega/\partial \mathbf{y}_t}{\partial \Omega/\partial C_t}(\mathbf{w}_t, \mathbf{u}_t)\frac{\partial U}{\partial \pi_t}(\pi_{t+1})$$
$$\left.\left.\frac{\partial \pi_t}{\partial C_{t-1}}(\mathbf{w}_{t+1}, \mathbf{u}_{t+1})\right]\right\} = 0 \quad \forall\ \mathbf{y}_t$$

and

$$E_t\left\{\frac{\partial U}{\partial \pi_t}(\pi_t)\frac{\partial \pi_t}{\partial \mathbf{z}_t}(\mathbf{w}_t, \mathbf{u}_t)\right. \tag{20}$$
$$+\frac{1}{1+\mu}\left[\frac{\partial U}{\partial \pi_t}(\pi_{t+1})\frac{\partial \pi_t}{\partial \mathbf{z}_{t-1}}(\mathbf{w}_{t+1}, \mathbf{u}_{t+1})\right.$$
$$-\frac{\partial \Omega/\partial \mathbf{z}_t}{\partial \Omega/\partial C_t}(\mathbf{w}_t, \mathbf{u}_t)\frac{\partial U}{\partial \pi_t}(\pi_{t+1})$$
$$\left.\left.\frac{\partial \pi_t}{\partial C_{t-1}}(\mathbf{w}_{t+1}, \mathbf{u}_{t+1})\right]\right\} = 0 \quad \forall\ \mathbf{z}_t$$

Equations (19) and (20) are generalizations of (16) and (17). If learning by doing is excluded by imposing $\partial \Omega/\partial \mathbf{y}_{t-1} = \mathbf{0}$, then (19) and (20) reduce to (16) and (17), respectively. In the rest of the current paper, we return to the special case of no technological change.

A further nested special case is also interesting. We acquire risk neutrality by setting $\rho = 1$. As is conventional under risk neutrality, discounting is acquired objectively by replacing the subjective rate of time discount, μ, by R_t.[14] One reason for interest in that special case is that, in general equilibrium theory, the assumption of complete contingent claims markets combined with perfect competition can be shown, under certain additional assumptions, to produce the conclusion that firms will be risk neutral, even if their owners are risk-averse. The risk aversion of the owners then is captured within the contingent claims prices, which are taken as given by the firms'

---

[14] While the risk-neutral case is acquired directly by making those substitutions in the original decision problem, the resulting Euler equations are not acquired simply by making those substitutions in the risk-averse Euler equations, (16) and (17). The reason is that a cancellation within the Euler equations that is produced when the rate of discount is the constant, μ, does not apply when the rate of discount becomes the variable, R_t. In particular, after replacing ρ with 1.0, and μ with R_t, it also is necessary to multiply the two terms within equation (17) by $1/(1+R_t)$ to get the risk neutral case Euler equations. No such adjustment is needed within equation (16), since no relevant factors cancelled out in the derivation of equation (16). This observation also is relevant to the risk-neutral Euler equations (80) and (81) below.

managers under perfect competition.[15]

While this theoretical issue is interesting, we do not consider it alone to be a convincing reason to impose risk neutrality on the management of an industry that behaves in a manner exhibiting clear risk aversion. However, we are interested in the fact that the Divisia index, along with virtually all of the literature on index number theory, is produced under the assumption of perfect certainty. This fact would suggest that the tracking ability of such index numbers may degrade as the level of risk aversion increases. Hence, we produce results both with and without risk neutrality imposed, as a means of exploring the extent to which the tracking ability of index numbers is degraded in the risk averse case relative to the risk-neutral case.

Under risk neutrality, our Euler equations reduce to[16]

$$E_t \left[P_t \frac{R_t(1 - k_{it}) - r_{it}}{1 + R_t} + P_t \frac{R_t}{1 + R_t} \frac{\partial \Omega / \partial y_{it}}{\partial \Omega / \partial C_t} \right] \quad (19')$$
$$= 0 \quad \forall \ y_{it}, \ i = 1, \ldots, I$$

and

$$E_t \left[P_t \frac{R_t}{1 + R_t} \frac{\partial \Omega / \partial z_{jt}}{\partial \Omega / \partial C_t} - w_{jt} \right] = 0 \quad \forall \ z_{jt}, \ j = 1, \ldots, J. \quad (20')$$

The assumption of perfect competition is itself sufficient for the existence of a representative firm. See Debreu 1959, p. 45, result 1. Hence, the theory acquired from our model can be applied with data aggregated over banks.[17]

2 Supply-Side Monetary Aggregation and a Weak Separability Test

Having formulated our dynamic model of financial firm production under uncertainty and having derived the Euler equations, we can proceed to inves-

---

[15]See, for example, Debreu (1959, ch. 7) and Duffie (1991, section 6.3). Regarding the complications produced by incomplete markets, see Magill and Shafer (1991, section 4).

[16]Observe that only one time subscript exists in the risk-neutral Euler equations, so that the solution becomes static. Once the nonlinear utility function has been removed from the objective function, the terms with common time subscripts can be grouped together. However, under risk aversion, even under our assumption of intertemporal strong separability, more than one time subscript exists within the utility function for each time period, since both current and lagged t appear as subscripts in equation (3) for each value of profit, π_t. Hence, the dynamics found within the objective function of equation (4) cannot be removed by regrouping terms.

[17]In fact, Debreu's theorem can be used to aggregate over all firms of all types in the economy to produce the aggregated technology of the country. The representative firm maximizes profits subject to that aggregated technology. However, we use the theorem only to aggregate over the firms in one industry. It should be observed that the ease of aggregation over firms under perfect competition is in marked contrast with the complexity of the theorems on aggregating over consumers.

tigate the exact supply-side monetary aggregates that are generated, if the firm's output monetary services are weakly separable from inputs.

2.1 Supply-Side Aggregation

Most money in modern economies is inside money, which is simultaneously an asset and a liability of the private sector. Inside money provides net positive services to the economy, as a result of the value added that is created by the financial intermediation that produces the inside money. In our model, the borrowed funds that are outputs produced by financial intermediaries are inside money. Inside money may take various forms such as demand deposits, interest-bearing checking accounts, small time deposits, and checkable money market deposit accounts. The sum of the dollar value in such accounts does not measure the services of inside money, any more than the sum of subway trains and roller skates measures transportation services, since the components of the aggregate are not perfect substitutes. The aggregation-theoretic exact quantity aggregate does, however, measure the service flow.[18]

The procedures involved in identifying and generating the exact quantity aggregates of microeconomic theory are described in detail by Barnett (1980a). The approach necessarily involves two steps: identification of the components over which exact aggregation is admissible and determination of the aggregator function defined over those components. The first step determines whether or not an exact aggregate exists, and the second step creates the exact aggregate that is consistent with microeconomic theory. The second step cannot be applied unless the first step succeeds in identifying a component cluster that satisfies the existence condition. That existence condition, which is the basis for the first stage clustering of components, is blockwise weak separability. In accordance with the definition of weak separability, a blocking of components is admissible if and only if the goods in the block can be factored out of the structure of an economy through a subfunction. In other words, it must be possible to formulate the economic structure in the form of a composite function, with the goods in the cluster being the sole variables entering into the inner function of the structure. If that condition is satisfied, an exact quantity aggregate exists over the goods in the cluster and the aggregator function that produces the exact aggregate over those goods is the inner function within the composite function.

Let $\mathbf{y} = (y_{1t}, \ldots, y_{It})'$ and $\mathbf{x} = (C_t, z_{1t}, \ldots, z_{Jt})'$ where $\mathbf{y}$ is the vector of the firm's outputs and $\mathbf{x}$ is the vector of the firm's inputs. The transformation function becomes

$$\Omega(\mathbf{y}, \mathbf{x}) = 0.$$

---

[18] See, for example, Blackorby, Schworm and Fisher (1986) regarding the importance of using appropriately aggregated output data from firms.

An exact supply-side aggregator exists over all of the elements of **y** if and only if **y** is weakly separable from **x** within the structure of Ω. Mathematically, that statement is equivalent to the existence of two functions H and y_0 such that

$$\Omega(\mathbf{y},\mathbf{x}) = H(y_0(\mathbf{y}),\mathbf{x}),$$

where $y_0(\mathbf{y})$ is a convex function of $\mathbf{y}$.[19] In aggregation theory, $y_0(\mathbf{y})$ is called the output aggregator function. Furthermore, suppose that $y_0(\mathbf{y})$ is linearly homogeneous in **y**. Under this assumption, if each y_i grows at the same common rate, the theoretical aggregate $y_0(\mathbf{y})$ will grow at that rate. Clearly, without that condition, $y_0(\mathbf{y})$ could not serve as a reasonable aggregate.[20]

As shown by Leontief (1947a, 1947b), the weak separability condition is equivalent to

$$\frac{\partial}{\partial x_k}\left(\frac{\partial \Omega(\mathbf{y},\mathbf{x})/\partial y_i}{\partial \Omega(\mathbf{y},\mathbf{x})/\partial y_j}\right) = 0 \quad \text{for all } k. \tag{21}$$

If a subset of the components of **y** were weakly separable from all of the other variables in Ω, then an exact output aggregate would exist only over the services of that subset of components and not over the services of all outputs. If we can test for the separability structure of the transformation function and acquire the functional form of $y_0(\mathbf{y})$, when **y** is weakly separable from **x**, then we could estimate the parameters of $y_0(\mathbf{y})$ to acquire an econometric estimate of the exact output aggregate.

Although aggregation theory can provide us with the tools to estimate the exact aggregator function, the resulting aggregate is specification and estimator dependent. Alternatively, the literature on statistical index number theory provides nonparametric approximations to aggregator functions when the existence of the aggregator can be demonstrated through a weak separability test. Statistical index numbers provide only approximations to the theoretical aggregate, however, and when uncertainty exists, little is known about the tracking ability of statistical index numbers as approximations to the exact aggregates of microeconomic theory. In this paper we consider the Divisia, simple-sum and CE indexes to explore their abilities to track the econometrically estimated exact output aggregate.[21] We produce our econometric estimate of the exact theoretical aggregate, for comparison with the

---

[19] See Barnett (1987).

[20] Without linear homogeneity of y_0, the exact aggregate would become the distance function, rather than y_0, and would reduce to y_0, only under linear homogeneity of y_0. We do not pursue that generalization in this study, but see Barnett (1980a) for details.

[21] The Divisia monetary aggregate index was introduced by Barnett (1978, 1980a). The simple-sum index is the traditional monetary index acquired by simply adding up the component quantities without weights. The CE index is the currency equivalence aggregate, originated by Rotemberg (1991) and Rotemberg, Driscoll and Poterba (1995). For an alternative interpretation of the CE index as an economic monetary stock index connected with the Divisia service flow, see Barnett (1991).

index numbers, by using generalized method of moments (GMM) estimation of the parameters of the Euler equations under rational expectations. We do the GMM estimation both under risk aversion and under the imposition of risk neutrality, to investigate sensitivity of our conclusions to risk aversion.

2.2 Flexibility, Regularity, and Weak Separability

In empirical applications, there are two widely used approaches to testing for the weak separability condition that is necessary for economic aggregation: the nonparametric, nonstochastic approach based upon revealed preference and the statistical, parametric approach.[22] Since we are working from within a parametric specification, the conventional parametric approach to testing the hypothesis is to be preferred. In fact, we shall see that weak separability will be a strictly nested null hypothesis within our parametric specification, and, hence, conventional statistical testing is available immediately. In addition, the nonparametric approach, at its current state of development, is nonstochastic and, hence, has unknown power.

Restrictive parametric specifications can bias inferences. As a result, flexible functional forms have been developed and are widely used in current studies. A flexible functional form, by definition, has enough free parameters to approximate locally to the second-order any arbitrary function.[23] However, using flexible functional forms creates a new problem. These models, unlike earlier, more restrictive models, may not globally satisfy the regularity conditions of economic theory, including the monotonicity and curvature conditions. It would be desirable to be able to impose global theoretical regularity on these models, but most of the models in the class of flexible functional forms lose their flexibility property, when regularity is imposed.[24] We use a model that permits imposition of regularity, without compromise of flexibility.

While flexibility and regularity are desirable in any neoclassical empirical study, weak separability in some blocking of the goods is also needed to permit aggregation over the goods in that block. We again are presented with the risk of losing flexibility by imposing a restriction, and in fact imposing weak

---

[22] See Swofford and Whitney (1987).

[23] The flexibility here is sometimes called Diewert-flexible or second-order flexible. See Diewert (1971). The flexibility applies only locally. However, Gallant (1981, 1982) introduced the Fourier semi-nonparametric functional form, which can provide global flexibility asymptotically. Barnett, Geweke, and Wolfe (1991a) have developed the alternative semi-nonparametric asymptotically ideal model (AIM), which is globally flexible asymptotically and has advantages in terms of regularity.

[24] See Gallant and Golub (1984), Lau (1978), and Diewert and Wales (1987). However, if we can choose a model whose regularity region contains the data, then the regularity will be satisfied without imposing additional restrictions.

separability on many flexible functional forms greatly damages the specifications' flexibility. For example, imposing weak separability on the translog function does great damage to its flexibility.[25] Because of the difficulties in imposing regularity and separability simultaneously without damage to flexibility, parametric tests of weak separability have been slow to appear and have been applied only to the static, perfect certainty case in which duality theory is available. In our case of dynamic uncertainty, very little duality theory is currently available.

In this section, we develop an approach that permits testing and imposing blockwise weak separability within a globally regular and locally flexible transformation function that is arising from a dynamic, stochastic choice problem. Our approach uses Diewert and Wales' (1995) symmetric generalized McFadden functional form to specify the technology of the firm.[26] In the discussion to follow, we first specify the model's form under the null hypothesis of weak separability in outputs. We then provide the more general form of the model that remains valid without the imposition of weak separability.

Using the notations defined previously, if $\mathbf{y}$ is weakly separable from $\mathbf{x}$, then

$$\Omega(\mathbf{y}, \mathbf{x}) = H(y_0(\mathbf{y}), \mathbf{x}).$$

We further assume that the transformation function is linearly homogeneous. Instead of specifying the form of the full transformation function Ω directly and thereafter imposing weak separability in $\mathbf{y}$, we impose weak separability directly by specifying $H(y_0, \mathbf{x})$ and $y_0(\mathbf{y})$ separately. We acquire our weakly separable form for Ω by substituting $y_0(\mathbf{y})$ into $H(y_0, \mathbf{x})$. Our specifications of $y_0(\mathbf{y})$ and $H(y_0, \mathbf{x})$ are both flexible, subject to the separability restriction.

We specify H to be the symmetric generalized McFadden functional form

$$H(y_0, \mathbf{x}) = a_0 y_0 + \mathbf{a}'\mathbf{x} + \frac{1}{2}[y_0, \mathbf{x}']\bar{\mathbf{A}}\left[\begin{pmatrix} y_0 \\ \mathbf{x} \end{pmatrix}\right]/\boldsymbol{\alpha}'\mathbf{x}, \qquad (22)$$

with $\boldsymbol{\alpha}'\mathbf{x} \neq 0$, where a_0, $\mathbf{a}' = (a_1, \ldots, a_n)$, and $\bar{\mathbf{A}}$ consist of parameters to be estimated. The matrix $\bar{\mathbf{A}}$ is $(n+1) \times (n+1)$ and symmetric. The vector $\boldsymbol{\alpha}' = (\alpha_1, \ldots, \alpha_n)$ is a fixed vector of nonnegative constants.[27] The division

---

[25] See Blackorby, Primont, and Russell (1977). Denny and Fuss (1977) propose a partial solution to avoid destroying flexibility. Their approach is to impose weak separability conditions at a point. However, local weak separability is not sufficient for the existence of a global aggregator function.

[26] Diewert and Wales (1987) alternatively also developed the generalized Barnett model. Although we have not used that model in this study, the generalized Barnett model has been applied to the analogous perfect-certainty case by Barnett and Hahm (1994). Regarding the merits of the generalized Barnett model in testing for weak separability, also see Blackorby, Schworm, and Fisher (1986).

[27] We use the term 'fixed constants' to designate constants that the researchers can select *a priori* and treat as constants during estimation.

by $\alpha'\mathbf{x}$ in (22) makes H linearly homogeneous in y_0 and $\mathbf{x}$.

To conform with the partitioning of the vector $(y_0, \mathbf{x}')$, we partition the matrix $\bar{\mathbf{A}}$ as

$$\bar{\mathbf{A}} = \begin{bmatrix} A_{11} & \mathbf{A}_{12} \\ \mathbf{A}_{21} & \mathbf{A} \end{bmatrix}$$

where A_{11} is a scalar, $\mathbf{A}_{12}$ is a $1 \times n$ row vector, $\mathbf{A}_{21}$ is an $n \times 1$ column vector, and $\mathbf{A}$ an $n \times n$ symmetric matrix. Since $\bar{\mathbf{A}}$ is symmetric, it follows that $\mathbf{A}_{12} = \mathbf{A}'_{21}$.

Let $(y_0^*, \mathbf{x}^*) \neq 0$ be the point about which the functional form is locally flexible. That point is selected by the researcher in advance, in a manner analogous to the selection of the point about which a Taylor series is expanded. Since the transformation function is assumed to be linearly homogeneous, the specification in the above form is not parsimonious, and hence, we further can restrict the model without losing the local flexibility property.[28] We therefore impose

$$\alpha' \mathbf{x}^* = 1, \qquad (23)$$

$$A_{11} y_0^* + \mathbf{A}_{12} \mathbf{x}^* = 0, \qquad (24)$$

and

$$\mathbf{A}'_{12} y_0^* + \mathbf{A} \mathbf{x}^* = \mathbf{0}_n, \qquad (25)$$

where $\mathbf{0}_n$ is an n-dimensional vector of zeros. Under (23), (24), and (25), it can be verified that the number of free parameters in equation (22) equals the minimum number of free parameters needed to maintain flexibility.

Solving (24) and (25) for A_{11} and $\mathbf{A}_{12}$, we have

$$\mathbf{A}'_{12} = -\mathbf{A} \mathbf{x}^* / y_0^* \qquad (26)$$

and

$$A_{11} = \mathbf{x}^{*'} \mathbf{A} \mathbf{x}^* / y_0^{*2}. \qquad (27)$$

Substituting (26) and (27) into (22) yields

$$H(y_0, \mathbf{x}) = a_0 y_0 + \mathbf{a}' \mathbf{x} + \frac{1}{2}(\alpha' \mathbf{x})^{-1} \mathbf{x}' \mathbf{A} \mathbf{x} \qquad (28)$$

$$- (\alpha' \mathbf{x})^{-1} \mathbf{x}^{*'} \mathbf{A} \mathbf{x} (y_0/y_0^*) + \frac{1}{2}(\alpha' \mathbf{x})^{-1} \mathbf{x}^{*'} \mathbf{A} \mathbf{x}^* (y_0/y_0^*)^2.$$

---

[28] A flexible functional form is parsimonious if it has the minimum number of parameters needed to maintain flexibility. Diewert and Wales (1988) have acquired the minimum number of parameters needed to provide a second-order approximation to an arbitrary function. If a specification for an arbitrary function with n variables is flexible, it must have at least $1+n+n(n+1)/2$ independent parameters. In our case, the linear homogeneity imposes $1+n$ extra constraints on the first and second derivatives of H, so the minimum number of parameters needed to acquire flexibility is reduced by $1+n$.

Diewert and Wales (1987) have proved that $H(y_0, \mathbf{x})$, defined by equation (28), is flexible at $(y_0^*, \mathbf{x}^*)$.

In a similar way, we define $y_0(\mathbf{y})$ to be

$$y_0(\mathbf{y}) = \mathbf{b}'\mathbf{y} + \frac{1}{2}\mathbf{y}'\mathbf{B}\mathbf{y}/\boldsymbol{\beta}'\mathbf{y}, \qquad (29)$$

with the parameters satisfying

$$\boldsymbol{\beta}'\mathbf{y}^* = 1, \qquad (30)$$

$$y_0^* = \mathbf{b}'\mathbf{y}^*, \qquad (31)$$

and

$$\mathbf{B}\mathbf{y}^* = \mathbf{0}_m, \qquad (32)$$

where $\mathbf{b}' = (b_1, \ldots, b_m)$, and the $m \times m$ symmetric matrix $\mathbf{B}$ consists of parameters to be estimated, $\boldsymbol{\beta}' = (\beta_1, \ldots, \beta_m)$ is a fixed vector of nonnegative constants, and $\mathbf{y}^* \neq 0$ is the point at which local flexibility of equation (29) is maintained.

Substituting (29) into (28), we get

$$\begin{aligned}\Omega(\mathbf{y}, \mathbf{x}) &= H(y_0(\mathbf{y}), \mathbf{x}) \qquad (33)\\ &= a_0(\mathbf{b}'\mathbf{y} + \frac{1}{2}(\boldsymbol{\beta}'\mathbf{y})^{-1}\mathbf{y}'\mathbf{B}\mathbf{y}) + \mathbf{a}'\mathbf{x} + \frac{1}{2}(\boldsymbol{\alpha}'\mathbf{x})^{-1}\mathbf{x}'\mathbf{A}\mathbf{x} \\ &\quad - (y_0^*\boldsymbol{\alpha}'\mathbf{x})^{-1}\mathbf{x}^{*'}\mathbf{A}\mathbf{x}(\mathbf{b}'\mathbf{y} + \frac{1}{2}(\boldsymbol{\beta}'\mathbf{y})^{-1}\mathbf{y}'\mathbf{B}\mathbf{y}) \\ &\quad + \frac{1}{2}(y_0^{*2}\boldsymbol{\alpha}'\mathbf{x})^{-1}\mathbf{x}^{*'}\mathbf{A}\mathbf{x}^*(\mathbf{b}'\mathbf{y} + \frac{1}{2}(\boldsymbol{\beta}'\mathbf{y})^{-1}\mathbf{y}'\mathbf{B}\mathbf{y})^2,\end{aligned}$$

which is a flexible functional form for $\Omega(\mathbf{y}, \mathbf{x})$ and satisfies weak separability in outputs.

Neoclassical curvature conditions require $\Omega(\mathbf{y}, \mathbf{x})$ and $y_0(\mathbf{y})$ to be convex functions, and neoclassical monotonicity requires $\partial \Omega / \partial \mathbf{y} \geq 0$ and $\partial \Omega / \partial \mathbf{x} \leq 0$. Diewert and Wales (1987), theorem (10), have shown that $H(y_0, \mathbf{x})$, defined by (28), and $y_0(\mathbf{y})$, defined by (29), are globally convex if and only if $\mathbf{A}$ and $\mathbf{B}$ are positive semidefinite. For $\Omega(\mathbf{y}, \mathbf{x})$ to be convex, we further need

$$\frac{\partial H(y_0, \mathbf{x})}{\partial y_0} \geq 0. \qquad (34)$$

If (34) holds, then $\Omega(\mathbf{y}, \mathbf{x})$ is globally convex in $(\mathbf{y}, \mathbf{x})$, when $H(y_0, \mathbf{x})$ is convex in $(y_0, \mathbf{x})$ and $y_0(\mathbf{y})$ is convex in $\mathbf{y}$.[29]

---

[29] See Diewert and Wales (1991) for the proof.

If the unconstrained estimates of **A** and **B** are not positive semidefinite symmetric matrices, positive semidefiniteness can be imposed without destroying flexibility by the substitution

$$\mathbf{A} = \mathbf{qq'} \tag{35}$$

and

$$\mathbf{B} = \mathbf{uu'}, \tag{36}$$

where **q** is a lower triangular $n \times n$ matrix and **u** is a lower triangular $m \times m$ matrix.[30] In estimation, we replace **A** and **B** by lower triangular matrices **qq'** and **uu'**, so that the function (33) is globally convex if (34) is true.

Monotonicity restrictions are difficult to impose globally. However, we can impose local monotonicity with simple restrictions. Differentiating (33) with respect to $(\mathbf{y}, \mathbf{x})$, we get

$$\frac{\partial \Omega}{\partial \mathbf{y}} = a_0[\mathbf{b} + \frac{1}{2}(2(\beta'\mathbf{y})^{-1}\mathbf{B}\mathbf{y} - (\beta'\mathbf{y})^{-2}\beta\mathbf{y}'\mathbf{B}\mathbf{y})] \tag{37}$$

$$-(y_0^*\alpha'\mathbf{x})^{-1}\mathbf{x}^{*'}\mathbf{A}\mathbf{x}[\mathbf{b} + \frac{1}{2}(2(\beta'\mathbf{y})^{-1}\mathbf{B}\mathbf{y} - (\beta'\mathbf{y})^{-2}\beta\mathbf{y}'\mathbf{B}\mathbf{y})]$$

$$+(y_0^{*2}\alpha'\mathbf{x})^{-1}\mathbf{x}^{*'}\mathbf{A}\mathbf{x}^*[\mathbf{b} + \frac{1}{2}(2(\beta'\mathbf{y})^{-1}\mathbf{B}\mathbf{y}$$

$$-(\beta'\mathbf{y})^{-2}\beta\mathbf{y}'\mathbf{B}\mathbf{y})](\mathbf{b}'\mathbf{y} + \frac{1}{2}(\beta'\mathbf{y})^{-1}\mathbf{y}'\mathbf{B}\mathbf{y})$$

and

$$\frac{\partial \Omega}{\partial \mathbf{x}} = \mathbf{a} + \frac{1}{2}[2(\alpha'\mathbf{x})^{-1}\mathbf{A}\mathbf{x} - (\alpha'\mathbf{x})^{-2}\alpha\mathbf{x}'\mathbf{A}\mathbf{x}] \tag{38}$$

$$-[(y_0^*\alpha'\mathbf{x})^{-1}\mathbf{A}\mathbf{x}^* - (y_0^*\alpha'\mathbf{x})^{-2}y_0^*\alpha\mathbf{x}^{*'}\mathbf{A}\mathbf{x}](\mathbf{b}'\mathbf{y} + \frac{1}{2}(\beta'\mathbf{y})^{-1}\mathbf{y}'\mathbf{B}\mathbf{y})$$

$$-\frac{1}{2}(y_0^{*2}\alpha'\mathbf{x})^{-2}y_0^{*2}\alpha\mathbf{x}^{*'}\mathbf{A}\mathbf{x}^*(\mathbf{b}'\mathbf{y} + \frac{1}{2}(\beta'\mathbf{y})^{-1}\mathbf{y}'\mathbf{B}\mathbf{y})^2.$$

If we evaluate these derivatives at $(\mathbf{y}^*, \mathbf{x}^*)$, we have

$$\frac{\partial \Omega}{\partial \mathbf{y}} = a_0 \mathbf{b} \tag{39}$$

and

$$\frac{\partial \Omega}{\partial \mathbf{x}} = \mathbf{a}. \tag{40}$$

---

[30] See Lau (1978) and Diewert and Wales (1987).

Applying the method of squaring technique, we impose on (39) and (40) the monotonicity conditions[31]

$$\frac{\partial \Omega}{\partial \mathbf{y}}(\mathbf{y}^*, \mathbf{x}^*) = a_0 \mathbf{b} \geq 0 \quad \text{and} \quad \frac{\partial \Omega}{\partial \mathbf{x}}(\mathbf{y}^*, \mathbf{x}^*) = \mathbf{a} \leq 0. \tag{41}$$

Equation (41) assures that the monotonicity conditions are satisfied locally at $(\mathbf{y}^*, \mathbf{x}^*)$.

We have shown that the functional form defined by equation (33) and restricted to satisfy equations (23), (30)–(32), (34)–(36), and (41) is flexible, locally monotone, and globally convex, provided that the assumed weakly separable structure is true. Although we do not impose global monotonicity, we do check and confirm that monotonicity is satisfied at each observation within our data. In the following discussion, we will define a more general flexible functional form that does not require weak separability.

The number of independent parameters in equation (33) is

$$1 + n + \frac{n(n+1)}{2} + m - 1 + \frac{m(m-1)}{2}. \tag{42}$$

We know that the minimum number of parameters required to maintain flexibility for a linearly homogeneous function with $n + m$ variables is

$$1 + n + m + \frac{(n+m)(n+m+1)}{2} - (1 + n + m). \tag{43}$$

Subtracting (42) from (43), we get $n(m-1)$, which is the number of additional parameters that must be introduced into equation (33) to acquire a flexible functional form for a general transformation function. Let

$$\Omega(\mathbf{y}, \mathbf{x}) = H(y_0(\mathbf{y}), \mathbf{x}) + \mathbf{c}'\mathbf{y} + \mathbf{y}'\mathbf{C}\mathbf{x}/(\boldsymbol{\gamma}'\mathbf{y} + \boldsymbol{\lambda}'\mathbf{x}), \tag{44}$$

where $\boldsymbol{\gamma}$ and $\boldsymbol{\lambda}$ are vectors of nonnegative fixed constants, the vector $\mathbf{c}' = (c_1, \ldots, c_m)$ and the $m \times n$ matrix $\mathbf{C}$ are new parameters to be estimated, and the division by $\boldsymbol{\gamma}'\mathbf{y} + \boldsymbol{\lambda}'\mathbf{x}$ makes Ω linearly homogeneous. Because of the linear homogeneity property, we have more free parameters than needed for flexibility and, hence, we can impose the following additional restrictions without losing local flexibility:

$$\boldsymbol{\gamma}'\mathbf{y}^* + \boldsymbol{\lambda}'\mathbf{x}^* = 1, \tag{45}$$

$$\mathbf{c}'\mathbf{y}^* = 0, \tag{46}$$

$$\mathbf{y}^{*'}\mathbf{C} = \mathbf{0}'_n, \tag{47}$$

---

[31] See Lau (1978a).

and
$$\mathbf{Cx}^* = \mathbf{0}_m, \tag{48}$$

where $(\mathbf{y}^*, \mathbf{x}^*)$ is the point at which local flexibility is maintained. Under equations (45)–(48), the number of new free parameters added into (44) is exactly equal to $n(m-1)$. Diewert and Wales (1991) have proved that the function (44) is a flexible functional form at $(\mathbf{y}^*, \mathbf{x}^*)$ for a general nonseparable transformation function.

Global convexity is difficult to impose in this case. However, we can derive the restrictions for local convexity at $(\mathbf{y}^*, \mathbf{x}^*)$. Deriving the Hessian matrix of (44) and evaluating at $(\mathbf{y}^*, \mathbf{x}^*)$, we have

$$\nabla^2 \Omega(\mathbf{y}^*, \mathbf{x}^*) = \begin{bmatrix} a_0 \mathbf{B} + \mathbf{b}\mathbf{b}'\mathbf{x}^{*'} \mathbf{A} \mathbf{x}^* / y_0^{*2} & \mathbf{C} - \mathbf{b}\mathbf{x}^{*'} \mathbf{A}/y_0^* \\ \mathbf{C}' - \mathbf{A}\mathbf{x}^* \mathbf{b}'/y_0^* & \mathbf{A} \end{bmatrix}. \tag{49}$$

If $\nabla^2 \Omega(\mathbf{y}^*, \mathbf{x}^*)$ is positive semidefinite, then $\Omega(\mathbf{y}^*, \mathbf{x}^*)$ is convex at $(\mathbf{y}^*, \mathbf{x}^*)$. Let

$$\mathbf{A} = \mathbf{q}\mathbf{q}', \tag{50}$$

$$\mathbf{C} = \mathbf{v}\mathbf{q}', \tag{51}$$

and
$$\mathbf{B} = a_0^{-1}[\mathbf{v}\mathbf{v}' + \mathbf{u}\mathbf{u}'], \tag{52}$$

where $\mathbf{q}$ and $\mathbf{u}$ are lower triangular matrices introduced for reasons described above, and $\mathbf{v}$ is an unrestricted $m \times n$ matrix. Then $\nabla^2 \Omega(\mathbf{y}^*, \mathbf{x}^*)$ is a positive semidefinite symmetric matrix.[32]

Using (50)–(52), we rewrite (47), (48), and (32) as

$$\mathbf{y}^{*'} \mathbf{v} = \mathbf{0}'_n, \tag{53}$$

$$\mathbf{v}(\mathbf{q}'\mathbf{x}^*) = \mathbf{0}_m, \tag{54}$$

and
$$\mathbf{u}'\mathbf{y}^* = \mathbf{0}_m. \tag{55}$$

The function defined by (44) and satisfying (23), (30)–(31), (45)–(46), and (50)–(55) is a flexible functional form for a general transformation function at $(\mathbf{y}^*, \mathbf{x}^*)$. In addition, local convexity is satisfied.

We now turn to imposing local monotonicity. Differentiating (44) with respect to $(\mathbf{y}, \mathbf{x})$ and evaluating at $(\mathbf{y}^*, \mathbf{x}^*)$, we have

$$\frac{\partial \Omega}{\partial \mathbf{y}} = a_0 \mathbf{b} + \mathbf{c} \tag{56}$$

---

[32] See Lau (1978a) and Diewert and Wales (1991).

and
$$\frac{\partial \Omega}{\partial \mathbf{x}} = \mathbf{a}. \tag{57}$$

As above, we use the method of squaring to impose nonnegativity on (56) and nonpositivity on (57). The estimated results then satisfy local monotonicity.

Comparing (33) with (44), we see that weak separability of outputs in (44) is equivalent to:

$$H_0 : \mathbf{c} = \mathbf{0}_m \quad \text{and} \quad \mathbf{v}_{m \times n} = \mathbf{0}_{m \times n}. \tag{58}$$

Note that under the null hypothesis, H_0, equation (44) reduces to (33). Hence, $\mathbf{y}$ is weakly separable from $\mathbf{x}$ if and only if H_0 is true.

We have derived two flexible functional forms with appropriate regularity properties. One structure holds in the general case and the other under the null hypothesis of weak separability. We now are prepared to test weak separability and to estimate the parameters of the transformation function. The basic tool is Hansen and Singleton's generalized method of moments (GMM) estimator.

Substituting the functional form given by either (33) or (44) into the Euler equations (16) and (17), we obtain our structural model, which consists of a system of integral equations. A closed form solution to such Euler equations rarely exists. However, GMM permits estimating nonlinear rational expectations models defined in terms of Euler equations. Hansen (1982) has proved that under very weak conditions, the GMM estimates are consistent and asymptotically normally distributed.[33]

In the GMM framework, there are two methods of testing hypotheses.[34] The first approach applies Hansen's asymptotic χ^2 statistic to test for no overidentifying restrictions. We impose the weak separability restrictions (58) on the flexible functional form (44), estimate the restricted system, and then run Hansen's test for no overidentifying restrictions. Since (44) reduces to (33) after imposing the weak separability restrictions, we can substitute equation (33) itself directly into the Euler equations to impose the null for testing. If the test of no overidentifying restrictions is rejected, then the restrictions imposed under the null hypothesis are rejected, where in our case the null is the weakly separable structure imposed on the transformation function.

The second approach to hypothesis testing with GMM is based on the asymptotically normal distribution of the GMM parameter estimators. Let θ be the vector of parameters to be estimated in equation (44). Then the

---

[33] Hansen (1982), Hansen and Singleton (1982), and Newey and West (1987) provide a detailed discussion of GMM estimation.

[34] See Mackinlay and Richardson (1991).

GMM estimator $\hat{\boldsymbol{\theta}}$ has an asymptotically normal distribution with mean $\boldsymbol{\theta}$ and covariance matrix Σ.

Let τ be an $[n(m-1)] \times 1$ vector which contains all $n(m-1)$ independent parameters in the vector $\mathbf{c}$ and the matrix $\mathbf{v}$. The hypothesis of weak separability can be rewritten now as $\tau = \mathbf{0}$ or equivalently as a set of linear restrictions of the form

$$\mathbf{S}\boldsymbol{\theta} = \tau = \mathbf{0}, \tag{59}$$

where $\mathbf{S}$ is an $[n(m-1)] \times [(n+m+1)/2]$ matrix whose elements are all zeros and ones.

From the known asymptotic distribution of $\hat{\boldsymbol{\theta}}$, we have

$$\sqrt{T}(\mathbf{S}\hat{\boldsymbol{\theta}} - \mathbf{S}\boldsymbol{\theta}) \stackrel{a}{\sim} N(\mathbf{0}, \mathbf{S}\Sigma\mathbf{S}'), \tag{60}$$

where T is the number of observations. Under the null hypothesis, $H_0 : \mathbf{S}\boldsymbol{\theta} = \mathbf{0}$, we have

$$\sqrt{T}\,\hat{\tau} \stackrel{a}{\sim} N(\mathbf{0}, \mathbf{S}\Sigma\mathbf{S}'),$$

where $\hat{\tau} = \mathbf{S}\hat{\boldsymbol{\theta}}$. We obtain the following χ^2 statistic

$$\begin{aligned}\phi &= (\sqrt{T}\,\hat{\tau})'[\mathbf{S}\Sigma\mathbf{S}']^{-1}(\sqrt{T}\,\hat{\tau}) \\ &= T\hat{\tau}'[\mathbf{S}\Sigma\mathbf{S}']^{-1}\hat{\tau} \stackrel{a}{\sim} \chi^2_{n(m-1)}.\end{aligned} \tag{61}$$

Although Σ is unknown, we can replace it by a consistent estimate without changing the asymptotic results. The test is one sided, with the null of separability rejected if ϕ is large.

3 Empirical Application

Barnett and Hahm (1994) and Hancock (1985, 1987, 1991) have analyzed monetary service production by the banking industry in detail, under the assumptions of perfect certainty and neoclassical joint production. The balance sheet of a bank consists of fund-providing functions and fund-using functions. The fund-providing functions include demand deposits, time deposits, and nondeposit funds.[35] The fund-using functions include investment, real estate mortgage loans, installment loans, credit card loans, and industrial loans. In our theoretical model, the sources of funds are the firm's borrowed funds,

---

[35] Demand deposits consist of checking accounts, official checks, money orders, treasury tax accounts and loan accounts. Time deposits consist of regular savings, money market deposit accounts, other time accounts, retirement accounts, and certificates of deposit under $100,000. Nondeposit funds consist of equity capital, federal funds purchased, borrowed money, capital notes and debentures, time deposits of $100,000 and over, other money market instruments, and other liabilities.

and the uses of funds are the firm's portfolio. The total available funds on the balance sheet are total assets minus premises and other assets.

On the average, demand deposits and time deposits account for over 85 percent of total available funds. The equity capital included in the nondeposit funds can be treated as a fixed factor that does not enter the variable profit function.[36] For these reasons, we only choose demand deposits and time deposits as borrowed funds in our model. Turning to inputs, excess reserves are total cash balances minus required reserves. Other real resource inputs are labor, materials, and capital.[37] Capital is treated as fixed, and we include only variable factors in the transformation function. An obvious direction for possible future extension of this research would be the incorporation of some or all capital as variable factors to produce inferences applicable to a longer run perspective than that implicit in our definition of variable and fixed factors.

Using equations (16) and (17), the Euler equations are

$$E_t \left\{ P_t k_{1t} \left(\frac{h}{1-\rho} \pi_t + d \right)^{\rho-1} \right. \tag{62}$$

$$+ P_t \frac{1}{1+\mu} \left[(1+R_t)(1-k_{1t}) - (1+h_{1t}) \right]$$

$$\left. + R_t \frac{\partial \Omega/\partial D_t}{\partial \Omega/\partial C_t} \right] \left(\frac{h}{1-\rho} \pi_{t+1} + d \right)^{\rho-1} \right\} = 0,$$

$$E_t \left\{ P_t k_{2t} \left(\frac{h}{1-\rho} \pi_t + d \right)^{\rho-1} \right. \tag{63}$$

$$+ P_t \frac{1}{1+\mu} \left[(1+R_t)(1-k_{2t}) - (1+h_{2t}) \right]$$

$$\left. + R_t \frac{\partial \Omega/\partial T_t}{\partial \Omega/\partial C_t} \right] \left(\frac{h}{1-\rho} \pi_{t+1} + d \right)^{\rho-1} \right\} = 0,$$

$$E_t \left\{ \left[P_t R_t \frac{\partial \Omega/\partial L_t}{\partial \Omega/\partial C_t} - (1+R_t) w_{1t} \right] \left(\frac{h}{1-\rho} \pi_{t+1} + d \right)^{\rho-1} \right\} = 0, \tag{64}$$

and

$$E_t \left\{ \left[P_t R_t \frac{\partial \Omega/\partial M_t}{\partial \Omega \partial C_t} - (1+R_t) w_{2t} \right] \left(\frac{h}{1-\rho} \pi_{t+1} + 1 + d \right)^{\rho-1} \right\} = 0, \tag{65}$$

---

[36]See Barnett (1987). Equity capital includes preferred and common stocks, surplus, undivided profits and reserves, and valuation reserves.

[37]Labor includes managerial labor and nonmanagerial labor. Materials include stationery, printing and supplies, telephone, telegraph, postage, freight and delivery.

Empirical Application

where D_t is demand deposits, T_t is time deposits, L_t is labor input, M_t is materials input, and w_{1t} and w_{2t} are the prices of labor and materials respectively.

Using the notations in section three, we can write

$$\mathbf{y}' = (D_t, T_t) \quad \text{and} \quad \mathbf{x}' = (C_t, L_t, M_t).$$

If the weakly separable structure of the transformation function is true, then equation (33) is the transformation function. As discussed in section three, the weak separability hypothesis can be tested by applying Hansen's χ^2 statistic.

The derivatives of Ω with respect to its arguments are given by equations (37) and (38). The fixed constants and the center of the local approximation need to be selected before estimation. We choose

$$y_0^* = 1, \quad \mathbf{y}^{*'} = (1,1), \quad \text{and} \quad \mathbf{x}^{*'} = (1,1,1)$$

as the center of approximation. To locate that center within the interior of the observations, we rescale the data about the midpoint observation

$$\begin{aligned} \tilde{x}_i^t &= x_i^t / x_i^{t*} \quad \forall\, i = 1,2,3 \quad \text{and} \\ \tilde{y}_i^t &= y_i^t / y_i^{t*} \quad \forall\, i = 1,2, \end{aligned} \tag{66}$$

where t^* represents the midpoint observation.[38] We correspondingly rescale each price by multiplication by the midpoint observation. That rescaling of prices keeps dollar expenditures on each good unaffected by the rescaling of its quantity.

We select the fixed nonnegative constants α_i and β_i such that

$$\alpha_i = |\bar{\tilde{x}}_i| / \sum_{j=1}^{3} |\bar{\tilde{x}}_j| \quad \forall i = 1,2,3 \tag{67}$$

and

$$\beta_i = |\bar{\tilde{y}}_i| / \sum_{j=1}^{2} |\bar{\tilde{y}}_j| \quad \forall i = 1,2, \tag{68}$$

where $\bar{\tilde{x}}$ and $\bar{\tilde{y}}$ are the sample means of $\tilde{x}$ and $\tilde{y}$ respectively. Note that α_i and β_i satisfy equations (23) and (30), as is required. With our data sample, we find $\alpha_1 = 0.33$, $\alpha_2 = 0.35$, $\alpha_3 = 0.32$, $\beta_1 = 0.58$, and $\beta_2 = 0.42$.

Before estimating the independent parameters, we need only impose the inequality restrictions. Equation (31) implies $b_2 = 1 - b_1$, and the monotonicity condition (41) requires $b_i \geq 0$. Hence, it also follows that $b_i \leq 1$.

---

[38] The data point at which all quantities are set to unity can be arbitrary.

Combining these conditions, we can replace b_1 and b_2 by

$$b_1 = \sin^2(\xi) \quad \text{and} \quad b_2 = \cos^2(\xi) \tag{69}$$

and estimate ξ. Since $\Omega(\mathbf{y}, \mathbf{x}) = 0$, we also normalize $a_0 = 1$.

The monotonicity condition (41) requires $a_i \leq 0$, which we impose by replacing a_i by $-\tilde{a}_i^2$ $\forall i = 1, 2, 3$, where $\tilde{a}_i$ $\forall i = 1, 2, 3$ are the new parameters to be estimated. The convexity conditions are imposed by replacing $\mathbf{A}$ and $\mathbf{B}$ by the lower triangular matrices $\mathbf{qq'}$ and $\mathbf{uu'}$ respectively, where $\mathbf{q}$ and $\mathbf{u}$ are

$$\mathbf{q} = \begin{bmatrix} q_{11} & 0 & 0 \\ q_{21} & q_{22} & 0 \\ q_{31} & q_{32} & q_{33} \end{bmatrix}$$

and

$$\mathbf{u} = \begin{bmatrix} u_{11} & 0 \\ u_{21} & u_{22} \end{bmatrix}.$$

Equation (32) implies

$$\begin{bmatrix} u_{11} & 0 \\ u_{21} & u_{22} \end{bmatrix} \begin{bmatrix} u_{11} & u_{21} \\ 0 & u_{22} \end{bmatrix} \begin{bmatrix} 1 \\ 1 \end{bmatrix} = \begin{bmatrix} 0 \\ 0 \end{bmatrix}. \tag{70}$$

Solving (70), we get $u_{21} = -u_{11}$ and $u_{22} = 0$. Substituting them into equation (36), we have

$$\mathbf{B} = u_{11}^2 \begin{bmatrix} 1 & -1 \\ -1 & 1 \end{bmatrix}. \tag{71}$$

The above discussion identifies all the independent parameters to be estimated in the specification of the transformation function. They are ξ, u_{11}, the lower triangular matrix $\mathbf{q}$, and the vector $\tilde{\mathbf{a}}' = (\tilde{a}_1, \tilde{a}_2, \tilde{a}_3)$.

The primary data source is the Federal Reserve's Functional Cost Analysis (FCA).[39] We got our data from the Federal Reserve Bank of St. Louis. The data used are the National Average FCA Report, which contains annual data from 1966 to 1990. Hence, there are a total of 25 observations in our annual data. Monthly data are not available from the FCA. From the FCA, we acquired banks' portfolio rate of return, the net interest rates on demand deposits and time deposits, and the nominal quantity of demand deposits, time deposits and cash balances.[40] The prices and quantities of labor and

---

[39] The Functional Cost Analysis program is a cooperative venture between the Federal Reserve Banks and the participating banks. This program is designed to assist a participating bank in increasing overall bank earnings as well as to improve the operational efficiency of each bank function.

[40] The net interest rate equals the interest paid minus service charges earned plus FDIC insurance premiums paid.

materials are aggregate producer prices and quantity indexes from the data in the FCA Report and the *Survey of Current Business*.[41] The required reserve ratio is from the *Federal Reserve Bulletin*. The implicit price deflator is the implicit GNP deflator from the Citibank data base. We deflate the nominal dollar balances of all financial goods to convert them into real balances.

4 Empirical Results

We use the GMM estimator in the TSP mainframe version (version 4.2) to estimate our model. In the disturbances we allow for conditional heteroskedasticity and second-order moving average serial correlation. Using the spectral density kernels in TSP, our estimated results are robust to heteroskedasticity, autocorrelation, and positive semidefinite weighting matrix. To use the GMM method, instrumental variables must be selected. We choose as instruments the constant, the federal funds rate, the discount window rate, the composite bond rate (maturities over 10 years), the holding cost of demand deposits and time deposits, the lagged banks' portfolio rate of return, excess cash reserves, and capital. In estimation, we replace h by h^2 to impose nonnegativity of the resulting h^2. That nonnegativity is needed for regularity in the definition of the HARA class.

The GMM parameter estimates, subject to imposition of weak separability of outputs from inputs, are reported in Table 1. All three parameters in the utility function are statistically insignificant at the 5 percent level. As a result of the very low precision of those three parameter estimates, it is clear that we have introduced risk aversion in a manner incorporating too many parameters for the available sample size. Hence, we need to restrict HARA to one of its less deeply parameterized special cases. As observed in the second section, the HARA class reduces to the popular power (CRRA isoelastic) utility function. We now test whether that popular special case is accepted.

Equation (61) in the third section provides a statistic to test that a set of parameters is jointly equal to zeros. When the set of parameters includes only one element, the χ^2 test statistic ϕ, given by equation (61), equals the number of observations multiplied by the square of the t-statistic of that parameter. We calculated that $\phi = 0.0033$, while the critical value is 6.635 at the one percent significance level. Hence, we cannot reject $d = 0$, and the power utility function is accepted. We reestimate the model using that specification.

---

[41] See Barnett and Hahm (1994) for a detailed discussion about the aggregation of labor and material.

TABLE 1
GMM Estimates Using the HARA Utility Function with Weak Separability in Outputs Imposed

Parameter	Estimate	Standard error	t-Statistic
h^2	0.003	0.122	0.024
$\rho - 1$	2.330	25.625	0.091
d	0.001	0.044	0.012
$\mu + 1$	1.090	0.165	6.602
ξ	58.382	0.201	290.459
u_{11}	0.232	0.418	0.555
q_{11}	0.186	0.078	2.372
q_{21}	0.418	0.106	3.931
q_{31}	0.105	0.048	2.178
q_{22}	0.477	0.101	4.725
q_{32}	0.120	0.162	0.743
q_{33}	0.116	0.505	0.230
$\tilde{a}_1$	0.323	0.035	9.117
$\tilde{a}_2$	0.436	0.058	7.523
$\tilde{a}_3$	0.280	0.038	7.448

To impose the inequality restriction $0 < \rho < 1$, which is sufficient for regularity of the power utility function special case, we replace ρ by $\sin^2(\tilde{\rho})$ and estimate $\tilde{\rho}$. In addition, to prevent the implausible possibility of a negative subjective rate of time discount, we replace μ by $\tilde{\mu}^2$ and estimate $\tilde{\mu}$.[42] The estimated results, subject to imposition of weak separability of outputs from inputs, are reported in Table 2.[43] All parameters are significantly different from zero at the 5 percent level except for $\tilde{\mu}$, u_{11}, and q_{33}. Monotonicity is necessarily satisfied at $(\mathbf{y}^*, \mathbf{x}^*)$, since local monotonicity was imposed at that point. We use the estimated parameters to determine whether monotonicity is satisfied elsewhere in the sample. Substituting the estimated parameters into equations (37) and (38), we find that $\partial \Omega / \partial \mathbf{y} > 0$ and $\partial \Omega / \partial \mathbf{x} < 0$ everywhere in the sample. Hence, no violations of monotonicity occurred

---

[42] Actually only the upper bound imposed on ρ is required by theory. Hence, if we had found that the lower bound implied by our substitution was binding, we would have switched to the more sophisticated substitution of $2 - \cosh(\tilde{\rho})$ in place of ρ. But in practice our estimate of ρ was strictly positive, so we did not have to resort to the introduction of hyperbolic functions. Furthermore, our imposition of nonnegativity on μ was equally as harmless, since no corner solutions were acquired on that inequality restriction either. In fact, in the HARA case, we did not impose nonnegativity on μ at all, since we got nonnegativity from our estimates without the need to impose it, and in retrospect it is evident that we could have done the same in the power utility case.

[43] The instrumental variables are the constant, the federal funds rate, the discount window rate, the composite bond rate (over 10 years), the three-month T-bill rate, the yields on demand deposits and time deposits, the lagged bank's portfolio rate of return, and capital.

Empirical Results

within the sample. Regarding curvature, we have imposed global convexity in $H(y_0, \mathbf{x})$ and $y_0(\mathbf{y})$. To verify global convexity of $\Omega(\mathbf{y}, \mathbf{x})$, we must check equation (34) at each data point.

TABLE 2
GMM ESTIMATES USING THE POWER UTILITY FUNCTION WITH WEAK SEPARABILITY IN OUTPUTS IMPOSED

Parameter	Estimate	Standard error	t-Statistic
$\tilde{\rho}$	−524.629	9.410	−55.754
$\tilde{\mu}$	0.351	0.187	1.877
ξ	60.692	0.019	3122.720
u_{11}	0.171	0.283	0.605
q_{11}	0.240	0.050	4.821
q_{21}	0.461	0.077	5.980
q_{31}	0.103	0.018	5.908
q_{22}	0.418	0.047	8.958
q_{32}	0.093	0.029	3.147
q_{33}	−0.025	0.412	−0.062
$\tilde{a}_1$	0.330	0.031	10.762
$\tilde{a}_2$	0.482	0.045	10.607
$\tilde{a}_3$	0.217	0.020	10.836

Differentiating $H(y_0, \mathbf{x})$ with respect to y_0, we get

$$\frac{\partial H(y_0, \mathbf{x})}{\partial y_0} = a_0 - (\boldsymbol{\alpha}'\mathbf{x})^{-1}\mathbf{x}^{*'}\mathbf{A}\mathbf{x}/y_0^* \quad (72)$$
$$+ (\boldsymbol{\alpha}'\mathbf{x})^{-1}\mathbf{x}^{*'}\mathbf{A}\mathbf{x}^* y_0/y_0^{*2},$$

where y_0 is given by equation (29). Substituting the estimated parameters into equation (72), we find that $\partial H(y_0, \mathbf{x})/\partial y_0 > 0$ at every data point. Convexity of Ω is satisfied throughout the sample.

The weak separability hypothesis is tested by using Hansen's χ^2 test for no overidentifying restrictions. His test statistic is

$$\Phi = TQ \sim \chi^2_{e-f}, \quad (73)$$

where T is the number of observations, Q is the value of the objective function, e is the number of orthogonal conditions, and f is the number of parameters estimated.[44] The calculated statistic is 27.6, while the critical value

---

[44] The value of the objective function is defined as $Q = G_N(\hat{\theta})'\hat{W}_N G_N(\hat{\theta})$, where $G_N(\hat{\theta})$ is the sample mean of the moment conditions and $\hat{W}_N$ is the weighting matrix that defines the metric in making $G_N(\hat{\theta})$ close to zero in the GMM estimation procedure.

is 41.64 at the 1 percent significance level. We cannot reject the weak separability hypothesis. Hence, the existence of a theoretical monetary aggregate over the outputs produced by banks is accepted.

Substituting the parameter estimate of ξ from Table 2 into equation (69), we obtain $b_1 = 0.76$ and $b_2 = 0.24$. The estimated theoretical aggregate then is acquired by substituting the estimated parameters and fixed constants into equation (29) to get

$$y_0(D_t, T_t) = 0.76 D_t + 0.24 T_t + \frac{1}{2}\left[\frac{.17^2(D_t - T_t)^2}{.58 D_t + 0.42 T_t}\right]. \tag{74}$$

It is important to recognize that this aggregator function should not be used for forecasting or simulation outside the region of the data, and hence its usefulness is limited to research within the sample. While we have confirmed monotonicity within the region of the data, this aggregator function is not globally regular for all possible nonnegative values of the variables outside that region.

Having our econometrically estimated theoretical supply-side monetary aggregate, we now proceed to investigate whether any of the well known nonparametric statistical index numbers can track the estimated exact aggregate adequately. By converting from $\tilde{\rho}$ back to ρ and then computing the degree of relative risk aversion, $1 - \rho$, we find that the degree of relative risk aversion is $1 - .07 = .93$. Since risk neutrality occurs only for zero values of relative risk aversion, we do not have risk neutrality. But there is no currently available theory regarding the tracking ability of nonparametric statistical index numbers when risk aversion exists. Hence, our only method of investigating the tracking ability of the more easily computed nonparametric statistical indexes is to estimate the exact index econometrically, as we just have done, and compare its behavior with that of the statistical index numbers.

In this paper, we compare the estimated theoretical aggregate with the Divisia, simple-sum, and CE indexes. Rotemberg, Driscoll, and Poterba (1995) have found that the growth rate of the CE index is very volatile with monthly data. Hence, they have proposed (see their footnote 11) a method of smoothing that index's growth rates by replacing the index's weights by 13-month, centered moving averages. Since we are using annual data, there already is a form of smoothing implicit in the data construction. Nevertheless, in addition to computing the annual contemporaneous CE index, we compute the smoothed index in accordance with the method selected by Rotemberg, Driscoll and Poterba.

To parallel the 13-month centered moving-average smoothing as closely as possible with annual data, we use a three-year centered moving average.

Empirical Results

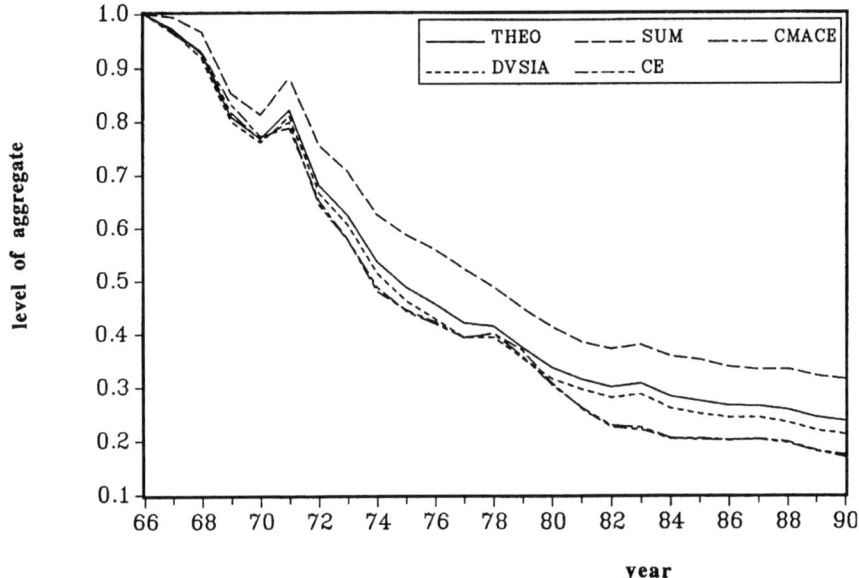

Note: THEO=level of estimated theoretical aggregate, DVSIA=level of Divisia index, SUM=level of simple-sum index, CE=level of CE index, CMACE=level of smoothed CE index, in which the weights are replaced by 3 year centered moving averages.

Figure 1: Levels of theoretical monetary aggregate, Divisia index, simple-sum index, CE index, and smoothed CE index. Parameters of theoretical monetary aggregate estimated with risk aversion permitted.

In a sense, our results with unsmoothed annual data slightly undersmooths relative to Rotemberg, Driscoll and Poterba's method, while the three-year centered moving average oversmooths relative to Rotemberg, Driscoll and Poterba's method. Nevertheless, as we shall see, the CE index's growth rate remains too volatile. A centered moving average is not defined at the start and end of a sample. Hence, a special method is needed to phase in the centered moving average at the start of the sample and phase it out at the end of the period. For that purpose, we use the procedure advocated by Rotemberg, Driscoll and Poterba. Figure 1 contains plots of the levels of all those aggregates. Figure 2 contains plots of their growth rates. We also separately plot the growth rate of each of the four statistical index numbers (simple-sum, Divisia, unsmoothed CE and smoothed CE), with the growth rate of the estimated theoretical path superimposed. These plots are given in Figures 3, 4, 5, and 6.

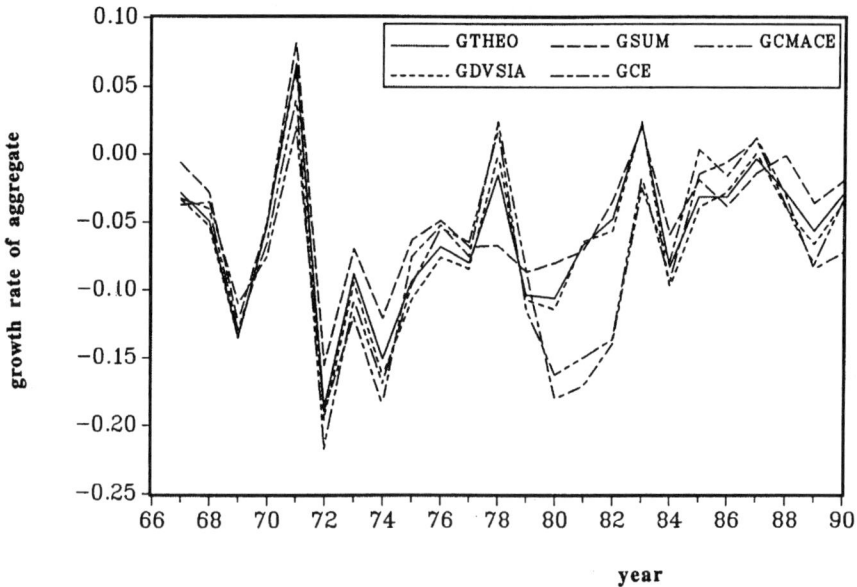

Note: GTHEO=growth rate of estimated theoretical aggregate, GDVSIA=growth rate of Divisia index, GSUM=growth rate of simple-sum index, GCE=growth rate of CE index, GCMACE=growth rate of smoothed CE index, in which the weights are replaced by 3 year centered moving averages

Figure 2: Growth rates of theoretical monetary aggregate, Divisia index, simple-sum index, CE index, and smoothed CE index. Parameters of theoretical monetary aggregate estimated with risk aversion permitted.

While no econometric estimation is needed to compute the Divisia index, it is important on the supply side to incorporate the required reserves implicit tax into the user cost formula, when computing the Divisia output index. The user-cost formula is needed to compute the prices of monetary services, since the Divisia quantity index is a function of prices as well as quantities. On that subject, also see Barnett and Hahm (1994), Barnett, Hinich, and Weber (1986), Hancock (1985, 1987, 1991), and Barnett (1987), who derive and supply the user cost of supplied monetary services, when required reserves yield no interest. The resulting real user-cost price for account type i is

$$\phi_{ift} = \frac{(1 - k_{it})R_t - r_{it}}{1 + R_t} \tag{75}$$

$$= \phi_{ict} - \frac{k_{it}R_t}{1 + R_t}, \tag{76}$$

Empirical Results

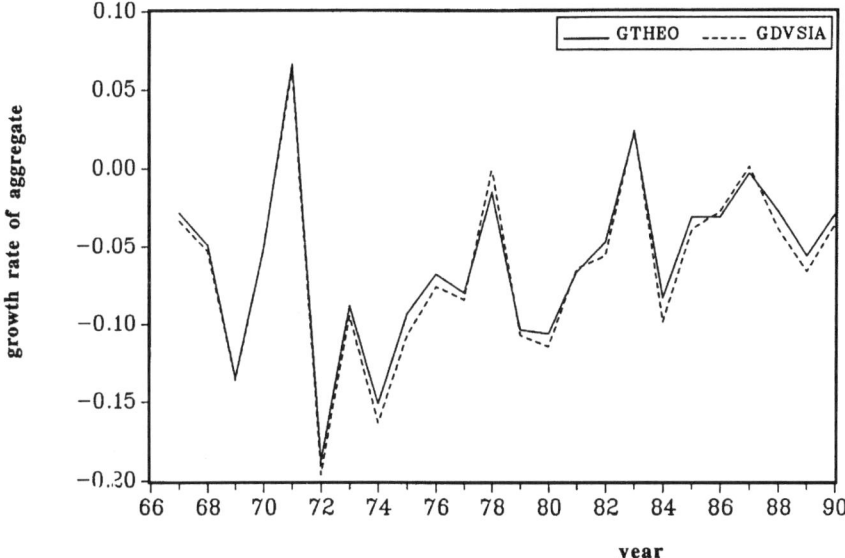

Note: GTHEO=growth rate of estimated theoretical aggregate, GDVSIA=growth rate of Divisia index

Figure 3: Growth rates of theoretical monetary aggregate and Divisia index. Parameters of theoretical monetary aggregate estimated with risk aversion permitted.

where r_{it} is the own rate of return defined in footnote 8, and where

$$\phi_{ict} = \frac{R_t - r_{it}}{1 + R_t}. \tag{77}$$

The nominal user cost is $P_t \phi_{ift}$. The second term on the right-hand side of equation (76) is the discounted implicit tax on banks resulting from the nonpayment of interest on required reserves. Equation (77) is the same form as the user-cost price paid on the demand side by depositors, where R_t is the benchmark yield on a pure investment asset producing no services other than its own yield, so that equation (77) is the discounted foregone interest given up by the depositor in return for the services provided by asset type i.

Clearly the Divisia index tracks the theoretical aggregate more accurately than any of the other two indexes. The smoothed and unsmoothed CE index's level paths are almost identical to each other, as shown in Figure 1, despite the improvement in the performance of the CE index's growth rate plot after smoothing. Before 1972, the Divisia and estimated theoretical index are almost identical. After 1972, a small gap opens between them.

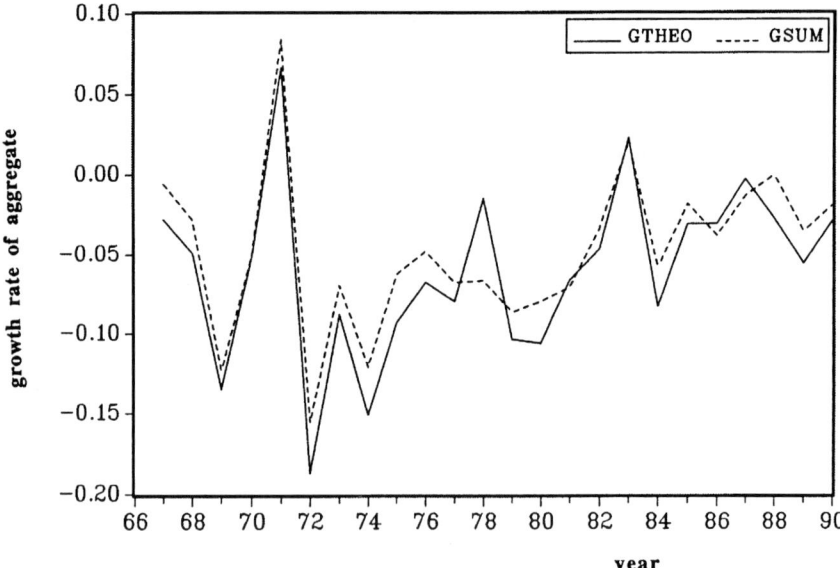

Note: GTHEO=growth rate of estimated theoretical aggregate, GSUM=growth rate of simple-sum index

Figure 4: Growth rates of theoretical monetary aggregate and simple-sum index. Parameters of theoretical monetary aggregate estimated with risk aversion permitted.

The CE index almost always underestimates the theoretical aggregate throughout the sample period, with the gap growing to be larger after 1980. The simple-sum index always overestimates the theoretical aggregate, with the gap growing to be large and remaining large after only a few years. In terms of levels, the tracking error of the CE index is smaller than that of the simple-sum index, especially early in the same period. However, the CE index is much more volatile than the theoretical aggregate, especially from 1979 to 1983. Comparing Figures 5 and 6, we see that the CE index with smoothed weights is less volatile than the unsmoothed index, but the volatility still remains larger than that of the estimated theoretical index. We could experiment with even more smoothing of the CE index than is advocated by Rotemberg, Driscoll, and Poterba, but we feel that further experimentation in that direction would produce an index having dynamics determined more by the ad hoc method of smoothing than by the theory that produces the index. Furthermore, we suspect that smoothing adequate to fix the index between 1979 and 1983 would oversmooth elsewhere. Hence,

Empirical Results

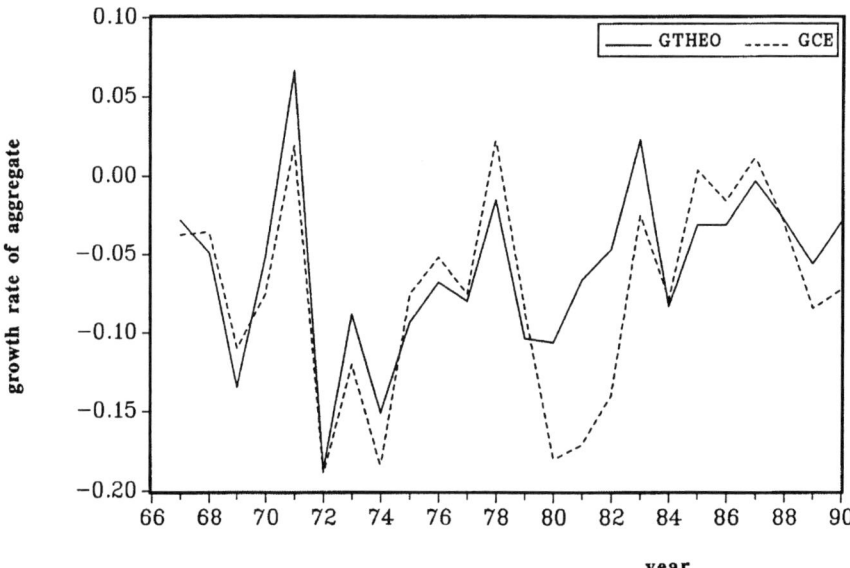

Note: GTHEO=growth rate of estimated theoretical aggregate, GCE=growth rate of CE index

Figure 5: Growth rates of theoretical monetary aggregate and CE index. Parameters of theoretical monetary aggregate estimated with risk aversion permitted.

it seems that there is no way that the CE index can track the growth rates adequately throughout the sample.

In short, as a measure of the level of the money stock, the simple-sum index performs most poorly, while in terms of growth rates, the CE index performs most poorly. In both cases, the Divisia index performs best. These results are in accordance with index number theory, although most of that theory is available in rigorous form only under the assumption of perfect certainty. Our weak separability test supports the existence of an inside-money output aggregate in banking, and our plots support the use of the Divisia index as the best currently available statistical index for tracking that output aggregate.

For comparison purposes, we repeat the above estimation and testing in the special case of risk neutrality. The Euler equations, (62)–(65), under risk

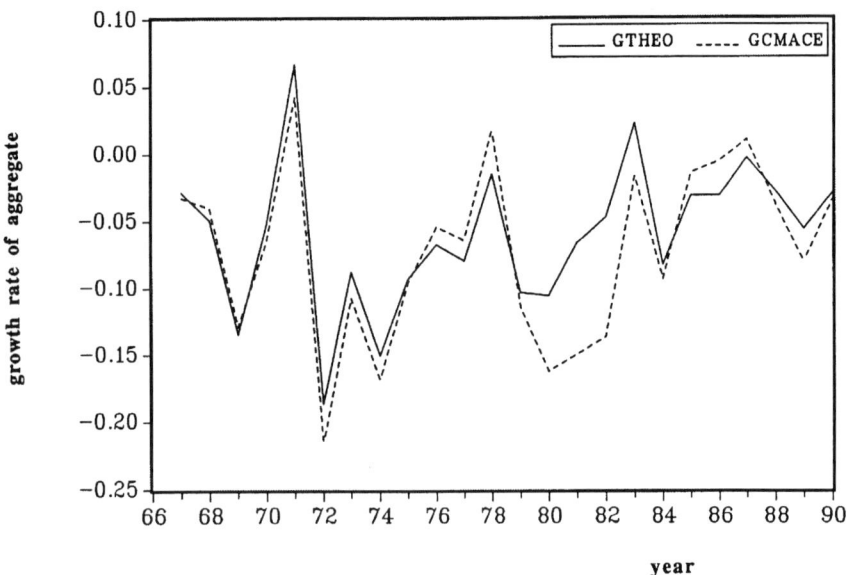

Note: GTHEO=growth rate of estimated theoretical aggregate, GCMACE=growth rate of smoothed CE index, in which the weights are replaced by 3 year centered moving averages

Figure 6: Growth rates of theoretical monetary aggregate and smoothed CE index. Parameters of theoretical monetary aggregate estimated with risk aversion permitted.

neutrality become[45]

$$E_t \left\{ P_t \frac{R_t(1-k_{1t}) - r_{1t}}{1+R_t} + P_t \frac{R_t}{1+R_t} \frac{\partial \Omega / \partial D_t}{\partial \Omega / \partial C_t} \right\} = 0, \qquad (78)$$

$$E_t \left\{ P_t \frac{R_t(1-k_{2t}) - r_{2t}}{1+R_t} + P_t \frac{R_t}{1+R_t} \frac{\partial \Omega / \partial T_t}{\partial \Omega / \partial C_t} \right\} = 0, \qquad (79)$$

$$E_t \left\{ P_t \frac{R_t}{1+R_t} \frac{\partial \Omega / \partial L_t}{\partial \Omega / \partial C_t} - w_{1t} \right\} = 0, \qquad (80)$$

and

$$E_t \left\{ P_t \frac{R_t}{1+R_t} \frac{\partial \Omega / \partial M_t}{\partial \Omega / \partial C_t} - w_{2t} \right\} = 0. \qquad (81)$$

---

[45] In producing equations (80) and (81) as special cases of the corresponding risk-averse Euler equations, recall footnote 14.

Empirical Results

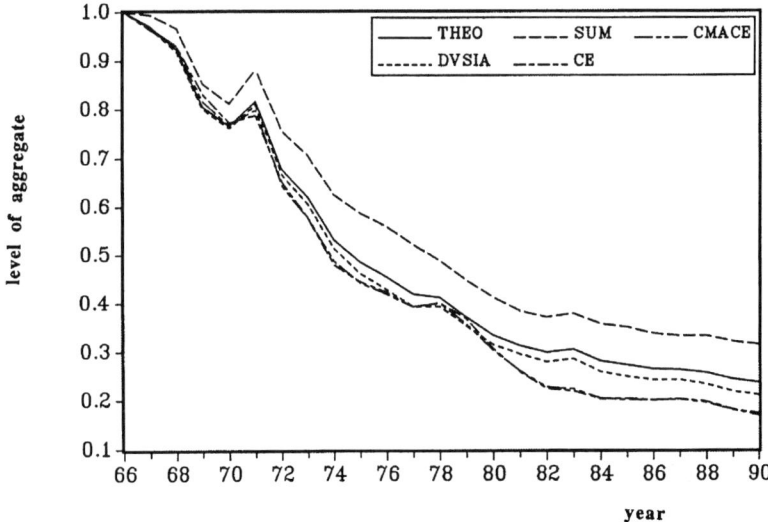

Note: THEO=level of estimated theoretical aggregate, DVSIA=level of Divisia index, SUM=level of simple-sum index, CE=level of CE index, CMACE=level of smoothed CE index, in which the weights are replaced by 3 year centered moving averages.

Figure 7: Levels of theoretical monetary aggregate, Divisia index, simple-sum index, CE index, and smoothed CE index. Parameters of theoretical monetary aggregate estimated subject to imposed risk neutrality.

TABLE 3
GMM Estimates with Weak Separability in Outputs and Risk Neutrality Imposed

Parameter	Estimate	Standard error	t-Statistic
ξ	61.82	0.005	11968.80
u_{11}	0.27	0.019	14.31
q_{11}	0.18	0.005	32.78
q_{21}	0.38	0.022	17.01
q_{31}	0.07	0.007	10.14
q_{22}	0.44	0.023	19.09
q_{32}	0.11	0.063	1.68
q_{33}	0.16	0.132	1.25
$\tilde{a}_1$	0.33	0.002	162.74
$\tilde{a}_2$	0.50	0.003	164.39
$\tilde{a}_3$	0.23	0.006	36.50

The parameter estimates acquired from GMM estimation under risk neu-

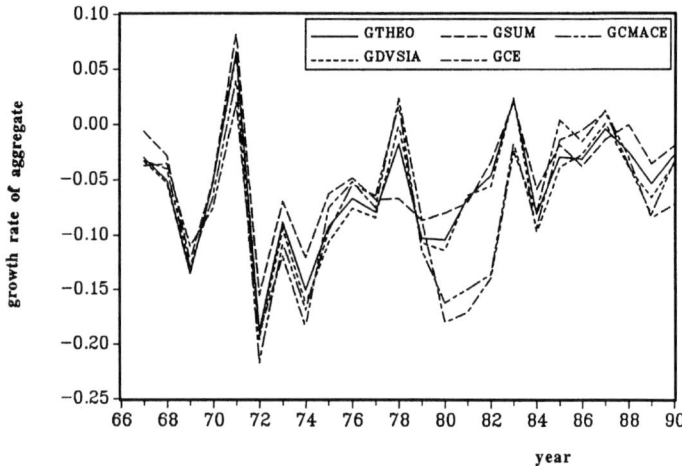

Note: GTHEO=growth rate of estimated theoretical aggregate, GDVSIA=growth rate of Divisia index, GSUM=growth rate of simple-sum index, GCE=growth rate of CE index, GCMACE=growth rate of smoothed CE index, in which the weights are replaced by 3 year centered moving averages

Figure 8: Growth rates of theoretical monetary aggregate, Divisia index, simple-sum index, CE index, and smoothed CE index. Parameters of theoretical monetary aggregate estimated subject to imposed risk neutrality.

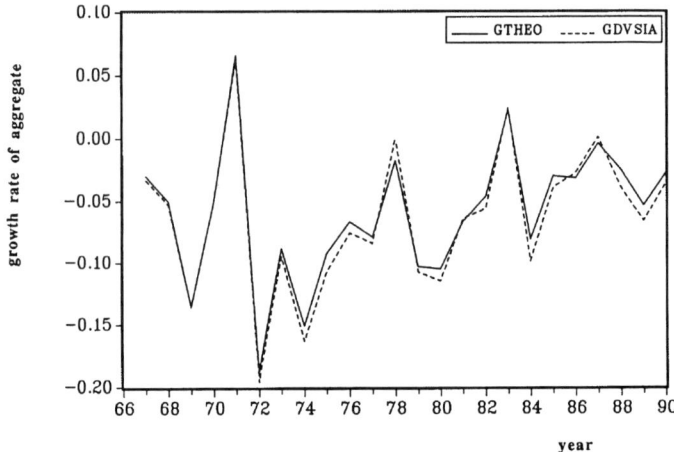

Note: GTHEO=growth rate of estimated theoretical aggregate, GDVSIA=growth rate of Divisia index

Figure 9: Growth rates of theoretical monetary aggregate and Divisia index. Parameters of theoretical monetary aggregate estimated subject to imposed risk neutrality.

Empirical Results

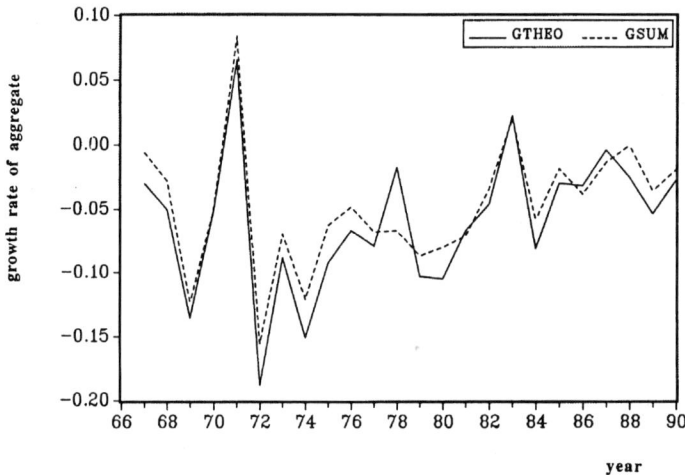

Note: GTHEO=growth rate of estimated theoretical aggregate, GSUM=growth rate of simple-sum index

Figure 10: Growth rates of theoretical monetary aggregate and simple-sum index. Parameters of theoretical monetary aggregate estimated subject to imposed risk neutrality.

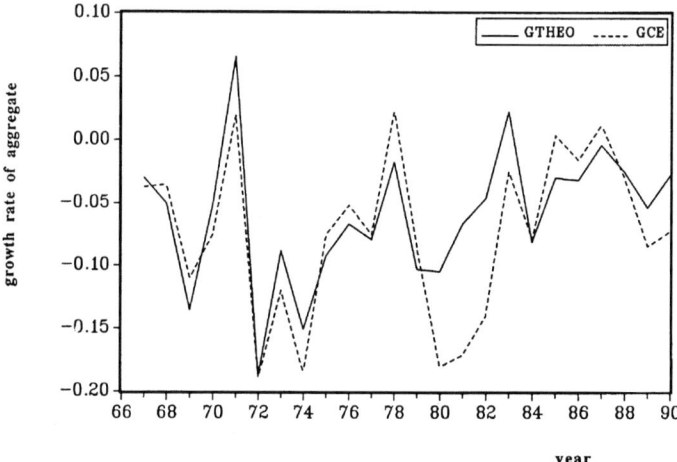

Note: GTHEO=growth rate of estimated theoretical aggregate, GCE=growth rate of CE index

Figure 11: Growth rates of theoretical monetary aggregate and CE index. Parameters of theoretical monetary aggregate estimated subject to imposed risk neutrality.

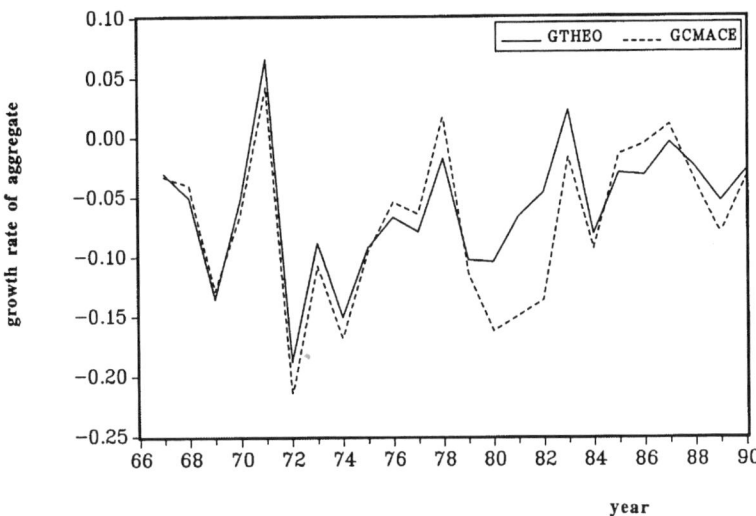

Note: GTHEO=growth rate of estimated theoretical aggregate, GCMACE=growth rate of smoothed CE index, in which the weights are replaced by 3 year centered moving averages

Figure 12: Growth rates of theoretical monetary aggregate and smoothed CE index. Parameters of theoretical monetary aggregate estimated subject to imposed risk neutrality.

trality, with weak separability in outputs imposed, are in Table 3.[46] Substituting the parameter estimate of ξ in the risk-neutrality case into equations (69), we obtain $b_1 = 0.777$ and $b_2 = 0.223$. The estimated theoretical aggregate then is acquired by substituting the estimated parameters and fixed constants into equation (29) to get

$$y_0(D_t, T_t) = 0.777 D_t + 0.223 T_t + \frac{1}{2}\left[\frac{.275^2(D_t - T_t)^2}{.58 D_t + 0.42 T_t}\right]. \tag{82}$$

The value of the weak separability test statistic, equation (73), is 9.25, while the critical value is 21.666 at the 1 percent significance level. We cannot reject the weak separability hypothesis and, hence, the existence of a theoretical monetary aggregate over the outputs produced by banks again is accepted. Furthermore, monotonicity and convexity again are accepted throughout the region on the data.

Figures 7–12 provide the risk-neutral plots analogous to those in Figures 1–6 under risk aversion. Imposing risk neutrality produced negligible gain in

---

[46]The instrumental variables are the constant, the discount rate, the lagged banks' portfolio rate of return, excess cash reserves, and capital.

tracking ability for any of the indexes. Hence, at least with this data, risk aversion does not seriously compromise index number theory.

5 The Regulatory Wedge

Although the imposition of risk neutrality did not improve the tracking ability of any of our indexes, the risk-neutral special case does permit especially simple graphical illustration of equilibrium phenomena through the use of separating hyperplanes. In particular, with risk neutrality and complete contingent claims markets, each consumer maximizes utility and each firm maximizes profits conditionally upon any fixed, realized contingency (i.e., state). Hence, perfect certainty methods of graphical illustration are available in the risk neutral case, with the understanding that the illustration is conditional upon the realization of all contingencies.

If no regulatory wedge exists between the demand and supply side, a hyperplane separates tastes from technology. But in the case of commercial banks, a regulatory wedge does indeed exist. This conclusion follows from the observation in footnote 8 that an implicit tax is imposed upon banks through the existence of noninterest bearing required reserves. Hence, the user cost price received by banks for the production of monetary services differs from the user cost price paid by depositors for the consumption of those services. The difference is the implicit tax.

The formulas for the user cost prices on each side of the market for produced monetary services was derived by Barnett (1978, 1980a, 1987) and computed by Barnett, Hinich, and Weber (1986). The result is most easily illustrated in the case of an economy with one consumer, who consumes all of the economy's monetary services, one financial intermediary, which produces all of the economy's monetary services, and two monetary assets. Equilibrium in the monetary sector of the economy at a fixed contingent state is illustrated in Figure 13, when no reserve requirements exist. Money market equilibrium at a fixed contingent state, when one or both of the monetary assets is subject to reserve requirements, is illustrated in Figure 14.

In Figure 13, equilibrium is produced by the familiar separating hyperplane. The separating hyperplane simultaneously supports an indifference curve from below and a production possibility curve from above. The axes represent quantities of each of the two monetary assets demanded and supplied. Equilibrium in the two markets exists at the mutual tangency of the separating hyperplane, the indifference curve, and the production possibility curve at a given optimal level of factor use. In equilibrium, the quantities demanded of each asset are equal to the quantities supplied at the equilibrium point $\mathbf{y}^e = (y_1^e, y_2^e)$. In addition, the gradient vector to the separating

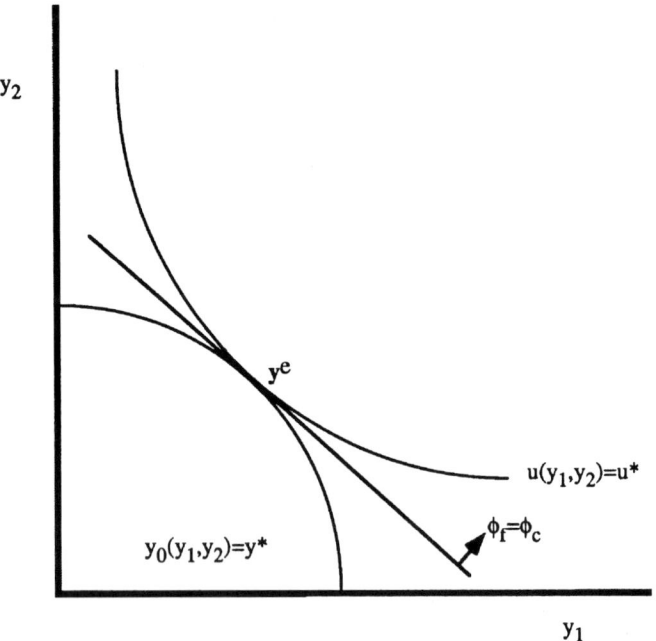

Figure 13: Equilibrium with no required reserves.

hyperplane produces the equilibrium user-cost prices. The vector of user-cost prices paid by the consumer, ϕ_c, are equal, in equilibrium, to the vector of user-cost prices received by the financial intermediary, ϕ_f. The user cost price of asset type i is defined by equation (77) above.

With factor employment assumed to be set in advance at its optimum, $\mathbf{x}^*$, the optimum level of aggregate monetary service production, y^*, is defined to be the solution for y^* to the equation $H(y^*, \mathbf{x}) = 0$, where $y^* = y_0(\mathbf{y})$ and where $\Omega(\mathbf{y}, \mathbf{x}) = H(y^*, \mathbf{x}) = H(y_0(\mathbf{y}), \mathbf{x})$, as explained in the subsection above. Hence, Figure 13 is drawn conditionally upon that fixed setting of y^*, so that the production possibility surface is the set $\{(y_1, y_2) : y_0(y_1, y_2) = y^*\}$.

However, the situation is very different, when required reserves exist. In that case, two different supporting hyperplanes exist in equilibrium. One supporting hyperplane exists for the financial intermediary, and another exists for the consumer. In Figure 14, the line with gradient prices, ϕ_c, is the consumer's supporting hyperplane, and it is his budget constraint in equilibrium. That line is tangent to the displayed indifference curve in equilibrium. The financial intermediary's supporting hyperplane has gradient equal to the

The Regulatory Wedge

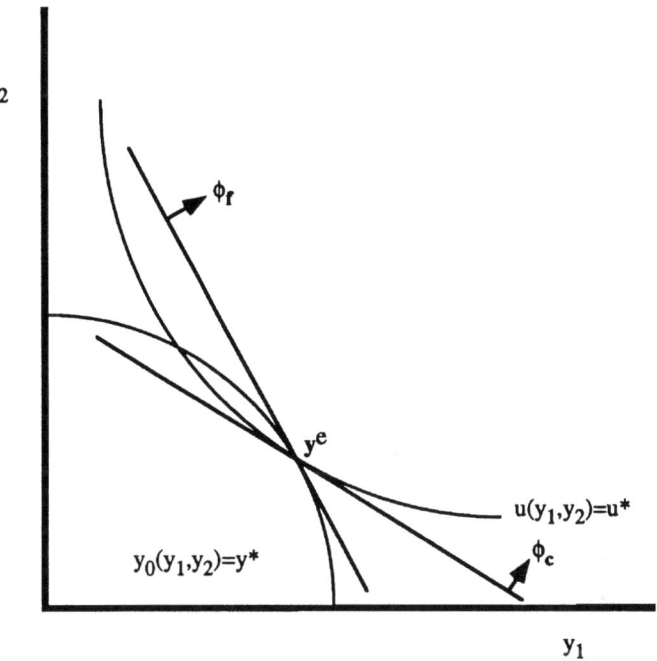

Figure 14: Equilibrium with required reserves.

financial intermediary's user-cost prices, ϕ_f. That hyperplane is the financial intermediary's iso-revenue line, which is tangent to the firm's production possibility curve at the equilibrium point. While the user-cost price paid by the consumer for the services of asset type i is still defined by equation (77), the user-cost price received by the bank for producing those services now is defined by equation (75), which does not equal equation (77) unless no required reserves exist.

The equilibrium point is the point $\mathbf{y}^e$ at which the two supporting hyperplanes intersect, and the angle between them is the regularity wedge produced by the implicit reserve requirement tax paid by the financial intermediary in the form of foregone interest on required reserves. At the equilibrium point both markets are cleared, and the consumer is maximizing utility subject to the displayed budget constraint, while the financial intermediary is maximizing revenue subject to the displayed production possibility curve.

6 The Errors-in-the-Variables Problem

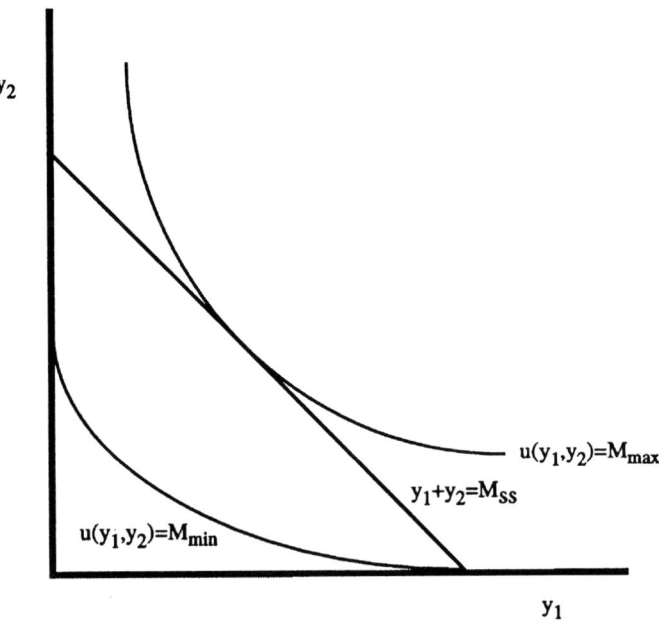

Figure 15: Demand side errors-in-variables.

This same figure also can be used to illustrate the magnitude of the errors-in-the-variables problem produced by the use of the simple-sum index as a measure of the flow of monetary services. Figure 15 illustrates the range of the error on the demand side, while Figure 16 does the same on the supply side. The same illustration could be produced on the supply side by replacing the two indifference curves that are convex to the origin with two production possibility curves, that are concave to the origin. The conclusion would be the same.

In both figures, the hyperplane represents the set

$$A = \{(y_1, y_2): y_1 + y_2 = M_{ss}\},$$

where M_{ss} is the measured level of the simple-sum index, while A is the set of possible values of the monetary asset component quantities (y_1, y_2) that are consistent with the measured level of the simple-sum index.

For any such measurement on the simple-sum index, the value of the demand-side monetary service flow received by asset holders could be any-

The Errors-in-the-Variables Problem

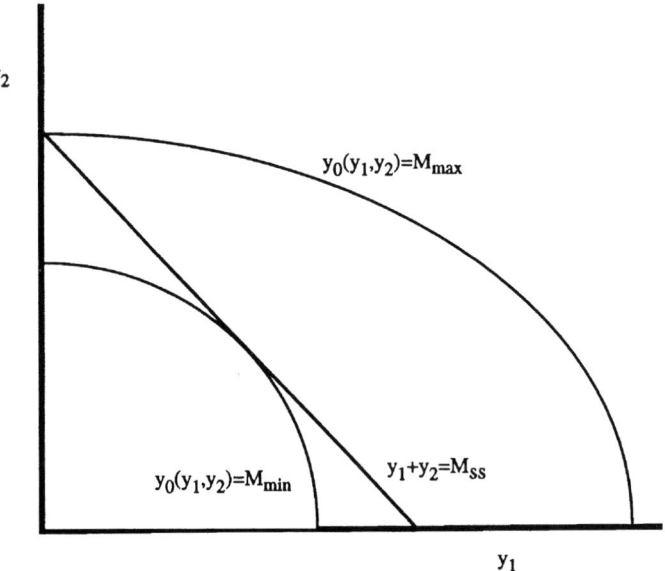

Figure 16: Supply side errors-in-variables.

where within the set

$$\{u(y_1, y_2) : (y_1, y_2) \in A\}. \tag{83}$$

The range of that set is the gap between the utility levels at which the two indifference curves are drawn in Figure 15. Clearly, the upper indifference curve is the one which intersects the hyperplane A at the highest possible utility level, while the lower indifference curve is the one which intersects the hyperplane A at the lowest possible utility level. We see that magnitude of the errors-in-the-variables problem in that illustration, when measured by the range of the set (83), is $M_{\max} - M_{\min}$. The same conclusion is produced on the supply side from Figure 16, but with set (83) replaced by[47]

$$\{y_0(y_1, y_2) : (y_1, y_2) \in A\}.$$

The simple-sum monetary aggregates produce a disturbingly large and entirely unnecessary errors-in-the-variables problem. Figures 15 and 16 illustrate the reason. Figures 1–12 illustrate the effect, under circumstances

---

[47] The magnitude of the gap, $M_{\max} - M_{\min}$, may differ, when a regulatory wedge is produced by required reserves, but the difference between the conclusions on the demand and supply side is not likely to be large. If the errors-in-the-variables problem is large on one side of the market, it is likely to be approximately as large on the other side of the market. See Barnett, Hinich, and Weber (1986) for relevant empirical evidence.

that are most favorable to the simple-sum aggregates: a low level of aggregation over assets having similar yields. With broader aggregation over assets having very different own rates of return, including currency with a zero rate of return, the continued use of simple-sum monetary aggregates by central banks becomes even more difficult to comprehend. The days when all monetary components had zero-own rates of return are long gone.

7 Conclusions

In this paper, we develop a theoretical model of monetary service production by financial firms. Earlier models either have permitted risk, but with minimal connection with neoclassical economic theory, or have made full use of neoclassical production theory, but under the assumption of perfect certainty. The latter case has been developed extensively by Barnett (1987), Barnett and Hahm (1994), and Hancock (1985, 1987, 1991). We extend that latter fully neoclassical production approach to the case of risk aversion, subject to Diewert and Wales's symmetric generalized McFadden technology. Our approach permits risk aversion without compromising second-order flexibility or neoclassical regularity of the specification. This is true with or without the imposition of global blockwise weak separability, which we therefore are able to test and to impose, when accepted. Using the resulting Euler equations, we explore exact output aggregation in this paper.

Although applicable to all financial intermediaries, we apply our approach only to the banking industry. While it is possible to impose regularity in curvature conditions upon the generalized McFadden specification, monotonicity can be imposed only locally without damaging the model's flexibility. Diewert and Wales' alternative specification, called the generalized Barnett model, is globally regular both in terms of curvature and monotonicity, and hence, that model was used by Barnett and Hahm (1994) in the perfect certainty case. However, in the current paper, using the generalized McFadden model, the estimated parameters satisfy the neoclassical monotonicity and convexity conditions for all observations, even though only convexity was imposed globally. Hence, we doubt that our conclusions would have been much different if we had used the generalized Barnett model in producing our estimated Euler equations. The hypothesis that banks' outputs are weakly separable from inputs is accepted. Hence, the existence of an exact supply-side theoretical monetary aggregate is accepted for banks. The resulting output aggregate is the banking industry's contribution to the economy's inside money services.

While our theory provides a means of econometrically estimating the exact supply-side monetary aggregate, no theory currently is available to support the use of a nonparametric statistical index number as an approximation to the parametrically estimated exact aggregate.[48] Considering the complexities of the GMM estimation involved in producing the estimated exact aggregate, a nonparametric statistical index would, in practice, be much easier to compute and use. We compute the currently most popular of those indexes and find that at least for our sample, the Divisia index tracks the estimated theoretical index more accurately than the others. This conclusion holds regardless of whether or not we impose risk neutrality during estimation of the exact theoretical aggregate. Risk aversion does not appear to produce appreciable degradation of the tracking ability of the Divisia index with our data.

We believe that the approach developed in this paper could be used to investigate technological change in banking, economies of scale and scope in banking, value added in banking and its connection with inside money creation, and the transmission mechanism of monetary policy. We have in fact taken a first step in the direction of producing one of those extensions: We have derived and supplied the Euler equations with learning by doing technological change included in technology. A longer-run framework for the theory also could be productive. In particular, some of the factors excluded from the variable cost function as fixed factors could be incorporated among the variable factors. Bank capital is one such example. Incorporating capital among the variable factors could permit integration of the model with economic growth theory, in which capital evolves endogenously in accordance with a law of motion. In short, this is just a start in a direction that we expect will be very productive for researchers interested in the role of financial institutions in the economy.

---

[48] While this was true at the time that this paper was originally published, the extension of index number theory to the case of risk aversion was subsequently accomplished by Barnett, Liu, and Jensen (1997) and further extended by Barnett and Xu (1998), which are reprinted in this book as chapters 12 and 13 respectively.

Chapter 22

Estimating Policy-Invariant Deep Parameters in the Financial Sector When Risk and Growth Matter

William A. Barnett, Milka Kirova, and Meenakshi Pasupathy*

1 Introduction

This paper provides and illustrates an approach to the estimation of technology parameters in the financial sector. The relevant technologies are those of the financial intermediaries that produce inside money as output services and the nonfinancial firms that demand financial services as inputs to production technology. We also display analogous results for consumer demand, but without the modeling and econometric details, which are available elsewhere. The problems that we seek to solve through our approach to modeling and Euler equation estimation are the 'Lucas Critique' and what Chrystal and MacDonald (1994, p. 76) recently have called the 'Barnett Critique.' We also explore the tracking ability of the Divisia monetary aggregate and simple sum monetary aggregate relative to the GMM estimated exact rational expectations monetary aggregate for each type of economic agent.

In this paper, we produce and estimate Euler equations for firms that demand or supply financial services as an illustration of the available approach, first advocated forcefully and convincingly for the financial sector by Poterba and Rotemberg (1987) with respect to consumer demand for financial services. We do not seek to integrate the three sectors into a complete economy, in which aggregation blockings would have to conform across sectors. In addition, we do not explore in detail the implications of our parameter estimates for the elasticities and other properties of technology, although the approach clearly is relevant to the creation of a small-scale macroeconomic model based upon the estimation of deep parameters, and is relevant to the investigation of demand and supply elasticities, economies of scale, and technological change. However, those objectives are beyond the scope of the current paper, which

---

*Reprinted by permission from the *Journal of Money, Credit, and Banking*, Vol. 27, No. 4 (November 1995). Copyright 1982 by Ohio State University Press. All rights reserved. This research was partially supported by NSF grant SES 9223557.

is an illustration of the available methodology, rather than a final modeling result.[1]

1.1 The Lucas Critique

According to the Lucas critique, private sector parameters and the parameters of central bank policy rules are confounded together within the demand and supply solution functions that typically are estimated in macroeconometric models. When modeled dynamically, those demand and supply functions are the feedback rules or contingency plans that comprise the solution functions to dynamic programming or optimal control decisions of consumers and firms. However, the central bank's policy process is among the laws of motion serving as constraints in the private sector's dynamic decision. Hence the feedback rules that solve the private sector's decision depend upon the parameters of those processes as well as of the private sector's own taste and technology parameters. Shifts in the parameters of the central bank's policy process will shift the private sector's solution feedback rules.

The source of this confounding is the solution to the first-order conditions (Euler equations) of the private sector's decision, since that solution cannot be acquired without augmenting the private sector's Euler equations with the government's policy rules. In particular, the central bank's policy rule, interest rate processes, and other governmentally influenced stochastic processes for variables that are in the private agent's decision, but are not under the control of that private decision maker, must be adjoined to private decision maker's Euler equations, before the solution for the feedback rules (demand and supply functions) can be found. But if the Euler equations of the private sector are estimated directly, the confounding problem is avoided. Hence in macroeconomics, there is wide acceptance of the idea that Euler equations should be estimated, rather than the demand and supply functions that are the solution to the augmented system. See, for example, Sims and Leeper (1994).

Despite the influence of Euler equation estimation and the Lucas critique in macroeconomics, a substantial portion of the literature on monetary economics has continued to use estimated money demand and money supply functions, which are vulnerable to the Lucas critique. In this paper, we estimate Euler equations in the financial sector for firms demanding monetary services and banks supplying monetary services.

---

[1]In addition, we do not seek to produce a closed-form algebraic solution for the gap between the Divisia monetary aggregate and the exact GMM estimated rational expectations monetary aggregator function, although a consumption CAPM beta solution for that gap recently has been derived by Barnett, Liu, and Jensen (1997), which is reprinted in this book as chapter 12.

1.2 The Barnett Critique

According to the Barnett critique, as defined by Chrystal and MacDonald (1994, p. 76), an internal inconsistency exists between the microeconomics used to model private-sector structure and the aggregator functions used to produce the monetary aggregate data supplied by central banks. The result can do considerable damage to inferences about private-sector behavior, when central bank monetary aggregate data are used. Chrystal and MacDonald (1994, p. 76) have observed the following regarding "the problems with tests of money in the economy in recent years .... Rather than a problem associated with the Lucas critique, it could instead be a problem stemming from the 'Barnett Critique.'" In fact, Barnett critique issues have been used to cast doubt upon many widely held views in monetary economics, as recently emphasized by Barnett, Fisher, and Serletis (1992), Belongia (1996), and Chrystal and MacDonald (1994). Based upon this rapidly growing line of research, Chrystal and MacDonald (1994, p. 108) conclude — in our opinion correctly — that: "Rejections of the role of money based upon flawed money measures are themselves easy to reject."

The Poterba and Rotemberg approach to inference about consumer behavior in the monetary sector circumvents the Barnett critique by nesting the monetary aggregator function within the consumer's utility function and estimating the aggregator function jointly with the other parameters of the consumer's decision. Hence Poterba and Rotemberg have extended Barnett's (1980a, 1987) perfect certainty theory to the case of risk.[2] An initial step in the direction of Euler equation estimation of technology in the financial sector with internally consistent nested monetary aggregation was taken by Barnett and Zhou (1994b), who produced a model for banking supply of monetary services with nested monetary output aggregation.[3] In this paper we extend the Barnett and Zhou model by weakening some of their assumptions, and we produce a similar model for manufacturing firms that demand monetary services as inputs.

It is important to recognize that the Lucas critique is neither necessary nor sufficient for the Barnett critique. The Barnett critique applies independently of whether or not Euler equation parameters or feedback rule parameters are

---

[2] Recently Feldstein and Stock (1996) have drawn further attention to the importance of risk by finding possible empirical gains from incorporating risky stock and bond mutual funds within weighted monetary aggregates, although Feldstein and Stock, unlike Poterba and Rotemberg, do not base their analysis upon formal aggregation theory.

[3] However, their paper introduced little dynamics into the decision of the commercial banks that they modeled. In the current paper, we introduce capital dynamics. The importance of investigating money demand function properties separately across sectors, including the manufacturing firm sector, has been emphasized in Drake and Chrystal (1994).

Introduction

estimated and is unrelated to the confounding produced by the use of feedback rule parameters. Similarly the Lucas critique applies independently of whether or not monetary aggregate index numbers are used that can track structurally separable monetary aggregator functions and is unrelated to the appearance of structural shift produced by estimating model parameters from models that are internally inconsistent with the theory implied by the monetary aggregate data used in the estimation. In short, the appearance of structural shift can be produced by either the Lucas critique or the Barnett critique or by both. We advocate an approach that simultaneously resolves both potential sources of faulty inference about structural shift.

1.3 The Two Critiques Combined

In our paper, we seek to respond to the Lucas critique and the Barnett critique jointly. Both relate to the connection between empirical research and economic theory and the misleading appearance of parameter shifts, when in fact the economy's structure has not changed. To the degree that index number theory is relevant to our paper, the index number needs to have known tracking ability relative to the economic aggregator function. That is the objective of economic index number theory. We estimate Euler equations to respond to the Lucas critique. We test for blockwise weak separability of component monetary assets, since weak separability is the existence condition for an aggregator function. Having found an admissible component group relative to that existence condition, we have existence of an aggregator function.

With the existence of an aggregator function, the resulting aggregate can be produced in one of two ways. One way is to estimate the parameters of the aggregator function jointly with the other parameters in the Euler equations. The other way is to use a nonparametric statistical index number to track the aggregator function approximately. We do both. The investigation of that nonparametric tracking ability under risk is the purpose of our use of statistical index numbers.

In economic aggregation theory, the aggregator function is a nonlinear function of component quantities and of parameters, and usually has the form of a production or utility function. Such aggregator functions have no easily identified 'weights.' We estimate the aggregator function nested in our model. Statistical index numbers designed to track aggregator functions sometimes can be manipulated into a form that permits some factors to be interpreted as weights. There are exceptions, such as the Fisher ideal index, which is rarely written in a form that lends itself to such an interpretation. But with all such conventional index numbers produced from index number theory, the index is nonparametric. In fact, that's the point of them — to track the aggregator functions of economic theory nonparametrically. The usual definition of a statistical index number is a nonparametric function of current and one-period-lagged prices and quantities, such that the resulting index has hopefully good tracking ability relative to the economic aggregator function being tracked. On this subject, see Diewert (1976), who defines a class of index numbers having the ability to track arbitrary aggregator functions up to a third-order remainder term.

The purpose of all scientific research is to reveal the truth, not to alter the data in a manner that may tend to justify some preconceived policy view. The purpose of data is to measure something that exists, that is, an aggregator function that is separable within the structure of the economy. The Barnett critique deals with the errors in inference produced by the use of aggregates that do not track an aggregator function implied by the model within which the aggregate is used. Those inference errors result from the fact that such aggregates internally contradict the structural theory on which the inferences are based.

2 Financial Intermediaries

One of the recent approaches to modeling financial intermediaries is to model them as profit-maximizing neoclassical multiproduct firms, which produce financial services such as demand deposits and time deposits as outputs. Early work that used this approach was based on the assumption of perfect certainty.[4] Barnett and Zhou (1994b) extended this approach to the case of uncertainty. In this paper we extend Barnett and Zhou's model by introducing capital accumulation and by relaxing the assumption of 'no retained earnings.' We also rigorously nest exact supply-side monetary output aggregates within the transformation function of the financial intermediary, so that supply-side monetary aggregation can be accomplished in a manner that circumvents the Barnett critique. We derive and estimate the Euler equations in a manner that circumvents the Lucas critique.

We view the resulting model as a step in the direction of exploring technological change and economies of scale and scope in financial intermediation in a manner that is invariant to central bank policy intervention, and in a manner that can produce inside money aggregates that are consistent with the theory that produced the policy invariant Euler equations.

---

[4]See Barnett (1987), Barnett and Hahm (1994), and the path-breaking work by Hancock (1985, 1987, 1991).

2.1 Financial Firm's Production

The financial firm uses real resources such as labor, capital, and other material inputs, plus monetary input in the form of cash in the production of the services of the produced liabilities. The output of the firm in our application consists of demand deposits and time deposits, which are liabilities to the firm.

Let Y_t be the real balances of the asset (loan) portfolio, $y_{i,t}$ the real balances of the ith produced account (liability) type, C_t the real balances of cash holdings, $z_{j,t}$ the quantity of jth real input (including labor), and K_t the quantity of capital stock of the financial firm at time t. In the model, $y_{i,t}$ constitute the outputs of the financial firm, while C_t, $z_{j,t}$ and K_t are the inputs. Let R_t be the portfolio rate of return, which is unknown at the beginning of period t, and let $h_{i,t}$ be the holding cost per dollar of the ith liability. All financial transactions are contracted at the beginning of the period. Interests on the deposits are paid at the end of the period. The cost per unit of the jth real input, $w_{j,t}$, is incurred at the beginning of the period. Let $P_{K,t}$ be the cost of capital and P_t be the general price index, which is used to deflate nominal to real terms.

We use Barnett's (1987) method of defining inputs and outputs, so that demand deposits and time deposits are categorized as outputs of the firm, while cash, labor, materials, and capital constitute the firm's inputs in the production process.[5] We extend Hancock's (1991) and Barnett and Zhou's (1994b) variable profit function as follows.[6] Variable profits (net of investment expenditure), π_t, at the beginning of period t, can be represented by

$$\pi_t = (1 + R_{t-1})Y_{t-1}P_{t-1} - Y_t P_t + C_{t-1}P_{t-1} - C_t P_t$$
$$+ \sum_{i=1}^{I}[y_{i,t}P_t - (1 + h_{i,t-1})y_{i,t-1}P_{t-1}] - \sum_{j=1}^{J} w_{j,t} z_{j,t} - P_{K,t} I_t. \quad (1)$$

---

[5]Barnett classifies demand and time deposits as outputs, while loans are not classified either as inputs or outputs, but rather as dependent functions of other variables. Hancock lets the estimated user costs determine whether a particular monetary good is an input or output.

[6]Hancock and Barnett differ in their specifications of the variable profit function. Barnett's (1987) formulation of the variable profit function is based upon the application of contemporaneous user cost functions. The resulting difference in the specification of the variable profit function causes the discounted value of the profit streams in the two models to differ, but only by a function of initial conditions that is invariant to the firm's decisions. Regarding that invariance result, see Barnett and Zhou (1994c). In Barnett and Zhou's (1994b) model under risk, the financial firm does not have any undistributed retained earnings. In the Barnett and Zhou model, dynamics are further constrained by the assumption that capital is a fixed factor. We eliminate Barnett and Zhou's assumptions of 100 percent dividend payout ratio and their assumption that no variable capital factors exist. Barnett and Zhou (1994b) is reprinted in this book as chapter 21.

The first two terms in the above equation represent the change in variable profits from rolling over the loan portfolio during period t. The third and fourth terms represent the change in the nominal value of excess reserves. The fifth term represents the change in the firm's variable profits from the change in the issuance of produced financial liabilities. The sixth term constitutes payments for real inputs, and the last term is the expenditure on investments.

Portfolio investment, Y_t, is constrained by total available funds. The constraint is given by

$$Y_t P_t = \sum_{i=1}^{I}[(1-k_{i,t})y_{i,t}P_t] - C_t P_t - \sum_{j=1}^{J} w_{j,t}z_{j,t} - P_{K,t}I_t, \qquad (2)$$

where $k_{i,t}$ is the required reserves ratio on the ith produced liability. Equation (2) implies that the total deposits $\sum_{i=1}^{I} y_{i,t}P_t$ are allocated to required reserves, excess reserves, payment for all real inputs used in production, investment in capital, and investment in loans.

The time-to-build approach is adopted to model capital dynamics. Capital accumulation based on this approach is given by

$$K_t = I_{t-1} + (1-\delta)K_{t-1}, \qquad (3)$$

where the depreciation rate δ is a constant and is assumed to be given. Gross investment at time $t-1$, I_{t-1}, becomes productive only in period t. Substituting equations (2) and (3) into equation (1) to eliminate investment in loans and investment in capital goods, we get the variable profits at time t to be

$$\pi_t = \sum_{i=1}^{I}[(1+R_{t-1})(1-k_{i,t-1}) - (1+h_{i,t-1})]y_{i,t-1}P_{t-1} + k_{i,t}y_{i,t}P_t$$

$$-R_{t-1}C_{t-1}P_{t-1} - (1+R_{t-1})\sum_{j=1}^{J} w_{j,t-1}z_{j,t-1}$$

$$+(1-\delta)(1+R_{t-1})K_{t-1}P_{K,t-1} - (1+R_{t-1})K_t P_{K,t-1}. \qquad (4)$$

The financial firm maximizes the expected value of the discounted intertemporal utility of its variable profits stream, subject to the firm's technological constraint. The firm's optimization problem is then given by

$$\max \quad E_t \left[\sum_{s=t}^{\infty} \left(\frac{1}{1+\mu}\right)^{s-t} U(\pi_s) \right] \qquad (5)$$

$$\text{s.t.} \quad \Omega(y_{1,s}, \ldots, y_{I,s}, C_s, z_{1,s}, \ldots, z_{J,s}, K_s) = 0 \qquad \forall s \geq t,$$

where E_t is the expectation at time t, μ is the subjective rate of time preference, U is the utility function, π_s is the variable profit at time s, and Ω is the transformation function.

The transformation function, Ω, is convex in its arguments. The derivatives of Ω with respect to the inputs and outputs are respectively given by

$$\frac{\partial \Omega}{\partial C_s} \leq 0, \quad \frac{\partial \Omega}{\partial K_s} \leq 0, \quad \frac{\partial \Omega}{\partial z_{j,s}} \leq 0 \quad \forall j = 1, \ldots, J \quad (6)$$

and

$$\frac{\partial \Omega}{\partial y_{i,s}} \geq 0 \quad \forall i = 1, \ldots, I. \quad (7)$$

We now specify the utility function, U, to be in the class of functions exhibiting hyperbolic absolute risk aversion (HARA). The HARA class functions can be represented by

$$U(\pi_t) = \frac{1-\rho}{\rho}\left(\frac{h}{1-\rho}\pi_t + d\right)^{\rho}, \quad (8)$$

where ρ, h and d are parameters to be estimated.

Using Bellman's method and the Benveniste and Scheinkman equation, we obtain the following set of Euler equations:

$$E_t\left\{\frac{\partial U}{\partial \pi_t}(\pi_t)k_{i,t}P_t + \frac{1}{1+\mu}\frac{\partial U}{\partial \pi_t}(\pi_{t+1})P_t\left[R_t\frac{\partial \Omega/\partial y_{i,t}}{\partial \Omega/\partial C_t}\right.\right.$$
$$\left.\left. + [(1+R_t)(1-k_{i,t}) - (1+h_{i,t})]\right]\right\} = 0 \quad \forall y_{i,t}, i = 1, \ldots, I. \quad (9)$$

$$E_t\left\{\frac{\partial U}{\partial \pi_t}(\pi_{t+1})\left[R_t P_t \frac{\partial \Omega/\partial z_{j,t}}{\partial \Omega/\partial C_t} - (1+R_t)w_{j,t}\right]\right\} = 0 \quad \forall z_{j,t}, j = 1, \ldots, J. \quad (10)$$

$$E_t\left\{\frac{\partial U}{\partial \pi_t}(\pi_t)[(1+R_{t-1})P_{K,t-1}]\right.$$
$$\left. -\frac{1}{1+\mu}\frac{\partial U}{\partial \pi_t}(\pi_{t+1})\left[R_t P_t \frac{\partial \Omega/\partial K_t}{\partial \Omega/\partial C_t} + (1-\delta)(1+R_t)P_{K,t}\right]\right\} = 0 \quad (11)$$

where

$$\frac{\partial U}{\partial \pi_t} = h\left(\frac{h}{1-\rho}\pi_t + d\right)^{\rho-1}. \quad (12)$$

2.2 Output Aggregation

In this section, we find the aggregation-theoretic exact quantity output aggregate that measures the firm's produced monetary service flow. Relative to the money markets, our aggregation in this case is on the supply side.

Generating the exact quantity aggregate consists of first identifying the components over which aggregation is admissible and then determining the aggregator function defined over the identified components. The condition for the existence of an admissible component group is *blockwise weak separability*. In accordance with the definition of weak separability, a component grouping is admissible if and only if the group can be factored out of the rest of the economy's structure through a subfunction. Then the economic structure can be represented in the form of a composite function, with the goods in the separable block being the only goods in the inner function of the structure. If this condition is satisfied, an exact quantity aggregate exists over the goods in the block, and the aggregator function that produces the exact quantity aggregate over those goods is the inner ('category') function itself. Without weak separability, no such inner function exists and hence no aggregate exists.

Let $\mathbf{y} = (y_{1,t}, \ldots, y_{I,t})'$ be the firm's output vector, and let $\mathbf{x} = (z_{1,t}, \ldots, z_{J,t})'$ be the input vector, changing the notation for inputs from $\mathbf{z}$ to $\mathbf{x}$. Then the transformation function can be written as $\Omega(\mathbf{y}, \mathbf{x}) = 0$. An exact supply-side aggregate exists over all of the firm's outputs if and only if $\mathbf{y}$ is weakly separable from $\mathbf{x}$ within the function Ω. There then exist two functions H and y_0 such that

$$\Omega(\mathbf{y}, \mathbf{x}) = H(y_0(\mathbf{y}), \mathbf{x}),$$

where the output aggregator function, $y_0(\mathbf{y})$, is a convex function of $\mathbf{y}$. Although weak separability alone is sufficient for the existence of an aggregate, a considerable (although unnecessary) simplification is available if we also assume that $y_0(\mathbf{y})$ is linearly homogeneous in $\mathbf{y}$.[7] If we can test for weak separability of the transformation function and then estimate the resulting aggregator function $y_0(\mathbf{y})$, we obtain the econometrically estimated exact output aggregate. The related literature on statistical index numbers, such as Divisia and Laspeyres, seeks to produce nonparametric approximations that can track the level of $y_0(\mathbf{y})$ over time without the need to estimate the parameters of the aggregator function y_0 itself.

---

[7] If the function y_0 is not assumed to be linearly homogeneous, then the aggregator function is no longer y_0 but rather becomes the distance function. The growth rate of the distance function is equal to that of y_0 only under the assumption of linear homogeneity, so that our use of y_0 as the aggregator function under the assumption of linear homogeneity is a strictly nested special case of the more general result, which is straightforward and will not be considered further in this paper. See Barnett (1980a) for details.

2.3 Testing for Weak Separability

We use a flexible functional form for technology.[8] Unfortunately flexible functional forms need not satisfy the regularity conditions imposed by economic theory, including the monotonicity and curvature conditions. Hence we must consider methods for testing and imposing those conditions, at least locally, as well as methods for testing and imposing global blockwise weak separability of the technology in its outputs. For existence of aggregator functions, the weak separability must be global. Hence we must test and impose weak separability globally. We use the generalized McFadden functional form to specify the technology of the firm.[9]

We assume that the transformation function, Ω, is linearly homogeneous. Instead of specifying the form of the full transformation function Ω, and then imposing weak separability in $\mathbf{y}$, we directly impose weak separability by specifying $H(y_0, \mathbf{x})$ and $y_0(\mathbf{y})$ separately. The specification for Ω is then obtained by substituting $y_0(\mathbf{y})$ into $H(y_0, \mathbf{x})$. Since $y_0(\mathbf{y})$ and $H(y_0, \mathbf{x})$ are both specified to be flexible, the full technology Ω is flexible, subject to the separability restriction.

The function H is specified to be the symmetric generalized McFadden functional form

$$H(y_0, \mathbf{x}) = a_0 y_0 + \mathbf{a}'\mathbf{x} + \frac{1}{2}[y_0, \mathbf{x}']\bar{\mathbf{A}} \begin{bmatrix} y_0 \\ \mathbf{x} \end{bmatrix} / \boldsymbol{\alpha}'\mathbf{x}, \qquad (13)$$

where $\boldsymbol{\alpha}'\mathbf{x} \neq 0$, and a_0, $\mathbf{a}' = (a_1, \ldots, a_n)$, and $\bar{\mathbf{A}}$ are parameters to be estimated. The matrix $\bar{\mathbf{A}}$ is $(n+1) \times (n+1)$ and symmetric. The vector $\boldsymbol{\alpha}' = (\alpha_1, \ldots, \alpha_n)$ contains all fixed nonnegative constants, which are chosen by the researcher. The matrix $\bar{\mathbf{A}}$ is partitioned as follows:

$$\bar{\mathbf{A}} = \begin{bmatrix} A_{11} & \mathbf{A}_{12} \\ \mathbf{A}_{21} & \mathbf{A} \end{bmatrix},$$

where A_{11} is a scalar, $\mathbf{A}_{12}$ is a $1 \times n$ row vector, $\mathbf{A}_{21}$ is an $n \times 1$ column vector, and $\mathbf{A}$ is an $n \times n$ symmetric matrix.

Let $(y_0^*, \mathbf{x}^*) \neq 0$ be the chosen point about which the functional form is locally flexible. Within the class of linearly homogeneous transformation

---
[8] The form of flexibility that we use is called Diewert-flexibility or second-order flexibility. See Barnett (1983c) for the definition and its connection with other definitions of parametric flexibility. The newer concept of global or Sobolev flexibility (see Barnett, Geweke, and Wolfe (1991a, b)) is beyond the scope of this paper.

[9] That specification, which also was used in the case of stochastic choice by Barnett and Zhou (1994b), was originated by Diewert and Wales (1987, 1995), who also originated the generalized Barnett functional form. That latter model was applied by Barnett and Hahm (1994) in the perfect certainty case, but has not yet been adapted to the case of stochastic choice.

functions, the specification given above is not parsimonious, and hence we can impose further restrictions on the model without losing local flexibility.[10] We impose the following restrictions, which reduces the number of free parameters in our specification to the minimum required number to maintain local flexibility.

$$\alpha' \mathbf{x}^* = 1,$$
$$A_{11} y_0^* + \mathbf{A}_{12} \mathbf{x}^* = 0,$$
$$\mathbf{A}'_{12} y_0^* + \mathbf{A} \mathbf{x}^* = \mathbf{0}_n.$$

Solving for A_{11} and $\mathbf{A}_{12}$, and then substituting into (13) results in

$$H(y_0, \mathbf{x}') = a_0 y_0 + \mathbf{a}' \mathbf{x} + \frac{1}{2}(\alpha' \mathbf{x})^{-1} \mathbf{x}' \mathbf{A} \mathbf{x} - (\alpha' \mathbf{x})^{-1} \mathbf{x}^{*'} \mathbf{A} \mathbf{x} (y_0/y_0^*)$$
$$+ \frac{1}{2}(\alpha' \mathbf{x})^{-1} \mathbf{x}^{*'} \mathbf{A} \mathbf{x}^* (y_0/y_0^*)^2, \tag{14}$$

which is flexible at $(y_0^*, \mathbf{x}^*)$.[11]

The aggregator function $y_0(\mathbf{y})$ is specified as:

$$y_0(\mathbf{y}) = \mathbf{b}' \mathbf{y} + \frac{1}{2} \mathbf{y}' \mathbf{B} \mathbf{y} / \boldsymbol{\beta}' \mathbf{y}, \tag{15}$$

where $\boldsymbol{\beta}' \mathbf{y} \neq 0$ and $\mathbf{b}' = (b_1, \ldots, b_m)$ and the $m \times m$ symmetric matrix $\mathbf{B}$ contain the parameters to be estimated, while $\boldsymbol{\beta}' = (\beta_1, \ldots, \beta_m)$ is the vector of fixed nonnegative constants chosen by the researcher. As similarly done above with H, we can impose the following restrictions on $y_0(\mathbf{y})$ without losing local flexibility:

$$\boldsymbol{\beta}' \mathbf{y}^* = 1,$$
$$y_0^* = \mathbf{b}' \mathbf{y}^*$$
$$\mathbf{B} \mathbf{y}^* = \mathbf{0}_m.$$

Substituting (15) into (14), we get the nested flexible functional form for $\Omega(\mathbf{y}, \mathbf{x})$, which satisfies the weak separability conditions:

$$\Omega(\mathbf{y}, \mathbf{x}) = H(y_0(\mathbf{y}), \mathbf{x})$$
$$= a_0(\mathbf{b}' \mathbf{y} + \frac{1}{2}(\boldsymbol{\beta}' \mathbf{y})^{-1} \mathbf{y}' \mathbf{B} \mathbf{y}) + \mathbf{a}' \mathbf{x} + \frac{1}{2}(\alpha' \mathbf{x})^{-1} \mathbf{x}' \mathbf{A} \mathbf{x}$$

---

[10] A flexible functional form is parsimonious, if it has the minimum number of parameters needed to maintain flexibility. Diewert and Wales (1987) show that a parsimonious specification of a flexible functional form, which provides second order approximation to any arbitrary function with n variables, must have $1 + n + n(n+1)/2$ free parameters.
[11] See Diewert and Wales (1987) for the proof of flexibility.

$$-(y_0^*\alpha'x)^{-1}x^{*'}\mathbf{A}x(b'y+\frac{1}{2}(\beta'y)^{-1}y'\mathbf{B}y)$$
$$+\frac{1}{2}(y_0^{*2}\alpha'x)^{-1}x^{*'}\mathbf{A}x^*(b'y+\frac{1}{2}(\beta'y)^{-1}y'\mathbf{B}y)^2. \qquad (16)$$

The neoclassical curvature conditions require $\Omega(\mathbf{y},\mathbf{x})$ and $y_0(\mathbf{y})$ to be convex functions. Monotonicity requires that $\partial\Omega/\partial\mathbf{y} \geq 0$ and $\partial\Omega/\partial\mathbf{x} \leq 0$. Convexity of $H(y_0,\mathbf{x})$ and $y_0(\mathbf{y})$ requires the matrices $\mathbf{A}$ and $\mathbf{B}$ to be positive semidefinite. Global convexity of $\Omega(\mathbf{y},\mathbf{x})$ further requires H to be nondecreasing in y_0.

Positive semidefiniteness of the matrices $\mathbf{A}$ and $\mathbf{B}$ can be imposed without loss of flexibility by substituting

$$\mathbf{A} = \mathbf{q}\mathbf{q}'$$

and

$$\mathbf{B} = \mathbf{u}\mathbf{u}',$$

where $\mathbf{q}$ is an $n \times n$ lower triangular matrix and $\mathbf{u}$ is an $m \times m$ lower triangular matrix.

The method of squaring technique can be used to obtain local monotonicity of $\Omega(\mathbf{y},\mathbf{x})$ at the point of approximation $(\mathbf{y}^*,\mathbf{x}^*)$. The first derivatives of $\Omega(\mathbf{y},\mathbf{x})$ are

$$\frac{\partial\Omega}{\partial\mathbf{y}} = a_0\left[\mathbf{b}+\frac{1}{2}(2(\beta'y)^{-1}\mathbf{B}y-(\beta'y)^{-2}\beta y'\mathbf{B}y)\right]$$
$$-(y_0^*\alpha'x)^{-1}x^{*'}\mathbf{A}x\left[\mathbf{b}+\frac{1}{2}(2(\beta'y)^{-1}\mathbf{B}y-(\beta'y)^{-2}\beta y'\mathbf{B}y))\right]$$
$$+(y_0^{*2}\alpha'x)^{-1}x^{*'}\mathbf{A}x^*\left[\mathbf{b}+\frac{1}{2}(2(\beta'y)^{-1}\mathbf{B}y-(\beta'y)^{-2}\beta y'\mathbf{B}y)\right]$$
$$\times(b'y+\frac{1}{2}(\beta'y)^{-1}y'\mathbf{B}y),$$

$$\frac{\partial\Omega}{\partial\mathbf{x}} = \mathbf{a}+\frac{1}{2}(2(\alpha'x)^{-1}\mathbf{A}x-(\alpha'x)^{-2}\alpha x'\mathbf{A}x)$$
$$-[(y_0^*\alpha'x)^{-1}\mathbf{A}x^*-(y_0^*\alpha'x)^{-2}y_0^*\alpha x^{*'}\mathbf{A}x]\left(b'y+\frac{1}{2}(\beta'y)^{-1}y'\mathbf{B}y\right)$$
$$-\frac{1}{2}(y_0^{*2}\alpha'x)^{-2}y_0^{*2}\alpha x^{*'}\mathbf{A}x^*(b'y+\frac{1}{2}(\beta'y)^{-1}y'\mathbf{B}y)^2.$$

At $(\mathbf{y}^*,\mathbf{x}^*)$ the value of the derivative reduces to

$$\frac{\partial\Omega}{\partial\mathbf{y}} = a_0\mathbf{b}$$

and
$$\frac{\partial \Omega}{\partial \mathbf{x}} = \mathbf{a}.$$

Imposing monotonicity at the point of approximation results in

$$\frac{\partial \Omega}{\partial \mathbf{y}}(\mathbf{y}^*, \mathbf{x}^*) = a_0 \mathbf{b} \geq 0 \quad \text{and} \quad \frac{\partial \Omega}{\partial \mathbf{x}}(\mathbf{y}^*, \mathbf{x}^*) = \mathbf{a} \leq 0. \qquad (17)$$

The transformation function $\Omega(\mathbf{y}, \mathbf{x})$ under the imposed restrictions is flexible, locally monotone at $(\mathbf{y}^*, \mathbf{x}^*)$, and globally regular, subject to the weak separability condition. Local monotonicity is verified empirically at each point within the data.

Testing for weak separability and estimating the parameters of the transformation function can be done by Hansen and Singleton's generalized method of moments (GMM) method. Substitute the functional form for Ω defined by equation (16) into the system of Euler equations. We obtain the structural model, which is a system of integral equations, which we estimate by GMM. We test for weak separability by using Hansen's asymptotic χ^2 statistic to test for no overidentifying restrictions.[12]

2.4 Empirical Application

The outputs of commercial banks in our application consist of demand deposits and time deposits.[13] The inputs used in the production process include both financial and nonfinancial inputs. The financial input in the form of cash is excess reserves. The nonfinancial inputs include labor, materials, and physical capital. The output vector is given by $\mathbf{y}' = (D_t, T_t)$, and the input vector is $\mathbf{x}' = (C_t, L_t, M_t, K_t)$, where D_t is demand deposits, T_t is time deposits, C_t is excess reserves, L_t is labor input, M_t is material inputs, and K_t is capital.

In our empirical application we use the power utility function, which is a nested special case of the general class of HARA utility functions, $U(\pi_t)$, given by equation (8). We use this simplification, since the available sample size does not permit the use of the more general form. The power utility function is obtained by setting $d = 0$, and by imposing the restriction $0 < \rho < 1$, in equation (8). The power utility function is then represented by

---

[12]Since the nested model was derived after imposing weak separability, the null hypothesis of weak separability is already imposed within the Euler equations. If the test of no overidentifying restrictions is rejected, then we reject the null hypothesis of weak separability. That rejection in turn would imply that no aggregator function exists over all of the outputs of the firm.

[13]As shown in Debreu (1959), perfect competition alone is a sufficient condition for the existence of a representative firm.

Financial Intermediaries

$U(\pi_t) = \pi_t^\rho/\rho$. Substituting this specification for the utility function into the Euler equations, we acquire the fully parameterized and estimable Euler equations:[14]

$$E_t\left\{(\pi_t)^{\rho-1}k_{1,t}P_t + \frac{1}{1+\mu}P_t(\pi_{t+1})^{\rho-1}\right.$$

$$\left.\times\left[R_t\frac{\partial\Omega/\partial D_t}{\partial\Omega/\partial C_t} + [(1+R_t)(1-k_{1,t}) - (1+h_{1,t})]\right]\right\} = 0.$$

$$E_t\{(\pi_t)^{\rho-1}k_{2,t}P_t + \frac{1}{1+\mu}P_t(\pi_{t+1})^{\rho-1}$$

$$\times[R_t\frac{\partial\Omega/\partial T_t}{\partial\Omega/\partial C_t} + [(1+R_t)(1-k_{2,t}) - (1+h_{2,t})]]\} = 0.$$

$$E_t\left\{(\pi_{t+1})^{\rho-1}\left[R_tP_t\frac{\partial\Omega/\partial L_t}{\partial\Omega/\partial C_t} - (1+R_t)w_{1,t}\right]\right\} = 0.$$

$$E_t\left\{(\pi_{t+1})^{\rho-1}\left[R_tP_t\frac{\partial\Omega/\partial M_t}{\partial\Omega/\partial C_t} - (1+R_t)w_{2,t}\right]\right\} = 0.$$

$$E_t\left\{(\pi_t)^{\rho-1}[(1+R_{t-1})P_{K,t-1}] - \frac{1}{1+\mu}(\pi_{t+1})^{\rho-1}\right.$$

$$\left.\times\left[R_tP_t\frac{\partial\Omega/\partial K_t}{\partial\Omega/\partial C_t} + (1-\delta)(1+R_t)P_{K,t}\right]\right\} = 0$$

where $h_{1,t}$ and $h_{2,t}$ are respectively the holding costs of demand deposits and time deposits, $k_{1,t}$ and $k_{2,t}$ are respectively the required reserves ratio on demand and time deposits, and $w_{1,t}$ and $w_{2,t}$ are respectively the prices of labor and material inputs.

The fixed nonnegative constants are chosen such that

$$\alpha_i = \frac{|\bar{\tilde{x}}_i|}{\sum_{j=1}^{4}|\bar{\tilde{x}}_j|} \quad \forall i = 1,2,3,4$$

---

[14] Before using Hansen's χ^2 statistic to test for weak separability in outputs, we have to choose the center of local approximation. We choose the unit vector, $y_0^* = 1$, $\mathbf{y}^{*'} = (1,1)$, and $\mathbf{x}^{*'} = (1,1,1,1)$, as the center of approximation. To locate the center within the interior of the observations, we rescale the data about the midpoint observation so that the rescaled data becomes $\tilde{x}_i^t = x_i^t/x_i^{t^*}$ for $i = 1,2,3,4$ and $\tilde{y}_i^t = y_i^t/y_i^{t^*}$ for $i = 1,2$, where t^* is the midpoint observation. Each price vector is correspondingly rescaled by multiplying by the midpoint observation. This rescaling of price leaves the dollar expenditure on various goods unaffected by the rescaling of the corresponding quantity.

and

$$\beta_i = \frac{|\bar{\tilde{y}}_i|}{\sum_{j=1}^{2} |\bar{\tilde{y}}_j|} \quad \forall i = 1, 2,$$

where $\bar{\tilde{x}}_i$ and $\bar{\tilde{y}}_i$ are the sample means of $\tilde{x}_i$ and $\tilde{y}_i$, respectively.

One of the model's implied restrictions is $b_1 + b_2 = 1$. There are also inequality restrictions to be imposed. They include $b_i \geq 0$ for $i = 1, 2$, and also $b_i \leq 1$ for all $i = 1, 2$. Combining these two conditions and the mathematical identity $\sin^2 \theta + \cos^2 \theta = 1$, we have the substitution $b_1 = \sin^2 \theta$ and $b_2 = \cos^2 \theta$, where the parameter θ must now be estimated.

We normalize $a_0 = 1$, and we impose the monotonicity conditions $a_i \leq 0$ for $i = 1, 2, 3, 4$, by replacing a_i by $-\tilde{a}_i^2$ for $i = 1, 2, 3, 4$, and estimating $\tilde{a}_i$. Positive semidefiniteness of the matrices **A** and **B**, as required by the convexity conditions, can be imposed without loss of flexibility by substituting $\mathbf{A} = \mathbf{qq}'$ and $\mathbf{B} = \mathbf{uu}'$, where **q** is an $n \times n$ lower triangular matrix and **u** is an $m \times m$ lower triangular matrix. In our two-output, four-input case, **q** and **u** are given by

$$\mathbf{q} = \begin{bmatrix} q_{11} & 0 & 0 & 0 \\ q_{21} & q_{22} & 0 & 0 \\ q_{31} & q_{32} & q_{33} & 0 \\ q_{41} & q_{42} & q_{43} & q_{44} \end{bmatrix} \quad \text{and} \quad \mathbf{u} = \begin{bmatrix} u_{11} & 0 \\ u_{21} & u_{22} \end{bmatrix}. \quad (18)$$

But the model's restrictions imply

$$\begin{bmatrix} u_{11} & 0 \\ u_{21} & u_{22} \end{bmatrix} \begin{bmatrix} u_{11} & u_{21} \\ 0 & u_{22} \end{bmatrix} \begin{bmatrix} 1 \\ 1 \end{bmatrix} = \begin{bmatrix} 0 \\ 0 \end{bmatrix},$$

which, when solved, produces the restrictions $u_{22} = 0$ and $u_{21} = -u_{11}$. Hence the matrix **B** must satisfy

$$\mathbf{B} = u_{11}^2 \begin{bmatrix} 1 & -1 \\ -1 & 1 \end{bmatrix}.$$

Following these substitutions, the parameters that remain to be estimated within technology are θ, u_{11}, **q**, $\tilde{\mathbf{a}} = (\tilde{a}_1, \tilde{a}_2, \tilde{a}_3, \tilde{a}_4)$. In addition the subjective rate of time discount μ and the risk aversion parameter ρ must be estimated.

The data used for estimating the model were mainly obtained from the Federal Reserve Bank Functional Cost Analysis (FCA) Program.[15]

---

[15]Data on the National Average Banks for the years 1966-1992 was used in the estimation. Labor inputs consist of two groups: managerial and nonmanagerial. Data on expenditure and quantity for the two categories of labor were obtained from FCA. Ma-

2.5 Results

The parameter estimates were obtained by estimating the system of Euler equations with technology specified in our nested generalized McFadden form. We used the GMM estimation procedure on mainframe TSP (version 7.02).[16] In the estimation, to ensure that $0 < \rho < 1$, we replace ρ by $\sin^2(\hat{\rho})$ and estimate $\hat{\rho}$. Similarly, to rule out negative values for the subjective rate of time preference, μ, we replace μ by $\bar{\mu}^2$ and estimate $\bar{\mu}$.

---

terial inputs are divided into three categories: printing and stationery, telephone and telegraph, and postage, freight, and delivery. Physical capital is made up of structures (bank buildings), furniture and equipment, and computers. Data on expenditure on the various types of material inputs and physical capital were obtained from the FCA, while the corresponding price indices were obtained from the *Survey of Current Business*. A quantity aggregate and the corresponding price aggregate must be constructed for each of the three nonfinancial inputs. For further details on data and data construction, refer to Hancock (1991) and Barnett and Hahm (1994).

If data on expenditure and price for the individual categories of each input are available, we first construct the Divisia price aggregate and then find the corresponding quantity aggregate using Fisher's factor reversal test. If on the other hand, we have data on expenditure and quantity, we first construct the Divisia quantity aggregate and then find the corresponding price aggregate.

Data on the nominal quantity of demand deposits and time deposits, net interest rate on demand deposits and time deposits, and the bank's portfolio rate of return were obtained from the FCA data set. Net interest rate is the interest paid on the deposit plus FDIC insurance premium paid minus service charges earned. The required reserves ratio was obtained from the Federal Reserve *Bulletin*. Nominal dollar balances of all financial goods were converted to real balances by deflating the nominal balances using Fisher's ideal price index. The Fisher ideal price index is used as a proxy for the *true cost of living index*. The Fisher ideal price index is equal to the geometric mean of the Laspeyres and Paasche index, where we approximate the former from the Bureau of Labor Statistic's consumer price index (CPI) and the latter from the Commerce Department's GDP implicit price deflator (IPD). Data on the CPI and IPD are from the Citibank Database.

[16]This estimation process allows for heteroskedasticity and autocorrelation in the disturbance terms. We specified a second-order moving average serial correlation. Bartlett kernels were specified for the kernel density. Discount window rate, federal funds rate, composite bond rate, lagged value of excess reserves, lagged value of the Fisher ideal price index, and a constant were chosen as instruments. The instruments were chosen to be variables that influence the decision of the firm, but are exogenous or predetermined in the firm's decision. We checked for robustness of the parameter estimates to alternative selections of instruments. Other instruments tried as substitutes for some of the instruments listed above were the interest rate on time deposits, the prime rate, and lagged values of capital. Although the parameters changed when instruments were changed, the parameter shifts were adequately small to support the conclusion of robustness of inferences to suitable choices of instruments.

TABLE 1
GMM Estimates of Parameters of Theoretical Aggregator Function Nested in Financial Firm's Technology

Parameter	u_{11}	θ
Estimate	.395	58.19
t-ratio	1.84	750.5

NOTE: The other parameters of technology, outside the monetary aggregator function, are $(\tilde{a}_1, \tilde{a}_2, \tilde{a}_3, \tilde{a}_4, \hat{\rho}, \hat{\mu}, q_{11}, q_{21}, q_{31}, q_{41}, q_{22}, q_{32}, q_{33}, q_{42}, q_{43}, q_{44})$, and were estimated to be $(.041, -.089, .052, .091, 263.9, .284, -.098, .024, .860, -.534, -1.10, 1.332, -1.936, -.451, 2.230, 1.069)$, respectively, with corresponding t-ratios of $(2.45, -1.38, .128, .268, 19.16, 3.02, -4.23, .05, 1.86, -1.12, -1.80, 2.06, -5.58, -1.70, 6.49, 6.08)$ respectively.

Monotonicity was imposed upon the monetary aggregator function at only one point. However, monotonicity of that function was checked at all points, and violations of monotonicity conditions within the aggregator function did not occur at any observation. Convexity of the monetary aggregator function was imposed globally. Monotonicity of the transformation function, Ω, was imposed at only one point but checked at all points. Monotonicity was satisfied at all data points for outputs, at all data points for cash, at all but four points for materials, at all but three points for labor, and at all but four points for capital. Convexity of Ω was satisfied at all data points.

As is evident from Table 1, the precision of the GMM estimates of the parameters of financial firm technology is extremely high for all of the parameters in the aggregator function $y_0(\mathbf{y})$. Figure 1 displays the levels of the estimated theoretical aggregate, the simple sum index, and the Divisia index. The aggregate is in real, rather than nominal, terms. Clearly the estimated theoretical and Divisia indices move closely together, while the simple sum aggregate tracks less well.

The estimated exact aggregate depends upon our choice of estimated aggregator function, but was estimated in a manner that permits risk. The Divisia index, on the other hand, does not depend upon the form of the aggregator function, but is derived under the assumption of perfect certainty. However, the damage to its tracking ability from risk has been shown in other research to become significant only when the degree of risk and of risk aversion are very high. Evidently the degree of risk and of risk aversion were not sufficiently large to do much damage to the tracking ability of the Divisia index. The violations of regularity reported in the footnote of Table 1 were few and did not seem to be a serious problem in modeling bank behavior.

We ran the test of weak separability of monetary assets from the other variables in technology.[17] The calculated test statistic is 9, and the critical value at the 10 percent level of significance is 12.07. Hence we cannot

---

[17] As described above, we ran that test using Hansen's χ^2 test for no overidentifying restrictions in the model with weak separability imposed through the structure of the

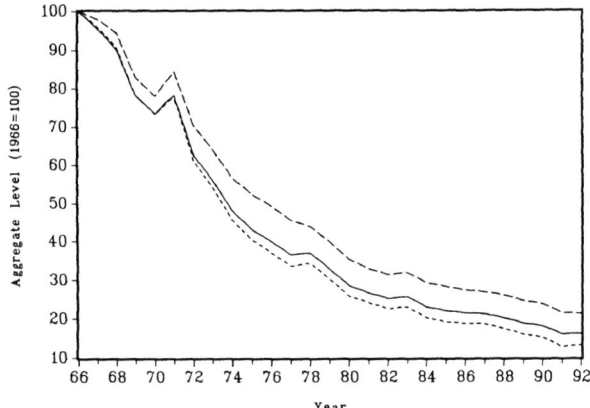

Figure 1: Levels of indices of the real monetary aggregate nested within the financial firm's transformation technology (—— = theoretical, – – = simple sum, and ···· = Divisia).

reject the hypothesis of weak separability of monetary assets. That weak separability condition is the existence condition for an economic monetary aggregate.

3 Manufacturing Firms

Compared to financial firms and consumers, manufacturing firms have been the subject of relatively little research through this modern approach of Euler equation estimation with nested monetary aggregation.[18] We now provide a model of a manufacturing firm that employs a monetary asset portfolio as inputs. We assume rational expectations under risk, and we investigate the existence of an exact aggregation-theoretic monetary asset input aggregate.

There is no unanimous agreement among economists about the specific role that money plays in the production process. But regardless of the explicit role of money in the operation of a manufacturing firm, a derived produc-

---

model. The test statistic is $\Phi = TQ$, where $T = 25$ is the sample size and $Q = 0.36$ is the value of the objective function in the GMM estimation. The test statistic is distributed as a χ^2 with $e - f = 7$ degrees of freedom, where e is the number of orthogonality conditions and f is the number of parameters.

[18] However, in the perfect certainty case, relevant theory is available in Barnett (1987) and a positive contribution to dynamic modeling of firm demand for money, although without nested exact quantity aggregation, has been made by Robles (1993). The potential importance of this under-researched area has been emphasized by Drake and Chrystal (1994).

tion function always exists that absorbs that motive into the firm's technology, even if no direct role exists for money inside the factory's production activities.[19] When we enter the monetary asset portfolio into the firm's technology as factors of production, the technology should be understood to be that derived technology of the firm, and not necessarily the physical technology of the factory.

3.1 The Model

Our model is based on Barnett's (1987) monetary aggregation-theoretic approach, extended to include uncertainty and capital accumulation. Perfect competition in all markets and risk neutrality of the firm are assumed. The objective of the firm is to maximize the expected discounted value of its future variable profit flow, subject to its technology. The firm uses L_t real units of labor, K_t real units of capital goods, a J dimensional vector $\boldsymbol{\varepsilon}_t$ of monetary assets, and an N-dimensional vector $\mathbf{x}_t$ of other variable inputs as factors of production in producing an I-dimensional vector $\mathbf{y}_t$ of real output quantities during period t. The firm's technology is given by the transformation function:

$$\Omega(y_{1t},\ldots,y_{It},L_t,K_t,x_{1t},\ldots,x_{Nt},\varepsilon_{1t},\ldots,\varepsilon_{Jt}) = 0. \qquad (19)$$

The transformation technology Ω is assumed to be convex in its arguments. In addition, the monotonicity conditions assumed to hold are that Ω is nondecreasing in all outputs and nonincreasing in all inputs, including labor, capital, financial inputs, and other variable inputs.

Let $p_t^{y_i}$ be the price of the ith real output y_{it}. Let $p_t^{x_n}$ be the price of the nth variable input x_{nt}, and let w_t be the labor wage rate, which is paid at the end of the period. Real balances $\boldsymbol{\varepsilon}_t$ are defined to equal nominal balances divided by p_t^*, the true cost of living index. The return on holding nominal

---

[19]It is with respect to that derived technology that Fischer (1974) concluded that "there is a well-defined sense in which real money balances may be said to be a factor of production." Fischer illustrates that conclusion with two types of models: a Baumol-Tobin inventory model, in which the firm holds real balances because it is cheaper to hold them temporarily than to buy bonds, and a vending machine model in which it is expensive for the firm to be short of cash. A re-interpretation of the Baumol-Tobin model, by regarding transaction costs as costs of hiring labor, brings in an interaction between production and financial decisions of the firm and justifies putting money as an input factor in the production function. In an empirical test of that hypothesis in a manufacturing model containing both money and credit, Betancourt and Robles (1989) find that treating money as a factor of production in a derived production function performs better than treating credit as a factor of production. We do not treat credit as a factor of production. A similar argument is involved in the use of a derived technology for financial intermediaries with excess reserves treated as a factor of production.

money balances of type j is r_{jt} and is paid to the firm at the end of the period.

As the firm operates over time, it retains part of the earnings and uses them to finance its expansion and development. It is assumed that there exist markets for new and used capital. Capital accumulation is given by

$$K_t = (1-\delta)K_{t-1} + I_t \tag{20}$$

where I_t is gross investment and δ is the physical depreciation rate of capital. Investment becomes productive instantaneously, but capital installation is costly to the firm. Thus the total costs of purchasing and installing I_t are given by $p_t^I[I_t + C(I_t)]$, where p_t^I is the price of capital goods and $C(I_t)$ is a convex function, representing the costs of adjustment associated with installing capital.[20]

Extending Barnett's (1987, eq. [4.3]) formula to include q theory capital dynamics, the firm's variable profits during period t are

$$\pi_t = \sum_i y_{it} p_t^{y_i} - \sum_n x_{nt} p_t^{x_n} - w_{t-1} L_{t-1}$$
$$+ \sum_j [(1+r_{jt-1}) p_{t-1}^* \varepsilon_{jt-1} - p_t^* \varepsilon_{jt}] - p_t^I[I_t + C(I_t)], \tag{21}$$

where $I_t = K_t - (1-\delta)K_{t-1}$. The first term represents revenues from production during period t. The second term is the cost of other variable inputs x_t, which is paid at the beginning of the period. The third term is the costs of labor supplied during the previous period, but paid its wage at the end of that period. The end of one period is assumed to coincide with the start of the next period, since time intervals are assumed to be closed on the left and open on the right. The fourth term in the equation represents the flow of funds from rolling over the firm's portfolio of monetary assets, where the first part of the term is the nominal value of the monetary asset portfolio available at the beginning of the period as a result of last period holdings. The last term is the total cost of purchasing and installing capital during the period.

It is assumed that the manufacturing firm chooses the levels of output and real factors of production to maximize the expected discounted intertemporal profit flow, subject to its technology. Under the assumption of complete markets, perfect competition, and risk neutrality of the owners of the firm,

---

[20] Note that our notation for the price of capital differs from that used in section 2. We here use the superscript I in the role used by K in section 2, since we shall wish to reserve the notation p_t^K below for the user cost price of capital services.

the problem can be presented as the following dynamic choice problem:

$$\max \quad E_t \left\{ \sum_{s=t}^{\infty} \frac{1}{\mu_s} \left\{ \sum_{i=1}^{I} y_{is} p_s^{y_i} - \sum_{n=1}^{N} x_{ns} p_s^{x_n} - w_{s-1} L_{s-1} \right. \right.$$

$$+ \sum_{j=1}^{J} [(1 + r_{js-1}) p_{s-1}^* \varepsilon_{js-1} - p_s^* \varepsilon_{js}]$$

$$\left. \left. - p_s^I [K_s - (1-\delta) K_{s-1} + C(I_t)] \right\} \right\}$$

s.t. $\quad \Omega(y_{1s}, \ldots, y_{Is}, x_{1s}, \ldots, x_{Ns}, L_s, K_s, \varepsilon_{1s}, \ldots, \varepsilon_{Js}) = 0$

$$\forall s \geq t \tag{22}$$

where E_t denotes expectations, given the information available at period t, and where the discount factor μ_s is defined such that $\mu_s = 1$ if $s = t$ and $\mu_s = \prod_{a=t}^{s-1}(1 + R_a)$ if $s > t$.

Substituting the quadratic function $\gamma I_t^2 / 2$ for the cost of adjustment function $C(I_t)$, the first-order conditions for optimal behavior by firms can be acquired. Using Bellman's method and the Benveniste and Scheinkman equation, the Euler equations are found to be

$$E_t \left\{ p_t^{y_i} + \frac{1}{1+R_t} w_t \frac{\partial \Omega / \partial y_{it}}{\partial \Omega / \partial L_t} \right\} = 0 \quad \forall y_{it}, \; i = 1, \ldots, I \tag{23}$$

$$E_t \left\{ p_t^{x_n} - \frac{1}{1+R_t} w_t \frac{\partial \Omega / \partial x_{nt}}{\partial \Omega / \partial L_t} \right\} = 0 \quad \forall x_{nt}, \; n = 1, \ldots, N \tag{24}$$

$$E_t \left\{ p_t^* - \frac{1}{1+R_t} \left[(1 + r_{it}) p_t^* + w_t \frac{\partial \Omega / \partial \varepsilon_{jt}}{\partial \Omega / \partial L_t} \right] \right\} = 0 \quad \forall \varepsilon_{jt}, \; j = 1, \ldots, J \tag{25}$$

$$E_t \left\{ p_t^I [1 + \gamma(K_t - (1-\delta)K_{t-1})] \right. \tag{26}$$

$$- \frac{p_{t+1}^I}{1+R_t} [1 - \delta + \gamma(1-\delta)(K_{t+1} - (1-\delta)K_t)]$$

$$\left. - \frac{w_t}{1+R_t} \frac{\partial \Omega / \partial K_t}{\partial \Omega / \partial L_t} \right\} = 0.$$

3.2 Demand-Side Monetary Aggregation and Weak Separability

By estimating the parameters of the Euler equations by GMM, we can investigate properties of technology, such as returns to scale. If the firm's monetary inputs are weakly separable from output, we also can investigate the resulting exact demand-side monetary aggregate. In this initial step in that direction, we shall limit ourselves to the latter objective.

The approach to identifying and generating an exact theoretical demand-side monetary aggregate for a manufacturing firm is described by Barnett (1987) in the case of perfect certainty. We extend his approach to the case of risk. Define $\mathbf{y}_{0t} = (y_{1t}, \ldots, y_{It}, x_{1t}, \ldots, x_{Nt}, L_t, K_t)'$. For a monetary asset aggregator function to exist, monetary assets ε_t must be weakly separable from $\mathbf{y}_{0t}$. Hence there must exist functions H and z_0 such that $\Omega(\mathbf{y}_{0t}, \varepsilon_t) = H(\mathbf{y}_{0t}, z_0(\varepsilon_t))$, where z_0 is the aggregator function over the monetary asset inputs ε_t. If the existence condition is satisfied, we can progress to the next step, which is estimation of the aggregator function $z_0(\varepsilon_t)$.

3.3 Flexible Functional Form Specification and Regularity Conditions

As in the case of the financial intermediary in section 2, we specify the technology of the firm to be Diewert and Wales's (1991) symmetric generalized McFadden flexible functional form, but now with exact nested input aggregation for financial assets rather than exact nested output aggregation. Except for the fact that the monetary aggregator function is on the input side rather than the output side, the functional form used for technology is identical for manufacturing firms and for financial intermediaries, and we use the same notation for the parameterization in both cases. The variables used within the parameterized technology differ as derived above. In addition, the utility function parameters (μ, ρ) do not appear in the manufacturing firm model, since we have assumed risk neutrality for manufacturing firms, in accordance with the known implications of complete contingent claims markets. Hence the manufacturing firm maximizes expected discounted profits rather than discounted expected utility of profits. Risk aversion was permitted in the case of financial intermediaries, since the assumption of complete contingent claims markets seems less acceptable in the case of banks than in the case of manufacturing firms. In addition, a new parameter appears in the case of manufacturing firms: the parameter γ in the Tobin q dynamics. In the financial firm case, that parameter did not appear, since we introduced capital dynamics for banks through time-to-build rather than q theory. The choice of the capital dynamics model in each case was dictated by our need for Euler equations in recursive form.

As with the financial firm, we use GMM to estimate the technology, and we use Hansen's χ^2 to test the imposed assumption of weak separability in monetary assets.[21]

3.4 Data and Results

The model is applied empirically to the aggregate U.S. manufacturing sector data for the period 1949–1988. Real input resources include capital, labor, and materials. Monetary inputs include two types of assets: cash on hand and in U.S. banks and U.S. government securities.[22] The following variables are used as instruments in the GMM estimation procedure: a constant, total U.S. population, and lagged values of the prices of capital and materials, of the rate of return on cash and securities, and of the Moody's Baa bond rate.[23]

---

[21] We do not repeat the details of the generalized McFadden specification in this section, since the parametric analogy with the parameterization for banks is immediate. However, the full specification using the notation for manufacturing firm variables is available in Barnett, Kirova, and Pasupathy, (1995), and Barnett, Hinich, and Yue (2000).

[22] The data comes primarily from two sources. Data on output and factor inputs in U.S. manufacturing for the period 1949–1988 is acquired from the Division of Multifactor Productivity of the Bureau of Labor Statistics. The data consists of quantity and price Törnqvist indices. Output is defined as gross sectoral output. Capital input is defined as the flow of services from physical assets, which include equipment, structures, inventories, and land. Labor input is defined as the paid hours of all persons engaged in the sector. Materials input consists of all commodity inputs exclusive of fuel inputs.

The source of data on money balances held by manufacturing firms is the *Quarterly Financial Report for Manufacturing, Mining, and Trade Corporations* for the period 1949–1988. To convert to real units, we deflate the nominal balances by the Fisher ideal index approximation to the true cost-of-living index, computed as in section 2 above. The rates of return on cash on hand and in banks and government securities are from the City Bank database. We use the six-month commercial paper yield as the rate of return on cash on hand and in banks, because this rate is available for the entire period 1949–1988. The reason for the nonzero rate of return for cash on hand and in banks is that it does not consist solely of currency. Cash on hand and in banks in our data source is defined to be the sum of manufacturing sector holdings of currency, demand deposits, and time deposits. Separate data on such holdings of currency are available only for the most recent observations. The three-month Treasury-bill rate is used as the rate of return on government securities, which in our data source are defined as short-term financial investments, including marketable and government securities. This very short-term yield is used because the rate of return on securities with longer duration is not available for the most early observations in the sample. In principle, it would be best if all rates of return were yield curve adjusted to the same holding period, as would be consistent with the model's discrete time conventions, but data limitations prevent that adjustment, which we believe would have little effect on the results in any case. Our data choices in that regard are consistent with those of Betancourt and Robles (1989).

We use an external nominal bond rate for the rate of return on capital, R_t, since data was unavailable to compute an internal rate of return. For a rigorous discussion of theoretical and empirical issues concerning the measurement of the rate of return on capital, see Harper, Berndt, and Wood (1989). Data on Moody's Baa bond rate is obtained from the City Bank database.

[23] Given the number of observations, a larger set of instruments would not be feasible. But the robustness of the parameter estimates was checked by excluding some of the

TABLE 2
GMM Estimates of Parameters of Theoretical Aggregator Function Nested in Manufacturing Firm's Technology

Parameter	u_{11}	θ
Estimate	.05	61.82
t-ratio	9.41	228,814

NOTE: The other parameters of technology, outside the monetary aggregator function, are $(\tilde{a}_1, \tilde{a}_2, \tilde{a}_3, \tilde{a}_4, \gamma, q_{11}, q_{21}, q_{31}, q_{41}, q_{22}, q_{32}, q_{33}, q_{42}, q_{43}, q_{44})$, and were estimated to be (1.22, .689, 1.617, 1.635, 3.98, −1.61, −3.19, 5.23, 4.59, −3.75, −3.33, 5.52, 5.76, .963, −.035.) respectively, with corresponding t-ratios of (9.8, 6.21, 7.84, 10.18, 1.01, −6.85, −7.32, 7.12, 10.42, −6.68, −2.32, 4.05, 10.74, 1.11, −.001) respectively.

Monotonicity was imposed upon the monetary aggregator function at only one point. However, monotonicity of that function was checked at all points, and violations of monotonicity conditions within the aggregator function did not occur at any observation. Concavity of the monetary aggregator function was imposed globally.

Monotonicity of the transformation function, Ω, was imposed at only one point but checked at all points. Monotonicity was violated for output at three points, for labor at three points, for materials at five points, for capital at fourteen points, and for cash and securities at thirty-two points. Convexity of Ω was violated at thirty-two data points.

As is evident from Table 2, the precision of the GMM estimates of the parameters of manufacturing firm technology is extremely high for all of the parameters in the aggregator function $z_0(\varepsilon_t)$. Figure 2 displays the level of the estimated theoretical aggregate, the simple sum index, and the Divisia index. The aggregate is plotted in real, rather than nominal, terms. Clearly the estimated theoretical and Divisia indices move closely together, while the simple sum aggregate tracks less well.

The violations of regularity reported in the footnote of Table 2 suggest the limitations of the generalized McFadden parametric specification of the firm's technology and perhaps suggest that our future research on manufacturing firm technology should be based upon the generalized Barnett model originated in Diewert and Wales (1987) rather than upon our current use of the generalized McFadden model, also originated in Diewert and Wales (1987). Unlike the generalized McFadden model, the generalized Barnett model is globally regular. However, in the current research we investigate only the properties of the estimated aggregator function of monetary assets, and as reported in the footnote to Table 2, the estimated monetary aggregator function was globally regular.

---

instruments listed above and using in their place other variables from the information set of the firm. The alternative instruments that were used are the lagged values of the prices of labor and of output. The parameter estimates were found to be robust to the changes in the instrument set.

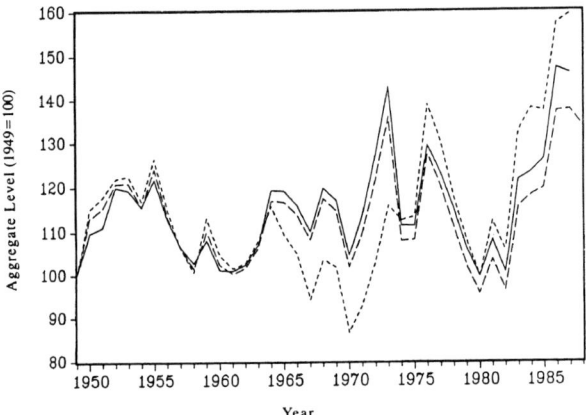

Figure 2: Levels of indices of the real monetary aggregate nested within the manufacturing firm's transformation technology (——— = theoretical, – – – = simple sum, and · · · · = Divisia).

We tested weak separability of monetary assets from the other variables in technology. We ran that test using Hansen's χ^2 test for no overidentifying restrictions in the model with weak separability imposed through the structure of the model.[24] The calculated test statistic is 14, and the critical value at the 1 percent level of significance is 27.69. Hence we cannot reject the hypothesis of weak separability of monetary assets.

4 Consumers

This line of research in monetary economics began with Barnett (1980a) in the perfect certainty case and Poterba and Rotemberg (1987) in the case of risk. Both papers were produced from models of consumer behavior. A long list of papers have been motivated by Barnett's perfect certainty model, and recently Poterba and Rotemberg's extension to risk has motivated papers by Barnett, Hinich, and Yue (1991) and by Rotemberg, Driscoll, and Poterba (1995). The ultimate objective of the current paper is to indicate the availability of an approach to estimating the deep parameters of a macroeconometric model, and this cannot be done without doing so for consumers as well as for firms.

---

[24]The test statistic is $\Phi = TQ$, where $T = 40$ is the sample size and $Q = .35$ is the value of the objective function in the GMM estimation. The test statistic is distributed as a χ^2 with $e - f$ degrees of freedom, where $e = 30$ is the number of orthogonality conditions and $f = 17$ is the number of parameters.

Since Euler equation parameter estimates for risk-averse consumers already exist, we use those estimates to produce the plots of estimated monetary aggregator functions for consumers and the approximating plots of Divisia and simple sum statistical index numbers. The specification is methodologically consistent with those used above for manufacturing firms and banks: the decision is stochastically dynamic, the exact monetary aggregator function is nested within the Euler equations, and the estimation by GMM is of deep Euler equation parameters, rather than of the parameters of the solution demand function parameters. The relevant theory, the data, and the parameter estimates can be found in various published and unpublished sources, although the resulting values of the estimated and approximating monetary aggregates have not previously been plotted.[25] Those plots are provided here in Figure 3 and are produced in a manner that is comparable to the plots produced for manufacturing firms and banks. The nominal per capita time paths of the three indexes, estimated theoretical, Divisia, and simple sum, are plotted for aggregates over M1 components and for aggregates over M2 components.

At the M1 level, Divisia M1 tracks the estimated theoretical aggregate rather well. At the M2 level, the growth rates of those two series diverged from September 1982 through April 1983, with the growth rate of the estimated theoretical aggregate being consistently higher than that of the Divisia aggregate throughout that time period. This phenomenon opened a gap between the plots of the levels of the two series. However, the two paths tracked parallel to each other after the eight months of diverging growth rates, since the growth rates of the two series returned to being very similar after April 1983.

The source of the divergence from September 1982 through April 1983 probably can be found in the unusual circumstances that existed in money markets. Many innovations in money markets evolved during that period, such as the introduction of super-NOW accounts and money-market deposit accounts at commercial banks.[26] There also was more than the usual degree

---

[25] The relevant theory and econometric specification can be found in Poterba and Rotemberg (1987), Barnett (1995), Barnett, Hinich, and Yue (1991), and Barnett, Kirova, Pasupathy, and Yue (1994). The data can be found in Barnett, Hinich, and Yue (1991), reproduced as chapter 11 of this book, and the parameter estimates can be found in Barnett, Hinich, and Yue (2000). In each of those papers, the monetary aggregator function nested within the Euler equations was CES (constant elasticity of substitution) and hence was not as flexible as the aggregator functions used above with manufacturing firms and banks.

[26] In particular, super-NOW accounts were introduced during January 1983 and money-market deposit accounts were introduced during December 1982. The period during which the growth rate of the estimated theoretic M2 aggregate diverged from the Divisia and simple sum M2 aggregates was September 1982 through April 1983.

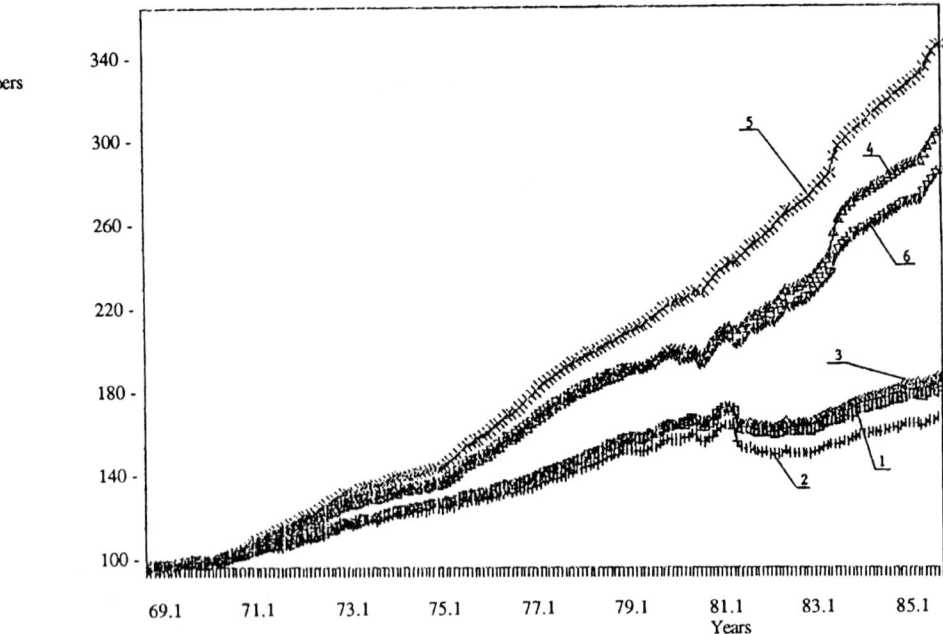

Figure 3: Levels of nominal per capita M1 and M2 monetary indices (1, M1 theoretic; 2, M1 simple sum; 3, M1 Divisia; 4, M2 theoretic; 5, M2 simple sum; 6, M2 Divisia).

of uncertainty regarding monetary policy, since that period immediately followed the termination of the Federal Reserve's 'monetarist experiment,' and the targets of monetary policy immediately following the termination of that experiment were unclear.

5 Conclusions

We conclude that both the Lucas critique and the Barnett critique can be circumvented by estimating Euler equations with weak separability tested and imposed prior to the construction of monetary aggregates in the financial sector. This conclusion applies to estimation of the technology of manufacturing firms, which demand monetary services as inputs, the tastes of consumers, who demand monetary services as inputs, and the technology of financial intermediaries, which supply financial services as outputs while contributing to the production of the economy's inside money supply. To avoid the need

Conclusions 557

to produce results that are conditional upon a particular motive for holding money, we assumed that money has positive value in equilibrium and then used the derived utility and production functions that must exist under that assumption. As has been proven in the general equilibrium theory literature, derived utility functions and derived production functions containing money exist, so long as money has positive value in equilibrium.[27] However, the same procedures illustrated in this paper are equally as applicable for models that are constructed conditionally upon a particular motive for holding money, and indeed we believe that these procedures should be introduced into that important literature. In such models the aggregator function becomes a weakly separable function within a constraint, which has not already been absorbed into an objective function.

The Divisia index is known to track exact aggregator functions without error under perfect certainty in continuous time, but that result does not apply under risk. While the Divisia index is not flawless under risk, we find that its tracking ability is better than that of other available statistical index numbers.[28] This advantage is most evident when the ratios of the user cost prices of the services of components differs substantially from 1.0. In fact, it can be shown that the Divisia index reduces to the simple sum if all user costs are equal, so that the components become perfect substitutes. The advantage of Divisia over simple sum is especially evident in the case of consumer demand, since our data in that case includes currency with a yield of zero, while the other assets in the consumer's portfolio yield a positive rate of return. In our results with manufacturing firms and with banks, no zero-yielding asset was among the components of the aggregate and hence the results are less dramatic.

The ultimate objective of this line of research is to permit investigation of various forms of policy intervention into asset markets and to investigate properties of tastes and technology. We agree with Poterba and Rotemberg's (1987) views on the direction that this research should take, and we have taken that line of research several steps further in this paper. Clearly much remains to be done, such as including returns to scale and learning-by-doing in technology and imposing consistent structure across economic agents such that aggregation will conform on both sides of markets. Market clearing in aggregates then can be imposed to produce a dynamic general equilibrium macroeconomic model in which the deep parameters can be estimated.

---

[27] See, for example, Arrow and Hahn (1971), Feenstra (1986), and Fischer (1974).

[28] The CAPM adjustment needed to remove the bias in the Divisia index under risk was only recently derived in Barnett, Liu, and Jensen (1997) and was not used in this paper.

PART 6: MONETARY POLICY WITH EXACT MONETARY AGGREGATION

Section 6.1: Editors' Overview of Part 6

William A. Barnett and Apostolos Serletis

The following table contains a brief summary of the contents of each chapter in Part 6 of this book. Since aggregation and index number theory are logically prior to macroeconomic modeling, this book largely avoids advocacy of any particular macroeconomic theory or policy. Data should not be "doctored" to help "confirm" a policy point of view. Nevertheless, this concluding section of the book does provide results having policy relevance.

Part 6 Section Contents
Monetary Policy with Exact Monetary Aggregation

Chapter Number	Chapter Title	Contents
23	Recent Monetary Policy and the Divisia Monetary Aggregates	Demonstrates that the Divisia monetary aggregates resolve the puzzles regarding the period of the "monetarist experiment" in the United States and that they predicted the recession that followed.
24	Which Road Leads to Stable Demand for Money?	An "*Economic Journal* Controversies" paper advocating the methodology developed in this book and demonstrating its power to resolve paradoxes.
25	Perspective on the Current State of Macroeconomic Theory	Opinion on the state of the field of macroeconomics.

Chapter 23:

Chapter 23 displays the fact that Divisia monetary aggregates grew at about half the rate of the simple sum monetary aggregates during the "monetarist experiment" in the United States. Barnett was at the Federal Reserve Board during most of that three year period. His experience and the evidence from the simple sum monetary aggregates suggest that the Federal Reserve Board was seeking to disinflate the economy in a manner that would not produce a severe contractionary shock and a subsequent recession. But the

Divisia monetary aggregates tell a very different story of an unintended strong negative shock, which was consistent with the recession that followed.

Chapter 24:

Chapter 24 originally appeared as a Controversies Section paper in the *Economic Journal*, and strongly advocates research based upon the approach developed in this book. As an illustration of the magnitude of the error that can be produced by the use of theoretically incoherent approaches, Chapter 24 provides plots of the simple sum and Divisia monetary aggregates in the early 1980s. The simple sum M2 monetary aggregate produced a huge growth rate spike in 1982. This observation led some monetarists to predict an unavoidable resurgence of inflation. The Divisia M2 data displayed no such spike, and indeed no resurgence of inflation followed.

Chapter 25:

Chapter 25 contains general commentary on the state of the field of macroeconomics.

Introduction

Section 6.2: Monetary Policy

Chapter 23

Recent Monetary Policy and the Divisia Monetary Aggregates

William A. Barnett*

> This article explains the currently available capability to use formal statistical index number theory to measure the economy's money supply accurately. The new procedure is illustrated by exploring the tightness of money during the recent three-year period of 'monetarist' Federal Reserve policy. When measured by a properly constructed statistical index number, the rate of growth of the money supply is found to have been lower and more volatile than when measured by the official simple sum monetary aggregates. As a result, targeting the simple sum aggregates may have induced a tighter and more volatile policy than was intended.

1 Introduction

A large body of literature exists on statistical index number theory, which provides formal means of aggregating over component goods to acquire aggregated price indexes and quantity indexes. The literature has led to the determination of a class of index numbers that have excellent statistical properties and excellent theoretical approximation properties; all elements of that

---

*Reprinted with permission from the *American Statistician*. Copyright (1984) by the American Statistical Association. The author's work on this article was partially supported by National Science Foundation Grant SOC8305162.

class, called the 'superlative' class, move in close concert (see Diewert 1976). In fact since the appearance of Fisher's (1922) early classic book on statistical index number theory, nearly all federal economic data series have been based on aggregation formulas from that literature. Well-known examples are the consumer price index (a Laspeyres price index), the implicit price deflator (a Paasche price index), and real GNP (a Laspeyres quantity index). An exception is the Federal Reserve Board's monetary aggregates, which are simple sum aggregates.[1]

Although aggregation by simple summation is in low repute in index number theory, the relationship between monetary theory and index number theory was not known until that theoretical linkage was derived in Barnett (1980a; 1981b, Ch. 7). As a result, statistical index number theory only recently became applicable to monetary aggregation. A survey of the earlier research on monetary aggregation, which was not based on statistical index number theory, can be found in Barnett (1990). The current article provides a brief exposition of the construction of Barnett's (1980a) index-number-theoretic monetary aggregates, based on the Divisia index formula. It then applies them to consideration of the degree of tightness of monetary policy from November 1979 to August 1982.

The Federal Reserve officially changed its operating procedures on October 6, 1979, by replacing the federal funds rate with nonborrowed bank reserves as the instrument of policy. The new instrument was to be used for targeting monetary growth rather than interest rates. The Federal Reserve thereby embarked on an experiment in monetarist policy designed to control the money supply and to permit interest rates to be determined, free of control, in the money markets. On October 9, 1982, Federal Reserve policy appeared to change again, as announced by Volcker (1982). General agreement does not yet exist on what the objectives and targets of monetary policy have been since that date. As a result, the monetary data from November 1979 to August 1982 are of particular importance.

In this article I compare the growth rates of the new Divisia monetary aggregates with those of the corresponding officially targeted simple sum aggregates from November 1979 to August 1982. I find that monetary policy during that period was considerably tighter and also more variable than the Federal Reserve Board thought, if the Board's views on monetary tightness were based on the official simple sum monetary aggregates.

---

[1] Following the original publication of this paper, the St. Louis Federal Reserve Bank began computing and supplying high quality Divisia monetary aggregate data. Regarding that source, see the appendix to the book.

2 The Tightness of Money

In virtually all widely held economic theories, the money supply appears in the economy's structure. The need to measure the money supply, therefore, exists within all such economic paradigms. It is well known in aggregation theory that aggregation by simple summation is valid only when aggregating over goods that are perfect substitutes. In other words, one can add apples and apples, but not apples and oranges. But the official monetary quantity indexes aggregate by summation over assets that are poor substitutes. In addition, at increasingly higher levels of aggregation (i.e., rising from M1 to M2 to M3), increasingly poor substitutes for pure money are incorporated into the monetary aggregates. As a result, the quality of the official simple sum aggregates deteriorates rapidly at higher levels of aggregation. In fact the simple sum M1 aggregate is the only official monetary aggregate whose behavior even remotely approximates that of a well-designed index number (see, e.g., Barnett, Offenbacher, and Spindt 1984). (See also Barnett and Spindt 1979, Barnett 1980b, 1981a, 1983a, b, 1990; Barnett, Offenbacher, and Spindt 1981; and Barnett, Spindt, and Offenbacher 1981). The ongoing deregulation of monetary assets is likely to result in an increased number of nearly equal market yields on some monetary assets. Since those assets will become close substitutes, simple sum subaggregation over such assets will result in less error than at present. With currency providing no yield, however, simple sum aggregation over any of the complete aggregates — M1, M2, or M3 — will become no better than at present. In fact deregulation will improve the quality of the Divisia aggregates by eliminating the need to impute implicit rates of return to regulated assets, such as demand deposits. Those yields appear in the Divisia weights.

Since the late 1950's, there has been increasing recognition of the importance of the growing array of new substitutes for money, such as passbook accounts at savings and loan associations and money market funds. During the past few years, the growth of that array has become dramatic, as a result of the introduction of money market deposit accounts, NOW accounts, and super-NOW accounts. A large number of monetary assets contribute, in varying degrees, to the economy's liquidity. As a result, the economy's monetary service flow cannot be measured reliably without the construction of a properly weighted quantity index number aggregating over all (or most) assets contributing to the economy's monetary service flow.

3 Statistical Index Number Theory

Statistical index number theory is now a highly developed field that provides easily implemented, well understood, and reliable means of constructing quantity and price aggregates over components whenever the prices and quantities of the components are known. Diewert (1976) unified economic aggregation theory with statistical index number theory, and Barnett (1980a) established the linkage between monetary theory and economic aggregation theory. As a result, the literature on statistical quantity index numbers is immediately applicable to monetary aggregation.

During period t let $\mathbf{q}_t$ be the vector of quantities consumed of the component goods over which we seek to aggregate, and let $\mathbf{p}_t$ be the corresponding vector of goods prices. Then a (chained) statistical index number is a function $f(\mathbf{p}_t, \mathbf{q}_t, \mathbf{p}_{t-1}, \mathbf{q}_{t-1})$ of current and lagged quantities and prices. If we seek a statistical price index, then we seek a function f such that $f(\mathbf{p}_t, \mathbf{q}_t, \mathbf{p}_{t-1}, \mathbf{q}_{t-1})$ can serve satisfactorily as the ratio of the correct price aggregate $P(\mathbf{p}_t)$ between periods t and $t-1$. That is, we wish to be able to use $f(\mathbf{p}_t, \mathbf{q}_t, \mathbf{p}_{t-1}, \mathbf{q}_{t-1})$ to approximate $P(\mathbf{p}_t)/P(\mathbf{p}_{t-1})$. If we seek a statistical quantity index, then we seek to find f such that $f(\mathbf{p}_t, \mathbf{q}_t, \mathbf{p}_{t-1}, \mathbf{q}_{t-1})$ can approximate $Q(\mathbf{q}_t)/Q(\mathbf{q}_{t-1})$, where $Q(\mathbf{q}_t)$ is the correct quantity aggregate.

The derivations of the exact economic quantity and price aggregates, $Q(\mathbf{q}_t)$ and $P(\mathbf{p}_t)$, respectively, are the subject of economic aggregation theory, which provides conditions for existence of a true economic aggregate. Statistical index number theory then provides estimators of the unknown exact aggregates of economic aggregation theory. The existence conditions in economic aggregation theory are factorability conditions (blockwise homogeneous weak separability), which permit the economy's structure to be written as a composite function of the quantity aggregator function Q. Given Q, the price aggregator function P is immediately available from economic duality theory. Since statistical index number theory, rather than economic aggregation theory, is the subject of this article, I will not discuss at length the sophisticated microeconomic theory on which economic aggregation theory is based. The fundamental theorem of economic aggregation theory, however, was presented as Theorem 4 in Green (1964), and the application of that theorem to monetary theory is contained in Barnett (1980a, 1982a) (see also Section 4).

It may appear to be paradoxical that f contains both prices and quantities as arguments, whereas P contains only prices and Q only quantities. The reason is that both P and Q also contain unknown parameters, whereas f does not. So the cost of using a nonparametric approach in index number theory is the need to use prices and quantities jointly as arguments of f, regardless of whether we seek to approximate $P(\mathbf{p}_t)/P(\mathbf{p}_{t-1})$ or $Q(\mathbf{q}_t)/Q(\mathbf{q}_{t-1})$.

The classical literature on statistical index numbers sought to classify various functions f in terms of their properties. To that end, good and bad properties were defined. For example, any commodity price or quantity aggregate should be linearly homogeneous. That is, if all component prices (or quantities) increase by the same percentage, then the price (or quantity) index should increase by that same percentage. Index number formulas f were then ranked in terms of the number of good and bad properties they possessed. The most famous book in that literature was Fisher's (1922), which extensively ranked hundreds of index numbers relative to their properties.

Two of Fisher's many good properties and both of his bad properties have become particularly famous. His two best-known good properties are the factor reversal test and the circularity test. The factor reversal test says that the product of the price and quantity indexes of an aggregated good should equal actual expenditure on the component goods. The circulatory test requires path independence of the index. Fisher defined only two bad properties — bias and freakishness. Suffice it to say that of the hundreds of index numbers classified by Fisher, only one had both bad properties. That index was the simple sum (or simple arithmetic) index. In fact Fisher virtually equated the two bad properties with the simple arithmetic index, saying, "There are two objections to ... the simple arithmetic, viz.: (1) that it is 'simple,' and (2) that it is arithmetic! ... that it is at once freakish and biased" (1922, p. 363). Fisher concluded that the simple sum index "produces one of the very worst of index numbers, and if this book has no other effect than to lead to the total abandonment of the simple arithmetic type of index number, it will have served a useful purpose" (1922, p. 29).

Prior to the publication of Fisher's book, most British economic data series were computed and published by the popular press rather than the government. All of those data series were computed as simple sums (or arithmetic averages). In the case of the British cost of living index, Fisher determined that "the bias alone reaches 36 percent!" (1922, p. 363).[2] Although Fisher found the simple sum index to be the worst known index number formula, the index that he found to be the best, in the sense of possessing the largest number of good statistical properties, has now become known as the Fisher ideal index. Another index found to possess a very large number of good properties was the Törnqvist discrete time approximation to the Divisia index. That index is commonly called the Törnqvist index or simply the Divisia index (in discrete time). I will use the latter term.

Let m_{it} be the quantity of the ith good (or asset) during period t, and let π_{it} be the price (or user cost or rental rate for a durable good or asset)

---

[2] For corrections to inaccurate representations in this paper about Fisher's statements regarding the simpls sum index, see footnotes 68 and 69 in chapter 2 of this book.

of that good during period t. Then the Fisher ideal index during period t is Q_t^F, where

$$Q_t^F = Q_{t-1}^F \left[\frac{\left(\sum_{i=1}^N \pi_{it} m_{it}\right)\left(\sum_{i=1}^N \pi_{i,t-1} m_{it}\right)}{\left(\sum_{i=1}^N \pi_{it} m_{i,t-1}\right)\left(\sum_{i=1}^N \pi_{i,t-1} m_{i,t-1}\right)} \right]^{1/2}. \qquad (1)$$

The Divisia index during period t is Q_t^D, where

$$Q_t^D = Q_{t-1}^D \prod_{i=1}^N \left(\frac{m_{it}}{m_{i,t-1}}\right)^{(1/2)(s_{it}+s_{i,t-1})}, \qquad (2)$$

with $s_{it} = \pi_{it} m_{it} / \sum_{k=1}^N \pi_{kt} m_{kt}$. Taking logarithms of each side, observe that

$$\log Q_t^D - \log Q_{t-1}^D = \sum_{i=1}^N s_{it}^* (\log m_{it} - \log m_{i,t-1}), \qquad (3)$$

where $s_{it}^* = \frac{1}{2}(s_{it} + s_{i,t-1})$, so the growth rate (log change) of the aggregate is the share-weighted average of the growth rates of the component quantities.

The primary advantage of the Fisher ideal index over the Divisia index is that the Fisher ideal index satisfies Fisher's factor reversal test, whereas the Divisia index fails that test. The magnitude of the error, however, is small (third order in the changes), and the Divisia index has the large advantage of possessing the easily interpreted functional form (3). The Fisher ideal index is a complicated geometric mean of two weighted averages; therefore, changes in the Fisher ideal index can be difficult to explain to policymakers and difficult to trace to underlying changes in individual components. As a result, the Divisia index, as a means of aggregating over quantities, has long been the most widely used statistical index number.

Another approach to the evaluation of statistical index number formulas is the information theoretic approach. The concept of Shannon information (from engineering) and the related concept of entropy (from physics) have produced large literatures in economics and statistics. Theil (1967) showed that the Divisia price and quantity indexes are naturally produced as the aggregation formulas in information theory.

4 Economic Aggregation Theory

Historically the literature on aggregation in economics was developed independently of the literature on statistical index number theory. Economic aggregation theory was related to estimation of economic theory's 'exact' aggregates, derived from utility and production functions. Economic aggregation theorists' views of statistical index number theory have not always been favorable. Green (1964) dismissed statistical (or 'atomistic') index number theory in his book on economic aggregation theory with the following brief statement:

> "The 'atomistic' approach, concerned with the satisfaction of 'chain' tests, 'base-reversal' tests and the like, is familiar from the work of Fisher (1922) and the statistics text books. Such analyses are not firmly based on economic theory; the same may be said of the celebrated Divisia indices (1925–6)." (p. 57)

Diewert (1976), however, succeeded in unifying economic aggregation theory and statistical index number theory. He identified a class of statistical index numbers, called *superlative* index numbers, that simultaneously possess good statistical properties (as defined by Fisher 1922) and always provide high quality (second order in the changes) approximations to the unknown exact aggregates of economic theory. Because all elements of the superlative class provide high quality approximations to the unique exact aggregate of economic theory, they also closely approximate each other. The choice among elements of the class can frequently be viewed as arbitrary, since they all usually move in close concert. The Divisia and Fisher ideal indexes are both in the superlative class.

In brief, the long statistical and economic literatures on aggregation have converged on the superlative class of index numbers, and the nearly interchangeable Fisher ideal and Divisia elements of that class now dominate the literature on index numbers. An excellent survey of the state of the art in index number theory is Diewert (1980); see also Barnett (1982b).

5 Monetary Aggregation

It has long been recognized that all components of the monetary aggregates do not contribute to the same degree to the economy's monetary service flow. Monetary services are defined to be the services valued in the asset holder's utility (or production) function. Since the yield paid by the asset appears in the budget constraint (or profit function) but not in the utility (or production) function, the asset's investment rate of return is not a monetary service. (See Barnett 1980a for the relevant formal model.) Clearly a dollar of currency provides far more monetary (transactions) services than a dollar of Series E bonds. Such observations motivated the construction of numerous ad hoc weighting schemes in monetary aggregation, such as weighting by bid-ask spreads, turnover rates, price variances, and denomination size. The research on such approaches did not, however, converge to any uniquely acceptable alternative to simple sum aggregation, because an infinite number of such potential ad hoc weighting schemes exist. (For a survey of much of that literature, see Barnett 1990.) In fact even with any single one of those vectors of weights, such as turnover rate weights, an infinite number of potential weighted aggregates exist. For example, the turnover rate weights could be applied linearly to levels or growth rates or geometrically to either. Furthermore, statistical index number theory is of no use in such selections because the functions f in index number theory contain only quantities and prices. The introduction of turnover rates, velocities, and so forth into f immediately renders the entire literature on index number and aggregation theory irrelevant. In short, ad hoc weighting schemes in monetary aggregation lead nowhere.

By contrast, the current preference for the Divisia index in the index number and aggregation theory literatures is far from arbitrary but, rather, is based on statistical theory, information theory, approximation theory, revealed preference theory, and neoclassical microeconomic theory. With Barnett's (1978, 1980a) derivation of the formula for the (user cost or rental) price of the services of a monetary asset, the values of π_{it} ($i = 1, \ldots, N$) became computable. The Divisia index from (2) or (3) then became available for aggregating directly over monetary asset growth rates. The Federal Reserve Board recently released the back data on the resulting Divisia monetary aggregates (see Barnett and Spindt 1982).

Figures 1 and 2 present the growth rates of Divisia and simple sum M2 and M3 from November 1979 to November 1982. (M1 contains currency, traveler's checks, demand deposits, and other checkable deposits. M2 contains M1, overnight repurchase agreements and Eurodollars, money market mutual fund balances, money market deposit accounts, and savings and small time deposits. M3 contains M2, large time deposits, term repurchase agreements, and institution-only money market mutual fund balances.) I included data for the three months following the sample period because it is not clear whether the change in policy announced by Volcker (1982) took effect instantaneously or was phased in over a few months.

I have not included graphs of M1 because the sample period preceded the recent secular decline of the growth rate of Divisia M1 to below that of simple sum M1. I believe that the real usefulness of Divisia M1 is just beginning, since NOW and super-NOW accounts have only recently become widely available. In addition, when computed as properly constructed Divisia aggregates, M2 and M3 are more useful than M1 (see Barnett 1982a). Nevertheless, it may be worth observing that although Divisia and simple sum M1 did not diverge greatly before August 1982, Cagan (1982) found Divisia

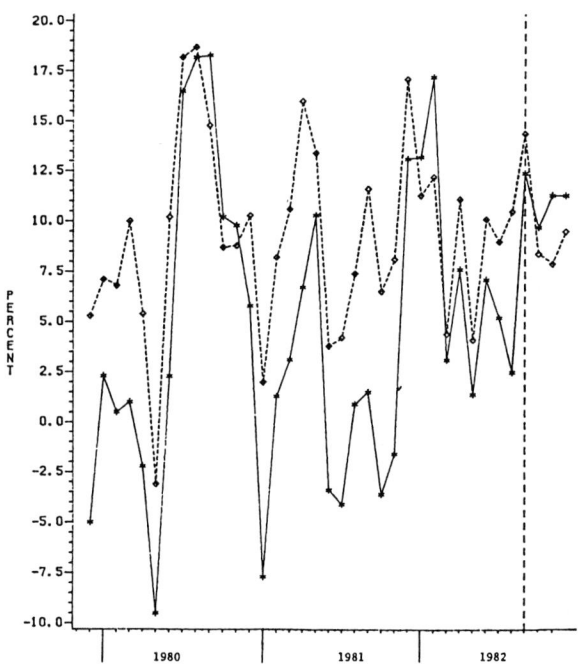

Figure 1: Annual rate of growth of M2. Montly data from November 1979 – November 1982 are seasonally adjusted. The diamonds connected by dashed lines designate the simple sum M2 growth rate; the asterisks connected by solid lines designate the Divisia M2 growth rate. The last three months of data are viewed as post-sample-period data and are plotted to the right of the vertical dashed line.

M1 preferable to simple sum M1 even before August 1982.

I used only publicly available sources (the updated data from Barnett and Spindt 1982) to assure that conclusions could be readily verified. Within the Federal Reserve System, however, there have been some recent minor data revisions that have slightly altered those aggregates. Table 1 contains the aggregates based on the most recent data available from the Federal Reserve Board. Although not discussed in this article, Table 1 is provided for reference purposes. It contains simple sum and Divisia M1, M2, and M3. The data date from January 1979, well before the beginning of our sample period, and extend up to the latest month available at the time of this writing. During the sample period of November 1979–August 1982, the conclusions of this article would be the same whether drawn from either Table 1 or Figures 1 and 2.

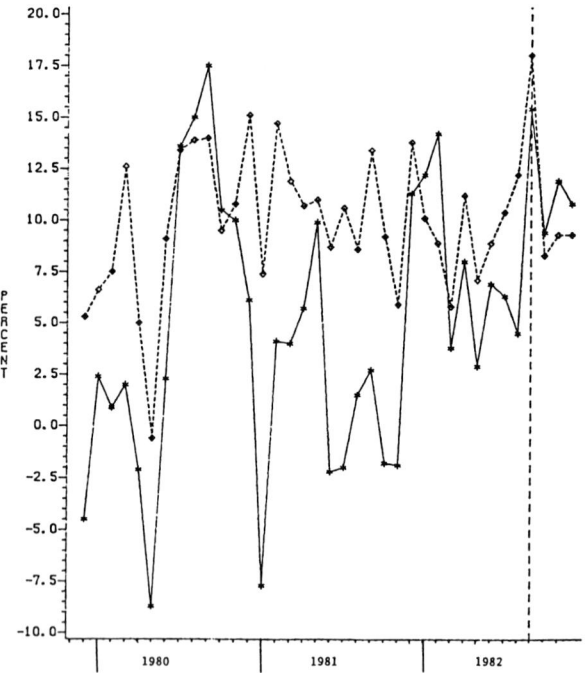

Figure 2: Annual rate of growth of M3. Monthly data from November 1979 – November 1982 are seasonally adjusted. The diamonds connected by dashed lines designate the simple sum M3 growth rate; the asterisks connected by solid lines designate the Divisia M3 growth rate. The last three months of data are viewed as post-sample-period data and are plotted to the right of the vertical dashed line.

Summary statistics based on the first- and second-order sample moments are provided in Table 2. The data used in constructing Table 2 are those displayed in Figures 1 and 2. Inspection of Figures 1 and 2 and of the summary statistics in Table 1 suggests that Federal Reserve policy during the sample period, as judged by the behavior of the official simple sum aggregates, did not appear unreasonable. The average growth rates of simple sum M2 and M3 were 9.3% and 10.0%, respectively. By those measures, monetary policy did not appear to have been particularly tight. With an inflation rate in the 10%–12% range, the policy appears moderately disinflationary. In fact it is surprising that such a severe recession could have been experienced during a period of such disinflationary gradualism. There is, however, some degree of controversy regarding the actual degree of severity of that recession. See Brunner (1983), who argued that the recession was less severe than it is frequently stated to have been.

TABLE 1
REVISED ANNUAL RATES OF GROWTH OF MONETARY AGGREGATES

Year and Month	M1		M2		M3	
	Divisia	Simple Sum	Divisia	Simple Sum	Divisia	Simple Sum
1979						
January	2.8	1.4	−2.7	4.6	−2.3	5.8
February	2.4	4.6	−.8	7.0	−.2	8.7
March	6.9	9.3	3.5	9.4	3.9	9.9
April	10.9	12.3	2.4	8.7	2.8	8.4
May	11.7	4.5	4.9	7.5	5.5	8.5
June	14.6	15.3	10.1	12.8	10.0	11.8
July	11.7	12.6	6.6	10.0	7.0	10.9
August	7.2	6.7	6.7	10.9	7.2	12.6
September	5.5	6.5	2.6	9.3	3.9	13.6
October	1.6	1.3	−4.7	3.0	−3.7	6.5
November	0.0	.4	−6.5	2.2	−6.4	1.3
December	4.7	7.6	−.6	5.2	−.3	5.2
1980						
January	8.3	7.4	.2	5.9	.6	6.2
February	10.0	12.7	2.8	11.7	3.7	13.2
March	2.2	−2.0	−3.2	5.7	−2.5	6.9
April	−13.1	−24.1	−15.7	−6.3	−14.4	−2.6
May	7.0	6.3	2.8	9.2	3.2	10.2
June	12.5	15.9	16.9	16.8	14.0	14.0
July	14.0	14.8	18.8	16.6	16.5	14.1
August	18.8	21.0	19.2	15.7	18.8	15.6
September	15.7	16.0	12.4	10.7	11.6	10.3
October	11.9	10.0	7.2	7.4	7.7	9.5
November	6.3	4.1	4.1	8.9	5.0	11.9
December	−6.1	−7.4	−11.1	−.2	−8.6	6.5
1981						
January	20.2	7.5	−1.5	5.8	.7	11.8
February	10.1	9.3	2.0	10.2	3.0	11.9
March	5.3	13.0	2.9	14.3	2.8	12.3
April	11.5	14.7	6.1	10.4	6.1	9.5
May	4.6	0.0	0.0	5.2	1.0	9.1
June	4.0	.5	1.6	8.5	3.1	12.4
July	4.8	5.8	3.8	10.2	5.0	12.5
August	1.7	5.2	1.8	14.6	3.1	15.8
September	0.0	−0.1	−2.0	7.0	−.3	9.9
October	2.0	−.5	−3.1	8.2	−2.4	8.1
November	12.0	7.0	10.3	11.4	10.5	12.1
December	15.5	12.9	11.5	9.6	11.4	10.0

TABLE 1 cont'd

Year and Month	M1 Divisia	M1 Simple Sum	M2 Divisia	M2 Simple Sum	M3 Divisia	M3 Simple Sum
1982						
January	17.5	19.4	13.8	10.1	11.6	7.7
February	5.8	.6	2.8	3.8	3.6	5.4
March	3.4	1.7	4.6	8.6	5.8	10.5
April	2.2	1.8	1.4	4.1	2.9	7.1
May	8.0	8.1	7.1	10.1	6.9	8.9
June	3.0	2.7	5.2	9.0	6.3	10.4
July	2.3	2.8	2.5	10.5	4.5	12.2
August	9.4	10.3	12.4	14.4	15.4	18.0
September	11.8	12.8	9.7	8.4	9.4	8.3
October	14.0	14.2	11.3	7.9	11.9	9.3
November	13.7	13.5	11.3	9.5	10.8	9.3
December	10.5	10.5	2.7	8.9	−.4	3.7
1983						
January	6.2	9.9	−4.2	30.6	−13.6	12.9
February	14.8	22.1	10.7	24.1	3.9	13.6
March	11.3	15.7	7.1	11.2	5.1	8.2
April	−4.0	−2.6	−.1	2.9	1.1	4.3
May	21.5	26.0	13.4	13.2	11.8	11.3

NOTE: All growth rates are percentage growth rates and are seasonally adjusted.

TABLE 2
SAMPLE MOMENTS OF REPORTED ANNUAL RATES OF GROWTH OF MONETARY AGGREGATES

Moment	Sample Period[a] Mean	Sample Period[a] Standard Deviation	Sample Plus Postsample Period[b] Mean	Sample Plus Postsample Period[b] Standard Deviation
Divisia M2	4.5	7.4	5.0	7.3
Simple Sum M2	9.3	4.8	9.3	4.6
Divisia M3	4.8	6.7	5.3	6.6
Simple Sum M3	10.0	3.6	9.9	3.5

[a] Monthly data on annual monetary growth rates from November 1979 to August 1982.
[b] Monthly data on annual monetary growth rates from November 1979 to November 1982.

The Divisia monetary aggregates, however, tell a very different story. The average growth rates of the Divisia aggregates were about half those of the corresponding simple sum aggregates, with the average growth rates of Divisia M2 and M3 being 4.5% and 4.8%, respectively. Comparing those results with the 10%–12% inflation rate reveals that the rate of growth of real monetary services was strongly negative. Monetary policy, as measured by the Divisia aggregates, was also much more volatile than was suggested by the simple sum aggregates. As Table 2 shows, the coefficients of variation for the Divisia aggregates were more than three times those of the corresponding simple sum aggregates. Inspection of Figures 1 and 2, however, suggests that volatility steadily declined during the sample period.

The three months of post-sample-period data would not materially alter the conclusions, as can be seen from the last three data points on Figures 1 and 2 and from the last four columns of Table 2.

6 Conclusions

Monetary policy during the sample period induced slower and more volatile monetary growth than was indicated by the official simple sum aggregates. It is interesting to observe, however, that both the tightness and volatility of monetary policy appeared to be steadily decreasing during the sample period, as suggested by inspection of the paths followed by the Divisia aggregates in Figures 1 and 2. Because monetary policy, as indicated by the Divisia monetary aggregates, was tighter than indicated by the official aggregates, our results provide an illustration of how inattention to well-established statistical theory can lead to policymaking that may be less effective than it might be.

At a given level of aggregation, both the simple sum and Divisia indexes are estimators of the same economic quantity aggregate, $Q(\mathbf{q}_t)$. The Divisia quantity index is known to possess very small error. In fact that error is typically less than the roundoff error with monetary data (see Barnett 1980a). As a result, the growth rates of the official simple sum M2 and M3 monetary aggregates were upwardly biased during the sample period and provided a deceptively high measure of the rate of growth of the corresponding exact economic monetary aggregate, $Q(\mathbf{q}_t)$. Monetary policy was tighter, as defined by the growth rate of $Q(\mathbf{q}_t)$ and measured by the growth rate of the Divisia index, than was indicated by the growth rate of the corresponding simple sum index in the cases of M2 and M3.

These conclusions should be qualified in two manners. The Federal Reserve Board was using multiple monetary targets (M1, M2, and M3) during the sample period. The conclusions are based on only two (M2 and M3) of the three, although M1 also played an important role in policy during that period. Nevertheless, consideration of M1 would not have affected our conclusions about the direction of the net indicator bias because no offsetting bias existed at the M1 level of aggregation. As can be seen from Table 1, the growth rate of simple sum M1 was not downwardly biased relative to the growth rate of Divisia M1. Although the direction of the net indicator bias is unambiguous, the magnitude of the effect on policy of the index number errors cannot be determined when multiple targets exist.

Another qualification concerns the distinction between stocks and flows. The Divisia monetary aggregates measure the flow of services produced by the component assets. The official simple sum aggregates measure the accounting stock. The elementary structural variables of economic theory are flows, not stocks, and accounting stocks in particular play no role in mainstream economic theory. Occasionally, however, the economic (rather than accounting) stock appears in economic theory. The nominal economic stock, often treated as proportional to the service flow, is the discounted present value of expected expenditure on the expected service flow from the current period through the lifetime of the component assets. Since those service flows are properly measured by the corresponding Divisia aggregates, the nominal stock is derived from a sequence of expected Divisia aggregates (and their dual user cost aggregates), and not from the accounting stock. In addition, if the expected service flow is constant over time, it can be proved that the nominal economic stock is proportional to the current Divisia monetary aggregate, although the proportionality factor, depending on the component user cost prices (which depend on interest rates), need not be constant (see, e.g., Barnett 1990).[3] The Divisia monetary aggregates, not the official simple sum aggregates, remain relevant.

The sort of analysis provided in this article is common in statistical index number theory. For example, policies and contracts indexed (or adjusted) by the Labor Department's consumer price index (CPI) or the Commerce Department's implicit price deflator (IPD), are known to produce policy errors or economic distortions because the CPI is a Laspeyres index, which is known to be upwardly biased, and the IPD is a Paasche index, which is known to be downwardly biased. The sign of the error with a simple sum index, whether used to aggregate over quantities or prices, is not always the same, but its magnitude is first order. The sign of the error with a Laspeyres or Paasche index is known in advance, but its magnitude is second order. The sign of the error with a Fisher ideal or Divisia index is not always the same, but its magnitude is third order. In short, the error with the simple sum monetary aggregates, as statistical quantity index numbers, is of variable sign but potentially of much larger magnitude than that for the CPI or IPD, as price indexes. The results given in this article illustrate that elementary fact from statistical index number theory and suggest the likely effect on monetary policy during the sample period.

---

[3]Barnett (1990) is reprinted in this book as chapter 14.

Chapter 24

Which Road Leads to Stable Money Demand?

*William A. Barnett**

1 The Broken Road

1.1 September 26, 1983

The date September 26, 1983 is of unusual significance to the field of monetary economics. The now widespread views on the 'instability of money demand' find their origins in a conspicuous error made on that day. On that day, *Newsweek* magazine published on p. 84 a misguided full page article that has dramatically altered the way in which the public, the press, and the economics profession look at monetary data. The article contains a photograph of its author and a title, 'A Case of Bad Good News.' At the center of the page is a highlighted statement in bold print stating: 'The monetary explosion leaves no satisfactory way out of our present situation.' The author explains in further detail within his article:

> "The monetary explosion from July 1982 to July 1983 leaves no satisfactory way out of our present situation. The Fed's stepping on the brakes will appear to have no immediate effect. Rapid recovery will continue under the impetus of earlier monetary growth. With its historical shortsightedness, the Fed will be tempted to step still harder on the brake — just as the failure of rapid monetary growth in late 1982 to generate immediate recovery led it to keep its collective foot on the accelerator much too long. The result is bound to be renewed stagflation — recession accompanied by rising inflation and high interest rates... The only real uncertainty is when the recession will begin."

The author of that article was Milton Friedman. Others who identified themselves as 'monetarists' at the time sounded the same alarm. The recession never came. 'Monetarism' has never recovered. While stability of

---

*Originally published in *The Economic Journal* 107 (1997), 1171-1185.

money demand is necessary but not sufficient for the 'monetarist' view, the damaged monetarist policy position was equated in the minds of many academic researchers with the view that the money demand function had 'broken down.'

The favored monetary aggregate among monetarists at that time, including especially Friedman, was simple sum M2. In retrospect, it is interesting to ask whether subsequent retroactive revisions in the Federal Reserve Board's simple sum monetary aggregate can shed any new light on the source of Friedman's September 26, 1983 public forecast error. The most recent such revision appears in a Federal Reserve Board staff working paper by Whitesell and Collins (1996), in which they provide plots of the old M2 and a revised simple sum M2 over the period of 1980–1987. Their paper displays the same immense spike in late 1982 and early 1983, as with the earlier unrevised series. The growth rate spike jumps from under 10% to over 30% and then back down again.

The monetarist view of the time was that a surge in inflation was unavoidably on the way, as the inflationary shock worked its way through the economy, and a subsequent recession produced by a Federal Reserve contractionary 'overreaction' was also unavoidable. The prediction of an unavoidable eventual recession is very much 'monetarist' and was therefore controversial among nonmonetarists, but the forecast of inflation seemed undeniable. Under virtually every view in macroeconomics, a correlation between money growth and neutral or near-neutral changes in nominal variables is predicted. Hence that aspect of Friedman's prediction should concern everyone.

There are only two possible conclusions: either money growth has no effect on prices, and hence all macroeconomic theory is wrong, or simple sum M2 is a terribly defective measure of monetary service flow.

1.2 September 26, 1983 Once Again

September 26, 1983 was indeed a significant date in the history of economic thought. But there is another reason to remember that day. On precisely that same day, another article appeared in a magazine with a public 'on the record' forecast by an economist, a photograph of that economist, and a boldface article title. The title of that article was 'What Explosion?' The article, which appeared on p. 196 of *Forbes* magazine on that day explains further

> "that people have been panicking unnecessarily about money supply growth this year. The new bank money funds and the super NOW accounts have been sucking in money that was formerly held in other forms, and other types of asset shuffling also have

occurred. But the Divisia aggregates are rising at a rate not much different from last year's... the 'apparent explosion' can be viewed as a statistical blip."

Yes, you have guessed it. The subject of the article was the Divisia monetary aggregates, which I had developed and advocated in earlier work, and which were the basis for my statements to *Forbes* magazine. A controlled 'experiment' of this sort is rare in the field of economics. Friedman and I went on the record on the exact same day with the dramatically different forecasts implied by the two different methods of monetary aggregation.[1]

While those magazine articles were both about M2, an even more enlightening illustration is now available from comparison of simple sum M2 with Divisia L, where L is the broadest monetary aggregate made available by the Federal Reserve System. As has been emphasized by Poterba and Rotemberg (1987) and Rotemberg et al.(1995), properly weighted monetary aggregates are most informative, when computed at the broadest level of aggregation, since such aggregates capture the contribution of all monetary assets to the economy's monetary service flow. On the other hand, simple sum aggregates deteriorate in quality as the level of aggregation increases, since growing amounts of nonmonetary services are included in those unweighted aggregates as distant substitutes for money are introduced into the aggregate. While the broadest simple sum monetary aggregates therefore have never been influential, and were not advocated by monetarists, we have no reason to exclude properly weighted distant substitutes for money in a Divisia monetary aggregate. In Figure 1, I provide plots of both simple sum M2 and Divisia L from the recently available new data made available online by the Federal Reserve Bank of St. Louis. The simple sum M2 giant spike is conspicuous, although Divisia L evidences no spike at all.[2]

It is unfortunate and perhaps puzzling that Milton Friedman's name has become attached to this dramatic failure of the simple sum monetary aggregates, since Friedman and Schwartz (1970, pp. 151–152) were among the

---

[1]The source of the spike in simple sum M2 is well known. Following the passage of the Depository Institution Deregulation and Monetary Control Act of 1980, money market deposit accounts (MMDAs) and super-NOW accounts were authorized in December 1982. The Divisia index or any other index produced from index number theory introduces new goods through a procedure explained by Diewert (1980a). Since the interest rates on MMDAs and super-NOWs were high at their introduction, their user cost prices (foregone interest) were low, and they were introduced smoothly with initially low weight, especially in the broadest aggregates, such as L. But MMDAs and super-NOWs were added directly into the simple sum monetary aggregates, which treat all included assets as perfect substitutes. For a history of the evolution of the official monetary aggregates and their components, see Anderson and Kavajecz (1994).

[2]Observe that Figure 1 plots monthly growth rates. The implied annualized growth rate at the peak of the simple sum spike exceeded 30% per year.

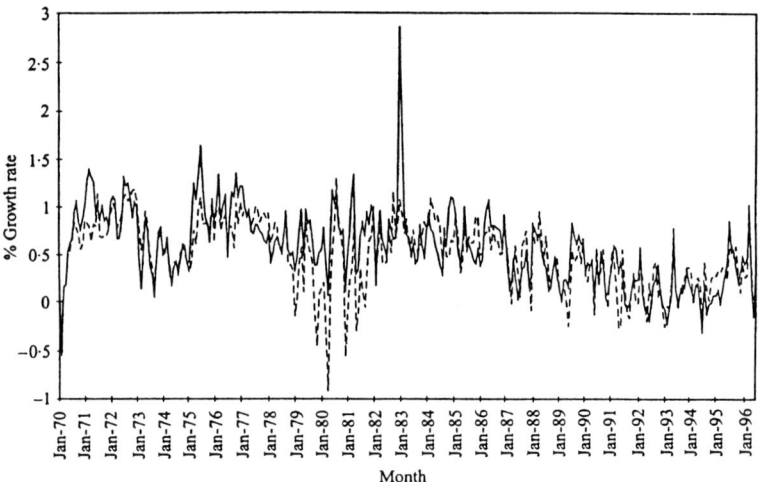

Figure 1: Monthly percentage growth rates of simple sum M2 (—) and Divisia L (- - -).

first to recognize the need for properly weighted monetary aggregates, and in recent tests of blockwise weak separability, Swofford (1995) has shown that Friedman and Schwartz's preferences in monetary component groupings were unusually astute.[3] In addition, the views contained in Friedman's *Newsweek* article were widely shared by the monetarists of the time. Rather than being too critical of the central bank, the monetarists were perhaps too trusting of the Federal Reserve, since the monetarists uncritically based their conclusions on data published by the Federal Reserve.

The direction in which monetary economists, the press, central banks, and public policy have moved since September 26, 1983 might have been very different, if the readership of *Forbes* exceeded the readership of *Newsweek*, rather than vice versa.

1.3 The 'Monetarist Experiment' of November 1979 to August 1982

It is perhaps worth asking why the field was so vulnerable and so fragile in 1983. While Friedman's forecast error was indeed conspicuous and created a disturbing anomaly to believers in simple sum monetary aggregation, economists historically have had a healthy (if unscientific) 'sense of humor'

---

[3]In fact Friedman and Schwartz's advocacy of research on weighted monetary aggregates has been widely quoted, as in Barnett, Fisher, and Serletis (1992, p. 2092).

about forecasts. But in fact the September 26, 1983 failure followed shortly after another serious blow to 'monetarism' and to advocates of stable simple sum money demand equations: the three year 'monetarist experiment' period of November 1979-August 1982. That experiment resulted in a serious recession, despite the fact that the behavior of the simple sum monetary aggregates during the period indicate an intent by the Federal Reserve to produce a gradual disinflation rather than a severe disinflationary shock.

I was on the staff of the Federal Reserve Board in Washington, DC from July 1973 to December 1981. As a result, I had more than average exposure to what led up to the 'monetarist experiment,' and I was a personal witness to many of the activities at the Federal Reserve during most of that period. Without unnecessarily getting into the controversies about what happened at the Federal Reserve during the 'experiment,' I do wish to observe that the data itself tells a very enlightening story, and it is that message from the data, rather than personal anecdotal information, that I shall discuss below.

As I reported in Barnett (1984), the growth rate of simple sum M2 during the period of the 'monetarist experiment' averaged 9.3%, while the growth rate of Divisia M2 during the period averaged 4.5%. Similarly the growth rate of simple sum M3 during the period averaged 10%, while the growth rate of Divisia M3 during the period averaged 4.8%. This period followed double digit growth rates of all simple sum and Divisia monetary aggregates. In short, believers in simple sum monetary aggregation, who had been the advocates of the 'monetarist experiment,' were put in the embarrassing position of witnessing an outcome (the subsequent recession) that was inconsistent with the intent of the prescribed policy and with the behavior of the simple sum monetary aggregates during the period. This unwelcome and unexpected outcome rendered vulnerable those economists who advocated a policy based upon the assumption of a stable simple sum demand for money function.

Friedman's very visible forecast error on September 26, 1983 followed closely on the heels of the end of the monetarist experiment in August 1982 and the recession that it produced. The road buckled and collapsed below the monetarists and those who believed in stable simple sum demand for money functions. Those two associated groups have never recovered.[4]

But the recession that followed the monetarist experiment was no surprise to anyone who had followed the Divisia monetary aggregates, since those

---

[4]There were other earlier shocks to the beliefs of the faithful, such as the 'missing money' issue. Those earlier problems seemed to have had little effect on policy, and were viewed as fixable, although there were differences of opinion about the right choice of fix. The real damage was done in the early 1980s. Those interested in the message from the high road about the earlier 'paradoxes' of the 1970s can find much of the relevant literature surveyed in Barnett, Fisher, and Serletis (1992), which is reprinted in this book as chapter 18.

aggregates indicated that a severe deflationary shock had occurred. To those who were using data based upon valid index number and aggregation theory, rather than the obsolete simple sum monetary aggregates, the road remained smooth — no bumps, no breaks. Nothing unexpected had happened.

2 The Low Road

2.1 Where is the Low Road?

The two dramatic failures of simple sum money demand theory set the stage for the 'controversy' that is the subject of the exchange in this issue of the *Economic Journal*. Badly shaken by the two failures in the early 1980s, monetary economists had two choices of roads to follow: the high road or the low road. Along the high road there were no paradoxes, no puzzles, no unexplained instabilities. There was, however, a very deep and difficult research agenda ahead, if the quality of monetary economics research was to be raised to a level consistent with principles accepted in other areas of economic research, such as index number and aggregation theory — two of the most disturbingly challenging areas of economic research. The high road insists upon internal coherence among data, theory, and econometrics, and it is that internal consistency that *defines* the high road. As I shall argue below, internal coherence is conspicuously lacking in the empirical literature on money demand 'instability.'

Along the low road, researchers can play fast and loose with data, theory, and econometrics. Paradoxes, puzzles, and 'controversies' appear at every turn. Most empirical monetary economists took the low road. In most other areas of applied economics, including capital theory, labor economics, consumer demand systems modeling, production modeling, economic growth modeling, and agricultural economics, the profession chose the high road long ago, and has remained there.

Pointing fingers at the drivers who took the low road is perhaps not constructive, but it indeed is worthwhile to understand the nature of the low road, so that it can be recognized when encountered. For that reason, this section will concentrate primarily upon a description of the low road, rather than a discussion of individual papers or authors. The basic point to be made is that the low road research is filled with internal logical inconsistencies, to a degree that is perhaps unparalleled in any other area of applied economic research. For reasons that I prefer not to try to rationalize, the route from the broken road to the low road seemed more convenient to some than the route from the broken road to the high road.

2.2 The Price of Money

To make this as clear as possible, let us begin by assuming that the simple sum monetary aggregates, which are the subject of most of this research, are correct. Let us then determine how a model could be structured so that the research would be internally consistent and methodologically coherent. First let us consider the correct price that should be imputed to a simple sum quantity index. As is well known in index number theory, every quantity index has a dual price index, and *vice versa*. For example, Laspeyres quantity indexes and Paasche price indexes are dual. In fact much governmental data is produced from those dual pairs. The simple sum quantity index is a special case (equal coefficients) of the linear index, and the price dual to the linear quantity index is the Leontief price index.[5] If we then set the coefficients of the linear quantity index equal to each other, so that the quantity index becomes simple sum, the dual Leontief price index becomes the minimum price over the set of prices of component goods.

This result should not be surprising. Linear quantity aggregator functions, whether for consumers or firms, imply perfect substitutability among components. In the special case of equal coefficients within the linear aggregator function, the isoquants or indifference curves of the quantity aggregator function will be at 45 degree angles to the axes. The components will not only be perfect substitutes, but will be perfect substitutes in identical ratios. In short, they will be indistinguishable. Corner solutions will result. Only the lowest priced component of an aggregate will be held or consumed.

To produce that dual price index, we need now to determine how to measure the price of a component monetary asset. The derivation is in Barnett (1978,1980a). The price of the services of a monetary asset is the asset's user cost, which is its opportunity cost. The formula for the user cost is in terms of foregone interest. In discrete time, that discounted foregone interest formula in real terms is $\pi_{it} = (R_t - r_{it})/(1 + R_t)$, where r_{it} is the own rate of return on monetary asset i, and R_t is the rate of return on the benchmark asset, defined to be that asset which is held solely as an investment.[6] In continuous time, the denominator does not appear in the real user cost formula, which reduces to the rate differential $R_t - r_{it}$. We conclude that the correct price to impute to the simple sum monetary aggregate is $\pi_t = \min\{\pi_{it} : i = 1, \ldots, n\}$, where n is the number of monetary assets included in the aggregate.

---

[5] With a linear quantity aggregator function, there will be a corner solution. On the duality between the simple sum index and the Leontief index, see Diewert (1976, p. 21).

[6] The benchmark asset provides no services other than its investment rate of return, R_t. Multiplication by the true cost of living index, p_t, would convert to the nominal user cost $p_t \pi_{it}$. The denominator of the formula discounts to present value from the end of the period to the start of the period, since interest is paid at the end of the period.

2.3 Ancient History

Many decades ago, 'money' was defined to include only monetary assets that yielded no interest. Those component monetary assets were currency plus demand deposits, and demand deposits yielded no interest.[7] Since interest yield is not a monetary service, any asset that yielded interest was excluded from consideration as a monetary aggregate's component. In that long-gone world, $r_{it} = 0$ for all i. Hence $\pi_{it} = R_t$ for all i in continuous time, and thereby the price of the simple sum monetary aggregate was $\pi_t = \min\{\pi_{it} : i = 1, \ldots, n\} = R_t$. The correct price to insert into the right hand side of a money demand function was R_t, which was the opportunity cost of money and was 'the' interest rate of classical macroeconomic theory.[8]

As we see, once upon a time long ago, the use of simple sum aggregation to aggregate over assets that all had the same zero yield made sense, since under those circumstances of continually equal user cost prices, the implicit assumption of perfect substitutability among components was credible, and under those same circumstances the use of 'the' interest rate as the price of money indeed was correct, at least in continuous time. But that was long, long ago. Yet most of the literature on the 'unstable' demand for money function is based upon the assumed duality between the simple sum as quantity aggregate and 'the' interest rate as its dual price.

2.4 We All Are Suffering from Delusions

As argued above, the measurement and modeling methods used in the literature on 'unstable' money demand made good sense in the financial environment that existed a long time ago (well over 40 years ago). But let us assume that somehow these models still are correct in the current world. We then must reason through the implications of the model when in fact many monetary assets yield interest, and the interest yields are not the same on all component monetary assets.

Again simple sum quantity aggregator functions imply perfect substitutability of one unit of any component for one unit of any other component. But in reality the component assets' yields are not the same. Hence we must conclude that there is a corner solution with only the highest yielding asset remaining in existence. All other assets are dominated and hence have disappeared from existence. We may think that we have observed the existence of more than one monetary asset, but we are deluded. Furthermore for the

---

[7]Imputation of implicit rates of return to demand deposits had not yet become an issue.

[8]In discrete time this is not really correct, since then $\pi_t = R_t/(1 + R_t)$, when $r_{it} = 0$ for all i. Hence some of our discussion to follow will implicitly relate to continuous time modeling so that $\pi_t = R_t$. Otherwise an attempt to rationalize the low road research becomes even more difficult.

user cost price $\pi_{it} = R_t - r_{it}$ of the one non-dominated asset i to be R_t, that asset's own rate of return r_{it} must be zero. Hence the dominated assets, that have disappeared from existence, must have even lower rates of return. In short, their nominal rates of return must be negative.

Large literatures exist on demands for nonmonetary goods, such as automobiles, food, services, physical capital, and labor. In none of those areas would economists take seriously a conclusion of function instability based upon theory implying mass delusions among economists and the public, although monetary economists who use a simple sum monetary aggregate with an interest rate as its price are implicitly accepting precisely such a view.

2.5 Income and Velocity

An income variable exists, along with 'the' interest rate, in most of the papers claiming instability of money demand. Such an income variable also is needed to define velocity in those studies that concentrate on velocity rather than money demand. The variable that most commonly appears in those equations as income is gross national product. But GNP does not appear as the right hand side of anyone's budget constraint. In addition, GNP does not include user-cost-evaluated expenditure on the services of monetary assets. Hence the right hand side of the 'constraint' does not include part of the left hand side. To make sense, a demand function that has income on its right hand side must imply the existence of a constraint containing that income variable on the right hand side of the constraint. The measure of income used in those models is internally inconsistent with the rest of the model.[9]

2.6 Functional Form

The demand for money studies that report unstable demand for money functions use an erroneous measure of monetary services on the left hand side and erroneous measures of the price of money and income on the right hand side. None of the variables used in these studies connects in a valid manner

---

[9]There is implied a constraint of the form:
$$\sum_{i=1}^{n} \pi_{it} m_{it} + \sum_{i=1}^{n} p_{it} c_{it} = I_t,$$
where m_{it} is the component monetary asset having user cost price π_{it}, and the second term on the left hand side is expenditure on other goods and services relevant to the decision of the economic agent, while I_t is the constraining 'income' or total expenditure variable. But GNP (or GDP) includes some forms of expenditure that do not appear on the left hand side of that constraint, while GNP does not include $\sum_{i=1}^{n} \pi_{it} m_{it}$ at all.

with economic theory. In addition, little if any consideration is given to the nonlinear functional forms implied by demand theory.

The usual rationalization for ignoring the implications of economic theory for functional structure is the potential damage to economic theory produced by aggregation over economic agents. Here we have another internal contradiction. It has long been well known in aggregation theory that the absence of distribution effects implies the existence of a representative consumer, where absence of distribution effects means that only the first moment of the income distribution appears in demand functions. If only per capita income or total income appears in demand functions and not any second or higher order moments of the distribution, we get the existence of a representative consumer 'for free.'[10] No further assumptions are needed.[11] Hence, if we assume away distribution effects, as is very common in the literature on 'unstable' money demand, there can be no justification for not using representative agent theory, since the maintained assumption is sufficient for the existence of a representative agent.

2.7 Evaluation of the Low Road

The techniques currently being used in the low road literature are to be preferred to those methods used to produce the broken road discussed in Section 1 above. But the faults that caused the road to break in the earlier literature remain in the low road literature. The low road empirical literature is so contaminated by bad data and internally inconsistent logic as to be devoid of scientific merit. Faced by such a disturbing literature, I am less than surprised by the growing 'rebellion' of some real business cycle theorists against much of current econometrics.[12]

A small group of economists have taken a detour off of the low road to a very old unpaved road. They have sought to emphasize outside money, the base, total reserves, or nonborrowed reserves. Those variables undoubtedly

---

[10] Oddly, many of the low road studies of demand for money do not even convert to per capita terms, but instead model total demand for money in terms of total income.

[11] If we do not wish to accept the existence of a representative consumer — and there are good reasons to be uncomfortable about that assumption — then we must include higher order moments of income distribution in our models. Few have ever attempted to estimate the integral equations produced by integrating demand systems over income distribution, as would be the valid approach without representative agent theory. For relevant theory and results in that challenging area of research, see Berndt, Diewert, and Darrough (1977) and Rios-Rull (1995).

[12] But the RBC literature, although far more theoretically tight than the 'low road' literature discussed above, is nevertheless not yet immune from these troubles. As has been correctly observed by Hansen and Heckman (1996, p. 101), 'It is remarkable to us that so little emphasis has been given to the transition from micro to macro in the real business cycle literature.'

have a connection with the transmission mechanism starting far back near its source at the central bank, but the demand for such a variable is no substitute in any reasonable macroeconomic model for the demand for money.[13]

3 The High Road

The message in Sections 1 and 2 above is a negative one, and unfortunately the alternative does not produce easy answers. The alternative is the high road, where the air is thin, and work is hard. The demand for money should be modeled using the same tools that are reputable in modeling the demand for other goods and services. No one who works in those areas would take seriously the statement that the demand for a good or service has 'broken down' based upon the research methods that have produced that view about money demand. As explained above, the root source of the failure of so many demand for money models is the payment of interest on monetary assets. Demand for money functions that ignore the theoretical implications of that fact have performed increasingly poorly as more and more deregulated, interest-bearing assets have been entered into monetary aggregates.[14]

3.1 The Dependent Variable

The use of simple sum monetary aggregates in demand for money functions has been indefensible for decades. Who would measure transportation services by adding subway trains and roller skates? A vast literature exists on capital aggregation, and is directly relevant to measuring the flow of monetary services, when some or all monetary assets yield interest. See, e.g., Barnett (1980a, 1987, 1995). On the general subject of capital aggregation, see Diewert (1978, 1980a). Recently vast data bases of Divisia monetary aggregate data have become available for many countries throughout the world.[15]

---

[13] Furthermore, a comparison between the vastly different behavior of money and of the base during the great depression clearly illustrates the dangers of using the base in any oversimplified policy prescription. The correct link between the base and the transmission mechanism is far from simple, as emphasized in Barnett (1987) and Barnett, Kirova, and Pasupathy (1994). Furthermore, questions have been raised about the monetary base data in recent years. See Anderson and Rasche (1997).

[14] Regarding the paradoxical empirical implications of adding increasingly distant substitutes for money into monetary aggregates, without any weighting, see Barnett and Zhou (1994a).

[15] The Bank of England publishes high quality monetary aggregate data based upon the use of the Divisia index formula and user cost prices. For details, see Fisher et al. (1993). An international Divisia monetary aggregate database, including data from many parts of the world, is maintained online at the University of Mississippi and can be accessed on the World Wide Web at no charge. See Belongia and Binner (2000) for a collection of

The basic principle upon which monetary index number theory operates is the following: at the margin, rational first-order conditions hold. The idea then is to remove from marginal services those that are not monetary services, and clearly investment yield is not a monetary service.[16]

The simple sum monetary aggregates extract nothing from the measured flow imputed to money, including interest yield. Since investment return therefore is counted as a monetary service, one must conclude that coal mines, land, education, and in fact the entire physical and human capital stock of the country is 'money.' See Barnett and Zhou (1994a) for a derivation of the confounding between investment rate of return and monetary services in the simple sum monetary aggregates and the ability of index number theory to remove the investment motive from the otherwise joint product.[17] Contrary to Cuthbertson's (1997) representations, Divisia monetary aggregation is not about isolating and measuring specific monetary services, but rather about removing from the simple sum monetary aggregates those services that clearly are not monetary services, with the investment rate of return being the most conspicuous example. In monetary index number theory, the services that are measured as 'monetary' are those services that remain after the non-monetary services are removed.

3.2 Independent Variables

In the literature on capital aggregation, much has been published on the derivation and computation of user-cost prices for the services of durables. That derivation method was applied to acquire the formula for the user cost of monetary assets by Barnett (1978, 1980a). Having the user cost prices measured for each component asset, aggregation over those user cost prices should be accomplished in a manner that is consistent with the manner in

---

articles covering the creation and analysis of these series for eleven countries and the core European Monetary Union area. Many of the authors of those articles are on the staffs of the central banks of those countries. High quality United States data on monetary services produced from Divisia aggregation is available from the Federal Reserve Bank of St. Louis and is updated and maintained routinely. See the appendix of this book regarding that data source and comparable international sources of Divisia monetary aggregate data.

[16] Hence monetary index numbers based upon valid index number theory remove the investment rate of return from the measured monetary services. To the degree that other nonmonetary services exist in the total services produced by an asset, those other nonmonetary services can be 'monetized' at the margin and used to augment the investment yield in the user cost formula. That user cost then is used as the price of the asset in a quantity index number from Diewert's (1976) superlative index number class. Among the infinite number of indexes in that class are the Fisher ideal index and the Törnqvist discrete-time approximation to the Divisia index. The adjusted user cost in the superlative index number formula removes the nonmonetary services from the measured service flow.

[17] Barnett and Zhou (1994a) is reprinted in this book as chapter 15.

which the quantity aggregate is aggregated over the services of the component quantities. That internal consistency is achieved by using the price index that is dual to the aggregate quantity of money services. The quantity of money index used to generate its price index dual can be Divisia, Fisher ideal, any other index in Diewert's (1976) class of superlative index numbers, or even Paasche or Laspeyres, but certainly not simple sum. Those dual monetary user cost price aggregates are available on the World Wide Web at the same locations as the Divisia monetary services index.

Many unsolved problems exist in durables aggregation and capital aggregation, and those problems continue to be the subject of expanding research. Advances in that research should be incorporated into monetary economics as those advances become available. One such example is the adjustments needed for risk, when contemporaneous prices are not known with perfect certainty.[18] Along the high road, the objective is to do the best that is possible at the current state of the art of economic theory. One can do no more.

The common practice of using an interest rate as the opportunity cost of money in demand for money equations makes no sense. It makes no sense for Divisia monetary aggregates. It makes no sense for Fisher ideal monetary aggregates. It makes no sense for simple sum monetary aggregates. It has made no sense for over 40 years, since 'money' began to yield interest.

3.3 Model Structure

Data, theory, and model structure all should be internally consistent and coherent. When this objective is met while recognizing that many monetary assets have yielded interest for decades, one is on the high road. An example of the high road is Barnett (1983a). That study assumes perfect certainty. The seminal study incorporating risk is Poterba and Rotemberg (1987), who emphasize the estimation of the deep parameters of Euler equations to avoid Lucas critique problems. Other examples include Belongia (1996a), Barnett and Hahm (1994), Barnett, Hinich, and Yue (1991), Barnett, Kirova, and Pasupathy (1995), Donovan (1978), Fisher and Fleissig (1994), Serletis (1991a), Swofford and Whitney (1987), and Yue (1991).[19] For a survey of other related

---

[18]Since interest rates are paid at the end of period, some degree of contemporaneous risk exists in monetary asset user costs, which depend upon those interest rates. Difficult research on that subject is ongoing, and recent progress can be found in Barnett, Liu, and Jensen (1997), Barnett et al. (1996), Poterba and Rotemberg (1987), and Rotemberg et al. (1995). This research at present is much complicated by the unresolved problems in consumption CAPM and the associated equity premium paradox, as well as by problems with the small sample properties of generalized method of moments (GMM) estimators.

[19]There also is a middle road, along which some but not all of the relevant theory is used. Only partial coherence is attained. See Barnett, Kirova, and Pasupathy (1984) and

work, see Barnett, Fisher, and Serletis (1992).[20]

While the real business cycle (RBC) literature has not yet come to grips with these issues, there are encouraging signs from recent developments in that literature.[21]

4 Misunderstandings

The high road builds on the foundation of existing microeconomic theory, including the theory of the firm, consumer theory, and the implied microeconomic aggregation and index number theory. Advances in those areas are accepted and absorbed in a coherent manner as research proceeds up the high road. Constructive criticism of the high road is based upon recognition of the existence of unsolved problems in the supporting areas of economic research and the need for further development in those areas to permit the high road to climb even higher. However in many cases, criticism unfortunately is based upon lack of understanding of the foundations of the high road research. For example, introduction of new goods into superlative index numbers is accomplished by a specialized procedure involving imputation of reservation prices and transitional use of the Fisher ideal index, as explained in Diewert (1980a). This procedure, while important to understanding the high road literature, is not widely known to nonspecialists in the field.

Misunderstandings produced from unawareness of specialized developments are not surprising; but some of the criticisms tend to be based upon misunderstandings of the relationship between elementary microeconomic theory and high road research. Perhaps the most persistent of those misunderstandings relates to the famous diamonds-versus-water paradox that is explained in most undergraduate microeconomic textbooks.[22] User costs of

---

Chrystal and MacDonald (1994) for noteworthy examples. For middle road detours to rather distant paths, see Spanos (1984), Roper and Turnovsky (1980), and Feldstein and Stock (1996).

[20] Barnett (1983a), Barnett and Hahm (1994), Barnett, Hinich, and Yue (1991), Barnett, Kirova, and Pasupathy (1995), and Barnett, Fisher, and Serletis (1992) are reprinted in this book as chapters 16, 20, 11, 22, and 18 respectively.

[21] Regarding the need for coherence between data and model structure, see the section 'Defining Consistent Measurements' in Cooley and Prescott (1995, pp. 17–20). It is unfortunate that these same principles of valid quantity aggregation are not yet being applied in the RBC literature to aggregation over monetary assets. Similarly, see Rios-Rull (1995) for an excellent discussion of aggregation over economic agents in the RBC literature, but again without consideration of the monetary aggregation issues discussed above.

[22] Diamonds are priced higher per unit than water, yet water is more valuable than diamonds, since the human race cannot survive without water. The answer to the paradox, of course, is that prices measure marginal utility and not total or average utility. In fact along a concave cardinal utility function, total utility and marginal utility move in opposite

monetary assets are the prices used in monetary index numbers. Prices do not measure total utility or average utility. User costs do not measure 'moneyness,' total services, or average services of monetary assets, although user cost prices do measure marginal services and opportunity costs at the margin. User costs are not weights in a Divisia index or in any other superlative index number. In the Divisia index, the weights are shares.

It is often stated that the increase in the own rate of return on a monetary asset decreases its user cost and thereby its 'moneyness' in a superlative monetary quantity index, such as a Divisia monetary aggregate. But in fact the share weights can either increase or decrease, when a user cost price decreases. In consumer theory, the direction of the change of the share of a good depends upon whether the good's own price elasticity is greater than or less than -1. In this volume, Laidler's (1997) well-meaning, but somewhat heuristic and loose explanation of superlative monetary aggregates, could lead a reader to fall into the diamonds-versus-water paradox error. While Laidler knows the relevant theory sufficiently well to avoid falling into that paradox's trap himself, the risks from lack of rigor in such statements of the relevant theory are made evident from Cuthbertson's comments (1997) in this *Economic Journal*. Cuthbertson falls straight into the diamonds-versus-water paradox error in his erroneous conclusions about the effect on Divisia monetary aggregates of payment of interest on checking accounts. He also comments on the new goods issue (relative to financial innovation via new accounts) in a manner that disregards Diewert's (1980a) correct approach mentioned above.

Responding to each such misunderstanding is a poor use of space in this *Economic Journal*, but references to relevant expository and clarifying articles can be found in Barnett, Fisher, and Serletis (1992).[23] It is worth repeating that the basic principle that distinguishes the high road from the low road is that the high road uses the relevant theory and insists upon internal coherence and consistency between the theory that produced the model, the inference methods used to estimate the model, and the theory implied by the data construction procedures. The basic principles of aggregation and index number theory are relevant to the objectives of the high road, and violations of those basic principles are the basis for what Chrystal and MacDonald (1994) have called the 'Barnett critique' in monetary economics. Criticisms of high road research necessarily fall into one of two possible groups: (1) refusal

---

directions. Sixty years ago these 'paradoxes' about the connection between microeconomic pricing and 'value' were fashionable topics in economic journals among critics of microeconomic theory. Oddly they keep being raised as 'criticisms' of the high road research in monetary economics, despite the fact that those 'paradoxes' were laid to rest in other areas of economics over a half century ago.

[23] Barnett, Fisher, and Serletis (1992) is reprinted in this book as chapter 18.

on the low road to recognize the existence of internal contradictions between the theory, econometrics, and data construction, and (2) misunderstandings of the high road. There are no other possibilities.

5 Conclusion

The broken road has been abandoned for over a decade. The low road is a dead end. From the vantage point of the high road, the subject of this Controversies section of the *Economic Journal* is the unstable non-demand function for a non-variable regressed on other non-variables through non-theory. The high road is a difficult road to travel, but it is the right road.

Section 6.3: Macroeconomic Policy

Chapter 25

Perspective on the Current State of Macroeconomic Theory

*William A. Barnett**

    Historically, microeconomics was the domain of scientific methodology in economics, while macroeconomics attracted less mathematically oriented economists. In recent years, the level of sophistication of macroeconomics has grown dramatically, and that field now attracts many of the most mathematically oriented economists. Nevertheless, the field's set of shared views (i.e., maintained hypotheses) has not grown. The purpose of the scientific method is to permit the maintained hypotheses within a field to grow by establishing a rigorous methodology for deductively deriving and empirically testing hypotheses. The field of macroeconomics has failed that test of scientific success during precisely the decades of most rapid growth in the use of scientific methodology. It is argued that the source of the paradox lies in the fact that the inroads of science into macroeconomics have been asymmetrical. Central to the definition and objectives of macroeconomics is dimension reduction and dynamics. Rigorous dimension reduction is impossible without formal aggregation, and complex dynamics is impossible without non-linearity.

---

*Originally published in the *International Journal of Systems Science* 25 (1994), 839-848.

Yet applications of formal aggregation theory and non-linear dynamics to macroeconomics have progressed very slowly, at a time when scientific methodology in other areas of macroeconomics has advanced rapidly. This asymmetry explains the paradox.

1 Introduction

The nature of macroeconomic theory has changed dramatically during the past decade. Some people say that macroeconomic theory is in crisis, and many detractors have argued that macroeconomic theorists are less willing to make policy recommendations with confidence than at any other time in this century. In fact the dramatic transformation of macroeconomics during the past decade has reflected the adoption of more scientific methodology than had previously characterized the field. A corollary is that conclusions are drawn more cautiously than earlier, as a natural result of the conservative nature of the scientific method itself. Hence, the caution characterizing macroeconomic policy conclusions should be viewed as positive evidence of the advancement of science in macroeconomics.

Prior to the recent transformation of macroeconomics, economists with strong mathematical and statistical leanings usually chose to work in microeconomic theory and microeconometrics. The use of formal mathematical logic was much deeper in microeconomics than in macroeconomics, and the most sophisticated econometric methods were more frequently applied to microeconometric analysis. However, during the past decade, macroeconomics has absorbed many of the most sophisticated methods of general equilibrium theory, dynamic programming, optimal control theory, stochastic choice theory, and game theory. As a result, a large percentage of the best and brightest young mathematical economists and econometricians now choose to work in macroeconomics.

Nevertheless, the divisions among macroeconomists are no less deep than before. In fact, the divisions may be deeper now than ever before, since the gap between real business cycle theorists and Keynesians is perhaps greater than the earlier gap between monetarists and Keynesians. For example, Keynesians and monetarists have always agreed that money matters, but real business cycle theorists frequently take the position that money matters little, if at all. In addition, monetarists and Keynesians have usually depended upon disequilibrium dynamics to explain the transmission mechanism of monetary policy, while real business cycle theorists often assume continuous market clearing. The differences of opinion between Keynesians and monetarists regarding long run macroeconomic policy now also divide Keynesians from real business cycle theorists, but those latter divisions now apply even to very short run analysis.

These divisions would appear to contradict the conclusion that macroeconomics is more scientific than before. The scientific method is intended to produce agreement on hypotheses that survive scientific tests and replications of those tests. While the state of the art in any science is always a contest between competing hypotheses, there normally is a non-controversial backlog of accepted hypotheses, shared by nearly all researchers in the field. Such is indeed the case in microeconomics. However, that backlog in macroeconomics has not grown over the years, even after the transformation of the field that has taken place during the past decade.

The purpose of the paper is to explore the reasons for this odd state of affairs.

2 Definition of Macroeconomics

All economics suffers from a shortage of experimental data. In other sciences, controlled experiments are used as an integral part of the scientific method. However, the economy is not a controlled experiment. Hence, it is not surprising that economic hypotheses are difficult to test in a manner that is satisfactory to all economists. This is no less the case for microeconomics than for macroeconomics. The source of the macroeconomic controversies must be found elsewhere.

Before we can look more deeply at these paradoxes, we need a formal mathematical definition of macroeconomics that can be contrasted rigorously with the definition of microeconomics. That distinction no longer can be found in the choice of tools, since microeconomists and macroeconomists use many of the same tools. It is sometimes argued that macroeconomics is 'what macroeconomist do,' while macroeconomists are defined in terms of their policy concerns regarding inflation, unemployment, the business cycle, and aggregate economic growth. While this definition does capture the reason for the existence of macroeconomics as a field, the definition is too informal to be useful for our purposes.

Here, the following definition is used: microeconomics is the economics of a high dimensional economy, while macroeconomics is the economics of a low dimensional economy. If the real world were low dimensional, the two fields would be identical, but except for some small island economies, the transition from microeconomics to macroeconomics unavoidably requires aggregation over economic agents and over goods to create such concepts as aggregate investment, consumption, savings, money, durables, and representative consumers. There also can be aggregation over time to produce overlapping generations models with consumers having two or three period lifetimes.

3   Aggregation Theory

There is indeed a formal literature on aggregation theory (for a survey of much of that literature, see Barnett (1987) and Diewert (1980a)). If macroeconomics were based entirely on formal aggregation theory, macroeconomics would be a subfield of microeconomics, since the tools of aggregation theory are microeconomic tools. Macroeconomic conclusions would be derived directly from microeconomics. Under those circumstances, the paradoxes described above would disappear. The growing collection of hypotheses embedded within the maintained hypotheses of microeconomics would be the hypotheses held in common among economists interested in macroeconomic policy, and the advancement of science in microeconomics and in macroeconomics would be directly linked through aggregation theory.

Unfortunately that is not the case. Macroeconomics has made remarkably little use of the tools of aggregation theory. For example, in microeconomic aggregation theory, weakly separable collections of goods are clustered into groups over which aggregation is then possible. Weak separability is a necessary condition for aggregation over a group of goods. Yet this test is rarely used in the macroeconomic literature. Goods are clustered together as 'durables', 'investment', 'capital', 'perishables' and other such aggregates without any consideration whatsoever to the separability condition needed to produce an aggregate admissible under aggregation theory.

Once a group of goods is selected to be the components of an aggregate, aggregation theory tells us how to find the exact aggregator function to use in aggregating over those goods. For a consumer, the aggregator function is the category (conditional) utility function over those goods. These aggregator functions are never linear, unless the components are perfect substitutes, since a utility function is linear if and only if the goods in the utility function are perfect substitutes. Yet the monetary aggregates used by nearly every central bank in the world are not only linear, but in fact are simple sums. To say that aggregation theoretic principles have not been used is an understatement (for an overview of the literature relevant to this peculiar phenomenon, see Barnett, Fisher, and Serletis (1992)).[1]

Regarding aggregation over economic agents, the situation is even more disturbing. Virtually the entire literature on macroeconomics is free from distribution effects. Mean preserving redistributions of income have no effects upon the macroeconomy. Only the first moment of the income distribution matters. However, it can be shown that freedom from distribution effects is

---

[1] Barnett, Fisher, and Serletis (1992) is reprinted in this book as chapter 18.

sufficient for the existence of a representative consumer. Hence, logical internal consistency would dictate that all macroeconomic models must assume the existence of a representative consumer, and therefore aggregate consumer demand systems must be integrable to the utility function of a representative agent. In an admirable display of deductive logic, most macroeconomists in recent years have asured that their models are integrable in that manner.

However, Gorman (1953) proved that a necessary condition for the existence of a representative agent is that all consumers have parallel linear Engel curves. Hence, all utility functions must either be identical homothetic functions or simple affine translations of that function. The resulting class of functions is called Gorman's polar form. Yet no one seriously believes that tastes are that uniform across consumers. Even as an approximation, the assumption appears to be much too strong. The assumption can be weakened somewhat by more complicated procedures that permit the existence of distribution effects, such as those derived by Muellbauer (1975) and Barnett (1979), but those sophisticated methods have not found their way into macroeconomics.

As a result of the unreasonable strength of the assumptions producing a representative consumer, macroeconomists directly involved in policy decisions, such as those in government and those employed by consulting firms, typically have used large scale macroeconomic models that are not integrable. No attempt is made to produce consistency with the existence of a representative consumer, since realism militates against accepting the existence of a representative consumer. The use of representative agent models in macroeconomics is limited to professional journal publications, where formal scientific rigour is more important than detailed empirical realism, as indeed should be the case in any scientific journal. The kinds of ad hoc methods that can easily produce 'better fit' have no place in science.

An internal inconsistency now arises. The macroeconometric models used by policy makers are usually free of distribution effects, even though those models are not integrable to a community utility function. Although such models dominate applied use of macroeconomics in government, such models rarely appear in the best published journals. In fact, no non-integrable macroeconomic models should be taken seriously by scientific journals, unless distribution effects are incorporated. The importance of the inclusion of distribution effects within large scale macroeconometric models does not appear to have been recognized by the builders of those models.

Clearly, the use of aggregation theory in macroeconomics is slight, at best. Hence, low dimensional macroeconomics cannot be derived from high dimensional microeconomics. The gap between low dimensional economics and high dimensional economics has not been filled. Without the discipline of aggregation theory imposed, macroeconomics floats free from important constraints. As argued below it is the lack of those logical constraints that produces many of the paradoxes in current macroeconomic research.

However, there are good reasons for some of the logical gaps described above. In particular, the literature on aggregating over economic agents is a very difficult one, and there exist many unsolved problems in that literature. Although it would be possible to improve upon the current macroeconomic literature by using the existing literature on aggregating over economic agents, the relevant results in aggregation theory are not adequate to permit full unification of microeconomics and macroeconomics. Without more progress in microeconomic aggregation theory, the aggregation theoretic gap between microeconomics and macroeconomics cannot be fully closed.

Aggregation over goods is another matter. That aspect of formal aggregation theory is highly developed. The fact that macroeconomics makes so little use of aggregation theory in aggregating over goods is a failing of the field of macroeconomics. As discussed by Barnett, Fisher, and Serletis (1992), the use of simple sum monetary aggregates by central banks, monetary economists, and macroeconomists is indefensible.

4 Dimension Reduction

If macroeconomics could be derived from microeconomics by using microeconomic aggregation theory, the resulting macroeconomic models undoubtedly would be very complex. The existence of distribution effects through higher order moments of the income distribution would be only one of the many complications that would enter into macroeconomic models. Theory would not rule out many such complications. Only econometric tests could be used to test for simplifying null hypotheses.

However, if microeconomic aggregation theory is ignored, the dimension reduction that defines macroeconomics can be accomplished in an infinite number of *ad hoc* ways. The theorist is free to emphasize whatever phenomenon he/she subjectively believes to be most important, at the expense of the phenomena that are assumed away.

Indeed, it is precisely that procedure that characterized all macroeconomics. For example, some models emphasize market imperfections, some emphasize the fundamental solution to rational expectations models, some emphasize bubbles, some emphasize continuous market clearing, some emphasize supply side shocks, some emphasize incomplete markets, some emphasize uncleared markets, and some emphasize chaos. Obviously the low dimension that defines macroeconomics cannot easily be attained while including all of those phenomena. Nevertheless, subject to the imposition of prejudiced priors excluding some of those phenomena, macroeconomic models currently appearing in the literature contain more scientific content than those models of earlier decades.

Convergence of views to produce a growing maintained hypothesis, as characterizes all science, cannot be attained within macroeconomics without the elimination of the prejudiced priors that emphasize one aspect of the economy at the expense of others; and the elimination of those controversial priors is impossible without the solution of the currently unsolved problems in formal microeconomic aggregation theory. Nevertheless, some of the recent advances in scientific methodology found in macroeconomics are surveyed below. Each of those advances is produced conditionally upon the imposition of a maintained hypothesis that has never been subjected to scientific testing.

5 Keynesian Discretion versus Open Loop Rules

Game theory has produced a much improved focus in the ongoing debate between rules versus discretion. It is now well understood that advocacy of open loop rules depends upon the assumption of the existence of time inconsistency in policy making, while advocacy of Keynesian discretion depends upon the assumption of reputational equilibrium. This conclusion is based upon the assumption that government knows the structure of the private sector's decision, while the private sector knows the announced plans of the government, but not the structure of the government's decision. The result is a Stackelberg game, with the government being the leader and the private sector being the follower.

It can be shown that in this game, the government's optimal solution is a non-recursive simultaneous one. To produce the optimal Stackelberg solution to the game, the government must produce its simultaneous intertemporal solution, announce it, and then stick with it as time passes. In short, once the government announces its optimal intertemporal solution path, the government must follow that path, so long as no new information is acquired that might change the optimum. The government must not replan as time passes, unless new information is acquired.

It can be shown (see, e.g., Calvo 1978) that continuous replanning, because of the simultaneous nature of the solution, will not produce the optimal path. Hence, the optimal intertemporal solution and the continuously replanned solutions differ. While it is the optimal intertemporal solution that needs to be followed to track the Stackelberg solution, there are incentives built into the game for the government to replan, while nevertheless announcing that it will follow the simultaneous solution. This odd phenomenon is called 'time inconsistency'. By fooling the private sector in that manner, the government feels that it can benefit everyone, but the private sector will eventually learn that the plans announced by the government are false, and then the private sector will adjust its own plans accordingly. The economy drops into an inferior solution.

In the macroeconomic literature, there are two solutions that are especially important. One is the rules solution, in which the government established its commitment to the optimal solution by imposing the solution on itself through a rule that cannot be broken. The optimal Stackelberg solution will then be attained. This solution supports the policy prescription of many monetarists and new classical economists, who advocate that the government should remove uncertainty about its plans by imposing its plans through an irreversible rule.

The other important solution is called 'reputational equilibrium'. The model is structured in a manner that eliminates the incentive for the government to lie. The private sector recognizes that fact and then believes all governmentally announced plans, regardless of how frequently they may be changed. This highly desirable solution is most likely to be attained if the government does not discount the future rapidly. If the government does in fact place much weight on the distant future, then the possible loss of reputation by the government in the distant future may be so important to the government that it will not take the risk of providing false information in the short run. The government will thereby resist the temptation to replan and will inevitably follow the optimal intertemporal path that it has announced. This solution leaves the government with the ability to run a discretionary policy without risking loss of public confidence, and is the solution often advocated by Keynesians.

6 Nonlinear Dynamics

In all areas of scientific research, nonlinear dynamics and the special case of chaotic dynamics have been growing in importance. Macroeconomics has been no exception. For example, Grandmont (1985) has demonstrated that even the most classical of economic models can produce either the stable solutions used in new classical economics or the unstable solutions characterizing much of Keynesian economics. The distinction between the two possibilities is found in the parameter settings. In some regions of the parameter space, the model produces stable solutions, while in other regions, the model produces more complex solutions, such as cycles or even chaos. Although the parameter settings are different in the two cases, the structure of the model is the same.

This conclusion contrasts with earlier views, in which different policy views were supported by models having different structures. We now find that even if all economists had the same structural models in mind, different economists could still have different views on policy, depending upon their views about the parameter values. This insight could prove to be unifying, since convergence on maintained features of economic structure could occur among economists who nevertheless have very different views on policy. In short, there can be agreement on theory, without agreement on empirical inferences regarding parameter values. The competition among different structural models may have resulted from the imposition of linearity on those models. Once modellers are freed from the linearity restriction, the need for alternative structural macroeconomic models may be replaced by empirical research regarding the values of the parameters in a single unifying model.

As a result of the potential importance of nonlinear dynamics in economics, there is a growing empirical literature on testing for nonlinear dynamics and chaos with economic data. At present only one such confirmed finding of chaos in economic data has been published (see Barnett and Chen 1988, Barnett and Hinich 1992, and Barnett, Gallant, Hinich, Jungeilges, and Jensen 1995).

7 Consequences

Clearly the introduction of deeply mathematical insights, such as those of nonlinear dynamics and time inconsistency, has strengthened the scientific foundations of macroeconomics. However, macroeconomics and microeconomics contain many such insights, and focusing on any one often requires assuming away others. The dimension reduction that is central to the definition of macroeconomics renders this fact unavoidable.

The question is whether the dimension reduction itself is conducted in a scientific manner. Science used conditionally upon non-science is non-science. If scientific methodology is applied conditionally upon a maintained unscientific approach to dimension reduction, the result is not science.

7.1 Time Inconsistency

It has been shown by Barnett (1993) that establishing reputational equilibrium is very difficult, when more than one monetary asset exists in the economy. The models that are currently used to establish reputational equilibrium contain only one monetary asset. However, with multiple monetary assets, exact monetary aggregation produces relevancy of at least two different monetary assets, including one to measure outside money and another to measure the flow of monetary services in the economy. Although money enters the economy primarily through the monetary service flow, outside money is relevant to measuring the magnitude of the seigniorage tax, which enters the government's budget constraint. With the existence of two or more different monetary aggregates in the economy, conflicting signals to the private sector are difficult to remove, and hence determining parameter settings that will assume the existence of reputational equilibrium is much more difficult than previously believed.

Establishing the conditions under which a discretionary Keynesian policy would not generate disbelief of government announcements may be very difficult. Similarly, selecting a satisfactory rule to be imposed under a monetarist policy could be very difficult, when two relevant monetary aggregates exist that serve important but sometimes uncorrelated roles in monetary policy.

In short, the dimension reduction produced by replacing multiple monetary assets by only one monetary asset masks the complexities that exist in policy selection under time inconsistent planning.

7.2 Nonlinear Dynamics

Similarly the literature on nonlinear dynamics in macroeconomics has tended to overlook important matters. For example, Grandmont's paper, which advocates an activist policy based upon the possibility of nonlinear dynamics, overlooks the related literature on social welfare. Since the structure of this model is fully classical, with no forms of market failure in existence, solutions in his model are Pareto optimal, regardless of the parameter settings. Hence, it can be argued that stabilizing governmental intervention into the economy could produce a Pareto loss, even if the solution without governmental intervention is chaotic. Pareto optimal chaos is to be preferred to Pareto inferior stability.

Attempts to produce a connection between chaos and market failure are just beginning, as in Woodford (1989). However, no necessary connection has yet been proven, and hence the connection between nonlinearity and policy views is not yet established. Related approaches based upon sunspot theory (Cass and Shell 1983) and bubbles have been attracting attention, because of their connection with possible market failure, but even with market failure in some of those models, questions exist about the possibility of Pareto improving market intervention. While all of this literature is important, the effects that they will have on policy views remain unclear.

7.3 Distribution Effects

As has been discussed above, there have been many advances in index number and aggregation theory. In addition, Diewert (1976) has unified the two fields by determining a class of index numbers, called superlative index numbers, that track the exact aggregates of microeconomic aggregation theory. Given that aggregation is central to the dimension reduction that defines macroeconomics, one would think that aggregation and index number theory would be fully absorbed in macroeconomics. Unfortunately that is not the case. The literature on aggregation over economic agents appears in macroeconomics only in terms of the simplest possible approach: Gorman's representative agent approach. The more sophisticated approaches, such as Pareto's method of integrating over distributions, have found no role in macroeconomics. Similarly, simple sum aggregation is still used to produce monetary aggregates by most central banks.

It would be comforting to be able to argue that ignoring advances in aggregation theory has little effect on macroeconomic conclusions, but that is not the case. Consider, for example, the representative agent approach. Under that approach, there are no distribution effects produced by macroeconomic policy. In fact in any model that contains only per capita income, without inclusion of any higher order moments of the income distribution, macroeconomic policy can have no distribution effects. Virtually every macroeconomic model currently in use contains only the first moment of the income distribution. Hence, regardless of whether or not the modellers have made conscious use of Gorman's method, those models implicitly accept Gorman's assumptions and thereby rule out distribution effects. Yet the connection between macroeconomic policies and political parties demonstrates that macroeconomic policies have strong distribution effects. Consider, for example, the effect of inflation on fixed income retirees.

The situation is even more surprising in the case of aggregation over monetary assets. Despite the existence of a large and sophisticated literature on exact aggregation over monetary assets, central banks throughout the world continue to fight a rear guard action resisting proper aggregation over monetary assets (see, e.g., Barnett, Fisher, and Serletis (1992) for a discussion of this odd paradox). Again the effects are far from trivial. For example, every few years the monetary economics literature is flooded with articles claiming that the demand for money function has shifted. Yet the parallel literature using the Divisia monetary aggregate has never found any such evidence. Furthermore, Barnett (1984) has shown that the recession produced by the Federal Reserve's 'monetarist experiment' was generated by a well intentioned policy, which unfortunately was biased towards restrictiveness by targeting an upwardly biased simple sum monetary aggregate.

8 Conclusion

Macroeconomics is economic theory with dimension reduction imposed. Conditionally upon that dimension reduction, current macroeconomic theory is far more strongly founded in the scientific method than the *ad hoc* macro models of a generation ago. However, the maintained dimension reduction upon which all of those models condition is problematic. It cannot be argued convincingly that the issues assumed away in the maintained hypothesis are less important than those left in the model after the dimension reduction. The dimension reduction is itself the source of many of the controversies that continue to plague the field. Advocates of Keynesian macroeconomics, new classical economics, chaos, sunspots, and other areas of active research in macroeconomics routinely assume away the issues viewed to be important by the competing schools of thought.

There are two alternatives that could avoid the resulting gridlock. One is to abandon macroeconomics and base all economics upon high dimensional microeconomics. Unfortunately, that approach would leave governmental decision makers with little access to advice from the economics profession, which would be forced to view most macroeconomic policy problems as being unsolved. The other alternative is to impose a scientific discipline upon the admissible approaches to dimension reduction: (1) either laboratory experimentation could be used to determine which maintained hypotheses can be defended, or (2) deductive logic, i.e., aggregation theoretic principles, could be imposed.

In addition to conditioning upon *ad hoc* dimension reductions, most macroeconomic models condition upon the maintained hypothesis of linearity, despite the fact that microeconomic theory rarely produces linear models. As argued above, that maintained linearity is as equally responsible for the divisions between macroeconomists as is the *ad hoc* dimension reduction. Within the class of linear models, differences in policy conclusions usually require differences in the structure of models. As a result, macroeconomists having different policy views have often proposed competing structural models, but once those macroeconomists are freed from the linearity restriction, differences in solution properties can be acquired from the same model at different parameter settings.

Convergence of views in macroeconomics is possible only through increased use of experimentation or of aggregation theory, to remove the arbitrariness of current approaches to macroeconomic dimension reduction, and through the removal of the linearity straight-jacket, which forces competing political groups to advocate different structural models. Without the imposition of any scientific discipline on dimension reduction and without the removal of the linearity restriction, macroeconomists can be expected to continue producing models that are increasingly sophisticated, but which reduce dimension and structure models in a manner that prejudices the results. The backlog of maintained hypotheses on which the profession agrees will continue not to grow, and hence macroeconomics will continue to fail the most fundamental criterion for judging scientific advancement.

DATA APPENDIX

Section A.1: Editors' Overview of Appendix

William A. Barnett and Apostolos Serletis

The St. Louis Federal Reserve Bank has produced a high quality source of monetary aggregate data that is consistent with the aggregation theoretic and index number theoretic principles in this book. The Federal Reserve calls the resulting index the MSI (monetary services index). When the data was first released, the St. Louis Federal Reserve Bank published a special report in an issue of the Federal Reserve Bank of St. Louis *Review*. That special report contained three papers explaining the theory, the background, the component data sources, and the data production procedures. Although all of the papers in that special report are valuable, we have reproduced in this index only one of the three papers: the introductory paper to the special report.

Those readers interested in all three of the papers can find them in Richard Anderson, Barry E. Jones, and Travis Nesmith, "Special Report: The Monetary Services Index Project of the Federal Reserve Bank of St. Louis," Federal Reserve Bank of St. Louis *Review*, vol. 79, no. 1, January/February 1997. That data source includes aggregation theoretic quantity indexes and their dual user cost prices along with the component quantities, user costs, and growth rate weights. The data can be downloaded from the web site maintained by the Federal Reserve Bank of St. Louis. In addition, the full text of the special report is maintained online at that site.

International Divisia monetary aggregate and dual user cost data are available for many countries throughout the world. References to many of the sources can be found in the survey paper in Chapter 18 of this book. In addition, an online database of international Divisia monetary aggregate data is maintained at the University of Mississippi. The sources for most of that data are staff members at the central banks of the various countries that have that data available. For research and details relevant to that international data, see Belongia and Binner (2000).

Links to the St. Louis Federal Reserve Bank's MSI data and the Mississippi international site are maintained in the data section of Barnett's web site, which can be found at:

http://wuecon.wustl.edu/~barnett/Welcome.html.

# Section A.2: St. Louis Federal Reserve Bank Data

Appendix A

Introduction to the St. Louis Monetary Services Index Project

Richard G. Anderson, Barry E. Jones, and Travis D. Nesmith[*]

Economists have long recognized that equilibrium between the demand for and supply of money is the primary long-run determinant of an economy's price level. There is far less agreement, however, on how to measure the aggregate quantity of money in the economy. The Federal Reserve Bank of St. Louis' monetary services index project seeks to provide researchers and policymakers with an extended database of new measures of monetary aggregates — the monetary services indexes (MSIs) — and related data.[1]

---

[*]Originally published in the Federal Reserve Bank of St. Louis *Review* 79 (1997), 25-29. Richard G. Anderson is an assistant vice president at the Federal Reserve Bank of St. Louis. Barry E. Jones and Travis D. Nesmith were Ph.D. candidates at Washington University in St. Louis and visiting scholars at the Federal Reserve Bank of St. Louis at the time that this paper was published. Barry Jones now is at the State University of New York at Binghamton, and Travis Nesmith is at the Board of Governors of the Federal Reserve System in Washington, D.C. We offer special thanks to Professor William A. Barnett, Washington University in St. Louis, for his generous and invaluable guidance during this project. We also thank Professors W. Erwin Diewert, University of British Columbia, and Adrian R. Fleissig, St. Louis University, for advice and comments; Mary C. Lohmann, Kelly M. Morris, and Cindy A. Gleit provided research assistance.

[1]Monetary services indexes have sometimes been referred to as Divisia monetary aggregates because their construction uses a discrete approximation to Divisia's (1925) continuous-time index. We label our monetary quantity indexes MSI to emphasize that they measure a flow of monetary services, not a stock of monetary assets.

The monetary services indexes differ considerably from the monetary aggregates that have been published by the Federal Reserve Board for more than 35 years, even though both begin with the same basic observation: Consumers hold monetary assets in equilibrium because the assets provide valuable services and hence increase utility.[2] The increased utility arises, in part, because some of the assets are media of exchange. Other things equal, a larger quantity of such assets reduces shopping time, permits immediate purchase of bargain-priced goods, provides a cushion against unanticipated expenses, and reduces the amount of time spent on cash management. Assets that are not media of exchange, such as mutual fund shares and savings and time deposits, may also increase utility, especially if they are readily convertible to an asset that is a medium of exchange. Samuelson (1947), for example, noted that

> "... it is a fair question as to the relationship between the demand for money and the ordinal preference fields met in utility theory. In this connection, I have reference to none of the tenuous concepts of money, as a numeraire commodity, or as a composite commodity, but to money proper, the distinguishing features of which are its indirect usefulness, not for its own sake but for what it can buy, its conventional acceptability, its not being 'used up' by use, etc., etc.
>
> Possession of an average amount of it [money] yields convenience in permitting the consumer to take advantage of offers of sale, in facilitating exchanges, in bridging the gap between receipt of income and expenditure, etc. The average balance is both used and at the same time not used; it revolves but is not depleted; its just being there to meet contingencies is valuable even if the contingencies do not materialize, *ex post*. Possession of this balance then yields a real service, which can be compared with the direct utilities from the consumption of sugar, tobacco, etc., in the sense that there is some margin at which the individual would be indifferent between having more tobacco and less of a cash balance, with all of the inconvenience which the latter condition implies (pp. 117–18)."

The monetary services indexes are based on microeconomic models of consumer and firm decision making that do not impose strong *ex ante* assumptions regarding the elasticities of substitution among monetary assets.

---

[2] See Anderson and Kavajecz (1994), Kavajecz (1994), and Whitesell and Collins (1996) for descriptions of the Federal Reserve Board's monetary aggregates.

Consumer demand for monetary assets, for example, can be modeled as arising from the choices made by a representative consumer maximizing a utility function, subject to a budget constraint, that includes both stocks of real monetary assets and quantities of non-monetary goods and services.[3] In this model, monetary assets are treated as durable goods that furnish a flow of monetary services to the consumer. The appropriate opportunity cost for a durable good is its rental equivalent price, or user cost. The consumer's user cost of a monetary asset is the present value of the interest foregone by holding the monetary asset, discounted to account for the payment of interest at the end of the period.

This decision problem may be formalized by assuming that the consumer maximizes the utility function, $U(m_1, \ldots, m_n, q_1, \ldots, q_m)$, subject to the budget constraint

$$\sum_{i=1}^{n} \pi_i m_i + \sum_{j=1}^{m} p_j q_j = Y,$$

where $\mathbf{m} = (m_1, \ldots, m_n)$ is a vector of the stocks of real monetary assets, $\boldsymbol{\pi} = (\pi_1, \ldots, \pi_n)$ is a vector of user costs of monetary assets, $\mathbf{q} = (q_1, \ldots, q_m)$ is a vector of quantities of non-monetary goods and services, $\mathbf{p} = (p_1, \ldots, p_m)$ is a vector of prices of non-monetary goods and services, and Y is the consumer's total current-period expenditure on monetary assets and on non-monetary goods and services. The solution to this problem yields demand functions for real monetary assets and for quantities of non-monetary goods and services:

$$m_i^* = f_i(\boldsymbol{\pi}, \mathbf{p}, Y), \quad \text{for} \quad i = 1, \ldots, n, \quad \text{and}$$
$$q_j^* = g_j(\boldsymbol{\pi}, \mathbf{p}, Y), \quad \text{for} \quad j = 1, \ldots, m.$$

The monetary aggregation problem is to combine the quantities of various individual monetary assets, $m_1, \ldots, m_n$, and their user costs, $\pi_1, \ldots, \pi_n$, into a smaller number of aggregate quantity and opportunity cost measures.

The monetary aggregates published by the Federal Reserve Board are constructed by summing the dollar values of the stocks of the monetary assets included in each aggregate. Summation implicitly assumes that the assets' owners regard them as perfect substitutes. Yet, according to microeconomic demand theory, if these assets were in fact perfect substitutes, rational consumers would choose to hold only a single asset, unless all the assets had the same user cost. Thus, measuring a monetary aggregate by summing the dollar values of the included assets is not generally consistent with the economic theory of consumer decision making.

---

[3]Note that the quantities of real, not nominal, monetary assets enter the utility functions. The stock of a real monetary asset equals its nominal dollar quantity, deflated by an index of the economy's overall price level, such as the CPI or the GDP deflator.

A method of aggregation that is consistent with microeconomic theory was suggested by Barnett (1980a). In his formulation, the consumer's utility function is assumed to have a special form, in which the quantities of monetary assets held during the current decision period are said to be *weakly separable* from the quantities of other goods and services. In this case, the utility function $U(m_1, \ldots, m_n, q_1, \ldots, q_m)$ may be written as $U[u(m_1, \ldots, m_n), q_1, \ldots, q_m]$. The function $u(m_1, \ldots, m_n)$, called a *category subutility function*, measures the amount of monetary services that the consumer receives from holding the monetary assets, $m_1, \ldots, m_n$. During any single period, the marginal rate of substitution between monetary assets m_i and m_j may be expressed in terms of the derivatives of $u(m_1, \ldots, m_n)$ as

$$\frac{\partial u(m_1, \ldots, m_n)}{\partial m_i} \bigg/ \frac{\partial u(m_1, \ldots, m_n)}{\partial m_j}$$

Note that these derivatives, and hence the consumer's willingness to substitute among monetary assets during the current period, do not depend on the quantities of the other goods consumed, $q_1, \ldots, q_m$, but solely on the quantities of monetary assets, $m_1, \ldots, m_n$, that the consumer holds during the current period.

Barnett's approach allows us to discuss the representative consumer's choice problem as if it were solved in two stages. In the first stage, the consumer selects (1) the desired total outlay on real monetary services (but not the quantities of individual monetary assets), and (2) the quantities of all nonmonetary individual goods and services. In the second stage, the consumer selects the quantities of the individual real monetary assets, $m_1, \ldots, m_n$, conditional on the total outlay on monetary services selected in the first stage, that provide the largest possible quantity of monetary services.

This two-stage budgeting model of consumer behavior implies that the category subutility function, $u(m_1, \ldots, m_n)$, is an *aggregator function* that measures the total amount of monetary services received from holding monetary assets. If we let $m_1^*, \ldots, m_n^*$ denote the optimal quantities of monetary assets chosen by the consumer, we can regard the aggregator function as defining a *monetary aggregate*, M, via the relationship $M = u(m_1^*, \ldots, m_n^*)$.[4] A major difficulty remains, however: The specific form of the aggregator function is usually unknown. Diewert (1976) and Barnett (1980a) have established that, in this model, the aggregator function at the optimal quantities, $M = u(m_1^*, \ldots, m_n^*)$, may be approximated by a statistical index number. The monetary services indexes presented in this issue of the *Review* are *superlative statistical index numbers*, as defined by Diewert (1976).[5]

---

[4] See Green (1964).
[5] Diewert (1992) provides a concise, authoritative survey of index number theory.

Our methodology for measuring the monetary services indexes lies solidly in the mainstream of current macroeconomic research. The theory and methods are the same as those that underlie the Department of Commerce's recently adopted measures of economic aggregates, such as GDP (Triplett, 1992; Young, 1992, 1993) and those suggested by the Advisory Commission to Study the Consumer Price Index (1996). Prior to recent revisions, the Department of Commerce measures were fixed-base Laspeyres index numbers; the new measures are chained superlative indexes. The Advisory Commission to Study the Consumer Price Index (1996) recommends that the Bureau of Labor Statistics calculate the CPI as a superlative index number, and that rental-equivalent user costs be used for consumer durable goods. The indexes presented in our article, 'Building New Monetary Services Indexes: Concepts, Methodology, and Data,' in this issue of the *Review*, are chained superlative indexes and hence have the same statistical properties as Commerce's new measures and those suggested by the Advisory Commission.

In addition to its consistency with other aggregation methods, a second advantage of the index-number approach to monetary aggregation is that it produces internally consistent dual opportunity costs. These cost measures are related to the monetary services indexes in the same way that the Department of Commerce's measure of the GDP deflator is related to GDP. Finally, we note that our methodology is consistent with the foundations of modern general-equilibrium business cycle theory, which often begins with the hypothesis of an optimizing microeconomic representative agent (Cooley and Hansen, 1995). As a result, the monetary services indexes may be a particularly valuable improvement in measurement that complements innovations in economic business-cycle modeling.

Recent empirical research suggests that conclusions regarding issues such as the interest and income elasticities of money demand, and the long-run neutrality of money, may be sensitive to the method of measurement of monetary aggregates. In other words, empirical conclusions may differ when money is measured by the flow of monetary services, rather than by summation of the dollar amounts of monetary assets (see Barnett, Offenbacher, and Spindt, 1984; Barnett, Fisher, and Serletis, 1992; Chrystal and MacDonald, 1994; and Belongia, 1996). Such findings have spurred the construction of MSI data for many countries. Academic studies include la Cour (1996), for Denmark; Janssen and Kool (1994), for the Netherlands; and Lim and Martin (1994), for Australia. Central bank studies include: Herrmann, Reimers, and Toedter (1994), for Germany; Ishida and Nakamura (1994), for Japan; Longworth and Atta-Mensah (1994), for Canada; and Fisher, Hudson, and Pradhan (1993), for the United Kingdom. Unique among central banks, the Bank of England publishes monetary services indexes alongside other monetary aggregates.

Although several previous measures of monetary services have been produced for the United States, our indexes are not extensions of previous series.[6] We have fully reexamined the sustainability and credibility of the assumptions and methodology used to construct previous indexes, retaining some and discarding others, to create the new measures presented in this issue. We also have reexamined the sources of the component data that were used in earlier indexes. Where we have been unable to document previously used data, we have replaced the data with series obtained or constructed from known, documented sources.

The first article following this introduction, 'Monetary Aggregation Theory and Statistical Index Numbers,' surveys the literature on the aggregation of monetary assets and summarizes theoretical results not readily available elsewhere. The article develops a dynamic, intertemporal consumer decision model and explains how monetary aggregation conditions may be obtained from a model of a competitive firm. Because the analysis is based on dynamic microeconomic theory, some aspects are necessarily technical.

Readers primarily interested in understanding the construction of the monetary services indexes and related series might prefer to move directly to the second article, 'Building New Monetary Services Indexes: Concepts, Data, and Methodology.' This article describes the indexes' construction in detail and provides a road map of the St. Louis MSI database. The database contains the MSIs and their dual price indexes; quantities, user costs, and own-rates of return for the indexes' components; the currency-equivalent (CE) monetary index suggested by Rotemberg, Driscoll, and Poterba (1995); heretofore unpublished second moments of the MSIs, which were suggested by Barnett and Serletis (1990) as useful measures of the amount of (statistical) aggregation error contained in the MSIs; and a measure of aggregate total expenditures on the services of monetary assets. In addition to these derived series, the database includes the computer programs used to construct the MSIs and related aggregates. To facilitate comparison with monetary aggregates published by the Federal Reserve Board, the MSIs and related data in the database are provided for the same groupings of monetary assets — M1, M2, M3, and L — as well as for other widely-used aggregates such as M1A (currency plus non-interest-bearing checkable deposits) and MZM (M2 less small time deposits). The indexes are provided at monthly, quarterly, and annual frequencies. The empirical properties of these data are explored in a third paper, 'The Monetary Services Index Numbers: Analysis and Extensions,' forthcoming in the *Review* later in 1997.

Our monetary services indexes and related data are available on the

---

[6] See Barnett (1980a, 1981b, 1987), Barnett and Spindt (1982), Farr and Johnson (1985), and Thornton and Yue (1992).

Federal Reserve Bank of St. Louis' server at www.stls.frb.org/research. The data will be updated and revised by the staff of the Federal Reserve Bank of St. Louis as new numbers become available. We hope that the indexes and related data provided by the St. Louis MSI project will stimulate further research on the aggregation of monetary and financial assets, and on the roles of such variables in the conduct of monetary policy. Further, the wide range of data included in the MSI database likely will allow researchers to develop better models of the demand functions for individual monetary assets, as well as for monetary aggregates.

Consolidated References

Advisory Commission to Study the Consumer Price Index, 1996. *Toward a More Accurate Measure of the Cost of Living*, Final Report to the Senate Finance Committee.

Ahlfors, L. V., 1966. *Complex Analysis*, New York: McGraw-Hill.

Akaike, H., 1969a. "Fitting Autoregressions for Prediction," *Annals of the Institute of Statistical Mathematics* 21, 243-247.

Akaike, H., 1969b. "Statistical Predictor Identification," *Annals of the Institute of Statistical Mathematics* 21, 203-217.

Allais, M., 1953. "Le comportement de l'homme rationnel devant le risque: critique de postulats et axiomes de l'école américaines," *Econometrica* 21, 503-546.

Allen, R. C. and W. E. Diewert, 1981. "Direct Versus Implicit Superlative Index Number Formulae," *Review of Economics and Statistics* 63, 430-435.

Allen, S. D., 1983. "A Note on the Implicit Interest Rate on Demand Deposits," *Journal of Macroeconomics* 5, 233-239.

Anderson, G. J. and R. W. Blundell, 1982. "Estimation and Hypothesis Testing in Dynamic Singular Equation Systems," *Econometrica* 50, 1559-1571.

Anderson, R. G. and K. A. Kavajecz, 1994. "A Historical Perspective on the Federal Reserve's Monetary Aggregates: Definition, Construction and Targeting," The Federal Reserve Bank of St. Louis *Review* 76, 1-31.

Anderson, R. G. and R. H. Rasche, 1996. "Measuring the Adjusted Monetary Base in an Era of Financial Change," The Federal Reserve Bank of St. Louis *Review* 78, 3-37.

Anderson, R. G., B. E. Jones, and T. D. Nesmith, 1997a. "Introduction to the St. Louis Monetary Services Index Project," The Federal Reserve Bank of St. Louis *Review* 79, 25-29.

Anderson, R. G., B. E. Jones, and T. D. Nesmith, 1997b. "Monetary Aggregation Theory and Statistical Index Numbers," The Federal Reserve Bank of St. Louis *Review* 79, 31-51.

Anderson, R. G., B. E. Jones, and T. D. Nesmith, 1997c. "Building New Monetary Services Indexes: Concepts, Data and Methods," The Federal Reserve Bank of St. Louis *Review* 79, 53-82.

Anderson, R. W., 1979. "Perfect Price Aggregation and Empirical Demand Analysis," *Econometrica* 47, 1209-1230.

Apostol, T. M., 1957. *Mathematical Analysis*, Reading, Mass.: Addison Wesley.

Arrow, K. J. and G. H. Hahn, 1971. *General Competitive Analysis*, San Francisco: Holden-Day.

Ashley, R., D. M. Patterson, and M. Hinich, 1986. "A Diagnostic Test for Nonlinear Serial Dependence in Time Series Fitting Errors," *Journal of Time Series Analysis* 7, 165-178.

Attfield, C. L. F. and M. J. Browning, 1985. "A Differential Demand System, Rational Expectations, and the Life Cycle Hypothesis," *Econometrica* 53, 31-48.

Balk, B. M., 1995. "Axiomatic Price Index Theory," *International Statistical Review* 63, 69-93.

Baltensperger, E., 1980. "Alternative Approaches to the Theory of the Banking Firm," *Journal of Monetary Economics* 6, 1-37.

Bansal, R., A. R. Gallant, R. Hussey, and G. Tauchen, 1994. "Computational Aspects of Nonparametric Simulation Estimation." In *Computational Techniques for Econometrics and Economic Analysis*, D. Belsley (ed.), Boston: Kluwer Academic, 3-22.

Bansal, R., A. R. Gallant, R. Hussey, and G. Tauchen, 1995. "Nonparametric Estimation of Structural Models for High-Frequency Currency Market Data," *Journal of Econometrics* 66, 251-287.

Barnett, W. A., 1976. "Maximum Likelihood and Iterated Aitken Estimation of Nonlinear Systems of Equations," *Journal of the American Statistical Association* 71, 354-360.

Barnett, W. A., 1977a. "Recursive Subaggregation and a Generalized Hypocycloidal Demand Model," *Econometrica* 45, 1117-1136.

Barnett, W. A., 1977b. "Pollak and Wachter on the Household Production Function Approach," *Journal of Political Economy* 85, 1073-1082.

Barnett, W. A., 1978. "The User Cost of Money," *Economics Letters* 1, 145-149. Reprinted in this book as Chapter 1.

Barnett, W. A., 1979a. "Theoretical Foundations for the Rotterdam Model," *Review of Economic Studies* 46, 109-130.

Barnett, W. A., 1979b. "The Joint Allocation of Leisure and Goods Expenditure," *Econometrica* 45, 1117-1136.

Barnett, W. A., 1980a. "Economic Monetary Aggregates: An Application of Aggregation and Index Number Theory," *Journal of Econometrics* 14, 11-48. Reprinted in this book as Chapter 2.

Barnett, W. A., 1980b. "Economic Monetary Aggregates: Reply," *Journal of Econometrics* 14, 57-59.

Barnett, W. A., 1981a. "The New Monetary Aggregates: A Comment," *Journal of Money, Credit, and Banking* 13, 485-489.

Barnett, W. A., 1981b. *Consumer Demand and Labor Supply: Goods, Monetary Assets, and Time*, Amsterdam: North-Holland.

Barnett, W. A., 1982a. "The Optimal Level of Monetary Aggregation," *Journal of Money, Credit, and Banking* 14, 687-710. Reprinted in this book as Chapter 7.

Barnett, W. A., 1982b. "Divisia Indices." In *Encyclopedia of Statistical Sciences*, N. Johnson and S. Kotz (eds.), New York: John Wiley, 412-415. Reprinted in this book as Chapter 5.

Barnett, W. A., 1983a. "New Indices of Money Supply and the Flexible Laurent Demand System," *Journal of Business and Economic Statistics* 1, 7-23. Reprinted in this book as Chapter 16.

Barnett, W. A., 1983b. "Understanding the New Divisia Monetary Aggregates," *Review of Public Data Use* 11, 349-355. Reprinted in this book as Chapter 4.

Barnett, W. A., 1983c. "Definitions of 'Second Order Approximation' and of 'Flexible-Functional Form'," *Economics Letters* 12, 31-35.

Barnett, W. A., 1984. "Recent Monetary Policy and the Divisia Monetary Aggregates," *American Statistician* 38, 165-172. Reprinted in this book as Chapter 23.

Barnett, W. A., 1985. "The Minflex Laurent Translog Flexible Functional Form," *Journal of Econometrics* 30, 33-44.

Barnett, W. A., 1987. "The Microeconomic Theory of Monetary Aggregation." In *New Approaches to Monetary Economics*, W. A. Barnett and K. J. Singleton (eds.), Cambridge: Cambridge University Press, 115-168. Reprinted in this book as Chapter 3.

Barnett, W. A., 1990. "Developments in Monetary Aggregation Theory," *Journal of Policy Modeling* 12, 205-257.

Barnett, W. A., 1991. "A Reply [to Julio J. Rotemberg]." In *Monetary Policy on the 75th Anniversary of the Federal Reserve System*, M. T. Belongia (ed.), Boston: Kluwer Academic, 232-244. Reprinted in this book as Chapter 14.

Barnett, W. A., 1993. "Monetary Policy and Credibility Under Exact Monetary Aggregation," In *Political Economy: Instistutions, Information, Competition and Representation*, W. A. Barnett, M. Hinich, and N. Schofield (eds.), Cambridge: Cambridge University Press, 465-486.

Barnett, W. A., 1994. "Perspective on the Current State of Macroeconomic Theory," *International Journal of Systems Science* 25, 839-848. Reprinted in this book as Chapter 25.

Barnett, W. A., 1995. "Exact Aggregation Under Risk." In *Social Choice, Welfare, and Ethics*, W. A. Barnett, H. Moulin, M. Salles, and N. Schofield (eds.), Cambridge: Cambridge University Press, 353-374. Reprinted in this book as Chapter 10.

Barnett, W. A., 1997. "Journal of Econometrics Fellow's Opinion: Econometrics, Data, and the World Wide Web," *Journal of Econometrics* 77, 297-302.

Barnett, W. A. and P. Chen, 1986. "Economic Theory as a Generator of Measurable Attractors," *Mondes en Developpement* 14, 5-20.

Barnett, W. A. and P. Chen, 1988. "The Aggregation Theoretic Monetary Aggregates are Chaotic and Have Strange Attractors: An Economic Application of Mathematical Chaos." In *Dynamic Econometric Modeling*, W. A. Barnett, E. Berndt, and H. White (eds.), Cambridge: Cambridge University Press, 199-245.

Barnett, W. A. and S. Choi, 1989a. "A Monte Carlo Study of Tests of Blockwise Weak Separability," *Journal of Business and Economic Statistics* 7, 363-377.

Barnett, W. A. and S. Choi, 1989b. "A Comparison between the Conventional Econometric Approach to Structural Inference and the Nonparametric Chaotic Attractor Approach." In *Economic Complexity: Chaos, Sunspots, Bubbles, and Nonlinearity*, W. A. Barnett, J. Geweke, and K. Shell (eds.), Cambridge: Cambridge University Press, 141-212.

Barnett, W. A. and J. H. Hahm, 1994. "Financial-Firm Production of Monetary Services: A Generalized Symmetric Barnett Variable-Profit-Function Approach," *Journal of Business and Economic Statistics* 12, 33-46. Reprinted in this book as Chapter 20.

Barnett, W. A. and M. J. Hinich, 1992. "Empirical Chaotic Dynamics in Economics," *Annals of Operations Research* 37, 1-15.

Barnett, W. A. and A. Jonas, 1983. "The Muntz-Szatz Demand System: An Application of a Globally Well Behaved Series Expansion," *Economics Letters* 11, 337-342.

Barnett, W. A. and Y. W. Lee, 1985. "The Global Properties of the Minflex Laurent, Generalized Leontief, and Translog Flexible Functional Forms," *Econometrica* 53, 1421-1437.

Barnett, W. A. and Y. Liu, 1995. "The CAPM-Extended Divisia Monetary Aggregate with Exact Tracking Under Risk," Discussion Paper #194, Department of Economics, Washington University at St. Louis. The contents of this working paper have now appeared in Barnett, Liu, and Jensen (1997).

Barnett, W. A. and Y. Liu, 2000. "Beyond the Risk Neutral Utility Function." In *Divisia Monetary Aggregates: Theory and Practice*, M. T. Belongia and J. E. Binner (eds.), London: Macmillan.

Barnett, W. A. and A. Serletis, 1989. "Prices, Output, and Money: An Application of Cointegration Techniques," Mimeo, Department of Economics, University of Texas at Austin.

Barnett, W. A. and A. Serletis, 1990. "A Dispersion-Dependency Diagnostic Test for Aggregation Error: With Applications to Monetary Economics and Income Distribution," *Journal of Econometrics* 43, 5-34. Reprinted in this book as Chapter 9.

Barnett, W. A. and P. A. Spindt, 1979. "The Velocity Behavior and Information Content of Divisia Monetary Aggregates," *Economics Letters* 4, 51-57.

REFERENCES

Barnett, W. A. and P. A. Spindt, 1980. "The Information Content of Divisia Monetary Quantity Indices," Special Studies Paper #146, Federal Reserve Board, Washington, D.C. The contents of this working paper have now appeared in Barnett, Offenbacher, and Spindt (1984).

Barnett, W. A. and P. A. Spindt, 1982. "Divisia Monetary Aggregates: Compilation, Data, and Historical Behavior," Staff Study #116, Federal Reserve Board, Washington, D.C.

Barnett, W. A. and P. Yue, 1988. "Seminonparametric Estimation of the Asymptotically Ideal Model: The AIM Demand System." In *Nonparametric and Robust Inference: Advances in Econometrics,* Vol. 7, G. F. Rhodes and T. B. Fomby (eds.), Greenwich, CT : JAI Press, 229-251.

Barnett, W. A. and P. Yue, 1989. "Monetary Aggregation with Risk Aversion," Mimeo, Department of Economics, University of Texas at Austin. The contents of this working paper have now appeared in Barnett, Hinich, and Yue (2000).

Barnett, W. A. and P. Yue, 1991. "Exact Monetary Aggregation under Risk," Discussion Paper #163, Department of Economics, Washington University at St. Louis. The contents of this working paper have now appeared in Barnett, Hinich, and Yue (2000).

Barnett, W. A. and G. Zhou, 1994a. "Commentary," Federal Reserve Bank of St. Louis *Review* 76, 53-61.

Barnett, W. A. and G. Zhou, 1994b. "Financial Firms' Production and Supply-Side Monetary Aggregation Under Dynamic Uncertainty," Federal Reserve Bank of St. Louis *Review* 76, 133-165. Reprinted in this book as Chapter 21.

Barnett, W. A. and G. Zhou, 1994c. "Response to Brainard's Commentary," Federal Reserve Bank of St. Louis *Review* 76, 169-174.

Barnett, W. A., D. Fisher, and A. Serletis, 1992. "Consumer Theory and the Demand for Money," *Journal of Economic Literature* 30, 2086-2119. Reprinted in this book as Chapter 18.

Barnett, W. A., J. Geweke, and M. D. Wolfe, 1991a. "Seminonparametric Bayesian Estimation of the Asymptotically Ideal Production Model," *Journal of Econometrics* 49, 5-50.

Barnett, W. A., J. Geweke, and M. D. Wolfe, 1991b. "Seminonparametric Bayesian Estimation of Consumer and Factor Demand Models." In *Equilibrium Theory and Applications,* W. A. Barnett, B. Cornet, C. D'Aspremont, J. Gabszewicz, and A. Mas-Colell (eds.), Cambridge: Cambridge University Press, 425-480.

Barnett, W. A., J. Geweke, and P. Yue, 1991. "Seminonparametric Bayesian Estimation of the Asymptotically Ideal Model: The AIM Consumer Demand System." In *Nonparametric and Semiparametric Methods in Econometrics and Statistics,* W. A. Barnett, J. Powell, and G. Tauchen, Cambridge: Cambridge University Press, 127-173.

Barnett, W. A., M. J. Hinich, and W. E. Weber, 1986. "The Regulatory Wedge between the Demand-Side and Supply-Side Aggregation-Theoretic Monetary Aggregates," *Journal of Econometrics* 33, 165-185. Reprinted in this book as Chapter 19.

Barnett, W. A., M. Hinich, and P. Yue, 1991. "Monitoring Monetary Aggregates under Risk Aversion." In *Monetary Policy on the 75th Anniversary of the Federal Reserve System*, M. T. Belongia (ed.), Boston: Kluwer Academic, 189-222. Reprinted in this book as Chapter 11.

Barnett, W. A., M. Hinich, and P. Yue, 2000. "The Exact Theoretical Rational Expectations Monetary Aggregate," *Macroeconomic Dynamics*, June, Vol. 4, no. 2, forthcoming.

Barnett, W. A., B. E. Jones, and T. D. Nesmith, 1996. "Divisia Second Moments: An Application of Stochastic Index Number Theory," *International Review of Comparative Public Policy* 8, 115-138.

Barnett, W. A., M. Kirova, and M. Pasupathy, 1995. "Estimating Policy-Invariant Deep Parameters in the Financial Sector when Risk and Growth Matter," *Journal of Money, Credit, and Banking* 27, 1402-1430. Reprinted in this book as Chapter 22.

Barnett, W. A., Y. W. Lee, and M. D. Wolfe, 1985. "The Three-Dimensional Global Properties of the Minflex Laurent, Generalized Leontief, and Translog Flexible Functional Forms," *Journal of Econometrics* 30, 3-31.

Barnett, W. A., Y. W. Lee, and M. D. Wolfe, 1987. "The Global Properties of the two Minflex Laurent Flexible Functional Forms," *Journal of Econometrics* 36, 281-298.

Barnett, W. A., Y. Liu, and M. J. Jensen, 1997. "CAPM Risk Adjustment for Exact Aggregation over Financial Assets," *Macroeconomic Dynamics* 1, 485-512. Reprinted in this book as Chapter 12.

Barnett, W. A., E. K. Offenbacher, and P. A. Spindt, 1981. "New Concepts of Aggregated Money," *Journal of Finance* 36, 497-505. Reprinted in this book as Chapter 8.

Barnett, W. A., E. K. Offenbacher, and P. A. Spindt, 1984. "The New Divisia Monetary Aggregates," *Journal of Political Economy* 92, 1049-1085. Reprinted in this book as Chapter 17.

Barnett, W. A., P. A. Spindt, and E. K. Offenbacher, 1981. "Empirical Comparisons of Divisia and Simple Sum Monetary Aggregates," Staff Study #158, Federal Reserve Board, Washington, D.C. The contents of this working paper have now appeared in Barnett, Offenbacher, and Spindt (1984).

Barnett, W. A., R. Gallant, M. J. Hinich, and M. J. Jensen, 1993. "Robustness of Non-Linearity and Chaos Tests to Measurement Error, Inference Method, and Sample Size," Discussion Paper #167, Department of Economics, Washington University at St. Louis. The contents of this working paper have now appeared in Barnett, Gallant, Hinich, Jungeilges, and Kaplan (1995).

REFERENCES

Barnett, W. A., M. Kirova, M. Pasupathy, and P. Yue, 1994. "Estimating Policy-Invariant Technology and Taste Parameters in the Financial Sector, When Risk and Growth Matter," Discussion Paper #193, Department of Economics, Washington University at St. Louis. The contents of this working paper have now appeared in Barnett, Hinich, and Yue (2000) and Barnett, Kirova, and Pasupathy (1995).

Barnett, W. A., A. R. Gallant, M. J. Hinich, J. A. Jungeilges, D. T. Kaplan, and M. J. Jensen, 1995. "Robustness of Nonlinearity and Chaos Tests to Measurement Error, Inference Method, and Sample Size," *Journal of Economic Behavior and Organization* 27, 301-320.

Barnett, W. A., A. R. Gallant, M. J. Hinich, J. A. Jungeilges, D. T. Kaplan, and M. J. Jensen, 1997. "A Single-Blind Controlled Competition among Tests for Nonlinearity and Chaos," *Journal of Econometrics* 82, 157-192.

Barnett, W. A., D. Beck, E. Ettin, J. Kalchbrenner, D. Lindsey, R. Porter, T. Simpson, and P. Tinsley, 1979. "A Proposal for Redefining the Monetary Aggregates," *Federal Reserve Bulletin* 65, 13-42.

Barro, R. J. and C. Sahasakul, 1983. "Measuring the Average Marginal Tax Rate from the Individual Income Tax," *Journal of Business* 56, 419-452.

Barro, R. J. and A. J. Santomero, 1972. "Household Money Holdings and the Demand Deposit Rate," *Journal of Money, Credit, and Banking* 4, 397-413.

Barten, A. P., 1969. "Maximum Likelihood Estimation of a Complete System of Demand Equations," *European Economic Review* 1, 7-73.

Barth, J. R., A. Kraft, and J. Kraft, 1977. "The 'Moneyness' of Financial Assets," *Applied Economics* 9, 51-61.

Basmann, R. L. and D. J. Slottje, 1987. "The Sensitivity of the True Cost of Living to Price-Induced and Income-Induced Changes in Aggregate Consumers' Tastes," *Journal of Business and Economic Statistics* 5, 483-498.

Batchelor, R., 1989. "A Monetary Services Index for the UK," Mimeo, Department of Economics, City University, London.

Baumol, W. J., 1952. "The Transactions Demand for Cash: An Inventory Theoretic Approach," *Quarterly Journal of Economics* 66, 545-556.

Baxter, M., 1991. "Approximating Suboptimal Dynamic Equilibria: An Euler Equation Approach," *Journal of Monetary Economics* 27, 173-200.

Baxter, M., M. J. Crucini, and K. G. Rouwenhorst, 1990. "Solving the Stochastic Growth Model by a Discrete State-Space, Euler Equation Approach," *Journal of Business and Economic Statistics* 8, 19-21.

Becker, W. E. Jr., 1975. "Determinants of the United States Currency-Demand Deposit Ratio," *The Journal of Finance* 30, 57-74.

Bell, F. W. and N. B. Murphy, 1968. "Costs in Commercial Banking: A Quantitative Analysis of Bank Behavior and Its Relation to Bank Regulation," Research Report #41, Federal Reserve Bank of Boston.

Belongia, M. T., 1985. "Money Growth Variability and GNP," *Federal Reserve Bank of St. Louis Review* 67, 23-31.

Belongia, M. T., 1995. "Weighted Monetary Aggregates: A Historical Survey," *Journal of International and Comparative Economics* 4, 87-114.

Belongia, M. T., 1996. "Measurement Matters: Recent Results from Monetary Economics Reexamined," *Journal of Political Economy* 104, 1065-1083.

Belongia, M. T. and J. E. Binner (eds.), 2000. *Divisia Monetary Aggregates: Theory and Practice*, London: Macmillan Press Ltd.

Belongia, M. T. and J. Chalfant, 1989. "The Changing Empirical Definition of Money: Some Estimates from a Model of the Demand for Money Substitutes," *Journal of Political Economy* 97, 387-398.

Belongia, M. T. and A. Chrystal, 1991. "An Admissible Monetary Aggregate for the United Kingdom," *Review of Economics and Statistics* 73, 497-503.

Benston, G. J., 1965. "Branch Banking and Economies of Scale," *Journal of Finance* 20, 312-341.

Benston, G. J., G. A. Hanweck, and D. B. Humphrey, 1982. "Scale Economies in Banking: A Restructuring and Reassessment," *Journal of Money, Credit, and Banking* 14, 435-456.

Benston, G. J., A. N. Berger, G. A. Hanweck, and D. B. Humphrey, 1983. "Economies of Scale and Scope in Banking," Mimeo, Federal Reserve Board, Washington, D.C.

Bernanke, B. and M. Gertler, 1987. "Banking and Macroeconomic Equilibrium." In *New Approaches to Monetary Economics*, W. A. Barnett and K. J. Singleton (eds.), Cambridge: Cambridge University Press, 89-111.

Berndt, E. R. and L. R. Christensen, 1973. "The Internal Structure of Functional Relationships: Separability, Substitution, and Aggregation," *Review of Economic Studies* 40, 403-410.

Berndt, E. R. and L. R. Christensen, 1974. "Testing for the Existence of a Consistent Aggregate Index of Labor Inputs," *American Economic Review* 64, 391-404.

Berndt, E. R. and M. S. Khaled, 1979. "Parametric Productivity Measurement and Choice among Flexible Functional Forms," *Journal of Political Economy* 87, 1220-1245.

Berndt, E. R. and N. E. Savin, 1975. "Estimation and Hypothesis Testing in Singular Equation Systems with Autoregressive Disturbances," *Econometrica* 43, 937-957.

Berndt, E. R., W. E. Diewert, and M. N. Darrough, 1977. "Flexible Functional Forms and Expenditure Distributions: An Application to Canadian Consumer Demand Functions," *International Economic Review* 18, 651-676.

Betancourt, R. and B. Robles, 1989. "Credit, Money, and Production: Empirical Evidence," *Review of Economics and Statistics* 71, 712-717.

Bhattacharya, S. and D. Gale, 1987. "Preference Shocks, Liquidity, and Central Bank Policy." In *New Approaches to Monetary Economics*, W. A. Barnett and K. J. Singleton (eds.), Cambridge: Cambridge University Press, 69-88.

Bisignano, J., 1974. "Real Money Substitutes," Discussion Paper #17, Federal Reserve Bank of San Francisco.

Blackorby, C., R. Davidson, and D. Donaldson, 1977. "A Homiletic Exposition of the Expected Utility Hypothesis," *Economica* 44, 351-358.

Blackorby, C., D. Primont, and R. R. Russell, 1977. "On Testing Separability Restrictions with Flexible Functional Forms," *Journal of Econometrics* 5, 195-209.

Blackorby, C., D. Primont, and R. R. Russell, 1978. *Duality, Separability, and Functional Structure*, Amsterdam: North-Holland.

Blackorby, C., W. Schworm, and T. Fisher, 1986. "Testing for the Existence of Input Aggregates in an Economy Production Function," Mimeo, Department of Economics, University of British Columbia.

Blanchard, O. J. and S. Fischer, 1989. *Lectures in Macroeconomics*, The MIT Press.

Bliss, C. J., 1975. *Capital Theory and the Distribution of Income*, Amsterdam: North-Holland.

Board of Governors of the Federal Reserve System 1979-1983. *Functional Cost Analysis*, Federal Reserve Board, Washington, D.C.

Board of Governors of the Federal Reserve System 1983. *Functional Cost Analysis: 1983 Average Banks*, Federal Reserve Board, Washington, D.C.

Bordo, M. D. and L. Jonung, 1981. "The Long-Run Behaviour of the Income Velocity of Money in Five Advanced Countries, 1870-1975: An Institutional Approach," *Economic Inquiry* 19, 96-116.

Bordo, M. D. and L. Jonung, 1987. *The Long-Run Behaviour of the Velocity of Circulation*, Cambridge: Cambridge University Press.

Bordo, M. D. and L. Jonung, 1990. "The Long-Run Behaviour of Velocity: The Institutional Approach Revisited," *Journal of Policy Modeling* 12, 165-197.

Box, G. E. P. and G. M. Jenkins, 1970. *Time Series Analysis, Forecasting and Control*, San Francisco: Holden-Day.

Boyle, G. W., 1990. "Money Demand and the Stock Market in A General Equilibrium Model with Variable Velocity," *Journal of Political Economy* 98, 1039-1053.

Brainard, W. and J. Tobin, 1963. "Financial Intermediaries and the Effectiveness of Monetary Controls," *American Economic Review* 53, 383-400.

Brainard, W. and J. Tobin, 1968. "Pitfalls in Financial Model Building," *American Economic Review* 58, 99-122.

Brennan, M. J. and E. S. Schwartz, 1979. "Savings Bonds: Theory and Empirical Evidence," *Monograph Series in Finance and Economics*, Monograph #1979-4, Salomon Brothers Center for the Study of Financial Institutions.

Bridge, J. L., 1971. *Applied Econometrics*, Amsterdam: North-Holland.

Brillinger, D. R., 1965. "An Introduction to Polyspectrum," *Annals of Mathematical Statistics* 36, 1351-1374.

Brock, W. A. and W. D. Dechert, 1988. "Theorems on Distinguishing Deterministic from Random Systems." In *Dynamic Econometric Modeling*, W. A. Barnett, E. Berndt, and H. White (eds.), Cambridge: Cambridge University Press, 247-265.

Brock, W. A., W. D. Dechert, B. LeBaron, and J. Scheinkman, 1996. "A Test for Independence Based on the Correlation Dimension," *Econometric Reviews* 15, 197-235.

Brockett, P. L., M. J. Hinich, and D. Patterson, 1988. "Bispectral-Based Test for the Detection of Gaussianity and Linearity in Time Series," *Journal of the American Statistical Association* 83, 657-664.

Brockett, P. L., M. J. Hinich, and G. R. Wilson, 1987. "Nonlinear and Non-Gaussian Ocean Noise," *Journal of the Acoustical Society of America* 82, 1386-1394.

Brown, M., 1980. "The Measurement of Capital Aggregates: A Postreswitching Problem." In *The Measurement of Capital*, D. Usher (ed.), Chicago: University of Chicago Press (for the NBER), 377-420.

Brown, R. S., D. W. Caves, and L. R. Christensen, 1979. "Modeling the Structure of Cost and Production for Multiproduct Firms," *Southern Economics Journal* 46, 256-273.

Brunner, K., 1979a. "Monetary Policy and the Road to a Stable Price Level," Shadow Open Market Committee Policy Statement and Position Papers, PPS-79-3.

Brunner, K., 1979b. "Our Perennial Issue: Monetary Policy and Inflation," Shadow Open Market Committee Policy Statement and Position Papers, PPS-79-6.

Brunner, K., 1983. "The Recession of 1981/1982 in the Context of Postwar Recessions," Shadow Open Market Committee Policy Statement and Position Papers, PPS-83-2, 43-44.

Brunner, K. and A. H. Meltzer, 1964. "Some Further Investigations of Demand and Supply Functions for Money," *Journal of Finance* 19, 240-283.

Brunner, K. and A. H. Meltzer, 1967. "The Meaning of Monetary Indicators." In *Monetary Process and Policy: A Symposium*, G. Horwich (ed.), Homewood: Richard D. Irwin, 187-217.

Brunner, K. and A. H. Meltzer, 1969. "The Nature of the Policy Problem." In *Targets and Indicators of Monetary Policy*, K. Brunner (ed.), San Francisco: Chandler, 1-26.

Brunner, K. and A. H. Meltzer, 1971. "The Uses of Money: Money in the Theory of an Exchange Economy," *American Economic Review* 61, 784-805.

Buck, R. C., 1965. *Advanced Calculus*, New York: McGraw-Hill.

Bullard, J. B., 1994. "Measures of Money and the Quantity Theory," Federal Reserve Bank of St. Louis *Review* 76, 19-30.

Burgess, D. F., 1974. "A Cost Minimization Approach to Import Demand Equations," *Review of Economics and Statistics* 56, 225-234.

Cagan, P., 1982. "The Choice Among Monetary Aggregates as Targets and Indicators for Monetary Policy," *Journal of Money, Credit, and Banking* 14, 661-686.

Caines, P. E., C. W. Keng, and S. P. Sethi, 1981. "Causality Analysis and Multivariate Autoregressive Modelling with an Application to Supermarket Sales Analysis," *Journal of Economic Dynamics and Control* 3, 267-298.

Calvo, G. A., 1978. "On the Time Consistency of Optimal Policy in a Monetary Economy," *Econometrica* 46, 1411-1428.

Carlson, J. A. and J. R. Frew, 1980. "Money Demand Responsiveness to the Rate of Return on Money: A Methodological Critique," *Journal of Political Economy* 88, 598-607.

Carlson, K. M., 1980. "Money, Inflation, and Economic Growth: Some Updated Reduced Form Results and Their Implications," Federal Reserve Bank of St. Louis *Review* 62, 13-19.

Cass, D. and K. Shell, 1983. "Do Sunspots Matter?," *Journal of Political Economy* 91, 193-227.

Caves, D. W., L. R. Christensen, and W. E. Diewert, 1982a. "The Economic Theory of Index Numbers and the Measurement of Input, Output, and Productivity," *Econometrica* 50, 1393-1414.

Caves, D. W., L. R. Christensen, and W. E. Diewert, 1982b. "Multilateral Comparisons of Output, Input, and Productivity Using Superlative Index Numbers," *Economic Journal* 92, 73-86.

Chetty, K. V., 1969. "On Measuring the Nearness of Near-Moneys," *American Economic Review* 59, 270-281.

Chetty, K. V., 1972. "On Measuring the Nearness of Near-Moneys: Reply," *American Economic Review* 62, 226-229.

Chew, S. H., 1989. "Axiomatic Utility Theories with the Betweenness Property," *Annals of Operations Research* 19, 273-298.

Choi, S. and K. Sosin, 1992. "Structural Change in the Demand for Money," *Journal of Money, Credit, and Banking* 24, 226-238.

Chow, G. C., 1966. "On the Long-Run and Short-Run Demand for Money," *Journal of Political Economy* 74, 111-131.

Christ, C. F., 1993. "Assessing Applied Econometric Results," Federal Reserve Bank of St. Louis *Review* 75, 71-94.

Christensen, L. R. and D. W. Caves, 1980. "Global Properties of Flexible Functional Forms," *American Economic Review* 70, 422-432.

Christensen, L. R., D. W. Jorgenson, and L. J. Lau, 1973. "Transcendental Logarithmic Production Frontiers," *Review of Economics and Statistics* 55, 28-45.

Christensen, L. R., D. W. Jorgenson, and L. J. Lau, 1975. "Transcendental Logarithmic Utility Functions," *American Economic Review* 65, 367-383.

Christiano, L. J., 1986. "Money and the U.S. Economy in the 1980s: A Break from the Past?," Federal Reserve Bank of Minneapolis *Quarterly Review* 10, 2-13.

Chrystal, A. K. and R. MacDonald, 1994. "Empirical Evidence on the Recent Behaviour and Usefulness of Simple-Sum and Weighted Measures of the Money Stock," Federal Reserve Bank of St. Louis *Review* 76, 73-109.

Clark, J. A., 1984. "Estimation of Economies of Scale in Banking Using a Generalized Functional Form," *Journal of Money, Credit, and Banking* 16, 53-75.

Clements, K. W., 1976. "A Linear Allocation of Spending-Power System: A Consumer Demand and Portfolio Model," *Economic Record* 52, 182-198.

Clements, K. W. and H. Y. Izan, 1980. "A Note on Estimating Divisia Index Numbers," *International Economic Review* 22, 745-747.

Clements, K. W. and H. Y. Izan, 1987. "The Measurement of Inflation: A Stochastic Approach," *Journal of Business and Economic Statistics* 5, 339-350.

Clements, K. W. and P. Nguyen, 1980. "Money Demand, Consumer Demand and Relative Prices in Australia," *Economic Record* 56, 338-346.

Clower, R. W., 1967. "A Reconsideration of the Microfoundations of Monetary Theory," *Western Economic Journal* 6, 1-8.

Cockerline, J. P. and J. D. Murray, 1981a. "Superlative Monetary Aggregation: Some Preliminary Results," Unpublished mimeograph, file #105-7-4, Bank of Canada.

Cockerline, J. P. and J. D. Murray, 1981b. "A Comparison of Alternative Methods of Monetary Aggregation: Some Preliminary Evidence," Technical Report #28, Bank of Canada.

Coen, R. M. and B. G. Hickman, 1970. "Constrained Joint Estimation of Factor Demand and Production Functions," *Review of Economics and Statistics* 52, 287-300.

Coleman, W. J., II 1990. "Solving the Stochastic Growth Model by Policy-Function Iteration," *Journal of Business and Economic Statistics* 8, 27-29.

Coleman, W. J., II 1991. "Equilibrium in a Production Economy with an Income Tax," *Econometrica* 59, 1091-1104.

Collins, S., 1991. "Do Banks Price Discriminate Among Their Retail Customers? A Test Based on Tiered Deposit Rates," Mimeo, Division of Monetary Affairs, Federal Reserve Board, Washington, D.C.

Collins, S. and C. L. Edwards, 1994. "An Alternative Monetary Aggregate: M2 Plus Household Holdings of Bond and Equity Mutual Funds," Federal Reserve Bank of St. Louis *Review* 76, 7-29.

Cooley, T. F. and G. D. Hansen, 1995. "Money and the Business Cycle." In *Frontiers of Business Cycle Research*, Thomas F. Cooley (ed.), Princeton: Princeton University Press, 175-216.

Cooley, T. F. and S. F. LeRoy, 1981. "Identification and Estimation of Money Demand," *American Economic Review* 71, 825-844.

Cooley, T. F. and E. D. Prescott, 1995. "Economic Growth and Business Cycles." In *Frontiers of Business Cycle Research*, Thomas F. Cooley (ed.), Princeton: Princeton University Press, 1-38.

Croushore, D., 1993. "Money in the Utility Function: Functional Equivalence to a Shopping-Time Model," *Journal of Macroeconomics* 15, 175-182.

Cuthbertson, K., 1997. "Microfoundations and the Demand for Money," *Economic Journal* 107, 1186-1201.

Day, R. H., 1992. "Complex Economic Dynamics: Obvious in History, Generic in Theory, Elusive in Data," *Journal of Applied Econometrics* 7, 19-23.

Deaton, A., 1979. "The Distance Function in Consumer Behaviour with Applications to Index Numbers and Optimal Taxation," *Review of Economic Studies* 46, 391-405.

Deaton, A. and J. N. Muellbauer, 1980. *Economics and Consumer Behavior*, Cambridge: Cambridge University Press.

Debreu, G., 1959. *Theory of Value*, Cowles Foundation Monograph 17, New Haven: Yale University Press.

Dekel, E., 1986. "An Axiomatic Characterization of Preferences Under Uncertainty: Weakening the Independence Axiom," *Journal of Economic Theory* 40, 304-314.

Den Haan, W. J., 1990a. "The Optimal Inflation Path in a Sidrauski-Type Model with Uncertainty," *Journal of Monetary Economics* 25, 389-409.

Den Haan, W. J., 1990b. "The Term Structure of Interest Rates in Real and Monetary Production Economies," Discussion Paper #91-30, Department of Economics, University of California, San Diego.

Den Haan, W. J. and A. Marcet, 1990. "Solving the Stochastic Growth Model by Parameterizing Expectations," *Journal of Business and Economic Statistics* 8, 31-34.

Den Haan, W. J. and A. Marcet, 1994. "Accuracy in Simulations," *Review of Economic Studies* 61, 3-17.

Denny, M. and M. Fuss, 1977. "The Use of Approximation Analysis to Test for Separability and the Existence of Consistent Aggregates," *American Economic Review* 67, 404-418.

Denny, M. and J. D. May, 1978. "Homotheticity and Real Value-Added in Canadian Manufacturing." In *Production Economics: A Dual Approach to Theory and Applications*, Vol. 2, M. Fuss and D. McFadden (eds.), Amsterdam: North-Holland, 53-70.

Denny, M. and C. Pinto, 1978. "An Aggregate Model with Multi-Product Technologies." In *Production Economics: A Dual Approach to Theory and Applications*, Vol. 2, M. Fuss and D. McFadden (eds.), Amsterdam: North-Holland, 247-267.

Diamond, D. W. and P. H. Dybvig, 1983. "Bank Runs, Deposit Insurance and Liquidity," *Journal of Political Economy* 91, 401-419.

Dickey, D. A., 1993. "Commentary," Federal Reserve Bank of St. Louis *Review* 75, 95-100.

Diewert, W. E., 1971. "An Application of the Shephard Duality Theorem: A Generalized Leontief Production Function," *Journal of Political Economy* 79, 481-507.

Diewert, W. E., 1973. "Functional Forms for Profit and Transformation Functions," *Journal of Economic Theory* 6, 284-316.

Diewert, W. E., 1974a. "Intertemporal Consumer Theory and the Demand for Durables," *Econometrica* 42, 497-516.

Diewert, W. E., 1974b. "Applications of Duality Theory." In *Frontiers in Quantitative Economics*, Vol. 2, M. Intriligator and D. Kendrick (eds.), Amsterdam: North-Holland.

Diewert, W. E., 1974c. "Intertemporal Consumer Theory and the Demand for Durables," *Econometrica* 42, 497-516.

Diewert, W. E., 1976. "Exact and Superlative Index Numbers," *Journal of Econometrics* 4, 115-145.

Diewert, W. E., 1978. "Superlative Index Numbers and Consistency in Aggregation," *Econometrica* 46, 883-900.

Diewert, W. E., 1980a. "Aggregation Problems in the Measurement of Capital." In *The measurement of Capital*, D. Usher (ed.), Chicago: University of Chicago Press (for the NBER), 433-538.

Diewert, W. E., 1980b. "Capital and the Theory of Productivity Measurement," *American Economic Review* 70, 260-267.

Diewert, W. E., 1980c. "Reply." In *The Measurement of Capital*, D. Usher (ed.), Chicago: University of Chicago Press (for the NBER), 538.

Diewert, W. E., 1981. "The Economic Theory of Index Numbers: A Survey." In *Essays in the Theory and Measurement of Consumer Behaviour in Honour of Sir Richard Stone*, A. Deaton (ed.), Cambridge: Cambridge University Press, 163-208.

Diewert, W. E., 1983. "The Treatment of Seasonality in a Cost-Of-Living-Index." In *Price Level Measurement*, W. E. Diewert and C. Montmarquette (eds.), Ottawa: Statistics Canada, 1019-1045.

Diewert, W. E., 1992a. "Index Numbers." In *The New Palgrave Dictionary of Money and Finance,* Vol. 2, P. Newman, M. Milgate, and J. Eatwell (eds.), Stockton Press, 364-379.

Diewert, W. E., 1992b. "Fisher Ideal Output, Input, and Productivity Indexes Revisited," *Journal of Productivity Analysis* 3, 211-248.

Diewert, W. E., 1993, "Symmetric Means and Choice Under Uncertainty." In *Essays in Index Number Theory*, Vol. 1, W. E. Diewert and A. O. Nakamura (eds.), Amsterdam: North Holland, 355-433.

Diewert, W. E., 1995a. "Axiomatic and Economic Approaches to Elementary Price Indexes," Discussion Paper #95-01, Department of Economics, University of British Columbia.

Diewert, W. E., 1995b. "Functional Form Problems in Modeling Insurance and Gambling," *The Geneva Papers on Risk and Insurance Theory* 20, 135-150.

Diewert, W. E., 1996. "Seasonal Commodities, High Inflation and Index Number Theory," Discussion Paper #96-06, Department of Economics, University of British Columbia.

Diewert, W. E. and A. M. Smith, 1994. "Productivity Measurement for a Distribution Firm," *Journal of Productivity Analysis* 5, 335-347.

Diewert, W. E. and T. J. Wales, 1987. "Flexible Functional Forms and Global Curvature Conditions," *Econometrica* 55, 43-68.

Diewert, W. E. and T. J. Wales, 1988. "A Normalized Quadratic Semiflexible Functional Form," *Journal of Econometrics* 37, 327-342.

Diewert, W. E. and T. J. Wales, 1995. "Flexible Functional Forms and Tests of Homogeneous Separability," *Journal of Econometrics* 67, 259-302.

Divisia, F., 1925. "L'Indice Monétaire et la Théorie de la Monnaie," *Revue d'Economie Politique* 39, 980-1008.

Dixon, P. B., 1975. *The Theory of Joint Maximization*, Amsterdam: North-Holland.

Donovan, D. J., 1977. *Consumption, Leisure, and the Demand for Money and Money Substitutes*, Ph.D. Thesis, University of British Columbia.

Donovan, D. J., 1978. "Modeling the Demand for Liquid Assets: An Application to Canada," International Monetary Fund *Staff Papers* 25, 676-704.

Dorfman, J. R., 1983. "What Explosion?," *Forbes* 132, 196.

Dowd, K., 1990. "The Value of Time and the Transactions Demand for Money," *Journal Money, Credit, and Banking* 22, 51-64.

Drake, L., 1992. "The Substitutability of Financial Assets in the U.K. and the Implication for Monetary Aggregation," *Manchester School of Economics and Social Studies* 60, 221-248.

Drake, L. and A. Chrystal, 1994. "Company-Sector Money Demand: New Evidence on the Existence of a Stable Long-Run Relationship for the United Kingdom," *Journal of Money, Credit, and Banking* 26, 479-494.

Dueker, M. J., 1993. "Can Nominal GDP Targeting Rules Stabilize the Economy?," Federal Reserve Bank of St. Louis *Review* 75, 15-30.

Dueker, M. J., 1995. "Narrow vs. Broad Measures of Money as Intermediate Targets: Some Forecast Results," Federal Reserve Bank of St. Louis *Review* 77, 41-51.

Duffie, D., 1991. "The Theory of Value in Security Markets." In *Handbook of Mathematical Economics*, Vol. 4, W. Hildenbrand and H. Sonnenschein (eds.), Amsterdam: North-Holland, 1615-1682.

Dutkowsky, Donald H., 1999. "Taxation and Monetary Aggregation," *Journal of Money, Credit, and Banking* 31, 811-817.

Dutton, D. and W. P. Gramm, 1973. "Transactions Costs, the Wage Rate, and the Demand for Money," *American Economic Review* 63, 652-65.

Eichhorn, W., 1976. "Fisher's Tests Revisited," *Econometrica* 44, 247-256.

Eichhorn, W., 1978. *Functional Equations in Economics*, Reading, MA: Addison-Wesley.

Enzler, J. J., L. Johnson, and J. D. Paulus, 1976. "Some Problems of Money Demand," *Brookings Papers on Economic Activity* 1, 261-280.

Epstein, L. G., 1992. "Behavior Under Risk: Recent Developments in Theory and Applications." In *Advances in Economic Theory*, J. J. Laffont (ed.), New York: Cambridge University Press.

Epstein, L. G. and S. E. Zin, 1990. "First Order Risk Aversion and the Equity Premium Puzzle," *Journal of Monetary Economics* 26, 387-407.

Epstein, L. G. and S. E. Zin, 1991. "The Independence Axiom and Asset Returns," NBER Working Paper #109, Cambridge, Mass.

Ewis, N. A. and D. Fisher, 1984. "The Translog Utility Function and the Demand for Money in the United States," *Journal of Money, Credit, and Banking* 16, 34-52.

Ewis, N. A. and D. Fisher, 1985. "Toward a Consistent Estimate of the Demand for Monies: An Application of the Fourier Flexible Form," *Journal of Macroeconomics* 7, 151-174.

Farr, H. T. and D. Johnson, 1985. "Revisions in the Monetary Services (Divisia) Indexes of the Monetary Aggregates," Staff Study #147, Federal Reserve Board, Washington, D.C.

Fase, M. M. G., 1985. "Monetary Control: The Dutch Experience: Some Reflections on the Liquidity Ratio." In *Monetary Conditions for Economic Recovery*, C. van Ewijk and J. J. Klant (eds.), Dordrecht: Martinus Nijhoff, 95-125.

Fayyad, S. K., 1986. *Monetary Asset Component Grouping and Aggregation: An Inquiry into the Definition of Money*, Ph.D. Thesis, University of Texas at Austin.

Feenstra, R. C., 1986. "Functional Equivalence Between Liquidity Costs and the Utility of Money," *Journal of Monetary Economics* 17, 271-291.

Feige, E. L. and D. K. Pearce, 1977. "The Substitutability of Money and Near-Monies: A Survey of the Time-Series Evidence," *Journal of Economic Literature* 15, 439-469.

Feige, E. L. and D. K. Pearce, 1979. "The Casual Relationship between Money and Income: Some Caveats for Time Series Analysis," *Review of Economics and Statistics* 61, 521-533.

Feldstein, M. and J. H. Stock, 1996. "Measuring Money Growth when Financial Markets are Changing," *Journal of Monetary Economics* 37, 3-27.

Fischer, S., 1974. "Money and the Production Function," *Economic Inquiry* 12, 517-533.

Fisher, D., 1978. *Monetary Theory and the Demand for Money*, London: Martin-Robertson.

Fisher, D., 1989. *Money Demand and Monetary Policy*, Ann Arbor: The University of Michigan Press.

Fisher, D., 1992. "Money-Demand Variability: A Demand Systems Approach," *Journal of Business and Economic Statistics* 10, 143-152.

Fisher, D. and A. Fleissig, 1994. "Money Demand in a Flexible Dynamic Fourier Expenditure System," Federal Reserve Bank of St. Louis *Review* 76, 117-128.

Fisher, D. and A. Serletis, 1989. "Velocity and the Growth of Money in the United States, 1970-1985," *Journal of Macroeconomics* 11, 323-332.

Fisher, F. M. and K. Shell, 1972. *The Economic Theory of Price Indices*, New York: Academic Press.

Fisher, F. M. and K. Shell, 1979. "The Theory of Price Indices and Subindices for Output and Input Deflation: Progress Report," CARESS Discussion Paper #79-02, University of Pennsylvania.

Fisher, F. M. and K. Shell, 1981. "Output Price Indices," CARESS Discussion Paper #81-05, University of Pennsylvania.

Fisher, I., 1911. *The Purchasing Power of Money*, London: Macmillan.

Fisher, I., 1922. *The Making of Index Numbers: A Study of Their Varieties, Tests, and Reliability*, Boston: Houghton Mifflin.

Fisher, P., S. Hudson, and M. Pradhan, 1993. "Divisia Indices for Money: An Appraisal of Theory and Practice," Working Paper Series #9, Bank of England.

Fixler, D., 1988. "Measuring Financial Services Output and Prices in Commercial Banking," Mimeo, Division of Price and Index Number Research, Bureau of Labor Statistics.

Fixler, D. and K. Zieschang, 1989a. "Measuring the Nominal Value of Financial Services in the National Income Accounts," Discussion Paper #193, Division of Price and Index Number Research, Bureau of Labor Statistics.

Fixler, D. and K. Zieschang, 1989b. "Output and Price Measurement in Commercial Banking," Mimeo, Division of Price and Index Number Research, Bureau of Labor Statistics.

Fixler, D. and K. Zieschang, 1989c. "User Costs, Shadow Prices, and the Real Output of Banks," Mimeo, Division of Price and Index Number Research, Bureau of Labor Statistics.

Ford, J. L. and F. Stark, 1967. *Long and Short Term Interest Rates*, New York: Augustus M. Kelley.

Freedman, C., 1981. "Monetary Aggregates as Targets: Some Theoretical Aspects," NBER Working Paper #775, Cambridge, Mass.

Friedman, M., 1969. "Interest Rates and the Demand for Money." In *The Optimum Quantity of Money, and Other Essays*, M. Friedman (ed.), Chicago: Aldine, 141-155.

Friedman, M., 1983. "Monetary Variability: United States and Japan," *Journal of Money, Credit, and Banking* 40, 339-343.

Friedman, M. and D. I. Meiselman, 1963. "The Relative Stability of Monetary Velocity and the Investment Multiplier in the United States, 1897-1958." In Commission on Money and Credit, *Stabilization Policies*, Englewood Cliffs, N.J.: Prentice Hall.

Friedman, M. and A. J. Schwartz, 1970. *Monetary Statistics of the United States: Estimates, Sources, Methods, and Data*, New York: Columbia University Press (for the NBER).

Frisch, R., 1930. "Necessary and Sufficient Conditions Regarding the Form of an Index Number Which Shall Meet Certain of Fisher's Tests," *Journal of the American Statistical Association* 25, 297-406.

Fuss, M. A., 1977. "The Demand for Energy in Canadian Manufacturing," *Journal of Econometrics* 5, 89-116.

Galbraith, J. K., 1979. "On Inflation," *Consumer Reports* 44, 87-98.

Gallant, A. R., 1981. "On the Bias in Flexible Functional Forms and an Essentially Unbiased Form: The Fourier Flexible Form," *Journal of Econometrics* 15, 211-245.

Gallant, A. R., 1982. "Unbiased Determination of Production Technologies," *Journal of Econometrics* 20, 285-323.

Gallant, A. R. and G. H. Golub, 1984. "Imposing Curvature Restrictions on Flexible Functional Forms," *Journal of Econometrics* 26, 295-321.

Gilbert, A. R., 1984. "Bank Market Structure and Competition: A Survey," *Journal of Money, Credit, and Banking* 14, 617-645.

Gilligan, T., M. Smirlock, and W. Marshall, 1984. "Scale and Scope Economies in the Multi-Product Banking Firm," *Journal of Monetary Economics* 13, 393-405.

Giovannini, A. and P. Labadie, 1991. "Asset Prices and Interest Rates in Cash-in-Advance Models," *Journal of Political Economy* 99, 1215-1252.

Goldfeld, S. M., 1973. "The Demand for Money Revisited," *Brookings Papers on Economic Activity* 3, 577-638.

Goldfeld, S. M., 1976. "The Case of the Missing Money," *Brookings Papers on Economic Activity* 3, 683-730.

Goldman, S. M. and H. Uzawa, 1964. "A Note on Separability in Demand Analysis," *Econometrica* 32, 387-398.

Gordon, R. J., 1984. "The Short-Run Demand for Money: A Reconsideration," *Journal of Money, Credit, and Banking* 16, 403-434.

Gorman, W. M., 1953. "Community Preference Fields," *Econometrica* 21, 63-80.

Gorman, W. M., 1959. "Separable Utility and Aggregation," *Econometrica* 27, 469-481.

Gorman, W. M., 1970. "Tricks with Utility Functions." In *Essays in Economic Analysis*, M. J. Artis and A. R. Nobay (eds.), Cambridge: Cambridge University Press, 211-243.

Gorman, W. M., 1981. "Some Engel Curves." In *Essays in the Theory and Measurement of Consumer Behaviour in Honor of Sir Richard Stone*, A. Deaton, (ed.), Cambridge: Cambridge University Press, 7-29.

Grandmont, J. M., 1985. "On Endogenous Competitive Business Cycles," *Econometrica* 53, 995-1045.

Granger, C. W. J. and P. Newbold, 1977. *Forecasting Economic Time Series*, New York: Academic Press.

Green, H. A. J., 1964. *Aggregation in Economic Analysis: An Introductory Survey*, Princeton, N.J.: Princeton University Press.

Guilkey, D. K. and C. A. K. Lovell, 1980. "On the Flexibility of the Translog Approximation," *International Economic Review* 21, 137-147.

Gul, F., 1991. "A Theory of Disappointment Aversion," *Econometrica* 59, 667-686.

Gurley, J. G., 1960. "Liquidity and Financial Institutions in the Postwar Economy," Study Paper #14, In *The Study of Employment, Growth, and Price Levels*, U.S. Government Printing Office, Washington, D.C.

Gurley, J. G. and E. S. Shaw, 1960. *Money in a Theory of Finance*, Washington, D.C.: Brookings.

Hall, R. E., 1973. "The Specification of Technology with Several Kinds of Output," *Journal of Political Economy* 81, 878-892.

Hall, T. E. and N. R. Noble, 1987. "Velocity and the Variability of Money Growth: Evidence from Granger-Causality Tests," *Journal of Money, Credit, and Banking* 44, 112-116.

Hamburger, M. J., 1970. "Indicators of Monetary Policy: The Arguments and the Evidence," *American Economic Review Papers and Proceedings* 60, 32-39.

Hamburger, M. J., 1980. "The Demand for Money in the United States: A Comment." In *On the State of Macro Economics*, K. Brunner and A. H. Meltzer (eds.), Carnegie-Rochester Conference Series on Public Policy 12, 273-281.

Hancock, D., 1985. "The Financial Firm: Production with Monetary and Non-Monetary Goods," *Journal of Political Economy* 93, 859-880.

Hancock, D., 1986. "A Model of the Financial Firm with Imperfect Asset and Deposit Elasticities," *Journal of Banking and Finance* 10, 37-54.

Hancock, D., 1987. "Aggregation of Monetary Goods: A Production Model." In *New Approaches to Monetary Economics*, W. A. Barnett and K. J. Singleton (eds.), Cambridge: Cambridge University Press, 200-218.

Hancock, D., 1991. *A Theory of Production for the Financial Firm*, Boston: Kluwer Academic.

Hansen, L. P., 1982. "Large Sample Properties of Generalized Method of Moments Estimators," *Econometrica* 50, 1029-1054.

Hansen, L. P. and J. J. Heckman, 1996. "The Empirical Foundations of Calibration," *Journal of Economic Perspectives* 10, 87-104.

Hansen, L. P. and T. J. Sargent, 1980. "Formulating and Estimating Dynamic Linear Rational Expectations Models," *Journal of Economic Dynamics and Control* 2, 7-46.

Hansen, L. P. and T. J. Sargent, 1981. "Linear Rational Expectations Models for Dynamically Interrelated Variables." In *Rational Expectations and Econometric Practice*, R. E. Lucas, Jr. and T. J. Sargent (eds.), Minneapolis: University of Minnesota Press, 127-156.

Hansen, L. P. and K. J. Singleton, 1982. "Generalized Instrumental Variable Estimation of Nonlinear Rational Expectations Models," *Econometrica* 50, 1269-1286.

Harper, M. J., E. R. Berndt, and D. O. Wood, 1989. "Rates of Return and Capital Aggregation Using Alternative Rental Prices." In *Technology and Capital Formation*, D. W. Jorgenson and R. Landau (eds.), Cambridge: The MIT Press, 331-372.

Haugh, L. D., 1972. *The Identification of Time-Series Interrelationships with Special Reference to Dynamic Regression*, Ph.D. Thesis, University of Wisconsin at Madison.

Hawtrey, R. G., 1930. "Money and Index Numbers," *Journal of the Royal Statistical Society* 93, 64-85.

REFERENCES

Herrmann, H., H. E. Reimers, and K. H. Toedter, 1994. "Weighted Monetary Aggregates for Germany," Mimeo, Deutsche Bundesbank.

Hicks, J. R., 1946. *Value and Capital*, Oxford: Oxford University Press.

Hill, R. J. and K. J. Fox, 1997. "Splicing Index Numbers," *Journal of Business and Economic Statistics* 15, 387-389.

Hinich, M. J., 1982. "Testing for Linearity and Gaussianity of a Stationary Time Series," *Journal of Time Series Analysis* 3, 169-176.

Hinich, M. J. and D. Patterson, 1985. "Identification of the Coefficients in a Non-Linear Time Series of the Quadratic Type," *Journal of Econometrics* 30, 269-288.

Hinich, M. J. and D. Patterson, 1989. "Evidence of Nonlinearity in the Trade-by-Trade Stock Market Return Generating Process." In *Economic Complexity: Chaos, Sunspots, Bubbles, and Nonlinearity*, W. A. Barnett, J. Geweke, and K. Shell (eds.), Cambridge: Cambridge University Press, 383-409.

Hinich, M. J. and W. E. Weber, 1984. "A Method for Estimating Distributed Lags when Observations are Randomly Missing," *Journal of the American Statistical Association* 79, 368-373.

Hinich, M. J. and W. E. Weber, 1986. "Estimating Linear Filters with Errors in Variables Using the Hilbert Transform," Staff Report #96, Federal Reserve Bank of Minneapolis.

Hoa, T. Y., 1985. "A Divisia System Approach to Modelling Monetary Aggregates," *Economics Letters* 17, 365-368.

Hodrick, R. J., K. L. Narayana, and D. Lucas, 1991. "The Variability of Velocity in Cash-in-Advance Models," *Journal of Political Economy* 99, 358-384.

Hulten, C. R., 1973. "Divisia Index Numbers," *Econometrica* 63, 1017-1026.

Humphrey, T. M., 1993. "The Origins of the Velocity Function," Federal Reserve Bank of Richmond *Economic Quarterly* 74, 1-17.

Hunter, W. C. and S. G. Timme, 1986. "Technical Change, Organizational Form, and the Structure of Bank Production," *Journal of Money, Credit, and Banking* 18, 152-166.

Hutt, W. H., 1963. *Keynesianism - Retrospect and Prospect*, Chicago: Regnery.

Ingersoll, J. E., 1987. *Theory of Financial Decision Making*, Totowa, NJ: Rowman and Littlefield.

Ishida, K., 1984. "Divisia Monetary Aggregates and the Demand for Money: A Japanese Case," *Bank of Japan Monetary and Economic Studies* 2, 49-80.

Ishida, K. and K. Nakamura, 1994. "Broad and Narrow Divisia Monetary Aggregates for Japan," Mimeo, Bank of Japan.

Jacklin, C. J. and S. Bhattacharya, 1988. "Distinguishing Panics and Information-Based Bank Runs: Welfare and Policy Implications," *Journal of Political Economy* 96, 568-592.

Janssen, N. G. J. and C. J. M. Kool, 1994. "The Measurement and Relevance of Weighted Monetary Aggregates in the Netherlands," Mimeo, Department of Economics, University of Limburg.

Jenkins, G. and D. Watts, 1968. *Spectral Analysis and its Applications*, San Francisco: Holden-Day.

Jensen, M., 1997. "A homotopy Approach to Solving Nonlinear Rational Expectations Problems," *Computational Economics* 10, 47-65.

Johannes, J. M. and R. Rasche, 1979. "Predicting the Monetary Multiplier," *Journal of Monetary Economics* 5, 301-325.

Jorgenson, D. W., 1967. "The Theory of Investment Behavior." In *Determinants of Investment Behavior*, R. Ferber (eds.), New York: Columbia University Press.

Jorgenson, D. W. and B. M. Fraumeni, 1981. "Relative Prices and Technical Change." In *Modeling and Measuring Natural Resource Substitution*, E. Berndt and B. Field (eds.), Cambridge: MIT Press, 17-47.

Jorgenson, D. W. and L. J. Lau, 1975. "The Structure of Consumer Preferences," *Annals of Economic and Social Measurement* 4, 49-101.

Jorgenson, D. W., L. J. Lau, and T. M. Stoker, 1982. "The Transcendental Logarithmic Model of Aggregate Consumer Behavior." In *Advances in Econometrics*, Vol. 1, R. L. Basmann and G. F. Rhodes (eds.), Greenwich, CT: JAI Press, 97-238.

Judd, J. P. and J. L. Scadding, 1982. "The Search for a Stable Money Demand Function," *Journal of Economic Literature* 20, 993-1023.

Kane, E. J., 1964. "Money as a Weighted Aggregate," *Zeitschrift fur Nationalokonomie* 25, 221-243.

Karni, E., 1974. "The Value of Time and the Demand for Money," *Journal of Money, Credit, and Banking* 6, 45-64.

Kavajecz, K. A., 1994. "The Evolution of the Federal Reserve's Monetary Aggregates: A Timeline," Federal Reserve Bank of St. Louis *Review* 76, 32-66.

Klein, B., 1974. "Competitive Interest Payments on Bank Deposits and the Long-Run Demand for Money," *American Economic Review* 64, 931-949.

Kloek, T., 1967. "On Quadratic Approximations of Cost of Living and Real Income Index Numbers," Report #6710, Econometric Institute, Netherlands School of Economics.

Konüs, A. A., 1924. "The problem of the true index of the cost-of-living," (in Russian), *The Economic Bulletin of the Institute of Economic Cojuncture*, Moscow 9-10, 64-71. English translation: *Econometrica*, 1939, Vol. 7, 10-29.

Labadie, P., 1989. "Stochastic Inflation and the Equity Premium," *Journal of Monetary Economics* 24, 277-298.

la Cour, L. F., 1996. "On the Measurement of Money: Results from the Experience with Divisia Monetary Aggregates for Denmark," Mimeo, Department of Economics, University of Copenhagen.

Laidler, D. E. W., 1993. "Commentary," Federal Reserve Bank of St. Louis *Review* 75, 101-102.

Laidler, D. E. W., 1997. "Notes on the Microfoundations of Monetary Economics," *Economic Journal* 107, 1213-1223.

Lancaster, K. J., 1971. *Consumer Demand: A New Approach*, New York: Columbia University Press.

Latane, H. A., 1954. "Cash Balance and the Interest Rate - A Pragmatic Approach," *Review of Economics and Statistics* 36, 456-460.

Lau, L. J., 1969. "Duality and the Structure of Utility Functions," *Journal of Economic Theory* 1, 374-396.

Lau, L. J., 1972. "Profit Functions of Technologies with Multiple Inputs and Outputs," *Review of Economics and Statistics* 54, 281-289.

Lau, L. J., 1974. "Applications of Duality Theory: a Comment." In In *Frontiers in Quantitative Economics*, Vol. 2, M. Intriligator and D. Kendrick (eds.), Amsterdam: North-Holland.

Lau, L. J., 1977. "Existence Conditions for Aggregate Demand Functions." Technical Report # 248, Institute for Mathematical Studies in the Social Sciences, Stanford University.

Lau, L. J., 1978a. "Testing and Imposing Monotonicity, Convexity, and Quasi-Convexity Constraints." *In Production Economics: A Dual Approach to Theory and Applications*, Vol. 1, M. Fuss and D. McFadden (eds.), Amsterdam: North-Holland, 409-453.

Lau, L. J., 1978b. "Applications of Profit Functions." In *Production Economics: A Dual Approach to Theory and Applications*, Vol. 1, M. Fuss and D. McFadden (eds.), Amsterdam: North-Holland, 133-215.

Lau, L. J., 1982. "A note on the Fundamental Theorem of Exact Aggregation," *Economics Letters* 9, 119-126.

Lee, T. H., 1972. "On Measuring the Nearness of Near Monies: Comment," *American Economic Review* 62, 217-220.

Leontief, W. W., 1947a. "An Introduction to a Theory of the Internal Structure of Functional Relationships," *Econometrica* 15, 361-373.

Leontief, W. W., 1947b. "A Note on the Interrelation of Subsets of Independent Variables of a Continuous Function with Continuous First Derivatives," *Bulletin of the American Mathematical Society* 55, 343-350.

LeRoy, S. F, 1984. "Nominal Prices and Interest Rates in General Equilibrium Money Shocks," *Journal of Business* 57, 177-195.

Lewbel, A., 1987. "Characterizing Some Gorman Engel Curves," *Econometrica* 44, 1451-1459.

Lewbel, A., 1988. "Exact Aggregation, Distribution Parameterizations, and a Nonlinear Representative Consumer." In *Nonparametric and Robust Inference: Advances in Econometrics,* Vol. 7, G. F. Rhodes and T. B. Fomby (eds.), Greenwich, CT: JAI Press, 253-290.

Lim, G. C. and V. L. Martin, 1994. "Weighted MonetaryAggregates: Empirical Evidence for Australia," Mimeo, Department of Economics, University of Melbourne.

Longworth, D. and J. Atta-Mensah, 1995. "The Canadian Experience with Weighted Monetary Aggregates," Working Paper #95-10, Bank of Canada.

Lucas, R. E., Jr., 1976. "Econometric Policy Evaluation: A Critique." In *The Philips Curve and Labor Economics*, K. Brunner and A. H. Meltzer (eds.), Carnegie-Rochester Series on Public Policy, 19-46.

Lucas, R. E., Jr., 1978. "Asset Prices in an Exchange Economy," *Econometrica* 46, 1429-1446.

Lucas, R. E., Jr. and N. L. Stockey, 1987. "Money and Interest in a Cash-in-Advance Economy," *Econometrica* 55, 491-513.

Machina, M., 1982. "'Expected Utility' Analysis without the Independence Axiom," *Econometrica* 50, 277-323.

MacKinlay, A. C. and M. Richardson, 1991. "Using Generalized Method of Moments to Test Mean-Variance Efficiency," *Journal of Finance* 46, 511-527.

Magill, M. and W. Shafer, 1991. "Incomplete Markets." In *Handbook of Mathematical Economics*, Vol. 4, W. Hildenbrand and H. Sonnenschein (eds.), Amsterdam: North-Holland, 1523-1614.

Mahoney, P. I., 1987. "Responses to Deregulation: Retail Deposit Pricing from 1983 through 1985," Staff Study #151, Federal Reserve Board, Washington, DC.

Maks, J. A. H., 1978. "Consistency and Consumer Behaviour in the Netherlands, 1921-1962," *European Economic Review* 11, 343-362.

Malmquist, S., 1953. "Index Numbers and Indifference Surfaces," *Tradajos de Estatistica* 4, 209-241.

Mehra, R. and E. C. Prescott, 1985. "The Equity Premium: A Puzzle," *Journal of Monetary Economics* 15, 145-161.

Marcet, A. and T. J. Sargent, 1989a. "Convergence of Least Squares Learning Mechanisms in Self-Referential Linear Stochastic Models," *Journal of Economic Theory* 48, 337-368.

Marcet, A. and T. J. Sargent, 1989b. "Convergence of Least-Squares Learning in Environments with Hidden State Variables and Private Information," *Journal of Political Economy* 97, 1306-1322.

Marcet, A. and K. J. Singleton, 1990. "Simulation Analysis of Dynamic Stochastic Models: Applications to Theory and Estimation," Mimeo, Department of Economics, Stanford University.

Marquez, J., 1986. "Money in Open Economies: A Divisia Application to the U.S. Case." In *New Approaches to Monetary Economics*, W. A. Barnett and K. J. Singleton (eds.), Cambridge: Cambridge University Press, 183-199.

Marshall, D. A, 1992. "Inflation and Asset Returns in a Monetary Economy," *Journal of Finance* 47, 1315-1342.

McFadden, D., 1978. "Cost, Revenue, and Profit Functions." In *Production Economics: A Dual Approach to Theory and Applications*, Vol. 1, M. Fuss and D. McFadden (eds.), Amsterdam: North-Holland, 3-109.

Mehra, R., and E. C. Prescott, 1985. "The Equity Premium: A Puzzle," *Journal of Monetary Economics* 15, 145-61.

Merton, R. C., 1990. "Capital Market Theory and the Pricing of Financial Securities." In *Handbook of Monetary Economics*, B. Friedman and F. Hahn (eds.), Amsterdam: North-Holland, 497-581.

Moorsteen, R. H., 1961. "On Measuring Productive Potential and Relative Efficiency," *Quarterly Journal of Economics* 75, 451-467.

Moroney, J. R. and B. J. Wilbratte, 1976. "Money and Money Substitutes," *Journal of Money, Credit, and Banking* 8, 181-198.

Mountain, D. C., 1988. "The Rotterdam Model: An Approximation in Variable Space," *Econometrica* 56, 47-484.

Muellbauer, J. N., 1975. "Aggregation, Income Distribution and Consumer Demand," *Review of Economic Studies* 62, 524-544.

Muellbauer, J. N., 1976. "Community Preferences and the Representative Consumer," *Econometrica* 44, 979-999.

Mullineaux, D. J., 1978. "Economies of Scale and Organizational Efficiency in Banking: A Profit-Function Approach," *Journal of Finance* 33, 259-280.

Murray, J. D. and R. W. White, 1983. "Economies of Scale and Economies of Scope in Multiproduct Financial Institutions: A Study of British Columbia Credit Unions," *Journal of Finance* 38, 887-902.

Newey, W. K. and K. D. West, 1987. "A Simple, Positive Semi-Definite, Heteroscedasticity and Autocorrelation Consistent Covariance Matrix," *Econometrica* 55, 703-708.

Niehans, J., 1978. *The Theory of Money*, Baltimore: Johns Hopkins University Press.

Offenbacher, E. K., 1979. *The Substitutability of Monetary Assets*, Ph.D. Thesis, The University of Chicago.

Offenbacher, E. K., 1980a. "The Substitutability of Monetary Assets," Mimeo, Federal Reserve Board, Washington, D.C.

Offenbacher, E. K., 1980b. "The Basic Functions of Money: An Application of the Input Independence Transformation," *Economics Letters* 5, 353-357.

Offenbacher, E. K., 1980c. "Economic Monetary Aggregates: Comment," *Journal of Econometrics* 14, 55-56.

Ohta, M., 1974. "A Note on the Duality between Production and Cost Functions: Rate of Returns to Scale and Rate of Technical Progress," *Economic Studies Quarterly* 25, 63-65.

Orphanides, A., B. Reid, and D. H. Small, 1994. "The Empirical Properties of a Monetary Aggregate that Adds Bond and Stock Funds to M2," Federal Reserve Bank of St. Louis *Review* 76, 31-51.

Parkin, J. M., R. J. Cooper, J. R. Henderson, and M. K. Danes, 1975. "An Integrated Model of Consumption, Investment, and Portfolio Decisions." In *Papers in Monetary Economics*, Vol. II, Reserve Bank of Australia.

Parks, R. W., 1969. "Systems of Demand Equations: An Empirical Comparison of Alternative Functional Froms," *Econometrica* 37, 629-650.

Patinkin, D., 1965. *Money, Interest, and Prices*, 2nd ed., New York: Harper and Row.

Pesek, B. P. and T. R. Saving, 1967. *Money, Wealth, and Economic Theory*, New York: Macmillan.

Phlips, L., 1978. "The Demand for Leisure and Money," *Econometrica* 46, 1025-1044.

Phlips, L. and F. Spinnewyn, 1982. "Rationality Versus Myopia in Dynamic Demand Systems." In *Advances in Econometrics*, R. L. Basmann and G. F. Rhodes (eds.), Greenwich, CT: JAI Press, 3-33.

Pierce, D. A. and L. D. Haugh, 1977. "Causality in Temporal Systems: Characterizations and a Survey," *Journal of Econometrics* 5, 265-293.

Pollak, R. A., 1976. "Habit Formation and the Long-Run Utility Function," *Journal of Economic Theory* 13, 272-297.

Poterba, J. M. and J. J. Rotemberg, 1987. "Money in the Utility Function: An Empirical Implementation." In *New Approaches to Monetary Economics*, W. A. Barnett and K. J. Singleton (eds.), Cambridge: Cambridge University Press, 219-240.

Prescott, E. C. and R. Mehra, 1980. "Recursive Competitive Equilibrium: The Case of Homogeneous Households," *Econometrica* 48, 1365-1380.

Priestley, M., 1981. *Spectral Analysis and Time Series*, New York: Academic Press.

Pudney, S. E., 1981. "An Empirical Method of Approximating the Separable Structure of Consumer Preferences," *Review of Economic Studies* 48, 561-577.

Quirk, J. D. and R. Saposnik, 1968. *Introduction to General Equilibrium Theory and Welfare Economics*, New York: McGraw-Hill.

Rios-Rull, J. V., 1995. "Models with Heterogeneous Agents." In *Frontiers of Business Cycle Research*, Thomas F. Cooley (ed.), Princeton: Princeton University Press, 98-125.

Richter, M. K., 1966. "Invariance Axioms and Economic Indexes," *Econometrica* 34, 739-755.

Robles, B., 1993. "The Optimal Demand for Money in U.S. Manufacturing: A Dynamic Micro Theoretic Approach," Mimeo, Department of Economics, University of Colorado at Boulder.

Roper, D. and S. J. Turnovsky, 1980. "The Optimum Monetary Aggregate for Stabilization Policy," *Quarterly Journal of Economics* 95, 333-355.

Rossiter, R. and T. H. Lee, 1987. "Implicit Returns on Conventional Demand Deposits: An Empirical Comparison," *Journal of Macroeconomics* 9, 613-624.

Rotemberg, J. J., 1991. "Commentary: Monetary Aggregates and Their Uses." In *Monetary Policy on the 75th Anniversary of the Federal Reserve System*, M. T. Belongia (ed.), Boston: Kluwer Academic, 223-231.

Rotemberg, J. J., J. C. Driscoll, and J. M. Poterba, 1995. "Money, Output, and Prices: Evidence from a New Monetary Aggregate," *Journal of Business and Economic Statistics* 13, 67-83.

Rothenberg, J., 1971. "Identification of Parametric Models," *Econometrica* 39, 577-592.

Rubinstein, M., 1976. "The Valuation of Uncertain Income Streams and the Pricing of Options," *Bell Journal of Economics* 7, 407-425.

Rush, M., 1980. "Comment and Further Evidence on 'Implicit Interest on Demand Deposits'," *Journal of Monetary Economics* 6, 437-451.

Russell, R. R., 1975. "Functional Separability and Partial Elasticities of Substitution," *Review of Economic Studies* 42, 79-86.

Samuelson, P. A., 1947. *Foundations of Economic Analysis*, Cambridge: Harvard University Press.

Samuelson, P. A., 1968. "Two Generalizations of the Elasticity of Substitution." In *Value, Capital, and Growth: Essays in Honour of Sir John Hicks*, J. N. Wolfe (ed.), Edinburgh: Edinburgh University Press, 467-480.

Samuelson, P. A. and R. Sato, 1984. "Unattainability of Integrability and Definiteness Conditions in the General Case of Demand for Money and Goods," *American Economic Review* 74, 588-604.

Samuelson, P. A. and S. Swamy, 1974. "Invariant Economic Index Numbers and Canonical Duality: Survey and Synthesis," *American Economic Review* 64, 566-593.

Santomero, A. M., 1984. "Modeling the Banking Firm: A Survey," *Journal of Money, Credit, and Banking* 14, 576-602.

Sargent, T. J., 1987. *Dynamic Macroeconomic Theory*, Cambridge: Harvard University Press.

Sato, K., 1975. *Production Functions and Aggregation*, Amsterdam: North-Holland.

Saving, T. R., 1971. "Transactions Costs and the Demand for Money," *American Economic Review* 61, 407-420.

Saving, T. R., 1977. "A Theory of the Money Supply with Competitive Banking," *Journal of Monetary Economics* 3, 289-303.

Schwarz, G., 1978. "Estimating the Dimension of a Model," *Annals of Statistics* 6, 461-464.

Schwert, G. W., 1979. "Tests of Causality: The Message in the Innovations." In *Three Aspects of Policy and Policy Making: Knowledge, Data and Institutions*, K. Brunner and A. H. Meltzer (eds.), Amsterdam: North-Holland, 55-96.

Serletis, A., 1984. *The Substitutability and Separability of Monetary Assets*, Ph.D. Thesis, McMaster University.

Serletis, A., 1987a. "Monetary Asset Separability Tests." In *New Approaches to Monetary Economics*, W. A. Barnett and K. J. Singleton (eds.), Cambridge: Cambridge University Press, 169-182.

Serletis, A., 1987b. "The Demand for Divisia M1, M2, and M3 in the United States," *Journal of Macroeconomics* 9, 567-591.

Serletis, A., 1988a. "The Empirical Relationship between Money, Prices, and Income Revisited," *Journal of Business and Economic Statistics* 6, 351-358.

Serletis, A., 1988b. "Translog Flexible Functional Forms and Substitutability of Monetary Assets," *Journal of Business and Economic Statistics* 6, 59-67.

Serletis, A., 1991a. "The Demand for Divisia Money in the United States: A Dynamic Flexible Demand System," *Journal of Money, Credit, and Banking* 23, 35-52.

Serletis, A., 1991b. "Modeling the Demand for Consumption Goods and Liquid Assets," *Journal of Macroeconomics* 13, 435-457.

Serletis, A. and D. Krause, 1996. "Nominal Stylized Facts of U.S. Business Cycles," Federal Reserve Bank of St. Louis *Review* 78, 49-54.

Serletis, A. and A. L. Robb, 1986. "Divisia Aggregation and Substitutability among Monetary Assets," *Journal of Money, Credit, and Banking* 18, 430-446.

Shephard, R. W., 1970. *Theory of Cost and Production Functions*, Princeton, NJ: Princeton University Press.

Shiller, R. J., 1979. "The Volatility of Long-Term Interest Rates and Expectations Models of the Term Structure," *Journal of Political Economy* 37, 1190-1219.

Siklos, P. L., 1993. "Income Velocity and Institutional Change: Some New Time Series Evidence, 1870-1986," *Journal of Money, Credit, and Banking* 25, 377-392.

Simpson, T. D. and R. D. Porter, 1981. "Some Issues Involving the Definition and Interpretation of Monetary Aggregates." In *Controlling Monetary Aggregates III*, Federal Reserve Bank of Boston Conference Series #24, Boston, Mass.

Sims, C. A., 1969. "Theoretical Basis for a Double Deflated Index of Real Value Added," *Review of Economics and Statistics* 51, 470-471.

Sims, C. A., 1972. "Money, Income, and Causality," *American Economic Review* 62, 540-542.

Sims, C. A. and E. M. Leeper, 1994. "Towards a Modern Macroeconomic Model Usable for Policy Analysis," NBER *Macroeconomics Annual*, S. Fischer and J. J. Rotemberg (eds.), Cambridge: The MIT Press, 81-118.

Sono, M., 1961. "The Effect of Price Changes on the Demand and Supply of Separable Goods," *International Economic Review* 2, 239-271.

Spanos, A., 1984. "Liquidity as a Latent Variable: An Application of the MIMIC Model," *Oxford Bulletin of Economics and Statistics* 46, 125-143.

Spencer, P., 1994. "Portfolio Disequilibrium: Implications for the Divisia Approach to Monetary Aggregation," *The Manchester School of Economic and Social Studies* 62, 125-150.

Spindt, P. A., 1984. "Modeling the Monetary Multiplier and the Controllability of the Divisia Monetary Quantity Aggregates," *Review of Economics and Statistics* 66, 314-319.

Spindt, P. A., 1985a. "Money Is What Money Does: Monetary Aggregation and the Equation of Exchange," *Journal of Political Economy* 93, 175-204.

Spindt, P. A., 1985b. "The Rates of Turnover of Money Goods under Efficient Monetary Trade: Implications for Monetary Aggregation," *Economics Letters* 17, 141-143.

Star, S. and R. E. Hall, 1976. "An Approximate Divisia Index of Total Factor Productivity," *Econometrica* 44, 257-264.

Startz, R., 1979. "Implicit Interest on Demand Deposits," *Journal of Political Economy* 37, 1190-1291.

Steinhauer, L. and J. Chang, 1972. "On Measuring the Nearness of Near-Moneys: Comment," *American Economic Review* 62, 221-225.

Stoker, T. M., 1986. "Simple Tests of Distributional Effects on Macroeconomic Equations," *Journal of Political Economy* 94, 763-795.

Stokey, N. L. and R. E. Lucas, Jr., 1989. *Recursive Methods in Economic Dynamics*, Cambridge: Harvard University Press.

Stone, C. C. and D. L. Thornton, 1987. "Solving the 1980's Velocity Puzzle: A Progress Report," Federal Reserve Bank of St. Louis *Review* 69, 5-23.

Strotz, R. H., 1957. "The Empirical Implications of a Utility Tree," *Econometrica* 25, 169-180.

Strotz, R. H., 1959. "The Utility Tree - A Correction and Further Appraisal," *Econometrica* 27, 482-488.

Svensson, L. E. O., 1985. "Money and Asset Prices in a Cash-in-Advance Economy," *Journal of Political Economy* 93, 919-944.

Swamy, P. A. V. B. and P. A. Tinsley, 1980. "Linear Prediction and Estimation Methods for Regression Models with Stationary Stochastic Coefficients," *Journal of Econometrics* 12, 103-142.

Swofford, J. L., 1995. "A Revealed Preference Analysis of Friedman and Schwartz Money," *Journal of Money, Credit, and Banking* 27, 154-164.

Swofford, J. L. and G. A. Whitney, 1986. "Flexible Functional Forms and the Utility Approach to the Demand for Money: A Nonparametric Analysis," *Journal of Money, Credit, and Banking* 18, 383-389.

Swofford, J. L. and G. A. Whitney, 1987. "Nonparametric Tests of Utility Maximization and Weak Separability for Consumption, Leisure, and Money," *Review of Economics and Statistics* 69, 458-464.

Swofford, J. L. and G. A. Whitney, 1988. "A Comparison of Nonparametric Tests of Weak Separability for Annual and Quarterly Data on Consumption, Leisure, and Money," *Journal of Business and Economic Statistics* 6, 241-246.

Swofford, J. L. and G. A. Whitney, 1994. "A Revealed Preference Test for Weakly Separable Utility Maximization with Incomplete Adjustment," *Journal of Econometrics* 60, 234-249.

Taggart, R. A., Jr., 1984. "Comment on Modeling the Banking Firm: A Survey," *Journal of Money, Credit, and Banking* 14, 612-616.

Tatom, J. A., 1981. "Energy Prices and Short-Run Economic Performance," Federal Reserve Bank of St. Louis *Review* 63, 3-17.

Taylor, J. B. and H. Uhlig, 1990. "Solving Nonlinear Stochastic Growth Models: A Comparison of Alternative Solution Methods," *Journal of Business and Economic Statistics* 8, 1-17.

Theil, H., 1954. *Linear Aggregation of Economic Relations*, Amsterdam: North-Holland.

Theil, H., 1967. *Economics and Information Theory*, Amsterdam: North-Holland.

Theil, H., 1968, "On the Geometry and the Numerical Approximation of Cost of Living and Real Income Indices," *De Economist* 116, 677-689.

Theil, H., 1971. *Principles of Econometrics*, New York: John Wiley.

Theil, H., 1975. *Theory and Measurement of Consumer Demand*, Vol. 1, Amsterdam: North-Holland.

Theil, H., 1976. *Theory and Measurement of Consumer Demand*, Vol. 2, Amsterdam: North-Holland.

Theil, H., 1980. *The System-Wide Approach to Microeconomics*, Chicago: University of Chicago Press.

Thornton, D. L., 1994. "Financial Innovation, Deregulation and the 'Credit View' of Monetary Policy," Federal Reserve Bank of St. Louis *Review* 76, 31-49.

Thornton, D. L. and P. Yue, 1992. "An Extended Series of Divisia Monetary Aggregates," Federal Reserve Bank of St. Louis *Review* 74, 35-52.

Thornton, J., 1995. "Friedman's Money Supply Volatility Hypothesis: Some International Evidence," *Journal of Money, Credit, and Banking* 27, 288-291.

Tinsley, P. A., B. Garrett, and M. E. Friar, 1980. "The Measurement of Money Demand," Special Studies Paper #133, Federal Reserve Board, Washington, D.C.

Tinsley, P. A., P. A. Spindt, and M. E. Friar, 1980. "Indicator and Filter Attributes of Monetary Aggregates: A Nit-Picking Case for Disaggregation," *Journal of Econometrics* 14, 61-91.

Tobin, J., 1956. "The Interest Elasticity of the Transactions Demand for Cash," *Review of Economics and Statistics* 38, 241-247.

Tobin, J., 1958. "Liquidity Preference as Behaviour Towards Risk," *Review of Economic Studies* 25, 65-86.

Tobin, J., 1961. "Money, Capital, and Other Stores of Value," *American Economic Review Papers and Proceedings* 51, 26-37.

Törnqvist, L., 1936. "The Bank of Finland's Consumption Price Index," Bank of Finland *Bulletin* 10, 1-8.

Triplett, J. E., 1976. "The Measurement of Inflation: A Survey of Research on the Accuracy of Price Indices." In *Analysis of Inflation*, P. H. Earl (ed.), Lexington, Mass.: D.C. Heath, 19-82.

Triplett, J. E., 1992. "Economic Theory and BEA's Alternative Quantity and Price Indexes," *Survey of Current Business* 72, 32-48.

Ullah, A. and H. D. Vinod, 1988. "Flexible Production Function Estimation by Nonparametric Kernel Estimators." In *Nonparametric and Robust Inference: Advances in Econometrics*, Vol. 7, G. F. Rhodes and T. B. Fomby (eds.), Greenwich, CT: JAI Press, 139-160.

Usher, D., 1980. "Introduction." In *The Measurement of Capital*, D. Usher (ed.), Chicago: University of Chicago Press (for the NBER), 1-21.

Varian, H. R., 1982. "The Nonparametric Approach to Demand Analysis," *Econometrica* 50, 945-973.

Varian, H. R., 1983. "Non-Parametric Tests of Consumer Behaviour," *Review of Economic Studies* 50, 99-110.

Varian, H. R., 1984. *Microeconomic Analysis*, 2nd ed., New York: W. W. Norton.

Vartia, Y. O., 1976. "Ideal Log Change Index Numbers," *Scandinavian Journal of Statistics* 3, 121-126.

Volcker, P. A., 1982. "Remarks on Monetary Policy," *Federal Reserve Bulletin* 68, 691-692.

Wales, T. J., 1977. "On the Flexibility of Flexible Functional Forms: An Empirical Approach," *Journal of Econometrics* 5, 183-193.

Wall, K. D., 1974. "Estimation of Rational Distributed Lag Structural Form Models," Mimeo, NBER, Cambridge, Mass.

White, H., 1980. "Using Least Squares to Approximate Unknown Regression Functions," *International Economic Review* 21, 149-170.

Whitesell, W. C. and S. Collins, 1996. "A Minor Redefinition of M2," Finance and Economics Discussion Series Paper #96-7, Federal Reserve Board, Washington, D.C.

Wiley, D. E., W. H. Schmidt, and W. J. Bramble, 1973. "Studies of a Class of Covariance Structure Models," *Journal of the American Statistical Association* 68, 317-323.

Wonnacott, T. H. and R. J. Wonnacott, 1. '/. *Introductory Statistics for Business and Economics*, 2nd ed., New York: John Wiley.

Woodford, M., 1989. "Imperfe' , Fi.ancial Intermediation and Complex Dynamics." In *Economic Co,   ty: Chaos, Sunspots, Bubbles, and Nonlinearity*, W. A. Barnett, J. Geweke, and K. Shell, Cambridge: Cambridge University Press, 309-338.

Woodland, A. D., 1978. "On Testing Weak Separability," *Journal of Econometrics* 8, 383-398.

Woodland, A. D., 1979. "Stochastic Specifications and the Estimation of Share Equations," *Journal of Econometrics* 10, 361-383.

Young, A. H., 1992. "Alternative Measures of Change in Real Output and Prices," *Survey of Current Business* 72, 32-48.

Young, A. H., 1993. "Alternative Measures of Change in Real Output and Prices: Quarterly Estimates for 1959-92," *Survey of Current Business* 73, 31-41.

Yue, P., 1991. "A Microeconomic Approach to Estimating Money Demand: The Asymptotically Ideal Model," Federal Reserve Bank of St. Louis *Review* 73, 36-51.

Yue, P. and R. Fluri, 1991. "Divisia Monetary Services Indexes for Switzerland: Are They Useful for Monetary Targeting?," Federal Reserve Bank of St. Louis *Review* 73, 19-33.

Index by Name*

Afriat, S. N., xxv, 14, 83
Ahlfors, L. V., 344, 357
Akaike, H., 174
Allais, M., xxvi
Allen, R. C., 78
Anderson, G. J., 25, 421, 579n
Anderson, R. G., 8n, 587n, 610–616
Apostol, T. M., 344
Arrow, K. J., 18, 52n, 60n, 137n, 154n, 197n, 227n, 248, 250n, 277n, 329, 397n, 436n, 557n
Ashley, R., 243
Attfield, C. L. F., 53n

Balk, B. M., xxvii, 402n
Baltensperger, E., 457
Bansal, R., 267
Barnett, W. A., xxiii, xxv, xxviii, 12n, 15n, 24n, 28n, 29n, 39n, 46n, 49n, 51n, 96n, 97n, 100n, 102n, 11–108, 127n, 129n, 130n, 137n, 138n, 140n, *146*, *147*, *148*, 113–150, 150n, 151n, 153n, 154n, 159n, 151–160, 173n, 188n, 189n, 191n, 195n, 211n, 219n, 220n, 221n, 223n, 224n, 225n, 228n, 231n, 232n, 238n, 239n, 245n, 246n, 247n, 264n, 267n, 269n, 270n, 275n, 278n, 279n, 303n, 308n, 318n, 167–319, 360n, 361n, 363n, 365n, 371n, 380n, 382n, 391n, 400n, 401n, 405n, 410n, 411n, 416n, 420n, 422n, 423n, 424n, 425n, 325–427, 427n, 434n, 436n, 437n, 439n, 440n, 482n, 483n, 485n, 486n, 488n, 496n, 497n, 498n, 506n, 509n, 527n, 433–529, 531n, 534n, 535n, 538n, 539n, 545n, 547n, 552n, 555n, 530–557, 557n, 580n, 581n, 587n, 588n, 589n, 563–605
Barro, R. J., 360n, 365
Barten, A. P., 187, 189, 189n, 475
Barth, J. R., 127n, 327, 361n

Basmann, R. L., 191n
Batchelor, R., 426n
Baumol, W. J., 372n
Baxter, M., 270
Beck, D., 37, 151n, 326
Behrens, K. H., 481
Bell, F. W., 458
Belongia, M. T., 121, 191n, 217n, 219, 230, 246n, 275n, 296n, 304, 318, 411n, 418, 426n, 464, 532, 587n, 589, 609
Benston, G. J., 458, 470, 473
Berger, A. N., 458, 470
Berndt, E. R., 75, 90n, 169, 187, 188, 425n, 437n, 440n, 462, 465, 552n, 586n
Betancourt, R., 548n, 552n
Binner, J. E., 587n, 609
Bisignano, J., 14n, 127n, 327, 361n
Blackorby, C., xxvi, 67, 75, 220n, 221, 345, 399, 414n, 462, 464–467, 475, 485n, 495n, 498n
Blanchard, O. J., 277n
Bliss, C. J., 89
Blundell, R., 421
Bordo, M. D., 275
Box, G. E. P., 240
Boyle, G. W., 280n, 282
Brainard, W., 11n, 482n, 484n
Bramble, W. J., 465
Bramlett, J., 481
Bridge, J. L., 93n
Brillinger, D. R., 241
Brock, W. A., 274
Brockett, P. L., 241
Brown, M., 99
Brown, R. S., 59n, 440n, 463, 467
Browning, M. J., 53n
Brunner, K., 95n, 138n, 150n, 397, 572
Buck, R. C., 341, 355, 356
Burgess, D. F., 465
Byron, R. P., 325n

Cagan, P., 142, *148*, 149, 384n, 418, 570
Calvo, G. A., 599
Carlson, K. M., 378
Cass, D., 602
Caves, D. W., 49n, 59n, 86, 87, 91, 328, 363, 437n, 440n, 463, 467, 473

---

*Page numbers appear in italics, when the referenced name is in either a figure or table. Page numbers are followed by n, when the referenced name is in a footnote.

Chalfant, J., 121, 191n, 219, 230, 304, 318, 411n, 418, 464
Chang, J., 127n, 326
Chen, P., 121, 125, 232, 274, 427n, 601
Chetty, K. V., 14n, 127n, 326, 349, 361n, 418n
Chew, S. H., xxvi
Choi, S., 191n, 220n, 304, 411n, 421n, 464
Chow, G. C., 421n
Christ, C. F., 282, 325n
Christensen, L. R., 49n, 59n, 75, 86, 87, 91, 328, 338, 339, 363, 413, 437n, 440n, 462–465, 467, 473
Christiano, L. J., 418
Chrystal, A. K., 219, 246, 246n, 426n, 530, 532, 532n, 547n, 590n, 591
Clark, J. A., 458
Clements, K. W., 11n, 14n, 89, 168n
Clower, R. W., 397n
Cockerline, J. P., 49n, 127n, 327, 330, 383n, 426n
Coen, R. M., 62
Coleman, W. J., 270
Collins, S., 307, 308, 315, 578
Cooley, T. F., 389n, 590n
Cooper, R. J., 14n
Croushore, D., 248
Crucini, M. J., 270
Cuthbertson, K., 588, 591

Danes, M. K., 14n
Darrough, M. N., 169, 187, 188, 425n, 586n
Davidson, R., xxvi
Day, R. H., 274
Deaton, A., 82, 83n, 95n, 189
Debreu, G., 89, 466, 494, 542n
Dechert, W. D., 274
Dekel, E., xxvi
Den Haan, W. J., 263, 263n, 266, 267
Denny, M., 36n, 59n, 86, 93n, 437n, 440, 462, 464, 465, 498n
Diamond, D. W., 484
Dickey, D. A., 282n
Diewert, W. E., xxv, xxvi, xxviii, 14n, 25, 38n, 39, 40, 45, 46n, 49, 49n, 55n, 62, 63, 66, 74n, 77, 78, 78n, 83, 84n, 86, 87, 87n, 88, 90n, 91, 91n, 93, 93n, 97, 98, 115, 119, 121, 127, 130n, 140, 150, 151n, 154, 155, 169, 171, 187–189, 218, 300, 302, 325n, 328, 330, 338, 339, 342, 344, 346, 352–355, 358, 360, 363, 363n, 402n, 403, 413, 423, 425n, 434, 437n, 465–467, 473, 483, 485n, 488n, 497n, 498, 499n, 500, 501n, 503, 528, 534, 539, 540n, 551, 553, 566, 569, 579n, 583n, 586n, 587, 588n, 589–591, 596, 603
Divisia, F., 102, 115, 120, 245, 247, 257, 402n
Dixon, P. B., 14, 39n
Donaldson, D., xxvi
Donovan, D. J., xxv, 11n, 14n, 15, 20n, 140, 152, 327, 331, 349, 361n, 398, 404, 418, 419n, 589
Dorfman, J. R., 361n
Dowd, K., 412n
Drake, L., 426n, 532n, 547n
Driscoll, J. C., 209, 311, 314, 405, 485n, 496n, 512, 513, 516, 554, 579, 589n
Dueker, M. J., 275
Duffie, D., 494n
Dutkowsky, D. H., 153
Dutton, D., 412n
Dybvig, P. H., 484
Dylan, B., 327

Edwards, C. L., 307, 308, 315
Eichhorn, W., 402n
Enzler, J. J., 13n, 368n
Epstein, L. G., xxv, xxvi
Ettin, E., 36, 151n, 326
Ewis, N. A., 49n, 121, 383, 418, 419n, 477

Fase, M. M. G., 426n
Fayyad, S. K., 194, 223, 412n, 419n, 433n, 436n, 443n
FCA Report, 509
Feenstra, R. C., xxiii, xxv, 197n, 227n, 248, 250n, 277n, 397n, 557n
Feige, E. L., 383
Feldstein, M., 248, 532n, 590n
Fischer, S., xxiii, xxv, xxvi, 60n, 213, 248, 277n, 397n, 436n, 548n, 557n
Fisher, D., xxiii, 49n, 121, 122, 219, 246n, 275n, 305, 318, 372n, 383,

418n, 419n, 420n, 389–427, 456, 477, 482n, 532, 580n, 581n 589–591, 596, 598, 603
Fisher, F. M., 61n
Fisher, I., xxiii, xxviii, 14, 36n, 38n, 39, 45, 45n, 46, 46n, 115, 140n, 151, 152, 362, 402, 427n, 564, 567, 569
Fisher, P., 587n
Fisher, T., 464–467, 475, 485n, 495n, 498n
Fixler, D., 219
Fleissig, A., 589
Fluri, R., 426n
Ford, J. L., 127n, 326
Fraumeni, B. M., 465
Friar, M. E., *147*, 367, 368n
Friedman, M., xxiv, 127n, 128, 149n, 275, 286, 326, 361n, 389, 396, 418, 577–580, 580n
Frisch, R., xxvi, 14, 15
Fuss, M. A., 25, 36n, 71, 71n, 437n, 462, 464, 465, 498n

Galbraith, J. K., 11
Gallant, A. R., 150n, 267, 267n, 325n, 328, 342, 346, 353, 401n, 415, 419, 419n, 497n, 601
Garrett, B., 368n
Geweke, J., 188n, 231n, 325n, 401n, 416n, 497n, 539n
Gilbert, A. R., 458
Gilligan, T., 458
Giovannini, A., 277n
Glasner, D., 118n
Goldfeld, S. M., 13n, 147, *147*, 368n, 389, 414, 421n, 426n
Goldman, S. M., 462
Golub, G. H., 497n
Gordon, R. J., 421n
Gorman, W. M., 83, 169, 211n, 329, 337, 399, 424, 467, 597
Gramm, W. M., 412n
Grandmont, J. M., 600, 602
Green, H. A. J., 66, 114, 137n, 141n, 142n, 153n, 464, 566, 569
Guilkey, D. K., 328
Gul, F., xxvi
Gurley, J. G., 127n, 309, 326

Hahm, J. H., xxiii, 454–481, 498n, 505, 509n, 514, 528, 534n, 539n, 545n, 589

Hahn, F., 397n
Hahn, G. H., 18, 52n, 60n, 154n, 197n, 227n, 248, 250n, 277n, 329, 436n, 557n
Hall, R. E., 59n, 72n, 77n, 465, 488n
Hall, T. E., 275n
Hamburger, M. J., 138n, 150n
Hancock, D., xxv, 57n, 121, 191n, 382n, 426, 434n, 438n, 439n, 456, 458, 459, 461, 464, 465, 477, 483, 484, 487, 505, 514, 528, 534n, 535, 535n, 545n
Hannaway, M., 481
Hansen, L. P., 224, 231, 267, 485, 504, 504n, 542, 586n
Hanweck, G. A., 458, 470, 473
Harper, M. J., 552n
Haugh, L. D., 365
Hawtrey, R. G., 127n, 128, 326, 361n
Heckman, J. J., 586n
Henderson, J. R., 14n
Hester, D., 11n
Hickman, B. G., 62
Hicks, J. R., 396
Hinich, M. J., xxiii, 49n, 121, 122, 223n, 217–244, 264, 265, 268, 270, 297, 298, 302, 304–306, 308, 382n, 391, 391n, 422n, 426, 433–453, 483, 484n, 514, 523, 527n, 552, 554, 555n, 589, 601
Hoa, T. Y., 426n
Hodrick, R. J., 277n
Hudson, S., 587n
Hulten, C. R., 39, 45n, 77, 115, 116, 130n, 247
Humphrey, D. B., 458, 470, 473
Humphrey, T. M., 11n
Hunter, W. C., 458
Hussey, R., 267
Hutt, W. H., 119, 209

Ingersoll, J. E., 491n
Ishida, K., 49n, 121, 426n
Izan, H. Y., 88, 168n

Jenkins, G., 240
Jensen, M., xxiii, 245n, 264n, 245–273, 283, 601
Jensen, M. J., 219, 220n, 227, 228n, 239n, 247n, 271, 529n, 531n, 557n, 589n

Johannes, J. M., 95n
Johnson, L., 13n, 368n
Johnson, N., 113n
Jonas, A., 188n, 267n, 351, 401n, 416n
Jones, B. E., 8n, 589n, 610–616
Jonung, L., 275
Jorgenson, D. W., 92, 169, 338, 339, 413, 465
Judd, J. P., 389
Jungeilges, D.T., 601

Kalchbrenner, J., 37, 151n, 326
Kane, E. J., 127n, 326
Karni, E., 412n
Kavajecz, K. A., 579n
Khaled, M. S., 90n, 440n
Kirova, M., xxiii, 220n, 224n, 232n, 262, 270n, 552n, 555n, 530–557, 587n, 589, 589n
Klein, B., 22n, 364, 473
Kloek, T., 86
Konüs, A. A., xxvi, 84
Kotz, S., 113n
Kraft, A., 127n, 327, 361n
Kraft, J., 127n, 327, 361n
Krause, D., 275n

Labadie, P., 277n
Laidler, D. E. W., 282n, 591
Lakota, K. L., 277n
Lancaster, K. J., 158
Latane, H. A., 276, 282
Lau, L. J., 92, 93n, 169, 338, 339, 412n, 413, 440n, 465, 467, 497n, 501, 502n
LeBaron, B., 274
Lee, T. H., 127n, 326
Lee, Y. W., 188n, 415
Leeper, E. M., 531
Leontief, W. W., 14, 399, 496
LeRoy, S. F., 282, 389n
Lewbel, A., 169
Lindsey, D., 37, 151n, 326
Liouville, J., 356
Liu, Y., xxiii 219, 220n, 227, 228n, 239n, 247n, 269n, 245–273, 283, 529n, 531n, 557n, 589n
Lovell, C. A. K., 328
Lucas, D., 277n
Lucas, R. E., 204n, 378n

MacDonald, R., 246, 246n, 530, 532, 590n, 591

Machina, M., xxvi
Magill, M., 494n
Maks, J. A. H., 15, 39n
Malmquist, S., 83n, 84
Mandel, M. J., 245
Marcet, A., 263, 263n, 266 267, 267n
Marquez, J., 49n
Marshall, D. A., 267, 280n
Marshall, W., 458
May, J.D., 93n
McFadden, D., 466
Mehra, R., xxvi, 224, 271n
Meiselman, D. I., 127n, 326
Meltzer, A. H., 95n, 138n, 397
Merton, R. C., 230, 302n
Modigliani, F., 11n
Moorsteen, R. H., 84
Moroney, J. R., 127n, 327, 361n
Moulin, H., 195n
Mountain, D. C., 188n
Muellbauer, J. N., 39n, 82, 95n, 137n, 169, 187, 189, 211n, 329, 337, 425n, 597
Mullineaux, D. J., 470
Murphy, N. B., 458
Murray, J. D., 49n, 127n, 327, 330, 383n, 426n, 458

Nesmith, T. D., 8n, 589n, 610–616
Newey, W. K., 504n
Nguyen, P., 14n
Niehans, J., 391
Noble, N. R., 275n

Offenbacher, E. K., xxiii, 14n, 22n, 31n, 44, 46, 46n, 49n, 100n, 106, 122, 127, 127n, 132, *146, 147*, 148, 159n, 151–160, 327, 334, 349, 360n, 361n, 365n, 371n, 380n, 360–388, 418, 419n, 434n, 565
Ohta, M., 90
Orphanides, A., 307, 308, 315

Parkin, J. M., 14n
Pasupathy, M., xxiii, 220n, 224n, 232n, 262, 270n, 552n, 555n, 530–557, 587n, 589, 589n
Patinkin, D., 396, 397n
Patterson, D. M., 240, 241, 243
Paulus, J. D., 13n, 368n
Pearce, D. K., 383

INDEX BY NAME

Pearce, J., 481
Pesek, B. P., 300, 309, 313
Philips, L., 397n
Phlips, L., 14n, 52n, 60n, 137n, 197n, 227n, 248, 250n, 329, 436n
Pierce, D. A., 365
Pinto, C., 59n, 437n, 440n, 462, 464, 465
Pollak, R. A., xxvi 21n, 29n
Porter, R. D., 37, 151n, 326, 368n
Poterba, J. M., 121, 209, 219–221, 223, 224, 228, 231, 238, 248, 265, 304–306, 308, 311, 314, 391n, 397n, 405, 422n, 483, 485n, 496n, 512, 513, 516, 530, 532, 532n, 554, 555n, 557, 579, 589, 589n
Pradhan, N., 587n
Prescott, E. C., xxvi, 224, 271n, 590n
Priestley, M., 240
Primont, D., 67, 75, 220n, 221, 328, 345, 399n, 414n, 462, 465, 498n
Pudney, S. E., 363n

Quirk, J. D., 18, 137n, 154n, 248, 250n, 329

Rasche, R. H., 11n, 95n, 587n
Reid, B., 307, 308, 315
Richter, M. K., 115
Rios-Rull, J. V., 586n, 590n
Robb, A. L., 49n, 419n
Robles, B., 483n, 547, 548n, 552n
Roper, D., 405, 590n
Rotemberg, J. J., 119, 121, 209, 219–221, 223, 224, 228, 230, 231, 238, 248, 265, 296, 297, 302, 303, 303n, 304–306, 308, 311, 314, 391n, 397n, 405, 422n, 483, 485n, 496n, 512, 513, 516, 530, 532, 532n, 554, 555n, 557, 579, 589, 589n
Rothenberg, J., 351
Rouwenhorst, K. G., 270
Rubinstein, M., 260n
Russell, R. R., 67, 75, 220n, 221, 328, 345, 399n, 414n, 462, 465, 498n

Sahasakul, C., 365
Salles, M., 195n
Samuelson, P. A., xxv, 14, 21, 29n, 49, 52n, 60, 80, 87n, 96, 248, 250n, 436n

Santomero, A. M., 456, 457
Saposnik, R., 18, 137n, 154n, 248, 250n, 329
Sargent, T. J., 198n, 204n, 267n, 489, 490n
Sato, K., 88, 92, 92n, 96, 96n
Sato, R., xxv, 52n, 60n, 436n
Saving, T. R., 96, 96n, 300, 309, 313, 412n
Scadding, J., 389
Scheinkman, J., 274
Schmidt, W. H., 465
Schofield, N., 195n
Schwartz, A. J., 127n, 128, 326, 361n, 396, 579, 580n
Schwarz, G., 174n
Schwert, G. W., *148*, 367
Schworm, W., 464–467, 475, 485n, 495n, 498n
Serletis, A., xxiii, xxviii, 49n, 121, 122, 167, 174n, 191n, 211n, 219, 221n, 223, 225n, 246n, 275n, 305, 318, 383, 391n, 419n, 389–427, 436n, 456, 464, 482n, 532, 580, 581n, 589–591, 596, 598, 603
Shafer, W., 494n
Shaw, E. S., 309
Shell, K., 61n, 602
Shephard, R. W., 59n, 65, 68, 72
Shiller, R. J., 160n
Simpson, T. D., 37, 151n, 326, 368n
Sims, C. A., 93, 366, 531
Singleton, K. J., 49n, 224, 231, 267, 485, 504, 504n, 542
Slottje, D. J., 191n
Small, D. H., 307, 308, 315
Smirlock, M., 458
Sono, M., 399
Sosin, K., 421n
Spanos, A., 590n
Spindt, P. A., xxiii, 44, 46, 46n, 49n, 97, 98, 100, 100n, 106, 107, 122, 127, 127n, 129n, 131, 132, 140n, *146–148*, 151–160, 326, 327, 332–334, 349, 360n, 361n, 365n, 371n, 380n, 381n, 360–388, 405, 418, 434n, 565, 570, 571
Spinnewyn, F., 52n, 60n, 137n, 197n, 227n, 248, 250n, 329, 397n, 436n

Star, S., 77n
Stark, F., 127n, 326
Startz, R., 159n
Steinhauer, L., 127n, 326
Stock, J. H., 248, 532n, 590n
Stoker, T. M., 169, 169n, 194
Stokey, N. L., 204n
Stone, C. C., 275
Strotz, R. H., 53n, 398
Survey of Current Business, 509
Swamy, P. A. V. B., 274, 276, 288, 290, 374, 375, 375n
Swamy, S., 14, 21, 29n, 49, 80, 87n
Swofford, J. L., 49n, 131, 191n, 308n, 411, 412n, 416n, 464, 497n, 580, 589

Taggart, R. A., 458
Tauchen, G., 267
Taylor, J. B., 263n, 266n, 267
Theil, H., 11n, 39, 45n, 86, 89, 115, 116, 158, 168n, 170n, 172, 173, 187, 189, 189n, 330, 338, 339, 363, 425n
Thornton, D. L., 275, 275n, 485n
Timme, S. G., 458
Tinsley, P. A., 11n, 37, *147*, 151n, 274, 276, 288, 290, 326, 367, 368n, 374, 375, 375n
Tobin, J., 372n, 391, 484n
Törnqvist, L., 39, 116, 363
Triplett, J. E., 26
Turnovsky, S. J., 405, 590n

Uhlig, H., 263n, 266n, 267
Usher, D., 95
Uzawa, H., 462

Varian, H. R., 137n, 411, 415, 468
Vartia, Y. O., 88
Volcker, P. A., 564n, 570

Wales, T. J., 328, 345, 465, 466, 485n, 497n, 498, 498n, 499n, 500, 500n, 501n, 503, 528, 539n, 540n, 551, 553
Wall, K. D., 366n
Watts, D., 240
Weber, W. E., xxiii, 49n, 121, 237–239, 382n, 426, 433–453, 483, 484, 514, 523, 527n
West, K. D., 504n

White, H., 328
White, R. W., 458
Whitesell, W. C., 578
Whitney, G. A., 49n, 121, 191n, 308n, 411n, 412n, 416n, 464, 497n, 589
Wilbratte, B. J., 127n, 327, 361n
Wiley, D. E., 465
Wilson, G. R., 241
Wolfe, M. D., 188n, 231n, 401n, 415, 416n, 497n, 539n
Wood, D. O., 552n
Woodford, M., 602
Woodland, A. D., 350, 464, 465

Xu, H., xxiii, 219n, 274–295, 529n

Yue, P., xxiii, 121, 122, 188n, 223n, 231n, 217–244, 264, 265, 267n, 268, 270, 297, 298, 302, 304–306, 308, 391n, 401, 401n, 416n, 420n, 422n, 426n, 483, 483n, 485n, 552n, 554, 555n, 589

Zellner, A., 325n
Zhou, G., xxiii, 220n, 223n, 248, 308n, 307–319, 481–529, 532, 534, 535, 535n, 539n, 587n, 588, 588n
Zieschang, K., 219
Zin, S. E., xxvi

Index by Subject*

Accounts. *See also* Deposits.
    checking, 495, 505n
    deposit, 32, 32n, 486, 505n
    loan, 505n
    money market deposits, 420, 495, 505n, 570, 579n
    money orders, 505n
    official checks, 505n
    passbook, 27, 34, 486
    regular savings, 505n
    retirement, 505n
    savings and loan passbook, 26, 30, 31
    savings bank passbook, 31, 32, 32n
    time deposits, 37, 505n
Additive preferences. *See* Separability (strong).
Adjustment costs, 28, 550
Affine transformation, 491n
Aggregates/aggregation (monetary), 217, 383, 388, 445, 568, 591. *See also* Aggregator functions; Aggregation theory; Divisia indexes/aggregates; Fisher ideal indexes; Monetary aggregate(s); Price aggregates; Quantity aggregates; Simple sum indexes/aggregates.
    bias, 169
    broad, 362, 579
    category utility, 251
    Cobb–Douglas, 264
    conditions, 37, 387
    conformable, 99
    demand side, 238, 441n
    economic, 12, 12n, 13, 15, 21, 23, 24, 31, 33n, 34, 44n, 45, 47, 51, 104, 114–116, 124, 135, 139, 141, 152, 153, 156, 157, 237, 269, 305, 330, 337, 391, 392, 424, 439, 441n, 566, 595
    error, 167–194, 380, 383, 388
    estimated theoretical, 246, 485, 512

    exact, 75, 84, 168, 169, 186, 193, *268*, 245–273, 495, 496, 603
    Hicksian approach, 59, 390, 396
    inexact, 167, 169
    input, 59
    labor, 509n
    Malmquist demand, 443n
    Malmquist supply, 443n
    material, 509n
    methodology, 143, 217
    multi-stage recursive, 75
    neoclassical, 456
    nonhomothetic, 63
    official, 142, 143n, 145, 365, 367, 373, 417
    output, 58, 59, 80, 482, 496, 517, 528
    parametric, 529
    passbook savings, 31
    perfect economic, 141
    recursive, 87
    stochastic, 168
    subaggregation, 75, 87–88, 90, 565
    supply side, 94, 238, 441n, 495–497, 538
    theoretical, 30n, 38, 45, 49, 53, 63–75, 327, 485, 496, *519, 520*, 522, 604
    under homogeneity, 63–75
    under risk, 195–216
    user cost, 24, 25, 34, 47, 65
    velocity, 98
    weighted, 396
Aggregation
    over consumers, 51, 88–90, 97, 153n, 167–169, 186–193, 328, 494n
    over economic agents, 167, 586, 590n, 596, 598, 603
    over factors of production, 62
    over firms, 88, 153n, 494n
    over goods, 14, 51, 54, 88–90, 97, 167, 168, 248, 391, 424, 479, 497, 595, 598, 603
    over outputs, 59
    over primary inputs, 93
Aggregation theory, 30n, 11–48, 80–85, 113–114, 118–120, 124, 126, 134, 135, 135n, 137n, 138, 138n, 139, 141, *146*, 147, 151–

---

*Page numbers appear in italics, when the referenced subject is in either a figure or table. Page numbers are followed by n, when the referenced subject is in a footnote.

154, 160, 211, 212, 239, 248, 249, 271, 304, 308, 327, 331, 360, 383, 390, 391, 394, 397, 400–407, 423, 425, 427, 434–437, 441n, 455, 462, 463, 496, 532n, 570, 582, 586, 596–598, 603, 604
and two-stage budgeting, 464
demand side, 433
economic, 124, 193, 329, 464, 483, 484, 566, 568
exact, 119, 482
macroeconomic, 597, 598
microeconomic, 596, 598, 599, 603
stochastic, 168
supply-side, 433, 434, 456
Aggregator functions, 29n, 11–49, 51, 74, 82, 113–115, 118, 138n, 139, 139n, 153, 154, 199, 201, 204, 206, 207, 209, 215–219, 221, 223, 227, 229, 230, 238, 239, 245, 246, 251, 253, 257, 264, 268, 272, 277, 300, 306, 329, 330, 387, 394n, 400, 400n, 401, 404, 408n, 410, 410n, 412, 415, 423, 454, 463–465, 476, 478–480, 495, 512, 531n, 532–534, 538, 538n, 540, 542n, 546, *546*, 551, 553, *553*, 555n, 557, 596. *See also* Category utility functions.
and homotheticity, 465, 466
demand side, 279n
direct, 412n
economic, 157, 220, 404n, 533
estimation of, 43, 44, 76, 218, 219, 246, 553, 555
exact, 12, 75, 76, 87, 114, 211, 237, 253, 262–264, 279n, 422, 424, 437, 496, 557
flexible, 114, 115, 466
global, 498n
indirect, 412, 412n
input, 59, 91
linear, 583
linear homogeneous, 114, 251, 423
nonlinear, 38, 248, 401
nonparametric approximations of, 496
output, 59, 463, 484, 496
price, 24, 66, 72, 74, 75, 116, 278
quantity, 24, 47, 66, 67, 74, 75, 80,

116, 154, 283, 437, 439n, 464, 566, 583, 583n, 584
rational expectations, 422
separable, 228, 484
simple sum, 273
supply side, 279n
theoretical, 220
tracking ability of, 268, 269, 534
tracking error of, 268
translog, 130n, 189
under perfect certainty, 247
under risk, 212, 248
user cost, 412
Akaike Information Criterion (AIC), 174, 174n, 418
Allen indexes and variants, 84, 84n, 86, 87, 476. *See also* Index numbers.
nonparametric approximations of, 86
Allen-Uzawa elasticities, *477*
Analytic functions, 328, 340–341, 355–357
Analytic part, 343–345, 355, 356
Approximation
and Weierstrass theorem, 341
center of, 507
error, 168, 340
exact aggregates, 496
in discrete time, 113, 140n, 154, 302, 440, 567
linear, 368
local, 344, 353, 355, 507
nonparametric, 76, 86, 496
of generalized Leontief, 344
of minflex Laurent, 353
of Taylor series, 328, 340–342, 344, 345, 348, 355–357
parameter-free, 330
remainder term of, 328
second order, 338–340, 342, 353–355, 497, 499n
statistical, 87
superlative, 423
Törnqvist-Theil, 77, 79, 102n, 103, 105, 116, 121, 140n, 302, 440, 567, 588n
Arrow-Pratt risk aversion. *See* Risk aversion.
Asset loan portfolio, 486
Asymptotically Ideal Model (AIM), 188, 189n, 401n, 416n, 497n

INDEX BY SUBJECT

Atomistic approach, 89
Autocorrelation, 509
Axioms. See Tests.

Balance sheets, 487, 505, 506
Bank of Canada, 330
Banking sector (industry), 90, 92, 483, 485, 494, 505, 515, 517, 522, 523, 528
  balance sheet, 505
  capital, 529
  commercial, 485
  earnings, 508n
  economies of scale, 529
  outputs, 512, 528
  runs on, 484
  scope, 529
  structural change, 97
  technological change, 529
  technology, specification of, 485
  value added, 529
Barnett and Zhou model, 535n
Barnett critique, 246, 246n, 530, 532–534, 556, 591
Barnett-Yue model, 223, 224, 228
Baumol-Tobin model, 548n
Bellman equations (method), 201–203, 205, 228, 252, 488–490, 537, 550
Bellman's principle, 201, 228, 490
Benchmark asset, 8n, 51, 52, 54, 119, 120, 196, 197, 197n, 226, 250, 256, 266, 304, 398, 398n, 413, 413n, 583, 583n
Benchmark rate (yield), 8n, 119, 123, 129, 140n, 160n, 198, 251, 256, 259, 259n, 261, 261n, 282, 304–305, 314, 318n, 436, 515
  risk adjusted, 259, 259n
Benveniste and Scheinkman equations, 203, 204n, 490, 537, 550
Blocking of components, 495
Bonds, 8, 17, 22, 334
Bretton-Woods system, 427
Budget constraint, 22n, 25n, 28, 35, 201, 248, 277n, 278, 279, 291, 398n, 442, 569, 602
Budget decision, 23n, 23–25. See also Two-stage decision (budgeting).

Cagan's velocity function, 148
Capital, 58, 62, 506

Capital Asset Pricing Model (CAPM), 245–273, 484, 531n, 557n. See also Risk; Risk aversion.
  consumption based (CCAPM), 256, 258–261, 261n, 262, 271
  risk adjusted, 260
Capital notes, 505n
Capital stocks, 95, *315–317*
Cash balances, 470, 472, 474–480, 486, 506, 508, 535
Cash flow, 487
Cash reserves, 472
Category production functions, 67, 74, 81, 329
  subproduction, 63, 87, 88, 93
Category utility functions, 18, 48, 74, 81, 84, 199, 209, 227, 251, 278, 538, 596. See also Utility functions (subutility).
  subutility, 17, 52, 67, 81, 83, 85, 87, 88
Causality tests, *146*, 169, 174n, 367, 371. See also Tests.
  Divisia moments to income, 175, *176*, 177
  Granger, 122, *148*, 174–177
  lag lengths in, 174
Central bank policy (instruments), 96, 273, 426, 528, 531, 603
Certainty equivalence assumption, 55n
Changing tastes, 86, 87
Checkable deposits. See Deposits.
Cobb-Douglas
  aggregates, 264
  model, 328
  utility function, 401
Cochrane-Orcutt technique, 378n
Commerce Department, 191, 348
Complete contingent claims market, 493, 523
Complex variables, 356
Component cluster, 495
Component quantity growth rates, 169
Composite function, 495. See also Separability.
Conditional allocation, 22. See also Two-stage decision (budgeting).
  current-period, 53n
Conjugate price and quantity, 83
Consistency conditions, 137
Consistency in aggregation. See Aggregates/aggregation (monetary).

Constant elasticity of substitution (CES), 31, 32, 264. *See also* Elasticities.
  functional form, 230, 555n
Constant relative risk aversion (CRRA), 491
Consumer demand for monetary assets (applied), 25–45, 143–149, 174–193, 230–237, 263–272, 288–290, 314–318, 325–359, 372–382, 410–421
Consumer demand for monetary assets (theory), 16–25, 51–54, 64–66, 76–78, 81–84, 86–90, 170–173, 195–216, 245–273, 276–288, 397–415
Consumer durables, 331
Consumer price index, 25, 26n, 108, 151, 191n, 217, 218, 221, 402, 545n, 564, 576
Consumers, 64–66, 483n
  expenditure, 31
  survival set, 357
Contingency, 523
  fixed, 523
Continuous time, 76, 115, 116, 121, 140n, 204, 245, 278, 437, 557, 583, 584, 584n
Control variables, 201, 205
Controllability, 334
Convexity, 511, 522, 528
  conditions, 508
  global, 500, 502, 503, 511
  local, 503
Convolution, 342
Corner solutions, 510n
Corporate office, 67, 68, 71
Cost functions, 64, 71n, 83, 85, 87. *See also* Duality; Subfunctions; Unit cost functions.
  subcost, 69
  unit cost, 65, 74, 75, 82, 83
Cost of living index, 18, 52, 82, 84, 87, 102, 140n, 152, 196, 217, 218, 221, 226, 250, 331, 364, 398, 398n, 436n, 459, 474, 545n, 548, 552n, 567, 583n
Costs
  holding, 486n
  real resource, 486
  variable, 460
Credit unions, 31n, 40

Currency, 12, 13, 55, 57, 123, 129, 159, 210, *231*, 249, 307, 313, 362, 392n, 420n, 459, 528, 552n, 569, 570, 584
Currency equivalent (CE) indexes, 209–211, 296, 312, *317*, 318, 318n, 405, 405n, 485, 485n, 496n, 512, *513, 514*, 515–517, *517, 519–521*. *See also* Rotemberg money stock index.
  growth rate of, 513
  M1, *315*
  M2, *316*
  M2+, *316*
  smoothed, 513, *513, 514*, 515, *518–520, 522*
  stock, *317*
  tracking ability of, 496
  unsmoothed, 513, 515
Curvature conditions, 455, 497, 500, 511, 539

Debentures, 505n
Debt/equity ratios, 62
Decentralizing, 67–71
Deflators
  input, 61n
  output, 61n
Demand deposits, 31n, 107, 123, 159, *231*, 299n, 307, 308, 313, 392, 411n, 420n, 456, 458, 470, 472–481, 486, 495, 505, 505n, 506–509, 510n, 534, 535, 535n, 542, 543, 545n, 552n, 565, 570, 584, 584n. *See also* Deposits.
  interest-bearing, 473
  money market, *231*
Demand for money functions, *146*, 148n, 169, 221, 222, 327, 334, 368, 369, 372–378, *386, 387*, 389–427, 483n, 532n, 577–592, 603
  single equation, 327
Demand functions, 14, 141, 327, 376, 389, 531, 586
  input, 462
  money. *See* Demand for money functions
Demand systems, 27, 186, 327, 328, 337, 341, *351*, 352, 391, 414, 421, 597. *See also* Cobb-Douglas; Generalized Leontief model; Laurent demand model; Trans-

INDEX BY SUBJECT 659

log model.
approach, 418–421
full Laurent, 346–348, 350, 351, 359
generalized Leontief, 345
Laurent, 325–328, 353
Müntz-Szatz, 351, 416n
Taylor, 326
Demand theory, 586
Deposits. See also Accounts; Demand deposits; Savings deposits; Time deposits.
checkable, 570
large time, 570
money market demand, *231*
multipliers, 483
small time, 570
Derived demand, 58
Deterministic point, 198, 200, 201, 227, 250, 272, 273. See also Utility functions.
Diewert indexes, 86, 116, 328, 483. See also Index numbers.
superlative, 140
Direct production function. See Aggregator functions; Production function.
Direct utility function. See Aggregator functions; Utility functions.
Discount factor, 19, 61
subjective rate of time, 493
Discount rate, 57n
Discrete time, 116, 121, 130n, 140n, 253, 263, 440, 584n
Disintermediation, 333
Dispersion measures, 168
macroeconomic effects of, 169
Dispersion-dependency diagnostic test, 189n, 167–194, 194n
Distance function, 82, 83, 85–87, 92, 173n, 443n, 538n
input, 87
output, 87
Distributions
first moments, 424
income, 167–194
second moments, 424
Dividends, 58, 487
Divisia approach, 170–173. See also Divisia indexes/aggregates.
Divisia indexes/aggregates, 41–44, 44n, 76, 79, 86, 88, 89, 100–108, 113–125, 128–130, 130n, 131–134, 140, 140n, 144n, 143–145, 145n, *146*, 148, *149*, 154–156, 158, 159, 168, 171, 174n, 181, 182, 185, 190, 194, 204, 205, 207–211, 211n, 212, 219, 223, 229, 231, 232, 237, 245–248, 252, 257, 258, 262, 263, 266, 268, *268-270*, 278, 283, 288, 297, 299, 299n, 300–305, 309, 318, 318n, 319, 330–334, 360–388, 391, 402n, 404, 404n, 405, 408–409, 411, 417, 418, 422–424, 425, 426n, 427, 427n, 434, 437, 441, 441n, 443, 443n, 449, 451, 474, 483, 485, 496n, 512, 513, *513-515*, 517, *519, 520*, 531n, 538, 546, *547*, 553, *554*, 555, 557, 563–576, 579, 579n, 581, 587, 587n, 588, 588n, 589, 591, 603. See also Divisia approach; Index numbers; Price (user cost) indexes; Quantity indexes; Törnqvist-Theil indexes and variants.
chained, 473
continuous time, 76, 77, 115–116, 121, 245, 363, 387, 437, 440
covariances, 169, 194
demand, 237, 238, 434, 435, 440, 441, 441n, 442, 443, 443n, 444–446, 448, *448*, 449, *449*, 450–453
discrete time, 79, 86, 113, 116–117, 121, 253, 330, 363, 404, 437, 440, 567
exact, 247
extended to account for risk, 245–247, 249, 257, 262, 264, 271, 283
first moments, 174, 175, *176*, 177, 194, 305
flow, 405n
generalized, 247, 253–258
implicit, 78, 80
L, 128, 132, 148, 150, *176, 178, 179, 181-185*, 333, 362, 366, 371, 373, *374*, 376, 378, 380–384, *387, 406*, 407, 579, *580*
M1, *176, 178, 179, 181*, 182, *182-185*, 288, 367, 373n, *374*, 376, 378, 381, 383, 384, 405, *406*,

418, 423n, 443, 444, 450, 555, *556*, 570, 571, *573, 574*, 576
M1B, 144, 144n, 148–150
M2, 144n, 150, *176, 178, 179, 181*, 182, *182–185*, 222, 366, 367, 373, *374*, 376, 378, 381, *386*, *406*, 443, 450, 453, 555n, *556*, 570, 571, *571, 573*, 574, *574*, 581
M3, 133, *135, 136*, 148, 150, 155, *176, 178, 179, 181–185, 336*, 366, *370*, 371, *371*, 372, 373n, *374*, 376, 378, 381, 382, *382*, 383, *386, 406, 407*, 443, 450, 570, 571, *572, 573*, 574, *574*, 581
M3+, 157
mean, 170–172, 174, 175, 177, 183, 193
multilateral, 473
non-risk neutrality case, 246
output, 514
price, 373, 403, 474, 545n, 568
price variance, 172
price-quantity covariance, 173
quantity, 80, 87, 106–108, 115, 127, 129n, 140n, 545n, 129–568
quantity variance, 172, 174, 387, 388
risk adjusted, 262, 263, 269, 271
risk aversion, 257–258
second moments, 169, 172–174, *176*, 177–188, 190, 193, 194, 305, 380, 383, 387, 388, *388*, 425
share mean, 173
share variance, 173, 388
share weights, 104, 106, 150n, 318n, 403, 591
subindices, 155
supply, 94, 96, 237, 238, 434, 435, 441, 441n, 443, 443n, 444–446, 448, *448*, 449–453
third or higher-order moments, 193, 194
tracking ability, 246, 258, 266, 268, 278, 302, 496, 529, 530, 546, 557
tracking error, 271, 302
unadjusted, 246
under perfect certainty, 246, 247
under risk, 257, 262
user cost, 89, 211, *369, 370*, 372–374, *386, 387*
user cost variance, 387
variances, 169, 175, 177, 181–184, 186, 187, 193, 194, 221n
velocity, 131, 155–157, 333
weights, 100, 101, 103–105, 155, 388, 565, 591
Double deflation, 93
Duality, 18, 23, 26, 47–48, 61n, 66, 73, 75, 80–84, 116–117, 141n, 195, 217, 219, 229, 238, 292, 295, 403, 436n, 466, 468, 473, 498, 566, 583, 583n, 584, 589
Durable goods, 95n, 331, 352
Dynamic (stochastic) choice problem, 265, 487, 498
Dynamic programming, 489n, 531, 594
Dynamic risk, 482–484
Dynamics, 421, 494, 516, 532
 nontrivial, 489n
 stochastic choice, 485
 uncertainty, 482–529

Economies of scale, 457, 529, 530, 534
Eisenpress, 349
Elasticities, 477
 Allen-Uzawa partial, *477*
 demand, 477, 530
 Hicks-Allen, 476, *478*
 income, *421*
 of substitution, 29, 31n, 33, 35–37, 137, 154, 230, 328, 342, 391, 401, 414, 418–420, *420*, 457, 476, 477, *477*
 of transformation, 476, 477, *477*
 price, 104, 457
 supply, 530
Engel curves, 32, 186, 424
 linear, 597
Equilibria, 523, *524*, 525, *525*
Equilibrium theory, 484n
Equity capital, 505n, 506, 506n
Errors in the variables, 314, 485, 527n, 526–528
 demand side, *526*
 supply side, *527*
Euler equations, 204, 204n, 207, 208, 228, 247, 252, 253, 257, 265–270, 483, 485, 488, 492, 493n, 494, 497, 504, 506, 517, 528–534, 537, 542, 542n, 543, 545, 547, 550, 551, 555, 555n, 556, 589

INDEX BY SUBJECT
661

risk averse, 493n, 518n
risk neutral, 493, 494n
under risk, 271
Exact index numbers. *See* Index numbers; Superlative indexes.
Existence condition, 135, 495
Expenditure distribution over consumers. *See* Income distribution; Total expenditure distribution.
Expenditure minimization, 65
Expenditure shares, 28, 116, 229, 252, 568
Explicit taxes, 439n

Factor demand, 463
  function, 58
  monetary, 61n
Factor intensities, 75
Factor markets, 60n
Factor prices, 58, 461
Factor productivity, 90
Factor requirements function, 59, 74, 85, 463
Factor reversal test (Fisher's), 48, 64–66, 71, 73, 78, 83, 83n, 87, 89, 98, 116, 229, 278, 283, 293, 295, 301, 350, 402n, 403, 408, 464, 473, 474, 545n, 568. *See also* Tests (Fisher's system).
Factors of production, 60, 61
  durable variable, 56
  fixed, 57n
  primary, 92
FDIC, 508n
Federal funds, 56, 505n
  rate, 56
Federal Reserve System/Board/Bank, 11, 56, 106, 126, 128, 142, 143, 144n, 145, 151, 151n, 191, 194, 221, 230, 262, 275, 288, 290, 296, 307, 307n, 325n, 326, 327, 337, 360, 361n, 362, 364, 382, 392, 392n, *393*, 404, 404n, 410, 433, 434n, 443n, 461, 470, 473, 474, 481, 482n, 485n, 508, 508n, 544, 545n, 556, 563, 564, 570–572, 575, 577–581, 588n, 603
  policy, 56, 97
Financial assets, 23n, 23–25, 245–273, 420n
Financial capital, 57n
Financial division, 67, 68, 71

Financial intermediaries, 55, 58, 72–74, 78–80, 85, 87, 224, 434, 438, 439, 439n, 440, 454–481, 484–486, 523, 524, 528, 529, 534–547, 551
  asset portfolio, 486
  behavior, 457, 472, 483
  capital stock, 535
  decision problem, 463
  implicit tax, 95, 439, 442, 450, 486n
  inputs, 55n, 535
  models, 224, 457–462, 483, 484
  opportunity cost, 486n
  outputs, 55n, 61n, 62, 73, 74, 78, 80, 85, 87, 438, 456–459, 482, 484, 535
  produced liabilities of, 486, 487
  production, 55, 79, 438, 452, 456–459, 476, 480, 483n, 482–529, 535–537
  production technology, 454, 455, 459, 462, 464, 466, 467, 469, 475, 478–481
  profits, 72, 460, 461, 486, 536
  reserves, 425, 441, 452, 486, 524, 525
  supply, 55–59
  technology, 58, 59, 91, 92, 457, 459, 466, 530, 546, 548n, 551, 556
  transformation technology, *547*
Financial intermediation, 55, 55n, 434, 454, 455, 459, 462, 482, 495
Financial markets
  primary, 486
Financial services, 67, 534
  demand, 530
  supply, 530
Financial transactions, 535
Firms, 56
  corporate office, 67
  financial. *See* Financial intermediaries.
  manufacturing, 60–63, 66–68, 74, 76, 79–85, 89, 97, 224, 483, 483n, 549, 551, 553, *554*, 555, 556. *See also* Manufacturing firms.
  multiple-output, 68
  multiproduct, 55
  technology, 469, 548, 553
Fisher ideal indexes, 26n, 39–41, 45, 77, 97, 98, 104, 108, 154, 218, 219,

309, 330, 361, 402–404, 404n, 405, 459, 474, 533, 552n, 567–569, 576, 588n, 589, 590. *See also* Index numbers.
   money stock, 365n
   price, 25, 191, 403, 459, 545n
   quantity, 403
Fisher's factor reversal test. *See* Factor reversal test (Fisher's).
Fisher's system of tests, 15, 402, 402n
Fixed factors, 460, 506
Flexibility properties, 221, 455, 469, 480, 485n, 499n, 497–505, 528, 539, 539, 540n, 544
   Diewert, 353, 539n
   global, 497n
   local, 499, 500, 503, 540
   Minflex Laurent, 358–359
   second-order, 539n
   Sobolev, 539n
Flexible functional forms, 27n, 188, 239, 267, 330, 337, 346, 353, 401, 404, 413, 414, 414n, 415, 418, 419, 419n, 427, 454, 485, 497, 497n, 498, 499n, 500, 502–504, 539, 540, 540n, 551–552
   and demand models, 341
   Asymptotically Ideal Model (AIM), 188, 188n, 497n
   Diewert's class, 341
   Fourier, 497n
   generalized Leontief, 413
   generalized McFadden, 498, 528
   generalized symmetric Barnett, 454–481
   generalized symmetric McFadden, 539, 545, 551, 553
   local, 328, 338, 342, 345–347, 358, 415
   quadratic, 114
   second order, 497n
   semi-nonparametric, 497n
   translog, 114, 189n, 401, 413, 415, 465
Flows, 107, 310
   current period service, 206
   investment yield, 312
   monetary service, 204, 215, 229, 248, 297, 299, 300, 310, 331, 362, 371, 382, 394, 434, 538, 565, 578
Forecasting, 512
   vector autoregression (VAR), 311, 318
Fourier functional form, 346, 401n, 415, 419, 419n, 497n
Fourier series expansion, 328, 346, 415. *See also* Series expansion.
Free parameters, 499, 503
Function valued estimator, 342
Functional approximation methods, 338–340
Functional cost analysis, 508, 508n
Functional forms, 585–586
   nonlinear, 586
Fund-providing functions, 505
Fund-using functions, 505
Funds
   bond, 309
   bond mutual, *317*, 532n
   borrowed, 486, 486n, 487, 495, 505, 506
   common stock, *317*
   money market mutual, *231*, 565, 570
   mutual, 307, 310, 313, *317*, 318
   non-deposit, 505, 505n, 506
   sources, 505
   stock, 309, 532n
   uses, 506

Gallant's model, 346
General equilibrium theory, 94–99, 485, 493
Generalized Barnett model, 189n, 193, 454–481, 498n, 528, 539n, 553
Generalized Leontief model, 344–347, 357, 413, 415
Generalized McFadden functional form, 498, 528, 539, 545, 551, 553
Generalized method of moments (GMM), 485, 497, 504, 504n, 509, *510*, *511*, 511n, 519, 529, 530, 542, 545, 546, 547n, 550–553, 554n, 555, 589n
Generating function, 327
Global behavior, 345
Global theoretical regularity conditions, 328, 347, 349, 351, *351*, 352, 353, 359, 512
Gorman's conditions/method, 169, 186–190, 280, 305, 425, 603
Gorman's polar form, 597
Government agencies, 330

INDEX BY SUBJECT 663

Granger causality tests, 122, *148*, 174–177, 193, 365–367, 418
   Akaike's FPE criterion, 174, 175n
   Divisia moments to income, 175, 177
   lag lengths, 174
   Schwarz's criterion, 174n
Gross National Product (GNP), 378, 585
Growth models, 373n, 489n, 529

Hansen and Singleton's estimator, 231
Hansen's asymptotic χ^2 statistic, 543n, 546n, 554
Heteroskedasticity, 509
Hicks-Allen elasticities, 476, *478*
Higher order terms, 340
Hilbert transformation estimator, 238, 382n, 435, *449*, 447–450, 453
Hinich test, 232
Hinich-Weber method, 448
Holding costs, 486n
Holding period yield, 8, 17, 102, 119, 129, 140n, 159, 160, 196, 197n, 226, 237, 250, 276, 297, 310, 318n, 364, 365, 398, 398n. *See also* Interest rate(s).
Homogeneity. *See also* Aggregator functions.
   linear, 21, 101, 102, 114, 208, 209, 211, 252n, 257, 278, 408, 408, 409n, 423, 441n, 443n, 464, 466, 468, 498, 499n, 502, 538, 538n, 539, 567
Homotheticity, 81, 400n, 410, 412n, 454, 465, 466, 480
   nonhomothetic aggregation, 63
   separability, 455
   taste and technology, 408n
Hotelling's lemma, 462
Humphrey-Hawkins targets, 223
Hyperbolic Absolute Risk Aversion (HARA) class, 491, 509, 510, *510*
Hyperbolic functions, 510n
Hypothesis testing, 37

Implicit function theorem, 463
Implicit GNP deflator, 509
Implicit interest rates, 159, 473, 584n
Implicit price deflator, 191, 191n, 509, 564, 576
Implicit price index, 78, 80, 403
Implicit quantity index, 87

Implicit taxes, 434, 435n, 439, 439n, 442, 450–452, *452*, 461, 486n, 514, 515, 523
   on financial intermediaries, 95
   on reserves, 461
Implied indexes. *See* Index numbers.
Income, 190, 585
Income distribution, 167–194
Income effects, 394
Income taxes, 54, 95
Index number theory, 11–50, 53, 76–80, 86–88, 114–115, 118–120, 126, 126n, 128, 131, 134, 139, *146*, 151–155, 160, 204, 211, 212, 238, 246–248, 308, 309, 327, 330–331, 365, 402–407, 425, 434–437, 437n, 438–440, 441n, 456, 483, 494, 533, 564, 567, 570, 582, 588, 588n, 590, 591, 603. *See also* Index numbers.
   Divisia, 170–173
   economic, 49, 118, 271
   nonparametric, 252
   risk extended, 248
   statistical, 119, 120
   stochastic, 172
Index numbers, 25, 26, 26n, 45, 116, 126n, 131, 140, 151, 154, 217, 220, 222, 304, 361, 362, 387, 397, 416–418, 533, 570, 588n. *See also* Allen indexes and variants; Consumer price index; Cost of living index; Currency equivalent (CE) indexes; Diewert indexes; Divisia indexes/aggregates; Fisher ideal indexes; Laspeyres indexes and variants; Leontief indexes; Index number theory; Malmquist indexes and variants; Paasche indexes and variants; Price (user cost) indexes; Quantity indexes; Simple sum indexes/aggregates; Statistical index numbers; Superlative indexes; Vartia indexes.
   chained, 86, 87, 303
   continuous time, 113, 140n
   dual, 84
   dual price, 34
   dual yield, 473
   errors, 576

exact, 84
fixed base, 35, 239, 302, 303
flow, 302
functional, 34, 114, 400
implied, 26
monetary services, 434n
monetary stock, 365n, 496n
Roper-Turnovsky, 405
Rotemberg. *See* Rotemberg money stock index.
smoothed, 512
superlative, 39, 41, 77, 119, 121, 140
theoretical, 49, 50, 76, 529, *547*, *554*, 555
tracking ability, 229, 246, 247, 253, 368, 494, 523, 533, 546
translog, 473
user cost (price), 31n, 34, 47, 48, 87, 349
value added, 93
velocity, 41
Indicators
monetary, 94
Indifference curve, 35, 443n
Indirect aggregator functions. *See* Aggregator functions.
Indirect utility function, 64, 75n, 101n
Industry
management, 494
Inflation rates, 20
Inner function, 495
Input requirement function, 73, 74, 79
Inputs
intermediate, 92, 92n
Instrumental variables, 509, 510n, 522n
Integrability, 31n
Integral equations, 504
Interest rate cycle, 333, 334
Interest rate spread, 486
Interest rate(s), 20, 35, 103, 141, 148, 207, 214, 286, 308, 311, 368, 372, 388. *See also* Holding period; Holding period yield; Yields.
bank's portfolio, 509, 510n
benchmark, 282
bond rate (yield), 17, 334, *335*
composite bond, 509, 510n
corporate bond, *335*, *336*, 369, *370*, *371*
covariances, 275, 290

discount, 56, 522n
discount window, 509, 510n
dual, 473
excess reserves, 56
federal funds, 509, 510n
free reserves, 56
holding period yield, 8, 17
implicit, 159, 473, 584n
investment, 313, 588
on required reserves, 515
own, 392n
real, 294
risk, 308
stochastic, 274, 275
stochastic volatility, 274–295
T-bill, 510n
uncertainty, 276, 286, 290, 294
yield, 313, 473
yield curve, 364
yield curve adjusted, 288n, 304, 318n
Intertemporal allocation (decision), 197
Intertemporal optimization, 398, 422
Introduction of new monetary assets. *See* Monetary assets.
Invariance tests. *See* Tests.
Investment, 58, 505
yield, 309, 310, 312

Joint Committee on Taxation, 350
Joint products, *315*, *316*, *317*, 307–319

Keynesian theory, 389, 594, 599–600, 602, 604
Konüs indexes and aggregates, 82, 83n, 84, 85, 87. *See also* Index numbers.

Labor, 8, 17, 56, 57, 475
input, 507
managerial, 506n
nonmanagerial, 506n
Labor quantities, 8, 17, 55, 460, 474
Divisia, 474
Laspeyres indexes and variants, 26, 26n, 29, 34, 44, 45, 104, 108, 118, 131, 151, 157, 191n, 217, 218, 239, 302, 302, 303n, 304, 309, *332*, 333, 348, 362, 402, 403n, 459, 474, 538, 545n, 564, 576, 583, 589. *See also* Index numbers.

INDEX BY SUBJECT 665

M3+, 157
price, 402
quantity, 157, 402
Laurent demand model, 325–359
Laurent series expansion, 325, 325n, 326, 343–346, 348, 351, 353, 357–358, 415
  basis, 348
  remainder term, 328
  second order, 328, 337
Laws of motion, 489n, 529
Learning by doing, 492, 493, 529
Lending rates, 62
Leontief indexes, 29, 35, 350, 583, 583n. *See also* Index numbers.
Liabilities, 505n
Likelihood ratio test, 30n, 366, 475, 479
Liquidity, 30, 30n, 158–160, 258, 261n, 307, 418
Loans, 55–58, 486
  asset portfolio, 486
  credit card, 505
  industrial, 505
  installment, 505
  portfolio, 487
  primary market, 56
  rates, 62
  real estate mortgage, 505
Lucas critique, 246, 530–534, 556, 589

Macroeconomic policy, 594
Macroeconomic theory, 94, 99, 593–605
  policy simulations, 94
Malmquist indexes and variants, 82, 83n, 84–87, 92, 363, 410n, 423, 423n, 436n, 439n, 443n. *See also* Index numbers.
  nonparametric approximations, 86
Manufacturing firms, 60–62, 66–68, 74, 76, 79–85, 89, 97, 224, 483, 549, 551, 553, *554*, 555, 556
  demand, 483, 483n
  returns to scale, 492
  technology, 60n, 553
Marginal tax rate. *See* Tax rates.
Markov process, 225, 489
Materials, 506n
Maximum likelihood (ML) estimator, 27, 29, 33, 33n, 34, 475, 476
Microeconomic theory, 49–99, 327, 397–410, 593–598, 601, 604
Miller-Modigliani theorem, 484

Minflex Laurent model, 188, 188, 189n, 346–348, 350, 351, 353, 358–359, 401n, 415
Monetarism, 577
Monetarist policy, 578, 580–582, 594, 602, 603
Monetary aggregate(s), 49–99, 101, 126, 131, 134, 145, *147*, 149, 160, 198–201, 206, 215–216, 220–222, 227, 256, 262, 282, 307, 308n, 318, 360, *379*, 390–392, 400, 401, 417, 455, 466–468, 480, 533, *546*, *547*, *554*, 556, 564, 587n, 596, 602, 603. *See also* Aggregates/aggregation (monetary); Divisia indexes/aggregates; Fisher ideal indexes; Monetary aggregation; Simple sum indexes/aggregates; Superlative indexes.
  aggregation theoretic, 433–453
  base multiplier, *133*, *333*
  broad, 309, 579
  demand side, 425, 426, 433–453
  economic, 11–48, 151, 153, 205, 547
  exact, 199, 208, 215, 227, 251, 252, 264, 272, 278, 279, 281, 282, 426, 483, 575, 601
  flow, 302–303
  for consumers, 198, 251
  growth rates, *573*, *574*
  L, 139n, *147*, 191, 362, 371, 374, 376, 378, 392, 409, 410, 579
  M1, 191, 315, *315*, 362, 372, *374*, 376, 380, 383, 392, 405, 409, 410, 411n, 416, *416*, 417, *417*, 423n, 445, 446, *556*, 565, 570, 575
  M1+, 411n
  M1B, 139n
  M2, 139n, *147*, 191, 313, 315, *316*, 362, 371, *374*, 376, 383, 392, 409, 410, 412n, 416, *416*, 417, 444, 447, *556*, 565, *571*, 575, 579
  M2+, *316*, 307–319
  M3, 139n, *147*, 362, *374*, 375, 376, 378, 392, 409, 410, 416, *416*, 417, 445, 451, *451*, 565, *572*, 575
  MQ, 97, 405, 435
  nested, 75

666 INDEX BY SUBJECT

official, 372, 374, 390, *393*, 579n
optimal, 126–150
stock, 302–303
supply side, 425, 426, 433–453, 455, 456, 482–529, 534, 538
theoretical, 212, 263, 266, 455, 512, *513–518, 521, 522*
under risk aversion, 217–244
weighted, 326, 532, 579
weights, 569, 570

Monetary aggregation, 124, 140, 151–160, 211, 212, 252, 263, 266, 327, 368n, 390, 402–403, 483, 564, 566, 569–575, 590n. *See also* Monetary aggregate(s).
demand-side, 483, 550–551
subaggregation, 409–410
supply-side, 279, 434n, 454, 455, 462–464, 480, 494–505, 528
theoretical, 279

Monetary assets, 8, 16, 17, 20–22, 25, 56, 57, 77n, 101, 119, 120, 137–139, 196, 198, 209, 226, 238, 249–251, 253, 258, 264, 276, 310, 311, 331, 361, 392, 397, 398, 439, 455, 456, 459, 463, 533, 547, 601, 602. *See also* Accounts; Aggregates/aggregation (monetary); Deposits.
consumer demand for, 225–227
currency, 55
demand for, 60–63, 250–252, 436, 452, 456
discounted present value, 214
introduction of, 16, 55–59, 90
linear homogeneity, 209
rates of return, 17, 249
real balances, 250, 459
services of, 107, 259, 585
stock, 297
substitutability, 154
supply of, 277, 454, 463
under risk, 254
user cost (price). *See* User cost of monetary assets.

Monetary base, 96

Monetary policy, 12, 158, 201, 205–206, 334, 387, 391, 427, 454, 556, 563–576, 594
transmission mechanism, 529

Monetary services, 35, 129, 152, 155, 159, 160, 211–213, 224, 237, 253, 254, 259, 277, 285, 300, 308–310, 313, 314, 364, 392, 398n, 399, 400, 404, 410, 412–415, 426, 436, 438, 440, 447, 452, 454, 456, 484, 485, 514, 569, 583–585, 588, 588n, 591
demand, 237, 246, 281, 450, 451, 483n, 531, 532, 556
discounted, 318
flow, 120, 122, 129, 132, 204, 229, 248, 300, 301, 307, 310, 318, 331, 362, 371, 382, 394, 405, 434, 473, 485, 538, 565, 578, 579, 602
growth, 318
indexes, 434n
marginal rate of substitution between consumption goods and, 284
marginal utility of, 309
price of, 404, 514
production of, 454–481, 483, 483n, 486, 505, 528
quantity, 589
real, 575
separability, 400
supply, 450, 451, 456, 531

Monetary substitutes, 156
Monetary targets/indicators, 94, 331
Monetary theory, 158, 167–194
Monetary wealth, 95, 229, 301. *See also* Rotemberg money stock; Money.

Money, 249, 277, 309, 390, 411
and GNP, 378
base, 58, 92, 95–97, 150, 206
base multiplier, *136*, 148, 150, 333, 334, *336*, 352, *381*, 382, *382*
borrowed, 505n
broader measures, 392
consumer demand for, 196–206
definition of, 392–397
degree of moneyness, 361, 390, 392, 396, 591
demand, 50, *146, 147*, 148n, 221, 305, 327, 334, 368, 369, 372–378, *386, 387*, 389–427, 435, 483n, 531, 532n, 586n, 577–592, 603
economy, 397–410
growth, 286, 287, 290, 378
high-powered, 58, 92, 93, 95

INDEX BY SUBJECT 667

holding, 249, 397n
inside, 92, 484–486, 495, 517, 528, 529
multiplier, 95, 97, 333
outside, 92, 601
price of, 15, 583, 585
role of, 138
Rotemberg stock, 230, 297–299, 299n, 301, 303, 304
stock, 229, 297, 299–301, 303, 310–312, 419, 517
superneutrality, 178, 179, 184
supply, 55, 276, 277, 325–359, 382, 435, 455, 456, 481, 531, 563, 565, 578
variable, 138
velocity, 12, 149, 274, 275, 280–288, 290
wealth, 299
Money market, 138, 141, 144n, 156, 157, 237, 371, 435n, *441, 442*, 538, 555, 565. *See also* Accounts; Demand deposits; Funds.
cleared, 94
equilibrium, 523
function shifts, 334
instruments, 472, 505n
new assets, 77n, 150
primary securities, 486
short maturity assets, 486
substitution, 156
supply-side, 462, 485
Monotonicity, 497, 500–502, 510, 512, 522, 528, 539, 541, 542, 544, *546, 553*
conditions, 508, 528, 548
local, 501–503, 510, 541
Monte Carlo studies, 191n, 345
Moral suasion, 56n
Moving average processes, 444, 445n, 512
centered, 512, 513
serial correlation, 509
smoothed, 512
MQ index, 97, 405, 435
Muellbauer's approach, 424, 425, 425n
Multi-stage decision, 23–25, 27n. *See also* Two-stage decision (budgeting).
N-level hierarchy, 75
N-stage decision, 75
Multiple products, 58. *See also* Financial intermediaries; Output aggregate(s).
Mutual funds. *See* Funds.

Nesting, 75
Net worth, 58
Neutrality/superneutrality of money, 178, 179, 184
New assets, 77, 150
Nonhomogeneous case, 85–88
Nonhomothetic approach, 63, 78–85, 91
Divisia, 86
Nonidentification
local, 351
Nonlinear dynamics, 600–602
Nonlinear functional forms. *See* Flexible functional forms.
Nonparametric approximation, 497
Nonparametric revealed preference procedure (NONPAR). *See* Revealed preference theory.
Nonseparability, 91
Normalization, 27n, 28, 349, 350
Normalizing restriction, 346

Official aggregates. *See* Aggregates/aggregation (monetary).
OLS estimation, 448, *449*
Opportunity cost, 365, 368, 369, 372, 373, 398, 486n, 583, 584, 589, 591
Optimal control problem, 224, 489n, 531, 594
stochastic, 488
Ordinality, 83
Ordinary least squares (OLS) estimators, 465
Output aggregate(s), 59, 483, 496
exact, 484, 496
theoretical, 484
Output aggregation, 55, 58, 78, 80, 85, 538
Outputs
by financial intermediaries. *See* Financial intermediaries.
demand, 61n
expected output prices, 61
output quantities, 60
Overidentifying restrictions, 504, 511

Paasche indexes and variants, 26, 104, 108, 118, 191n, 217, 218, 309, 402, 403n, 459, 474, 545n, 564, 576, 583, 589. *See also* Index numbers.

price, 402
Parameterized Expectations Approach (PEA), 266, 267
Parametric stability, 374–378, 380
Pareto optimality, 602
Pareto's stratification approach, 424, 602, 603
Passbook deposits, 34
Perfect competition, 489, 493, 494, 494n, 548, 549
Perfect substitutes, 15, 29, 35, 100, 104, 107, 124, 129, 130, 142, 143, 154, 201, 210, 216, 248, 249, 268, 277, 360, 362, 383, 394, 394n, 396, 396n, 400, 401, 495, 557, 565, 583, 584, 596
Planning horizon, 21, 51, 53, 214, 226, 227, 297, 311. *See also* Utility functions.
  finite, 51–225
  infinite, 53–54, 198, 201
Policy criteria, 327
Policy simulations
  macroeconomic, 94
Power functions, 491n
Price (user cost) indexes, 15, 23–26, 28, 29, 31n, 34, 47, 80, 105–107, 116–118, 217, 349, 474, 486, 563, 566, 567, 583, 589. *See also* Index numbers; Divisia indexes/aggregates; Fisher ideal indexes; Konüs indexes and aggregates; Laspeyres indexes and variants; Leontief indexes; Paasche indexes and variants; Price aggregates; Simple sum indexes/aggregates; Statistical index numbers; Törnqvist-Theil indexes and variants; Vartia indexes.
  Divisia, 78, 80, 89, 108, 128, 169, 172, 173, 211, 219, *370*, 372–374, *386*, 387, 403, 474, 568, 589
  dual, 78, 350, 408, 473
  Fisher ideal, 25, 26, 108, 191, 219, 403, 459, 474, 545, 545n, 589
  implied, 403
  Könus, 82–85, 87
  Laspeyres, 25, 26, 108, 151, 191, 217, 218, 239, 402, 459, 474, 545n, 564, 576, 589
  Leontief, 29, 35, 350, 583

Paasche, 26, 108, 191n, 402, 403n, 459, 474, 545n, 564, 576, 583, 589
Törnqvist-Theil, 103, 116, 552
Vartia, 88
Price aggregates, 74, 80, 118, 141, 141n, 229, 280, 292, 295, 545n, 566. *See also* Aggregates/aggregation (monetary); Divisia indexes/aggregates; Konüs indexes and aggregates; Monetary aggregate(s); Price (user cost) indexes; Simple sum indexes/aggregates.
  dual, 82
  dual monetary, 74
  dual user cost, 74, 75
  economic, 71, 151
  exact, 64, 83, 204, 252n
  output, 73, 74, 85, 464
  user cost, 67, 278, 282, 301, 337
Price function, 65
Price of leisure, 51n
Price of money, 15, 24, 103, 583–585. *See also* User cost of monetary assets.
Primary securities, 55
Principal part, 343, 344
Produced financial liabilities, 486, 487
Produced monetary asset, 57
Producer price indexes. *See* Price (user cost) indexes.
Producer's cost functions. *See* Cost functions; Costs.
Producer's variable profit function. *See* Variable profit.
Production, 455, 459, 462, 464, 466, 475, 477, 478, 480–529, 535–537. *See also* Financial intermediaries.
  factors of, 548, 548n, 549
  joint, 505
  technology, 530
  theory for the financial firm, 55
  under uncertainty, 484
Production cost models, 457
Production function, 14, 59, 71n, 113, 137, 213, 329, 463, 464, 548, 548n, 569. *See also* Aggregator functions; Duality.
  community, 337
  derived, 60n, 329

economy-wide, 88
output, 59, 463
subproduction, 436. *See also* Category production functions.
utility, 95–96
Production possibility set, 459
Production technology, 55, 454, 455, 457, 459, 462, 464, 466, 467, 469, 475, 478–481, 530
Production transformation surfaces, 88
Production tree, 75, 87
Productivity measurement. *See* Divisia indexes/aggregates; Index numbers.
Profit, 58
variable, 56, 57, 57n, 58, 62, 459
Profit function, 467, 487, 569
translog, 465
variable, 454
Profit maximization problem, 463, 464, 468
expected, 55n
second-order conditions, 492

Quadratic function, 114
Quantity aggregates, 24, 30, 33n, 36, 38, 47, 66, 74, 101, 103, 116, 118, 141, 252, 278, 288, 292, 361, 423, 437, 440, 441, 443n, 545n, 565, 566, 589. *See also* Aggregates/aggregation (monetary); Divisia indexes/ aggregates; Monetary aggregate(s); Quantity indexes; Simple sum indexes/ aggregates.
aggregation theoretic, 495, 538
demand side, 443n
economic, 34, 47, 90, 101, 104, 114, 130, 131, 151–153, 329, 408, 436, 439, 464, 575
exact, 64, 71, 74, 83, 204, 282, 495, 538
exact monetary, 74
nonlinear, 427
output, 73, 74, 464
supply side, 443n
Quantity equation, 98
Quantity indexes, 14, 25, 25n, 26, 28, 29, 31n, 34, 48, 84, 104–107, 114, 116, 118, 119, 128, 131, 139–141, 143n, 145, 153, 158, 217, 329–332, 394, 400, 437, 444, 473, 474, 563, 565, 567. *See also* Allen indexes and variants; Divisia indexes/aggregates; Fisher ideal indexes; Index numbers; Laspeyres indexes and variants; Malmquist indexes and variants; Quantity aggregates; Simple sum indexes/aggregates; Statistical index numbers; Törnqvist-Theil indexes and variants.
Allen, 84, 86, 87
Diewert's superlative class, 360
discrete time, 437
Divisia, 80, 87, 100, 106–108, 115, 127, 129, 129n, 130, 131, 140, 145, 151, 155, 169, 172–174, 190, 211, 219, 231, 232, 295, 309, 330, 331, 333, 337, 352, 361, 364, 380, 383, 387, 388, 403, 437, 440, 442–445, 450, 473, 474, 514, 538, 545n, 568, 575, 588n
dual, 84
economic, 15, 35
Fisher ideal, 39, 40, 98, 104, 219, 309, 361, 403, 568, 588n
Laspeyres, 29, 45, 104, 131, 157, 309, 333, 348, 362, 402, 403n, 538, 564, 583
linear, 583
Malmquist, 82, 84, 86, 436n, 439n, 443n
nonparametric, 84
Paasche, 104, 309
simple sum, 35, 131, 192, 232, 333, 337, 350, 352, 383, 402, 575, 576, 583, 584
statistical, 437, 566, 576
Törnqvist-Theil, 39, 40, 86, 154, 192, 437, 440, 473, 552, 588n
Vartia, 88

Radius of convergence, 356, 357
Rate of time discount, 493n
subjective, 493
Rate of time preference, 227, 250, 537
subjective, 53, 488
Rational expectations, 53n, 302, 392, 497
nonlinear, 504
Real business cycle, 586, 586n, 590, 590n, 594

Real resource costs, 486
Real resource models, 457. *See also* Production cost models.
Recursive structures, 16
Reduced form equations, 95, *147*, 177–185, *379*
Reduced form estimation, 169, 378–382
    constrained, *147*
    unconstrained, *147*
Reference input vector, 85
Reference prices, 93
    user cost vector, 84
Reference utility level, 86
Region of convergence, 342, 343, 348, 355, 357
Region of divergence, 356
Regularity, 528
    conditions/constraints, 267, 491, 497, 497n, 505, 551–552
    properties, 485n, 497n, 497–539
Regulatory wedge, 425, 435n, 433–453, 523–525, 527n
Remainder term, 189, 338–345, 355
    big O order, 339
    little O order, 339
Rental market, 331
Rental price of monetary assets, 331. *See also* User cost of monetary assets.
Replanning, 52
Representative consumer/agent, 18, 97, 101, 189, 193, 225, 250, 263, 276, 277, 279, 280, 287, 305, 398n, 424, 586, 586n, 597, 603
    Gorman's, 425
    Muellbauer, 425, 425n
Representative firm, 494, 494n, 542n, 603
Required reserves, 434, 435n, 439, *441, 442*, 450, 483n, 486n, 487
    reserve ratio, 461
Rescaling
    of prices, 507
    of quantities, 507
Reservation price, 78n
Reserve requirements, 55, 58, 80, 95, 124, 440, 441n, 442, 452, *452*, 459, 461, 472, 473, 486n, 515, 523, 536, 543, 545n
    implicit tax, 525
    ratio, 438, 484, 487, 509
Reserves, 56, 472, 506n
    cash, 472

excess, 55–57, 459, 461, 472, 486, 487, 506, 509, 522n, 536, 542, 545n, 548n
free, 56
required, 56, 58, 425, 483n, 487, 506, 514, 515, 523, 524, *524*, 525, *525*, 536
valuation, 506n
Restricted cost function. *See* Cost functions; Expenditure shares.
Restricted profit function. *See* Profit function; Variable profit.
Returns to scale, 492
    constant, 466
Revealed preference theory, 76, 106, 497
    nonparametric revealed preference procedure (NONPAR), 411, 411n, 412
Revenue, 72, 85, 87, 460
    maximizing problem, 461, 466
    unit, 73–75
    variable, 56–58, 459
Reversal tests. *See* Factor reversal test (Fisher's); Tests.
Risk, 55n, 195–216, 245, 246, 251, 308, 482, 483, 528, 532, 532n, 546, 557, 589n. *See also* Uncertainty; Capital Asset Pricing Model (CAPM).
    behavior, 491n
    dynamic, 483, 484
    nominal, 280–282
    risky assets, 256, 261n
    risky investments, 256
    tracking ability, 533
Risk aversion, 195, 196, 204, 205, 207, 208, 217–244, 246, 247, 253–260, 260, 261n, 266, 267, 269, 271, 276, 278, 282, 285, 286, 288, 290, 302, 304, 308, 392, 422, 493, 494, 494n, 497, 509, 512, *513*, 514, *515–518*, 518n, 522, 528, 529, 544, 546, 551, 555
    absolute, 259
    hyperbolic absolute, 491, 509, 510n
    relative, 261, 264, 268, 280, 512
Risk neutrality, 195, 206–207, 209, 219–221, 228–230, 237, 239, 246, 254, 255, 258, 269, 308, 311, 422, 422n, 491, 493, 493n, 494, 497, 512, 517, 518, *519–521*,

522, *522*, 523, 529, 548, 549
Role of money, 138. *See also* Money.
Roper-Turnovsky indexes. *See* Index numbers.
Rotemberg money stock index, 230, 296–306. *See also* Currency equivalent (CE) index; Index numbers; Money.
Rotterdam model, 187, 187n, 188–193, 328, 412n
Roy's identity/theorem, 189n, 337, 414, 414n, 415, 419n

Savings and loans, 26, 31, 37
Savings deposits, 16n, 23, 32, 32n, 33, *231*, *395*, 420
Schwartz's criterion, 174n
Seasonally adjusted data, 78n, *571*, *572*
Separability, 59, 67, 71n, 104, 123, 135, 138, 141, 206, 227, 230, 399, 399n, 400, 411, 412, 414n, 420n, 424n, 455, 462, 464–469, 479, 498, 505, 533, 534. *See also* Weak separability (blockwise).
   additively, 487
   blockwise homogeneous, 337
   homothetic, 412n, 455
   in currency, 209–211
   intertemporal strong, 494n
   of technology, 462–464
   output, 91
   strong, 19, 104, 209–211, 226, 251, 251n, 422
   tests, 467, 468
   weak, 422
Separability conditions, 14, 469
   technology, 62–63
Separating hyperplane, 523
Series expansion, 338. *See also* Fourier series expansion; Laurent series expansion; Remainder term; Taylor series expansion.
   globally regular, 352
   remainder term, 338
   second order, 357
Service (monetary) flows, 107, 122, 124, 131, 140, 141, 206, 215, 297, 299, 300, 302, 303, 313, 382, 576, 588n. *See also* Monetary services.
Service charges, 486n, 508n
Shifts in structural functions, 334

Simple sum indexes/aggregates, 12, 16, 26, 27n, 29, 30, 30n, 31, 34, 35, 37, 43, 44, 44n, 45, 46n, 106, 107, 118, 121–124, 127, 128, 130–134, 139, 140, 142, 143, 143n, 144–145, 145n, *146*, 149, *149*, 152, 154, 155, 157, 159, 192, 201, 206, 212, 216, 223, 231, 232, 237, 239, 248, 249, 264, 273, 277, 281, 282, 299, 299n, 300, 303, 305, 312, 313, *317*, 318, 326, 327, 329–334, 348, 350, 352, 362, 365, 366, 372–376, 378, 380, 383, *384*, 390, 392, 394, 394n, 396, 397, 401, 402, 404, 405n, 416, 417, 418n, 419, 420, 427, 443, 444, 450, 452, 480, 485, 496n, 512, 513, *513*, *514*, 516, *516*, 517, *519–521*, 526–528, 546, *547*, 553, *554*, 555, 557, 563–565, 567, 570, 572, 574–576, 579–583, 583n, 584, 585, 587–589, 596, 598, 603. *See also* Index numbers; Monetary aggregate(s); Quantity aggregates; Quantity indexes.
   L, 128, 132, 149, 333, 374, 376, 380, 381, *387*, *406*, *407*
   M1, 313, 314, *315*, 373n, 374, *374*, 376, 378, 381, 383, *406*, 423, *556*, 565, 570, 571, *573*, *574*, 576
   M1B, 144, 144n, 149, 150
   M2, 143, 144n, 148–150, 222, 313, 315, *316*, 366, 367, *374*, 376, 378, 381, 383, *386*, *406*, 555n, *556*, 570, 571, *571*, 572, *573*, *574*, 575, 578, 579, 579n, *580*, 581
   M2+, *316*
   M3, *134*, *136*, 143n, 148, 149, 155, 156, 334, *335*, *336*, *369*, *370*, 371, *374*, 376, 381, *381*, 382, *386*, *406*, *407*, 570–572, *572–574*, 575, 581
   M3+, 157
   official, 97, 127, 143, 360, 367, 373, 374
   over currency, 249
   quantity, 131, 333, 337
   stock, *317*

tracking ability, 496, 530
velocity, 41–43, 131, 155, 157
weighted, 396
Simpson's rule, 437
Sims test, 366, 366n, 384
Simulation, 512
Simultaneity bias, 353
Simultaneous equations structure, 391
Simultaneous equations systems, 475
Singular point, 340, 343, 348, 355–357
Smoothing, 512, 515, 516
    moving average, 512
    weights, 516
Specification error, 167, 368
Stackelberg solution/game, 599, 600
State variables, 201, 202, 205, 265
Statics, 421
Stationarity, 240
Stationary expectations, 302, 312
Statistical index numbers, 38–45, 45n, 114–115, 118–120, 154, 218–220, 223, 239, 247, 401–403, 422, 423, 440, 496, 512, 533, 534, 538, 557, 563, 564, 566–570. *See also* Divisia indexes/aggregates; Fisher ideal indexes; Index numbers; Price (user cost) indexes; Quantity indexes; Simple sum indexes/aggregates.
    continuous-time, 25, 113
    discrete-time, 25, 113, 116
    nonparametric, 212, 217, 512, 528
    nonparametric quantity, 84
    parameter-free, 16
    quantity, 154
    theory, 118, 437, 496, 513, 569
    tracking ability, 247, 404, 496, 512
Step-wise estimation, 341
Stochastic decision problem, 225
Stochastic process, 200, 201, 227, 265, 311
Stockholder capital, 58
Stocks, 107, 318, 331
    common, 506n
    economic, 311
Strong separability. *See* Separability.
Strotz consistent planning, 53
Subfunctions, 75, 75n, 495. *See also* Category production functions; Category utility functions; Separability.
    subcost, 69

    subutility, 278
    weakly separable, 75
Substitutability, 159, 268, 480
    perfect, 154
Substitution effects, 43, 45, 131, 156, 157, 266, 390, 394, 419, 477
Superlative indexes, 39, 41, 43, 44, 44n, 49, 77, 79, 80, 86, 88, 116, 119, 121, 140, 145, 218, 220, 239, 330, 352, 361, 404, 434, 473, 483, 569, 588n, 589–591, 603. *See also* Divisia indexes/aggregates; Fisher ideal indexes; Index numbers.
    Diewert's class, 140, 300, 360, 363
    quantity, 591
    velocity, 43, 43n
Supply functions, 58, 464, 531. *See also* Financial intermediaries.
    aggregates, 94
    money, 382, 456, 481
    multiplier type, 96
    of money, 55, 95
    output, 462
Supporting hyperplane, 524
Symmetry tests. *See* Tests.
System-wide modeling, 326, 327

Tax rates, 58, 62, 63, 461
    explicit, 54
    implicit, 434, 435n, 451, 452
    marginal, 54, 331, 350, *351*, 352
    reserve requirement, 80
Taylor series expansion, 325, 326, 328, 340–344, 346, 355–358, 415, 499
    second order, 339
Taylor series local approximation, 328, 340–342, 344, 348, 355–357
    remainder term, 340–342, 344
    second order, 340, 345
Technical change, 58, 86, 87, 91n, 90–92, 493, 530, 534
    in banking, 529
    learning by doing, 492, 529
    nonneutral, 92
    progress. *See* Production.
    rate of, 92
    rate of disembodied, 90, 91, 91n
    regress, 91n
Technological constraint, 536

INDEX BY SUBJECT

Technology, 59, 60, 455, 459, 462, 464, 466, 475, 478, 480, 481, 548, 550, 551, 553, 554
   aggregated, 494n
   financial firm, 454, 469, 546. *See also* Financial intermediaries.
   firms, 548
   intertemporal, 60
   production, 530
Tests
   Belongia and Chalfant, 418
   Den Haan and Marcet (DHM), 267
   detrending, 244
   Fisher's system, 402, 402n
   Granger causality, 365–367, 418
   Hansen's asymptotic χ^2, 504, 507, 511, 554
   Hinich, 232, 240–241, 243, 244
   hypothesis, 37, *180, 181, 184, 185*
   likelihood ratio, 366, 475, 479
   nonparametric approach, 497
   parametric approach, 497
   separability, 411, 467, 468
   Sims, 366, 384
   simulated forecasting, *180, 181, 184, 185*
   weak separability, 485, 494–505, 539–542. *See also* Weak separability (blockwise).
Theil's approach, 158
Third order moments, 240, 241
Time deposits, 12, 13, 37, *231*, 411, 420n, 456, 470, 472, 474–481, 495, 505, 505n, 506–509, 510n, 534, 535, 535n, 542, 543, 545n, 552n
   large, 570
   small, 570
Time shift, 489
Time trends, *136*
   linear, 133
Törnqvist-Theil indexes and variants, 39, 40, 43–45, 45n, 77, 116, 118, 121, 154, 155, 160, 189, 192, 218, 239, 253, 330, 363, 403, 473, 552n, 567, 588n. *See also* Index numbers; Translog model.
   approximation, 77, 102, 103, 105, 116, 121, 140, 302, 440
   discrete-time, 86, 116, 402, 437
Total cost diminution
   rate of, 90n
Total expenditure distribution. *See also*

Income distribution.
   moments of, 169
Tracking ability, 229, 283, 533, 534, 546, 557
Transactions
   approaches, 391
   balances, 16, 31n, 32n, 31–35, 40, 44, 47, 144n, 155, 159
   Baumol-Tobin model, 60n
   constraint, 329
   costs, 57n, 439n, 453, 461, 548n
   services, 454, 458, 569
   technology, 52n, 60n, 68, 101, 129, 135, 137, 137n, 141, 249, 329, 362n, 368n, 458, 480
Transformation function, 55, 213, 215, 241, 436, 438, 455, 459, 462, 464, 466, 467, 469, 485, 488, 489, 492, 495, 496, 498, 499, 503, 504, 507, 508, 534, 537–540, 542, *546, 547*, 548, *553*
   globally regular, 498
   intertemporal, 436
   locally flexible, 498
   nonseparable, 503
   variable factors, 506
Transformation technology, 548, *554*
Transition equations, 202, 203, 489, 489n
Translog indexes and variants. *See* Index numbers; Törnqvist-Theil indexes and variants.
Translog model, 77, 86, 91–93, 159, 415, 419. *See also* Aggregator functions; Demand systems; Flexible functional forms; Profit function; Variable profit; Weak separability (blockwise).
   dynamic, 421
   function, 79, 86, 87, 114, 189, 353, 356, 401, 404, 413, 415, 465, 466, 498
   profit function, 465
Transmission mechanism, 94, 426, 454, 529, 587, 594
Transversality condition, 251, 273
Turnover rates, 97, 98
Two-stage decision (budgeting), 23, 23n, 24, 47, 66–72, 75, 205, 206, 219, 228, 251, 398, 413, 422, 463. *See also* Multi-stage decision.
   decentralized, 464

674   INDEX BY SUBJECT

Uncertainty, 482–529, 600. See also Risk.
  dynamic, 483, 485, 486
Unit cost functions, 74, 75, 82, 83, 204.
  See also Cost functions; Duality.
Unit revenue functions, 73–75
User cost of monetary assets, 20, 20n, 22, 24, 25, 29, 30n, 31, 34, 38, 47, 48, 53, 57n, 58, 62, 80, 84, 101, 103–105, 107, 119–121, 123, 127n, 129, 130, 140, 145, 152–153, 156, 158, 159, 171, 204, 212, 228, 229, 237, 245, 247, 248, 252, 253, 255, 257, 261, 261n, 266, 271, 278, 280–283, 287, 295, 301, 309, 330–332, 364, 365, 368, 392n, 396, 398, 398n, 406–408, 412–414, 416–418, 420, 425, 435, 436, 439, 440, 440, 441n, 442, 453, 455, 456, 459, 461, 473, 474, 480, 483n, 514, 523, 535n, 549n, 557, 570, 583–585, 585n, 588, 588, 589n, 590, 591. See also Aggregates/aggregation (monetary); Price aggregates; Rental price of monetary assets.
  CCAPM adjustment, 271
  current period, 205, 364
  equilibrium, 524
  generalized, 284
  Hancock's, 439n
  Jorgensonian, 15, 16, 20
  nominal, 53, 54, 57, 206, 252, 398n, 460, 461, 583n
  real, 53, 120, 207, 228, 252, 253, 436, 438, 583
  risk adjusted, 253–258, 260, 261, 261n, 269
  under perfect certainty, 258
Utility, 19, 28, 248, 510n
  intertemporal, 487
  linearly homogeneous, 424
  marginal, 309, 590n
  total, 590n
Utility functions, 14, 15, 17, 18, 18n, 22–25, 26n, 36, 47, 64, 65, 103, 113, 137, 197, 197n, 199, 250, 251, 254, 264, 272, 277–279, 329, 363, 397, 398, 422n, 423, 423n, 436, 441n, 443n, 569. See also Aggregator functions;
  Constant relative risk aversion (CRRA); Duality.
  category. See Category utility functions.
  Cobb-Douglas, 401
  community, 337
  community indirect, 337
  community reciprocal indirect, 337
  concave cardinal, 590n
  constant elasticity of substitution (CES), 31, 32
  derived, 52n, 60n, 248, 249, 250n, 329
  generalized Leontief reciprocal indirect, 345, 347
  HARA, 509, *510*
  implied, 251
  indirect, 75n, 101n, 412, 414, 414n, 415
  intertemporal, 226, 397, 422
  isoelastic case, 491
  minflex Laurent reciprocal indirect, 347
  money in, 248–249, 277
  power, 491
  power (CRRA isoelastic), 509, 510, *511*
  representative consumer, 18, 101. See also Representative consumer/agent.
  social, 88
  subutility, 17, 413–414, 436. See also Category utility functions.
  under risk aversion, 255
Utility tree, 75, 87

Value added, 55, 92n, 92–93, 486, 495
  in banks, 529
  index, 93
  true index of real, 93
Value added function, 58
Variable cost, 57, 58, 68, 69, 460, 466, 467
Variable factor, 58, 461, 506
  cost, 69
Variable indirect utility function. See Duality.
Variable profit, 56, 57, 57n, 58, 59, 62, 72, 92, 93n, 454–481, 487, 488, 506, 535, 535n, 536, 537, 549
  conditional, 467–469
  translog, 465

INDEX BY SUBJECT   675

Variable revenue, 56–58, 459, 460
    from loans, 57
Varian's nonparametric revealed preference procedure (NONPAR). *See* Revealed preference theory.
Vartia indexes, 88
Velocity, 13, 41, 44, 97, 131, *147*, 148, *148*, 155–157, 282, 333, 352, 369, 418, 585
    behavior, *146*
    Divisia, 131, 155–157, 333, *335, 370, 371*, 368–372
    nonlinearity, 274–295
    of M3, 132, 334
    of monetary base, 97, 274
    of money, 12, 13, *132, 146*, 149, 274–276, 280–288, *289*, 290, 291
    simple sum, 41–43, 131, 155, 157, *335, 369, 370*
    superlative index, 43, 43n
    transactions balances, 156
Velocity function, 96–98, 145, *147*, 148, 282, 286–288, *289*, 290, 291, 327, 334
    Cagan, 148
Vending-machine model, 60n
Volatility, 516

Wage rates, 8, 17, 57, 460
Weak separability (blockwise), 14, 17–19, 22, 23, 35, 36, 52, 75, 135n, 137n, 153, 153n, 191, 191n, 199, 201, 205, 208, 215, 220, 222, 224n, 227, 230, 251, 251n, 257, 262, 264, 272, 304, 308n, 329, 349, 363n, 364, 399, 400, 409, 410, 410n, 411, 411n, 412, 413, 422, 423n, 424, 424n, 436, 438, 444n, 454, 455, 457, 458, 462, 464, 479–481, 484, 485, 485n, 495–505, 528, 533, 538–540, 542, 542n, 546, 546n, 550–551, 554, 556, 557, 566, 580, 596. *See also* Separability.
    conditions, 496, 498n, 547
    global, 528, 539
    in outputs, 498n, 500, *510, 511*, 522
    local, 498n
    nesting, 75
    of outputs, 509, 510

    of translog, 498
    parametric tests, 498
    tests, 498n, 494–505, 539–542, 543n
Wealth, 19, 62, 299, 301. *See also* Monetary wealth.
    stock, 229
Wealth constraints, 21, 22, 229, 298, 302
Wealth effect, 92
Wedges, 95
Weierstrass approximation theorem, 341
Weighting schemes, 327
Weights, 103, 104, 106, 130, 150, 309, 364, 365, 388, 409, 496n, 591
    continuous time, 437
    Divisia index, 100, 101, 103–105, 155
    equal, 394
    linear, 394
    share, 106, 591
    smoothed, 516

Yield curve adjustment, 364
Yields, 103, 313
    curve, 364
    holding period, 129, 140n, 159, 160, 364